The Life of Muḥammad

The Life of
Muḥammad

by
Muḥammad Ḥusayn Haykal

Translated from the
8th Edition
by

Isma'īl Rāgī A. al Fārūqī

Copyright © 1976 by North American Trust Publications
Library of Congress Catalog Card Number: 76–4661
International Standard Book Number: 0–89259–002–5

Printed in the United States of America

DEDICATION

TO THOSE WHO SEEK THE TRUTH FOR THE SAKE OF THE TRUTH

Foreword to the English Edition

The book, *Ḥayāt Muḥammad*, by Dr. Muḥammad Ḥusayn Haykal is well known to the Arabic reader. It is a biography of the Holy Prophet, *sallā Allahu 'alayhi wa sallam*, written in light of all the rules and requirements of modern, exacting scholarship. As its author has said, it is a renewed effort to establish the historical truth of the details of the Prophet's life in accordance with these rules, as well as to refute, by the same means, the false allegations against Islām and its Apostle. It has derived its materials from genuine sources and treated them with a mind unshackled by *parti pris* or superstition, by ignorance or false hopes. We trust that it will be followed by the research works of many other scholars; for the English readers stand in great need for books to enlighten them in the nature and history of Islām.

Fortunately, Islāmic sanity has persistently resisted all attempts at deifying the Prophet's person. Despite the fact that no human being has ever commanded as much respect, and none has ever been object of so much affection by his followers, Muslims have rejected every suggestion imputing to the Prophet superhuman power or characteristics. By itself, and when compared with the conceptions of the careers of charismatic founders and leaders of other religions in history, the Muslims' insistence on Muḥammad's humanity remains a miracle, a genuine triumph

vii

of the Muslim's historical sense. This book is a tribute to the Muslim's critical attitude in religious matters.

This is the fact which makes the quest of the historical Muhammad not only possible, but certain of achieving its objectives. It underlies this book and blesses its findings, as it invites further research and offers greater promise. Biography was never a critical science (it may even be contended that it ever existed!) before the Muslims began to sift the oral and written traditions concerning the Prophet. They undertook this task with a mind unwaveringly committed to Muhammad's humanity, absolutely convinced of his fulfillment of his mission under the full light of history.

It was these Muslim endeavors that produced the science of textual criticism. Firstly, the language, style, form, redaction and vocabulary of every reported tradition was subjected to the most complete analysis. Secondly, the ideational content of every tradition was subjected to critical tests of internal and external coherence (*i.e.*, with itself, with the Holy Qur'ān, with other traditions, with other established historical data). That content was further tested for historical relevance and relationality, and for reasonableness or systematic correspondence with reality. Finally, every *isnād* (or chain of reporters) was subjected to the most exacting tests of historicity and verification, giving birth to *'Ilm al Rijāl*, or the critical establishment of the minutest details of the personal lives of thousands of Muhammad's companions and contemporaries. This was Islāmic "Criticism"—a whole millennium ago! It was objective and scientific textual research such as the world has never seen nor probably ever will, despite the tremendous advances the science of criticism has made in modern times. This academic sophistication has made of Islām the scholarly, modernist, critical religion long before the priesthood, not to speak of the laity, of other religions achieved the minimum standards of literacy. Unfortunately for humanity as a whole, this critical and scientific spirit was lost to the Muslims with their decline.

How refreshing it is to see in this book evidence of awakening and reactivation of this spirit which Islām, the foremost champion of natural religion, of reasonableness in religion, has nurtured through the centuries! Great as the achievements of our ancestors are, it is our duty to make ourselves worthy of them. Benefit from their achievement, we certainly must. Indeed, inspired by their example, we ought to move and aspire to match and surpass them. Muḥammad Ḥusayn Haykal's *Ḥayāt Muḥam-mad* is a fair step in that direction.

This book has another value. For centuries, the English reader has been presented with prejudiced literature about Islām and the Prophet. Such polemics has prevented the non-Muslim from appreciating the genuine light of revelation, the beneficial contribution Islām can make to the solution of humanity's spiritual and social ills in modern times. It is certainly high time for the voice of Islām to be raised against the forces of atheism and materialism which have blinded modern man and dissipated his effort at finding the truth. Allah, *subḥānahu wa taʿālā*, does not wish man to be lost in skepticism, to be corrupted by injustice, alienation and ethnocentrism. On the contrary, He wishes him to realize universal brotherhood through justice, truth, dignity and mercy; to restore to him his lost poise and equilibrium; to guide him towards peace, well-being and happiness. It is He Who said in His Holy Book:

$$\text{يَٰٓأَيُّهَا ٱلنَّاسُ إِنَّا خَلَقْنَٰكُم مِّن ذَكَرٍ وَأُنثَىٰ وَجَعَلْنَٰكُمْ شُعُوبًا وَقَبَآئِلَ لِتَعَارَفُوٓا۟}$$

"O mankind! We created you from a single (pair) of male and female, and made you into nations and tribes, that ye may know and cooperate with one another" (49:13).

$$\text{يَٰٓأَيُّهَا ٱلنَّاسُ ٱتَّقُوا۟ رَبَّكُمُ ٱلَّذِى خَلَقَكُم مِّن نَّفْسٍ وَٰحِدَةٍ وَخَلَقَ مِنْهَا زَوْجَهَا}$$
$$\text{وَبَثَّ مِنْهُمَا رِجَالًا كَثِيرًا وَنِسَآءً وَٱتَّقُوا۟ ٱللَّهَ ٱلَّذِى تَسَآءَلُونَ بِهِۦ وَٱلْأَرْحَامَ إِنَّ ٱللَّهَ}$$
$$\text{كَانَ عَلَيْكُمْ رَقِيبًا}$$

"O mankind! Reverence your Guardian Lord, Who created you from a single person; Who created the first person's mate of like nature; Who created from them twain all men and women on earth" (4:1).

$$\text{إِنَّمَا ٱلْمُؤْمِنُونَ إِخْوَةٌ}$$

"The believers are but a single brotherhood" (49:9).

إِنَّ اللَّهَ يَأْمُرُ بِالْعَدْلِ وَالْإِحْسَانِ وَإِيتَآئِ ذِى الْقُرْبَى وَيَنْهَى عَنِ الْفَحْشَآءِ وَالْمُنْكَرِ وَالْبَغْىِ يَعِظُكُمْ لَعَلَّكُمْ تَذَكَّرُونَ ۞

"God commands justice, the doing of the good, and liberality to kith and kin. He forbids all shameful deeds, injustice and rebellion. Thus does He instruct you, that you may receive admonition" (16:90).

The Prophet of Islām (*salla Allahu 'alayhi wa sallam*) has said:

النَّاسُ سَوَاسِيَةٌ كَأَسْنَانِ الْمِشْطِ

"All Muslims are equal like the teeth of a comb."

الْمُسْلِمُ لِلْمُسْلِمِ كَالْبُنْيَانِ يَشُدُّ بَعْضُهُ بَعْضًا

"In relation to one another, the Muslims are like a building: every unit reinforces and is reinforced by all others."

These values of Islam are indeed the only ones capable of saving humanity from its certain collapse. The life of the Prophet is the guide and key. His conduct is the example for everyone to follow at all times and places.

It is of the essence of rational religion, as it is of the truth, to convince and to persuade its audience by mere presentation. But presentation must be honest and critical, thorough and substantiated, as well as alive and appealing. It is by Allah's grace that Professor Isma'īl Rājī al Fārūqī completed translation of this volume. He is a Muslim scholar of great renown, gifted with deep Islāmic knowledge and commitment.

Recognition is equally due to the World Assembly of Muslim Youth and to the Muslim Students Association of the United States and Canada for their part in bringing this project to fulfillment. We pray that Allah may continue to guide them, as well as all other organizations and Islāmic academic establishments dedicated to Islām, and assist them in their work for the salvation of mankind.

Allah alone is our help! He alone is Witness of our commitment and Judge of our deed!

Riyāḍ, Dhū al Ḥijjah 1395

> Ḥasan ibn 'Abdullah Āl al Shaykh
> President, World Assembly of
> Muslim Youth
> Minister of Higher Education
> Kingdom of Saudi Arabia

Translator's Preface

Haykal's *Ḥayāt Muḥammad* has a long and strange story. Its translation into English and publication by the University of Chicago Press was discussed by numerous western experts in the forties and early fifties. Obvious as the need for a scholarly sympathetic biography of the Prophet may be, negotiations took years to complete. Agreement, however, was not reached until 1964. When in 1968 the translation was completed, approved by the Supreme Council of Islāmic Affairs, Cairo, Egypt, and the University of Chicago Press, the manuscript copy edited, and its actual production begun, mysterious forces intervened and the University of Chicago Press unilaterally withdrew from its agreement.

Another agreement was negotiated *de novo* between the same parties and Temple University Press, on practically the same terms as Chicago, in 1969. Five years passed with little or no action. Then, mysterious forces again intervened and resulted in the unilateral withdrawal of Temple University Press from its agreement.

This Determined opposition to the publication of the work did not dissuade the translator from preparing this new translation with the encouragement of the Muslim Students' Association of the United States and Canada, an agency interested in the promotion of Islāmic scholarship.

Temple University   Isma'īl Rājī al Fārūqī
Philadelphia
Safar 1396 / February 1976

Translator's
Acknowledgments

The assistance of the Supreme Council of Islāmic Affairs, Arab Republic of Egypt, in making the translation of this work possible; of Professor Roger Parsell in copy editing; of Professor Erdogan Gurmen, Sr. Freda Shamma, Miss Andrée Coers, Mrs. Margaret Peirce, Dr. Lois Lamiyā' al Fārūqī, and Dr. Kaukab Siddique in proofreading; of Sr. Anmār al Fārūqī in preparing the index; of Dr. Lois Lamyā' al Fārūqī in preparing the maps and illustrations; and of the North American Islāmic Trust in the production of this book is gratefully acknowledged.

I wish to acknowledge with thanks the financial help and encouragement extended to this work by the World Assembly of Muslim Youth, Saudi Arabia.

*The reprinting of this Edition
has been financed by the Islamic Call Society
The Socialist Peoples Libyan Arab Jamahiriyah.*

Contents

List of Illustrations

The Life of Muhammad

Foreword to the First Edition

Ever since man appeared on earth he has been anxious to penetrate the universe and discover its laws and secrets. The more he came to know, the more he wondered at its greatness, the weaker he appeared to himself and the less reason he saw for vanity. The Prophet of Islām—may God's peace be upon him—is very much like the universe. From the very beginning, scholars worked hard to uncover various aspects of his great humanity, to grasp the realization of the divine attributes in his mind, character and wisdom. Certainly they achieved a fair measure of knowledge. Much however has escaped them; and there still lies ahead a long and indeed infinite road.

Prophethood is a gift which cannot be acquired. In His wisdom God grants it to whosoever stands prepared for it and is capable of carrying it. He knows best when and where it will be of most benefit. Muḥammad—may God's peace and blessing be upon him—was indeed prepared to carry the prophetic message unto all the races of mankind. He was equipped to carry the message of the most perfect religion, to be the final conclusion of prophethood, the unique light of guidance for ever and ever.

The infallibility of the prophets in the conveyance of their message and the performance of their divine trust is a matter on which the scholars have agreed for a long time. Once they are chosen for their task, the prophets' conveyance of their message and their performance of the duties entrusted to them carry no reward. Their work is a necessary consequence of such divine revelation. Like all men, prophets are truly fallible; their distinction lies in that God does not leave them in their error. He corrects them and often even blames them therefor.

Muḥammad—may God's peace and blessing be upon him—was commanded to convey a divine message. But he was not shown how to carry it out nor how to protect the fruits of his work. It was left to him as any rational and sentient being to conduct his affairs as his intelligence and wisdom might dictate. The revelation which he received was absolutely precise and clear in all that concerns the essence, unity, attributes and worship of God. But this was not the case as regards the social institutions of family, village and city, the state in its relations with the said institutions and with other states. There is hence wide scope for research on the Prophet's greatness before his commission as prophet, as there is after his commission had taken place. He became a messenger for his Lord, calling men unto Him, protecting the new faith and guaranteeing the freedom and security of its preachers. He became the ruler of the *Ummah* of Islām,[1] its commander in war and teacher, the judge and organizer of all its internal and foreign affairs. Throughout his career he established justice and reconciled hopelessly disparate and hostile nations and groups. His wisdom, farsightedness, perspicacity, presence of mind and resoluteness are evident in all that he said or did. From him streams of knowledge have sprung and heights of eloquence have arisen to which the great bend their heads in awe and wonder. He departed from this world satisfied with his work, assured of God's pleasure and crowned with the gratitude of men.

All these aspects of the Prophet's life deserve special study and research. It is not possible for any one scholar to give them their due; nor to exhaust the meanings inherent in any one of them.

Like that of any other great man, the biography of Muḥammad—may God's blessing be upon him and upon his house—has been expanded by many an imaginary story, whether innocently or with ulterior motive, deliberately or accidentally. Unlike all other biographies, however, a great portion of it has been included in the divine revelation and has thus been preserved forever in the pure Qur'ān. Another fair portion has been safely preserved for us by trustworthy narrators. From these unmistakable sources the biography of the Prophet should be constructed, and on their basis its hidden meanings and complicated problems should be investigated, and its moral established. Its constitutive materials should be subjected to objective and scholarly analysis taking well into consideration the circumstances of time and environment as well as the prevalent beliefs, institutions and customs.

In his book, *The Life of Muḥammad*, Dr. Haykal gave us the biography of the Prophet—may God's peace and blessings be upon him—which I have had the pleasure of reading in part before printing. Dr. Haykal is well known to the Arabic reader; his many books obviate the need for an introduction. He studied law and familiarized himself with logic and philosophy. His personal circumstances and career enabled him to study ancient as well as modern culture and to learn a great deal from both. He lectured on and debated, attacked and defended many questions of belief, of social organization and politics. The maturity of his mind is matched by the perfection of his knowledge, and the wide range of his readings. He debates with powerful, convincing arguments and he treats his subject with sound logic and a style all his own. Such preparation stands behind Dr. Haykal's book. In his Preface, Dr. Haykal wrote: "No one should think that research in the life of Muhammad is completed with this work; and I am far from making any such claim. It is closer to the truth for me to say that my work is really only the beginning of scientific research in this field in Arabic."[2] The reader might be surprised if the strong resemblance of the modern scientific method to the call of Muhammad is pointed out. The former demands that the investigator suspend his own beliefs and refrain from prejudgment, to begin his investigation with observation of the data, and then to proceed to experimentation, comparison, classification and finally to conclusion based upon these objective steps. A conclusion thus arrived at is scientific in that it is itself subject to further testing and critical analysis. It is reliable only as long as further scientific investigations do not disprove any of the premises on which it is based. True, the scientific method is the highest achievement of the human race in its effort to liberate man's thought, but it is precisely the method of Muhammad and the foundation of his call.

Dr. Haykal's new method is truly Qur'ānic. For he has made reason the judge, and evidence the foundation, of knowledge. He has repudiated conservatism and castigated the conservatives. Agreeing with the Qur'ānic principle "opinion and speculation are no substitute for true knowledge" (Qur'ān, 53:28), Dr. Haykal has chastised those who speculate without evidence; who regard the old purely for its age, as sacred. He has imposed the teaching of the truth upon all those who have the capacity to grasp it. "Muhammad—may God's peace and blessing be upon him—had only one irresistible miracle—the Qur'ān. But it is not irrational. How eloquent is the verse of al Busayrī: 'God did not try us with anything irrational. Thus, we fell under neither doubt nor illusion.' "

As for Dr. Haykal's claim that this method is a modern method, that is rather questionable. In holding such a claim, Dr. Haykal was reconciling the scholars who are his would-be critics. He himself has acknowledged that this method was the method of the Qur'ān. It is also the method of Muslim scholars of the past. Consider the books of kalām.[3] Some of them insisted that the first duty of the adult is to know God. Others held that the first incumbent duty is to doubt; for there is no knowledge except by means of proof and argument. Although the process of verification is a kind of deduction, the premises of such reasoning must be either self evident, mediately or immediately given to sense, or dependent upon unmistaken experimentation and generalization, following the rules of logic. The slightest error in any premise or in the form of reasoning vitiates the whole proof.

Al Ghazzālī, the great teacher, followed exactly the same method. In one of his books, he reported that he had decided to strip his mind bare of all former opinions, to think and to consider, to compare and to contrast, then to rethink all the proofs and all the evidence step by step. After all this reconstruction he reached the conclusion that Islām is true, and thus established a number of views and arguments regarding its nature. He did all this in order to avoid conservatism, to achieve faith with certitude, founded upon truth and argument. It is this kind of faith arising from rational conviction which, all Muslims agree, cannot but be true and bring about salvation.

The same method or deliberate repudiation of all creeds, as a preliminary to investigation and scholarly study, is found in most books of kalām. Doubt is indeed an old method; and so is experimentation and generalization. The latter is founded upon observation; and it is not new with us at all. Neglected and forgotten in the orient since it took to conservatism and irrationalism, this old method was taken up by the West, purged clean, and used with great benefit to science and industry. We are now taking it back from the West thinking that we are adopting a new method of scientific research.

This method then is both old and new. However, to know a method is easy; to apply it is difficult. Men do not differ much in their knowledge of a certain law; but they stand widely apart in their application of it.

To suspend all prejudices, to observe, to experiment, to compare, to deduct and to extrapolate are all easy words. But for man standing under an inheritance of heavy biological and mental burdens, struggling against an oppressive environment of home, village, school, city and country, suffering under the tremendous weight of conditioning by temperament, health, disease and passion—how could it be easy for him to apply the law? That is the question, whether in the past or in the present. That is the reason for the proliferation of views and doctrines. That is the reason for the movement and change of these views from country to country and people to people. With every generation, philosophy and literature don new robes very much like women do. Hardly any theory or principle stands beyond attack, and none is an impregnable fortress. Change has even attacked the theories of knowledge which were venerated during long ages. The theory of relativity brought a whirlwind to accepted scientific principles. But soon, it too was put under attack. Likewise, the theories of nourishment and disease, of their causes and cures, are undergoing continual change. A closer look, therefore, will convince us that there is no security for the productions of our minds unless they are supported by convincing proofs. But what is the proportion of such secure productions of the mind to the long parade of theories which are produced by fancy, projected by sick minds, imposed by politics, or created by scientists who simply love to differ from their peers? This thought may perhaps sober such men of knowledge and science who are too proud of reason and depend on it alone. Such a thought may yet guide them one day toward the truth, to take shelter under the absolute conviction which it provides, the conviction of true revelation, of the holy Qur'ān and the veritable *Sunnah*.[4]

Let us now turn to Dr. Haykal and his book. A number of *mutakallimūn*[5] have held that the knowledge which astronomy and the dissection of the human body provide clearly points to the fact that divine knowledge includes the most minute details of existence. I concur that the discovery and establishment of the laws and secrets of nature will, besides helping the human mind to penetrate what was incomprehensible before, finally support religion. In this vein, God said, "We shall show them

Our signs in the horizons as well as within themselves, and We shall continue to do so until they realize that Our revelation is the truth. Is it not sufficient that your Lord witnesses everything?" (Qur'ān, 41:53). The discovery of electricity and all the theories and inventions to which it has led has made it possible for us to understand how matter may be transformed into energy and energy into matter. Spiritualism has helped us to understand the transcendent nature of the soul and shed light on the possibility of its separate existence, of its capacity to travel through space and time. It has helped explain many matters on which men differed in ignorance. Dr. Haykal has used this new knowledge in his novel explanation of the story of Muḥammad's Isrā'.[6]

To list the good points which Dr. Haykal has made in his book would take many long pages. Suffice it then to point to these contributions in a general way. Undoubtedly, the reader will realize the worth of this work and will learn much from Dr. Haykal's well documented arguments, fine logic, and penetrating insight. The reader will realize that Dr. Haykal's whole devotion has been to the truth alone, and that he has approached his task with a heart replete with the light and guidance of the revelation of Muḥammad, as well as with great awe for the beauty, majesty, greatness, and moral height of the life of Muḥammad—may God's peace and blessing be upon him. Dr. Haykal is fully convinced that this religion of Muḥammad will surely deliver mankind from doubt, from dark materialism, and will open their eyes to the light of conviction, guide them to the divine light with which they will come to know God's infinite mercy. Dr. Haykal is confident that men will thereby come sooner or later to acknowledge the glory of God as heaven and earth already do, and praise the divine might before which all beings become humble. Indeed, he writes: "Indeed, I would even go further. I would assert that such a study may show the road to mankind as a whole to the new civilization to which it is currently groping. If western Christendom is too proud to find the new light in Islām and in its Prophet but willingly accepts it from Indian theosophy and other religions of the Far East then it devolves upon the Orientals themselves, Muslims, Jews or Christians, to undertake this study in all objectivity and fairness in order to reach and establish the truth. Islamic thought rests on a methodology that is scientific and modern as regards all that relates man to nature. In this respect it is perfectly realistic.

But it becomes personalist the moment it leaves nature to consider the relationship of man to the cosmos as a whole and to his creator."[7] Dr. Haykal goes on to say that "the pioneer fighters against this all-embracing paganism of modern times, however, are clearly distinguishable under close observance of the current flow of events. Perhaps, these pioneer forces will grow and become surer of themselves when scholarship has found answers to these spiritual problems through the study of the life of Muhammad, of his teachings, of his age, and of the spiritual world revolution which he incepted."[8]

Dr. Haykal's firm conviction is corroborated by real events. What we have witnessed today of the West's concern for the study of our heritage and the care with which western scholars study the legacy of Islām, its various contents, its ancient and modern history and peoples, of the fair treatment that some of them give to the career of the Prophet—may God's peace and blessing be upon him—and finally, what we know by experience of the necessary final victory of truth—all this leads to the consideration that Islām will spread all over the world. In this process, the strongest protagonists of Islām may well be its strongest enemies whereas its present alien antagonists may be Islām's adherents and defenders. As in the early period the strangers have supported Islām, strangers may yet help it achieve its final victory. It is said that "Islām began as a stranger and will return as a stranger. God bless the strangers!"

Since the Prophet—may God's peace and blessing be upon him—was the last of the prophets, and the world is to have no prophet after him, and since, as the revealed text has said, his religion is the most perfect, it is not possible that the *status quo* of Islām will last. Its light must necessarily eclipse all other lights as the rays of the sun eclipse those of the stars.

Dr. Haykal related the events of the Prophet's life closely to one another. His book therefore presents a closely knit argument. In every case, he has elaborated strong evidence and articulated it clearly and convincingly. His work is not only persuasive; it is pleasant reading and it moves the reader to keep on reading to the very end.

Furthermore, the book contains many studies which do not properly belong to the biography of the Prophet but are necessitated by the author's pursuit of questions related thereto. Finally, let me conclude this prefatory note with the prayer of the master of all men—may God's peace and blessing be upon him, his house, and his followers: "God, I take shelter under the light of Your face before Whom darkness became light, by Whose command this world and the next were firmly established. Save me from Your wrath and displeasure. To You alone belongs the judgment, harsh as it may be when You are not pleased. There is neither power nor strength except in You."

15 February, 1935   Muḥammad Muṣṭafā al Marāghī
                                       Grand Shaykh of al Azhar

"God and His angels bless the Prophet. O men who have
believed: Invoke God's peace and blessing upon him"

Qur'ān, 33:56

In the name of God, the Merciful, the Compassionate

Praise be to God, Lord of the universe,
The Gracious, the Merciful,
Master of the Day of Judgment.
You alone we worship; You alone we implore for help.

Guide us unto the straight path—
The path of those whom You have blessed,
Those who have not incurred Your displeasure,
Those who have not gone astray.

Amen

Qur'ān, 1:1–7

Preface to the
First Edition

Muḥammad, God's peace and blessing be upon him! This noble name has been on the lips of countless millions of men. For almost fourteen centuries, millions of hearts have palpitated with deep emotion at the pronouncement of it. Many more millions of people for a period as long as time, will pronounce it, and will be deeply moved thereby. Every day, as soon as the black thread becomes distinguishable from the white, the muezzin will call men to prayer. He will call them to the worship of God and the invocation of blessing upon His Prophet, a task the fulfillment of which is better for them than their sleep. Thousands and millions of men in every corner of the globe will undoubtedly respond to the muezzin's call, springing to honor through their prayers God's mercy and bounty, richly evidenced for them with the break of every new day. At high noon, the muezzin will call again for the noon prayer; then at mid-afternoon, at sunset, and after sunset. On each of these daily occasions Muslims remember Muḥammad, the servant of God and His Prophet, with all reverence and piety. Even in between these prayers the Muslims never hear the name of Muḥammad but they hasten to praise God and His chosen one. Thus they have been, and thus they will be until God vindicates His true religion and completes His bounty to all.

Muḥammad did not have to wait long for his religion to become known, or for his dominion to spread. God has seen fit to complete the religion of Islām even before his death. It was he who laid down the plans for the propagation of this religion. He

had sent to Chosroes, to Heraclius and other princes and kings
of the world inviting them to join the new faith. No more than
a hundred and fifty years passed from then until the flags of
Islām were flying high between Spain in the west and India,
Turkestan and indeed China in the east. Thus by joining Islām,
the territories of al Shām[1] Irāq, Persia, and Afghanistan have
linked the Arabian Peninsula with the kingdom of "the Son of
Heaven."[2] On the other hand, the Islāmization of Egypt, Burqah,
Tunisia, Algeria and Morocco have linked the native land of
Muhammad—may God's peace and blessing be upon him—with
Europe and Africa. From that time until our day Islām remains
supreme throughout all these territories. It withdrew from Spain
only under the attack of Christendom which inflicted upon the
people of Spain all kinds of suffering and persecution. As the
people could not bear these tragedies, some of them returned to
Africa. Others under the threats of fear and panic apostasized,
withdrew from the religion of their ancestors, and entered into
that of the tyrants and conquerors.

What Islām had lost in Spain and in western Europe was regained when the Ottomans conquered Constantinople and established the religion of Muhammad therein. From there, Islām
spread throughout the Balkans into Russia and Poland and
spread over territories many times wider than Spain. From the
day of its initial conquest until now, no religion has ever conquered Islām despite the fact that its people have fallen under
all kinds of tyrannies and unjust governments. Indeed, reduction
of their worldly power has made the Muslims more strongly
attached to their faith, to their Islāmic way of life, and to their
Islāmic hope.

Islām and Christianity

The power with which Islām quickly spread brought it face to
face with Christianity and involved the two religions in a *guerre
à outrance*. Muhammad vanquished paganism and eliminated it
from Arabia just as his early successors pursued it across Persia, Afghanistan and a good portion of India and eliminated it
from these territories. Later on the successors of Muhammad
conquered Christianity in Hīrah, Yaman, Syria, Egypt, and even
in the capital of the Christian empire, Constantinople. Was
Christianity then to receive the same fate of extinction which
befell paganism despite the fact that Muhammad had praised it

and confirmed the prophethood of its founder? Were the Arabs, coming out of their arid desert peninsula, destined to conquer the gardens of Spain, of Byzantium, and all Christendom? "No! Death rather than such a fate!" Thus the fight continued for many centuries between the followers of Jesus and the followers of Muḥammad. The war was not limited to swords and guns. It spread out to the fields of debate and controversy where the contenders contended in the names of Muḥammad and Jesus. No means were spared to sway the community, to arouse the populace and to stir the passions of the people.

The Muslims and Jesus

Islām, however, prevented the Muslims from attacking the person of Jesus. It held that Jesus was a servant of God endowed with scripture and appointed as prophet. It also held that Jesus was always blessed; that he was enjoined as long as he lived to hold prayer and to give *zakāt;*[3] that his mother was innocent and that he was neither unjust nor unfortunate. It asserted that Jesus was blessed on the day of his birth, on the day of his future death as well as on the day of his resurrection. Many Christians, on the other hand, have attacked the person of Muḥammad and attributed to him the most unbecoming epithets—thereby giving vent to their resentment and sowing the seeds of hatred and hostility. Despite the commonly held view that the Crusades have long been finished and forgotten, fanatic Christian antagonism still continues to rage against Muḥammad. The present situation has not changed except perhaps for the worse. Moved by the same fanaticism, the missionaries resort to immoral and depraved means in their struggle against Islām. This fanaticism was never exclusive to the Church. It stirred and inspired many writers and philosophers in Europe and America who are not related to the Church.

CHRISTIAN FANATICS AND MUḤAMMAD

One may wonder why Christian fanaticism against Islām continues to rage with such power in an age which is claimed to be the age of light and science, of tolerance and *largeur de cœur*. This fanaticism is all the more surprising when one remembers that the early Muslims were overjoyed at the news of the victory

of Christianity over Zoroastrianism, when the armies of Heraclius carried the day against those of Chosroes. Persia had a dominant influence in South Arabia ever since the Persians expelled
the Abyssinians from Yaman. Chosroes had sent his army in
614 C.E. under the command of his general named Shahrbarāz[4]
to conquer Byzantium. When their armies met in Adhri'at and
Busrā, territories of al Shām close to Arabia, the Persians inflicted upon the Byzantines heavy losses in lives and destroyed
their cities and orchards. The Arabs, especially the people of
Makkah, used to follow the news of this war with great anxiety.
At the time, the two hostile powers were the greatest on earth.
The Arabs adjoined both powers and had territories which fell
under the suzerainty of both. The Makkan idolaters rejoiced at
the defeat of the Christians and celebrated the event. They regarded them as people with a scripture, very much like the Muslims, and they even attempted to attribute their defeat to their
religion. For the Muslims, it was hard to believe the defeat of
the Byzantines for the same reason, namely that like them they
were a people with scripture. Muhammad and his companions
especially hated to see the Zoroastrians victorious. This difference in the views of the Muslims and the idolaters of Makkah
led to open contention between the two groups. The Muslims
were ridiculed for holding such opinions. One of them was so
bold in his show of joy in front of Abū Bakr that the latter,
known for his great calm and friendliness, was prompted to say:
"Don't take to joy too soon. The Byzantines will avenge themselves." When the idolater rejoined, "This is a lie," Abū Bakr
became angry and said: "You are the liar, O Enemy of God:
I wager ten camels that the Byzantines will win against the Zoroastrians within the scope of a year." When this came to the notice of Muhammad, he advised Abū Bakr to increase the amount
of the wager and to extend its term. Abū Bakr then raised the
wager to one hundred camels and extended the time to nine years.
In 625 C.E. Heraclius was victorious. He defeated Persia and
wrenched from it the territory of Syria as well as the cross of
Christ. Abū Bakr won his wager and the prophesying of Muhammad was confirmed in the following Qur'ānic revelation:
"The Byzantines have been defeated in the land nearby. However, they shall win in a few years. To God belongs the command
before and after. Then will the believers rejoice at the victory
which God has sent. God, the Mighty and Merciful, gives His

victory'to whomsoever He wishes. He never fails in His promise. Most men however do not know."[5]

The First Principles of the Two Religions

Muslim rejoicing at the victory of Heraclius and his Christian armies was great. Despite the many controversies that had taken place between the followers of Muḥammad and those who believed in Jesus, their friendly and fraternal relationships continued to be strong throughout the life of the Prophet. It was otherwise with the relationships of Muslims and Jews. There had been an armistice followed by alienation and war with consequences so disastrous and bloody that the Jews had to be moved out of the Arabian Peninsula altogether. The Qur'ān confirms the bond of friendship between Muslims and Christians and denounces the enmity of the Jews. It advises the Muslims, "You will find greater enmity to the believers among those who are Jews and idolaters; but you will find greater friendliness among those who say, 'We are Christians.' For they, especially the monks and priests among them, do not take to false pride."[6]

Indeed Christianity and Islām entertain the same view of life and ethics. Their view of mankind and of creation is one and the same. Both religions believe that God created Adam and Eve, placed them in paradise and commanded them not to listen to Satan, and that eating of the tree thereby caused them to be discharged. Both religions believe that Satan is the enemy of mankind who, according to the Qur'ān, refused to prostrate himself to Adam when commanded to do so by God and, according to Christian scripture, refused to honor the word of God. Satan whispered to Eve and deceived her, and she in turn deceived Adam. They ate from the tree of eternal life, discovered their nakedness, and then pleaded to God to forgive them. God sent them to earth, their descendants enemies of one another, forever open to the deception of Satan, some of them liable to fall under this deception and others capable of resisting it to the end. In order to transcend man's war against this deception, God sent Noah, Abraham, Moses, Jesus and the other prophets, commissioning every one of them to convey in the tongue of his people a book which confirms, elaborates, and makes evident the revelations received from his predecessor-prophet. As Satan is assisted by his helpers among the evil spirits, the angels praise the

Lord and adore Him. Both the good and the evil powers therefore compete to win mankind until the Day of Judgment when every soul will receive that which it has earned and when everyone will be responsible for himself alone.

The Difference between Them

Not only has the Qur'ān mentioned Jesus and Mary, but it has honored them and presented them in such light that the readers cannot but feel this fraternal feeling towards Christianity when they read its verses. It is all the more perplexing, therefore, that the Muslims and Christians have continued to fight each other century after century. The confusion disappears however, when we learn that Islām has differed from Christianity in many fundamental matters which were subjects of strong controversy, without ever leading to hatred and hostility. Christianity does not acknowledge the prophethood of Muhammad as Islām acknowledges the prophethood of Jesus. Moreover, Christianity upholds trinitarianism whereas Islām strongly rejects anything but the strictest monotheism. The Christians apotheosize Jesus and, in their argument with Muslims, seek confirmation of his divinity in the Qur'ānic assertion that he spoke out in the cradle (19:29–34) and in the many miracles which he alone had been favored by God to perform. During the early days of Islām, the Christians used to dispute with the Muslims in the following vein: Doesn't the Qur'ān itself, which was revealed to Muhammad, confirm our view when it says:

اِذْ قَالَتِ الْمَلَائِكَةُ يَمَرْيَمُ اِنَّ اللهَ يُبَشِّرُكِ بِكَلِمَةٍ مِّنْهُ ٱسْمُهُ الْمَسِيحُ عِيسَى ابْنُ مَرْيَمَ وَجِيهًا فِى الدُّنْيَاوَ الْاٰخِرَةِ وَمِنَ الْمُقَرَّبِينَ۞ وَيُكَلِّمُ النَّاسَ فِى الْمَهْدِ وَكَهْلًا وَّمِنَ الصّٰلِحِينَ۞ قَالَتْ رَبِّ اَنّٰى يَكُونُ لِى وَلَدٌ وَّلَمْ يَمْسَسْنِى بَشَرٌ قَالَ كَذٰلِكِ اللهُ يَخْلُقُ مَايَشَآءُ اِذَا قَضٰى اَمْرًا فَاِنَّمَا يَقُولُ لَهُ كُنْ فَيَكُونُ۞ وَيُعَلِّمُهُ الْكِتٰبَ وَالْحِكْمَةَ وَالتَّوْرٰىةَ وَالْاِنْجِيْلَ۞ وَرَسُولًا اِلٰى بَنِى اِسْرَآءِيْلَ ةَ اَنِّى قَدْ جِئْتُكُمْ بِاٰيَةٍ مِّنْ رَّبِّكُمْ اَنِّى اَخْلُقُ لَكُمْ مِّنَ الطِّينِ كَهَيْئَةِ الطَّيْرِ فَاَنْفُخُ فِيْهِ فَيَكُونُ طَيْرًا بِاِذْنِ اللهِ وَاُبْرِئُ الْاَكْمَهَ وَالْاَبْرَصَ وَاُحْىِ الْمَوْتٰى بِاِذْنِ اللهِ وَاُنَبِّئُكُمْ بِمَا تَأْكُلُونَ وَمَا تَدَّخِرُونَ فِى بُيُوتِكُمْ اِنَّ فِى ذٰلِكَ لَاٰيَةً لَّكُمْ اِنْ كُنْتُمْ مُّؤْمِنِينَ

"The angels said, 'O Mary God announces to you His command that a son will be born to you whose name shall be the Messiah, Jesus, Son of Mary, and who will be honored in this world and in the next and be close to God. He will speak as a baby in the cradle and he will be righteous throughout his long age.' Mary asked: 'How can I have a son when no human has touched me?' The angel answered: 'Thus God creates whatever He wills. He commands a thing to be and it is.' God will teach Jesus the scripture, wisdom, the Torah and the Evangel. He will send him a prophet of Israel, and charge him with the conveyance of a new revelation from God. He will confirm him by giving him the power to blow life into birds which he could fashion out of clay, to give vision to the blind, to heal the leper, to resurrect the dead, and to prophesy about what the Jews eat and what they hide in their houses—all with God's permission—that the Jews may believe in him and thereby prove their faith."[7]

The Qur'ān then did declare that Jesus would resurrect the dead and give vision to the blind and heal the leper, create birds out of clay and prophesy—all of which are divine prerogatives. Such was the view of the Christians who, at the time of the Prophet, were disputing and arguing with him that Jesus was a god besides God. Another group of them apotheosized Mary on the grounds that she had been the recipient of God's command. The Christian adherents to this view regarded Mary as a member of a trinity which included the Father, the Son and the Holy Ghost.[8] However, those who held that Jesus and his mother were divine were but one of the many sects into which Christianity was divided in those days.

Debate of the Christians with the Prophet

The Christians of the Arabian Peninsula debated with Muhammad on the basis of their diverse views. They argued that Jesus was God, that Jesus was the Son of God, that Jesus was the third person of the trinity. The apotheosizers of Jesus had recourse to the foregoing argument. Those who held the view that Jesus was the Son of God argued that he had no known father, that he had spoken out in the cradle as no other human had ever done. Those who held that he was the third person of the trinity argued that God referred to Himself as "We" in His acts of creation, of commanding and providing, and that this was evidence for His plurality—for otherwise He would have referred to Himself as "I." Muhammad used to listen to all these arguments and debate with them in kindness. He never showed

in his debates the hardness and severities which characterized
his debates with the associationists⁹ and the worshipers of idols.
Rather, he argued with them on the basis of revealed scripture
and based himself on what could be deduced therefrom. God said:
"Blasphemous are those who claim that God is Jesus, the son of
Mary. Say, 'Who is capable of anything should God desire to
destroy Jesus, the son of Mary, as well as his mother and all that
is on the face of the earth? To Him alone belongs the dominion
of heaven and earth and all that is in between. He, the Omnipotent, creates what He wills.' Both Jews and Christians claim that
they are the sons of God and His favorite people. Say, 'Why does
He then punish you for your sins? Rather, you are all humans,
on a par with all other men He has created. God forgives
whomsoever He wills and punishes whomsoever He wills.' "¹⁰
God said: "Blasphemous are those who claim that God is Jesus,
the son of Mary. Jesus said: 'O Children of Israel, worship God
alone, your Lord and my Lord. Whoever associates aught with
God, God will exclude from paradise and punish in hell. Such
unjust people will have no helper.' Blasphemous are those who
claim that God is the third person of a trinity. There is no God
other than God, the One. Unless they stop this blasphemy, God
will inflict upon them a painful punishment."¹¹ He, to Whom is
the glory, also said: "God asked Jesus, son of Mary: 'Did you
ask the people to take you and your mother as two gods beside
God?' Jesus answered: 'Praise be to You alone, I had not said
but that which I was commanded to say. You surely know
whether I am guilty of such blasphemy, for You know all that
is in my thoughts, and I know none of what is in Yours. You
alone are omniscient. I did convey to them that which You commanded me to convey, namely, that they ought to worship God
alone, my Lord and their Lord. In their midst, I have been a
witness unto You throughout my life. And when You caused me
to die, knowledge of what they did was Yours for You are the
witness of everything. If You punish them, they are Your creatures and servants: if You choose to forgive them, You are the
Mighty and Wise.' "¹²
    Christianity upholds the trinitarian view and claims that Jesus
is the Son of God. Islām, on the other hand, categorically denies
that God could possibly have a son. "Say," God commands Muḥammad, "God is one. God is eternal. He has neither progeny
nor ancestry. He is absolutely without parallel."¹³ "It is not possible for God—may He be praised—to take unto Himself a

son."[14] "Jesus is to God as Adam was to Him, a creature made out of dust that had come to be at God's command."[15] Islām is monotheistic *par excellence;* the unity of God it teaches is the most categorical, the clearest, the simplest, and therefore the strongest. Whatever casts the slightest doubt upon the unity of God is strongly rejected by Islām and declared blasphemous. "God does not forgive that He be associated with anyone, but He will forgive anything lesser than that to whomsoever He wills."[16] Whatever connection Christianity may have had with ancient religions as far as its trinitarian doctrine is concerned furnished no justification at all in the eye of Muḥammad. The truth is that God is one and unique, that He has no associates, that He has neither progeny nor ancestry and that He is absolutely without parallel. It is no wonder therefore that controversy arose between Muḥammad and the Christians of his time, that he debated with them in kindness, and that revelation confirmed Muḥammad with the foregoing Qur'ānic corroborations.

The Question of Jesus' Crucifixion

Another problem in which Islām differed from Christianity and which aroused controversy at the time of the Prophet is that of the crucifixion of Jesus as atonement for the sins of mankind. The Qur'ān clearly denies that the Jews had killed or crucified the Messiah. It says: "As for the Jews' claim that they killed the Messiah, Jesus, son of Mary, the Prophet of God, the truth is that they have not killed him, nor have they crucified him, but that that appeared to them to be the case; whereas those who contend concerning this matter have no certain knowledge at all but merely conjecture. None of them is absolutely certain that they killed Jesus. Rather, God the Mighty and Wise raised Jesus unto Himself."[17]

Despite the fact that the idea of the Messiah's sacrifice and his atonement for the sins of mankind with his own blood is undoubtedly beautiful and the writings it had inspired are worthy of poetical, moral, and psychological analysis, Islām founded itself upon the principle that moral guilt is non-transferable and that on the Day of Judgment justice shall be meted out to each according to his due. This fact rules out any logical rapprochement between the two doctrines. The *logique* of Islām is so precise on this matter and so clear and distinct that the difference between it and Christianity cannot be composed. The doctrine

of sacrificial atonement runs diametrically counter to that of
personal justice. "No father may bear the guilt of his son, and
no son may earn anything for his father."[18]

Byzantines and Muslims

Did any Christians at the time consider this new religion and
ponder the possibility of harmonizing its "unization"[19] of God
and their revelation of Jesus? Indeed! And many of them
joined it as a result. The Byzantines, however, whose victory the
Muslims had celebrated and regarded as the victory of the scriptural religions, did not take the trouble to investigate this new
religion. Rather, they looked at it from a political angle, and
worried about their dominion should the new religion carry the
day. They therefore began to attack it and its people and sent an
army of a hundred thousand soldiers (or of two hundred thousand according to another report) against it. This led to the
conquest of Tabūk by the Muslims and the retreat of the Byzantines in front of the army which rallied around Muhammad to
repulse the aggression with such power and determination as it
deserved.

Ever since then, Muslims and Christians have followed a policy of hostility towards each other; for many centuries victory
was on the side of the Muslims, enabling them to extend their
empire from Spain in the west to India and China in the east.
Most of the inhabitants of this empire joined the new faith and
adopted its Arabic language. When history came full cycle, the
Christians forced the Muslims from Spain, launched the Crusades against them, and began to attack their religion and
Prophet with falsehoods, lies, and forgeries. In their prejudice,
they forgot the great respect and honor accorded to Jesus—may
God's blessing be upon him—by Muhammad—may God's blessing be upon him—as the tradition has reported and the Qur'ān,
the revelation to Muhammad, has stated.

Christian Scholars and Muhammad

In presenting the views Christian scholars had of Muhammad
during the first half of the nineteenth century, the French *Ency-
clopédie Larousse* stated: "Muhammad remained in his moral
corruption and debauchery a camel thief, a cardinal who failed

to reach the throne of the papacy and win jt for himself. He therefore invented a new religion with which to avenge himself against his colleagues. Many fanciful and immoral tales dominated his mind and conduct. The *Life of Muhammad* by Bahomet is an example of this kind of literature. Other books on Muhammad, such as those published by Renault and François Michel in 1831, illustrate the idea of Muhammad prevalent in the Middle Ages. In the seventeenth century, Peel looked at the Qur'ān from a historian's point of view. But he refused to divulge his conclusions to his readers though he acknowledged that the ethical and social system of Muhammad does not differ from the Christian system except in the theory of punishment and polygamy."

Emil Dermenghem, the French writer, was one of the few orientalists who investigated the life of Muhammad with some objectivity. Quoting some of the writings of his colleagues, he wrote: "After the war between Islām and Christianity had been going on for centuries, the misunderstanding naturally increased and we are forced to admit the most serious ones were on the side of the Occidentals. Numerous were the Byzantine polemists who covered Islām with their contempt without taking the trouble to study it (with perhaps the exception of St. John of Damascus), as well as the writers and minstrels who fought the Saracens with only ridiculous calumnies. They portrayed Mahomet as a camel-thief, a rake, sorcerer, a brigand chief, and even as a Roman cardinal furious at not having been elected pope . . . they showed him as a false god to whom the faithful made human sacrifices.

"The worthy Guibert de Nogent himself tells us that he (Muhammad) died through excessive drunkenness and that his corpse was eaten by pigs on a dunghill, explaining why the flesh of this animal and wine are prohibited . . . .

"The opposition of the two religions had not, in the main, any more serious foundations than the affirmations of heroic songs portraying Mahomet, the iconoclast, as a golden-idol, and Mussulman mosques as pantheons filled with images! The *Song of Antioch* describes, as if the author had seen it, a massive idol, Mahom, in gold and silver enthroned on the mosaic seat of an elephant. The *Song of Roland,* which shows Charlemagne's horsemen throwing down Mussulman idols, tells us that the Saracens worshiped a Trinity composed of Termagant, Mahom and Apollo. The *Roman de Mahomet* asserts the Islām permitted polyandry . . . .

"Hate and prejudice were tenacious of life. From the time of Rudolph de Ludheim (620) until the present, Nicholas de Cuse, Vives, Maracci, Hottinger, Bibliander, Prideaux, etc. present Mohamet as an impostor, Islām as the cluster of all the heresies and the work of the devil, the Mussulmans as brutes, and the Koran as a tissue of absurdities. They declined to treat such a ridiculous subject seriously. However, Pierre le Vénérable, author of the first Occidental treatise against Islām, made a Latin translation of the Koran in the twelfth century. Innocent III once called Mahomet Antichrist, while in the Middle Ages he was nearly always merely looked upon as a heretic. Raymond Lull in the fourteenth century, Guillaume Postel in the sixteenth, Roland and Gagnier in the eigteenth, the Abbé de Broglie and Renan in the nineteenth give rather varied opinions. Voltaire, afterwards, amended in several places the hasty judgment expressed in his famous tragedy. Montesquieu, like Pascal and Malebranche, committed serious blunders on the religion, but his views of the manners and customs of the Mussulmans are well-considered and often reasonable. Le Comte de Boulainvilliers, Scholl, Caussin de Perceval, Dozy, Sprenger, Barthélemy, Saint-Hilaire de Castries, Carlyle, etc., are generally favorable to Islām and its Prophet and sometimes vindicate him. In 1876 Doughty nonetheless called Mahomet 'a dirty and perfidious nomad,' while in 1822 Foster declared that 'Mahomet was Daniel's little goat's horn while the Pope was the large one.' Islām still has many ardent detractors."[20]

What a nether world of degradation have the writers of the West sunk to! What chronic, centuries-old obstinacy to go astray and to stir hatred and hostility between men! Many of the aforementioned men belonged to the Age of Enlightenment, the century of science, of free thought and research, and of the establishment of brotherhood between man and man. Perhaps the gravity of this unfortunate chronicle is somewhat attenuated by the fact that a number of objective scholars, mentioned by Dermenghem, have accepted the truthfulness of Muhammad's faith in the message which God had revealed to him, have commended the spiritual and moral greatness of Muḥammad, his nobility and virtue, or have written about all these matters in literary and eloquent style. On the whole, however, the West continued to attack Islām and its prophet in the harshest possible terms. Indeed, western impertinence has gone so far as to spread Christian missionaries throughout the Muslim World, to urge them to dig their claws into its body, to dissuade the Muslims from their religion and to convert them to Christianity.

The Cause of Hostility between Islām and Christianity

We must search for the cause of this stormy hostility and fierce war which Christianity has been waging against Islām. We believe that western ignorance of the truth of Islām and of the life of its Prophet constitutes the first cause of this hostility. Without a doubt, ignorance is one of the most chronic causes of lethargy, conservatism and prejudice; and it is the most difficult to correct.

Ignorance and Fanaticism

This ignorance is centuries old. Over the years it has set up in the souls of generations idols of its own whose destruction will require a spiritual strength as great as that which characterized Islām when it first made its appearance. However, it is our opinion that there is yet another cause behind this fanaticism of the West and the terrible war it has waged and still wages against the Muslims, century after century. We are not here referring to political ambitions, or to the will of states to subjugate people for the purpose of exploiting them. In our opinion this is the result and not the cause of the fanaticism which goes beyond science and all its researches.

Christianity Does Not Accord with the Nature of Western Man

This deeper lying cause, we think, is the fact that Christianity—with its call for asceticism, other-worldliness, forgiveness, and the high personalist values—does not accord with the nature of western man whose religious life had for thousands of years been determined by polytheism and whose geographic position had imposed upon him the struggle against extreme cold and inclement nature. When historical circumstances brought about his Christianization, it was necessary for him to interpret it as a religion of struggle and to alter its tolerant and gentle nature. Thereby western man spoiled the spiritual sequence, completed by Islām, in which Christianity stood as a link in the chain. This spiritual continuum reconciles the claims of the body with those of the spirit; it synthesizes in harmony emotion and reason. It is a system which integrates the individual, indeed mankind, as a natural part of the cosmos and co-existent with it in its infinity of space and time. In our view, this spoiling is the cause of the fanaticism of the West *vis-à-vis* Islām and the cause of an attitude which Christian Abyssinia found beneath its dignity to adopt when the Muslims sought its protection at the beginning of the Prophet's career.

It is with reference to this cause that we can explain the exaggerated religiosity of western man as well as his extremist irreligiosity. For here too western fanatacism and hostility know neither tolerance nor temperance. Admittedly, history has known many saints among western men who in their lives have followed the example of Jesus and his disciples. But it cannot be denied that this same history affirms the life of the western people to be one of struggle, power, antagonism, and bloody war in the name of politics or religion. Nor can it be denied that the popes of the Church as well as the secular rulers have always engaged one another in strife: that one or the other was one day conqueror and the other vanquished. As secular power emerged victorious in the nineteenth century, it sought to stamp out the life of the spirit in the name of science, claiming that the latter should replace religious faith in human spirituality. Nowadays, after a long struggle, the West has come to realize its error and the impossibility of what it sought to achieve. Voices are now being heard from all sides demanding to regain the lost spirituality by looking for it in the new theosophic and other schools.[21] Had Christianity accorded with the instinct of strife which among westerners is the law of life, they would have realized the bankruptcy of materialism to furnish them with the needed spiritual power. They then would have returned to the noble Christian religion of Jesus, son of Mary, unless God were to guide them toward Islām. They would not have needed to emigrate to India and other places to obtain a necessary spiritual life. Such spirituality is of the essence of the religion of Jesus, indeed its very nature and being.

Colonialism and Christian Mission against Islām

Western colonialism helped the West to continue its war against Islām and Muḥammad. It encouraged the West to proclaim that Islām is the cause of the decadance of its adherents and their subjugation by others. Many western scholars still subscribe to this claim unaware that by doing so they cede the point to the Makkans who proclaimed thirteen centuries ago that Chritianity is responsible for the shameful defeat of Heraclius and Byzantium by Persia, as well as to anyone who wishes to make use of the argument to explain Christendom's retreat under the blows of the Muslims. One fact alone is sufficient to refute such an obvious piece of falsehood. That is the fact that the civilization of Islām was dominant in, and its people sovereign over, the whole known world for many centuries; that in the Muslim world arose greater men of science and knowledge who lived and worked in an atmosphere of freedom which the West was not to know until very recently. If it were at all possible to attribute to a religion the decay of its adherents, no such imputation is possible in the case of Islām which aroused the Bedouins of the Arabian Peninsula and enabled them to dominate the world.

Islām and the Present State of the Islāmic Peoples

Those who impute to Islām responsibility for the decay of the Islāmic peoples are partially right in the fact that there was added to the religion of God much which neither God nor His Prophet would have approved of. Such additions soon became integral to the religion, and whoever denied them was declared a heretic. Apart from the doctrine itself, let us take a close look at the biography of the Prophet of Islām—may God's blessing be upon him. Most of his biographies have narrated stories which no reason would accept and which no confirmation of Muḥammad's prophethood needed. It was from such additions that the western orientalists and critics of Islām, of its Prophet and of the Muslim peoples, drew their conclusions and formed their unjust and revolting attacks. After basing themselves on these incoherent assumptions, they launched further attacks and claimed for what they wrote the status of modern scientific research. The scientific method demands that events, people, and heroes be presented objectively, that the author's judgment be given only in light of the given evidence. The writings of these authors, however, were dictated by their passion for controversy and vituperation. They were aptly cast in expressions which deluded their co-religionists into believing that they were scientific, and that they were made in seeking after truth alone. Nonetheless, God did grant His peace to a number of contented souls, for among them there were men of letters, men of science, and other free thinkers who came closer to justice and fairness.

Conservatism and Ijtihād among the Muslims

A number of 'ulamā'[23] in different circumstances responded to the claims of these western fanatics. The name of Muḥammad 'Abduh shines most in this regard. But they have not observed the scientific method which the European writers and historians claim to have observed. Their argument would not have the same power as that of their opponents. Moreover, the same Muslim scholars—Muḥammad 'Abduh above all others—were accused of heresy and blasphemy—a fact which weakened their argument before the opponents of Islām. Such accusations as were directed at them left deep impressions in the hearts of educated Muslim youths. These young men felt that for a group of Muslim 'ulamā' adjudication by reason and logic amounts to heresy, that heresy is the twin of ijtihād, and that īmān[24] is the twin of conservatism. Hence their minds panicked, and they rushed to the books of the West seeking to learn the truth which they believed was not to be found in the books of Muslim authors. They did not at all consider the books of Christianity and of Christian history. Instead, they turned to the books of philosophy to quench their burning thirst for the truth. In western logic and scientific method they sought the light with which to illuminate their human souls, and the means by which to communicate with the universe. In the western products of pure philosophy, literature, and allied fields, these men found many great ideas by which they were deeply impressed. The methods of their presentation, the precision of their logic and their authors' candidness in the search for the truth added all the more to their attractiveness. That is why our youths' thinking was drawn away from all the religions in general and from the methods of Islām and its carriers in particular.

They were anxious not to stir a war with conservatism which they were not confident they could win, and they did not realize that spiritual intercourse with the universe is the necessary requisite of any human realization of perfection, of that moral power which is strong enough to withstand the storms.

Western Science and Literature

Our young men were thus drawn away from serious confrontation with the Islāmic message and its carriers. In this they were encouraged by what they observed of positive science and positivist philosophy, ruling for them that religious questions are not subject to logic, that they do not fall within the realm of scientific thinking, and that the metaphysical assumptions implied in those questions fall outside the realm of the scientific method. Our men have also observed the clear separation of state and church in the western countries. They learned that despite the fact that the constitutions of these countries prescribe that their kings are the protectors of Protestantism or Catholicism, or that the official religion of the state is Christianity, the Western states do not mean any more than to subscribe to the public observance of the feasts and other occasions of the Christian calendar. Hence they were encouraged to enter into this line of scientific thinking and to derive therefrom, as well as from the related philosophy, literature and art, all the inspiration possible. When the time came to transfer their attention from study to practical life, their occupations pulled them away further from those problems which they could not solve even at the time of their study. Their minds, therefore, continued to run in their original courses. They looked at conservatism with contempt and pity and drew their nourishment from the lifeline of western thought and philosophy. Remembering this lifeline as the source from which they obtained their nourishment in their youth, they continued to find therein their intellectual pleasure; their admiration for it was always growing.

Nevertheless, the Orient stands today in great need of learning from western thought, literature and art. The present of the Orient is separated from its past by centuries of lethargy and conservatism which have locked its old healthy mind in ignorance and suspicion of anything new. Anyone who seeks to dissolve this thick curtain must needs be assisted by the most modern thinking in the world if he is to forge anew the link between the live present and the great legacy of the past.

Efforts of Islāmic Reform

It is undeniable that we must acknowledge the worthy western achievements in Islāmic and Oriental studies. These have prepared the road for Muslims as well as Orientals to enter these fields of research with greater promise than was open to their western colleagues. The Muslims and Orientals are naturally closer to the spirit of Islām and the Orient which they are seeking to penetrate. As long as the new leadership in this field has come from the West, it is the Muslim's and Oriental's duty to look into the products of the West, to correct their mistakes, and to give to the discipline the proper orientation which will re-establish the unity of the old and the new. This should not be done merely on paper, for it is a living legacy, spiritual and mental, which the heirs ought to represent to themselves, to add thereto, and to illumine with their own vision and understanding of the central realities.

Many of our young men have succeeded in their undertaking of scientific researches on these lines. The orientalists have often appreciated their work and complimented them on their contributions to scholarship.

Western Missionaries and Muslim Conservatives

Scientific cooperation in Islāmics between Muslim and Oriental scholars on one hand, and western scholars on the others, is worthy of great promise. Although it has just begun to make progress, we yet notice that the Christian missionaries continue their attacks against Islām and Muḥammad with the same ferocity as their predecessors to whom we have alluded earlier. In this they are encouraged and supported by the western colonialist powers in the name of freedom of opinion. These very missionaries were themselves thrown out of their countries by their own governments because they were not trusted by them to implant true faith in the hearts of their own co-religionists at home.[25] Moreover this colonialism assists the leaders of conservatism among the Muslims. Colonialism in fact has brought about a coalescence of the two tendencies; on the one hand it confirms the infusion of Islām with that which is not Islāmic, such as the irrational and unrefined superstitions added to the life of the Prophet; on the other hand, it confirms the antagonists of Islām in their attacks against these forgeries.

The Idea and Plan of This Book

The circumstances of my life have enabled me to observe all these maneuvers in the various countries of the Islāmic East, indeed throughout the Muslim World, and to discover their final purpose. The objective of colonialism is to destroy in these countries the freedom of opinion, the freedom to seek the truth. I have come to feel that I stand under the duty to foil these maneuvers and spoil their purpose, for they are certainly harmful to the whole of mankind, not only to Islām and the Orient. What greater damage could befall humanity than to have its greater half, the half which has throughout history been the carrier of civilization, to wallow in sterility and conservatism? It was this consideration which led me at the end of the road of life to the study of the life of Muḥammad, the carrier of the message of Islām and the target of Christian attacks on one side and of Muslim conservatives on the other. But I have resolved that this will be a scientific study, developed on the western modern method, and written for the sake of truth alone.

I began to study the history of Muḥammad and to look more closely into the *Sīrah* of Ibn Hishām, the *Tabaqāt* of Ibn Saʻd, the *Maghāzi* of Wāqidī, and *the Spirit of Islam* of Sayyid Ameer Ali. Then I took care to study what some orientalists have written on the subject such as the work of Dermenghem, and also that of Washington Irving. The winter of 1932 at Luxor provided me with the occasion to begin my writing. At that time I was quite hesitant to publish my thoughts because I feared the storm which the conservatives and their followers who believe in superstitions might raise. But I was encouraged by a number of professors in the Islāmic institutions of learning, many of whom took such care in studying my writing and making pertinent observations on it that I resolved to follow my scientific treatment of the life of Muḥammad to a conclusion. It was the encouragement of these men that stirred me to search for the best means by which to analyze the biography of the Prophet.

The Qur'ān as the Most Reliable Source

I discovered that the most reliable source of information for the biography of Muḥammad is the Holy Qur'ān. It contains a reference to every event in the life of the Arab Prophet which can serve the investigator as a standard norm and as a guiding

light in his analysis of the reports of the various biographies and
of the *Sunnah*. As I sought to understand all the Qur'ānic references to the life of the Prophet, Professor Aḥmad Luṭfī al
Sayyid, of Dār al Kutub al Miṣriyyah, offered me great assistance by letting me use a topically arranged collection of all the
verses of the Qur'ān. While analyzing these verses, I began to
realize that it was necessary to discover the causes and occasions
of their revelation. I acknowledge that despite all the effort I
put in that direction I was not always successful. The books of
exegesis sometimes refer to these relations but often overlook
them. Al Wāḥidī's *Asbāb al Nuzūl*, and Ibn Salāmah's *al Nāsikh
Wa al Mansūkh* treat this matter very precisely but, unfortunately, very briefly. In these as well as other books of exegesis,
I discovered many facts which helped me in my analysis of the
claims various biographies have made as well as the many other
facts worthy of being considered and investigated by all scholars
of the Qur'ān and *Sunnah*.

Candid Advice

As my research progressed I found candid advice coming to me
from all directions, especially from the professors of Islām and
the learned men of religion. Dār al Kutub al Miṣriyyah and its
officers were responsible for the greatest assistance. No expression of appreciation of their work is adequate. Suffice it here to
mention that, encouraged by his director and other senior officers, Professor 'Abd al Raḥīm Maḥmūd, Editor in the Division
of Literature, used often to save me from great trouble by borrowing for me all the needed books. Whenever I did manage to
go to Dār al Kutub, all the employees were delightfully ready to
assist me in my search. Some of these men were personally
known to me and others were not. I referred many a question
which was opaque or presented difficulties to those of my friends
whom I knew would shed some light thereon; and more often
than not the confusion or opaqueness was cleared. This was many
times the case with the Grand Shaykh Muḥammad Muṣṭafā al
Marāghī, along with my expert friend, Ja'far Pasha Waliy, who
lent me several of his books, such as the *Ṣaḥīḥ of Muslim* and the
histories of Makkah, and who guided me in many problems.
Makram 'Ubayd Pasha, another 'friend of mine, lent me Sir
William Muir's *The life of Muḥammad* and Father Lammens's
Islam. This valuable assistance is all in addition to that which I

found in the writings of the contemporary authors such as *Fajr al Islām* by Aḥmad Amīn, *Qiṣaṣ al Anbiyā'* by 'Abd al Wahhāb al Najjār, *Fī al Adab al Jāhilī* by Ṭaha Ḥusayn, *The Jews in Arabia* by Israel Wolfenson, and many other contemporary works mentioned in my list of old and new references used in the preparation of this book.

As I progressed in my research more and more complicated problems emerged which overtaxed my powers. Throughout, the biographies of Muḥammad and the books of exegeses as well as the works of the orientalists have assisted me in achieving a measure of certainty of purpose. I found myself compelled to limit my investigation to the events in the life of Muḥammad and to refrain from tackling a number of side issues connected therewith. Had I allowed myself to indulge in the discussion of all these problems, I would have needed to write many volumes of this size or larger. Let me mention in passing that Caussin de Perceval wrote three volumes under the title *Study in Arab History*, of which he devoted the first two to the history and life of the Arab tribes and the third to the history of Muḥammad and his first two successors, Abū Bakr and 'Umar. Likewise, the *Ṭabaqāt of Ibn Saʻd* devoted one of its many volumes to the life of Muḥammad and all the others to the lives of his companions. My purpose in this work has never gone beyond the investigation of the life of Muḥammad itself; therefore, I did not allow myself the liberty to investigate the other problems involved.

Restriction to the Life of Muḥammad

Another consideration restricted me to the frontiers of the life of Muḥammad—the greatness, majesty, and brilliance which make his life unique among all others. How great was Abū Bakr! And how great was 'Umar! Each was a great sun eclipsing all others around him. How great, too, were the first Muslims, the companions of Muḥammad, who are remembered from generation to generation with the greatest pride. All these men, however, stood beneath Muḥammad, reflecting his light and his glory. It is not easy therefore for the investigator to restrict himself to the life of Muḥammad alone. This is all the more so if the investigation is to follow the modern scientific method, and thereby present the greatness of that life with all its strength and moving appeal in a manner which both Muslims and non-Muslims may accept and admire.

If we were to disregard those foolish fanatics, such as the missionaries and their like, whose purpose never goes beyond vituperation of Muhammad, we could still find a clear and distinct respect for greatness in the life of Muhammad in the works of the western orientalists. In his *On Heroes and Hero Worship*, Thomas Carlyle devoted a chapter to Muhammad in which he described the revelation of Muhammad as issuing from a spark that is divine and holy. He understood Muhammad's greatness and portrayed it in its whole strength. Likewise, Muir, Irving, Sprenger, and Weil, among other orientalists, eloquently described the greatness of Muhammad. A lack of vision, penetration, and critical skill prevented some of them from regarding one point or another of Muhammad's life as other than blameworthy. It is probable that they had relied in their investigation on unreliable biographies and books of exegesis of the Prophet, forgetting that the earliest biography was not written down until two centuries after Muhammad's death, and that during this time a great number of Israelitisms and other forgeries were forced into his biography and into his teachings. Generally, western orientalists acknowledge this fact even though they attribute to the Prophet materials which the least investigation would reject as superfluous. The cases of the goddesses of Makkah, of Zayd and Zaynab, of the wives of the Prophet, constitute examples of such superfluous materials as I have had the occasion to investigate in this book.

This Book as Mere Beginning of Research

No one should think that research in the life of Muhammad is completed with this work. It is closer to the truth for me to say that my work is really only the beginning of scientific research in this field in Arabic and that all my efforts in this regard do not make my work any more than a mere beginning in the scientific as well as Islāmic undertaking of this grave subject. As many scholars have devoted all their energies to the study of one period of history, even as Aulard has specialized in the study of the French Revolution, some scholars and historians ought to devote themselves to the study of the Age of Muhammad. The life of Muhammad is certainly worthy of being studied in a scientific and academic manner by more than one specialist or by more than one competent scholar. I have no doubt that any efforts spent on such scientific study of this brief period in the history of Arabia and on investigating the relations of Arabia to other countries during that age will prove beneficial to mankind as a whole, not merely to Islām or the Muslims. Such a study will clear many psychological and spiritual problems and prepare them for scholarly research. It will shed great light on the social moral and legislative life of Arabia and thus illuminate areas which so far science has been unable to penetrate on account of the religious conflict between Islām and Christianity. Such a study would dissipate the futile attempt at westernizing the Orientals or Christianizing the Muslims in a way that history has proven to be impossible and harmful to the relations of the various parts of mankind with one another.

Universal Benefits of the Study

Indeed, I would even go further. I would assert that such a study may show the road to mankind as a whole to the new civilization to which it is currently groping. If western Christendom is too proud to find the new light in Islām and in its Prophet but willingly accepts it from Indian theosophy and other religions of the Far East, then it devolves upon the Orientals themselves, Muslims, Jews or Christians, to undertake this study in all objectivity and fairness in order to reach and establish the truth. Islāmic thought rests on a methodology that is scientific and modern as regards all that relates man to nature. In this respect it is perfectly realistic. But it becomes personalist the moment it leaves nature to consider the relationship of man to the cosmos as a whole and to his creator. Moreover, in the psychological and spiritual fields Islāmic thought made contributions which science has not yet been able either to confirm or to deny. Although science may not regard these discoveries as facts in the scientific sense of the terms, they still remain the constituents of man's happiness and the determinants of his conduct in the world. What then is life? And what is man's relation to this world? How shall we explain his concern for life? What is the common faith which inspires human groups and by which their morale is raised to high pitch or dissolved? What is being? And what is the unity of being? What is the place of man in this being and in its unity? These are problems of metaphysics and a whole literature has arisen around them. Answers far nearer human understanding and implementation than are usually found in the literature of metaphysics are found in the life of Muḥammad and his teachings. Ever since the 'Abbāsī period, Muslim thinkers have spent centuries looking for metaphysical answers.

lvi   THE LIFE OF MUHAMMAD

Likewise western thinkers have spent three centuries, from the
sixteenth through the nineteenth, to lead the West to modern
science in the same manner as the Muslims have done in the past.
Once more, science stands today as it stood in the past as failing
to realize human happiness on earth. Such happiness is impossible to realize unless we resume research for a correct understanding of the personal relationship of man to the cosmos and
to the creator of the cosmos, and unless such understanding is
sought on the basis of a divine unity, which is eternal and immutable, and with regard to space and time in relation to our short
life. The life of Muhammad provides us with the best example of
personalist communion with being as well as the best materials
for a scientific study of this relationship. The same materials
may equally be the object of practical study for those who are
endowed therefore but naturally removed from achieving such
communion with God as the Prophet had achieved. It is most
likely that the scientific study, and the practical study, if felic-
itously undertaken, may yet shake our world loose from the
paganism into which it has fallen in spite of its religious creeds
and scientific doctrines. It may yet save the world from its present monolatry of wealth that has made all science, art, and ethics
its servants and conscripted all man's powers to do its bidding
and sing its praises. Such hopes may still be far from realization.
However, the beginning of the end of this all-embracing paganism of modern times is clearly distinguishable under close
observance of the current flow of events. Perhaps, these humble
beginnings will grow and become surer of themselves when
scholarship has found answers to these spiritual problems
through the study of the life of Muhammad, of his teachings,
of his age, and of the spiritual world revolution which he
incepted. Should such scientific and scholarly research uncover
for man his stronger bonds with the higher reality of the world,
it would have then provided the new civilization with its first
foundation.

As I said already, this book is only a mere beginning on this
road. It will prove sufficient reward for me if it should succeed
in convincing the reader of the validity of its assertions, and the
scholars and researchers of the need for dedication and special-
ization if the final end of the study is to be reached. God will
surely reward the good doers.

Muhammad Husayn Haykal

Preface to the
Second Edition

The speed with which the first edition of this work was exhausted has exceeded all expectations. Ten thousand copies were printed of which one-third were sold before the book came off the press. The remaining copies were sold during the first three months following its publication. If this is any indication, the reader must have been quite interested in its contents. A second printing, therefore, is as imperative as the reconsideration of those contents.

An Observation

Without a doubt, the title of the book attracted the reader most. The attraction may also have been due to the method with which the subject was treated. Whatever the reason, the thought of a second edition has occasioned the question of whether or not I should allow the book to be reprinted without change or have it corrected, considering that a need for correction, clarification, or addition has in the meantime seemed to me evident. Some, whose counsel I certainly value, have advised me to make the second edition an exact copy of the first in order to achieve equality between the earlier and later buyers and to allow myself longer time for revision thereafter. This view almost convinced me. Had I followed it, this second edition would have been put in the hands of the readers many months ago. But I hesitated to accept this advice and finally decided in favor of revisions which many considerations had made necessary. The first of such considerations concerned a number of observations which Muḥammad Musṭafā al Marāghī, Grand Shaykh of al Azhar, had kindly made when he read the first parts of the book as they came from the press, and kindly decided to write the foreword. When the book made its appearance, a number of 'ulamā' and other scholars spoke and wrote about it. Their observations were all preceded by numerous compliments for the achievement of this work, indeed more than the book actually deserved. These observations were based upon the understanding that a book about the Arab Prophet, which is so well written that it has won their approval and appreciation, ought to be absolutely free of all shortcomings. It is therefore necessary for me to take them into account and give them the consideration due.

It was perhaps this very approval and appreciation of the readers which moved them to make observations on incidental matters related neither to the essence of the book nor to its main themes. Some of them, for instance, pleaded for further clarification of certain points. Others called for closer scrutiny of my use of prepositions. Still others suggested different words better to express the meanings I intended. A number of them did focus on the themes of the book and therefore caused me to review what I have written. I certainly wish that this second edition will come closer to satisfying all these writers and scholars. All this notwithstanding, I still believe that this book provides no more than a mere beginning in the Arabic language of such studies using the modern scientific method.

A further consideration caused me to review the first edition. Having read the many observations made, most of which were not new, I became convinced as I read my work again that I ought to add, where relevant, a discussion of the points to which the observations referred in order at least to convince their authors of my point of view and of the veracity of my arguments. My reconsideration of some of these points opened new vistas which any student of the biography of the Arab Prophet will have to study. Although I am proud that the first edition did in fact deal with the points raised in the reviews, I am more proud yet today to present to the reader this second edition in which the same points have been treated more fully. No study, however, can be full or perfect which undertakes the investigation of the life of the greatest man history has known—the Seal of the Prophets and of the Messengers from on high—may God's peace and blessing be upon him.

In this edition, I have tried to address myself to a number of observations made regarding my method of investigation. I have added to the book two new chapters in which I have dealt with matters which have been only slightly referred to toward the end of the preface of the first edition. I have also re-edited the work wherever it needed editing, and added to its various sections and paragraphs such points as my rethinking has made necessary.

Answering the Followers of Western Orientalists

I want first to address myself to a letter I received from an Egyptian writer. He claimed that his letter is an Arabic translation of an article he wrote for a German Orientalist magazine in criticism of this book. I have not published this letter in the Arabic press because it contains many unfounded attacks; and I thought that its author had better bear the responsibility of publishing it if he wished to. Nor will I mention his name here because I believe he will repudiate his old views when he reads the critical analysis that follows. The substance of the letter is that my *The Life of Muḥammad* is not a scientific one in the modern sense. He argues that I have depended upon Arabic sources alone and have not consulted the studies of German orientalists such as Weil, Goldziher, Nöldeke, and others, and have not adopted their conclusions. The letter also blames me for regarding the Qur'ān as a certain historical document, whereas the investigations of the foregoing orientalists have proven that it has been tampered with and been changed after the death of Muḥammad in the first century A.H. It reported that these investigations have discovered that the name of the Prophet is a case in point; that having once been "Qutham" or "Quthāmah," it was later changed to "Muḥammad" in order to accord with the verse, "Jesus said: O Children of Israel, I am the Prophet of God sent to you to confirm the scripture that is already in my hand and to announce to you the advent of a prophet after me whose name shall be Aḥmad."[1] This fabrication was deemed desirable in order to forge a link between the Prophet and the Evangel's announcement of a prophet coming after Jesus. Moreover, the letter added, the researches of the orientalists have revealed that the Prophet suffered from epilepsy, that his so-called revelations were really effects of his epileptic attacks; that the symptoms of epilepsy—loss of consciousness, perspiration, convulsion, foam around the mouth—were all apparent in his

case. It was after he recovered from these fits that he claimed
that the revelation had come to him, recited it to the believers,
and claimed that it had come from God.

By itself, this letter is not worthy of attention or investigation.
Its author, however, is a Muslim and an Egyptian. Had he been
an orientalist or a missionary, I would have let him alone to rave
as he pleased. What I have said in the preface to the first edition
in this regard is sufficient refutation for such people and views.
The author of this letter, however, is an example of a class of
young Muslims who are too ready to accept what the orientalists
say and regard it as true knowledge. It is precisely to this class
of people that I want now to address myself and warn them of
the errors in which the orientalists fall. Some of these orientalists are candid and scholarly despite their errors. Error nonetheless finds its way into their conclusions either because of their
lack of mastery of the nuances of the Arabic language, or of their
prejudice against religion as such, or Islām in particular, which,
in turn, conditions them to seek to destroy the fundamental basis
of religion. Both shortcomings are unworthy of scholars and it
behooves them to seek a remedy therefor. We have seen Christian
thinkers who, moved by this same antagonism, denied that Jesus
ever existed in history; and we have seen others who have gone
further and have even written about the madness of Jesus. The
western thinker's innate antagonism to religion was generated
by the struggle between the Church and the state and this led
both the men of science and the men of religion to pull in different directions in order to wrench power from the other side and
seize it for themselves. Islām, on the other hand, is free of such
strife; Muslim scholars, therefore, should not be affected by it as
their western colleagues have been. In most cases, to fall under
such a complexus would vitiate the research. Muslim readers
therefore, should watch out more carefully when they read a
religious study by a westerner. They should scrutinize every
claim these studies make for the truth. A large measure of their
researches are deeply affected by this past strife which the men of
religion and the men of science had waged against one another
during long centuries.

Dependence upon the Muslim Biographers

The case of the letter from the Egyptian Muslim colleague
clearly points to the need for such care. His first criticism con-

cerned my dependence upon Arabic and Islāmic sources. Of course this is not denied. But I have also consulted the books of the orientalists mentioned in my list of references. The Arabic sources, however, constituted my primary sources as they constituted the primary sources for orientalists before me. That is natural. For these sources, and the Qur'ān above all, were the first ones ever to discuss the life of the Arab Prophet. There is nothing objectionable if such early historical documents are taken as primary sources for any modern and scientific biographical study of the Prophet. Nöldeke, Goldziher, Weil, Sprenger, Muir, and other orientalists have all taken the same works as primary sources for their studies, just as I have done. I have also allowed myself as much liberty in scrutinizing the reports of these works as they did. And I have also not omitted to consult some of the early Christian books which the orientalists had consulted despite the fact that they were products of Christian fanaticism rather than of scholarly research and criticism. If anybody were to criticize my work on the grounds that I have allowed myself to differ from some orientalists and have arrived at conclusions other than their own, he would in fact be calling for intellectual stagnation—a conservatism not less reactionary or retrogressive than any other conservatism we have known. It is unlikely that any of the orientalists themselves agree with such call; for to do so implies approval of religious stagnation. Neither for me nor for any scholarly student of history is such a stand viable. Rather, I should ask myself, as well as any other scholar, to scutinize the work of his colleagues. Unless he is convinced by clear evidence and incontestable proofs, he should seek other ways to the truth. To this task I call those of us, particularly the youth, who admire the researches of the Orientalists. This has also been my task. Mine is the reward where I have in fact arrived at the truth; and mine is the apology where I have erred despite my good intentions.

The Orientalists and the Bases of Religion

The aforesaid Muslim Egyptian's letter gives evidence of the western orientalists' extreme care to destroy the basis of religion. They claim that their researches have established that the Qur'ān is not a historical document devoid of doubt but that it has been tampered with and edited, and many verses added to it for religious or political ulterior purposes in the first century after

the death of the Prophet of Islām. I am not questioning the
author of the letter from an Islāmic point of view but arguing
with him, as it were, as a fellow Muslim, the veracity or otherwise of the Islāmic conviction that the Qur'ān is the work of
God and that it is impossible for it to be forged. The stand from
which he wrote his letter is clearly that of the orientalists who
hold that the Qur'ān is a book written by Muḥammad. According to a number of orientalists, Muḥammad wrote the Qur'ān
in the belief that it was God's revelation to him; according to
others, Muḥammad claimed that the Qur'ān was the revelation
of God merely in order to prove the genuineness of his message.
Let me then address the author of this letter in his own language
assuming that he is one of those free thinkers who refuse to be
convinced except by scientific, apodeictic proof.

The False Charge of Forgery

Our young author depends upon the western orientalists and
their views. A number of these do think of the Qur'ān in the
manner this young author exemplified. Their claim is based upon
flagrant motives which stand at the farthest possible remove
from science and the scientific method. Suffice it to expose the
incoherence of their arguments that the phrase, "and announcing the advent of a prophet after me whose name shall be
Ahmad"[2] was added to the Qur'ān after the death of the
Prophet in order to establish proof of Muḥammad's prophethood based upon the scriptures preceding the Qur'ān. Had
these orientalists who make this claim truly sought to serve the
purpose of science, they would not have recoursed to this cheap
propaganda that the Torah and the Evangel are truly revealed
books. Had they honored science for its own sake, they would
have treated the Qur'ān on a par with the scriptures antecedent
to it. Either they would have regarded the Qur'ān as sacred
as these scriptures—in which case it would have been natural
for it to refer to its antecedents—or, they would have regarded
all these books as they did the Qur'ān and imputed to them the
same kind of doubtful nature as they did to it, holding as well
their authors to have forged or written them in satisfaction of
ulterior religious or political purposes. Had the orientalists held
such a view, logic would rule out their claim that the Qur'ān
had been tampered with and forged for political and religious
purposes. It is inadmissible that the Muslims would have sought
such confirmation of Muḥammad's claim to prophethood from

these scriptures after Muslim dominion had been established, the Christian empire vanquished, so many other peoples of the earth subjugated and, indeed, after the Christians themselves had entered into Islām *en masse*. The inadmissibility of these orientalists' claims is demanded by genuine scientific thought. Furthermore, the claim that the Torah and the Evangel are sacred whereas the Qur'ān is not is devoid of scientific support. Therefore, the claim that the Qur'ān had been tampered with and forged in order to seek confirmation of Muḥammad's prophethood on the basis of the Torah and the Evangel is a piece of sheer nonsense unacceptable to either logic or history.

Those western orientalists who have made this false claim are very few and belong to the more fanatic group. The majority of them do believe that the Qur'ān which is in our hands today is precisely the Qur'ān which Muḥammad had recited to the Muslims during his lifetime; that it has neither been tampered with nor forged. They admit this explicitly in their writings while criticizing the method by which the verses of the Qur'ān were collected and its chapters arranged—a matter of discussion which does not belong here. The Muslim students of the Qur'ān did in fact study these criticisms and exposed their errors. As for our purpose here, suffice it to look at some orientalists' writing on this subject. Perhaps our young Muslim Egyptian author would thereby be convinced and, perhaps, he would convince those of his fellows who think like him.

Muir Rejects the Forgery of the Qur'ān

The orientalists have written a great deal on this subject. We can select a passage by Sir William Muir from his book, *The Life of Mahomet*, in the hope that those who claim that the Qur'ān has been forged will realize wherein they have erred, to the detriment of both the truth and their own scholarship. It should be remembered that our author, Muir, is a Christian, an *engagé* and proud Christian, as well as a missionary who never misses occasion to criticize the Prophet of Islām or its scripture.

When he came to speak of the Qur'ān and the veracity and precision of its text, he wrote:

"The divine revelation was the corner-stone of Islam. The recital of a passage from it formed an essential part of daily prayer public and private; and its perusal and repeti-

tion were enforced as a duty and a privilege fraught with
religious merit. This is the universal voice of early tradition,
and may be gathered also from the revelation itself. The
Coran was accordingly committed to memory more or less
by every adherent of Islam, and the extent to which it could
be recited was one of the chief distinctions of nobility in
the early Moslem empire. The custom of Arabia favoured
the task. Passionately fond of poetry, yet possessed of but
limited means and skill in committing to writing the effu-
sions of their bards, the Arabs had long been habituated to
imprint these, as well as the tradition of genealogical and
other tribal events, on the living tablets of their hearts.
The recollective faculty was thus cultivated to the highest
pitch; and it was applied, with all the ardour of an awakened
spirit, to the Coran. Such was the tenacity of their memory,
and so great their power of application, that several of
Mahomet's followers, according to early tradition, could,
during his life-time, repeat with scrupulous accuracy the
entire revelation.

·   ·   ·   ·   ·   ·

"However retentive the Arab memory, we should still have
regarded with distrust a transcript made entirely from that
source. But there is good reason for believing that many
fragmentary copies, embracing amongst them the whole
Coran, or nearly the whole, were made by Mahomet's followers during his life. Writing was without doubt generally
known at Mecca long before Mahomet assumed the propheti-
cal office. Many of his followers are expressly mentioned as
employed by the Prophet at Medina in writing his letters or
despatches . . . Some of the poorer Meccan captives taken
at Bedr were offered their release on condition that they
would teach a certain number of the ignorant citizens of
Medina to write. And although the people of Medina were
not so generally educated as those of Mecca, yet many are
distinctly noticed as having been able to write before Islam.
The ability thus existing, it may be safely inferred that the
verses which were so indefatigably committed to memory,
would be likewise committed carefully to writing.

"We also know that when a tribe first joined Islam,
Mahomet was in the habit of deputing one or more of his
followers to teach them the Coran and the requirements of

the faith. We are frequently informed that they carried written instructions with them on the latter point, and they would naturally provide themselves also with transcripts of the more important parts of the Revelation, especially those upon which the ceremonies of Islam were founded, and such as were usually recited at the public prayers. Besides the reference in the Coran to its own existence in a written form, we have express mention made in the authentic traditions of Omar's conversion, of a copy of the 20th Sura being used by his sister's family for social and private devotional reading. This refers to a period preceding, by three or four years, the emigration to Medina. If transcripts of the revelations were made, and in common use, at that early time when the followers of Islam were few and oppressed, it is certain that they must have multiplied exceedingly when the Prophet came to power, and his Book formed the law of the greater part of Arabia.

.   .   .   .

"Such was the condition of the text of the Coran during Mahomet's life-time, and such it remained for about a year after his death, imprinted upon the hearts of his people, and fragmentary transcripts increasing daily. The two sources would correspond closely with each other; for the Coran, even while the Prophet was yet alive, was regarded with a superstitious awe as containing the very words of God; so that any variations would be reconciled by a direct reference to Mahomet himself, and after his death to the originals where they existed, or copies from the same, and to the memory of the Prophet's confidential friends and amanuenses.

"It was not till the overthrow of Moseilama, when a great carnage took place amongst the Moslems at Yemama, and large numbers of the best reciters of the Coran were slain, that a misgiving arose in Omar's mind as to the uncertainty which would be experienced regarding the text, when all those who had received it from the original source, and thence stored it in their memories, should have passed away. 'I fear,' said he, addressing the Caliph Abu Bakr, 'that slaughter may again wax hot amongst the reciters of the Coran, in other fields of battle; and that much may be lost therefrom. Now, therefore, my advice is, that thou shouldest

give speedy orders for the collection of the Coran.' Abu
Bakr agreed, and thus made known his wishes to Zeid ibn
Thabit, a citizen of Medina, and the Prophet's chief aman-
uensis: 'Thou art a young man, and wise; against whom
no one amongst us can cast an imputation; and thou wert
wont to write down the inspired revelations of the Prophet
of the Lord. Wherefore now search out the Coran, and
bring it together.' So new and unexpected was the enter-
prise that Zeid at first shrank from it, and doubted the
propriety, or even lawfulness, of attempting that which
Mahomet had neither himself done nor commanded to be
done. At last he yielded to the joint entreaties of Abu Bakr
and Omar, and seeking out the fragments of the Coran from
every quarter, 'gathered it together, from dateleaves, and
tablets of white stone, and from the breasts of men.' By
the labours of Zeid, these scattered and confused materials
were reduced to the order and sequence in which we now
find them, and in which it is said that Zeid used to repeat
the Coran in the presence of Mahomet. The original copy
prepared by Zeid was probably kept by Abu Bakr during
the short remainder of his reign. It then came into the possession of Omar who . . . committed it to the custody of
his daughter Haphsa, the Prophet's widow. The compilation
of Zeid, as embodied in this exemplar, continued during
Omar's ten years' Caliphate to be the standard and authori-
tative text.

"But variety of expression either prevailed in the previous
transcripts and modes of recitation, or soon crept into the
copies which were made from Zeid's edition. Mussulmans
were scandalised. The Coran sent down from heaven was
ONE, but where was now its unity? Hodzeifa, who had
warred both in Armenia and Adzerbaijan and had observed
the different readings of the Syrians and of the men of Irac,
alarmed at the number and extent of the variations, warned
Othman to interpose, and 'stop the people, before they should
differ regarding their Scripture, as did the Jews and Christians.' The Caliph was persuaded, and to remedy the evil
had recourse again to Zeid, with whom he associated a
syndicate of three Coreish. The original copy of the first
edition was obtained from Haphsa's depository, the various
readings were sought out from the different provinces, and
a careful recension of the whole set on foot. In case of dif-

ference between Zeid and his coadjutors, the voice of the latter, as conclusive of the Coreishite idiom, was to preponderate; and the new collation was thus assimilated exclusively to the Meccan dialect, in which the Prophet had given utterance to his inspiration. Transcripts were multiplied and forwarded to the chief cities in the empire, and the previously existing copies were all, by the Caliph's command, committed to the flames. The old original was returned to Haphsa's custody.

"The recension of Othman had been handed down to us unaltered. So carefully, indeed, has it been preserved, that there are no variations of importance—we might almost say no variations at all—among the innumerable copies of the Coran scattered throughout the vast bounds of the empire of Islam. Contending and embittered factions, taking their rise in the murder of Othman himself within a quarter of a century from the death of Mahomet, have ever since rent the Mahometan world. Yet but ONE CORAN has been current amongst them; and the consentaneous use by them all in every age up to the present day of the same Scripture, is an irrefragable proof that we have now before us the very text prepared by command of the unfortunate Caliph. There is probably in the world no other work which has remained twelve centuries with so pure a text. The various readings are wonderfully few in number, and are chiefly confined to differences in the vowel points and diacritical signs. But these marks were invented at a later date. They did not exist at all in the early copies, and can hardly be said to affect the text of Othman.

"Since, then, we possess the undoubted text of Othman's recension, it remains to be enquired whether that text was an honest reproduction of Abu Bakr's edition, with the simple reconcilement of unimportant variations. There is the fullest ground for believing that it was so. No early or trustworthy traditions throw suspicion upon Othman of tampering with the Coran in order to support his own claims. The Sheeahs of later times, indeed, pretend that Othman left out certain Suras or passages which favoured Ali. But this is incredible. . . .

"When Othman's edition was prepared, no open breach had taken place between the Omeyads and the Alyites. The unity of Islam was still complete and unthreatened. Ali's pretensions were as yet undeveloped. No sufficient object can, therefore, be assigned for the perpetration by Othman of an offence which Moslems regard as one of the blackest dye . . . At the time of the recension, there were still multitudes alive who had the Coran, as originally delivered, by heart; and of the supposed passages favouring Ali—had any ever existed—there would have been numerous transcripts in the hands of his family and followers. Both of these sources must have proved an effectual check upon any attempt at suppression. Fourth: The party of Ali shortly after assumed an independent attitude, and he himself succeeded to the Caliphate. Is it conceivable that either Ali, or his party, when thus arrived at power, would have tolerated a mutilated Coran—mutilated expressly to destroy his claims? Yet we find that they used the same Coran as their opponents, and raised no shadow of an objection against it. The insurgents are indeed said to have made it one of their complaints against Othman that he had caused a new edition to be made, and had committed the old copies of the sacred volume to the flames; but these proceedings were objected to simply as unauthorised and sacrilegious. No hint was dropped of alteration or omission. Such a supposition, palpably absurd at the time, is altogether an after-thought of the modern Sheeas.

"We may then safely conclude that Othman's recension was, what it professed to be, namely, the reproduction of Abu Bakr's edition, with a more perfect conformity to the dialect of Mecca, and possibly a more uniform arrangement of the component parts—but still a faithful reproduction. The most important question yet remains, viz., Whether Abu Bakr's edition was itself an authentic and complete collection of Mahomet's Revelations. The following considerations warrant the belief that it was authentic and in the main as complete as at the time was possible.

"First.—We have no reason to doubt that Abu Bakr was a sincere follower of Mahomet, and an earnest believer in the divine origin of the Coran. His faithful attachment to the Prophet's person, conspicuous for the last twenty years of his life, and his simple, consistent, and unambitious deportment as Caliph, admit no other supposition. Firmly believing the revelations of his friend to be the revelations of God himself, his first object would be to secure a pure and complete transcript of them. A similar argument applies with almost equal force to Omar and the other agents in the revision. The great mass of Mussulmans were undoubtedly sincere in their belief. From the scribes themselves, employed in the compilation, down to the humblest Believer who brought his little store of writing on stones or palm-leaves, all would be influenced by the same earnest desire to reproduce the very words which their Prophet had declared as his message from the Lord. And a similar guarantee existed in the feelings of the people at large, in whose soul no principle was more deeply rooted than an awful reverence for the supposed word of God. The Coran itself contains frequent denunciations against those who should presume to 'fabricate anything in the name of the Lord,' or conceal any part of that which He had revealed. Such an action, represented as the very worst description of crime, we cannot believe that the first Moslems, in the early ardour of their faith and love, would have dared to contemplate.

"Second.—The compilation was made within two years of Mahomet's death. We have seen that several of his followers had the entire revelation . . . by heart; that every Moslem treasured up more or less some portions in his memory; and that there were official Reciters of it, for public worship and tuition, in all countries to which Islam extended. These formed a living link between the Revelation fresh from Mahomet's lips, and the edition of it by Zeid. Thus the people were not only sincere and fervent in wishing for a faithful copy of the Coran: they were also in possession of ample means for realising their desire, and for testing the accuracy and completeness of the volume placed in their hands by Abu Bakr.

"Third.—A still greater security would be obtained from the fragmentary transcripts which existed in Mahomet's life-time, and which must have greatly multiplied before the Coran was compiled. These were in the possession, probably, of all who could read. And as we know that the compilation of Abu Bakr came into immediate and unquestioned use, it is reasonable to conclude that it embraced and corresponded with every extant fragment; and therefore, by common consent, superseded them. We hear of no fragments, sentences, or word intentionally omitted by the compilers, nor of any that differed from the received edition. Had any such been discoverable, they would undoubtedly have been preserved and noticed in those traditional repositories which treasured up the minutest and most trivial acts and sayings of the Prophet.

"Fourth.—The contents and the arrangement of the Coran speak forcibly for its authenticity. All the fragments that could be obtained have, with artless simplicity, been joined together. The patchwork bears no marks of a designing genius or moulding hand. It testifies to the faith and reverence of the compilers, and proves that they dared no more than simply collect the sacred fragments and place them in juxtaposition.

"The conclusion, which we may now with confidence draw, is that the editions of Abu Bakr and of Othman were not only faithful, but, so far as the materials went, complete; and that whatever omissions there may have been, were not on the part of the compilers intentional . . . we may upon the strongest presumption affirm that every verse in the Coran is the genuine and unaltered composition[3] of Mahomet himself."[4]

The Slanderers of Islām

We have quoted Sir William Muir at length. Hence, we do not need to bring further quotations from the work of Father Lammens, Von Hammer, and other orientalists who hold this view. All these are absolutely certain that the Qur'ān which we recite today contains all that Muḥammad reported in all candidness as having been revealed to him from his Lord. If a certain group of orientalists do not agree and insist that the Qur'ān is forged without regard to these rational proofs which Muir had listed and which most orientalists had in fact taken from Muslim historians and scholars, it is in order to slander Islām and its Prophet. Such is the dictate of hate and resentment. However clever and adept such orientalists may be in formulating their slander, they will never be able to pass it as genuine scientific research; nor will they ever be able to fool any Muslims, except perhaps those young men deluded enough to think that free research demands of them the denial of their tradition and the naive acceptance of any nicely presented falsehood and attacks against their legacy, regardless of the validity or falsity of its premises and assumptions.

We could have quoted these same arguments of Sir William Muir and other orientalists directly from their primary Muslim sources as written by the scholars of Islām. But we have preferred to quote them in the words of an orientalist in order to show those of our youths who are spellbound by western works that precision in scientific research and a candid desire to seek the truth are sufficient to lead anyone to the ultimate facts of history. It was also our intention to show that the investigator ought to be very exact and precise in his investigation if he is to arrive at an understanding of his objective unaffected by ulterior motives or prejudice. Some orientalists undoubtedly arrive at the truth in some cases; others have not been as fortunate. The research which we have conducted in the writing of this book has convinced us that as regards the problem which the life of the Prophet poses to the scholar most of the orientalists have indeed erred.

Proper Methodology

It behooves us here to remember that the researcher should never assert or deny a thesis until his research and analysis have led him to perfect conviction that he has actually grasped all there is to know concerning the given problem. Here, the historian stands in the same predicament as his colleague researcher in the natural sciences. Such is his duty regardless of whether the material he analyzes is the work of an orientalist or that of a Muslim scholar. If we sincerely seek the truth, our duty is to scrutinize critically all that the Arab and the Muslim scholars have written in the fields of medicine, astronomy, chemistry and other sciences, and to reject all that does not hold its ground before the tribunal of science and to confirm that which does. The search for truth imposes upon us such exactitude in historical matters even though they may be related to the life of the Prophet—may God's peace and blessing be upon him. The historian is not a mere reporter. He is also a critic of what he reports, analyzing it and ascertaining the truth that it contains. There is no criticism without analytic scrutiny; and science and knowledge constitute the foundation of such criticism and analysis.

The exacting analysis which we have quoted in the foregoing pages regarding the Qur'ān is not enough. It does not obviate the need to respond to the letter of that Egyptian Muslim who naively believes all the writings of the orientalists, more particularly their claim that verses have been added to the Qur'ān regarding the name of the Prophet, that it was once "Qutham" or "Quthāmah." This claim is false, and it is motivated by the same ulterior motive that stands behind the charge of the forgery of the Qur'ān.

Let us then return to the last point in the letter of our young Muslim Egyptian author. He says that the investigations of the orientalists have established that the Prophet suffered from epilepsy, that the symptoms of the disease were all present in him and that he used to lose consciousness, perspire, fall into convulsions and sputter. After recovering from such seizures, the claim continues, Muhammad would recite to the believers what he then claimed to be a revelation from God, whereas that was only an aftereffect of the epileptic fits which he suffered.

The Slander of Epilepsy

To represent the phenomenon of Muhammad's revelations in these terms is, from the standpoint of scientific research, the gravest nonsense. The fit of epilepsy leaves the patient utterly without memory of what has taken place. In fact, the patient completely forgets that period of his life and can recollect nothing that has happened to him in the meantime because the processes of sensing and thinking come to a complete stop during the fit. Such are the symptoms of epilepsy as science has established them. This was not the case at all with the Prophet at the moment of revelation, for his cognitive faculties used to be strengthened—rather than weakened—and do so to a superlative degree hitherto unknown by the people who knew him most. Muhammad used to remember with utmost precision what he received by way of revelation and recited it to his companions without a flaw. Moreover, revelation was not always accompanied by paroxysms of the body. Much of it took place while the Prophet was perfectly conscious, during his usual wakefulness. We have advanced sufficient evidence for this in our discussion of the revelation of the *surah* "al Fath" upon return of the Muslims from Makkah to Yathrib after signing the Pact of Hudaybiyah.[5]

Scientific investigation therefore reveals that the case of Muhammad was not one of epilepsy. For this reason very few orientalists have upheld this claim and these turn out to be the same authors who upheld the charge of forgery against the Qur'ān. Obviously, in charging Muhammad with epilepsy, their motivation was not the establishment of historical fact but the derogation of the Prophet in the eyes of his Muslim followers. Perhaps, they thought, propagation of such views would cast some suspicion upon his revelation, for it was precisely the revelation that came as a result of the so-called epileptic fits. This, of course, makes them all the more blameworthy and, from the standpoint of science, positively in error.

Return to Science

Had these western orientalists been candid, they would not have presented their non-scientific claims in the name of science. They did so in order to delude the ignorant who, ignorant though they be of the symptoms of the epileptic disease, are prevented by their own naïveté from checking the orientalists' claims against the writings and opinions of the men of the medical sciences. A consultation of medical literature would have quickly exposed the errors of the orientalists, deliberate or accidental, and convinced them that in an epileptic fit all the intellectual and spiritual processes come to an absolute stop. When in a fit, the epileptic patient is either in a ridiculously mechanical state of motion or on a rampage injurious to his fellow men. He is utterly unconscious, unknowing of what he himself does, or of what happens to him, very much like the somnambulant who has no control over his movements during his sleep and who cannot remember them when he wakes up. A very great difference separates an epileptic fit from a revelation in which an intense and penetrating consciousness establishes, in full knowledge and conviction, a contact with the supernal plenum that enables the prophet to report and convey his revelation. Epilepsy, on the other hand, stops cognition. It reduces its patient to a mechanical state devoid of either feeling or sensation. Revelation is a spiritual heightening with which God prepares His prophet to receive from Him the highest and apodeictic cosmic truths that he may convey them to mankind. Science may eventually reach some of these truths and discover the secrets and laws of the universe. The rest may never become object of human knowledge until existence on this earth has come to an end. Nonetheless, these truths are apodeictically certain, furnishing true guidance to the earnest believer though they remain opaque to the ignorant whose hearts are locked and whose vision is dim.

Incapacity of Science in Some Fields

We would have understood and appreciated the western orientalists having said: "Revelation is a strange psychic phenomenon inexplicable in terms of contemporary science." Such a statement would mean that despite its wide scope and penetration, our science is still unable to explain many spiritual and psychic phenomena of which revelation is one. This statement is neither objectionable nor strange. Science is still unable to explain many natural, cosmic phenomena. The nature of the sun, moon, stars, and planets is still largely a matter for hypothesis. These heavenly bodies are only some of what the human eye, whether naked or through the telescope, reveals to us of the cosmos. Many of the inventions of the twentieth century that we presently take for granted were regarded by our predecessors in the nineteenth century as pure fiction. Psychic and spiritual phenomena are now subject to careful scientific study. But they have not yet been subject to the dominion of science so that it could be made to reveal their permanent role. We have often read about phenomena witnessed by the men of science and ascertained by them without explanation in terms coherent with scientific knowledge. Psychology, for instance, is a science which is not yet certain of the structures of many areas of psychic life. If this uncertainty is true of everyday phenomena, the demand to explain all the phenomena of life scientifically must be a shameful and futile exaggeration.

The revelations of Muḥammad were phenomena witnessed by his Muslim contemporaries. The more they heard the Qur'ān, the more convinced they became of the truth of these revelations. Among these contemporaries were many of extreme intelligence. Others were Jews and Christians who had argued with the Prophet for a long time before, and they believed in his mission and trusted his revelation in every detail. Some men of Quraysh had accused Muḥammad of magic and madness. Later, convinced that he was neither a magician nor a madman, they believed in and followed him. Since all these facts are certain, it is as unscientific to deny the phenomenon of revelation as it is unworthy of the men of science to speak of it in derogative terms. The man of science candid in his search for the truth will not go beyond asserting that his discipline is unable to explain the phenomenon of revelation according to the materialistic theory. But he will never deny the factuality of revelation as reported by the companions of the Prophet and the historians of the first century of Islām. To do otherwise would be to fall under prejudice and betray the spirit of science.

Slander against Muḥammad Is Argumentum ad Hominem

Such obstinate prejudice only proves the determined concern of its author to arouse suspicion in Islām itself. Such people have been incapable of arguing against Islām because they had found it sublimely noble, simple, and easy to understand, and realized that these qualities are the sources of its strength. They hence resort to the trick of the impotent who shifts attention from the great idea beyond his reach to the person advocating it. That is the *argumentum ad hominem* fallacy which every scholar should seek to avoid. It is natural for men to concern themselves with ideas and not with the personal circumstances of their authors and advocates. Men do not give themselves the trouble to investigate the roots of a tree whose fruits they had found delectable, nor the fertilizer which had helped it to grow, as long as their purpose is not to plant a similar or better tree. When they analyze the philosophy of Plato, the plays of Shakespeare, or the paintings of Raphael, and find nothing objectionable in them, they do not look for blameworthy aspects in the lives of these great men who constitute humanity's glory and pride. And if they try to fabricate charges against these persons, they will never succeed in convincing anyone. They only succeed in betraying themselves and exposing their ulterior motives. Casting resentment in the form of scientific research does not alter it from being what it is: namely resentment. Resentment refuses to recognize the truth; and the truth will always be too proud to allow resentment to be its source or associate. Such is the case of the orientalists' charges against the person of the Arab Prophet Muḥammad, Seal of the Prophets; and that is why their charges fall to the ground.

That is all I have to say by way of response to those orientalists to whom the letter of the Egyptian Muslim had referred. Having thus refuted their views, let me now direct my attention to a number of observations made on the first edition of this book by the Islāmicists at home.

It is my earnest hope that such base charges unworthy of science and unacceptable to scholars will never be repeated again. Perhaps, hitherto, the orientalists felt themselves excused on the grounds that they were writing for the consumption of their fellow Christians and Europeans and that they were actually discharging a national or religious duty imposed upon them by a patriotism or faith which requires scholarly form to make its propaganda palatable. Our day, however, is different. Communication between the various corners of the globe by means of radio broadcasting and the press has made it possible for anything said or published in Europe or America today to become known throughout the Orient in that same day or even the same hour. It is therefore the duty of those who assume the scholarly profession and the pursuit of truth to tear away from their hearts and eyes every curtain of national, racial, or religious isolation. They should realize that whatever they say or write will soon reach the ears of all men throughout the world and will be subject to universal criticism and scrutiny. The absolute and unconditional truth should be the objective of every one of us; and let us all take due care to connect the present reality of mankind with its past, to regard humanity as one great unit undivided by nationality, race or religion. Let such connection be the bond of free fraternity in the pursuit of truth, goodness, and beauty, and the noblest ideal that humanity has ever known. Such a bond is alone capable of guiding humanity in its quick march toward happiness and perfection.

Observations of Muslim Islāmicists

Whereas the naive believers in the exaggerations of the orientalists blame us for having recourse to the Arabic sources and depending upon them, a number of Muslim Islāmicists blame us for turning to the writings of the orientalists rather than limiting ourselves to the Islāmic biographies and books of Ḥadīth. The latter have also criticized us for not following the same method as these ancient books.

It was on this basis that some of them made friendly observations in hope of reaching the fact of the matter in question. Others made observations which betray such ignorance or prejudice as no scholar would wish to associate himself with. The former took note of the fact that we have not reported the miracles of Muhammad as the biographies and Ḥadīth have done. In this regard we wrote in the conclusion of our first edition: "The Life of Muhammad, therefore, has realized the highest ideals possible to man. Muhammad—may God's peace and blessing be upon him—was very careful that the Muslims should think of him as a human to whom revelation came. He never accepted that any miracle be attributed to him other than his association with the advent of the Qur'ān, and actually told this much to his companions." As regards the story of the splitting of Muḥammad's chest we wrote: "Orientalists as well as Muslim scholars take their attitude towards this event in the life of Muḥammad on the grounds that Muḥammad's whole life was all too human and noble and that he never resorted to miracles as previous prophets had done, in order to prove the veracity of his revelation. In taking this attitude, the above-mentioned thinkers rely upon the Arab and Muslim historians who share their view and who deny any place in the biography of the Arab Prophet to all that is irrational. They regard their stand as being in perfect accord with the Qur'ān's call to man to study the creation of God and discover therein His immutable laws. They find the claim for miracles incoherent with the Qur'ān's condemnation of the associationists as men who do not reason, as men who have no faculties with which to reason." Other more considerate critics criticized us for having mentioned at all the orientalists' attacks upon the Prophet, though we did so but to refute them. In their opinion, this procedure does not accord with the veneration due to the person of the Prophet—may God's blessing be upon him. Lastly, there is the class of prejudiced critics who were known even before the first edition of this book had appeared and, indeed, even before my researches had been collected in book form. Their strongest criticism was that I have given my work the title, "The Life of Muḥammad," without joining it to an invocation of peace and blessing upon him. Such invocations occur frequently in the course of the book. I had thought, nonetheless, that they would discover their prejudice once the title page of the first edition came out decorated, as it was, with the verse: "God and his angels bless the Prophet. O you who believe, invoke God's peace and blessing upon him and salute him with the salutation of peace."⁶ I had also thought that the method used in this book would itself dissolve their prejudice. By insisting as they did, however, they betrayed their ignorance of Islāmic truths and their satisfaction with the imitation of their ancestors.

Let us begin by answering their false criticism in the hope that neither they nor any others will repeat it regarding this or any other book. We shall refuse their criticism by turning to the books of the classical leaders of Islāmic knowledge. Everyone will then realize the free stand Islām has taken *vis-à-vis* all verbal restrictions and will then appreciate the *ḥadīth*, "This religion is indeed sound. Analyze it as you wish, but gently. You will never find a flaw therein." Abū al Baqā' wrote in his book, *Al Kulliyyāt:* "Writing the invocation of peace and blessing on Muḥammad at the beginning of a book occurred during the 'Abbāsī period. That is why the *Ṣaḥīḥ* of al Bukhārī and others are devoid of it."[7] The majority of the great men of Islāmic knowledge agree that the invocation of peace and blessing upon the Prophet need not be made by the Muslim more than once in his lifetime. In his book *Al Baḥr al Rā'iq,* ibn Nujaym wrote: "The religious imperative implied in the divine command, 'Invoke upon him God's peace and blessing,' is that it should be made at least once in a lifetime whether during or outside the prayer. For no command by itself implies repetition. On this there is no disagreement." Likewise, al Shāfi'ī contended with his colleagues on "whether or not the invocation of God's peace and blessing on the Prophet is imperative during the prayer or outside of it. Prayer is itself invocation. As it stands in the above mentioned verse, to invoke God's peace and blessing upon the Prophet simply means that one should ask God to bless the Prophet and to salute him the salutation of peace." That is the lesson which the Muslim men of knowledge and their leaders have taught in this regard. It proves that those who claim that this invocation is imperative whenever the name of the Prophet is mentioned or written are simply exaggerating. Had they known the foregoing facts, and that the greatest traditionists had not written such an invocation regarding the Prophet on the title pages or beginnings of their collections of *ḥadīths,* they would perhaps have avoided falling into their present error.

Refutation of the Orientalists and Its Method

As to those who claim that it does not become a Muslim scholar to repeat the attacks of the Orientalists and the missionaries against the Prophet even in order to refute them, they have really nothing to stand upon except an Islāmic emotion which we salute. From the religious as well as scholarly points of view, they simply have no argument at all. The Holy Qur'ān itself reported much of what the associationists of Makkah used to say about the Prophet and refuted them with clear and eloquent argument. The Arabic style of the Qur'ān is the highest and its morals the noblest.[8] It mentioned the accusation of the Quraysh that Muḥammad was either possessed or a magician. It said: "We do know that they say that it is only a man who teaches Muḥammad the Qur'ān. But the tongue of him to whom they refer by this insinuation is foreign whereas this Qur'ān is in the Arabic tongue, plain and clear."[9] There are many such statements in the Qur'ān. Moreover, an argument is not scientifically refuted unless it is honestly and precisely stated. In writing this book, my purpose has been to reach objective truth by means of scholarly research. And I have written my book so that both Muslims and non-Muslims may read it and be convinced of this objective truth. Such a purpose cannot be achieved unless the scholar be honest in his pursuit. He should never hesitate to acknowledge the truth whencesoever it may come.

Biographies and Ḥadīth Books

Let us return to the first criticism the Muslim students of Islām have kindly directed to our work, namely, that we have not taken into consideration the Islāmic biographies and Ḥadīth books and that we have not followed the same methodology as these ancient works. It should suffice to say in reply to this criticism that I have resolved to follow the modern scientific method and to write in the style of the century and that I have taken this resolution because it is the only proper one in the eyes of the contemporary world, whether for historiography or any other discipline. This being the case, ancient methods are ruled out *a priori*. Between these and the methods of our age there is great difference, the most obvious of which is the freedom to criticise. Most of the ancient works were written for a religious purpose and as devotional exercises, whereas contemporary writers are interested only in scientific analysis and criticism. To say this much concerning my method and work should be sufficient answer to their criticism. But I see the need for a more detailed treatment in order to show the reasons why our classical scholars of the past did not, and those of the present should not, assume in wholesale fashion the veracity of all that the books of biography and Ḥadīth have brought. It is also my intention to clarify the reasons why we ought to observe

the rules of scientific criticism as closely as possible in order
to guard against all possible errors.

The Difference between These Books

The first of these reasons is the difference of these books in
their reporting of events supposed to have taken place in the life
of the Arab Prophet. Those who studied these books have observed that the miracles and extraordinary events reported increased or decreased for no reason other than the change in
the time when they were written. The earlier report fewer
miracles than the later; and the miracles they do report are less
unreasonable than those reported in later books. The oldest
known biography, namely, that of ibn Hishām for example,
has far less material than the Tārīkh of Abū al Fidā', than
Al Shifā' of Qāḍī 'Ayyad and of most later writings. The same
is true of the books of the Ḥadīth. Some of them tell a story
and others omit it, or they report it and point out that it is not
trustworthy. The objective researcher investigating these books
must therefore have a standard by which he can evaluate the
various claims. That which agrees with the standard he would
find acceptable and that which does not, he would subject to
closer scrutiny wherever possible.

Our ancestors have followed this method in their investigations
at times, and they have omitted doing so at others. An example of
their omission is the story of "the daughters of God." It is told
that when the Prophet, under ever-increasing oppression of
Quraysh, recited the Qur'ānic surah "al Najm" and arrived at the
verse: "Consider al Lāt and al 'Uzzā; and Manāt, the third goddess,"[10] he added: "Those are the goddesses on high; their intercession with God is worthy of our prayers." He then went on
reciting the surah to its end and when he finished, he prostrated
himself in worship, and Muslims and associationists joined him
and did likewise. This story was reported by ibn Sa'd in his
Al Ṭabaqāt al Kubrā without criticism. It also occurs with little
variation in some books of Ḥadīth. Ibn Isḥāq, however, reported
the story and judged it as being the fabrication of zindīqs.[11]
In his Al Bidāyah wa al Nihāyah fī al Tarīkh, ibn Kathīr
wrote: "They mentioned the story of the goddesses of Makkah,
whereas we have decided to omit it for fear that the uninstructed
may naively accept it as truth. The story was first reported in
the books of Ḥadīth." He then reported a tradition from

Bukhārī in this regard and qualified it as being "unique to Bukhārī, rejected by Muslim." As for me, I did not hesitate to reject the story altogether and to agree with ibn Ishāq that it was the fabrication of *zindīqs*. In analyzing it I brought together several pieces of evidence. In addition to its denial of the infallibility of the Prophets in their conveyance of their divine messages, this story must also be subject to modern scientific criticism.

The Age of These Books

The books of the ancestors should be closely scrutinized and criticised in a scientific manner because the most ancient of them was written a hundred or more years after the death of the Prophet. At that time, many political and religious movements were spreading throughout the Islamic Empire, each of which fabricated all kinds of stories and *hadīths* to justify its own cause. The later books, written during even more turbulent and unsettled times, are more vulnerable. Political struggles caused a great deal of trouble to the collectors of Hadīth because they took utmost care in scrutinizing these various reports, rejecting the suspicious, and confirming only those which passed the severest tests. It is sufficient to remember here the travails of al Bukhārī in his travels throughout the Muslim World undertaken for this purpose. He told us that he had found some six hundred thousand *hadīths* current, of which only 4,000 he could confirm as true. The ratio is that of one to 150 *hadīths*. As for Abū Dāwūd, he could confirm 4,800 *hadīths* out of half a million. Such was the task of all collectors of *hadīths*. Nonetheless, many of the *hadīths* which they had found true after criticism were found untrue by a number of other scholars under further criticism. Such was the case of the goddesses. If such is the case of Hadīth, despite all the efforts spent by the early collectors, how trustworthy can the later biographies of the Prophet be? How can their reports be taken without scientific scrutiny?

Effects of Islāmic Political Strife

In fact, the political struggles of the first century of Islām caused the various parties to invent, and press into their service, a great number of stories ánd *hadīths*. No Hadīth has been committed to writing until the last years of the Umawī period. It was 'Umar ibn 'Abd al 'Azīz who ordered its collection for the first time. The job, however, was not completed until the reign of al Ma'mūn, the time when "the true *hadīth* was as discernible from the false as a white hair is in the fur of a black bull," to borrow the phrase of Dāraqutnī. The Ḥadīth was not collected in the first century of Islām perhaps because of the reported command of the Prophet: "Do not write down anything I say except the Qur'ān. Whoever has written something other than the Qur'ān, let him destroy it." Nonetheless, the *hadīths* of the Prophet were current in those days and must have been varied. During his caliphate, 'Umar ibn al Khaṭṭāb once tried to deal with the problem by committing the Ḥadīth to writing. The companions of the Prophet whom he consulted encouraged him, but he was not quite sure whether he should proceed. One day, moved by God's inspiration, he made up his mind and announced: "I wanted to have the traditions of the Prophet written down, but I fear that the Book of God might be encroached upon. Hence I shall not permit this to happen." He therefore changed his mind and instructed the Muslims throughout the provinces: "Whoever has a document bearing a prophetic tradition shall destroy it." The Ḥadīth therefore continued to be transmitted orally and was not collected and written down until the period of al Ma'mūn.

The Standard of Ḥadīth Criticism

Despite the great care and precision of the Ḥadīth scholars, much of what they regarded as true was later proved to be spurious. In his commentary on the collection of Muslim, al Nawawī wrote: "A number of scholars discovered many *hadīths* in the collections of Muslim and Bukhārī which do not fulfill the conditions of verification assumed by these men." The collectors attached the greater weight to the trustworthiness of the narrators. Their criterion was certainly valuable, but it was not sufficient. In our opinion, the criterion for the Ḥadīth criticism, as well as standard for materials concerning the Prophet's life, is the one which the Prophet himself gave. He said: "After I am gone differences will arise among you. Compare whatever is reported to be mine with the Book of God; that which agrees therewith you may accept as having come from me; that which disagrees you will reject as a fabrication." This valid standard is observed by the great men of Islām right from the very beginning. It continues to be the standard of thinkers today. Ibn Khaldūn wrote: "I do not believe any *hadīth* or report of a companion of the Prophet to be true which differs from the common sense meaning of the Qur'ān, no matter how trustworthy the narrators may have been. It is not impossible that a narrator appears to be trustworthy though he may be moved by ulterior motive. If the *hadīths* were criticised for their textual contents as they were for the narrators who transmitted them a great number would have had to be rejected. It is a recognized principle that a *hadīth* could be declared spurious if it departs from the common sense meaning of the Qur'ān from the recognized principles of the Sharī'ah,[12] the rules of logic, the evidence of sense, or any other self-evident truth." This criterion, as given by the Prophet as well as ibn Khaldūn, perfectly accords with modern scientific criticism.

True, after Muḥammad's death the Muslims differed, and they fabricated thousands of *hadīths* and reports to support their various causes. From the day Abū Lu'lu'ah, the servant of al Mughīrah, killed 'Umar ibn al Khattāb and 'Uthmān ibn 'Affān assumed the caliphate, the old pre-Islāmic enmity of Banū Hāshim and Banū Umayyah reappeared. When, upon the murder of 'Uthmān, civil war broke out between the Muslims, 'Ā'ishah fought against 'Alī and 'Alī's supporters consolidated themselves into a party, the fabrication of *hadīths* spread to the point where 'Alī ibn Abū Tālib himself had to reject the practice and warn against it. He reportedly said: "We have no book and no writing to read to you except the Qur'ān and this sheet which I have received from the Prophet of God in which he specified the duties prescribed by charity." Apparently, this exhortation did not stop the Hadīth narrators from fabricating their stories either in support of a cause they advocated, or of a virtue or practice to which they exhorted the Muslims and which they thought would have more appeal if vested with prophetic authority. When the Banū Umayyah firmly established themselves in power, their protagonists among the Hadīth narrators deprecated the prophetic traditions reported by the party of 'Alī ibn Abū Tālib, and the latter defended those traditions and propagated them with all the means at their disposal. Undoubtedly they also deprecated the traditions reported by 'Ā'ishah, "Mother of the Faithful." A humorous piece of reportage was given us by ibn 'Asākir who wrote: "Abu Sa'd Isma'īl ibn al Muthannā

al Istrabādhī was giving a sermon one day in Damascus when a
man stood up and asked him what he thought of the *hadīth* of
the Prophet: 'I am the city of knowledge and 'Alī is its gate.'
Abu Sa'd pondered the question for a while and then replied:
'Indeed! No one knows this *hadīth* of the Prophet except those
who lived in the first century of Islām. What the Prophet had
said, he continued, was, rather, "I am the city of knowledge;
Abū Bakr is its foundation; 'Umar, its walls; 'Uthmān its ceiling; and 'Alī its gate.' The audience was quite pleased with his
reply and asked him to furnish them with its chain of narrators.
Abu Sa'd could not furnish any chain and was terribly em-
barrassed." Thus *hadīths* were fabricated for political and other
purposes. This wanton multiplication alarmed the Muslims because many ran counter to the Book of God. The attempts to
stop this wave of fabrication under the Umawīs did not succeed.
When the 'Abbāsīs took over, and al Ma'mūn assumed the
caliphate almost two centuries after the death of the Prophet,
the fabricated *hadīths* numbered in the thousands and hundreds
of thousands and contained an unimaginable amount of contradiction and variety. It was then that the collectors applied
themselves to the task of putting the Hadīth together and the
biographers of the Prophet wrote their biographies. Al Wāqidī,
ibn Hishām and al Madā'inī lived and wrote their books in the
days of al Ma'mūn. They could not afford to contradict the
caliphate and hence could not apply with the precision due the
Prophet's criterion that his traditions ought to be checked
against the Qur'ān and accepted only if they accorded therewith.

Had this criterion, which does not differ from the modern
method of scientific criticism, been applied with precision, the
ancient masters would have altered much of their writing.
Circumstances of history imposed upon them the application of
it to some of their writings but not to others. The later generations inherited their method of treating the biography of the
Prophet without questioning it. Had they been true to history,
they would have applied this criterion in general as well as in
detail. No reported events disagreeing with the Qur'ān would
have been spared, and none would have been confirmed but
those which agreed with the Book of God as well as the laws
of nature. Even so, these *hadīths* would have been subject to
strict analysis and established only with valid proof and incontestable evidence. This stand was taken by the greatest Muslim
scholars of the past as well as of the present. The grand Shaykh

of al Azhar, Muḥammad Muṣṭafā al Marāghī, wrote in his foreword to this book: "Muḥammad—may God's peace and blessing be upon him—had only one irresistible miracle—the Qur'ān. But it is not irrational. How eloquent is the verse of al Buṣayrī: 'God did not try us with anything irrational. Thus, we fell under neither doubt nor illusion.' "[13]

The late Muḥammad Rashīd Riḍā, editor of *al Manār*, wrote in answer to our critics: "The most important objection which the Azharīs and the Ṣufīs raise against Haykal concerns the problem of the miracles. In my book, *Al Waḥy al Muḥammadī*, I have analyzed the problem from all aspects in the second chapter and the second section of the fifth chapter. I have established there that the Qur'ān alone is the conclusive proof of the prophethood of Muḥammad—may God's peace and blessing be upon him—as well as of the other prophets of their messages and prophecies regarding him. In our age it is impossible to prove any work of the Prophet except by the Qur'ān. From its standpoint, supernatural events are *ipso facto* doubtful. Besides the ubiquitous reports of their occurrence in all ages and places, they are believed in by the superstitious of all faiths. I have also analyzed the causes of this predeliction for belief in miracles and distinguished the miraculous from the spiritual and shown the relationship of both to cosmic laws."[14]

In his book, *Al Islām wa al Nasrāniyyah*, Muḥammad 'Abduh, the great scholar and leader wrote: "Islām, therefore, and its demand for faith in God and in His unity, depend only on rational proof and common sense human thinking. Islām does not overwhelm the mind with the supernatural, confuse the understanding with the extraordinary, impose acquiescent silence by resorting to heavenly intervention, nor does it impede the movement of thought by any sudden cry of divinity. All the Muslims are agreed, except those whose opinion is insignificant, that faith in God is prior to faith in prophethood and that it is not possible to believe in a prophet except after one has come to believe in God. It is unreasonable to demand faith in God on the ground that the prophets or the revealed books had said so, for it is unreasonable to believe that any book had been revealed by God unless one already believed that God exists and that it is possible for Him to reveal a book or send a messenger."

I am inclined to think that those who wrote biographies of the Prophet agreed with this view. The earlier generation of them could not apply it because of the historical circumstances

in which they lived. The later generation of them suspended the
principle deliberately on account of their belief that the more
miraculous their portrayal of the Prophet, the more faith this
would engender among their audience. They assumed, quite
naively, that the inclusion of these extraneous matters into his
biography achieved a good purpose. Had they lived to our day
and seen how the enemies of Islām had taken their writings as
an argument against Islām and its people, they would have
followed the Qur'ān more closely and agreed with al Ghazzālī,
Muḥammad 'Abduh, al Marāghī, and all other objective scholars.
And had they lived in our day and age, and witnessed how
their stories have alienated many Muslim minds and hearts instead of confirming their faith, they would have been satisfied
with the indubitable proofs and arguments of the Book of God.

Reports Condemned by Reason and Science

Now that the defect of reports condemned by reason and
science has become obvious, scientific and critical analysis of
the materials involved is demanded. This is equally the demand
of Islām and a service to it as well as to the history of the Arab
Prophet. It is a necessary requisite if that history is to illuminate
the road of mankind towards high culture and civilization.

The Qur'ān and Miracles

We will quickly agree with the views of the objective Muslim
scholars as soon as we compare a number of narratives from
the biography and Ḥadīth books with the Qur'ān. The latter
told us that the Makkans had asked the Prophet to perform
some miracles if they were to believe in him; it mentioned specifically their demands, and refuted them. God said:

وَقَالُوا لَن نُّؤْمِنَ لَكَ حَتَّى تَفْجُرَ لَنَا مِنَ الْأَرْضِ يَنْبُوعًا ۞ أَوْ تَكُونَ لَكَ جَنَّةٌ مِّن نَّخِيلٍ وَعِنَبٍ
فَتُفَجِّرَ الْأَنْهَارَ خِلَالَهَا تَفْجِيرًا ۞ أَوْ تُسْقِطَ السَّمَاءَ كَمَا زَعَمْتَ عَلَيْنَا كِسَفًا أَوْ تَأْتِيَ بِاللَّهِ وَالْمَلَائِكَةِ قَبِيلًا ۞
أَوْ يَكُونَ لَكَ بَيْتٌ مِّن زُخْرُفٍ أَوْ تَرْقَى فِي السَّمَاءِ وَلَن نُّؤْمِنَ لِرُقِيِّكَ حَتَّى تُنَزِّلَ عَلَيْنَا كِتَابًا نَّقْرَؤُهُ
قُلْ سُبْحَانَ رَبِّي هَلْ كُنتُ إِلَّا بَشَرًا رَّسُولًا

"They said that they will never believe in you unless you cause
a fountain to spring forth from the earth; or create for yourself
a garden of big trees and vines and cause abundant streams of

water to run from one side of it to the other, or cause heaven to fall upon them in pieces as you had claimed, or bring God and His angels before them face to face, or create for yourself a beauteous palace, or ascend to heaven in front of them. 'Nay,' they said to Muḥammad, 'we will not believe in your ascension unless you send down upon us a book confirming that you have done all these things clearly and unequivocally.' Answer: 'Praised be my Lord: Have I ever claimed to be anything but a human and a messenger?' "[15]

God also said: "They swore their strongest oaths that if they could witness a miracle they would believe. Answer: 'Miracles are God's prerogative, not mine.' But what would convince you [Muḥammad] that they will not believe even if such miracles were to take place? Let their mind and understanding remain as confused as ever. Let them wander aimlessly in their misguidance. Indeed, unless of course God wills for them to believe, they will not believe even if We sent them the angels, caused the dead to speak to them, and placed everything squarely before them. But most of them are ignorant."[16] There is no mention in the whole Qur'ān of any miracle intended to support the prophethood of Muḥammad except the Qur'ān, notwithstanding its acknowledgment of many of the miracles performed with God's permission by the prophets preceding Muḥammad and description of the many other favors which God has bestowed upon him. What the Qur'ān did report about the Arab Prophet does not violate any of the laws of nature in the least degree.

The Greatest Miracle

Since this is the logic of the Book of God and is demanded by the advent of His Prophet, what reason could have caused some of the Muslims of the past, and still cause some of them in the present, to attribute miracles to Muḥammad? It must be their reading in the Qur'ān of miracles performed by prophets preceding Muḥammad and their jumping to the conclusion that such supernatural occurrences are necessary for prophethood. They thus believed the stories circulating about Muḥammad's miracles despite the fact that they could not find any confirmation of them in the Qur'ān. They mistakenly believed that the more of them they could muster the more convinced they and their audiences would be of their faith. To compare the Arab Prophet with his predecessor prophets is to compare the incom-

parable. For he was the last of the prophets and the first one
sent by God unto all mankind rather than unto any specific
people alone. That is why God desired that the "miracle" of
Muhammad be human and rational, though unmatchable by any
humans or genii. This miracle is the Qur'ān itself, the greatest
that God permitted. He—may His glory be praised—willed that
His Prophet's mission be established by rational argument and
clear proof. He willed that His religion achieve victory in the
life of His prophet and that men might see in his victory the
might and dominion of God. Had God willed that a material
miracle force the conversion of Makkah, the miracle would
have occurred and would have been mentioned in the Qur'ān.
But some men do not believe except in that which their reason
understands and corroborates. The proper way to convince them
would be to appeal to their understanding and reason. God
made the Qur'ān Muhammad's convincing argument, a miracle
of the "illiterate Prophet." He willed that men's entry into Islām
and the sense of their faith in Him be dependent upon true
conviction and apodeictic evidence. A religion thus founded
would be worthy of the faith of all men in all times whatever
their race or language.

Should a people convert to Islām today who did not need any
miracle beside the Qur'ān, this fact would neither detract from
their faith nor from the worth of their conversion. As long as a
people is not itself recipient of a revelation, it is perfectly
legitimate to subject all the reports of such revelation to the
closest scrutiny. That which unquestionable proof confirms is
acceptable; the rest may validly be put to question. To believe
in God alone without associate does not need recourse to a
miracle. Nor does it need more than consideration of the nature
of this universe which God created. On the other hand, to believe
in the Prophethood of Muhammad who, by command of God,
called men precisely unto such faith, does not need any miracles
other than the Qur'ān. Nor does it need any more than the
presentation of the revealed text to consciousness.

Were a people to believe today in this religion without the
benefit of any miracle other than the Qur'ān, its faithful would
belong to one of the following kinds: the man whose mind and
heart does not oscillate but is guided by God directly to the
object of his faith, as was the case with Abū Bakr who believed
without hesitation; and, the man who does not seek his faith in
the miraculous but in the natural (*i.e.*, the created world, un-

limited in space or time and running perfectly in accordance with eternal and immutable laws), and whose reason guides him from these laws of nature to the creator and fashioner thereof. Even if miracles did exist, they would constitute no problem for either kind of believer who regards them as mere signs of divine mercy. Many leaders of Islāmic knowledge regard this kind of faith as indeed the highest. Some of them even prescribe that faith should not stand on a foundation of fear of God's punishment or ambition to win His reward. They insist that it should be held purely for the sake of God and involve an actual annihilation of self in God. To Him all things belong; and so do we. To Him, we and all things shall return.

The Believers during the Life of the Prophet

Those who believe today in God and in His Prophet and whose faith does not rest on miracles are in the same position as those who believed during the life of the Prophet. History has not reported to us that any one of those early companions had entered the faith because of a miracle he witnessed. Rather, it was the conclusive divine argument conveyed through revelation and the superlatively noble life of the Prophet himself which conduced those men to their faith. In fact, all biographies mention that a number of those who believed in Muḥammad before the *Isrā'* abandoned their faith when the Prophet reported to them that he had been transported during the night from the Mosque of Makkah to the Blessed One of Jerusalem. Even Ṣurāqah ibn Ju'shum, who pursued Muḥammad on the latter's flight to Madīnah in order to capture him dead or alive and win the prize the Makkans had placed on his head, did not believe despite the miracle which the biographers have reported to have taken place on his way there. History has not reported a single case of an associationist who believed in Muḥammad because of a miracle performed. Islām has no parallel to the case of the magicians of Pharaoh whose rods were swallowed up by that of Moses.[17]

The Goddesses and Tabūk

The classical biographies are not unanimous in their reportage of the so-called miracles. Many a time their narratives were subject to strong criticism despite their corroboration by the

books of Ḥadīth. We have already referred to the question of
the goddesses in this preface, and we have also treated the
problem in detail in the course of this work. The story of the
opening of Muḥammad's chest as reported by Ḥalīmah,
Muḥammad's wet nurse, is equally inconclusive.[18] There is a
difference of opinion concerning Ḥalīmah's reports as well as
the age of Muḥammad at which the story has supposedly taken
place. Likewise, the reports of the biographies and of the Ḥadīth
concerning Zayd and Zaynab are' devoid of foundation, as we
shall have occasion to see later.[19] Similar disagreement exists
as regards the story of the military expedition to Tabūk (Jaysh
al 'Usrah). In his *Ṣaḥīḥ*, Muslim reported from Mu'ādh ibn
Jabal that "the Prophet told ibn Jabal and his companions who
were marching to Tabūk: 'Tomorrow, but not before mid-day,
you will, with God's leave, reach the spring of Tabūk. You will
not, however, touch its waters until I come.' When we arrived,
we found that two of our men had reached it before us and the
spring had very little water. The Prophet asked the two men
whether they had touched the water of the spring, and they
confessed. He—may God's peace and blessing be upon him—
criticized and scolded them as he should. They then filled a
container with water from the spring. Mu'ādh said: 'The Prophet
of God—may God's peace and blessing be upon him—washed
his face and his hands and poured the water back into the spring
whereupon the spring gushed forth abundantly (he might have
said 'profusely') until all men drank and were satisfied. The
Prophet then said: 'If you were to live long enough, O Mu'ādh,
you would see this place full of gardens.' "[20]

In the biographies, on the other hand, the story of Tabūk is
told in a different way without mention of any miracles. Thus
we read in Ibn Hishām's *The Life of Muḥammad*: "When, in
the morning, the men discovered they had no water, they complained to the Prophet—may God's peace and blessing be upon
him. He prayed to God, who then sent a rain cloud. So much
rain fell that everybody drank his fill and filled his skin. Ibn
Ishāq said: 'Āṣim ibn 'Umar ibn Qatādah, reporting from
Maḥmūd ibn Labīd, who in turn was reporting what he heard
from some men of the Banū 'Abd al Ashhal tribe, said: 'I said
to Maḥmūd, 'Did these Muslims know that some hypocrites were
among them'? He answered, 'Yes. Sometimes a man would tell
a hypocrite even if he were his brother, father, uncle or fellow
tribesman; at other times he would not be able to differentiate
between them.' Maḥmūd continued: 'A fellow tribesman told

me of a well-known hypocrite who used to accompany the
Prophet of God—may God's peace and blessing be upon him—
wherever he went, and who was present at this expedition. After
the miracle had taken place, we went to him and asked: 'Are
you still in doubt after what you saw with your own eyes?' He
answered, 'It was but a passing cloud.' "

Such a wide range of difference as separates the classical accounts of this story makes it impossible for us to affirm it conclusively. Those who apply themselves to the study of it should
not stop at probable solutions which neither confirm nor deny
the classical reports. Whenever they are confronted by a story
not supported by positive evidence, the least they can do is to
discard it. Should other investigators later on discover the required evidence, the duty of presenting the story with its proof-
claims would devolve upon them.

My Methodology

This is the method which I have followed in my study of the
life of Muḥammad, the Prophet of the Islāmic mission to mankind. It characterizes my work throughout; for ever since I
decided to undertake this study I resolved that it would be
conducted in accordance with the modern scientific method in all
sincerity and for the sake of truth alone. That is what I announced in the preface of this book and prayed, in the conclusion
of its first edition, that I may have accomplished, thereby paving
the way for deeper and wiser investigations. I had hoped that
this and similar studies would clear for science a number of
psychic and spiritual problems and establish facts which would
guide mankind to the new civilization for which it is groping.
There is no doubt that deepening of analysis and extending the
scope of the investigation would unlock many secrets which
many people have thought for a long time to lie beyond scientific
explanation. The clearer the understanding mankind achieves of
the psychological and spiritual secrets of the world, the stronger
man's relation to the world will become and, hence, the greater
his happiness. Man will then be better able to rehabilitate himself in the world when he knows its secrets, just as he became
better able to enjoy it when he understood the latent forces of
electricity and radio.

It therefore behooves any scholar applying himself to such
a study to address his work not only to the Muslims but to
mankind as a whole. The final purpose of such work is not, as

some of them think, purely religious. Rather, it is, following the example of Muḥammad, that all mankind may better learn the way to perfection. Fulfillment of this purpose is not possible without the guidance of reason and heart, and the conviction and certainty they bring when founded on true perception and knowledge. Speculative thinking based upon imprecise knowledge which is not conditioned by the scientific method is likely to go astray and point to conclusions far removed from the truth. By nature, our thinking is deeply influenced by temperament. Men with equal training and knowledge, common purpose and resolution, often differ from one another for no reason other than their difference in temperament. Some are passionate, deeply perceptive, over-hasty in their conclusions, mystical, stoic, ascetic, inclined towards matter, or utterly conditioned by it. Others are different, and their views of the world naturally separate them from one another. As far as artistic expression and practical living are concerned, this variety of the human kind is a great blessing. It is, however, a curse in the field of scientific endeavor which seeks to serve the higher benefit of mankind as a whole. The study of history should search for high ideals within the facts of human life. Anyone who applies himself to this search should therefore be free from passion and prejudice. No method succeeds as well in avoiding these pitfalls as the scientific method, and no method will more surely lead to error than that which uses the materials of history to propagate a certain view or bends them to corroborate a certain prejudice.

The Works of Orientalists

Many western Orientalists have been affected in their so-called scientific research by their preconceptions and passions. The same is true of many Muslim authors as well. More surprising in both is the fact that each had taken the passionate and prejudiced propaganda of the other as basic sourcework, and each had claimed for his writing the objectivity which belongs to a research done for the sake of truth alone. Neither realized how deeply affected he was by his own vehement reaction to the propaganda of the other. Had either party taken the trouble to analyze objectively the work of the other, the respective claims would have dissolved and crumbled. Had any author kept his own predelictions at bay, immunizing himself against them by applying scientific principles, his writings would have had a more lasting

Apostasy, the so-called "differences over the caliphate." After the murder of 'Uthmān, disagreement spread among the Muslims; civil war was declared between 'Alī and Mu'āwiyah; insurgence and rebellion continued; and politics played a serious role even in the religious life itself. In order to help the reader appreciate this difference, let us compare the principles implied in the accession speeches of Abū Bakr and al Manṣūr al 'Abbāsī. The former said: "O men! Here I have been assigned the job of ruling over you while I am not the best among you. If I do well in my job, help me. If I do wrong, redress me. Truthfulness is fidelity, and lying is treason. The weak shall be strong in my eye until I restore to them their right, and the strong shall be weak in my eye until I have dispossessed them of that right. No people give up fighting for the cause of God but He inflicts upon them abject subjection; and no people give themselves to lewdness but He envelops them with misery. Obey me as long as I obey God and His Prophet. But if I disobey God's command or His Prophet, then no obedience is incumbent upon you. Rise to your prayer so he may have mercy on you." The other said: "O men! I am the power of God on His earth. I rule you with His guidance and confirmation. I am the guardian over His wealth and I manage it by His will and in accordance with His pattern. I disburse from it with His permission, for He has made me the lock. If He chooses to open me so that you may receive therefrom and be provided for, He will. And if He chooses to keep me locked, He will. . . ." A comparison of these two speeches is sufficient to realize the great change which had taken place in the basic rules of Muslim life in less than two centuries. It was a change from the rule of *shūrā*[21] to that of absolute power derived from divine right.

Revolts and successive changes of government and political principles were the cause of the retrogression and decay of the Islāmic state. Despite the fact that Islām and the civilization to which it gave birth continued to blossom two centuries after the murder of 'Uthmān, and despite the fact that after the first decay the Islāmic state was energized again to conquer many provinces and kingdoms first by the Saljūqs and then by the Moghuls, it was during the first period which came to an end with the murder of 'Uthmān that the true principles of Islāmic public life were established and crystallized. Therefore, one must look to that period alone if he seeks certitude regarding these principles. Later on, despite the blossoming of knowledge and science during effect on his readers. In this preface I have attempted to expose as briefly as possible some of the errors of both parties; I hope I have done so with fairness and objectivity.

It is not possible to expect the western Orientalists to carry out their researches in Islāmic matters with such precision and fairness, however sincere and scientific they may be. It is especially difficult for them to master the secrets of the Arabic language and to know its usage, its nuances and rules. Moreover, they are inevitably affected by the history of western Christianity which makes them regard all other religions with suspicion. The history of the struggle between Christianity and science affects equally the very few Orientalists who are still Christians. It causes them in their Islāmic studies to fall under the same prejudice which generally characterizes all their Christian or religious research: namely, that one or the other party's line must be vindicated against its opposite. The candid Orientalists, however, cannot be blamed for this. For no man can completely escape the conditioning of his time and place. Nonetheless, this conditioning vitiates their Islāmic researches and clouds their vision of the truth. All this imposes upon the Muslim scholars, whether in the religious or other fields of Islāmic research, the very grave burden of studying their legacy with precision and exactitude, according to the scientific method. Assisted as they are by their mastery of the Arabic language and understanding of Arab life in general, their researches should convince all or some Orientalists of their errors; these researchers should also persuade them to accept the new results readily and with intellectual satisfaction.

The Muslims and Research

Such results will not be easy to achieve, nor are they impossible or altogether difficult. Patience, perseverance in study and research, sound judgment, and free thinking are all required. Moreover, this is an extremely grave matter, grave in its promise for or threat to the future of Islām, as well as mankind. It seems to me that to undertake it well, one must distinguish between two periods of Muslim history: the first begins with Muhammad and ends with the murder of 'Uthmān; the second begins with the murder of 'Uthmān and ends with the closing of the gates of *ijtihād*. In the first period, Muslim agreement was complete. It stood unaffected by the conquest of foreign lands, the War of rest of time, absolutely pure and unadulterated. The purity of the Qur'ānic text is and will forever remain the greatest miracle of all history. God said of it: "It is We who have revealed it and it is We who will guard it."[23] The Qur'ān will always remain as it once was, the only miracle of Muḥammad. Of all that concerns his life, that is true which accords with the Qur'ān, and that is false which does not. I have attempted to heed this principle in this elementary study as precisely as I could. In going over the first edition of this work I praise God and thank Him for His guidance and pray that He will guide and provide for the continuation of the scientific study of the life of the Prophet.

"Oh God! It is upon You that we depend, to You that we have recourse, and to You that we shall return."[24]

the Umawī and especially the 'Abbāsī periods, these normative principles were tampered with and often replaced by others which did not accord with the spirit of Islām. For the most part, this was done in pursuit of political *shu'ūbī* reasons.[22] It was the insincere converts from Judaism and Christianity as well as the Persians who propagated these new principles. They had no inhibition against the fabrication of *ḥadīths* and their attribution to the Prophet—may God's peace be upon him—nor against the fabrication of tales about the early caliphs contrary to what is known of their biographies and temperament.

None of the materials which have come to us from this late period can be depended upon without the strictest scrutiny and criticism; none may be scientifically accredited without subjection to impersonal analysis, absolutely free of prejudice. The first requirement consists of referring all controversial material concerning the Arab Prophet to the Qur'ān and of discarding all that disagrees therewith. As for the rest of the period ending with the murder of 'Uthmān, scientific and critical analysis should accredit the materials that have come to us and thus enable us to use them as reference in our analysis of later materials. If we do this with scientific precision, we may gain a true picture of the genuine principles of Islām and of early Islāmic life. We will grasp the mind and spirit of Islām which achieved such heights of power and vision that the Arab Bedouins who were caught by it sallied forth into the world to spread in a few decades the noblest humanism that history has ever known. Success in this task would lay bare for the benefit of humanity new horizons capable of leading it to communion with the realm of soul and spirit and the achievement of happiness and felicity, just as man's knowledge of electricity and radio and his resultant communion with the forces of nature have led to his greater enjoyment of his life on earth. Furthermore, our success in this undertaking would bring to Islām the same honor which belonged to it in its early history when the Arabs carried forth its high principles from the Peninsula to the farthest reaches of the earth.

If we are to serve truth, science and humanity, one of our foremost requirements is to deepen our study of the biography of the Arab Prophet in order to uncover therein the guidance mankind seeks. The Qur'ān is unquestionably the truest and most reliable source for such a study. It is the book which is absolutely free of error and which no doubt can penetrate. It is the only book whose text has remained for thirteen centuries, and will remain for the

Preface to the Third Edition

This edition does not differ from the second except in a few words and phrases as demanded by clarity or syntactical precision. The changes are unnoticeable except in *verbatim* comparison. Hence, there is no need to mention them.

My reticence to undertake more serious emendation of the text is not due to any judgment on my part that in its second edition the book is perfect. I do not tire of repeating here what I said in the preface to the first edition, namely, that this book is merely the beginning of scientific Islāmic research in an important field. I have discussed many problems attendant upon such research in my book *Fī Manzil al Waḥy* ["At the Locus of Revelation"] written after my pilgrimage and following the traces of the Prophet through Ḥijāz and Tihāmah. I therefore refer the reader to it. Preoccupied with other things during the last eight years I have not been able to pursue my study of the life of the Prophet, of his teaching, and the careers of his companions, nor to analyze in detail the general assertions of the concluding chapters of the second edition. But I hope God will grant me the power to do so in a separate book devoted entirely to the subject. Perhaps, after reading the conclusion of the present edition, the reader might even share this hope with me.

Finally, I thank God for the appreciation with which this book has been met by Muslim as well as non-Muslim readers, and for the reviews and announcements of it in the publications of East and West. I pray Him to guide those who undertake the continuation of this research that they may be capable of bringing it to its ultimate purpose of service to the truth.

The Life of Muḥammad

1

Arabia before Islām

The Cradle of Human Civilization

The problem of the origin and development of human civilization continues to baffle the student in modern times. Scholars have long thought that Egypt was the cradle of civilization six thousand years ago and that the earlier ages consisted of a proto-history of which no scientific knowledge was possible. Today, however, archeologists have been at work in 'Irāq and Syria in the hope of discovering clues regarding the origins of the Mesopotamian and Phoenician civilizations, of establishing whether they are anterior or posterior to Egyptian civilization, and of determining the influence of one upon the other. Whatever the results of archeological research on this period of history, one fact has never been challenged by any archeological find in China or the Far East: that is the fact that the cradle of the earliest human civilization, whether in Egypt, Phoenicia, or Mesopotamia, was connected with the Mediterranean Sea. It is equally indubitable that Egypt was the first to export its civilization to Greece and Rome, and that modern civilization is very closely related to that antiquity. Whatever archeological study of the Far East may reveal concerning the civilizations of that region, it can hardly establish that any determining relationship existed between those civilizations and Egypt, Mesopotamia, and Greece. It is no more questioned whether these ancient civilizations of

3

the Near East were influenced by the civilization of Islām. Indeed, the latter was the only civilization which has altered its course as soon as it came into contact with them. The world civilization of the present which is dominating the four corners of the globe is a result of the influences of the civilizations of the ancient Near East and that of Islām upon one another.

The Mediterranean and Red Sea Basins

The civilizations which sprang up several thousand years ago on the shores of the Mediterranean Sea or in proximity thereto— in Egypt, Mesopotamia and Greece—reached heights of achievement which elicit our wonder and admiration today, whether in the fields of science, industry, agriculture, trade, war, or any other human activity. The mainspring of all these civilizations which gave them their strength is religion. True, the figurations of this mainspring changed from the trinitarianism of ancient Egypt expressed in the myth of Osiris, Isis and Horus, and representing the continuity of life in death and resurrection and permanence through generation, to the paganism of Hellas expressed in the sensory representation of truth, goodness, and beauty. It changed, likewise, in the succeeding periods of decay and dissolution to levels where the sensory representations of Hellas became gross. Regardless of these variants, religion has remained the source which has fashioned the destiny of the world; and it plays the same role in our age. Present civilization has sometimes opposed religion, or sought to get rid of and discard it; and yet from time to time, it has inclined towards religion. On the other hand, religion has continued to court our civilization and, perhaps, one day, may even assimilate it.

In this environment where civilization has rested for thousands of years on a religious base, three well known world religions arose. Egypt saw the appearance of Moses. He was brought up and disciplined in Pharaoh's house, instructed in the unity of divine being and taught the secrets of the universe by Pharaoh's priesthood. When God permitted Moses to proclaim His religion to the people, Pharaoh was proclaiming to them: "I am your Lord supreme" (Qur'ān, 79:24). Moses contended with Pharaoh and his priesthood until he finally had to emigrate with the children of Israel to Palestine. In Palestine there appeared Jesus, the spirit and word of God given unto Mary. When God raised Jesus unto Himself,[1] his disciples preached his religion and met in the process the strongest prejudice and opposition. When God permitted Christianity to spread, the Emperor of Rome,[2] then sovereign of the world, converted to the new faith and adopted its cause. The Roman Empire followed, and the religion of Jesus spread through Egypt, Syria, and Greece. From Egypt it spread to Abyssinia, and for centuries it continued to grow. Whoever sought Roman protection or friendship joined the ranks of the new faith.

Christianity and Zoroastrianism

Facing this Christian religion which spread by Roman influence and power, stood the religion of Persia supported by the moral power of India and the Far East. The civilization of Egypt, extending to Phoenicia, and that of Mesopotamia had for many ages separated the East from the West and prevented any grave confrontation of their ideologies and civilizations. The entry of Egypt and Phoenicia into Christianity dissolved this barrier and brought the Christianity of the West and the Zoroastrianism of the East face to face. For centuries East and West confronted each other without intermingling between their religions. Each felt such fear of the other party's religion that a moral barrier came to replace the old barrier provided by the ancient Near Eastern civilizations. Each was thus compelled to direct its religious expansion to its own hinterland, away from the other's territory. Despite the numerous wars they fought, each exhausted its power without being able to confront the other on the religious or civilizational level. Although Persia conquered and ruled Syria and Egypt and the approaches of Byzantium, its kings never thought of spreading their religion or of converting the Christians. On the contrary, the conquerors respected the religions of the conquered and assisted them in reconstructing the temples which war had ravished. They granted them the liberty of upholding their religious rituals. The farthest the Persians had gone in infringing on their subjects' religion was to seize the "Holy Cross" and to keep it in Persia. When the tables were turned and the Byzantines won, they took the cross back. Thus the spiritual conquests of the West were restricted to the West, and those of the East were restricted to the East. The moral barrier separated them as decisively as the geographic civilizational one had done. Spiritually speaking, the two paths were equivalent and their equivalence prevented any clash between them.

Byzantium, the Heir of Rome

This situation remained without significant change until the sixth century of the Christian Era. In the meantime, competition between the East and West Roman empires was intensified. Rome, which had ruled the West as far as Gaul and England for many generations, and which looked proudly back to the age of Julius Caesar, began to lose its glory gradually. The glory of Byzantium was increasing and, after the dissolution of Roman power following the raids of the Vandals and their conquest of Rome itself,[3] it became in fact the only heir of the wide Roman World. Naturally, these events were not without influence on Christianity, which arose in the lap of Rome where the believers in Jesus had suffered tyranny.

Christian Sects

Christianity began to divide into various sects, and every sect began in turn to divide into factions, each of which held a different opinion concerning the religion and its principles and bases. In the absence of commonly held principles, in terms of which these differences could be composed, the various sects became antagonistic toward one another. Their moral and mental backwardness transformed the opposing doctrines into personal antagonisms protected by blind prejudice and deadening conservatism. Some of them denied that Jesus ever had a body other than a ghostly shadow by which he appeared to men. Others regarded the person and soul of Jesus as related to each other with such extraordinary ties that only the most fastidious imagination could grasp what they meant. While some worshiped Mary, others denied that she remained a virgin after the birth of Christ. Thus the controversies dividing the followers of Jesus were typical of the dissolution and decadence affecting any nation or age; that is to say, they were merely verbal disputes arising from the assignment to words of secret and esoteric meanings removed from their commonsense connotations, oppugnant to reason and tolerated only by futile sophistry.

One of the monks of the Church wrote describing the situation of his day: "The city and all its precincts were full of controversy—in the market place, in the shops of apparel, at the changers, in the grocery stores. You ask for a piece of gold to be changed at the changer's and you find yourself questioned about that which in the person of Jesus was created and that which was not created. You stop at the bakery to buy a loaf of bread and ask concerning the price, only to find the baker answer: 'Will you agree that the Father is greater than the Son and the Son is subordinate to the Father?' You ask your servant about your bath, whether or not the water is warm, and your servant answers you: 'The Son was created from nothing.' "

The decay which befell Christianity and caused it to split into factions and sects did not shake the political foundations of the Imperium Romanum. The Empire remained strong and closely knit while the sects disputed their differences with one another and with the councils which were called from time to time to resolve them. For some time at least no sect had enough power to coerce the others into agreement. The Empire protected them all and granted them the freedom to argue their doctrines with one another, a measure which increased the civil power of the Emperor without reducing his religious prestige. Each faction sought his sympathy and encouragement; indeed, each claimed that the emperor was its patron and advocate. It was the cohesion of the Empire which enabled Christianity to spread to the farthest reaches of imperial authority. From its base in Roman Egypt, Christianity thus reached to independent Abyssinia and thence to the Red Sea which it then invested with the same importance as the Mediterranean. The same imperial cohesion also enabled Christianity to move from Syria and Palestine once it had converted their people to the adjoining Arab tribe of Ghassān and the shores of the Euphrates. There it converted the Arabs of Ḥīrah, the Banū Lakhm, and Banū Mundhir who had migrated thence from the desert but whose history has been divided between independence and Persian tutelage.

The Decay of Zoroastrianism

In Persia, Zoroastrianism was attacked by the same kind of decay. Although fire worship continued to give the various factions a semblance of unity, the religion and its followers divided into sects which contended with one another. Apparently unaffected by the religious controversy around the divine personifications and the meanings behind them, the political structure of the land remained strong. All sects sought the protection of

the Persian emperor, and the latter readily gave it to them if
only to increase his own power and to use them one against the
other wherever a political gain for him was to be made or a
political threat from any one section was to be avoided. The two
powers, Christianity and Zoroastrianism, the West and the East,
each allied with a number of smaller states which it held under
its influence, surrounded the Arabian Peninsula at the beginning
of the sixth century C.E. Each entertained its own ideas of colonialism and expansion. In each camp, the men of religion exerted
great efforts to spread the faith and doctrine in which they believed. This proselytizing notwithstanding, the Arabian Peninsula remained secure against conquest except at the fringes. Like
a strong fortress it was secure against the spread of any religious
call, whether Christian or Zoroastrian. Only very few of its tribes
had answered the call, and they did so in insignificant numbers—
a surprising phenomenon in history. To understand it we must
grasp the situation and nature of Arabia and the influence that
nature had exerted upon the lives, morals and thought of its
people.

The Geographic Position of the Peninsula

The Arabian Peninsula has the shape of an irregular rec-
tangle. On the north it is bounded by Palestine and the Syrian
desert; on the east by the kingdom of al Ḥīrah, the Euphrates
and Tigris and the Persian Gulf; on the south by the Indian
Ocean and the Gulf of 'Adan; and to the west by the Red Sea.
The natural isolation of the Peninsula combined with its size to
protect it against invasion. The Peninsula is over a thousand
kilometers long and as wide. Moreover, this vast expanse is utterly uncultivable. It does not have a single river nor a depend-
able rainy season around which any agriculture could be organized. With the exception of fertile and rainy Yaman in the
southwest, the Peninsula consists of plateaus, valleys and deserts
devoid of vegetation and an atmosphere so inclement that no
civilization could prosper therein. The Arabian Peninsula allows
only desert life; and desert life demands continuous movement,
adoption of the camel as means of transportation, and the pursuit
of thin pasture which is no sooner discovered than it is exhausted
and another movement becomes imperative. These well sought-
after pastures grow around springs whose waters have collected

from rainfall on the surrounding rocky terrain, allowing a
scarce vegetation to grow in the immediate vicinity.

Except Yaman the Arabian Peninsula Is Unknown

In a country such as this, or such as the Sahara of Africa, it
is natural that no people would seek to dwell and that it have a
scarce population. It is equally natural that whoever settles in
such a desert has done so for the sake of the refuge the desert
provides and that he entertains no purpose beyond survival. The
inhabitants of the oasis, on the other hand, may envision a different purpose. But the oases themselves remain unknown to any
but the most daring adventurer prepared to venture into the
desert at the risk of his own life. Except for Yaman, the Arabian
Peninsula was literally unknown to the ancient world.

The geographic position of the Peninsula saved it from de-
population. In those ancient times, men had not yet mastered
navigation and had not yet learned to cross the sea with the confidence requisite for travel or commerce. The Arabic proverbs
which have come down to us betray the fact that men feared the
sea as they feared death. Trade and commerce had to find another
road less dangerous than the sea. The most important trade
route was that which extended from the Roman Empire and
other territories in the west to India and other territories in the
east. The Arabian Peninsula stood astride the two roads connecting East and West, whether by way of Egypt or by way of the
Persian Gulf. Its inhabitants and masters, namely the Bedouins,
naturally became princes of the desert routes just as the maritime people became princes of the sea lanes when sea communications replaced land communications. It was equally natural that
the princes of the desert would plan the roads of caravans so as
to guarantee the maximum degree of safety, just as the sea navi-
gators were to plan the course of ships away from tempests, and
other sea dangers. "The course of the caravan," says Heeren,
"was not a matter of free choice, but of established custom. In
the vast steppes of sandy desert which the caravans had to cross,
nature had sparingly allotted to the traveler a few scattered
places of rest where, under the shade of palm trees and beside
cool fountains, the merchant and his beast of burden might re-
fresh themselves. Such places of repose became *entrepôts* of commerce and, not infrequently, sites of temples and sanctuaries

under the protection of which the merchant pursued his trade
and to which the pilgrim resorted."[4]

The Two Caravan Routes

The Arabian Peninsula was criss-crossed with caravan routes.
Of these, two were important. The first ran alongside the Persian Gulf, then alongside the Tigris[5] and then crossed the Syrian
desert towards Palestine. It was properly called "the eastern
route." The other route ran along the shore of the Red Sea and
was properly called "the western route." On these two main
routes, world trade ran between East and West carrying products
and goods in both directions. These two routes provided the desert
with income and prosperity. The peoples of the West, however,
lived in total ignorance of the routes which their own trade took.
None of them, or of their eastern neighbors, ever penetrated the
desert territory—unless it be the case of an adventurer who had
no concern for his own life. A number of adventurers perished
in trying the desert labyrinth in vain. The hardships which such
travel entailed were unbearable except to those who had been
accustomed to desert life from a tender age. A man accustomed
to the luxuries of town living cannot be expected to bear the discomfort of these barren mountains separated from the Red Sea
only by the narrow passages of Tihāmah,[6] and leading through
naked rocks to the apparently infinite expanse of most arid and
desolate desert. A man accustomed to a political order guaranteeing the security of all inhabitants at all times cannot be expected to bear the terror and lawlessness of the desert, devoid as
it is of political order, and whose inhabitants live as utterly independent tribes, clans—nay individuals—except where their relations to one another come under the jurisdiction of tribal law, or
some ad hoc convention of a strong protector. The desert had
never known any urban order such as we enjoy in our modern
cities. Its people lived in the shadow of retributive justice. They
repelled attack by attack, and they sought to prevent aggression
by the fear of counteraggressions. The weak had no chance unless somebody took them under protection. Such a life does not
encourage anyone to try it, nor does it invite anyone to learn of
it in any detail. That is why the Arabian Peninsula remained an
unknown continent throughout the world until the circumstances
of history permitted its people, after the advent of Muhammad
—may God's peace and blessing be upon him—to migrate and

thus tell about their country and give the world the information it lacked.

The Civilization of Yaman

The only exception to this universal ignorance of the Arabian Peninsula concerns Yaman and the coast line of the Persian Gulf and Arabian Sea. This exception is not due merely to their near location to the sea and ocean but to their radical difference from the rest of the Arabian Peninsula. Rather than being a barren desert profitless to befriend, explore, or colonize, these lands were fertile and had well-defined seasons with a fair amount of rainfall. They had an established civilization with many urban centers and long-lasting temples. Its people, the Banū Ḥimyar, were well-endowed and intelligent. They were clever enough to think of ways of saving rain water from running down to the sea and of making good use of it. They built the dam of Ma'rib and thereby changed the course which water would have naturally followed to courses such as settled life and intensive agriculture required. Falling on high mountains, rain water would gather in a 400 meters wide valley flanked by two mountains east of the city of Ma'rib. It would then divide into many streams and spread over a wide plain that is very much like the Nile in the dam area in upper Egypt. As their technological and administrative skill developed, the people of Yaman constructed a dam at the narrowest point between the two mountains with gates which allowed controlled distribution of water. By putting the resources of their country to good use, they increased the fertility of the land and the prosperity of the people. What has so far been discovered— and is still being discovered—by way of remains of this Ḥimyarī civilization in Yaman, proves that it had reached an impressive height and was strong enough to withstand not only a number of great political storms but even war.

Judaism and Christianity in Yaman

This civilization, founded upon agricultural prosperity and settled life, brought upon Yaman great misfortune, unlike the desert whose barrenness was for it a sort of protector. Sovereigns in their own land, Banū Ḥimyar ruled Yaman generation after generation. One of their kings, Dhū Nuwās, disliked the paganism of his people and inclined toward the Mosaic religion. In time, he

was converted to this faith by the Jews who had migrated to
Yaman. Historians agree that it was to this Ḥimyarī king that
the Qur'ān referred in the "story of the trench," reported in the
following verses:

$$\text{قُتِلَ اَصْحَبُ الْاُخْدُوْدِ ۞ النَّارِ ذَاتِ الْوَقُوْدِ ۞ اِذْ هُمْ عَلَيْهَا قُعُوْدٌ ۞ وَّ هُمْ عَلَى مَا يَفْعَلُوْنَ}$$
$$\text{بِالْمُؤْمِنِيْنَ شُهُوْدٌ ۞ وَمَا نَقَمُوْا مِنْهُمْ اِلَّا اَنْ يُّؤْمِنُوْا بِاللّٰهِ الْعَزِيْزِ الْحَمِيْدِ}$$

"Cursed be the fellows of the trench who fed the fire with fury,
sat by it and witnessed the burning of the believers whom they
threw therein. They executed the believers only because the latter
believed in God, the Almighty, the Praiseworthy."[7]

The story is that of a pious Christian, Qaymiyūn by name, who
emigrated from Byzantium, settled in Najrān, and converted
the people of that city by his piety, virtue, and good example.
When the news of the increasing converts and widening influence of Christianity reached Dhū Nuwās, he went to Najrān
and solemnly warned its people that they must either convert to
Judaism or be killed. Upon their refusal to apostasize, the king
dug a wide trench, set it on fire, and threw them in. Whoever
escaped from the fire was killed by the sword. According to the
biographies, twenty thousand of them perished in this manner.
Some nonetheless escaped, sought the Byzantine Emperor Jus-
tinian and asked for his help against Dhū Nuwās. Byzantium
was too far from Yaman to send any effective assistance. Its emperor therefore wrote to the Negus of Abyssinia to avenge the
Christians of Yaman. At the time—the sixth century C.E.—Abyssinia was at the height of its power, commanding a wide sea
trade protected by a strong maritime fleet and imposing its influence upon the neighboring countries.[8] The Abyssinian kingdom
was the ally of the Byzantine Empire and the protagonist of
Christianity on the Red Sea just as the Byzantine Empire was its
protagonist on the Mediterranean. When the Negus received the
message of the Byzantine emperor, he sent with the Yamanī,
who carried the emperor's message to him, an Abyssinian army
under the command of Aryāṭ. One of the officers of this expeditionary force was Abraha al Ashram.[9] Aryāṭ conquered Yaman
and ruled it in the name of the negus of Abyssinia. Later on he
was killed and succeeded by Abraha, "the general with the ele-

phant," who sought to conquer Makkah and destroy the Ka'bah but failed, as we shall see in the next chapter.[10]

The successors of Abraha ruled Yaman tyrannically. Seeking relief from the yoke the Ḥimyarī Sayf ibn Dhū Yazan approached the Byzantine emperor complaining against the Abyssinians and pleading for a Byzantine governor to be sent to establish justice. He was turned down because of the alliance between Byzantium and Abyssinia. Disappointed, he stopped on his way back at the court of Nu'mān ibn al Mundhir, Viceroy of Chosroes for al Ḥīrah and surrounding lands of 'Irāq.

Conquest and Rule of Yaman by Persia

When al Nu'man entered the audience hall of Chosroes, he was accompanied by Sayf ibn Dhū Yazan. Chosroes received them at his winter residence, sitting on the throne of Darius in the great *iwān* decorated with the pictures of the Zodiac. The throne was surrounded with a curtain made of the most precious furs which served as background for golden and silver chandeliers filled with warm water and for his golden and silver crown filled with rubies, beryls and pearls which, being too heavy to rest on his head, was attached to the ceiling by a golden chain. His clothes were of a golden weave, and he decorated himself with gold. So brilliant was this spectacle that any person was seized with awe at the mere sight of it. Surely, such was the case of Sayf ibn Dhū Yazan. When he came back to himself and felt reassured, he was asked by Chosroes about his mission and told the emperor the story of Abyssinia's conquest and tyrannous rule. Chosroes hesitated at the beginning, but then decided to send to Yaman an army under the command of Wahrīz, one of the noblest and bravest commanders of Persia. The Persian army arrived in Yaman, vanquished the Abyssinians and expelled them after a rule of seventy-two years. Yaman remained under Persian rule until the advent of Islām and the succeeding entry of all Arab countries into the religion of God as well as into the Islāmic Empire.

Cyrus's Rule of Persia

The Persians who ruled Yaman did not come directly under the authority of the Persian Emperor, particularly after Cyrus

had killed his father Chosroes and succeeded to his throne. The
new emperor seemed to think that the whole world ran according to his wishes and that the kingdoms of the world existed only
to fill his treasury and to increase his affluence and luxury. Because he was a young man, he neglected most of the affairs of
state in order to devote himself to his pleasures and pastimes.
The pageantry of his hunting trips was greater than any imagination could possibly conceive. He used to go out surrounded by
a whole troop of youthful princes clad in red, yellow, and violet;
carriers of falcons and servants held back their muzzled pan-
thers, perfume-carrying slaves, fly-fighters and musicians. In order to give himself a feeling of spring in the midst of winter, he
used to sit surrounded by the members of his house on an immense carpet on which were drawn the roads and highways of
the kingdom, the orchards, and gardens full of flowers, the for-
ests and greenwoods and the silvery rivers—all in a state of
blossoming spring. Despite Cyrus's extravagance and addiction
to pleasure, Persia maintained its glory and strong resistance to
Byzantium and prevented the spread of Christianity further east.
It was clear, however, that the accession of Cyrus to the throne
was the beginning of the decline of this empire and a preparation for its conquest by the Muslims and the spread of Islām
therein.

Destruction of the Dam of Ma'rib

The conflict of which Yaman had been the theatre ever since
the fourth century C.E. influenced the distribution of population
in the Arabian Peninsula. It is told that the dam of Ma'rib, by
means of which the Ḥimyarīs changed the course of nature to
benefit their country, was destroyed by the great flood, *"Sayl al
'Arim,"* with the result that large sections of the inhabitants had
to migrate. Apparently the continuing political conflicts so distracted men and governments from attending to the repair and
maintenance of the dam that when the flood came it was incapable of holding the water. It is also told that the shift in population was due to the fact that the Byzantine emperor, realizing
the threat to his trade by the conflict with Persia over Yaman,
built a fleet of ships to ply the Red Sea and thereby avoid the
caravan routes of Arabia. Historians agree on the historicity of
the immigration of the Azd tribes from Yaman to the north but
disagree in explaining it. Some attribute it to the loss of trade,

and others to the destruction of the dam of Ma'rib and the resultant loss in food production. Whatever the explanation, the historicity of the event is beyond doubt. It was at the root of the
blood relation of the Yamanīs with the northern Arabs and their
involvement in the history of the north. Even today the problem
is still far from solved.

The Social Order of the Peninsula

As we have just seen, the political order of Yaman was disturbed because of the geographic circumstances of that country
and the political wars of conquest of which it had been the object. *Per contra,* the Arabian Peninsula was free from any such
disturbances. Indeed, the political system known in Yaman, as
well as any other political system—whatever the term may mean
or may have meant to the civilized peoples of old—was literally
unknown in the areas of Tihāmah, Ḥijāz, Najd, and other wide
spaces constituting the Arabian Peninsula. The sons of the desert
were then, as most of them are today, nomads who had no taste
for settled life and who knew no kind of permanence other than
perpetual movement in search of pasture and satisfaction of the
wish of the moment. In the desert, the basic unit of life is not
the state but the tribe. Moreover, a tribe which is always on the
move does not know of any universal law nor does it ever subject
itself to any general political order. To the nomad, nothing is
acceptable that falls short of total freedom for the individual,
for the family, and for the tribe as a whole. Settled land farmers,
on the other hand, agree to give up part of their freedom,
whether to the group as a whole or to an absolute ruler, in exchange for peace, security, and the prosperity which order
brings. But the desert man who disdains the prosperity and
security of settled life and derides the comforts of urban living
cannot give any of his freedom for such "gains." Neither does he
accept anything short of absolute equality with all the members
of his tribe as well as between his tribe and other tribes. Naturally, he is moved like all other men by the will to survive and
to defend himself, but such will must accord with the principles
of honor and integrity demanded by the free life of the desert.
Therefore, the desert people have never suffered with patience
any injustice inflicted upon them but resisted it with all their
strength. If they cannot throw off the injustice imposed upon
them, they give up the pasture and move out into the wide ex-

panse of the desert. Nothing is easier for them than recourse to
the sword whenever a conflict seems insoluble under the conventional desert rules of honor, nobility, and integrity. It was these
very conditions of desert living which led to the cultivation and
growth of the virtues of hospitality, bravery, mutual assistance,
neighbor protection, and magnanimity. It is not by accident that
these virtues are stronger and more popular in the desert and
weaker and more scarce in the cities. For the above mentioned
economic reasons neither Byzantium nor Persia entertained any
ideas of conquering the Arabian Peninsula with the exception of
Yaman. For they know that the people of the Peninsula would
prefer emigration to the life of subjection and that they would
never yield to any established authority or order.

These nomadic characteristics influenced in large measure the
few small towns which grew up in the Peninsula along the caravan routes. To these centers the traders used to come in order to
rest. In them they found temples wherein to give thanks to the
gods for bringing them safely through their travels and for safeguarding their goods while in transit. Such were Makkah, Ṭā'if,
Yathrib, and others scattered between the mountains of the west
coastland and the desert sands. In their order and organization
these towns followed the pattern and laws of the desert. Indeed,
their being closer to the desert than they were to civilized life
was reflected in the system of their tribes and clans, in their
morals and customs, and in their strong resistance to any imposition upon their freedom, despite the fact that settled life had
somewhat restricted their movements in comparison with their
desert cousins. We shall witness more of this in the coming chapters when we talk about Makkah and Yathrib.

Arab Paganism and Its Causes

This state of nature and the moral, political, and social order
it implied were equally consequential for religion. Was Yaman
influenced by Byzantine Christianity or Persian Zoroastrianism,
and did it influence in turn the Arabian Peninsula? It would
seem so, especially in the case of Christianity. The missionaries
of Christianity were as active in those days as they are today.
Moreover, unlike the life of the city, desert life is especially conducive to the rise of religious consciousness. In the desert, man is
in constant touch with the universe as a whole. He senses the
infinity of existence in all its forms and is thereby prompted to

order his relationship with the infinite. The city man, on the other hand, is distracted from the consciousness of infinity by his constant occupation. He is protected from the *angst* and dread such consciousness of the infinite brings by the group to which he gave up part of his freedom. His submission to political authority and the consequent security arising from this submission prevent him from establishing a direct contact, beyond the civil power, with the spiritual powers of the world, and weaken his speculative thinking about them. In the case of the desert man, on the other hand, nothing impedes his speculation over religious meanings and problems to which the life of the desert naturally leads.

And now we may ask, did Christianity, with all its missionary activity, benefit from these circumstances to spread and propagate itself? Perhaps it would have done so had it not been that other factors went into play and enabled the Peninsula as a whole to preserve its paganism, the religion of its ancestors. Only a very few tribes therefore responded favorably to the Christian call.

Christianity and Judaism

The greatest civilization of the day stood in the basins of the Mediterranean and the Red Sea. The religions of Christianity and Judaism divided this civilization, and though they were not at war with each other, they were surely not friendly to each other. The Jews then remembered, as they still do, the rebellion Jesus had launched against their religion. As much as they could, therefore, they worked secretly to stop the flow of Christianity, the religion which forced them out of the promised land and assumed the Roman color as its own throughout the Empire. There were large communities of Jews living in Arabia, and a good number of them had settled in Yaman and in Yathrib. Zoroastrianism, on the other hand, was anxious to prevent Christianity from crossing the Euphrates. Hence, it lent its moral support to paganism while overlooking, or being mindful of, its spiritual and moral degradation. The fall of Rome and the passing of its power under all forms of dissolution encouraged the multiplication of sects in Christianity. These were not only becoming numerous and varied but were also fighting desperately with one another. Indeed, the Christian sects fell from the high level of faith to that of controversy regarding forms, figures, and words which related to the holiness of Mary and her priority to her son,

the Christ. The sectarian controversies of Christianity betray
the level of degradation and decay to which Christian thought
and practice had sunk. It takes a truly decadent mind to discard
content in favor of external form, to attach so much importance
to externalities that the essence disappears under their opaque
weight. And that is precisely what the Christian sects did.

The subjects under controversy varied from place to place; the
Christians of al Shām[11] disputed other questions than those of
Hīrah or Abyssinia. In their contact with the Christians, the
Jews did nothing to calm the raging controversies or to temper
the generated antagonism. The Arabs, on the other hand, were
on good terms with the Christians of Damascus and Yaman with
whom they came into contact during the winter and summer
caravan trips, as well as with the Abyssinian Christians who
visited them from time to time. It was natural for them to refrain from taking sides with any Christian party against another. The Arabs were happy with their paganism, contented to
follow in the footsteps of their ancestors, and prepared to leave
both Christians and Jews alone as long as these were not interfering with their religion. Thus, idol worship continued to flour-
ish among them and even spread to the centers inhabited by their
Christian and Jewish neighbors, namely Najrān and Yathrib.
The Jews of Yathrib tolerated idol worship, co-existed with it,
and finally befriended it as the trade routes linked them to the
pagan Arabs with mutually beneficial relations.

The Spread of Paganism

Perhaps the desperate struggle of the Christian sects against
one another was not the sole cause of why the Arabs remained
pagan. Varieties of paganism were still adhered to even by the
people who had converted to Christianity. Egyptian and Greek
paganism was quite apparent in the ideologies and practices of
many Christian sects. Indeed, they were apparent in some of the
views of orthodox Christianity itself. The school of Alexandria
and its philosophy still enjoyed a measure of influence, though it
was naturally reduced from that which it enjoyed during the time
of the Ptolemies, at the beginning of the Christian Era. At any
rate, this influence was deeply imbedded in the consciousness of
the people, and its brilliant logic, though sophistic in nature, still
exercised appeal for a polytheistic paganism of human deities so
close and lovable to man. It seems to me that polytheism has been

the strongest appeal of paganism to weak souls in all times and places. The weak soul is by nature incapable of rising high enough to establish a contact with total being and, in a supreme moment of consciousness, to grasp the unity of total being represented in that which is greater than all that exists, in God, the Lord of Majesty. The weak soul therefore stops at one of the differentiated phenomena of total being, like the sun or the moon or the fire, and awkwardly withdraws from rising beyond it to the unity of being itself.

What poverty of spirit characterizes those souls who, arrested by their grasp of a confused, insignificant little meaning of total being in an idol, commune with that object and wrap it with a halo of sanctity! We still witness this phenomenon in many countries of the world despite all the claims this modern world makes for its advances in science and civilization. Such is what the visitors see at St. Peter's cathedral in Rome where the foot of a statue of a certain saint is physically worn out by the kisses which the saint's worshipers proffer to it, so that the church has to change it for a new foot every now and then. If we could keep this in mind, we would excuse those Arabs whom God had not yet guided to the true faith. We would be less quick to condemn them for their continued idolatry and following in the footsteps of their ancestors when we remember that they were the witnesses of a desperate struggle of Christian neighbors against one another who had not yet liberated themselves completely from paganism. How can we not excuse them when pagan conditions are still with us and seem to be inextricably rooted in the world? How can we not excuse the pre-Islāmic Arabs when paganism is still evident in the idolatrous practices of so many Muslims of the present world despite the fact that Islām, the one unflinching enemy of paganism that had once succeeded in sweeping away every other worship besides that of God, the Lord of majesty, is their professed religion?

Idol Worship

In their worship of idols, the Arabs followed many ways difficult for the modern researcher to discover and understand. The Prophet destroyed the idols of the Ka'bah and commanded his companions to destroy all idols wherever they might be. After they destroyed the idols' physical existence, the Muslims launched a campaign against the very mention of idols and sought to wipe

them out from history, literature, and, indeed, from consciousness itself. The evidence the Qur'ān gives for the existence of
idolatry in pre-Islāmic times as well as the stories which circulated in the second century A.H. concerning idolatrous practices,
prove that idolatry once enjoyed a position of tremendous importance. The same evidence proves that it was of many kinds,
that idolatrous practices were of great variety and that idols differed widely in the degree of sacralization conferred upon them.
Every tribe had a different idol which it worshiped. Generally,
objects of worship belonged to three genres: metal and wooden
statues, stone statues, and shapeless masses of stone which one
tribe or another consecrated because its origin was thought to
be heavenly, whereas in reality it was only a piece of volcanic
or meteoric rock. The most finely made statues were those which
belonged to Yaman. No wonder, for the Yamanīs were more advanced in technology than the people of Ḥijāz, Najd, or Kindah.
The classical works on pre-Islāmic idols, however, did not report
to us that any fine statues existed anywhere, except perhaps
what they reported concerning Hubal, namely that it was made
out of carnelian in the likeness of man, that its arm once broke
off and was replaced by another contributed by Quraysh and
made of solid gold. Hubal was the greatest member of the Arab
pantheon and resided in Makkah, inside the Ka'bah. Pilgrims
came to its shrine from all corners. Still unsatisfied by these
great idols to which they prayed and offered sacrifices, the Arabs
used to adopt other statues or sacred stones for domestic worship and devotion. They used to circumambulate the "holy" precincts of these gods both before leaving on a trip and upon returning home. They often carried their idols with them when
they traveled, presuming that the idol had permitted its worshiper to travel. All these statues, whether in the Ka'bah, around
it or scattered around the tribes or the provinces, were regarded
as intermediaries between their worshipers and the supreme god.
They regarded the worship of them as a means of rapprochement
with God even though in reality that same worship had caused
them to forget the true worship of God.

Makkah's Place in Arabia

Despite the fact that Yaman was the most advanced province
in the Arabian Peninsula and the most civilized on account of its
fertility and the sound administration of its water resources, its

religious practices never commanded the respect of the inhabitants of the desert. Its temples never constituted a single center of pilgrimage. Makkah, on the other hand, and its Ka'bah, the house of Isma'īl, was the object of pilgrimage ever since Arab history began. Every Arab sought to travel to it. In it the holy months were observed with far more ado than anywhere else. For this reason, as well as for its distinguished position in the trade of the Peninsula as a whole, it was regarded as the capital. Further, it was to be the birthplace of Muḥammad, the Arab Prophet, and became the object of the yearning of the world throughout the centuries. Its ancient house was to remain holy forever. The tribe of Quraysh was to continue to enjoy a distinguished and sovereign position. All this was to remain so forever despite the fact that the Makkans and their city continued to lead a life closer to the hardness of bedouin existence which had been their custom for many tens of centuries.

Makkah, the Ka'bah, and the Quraysh

Geographic Position of Makkah

About eighty kilometers east of the shore of the Red Sea a number of mountain chains run from north to south paralleling the shore line and dovetailing with the caravan route between Yaman and Palestine. These chains would completely enclose a small plain, were it not for three main outlets connecting it with the road to Yaman, the road to the Red Sea close to the port town of Juddah and the road leading to Palestine. In this plain surrounded by mountains on all sides stands Makkah. It is difficult to trace its origins. In all likelihood these origins lie thousands of years in the past. It is certain that even before Makkah was built the valley on which it stands must have been used as a resting point for the caravan routes. Its number of water springs made it a natural stopping point for the caravans going south to Yaman as well as for those going north to Palestine. Ismā'īl, son of Ibrahīm, was probably the first one to dwell there permanently and establish it as a permanent settlement after it had long been a resting station for transient caravans and a marketplace in which the north-bound and south-bound travelers exchanged their goods.

Ibrahīm—May God's Peace be upon Him

Granted that Isma'īl was the first to make of Makkah a permanent habitat, the history of the city before Isma'īl is rather obscure. Perhaps it can be said that Makkah was used as a place of worship even before Isma'īl had migrated there. The story of the latter's migration to Makkah demands that we summarize the story of his father, Ibrāhīm—may God's peace be upon him. Ibrāhīm was born in 'Irāq to a father whose occupation was carpentry and the making and selling of statues for worship. As Ibrāhīm grew up and observed his father making these statues out of pieces of wood, he was struck by his people's worship and consecration of them. He doubted these deities and was troubled by his doubt. One day he asked his father to explain how he could worship that which his hand had wrought. Unsatisfied by his father's answer, Ibrāhīm talked about his doubts to his friends, and soon the father began to fear the consequences for the security of his son as well as for his own trade. Ibrāhīm, however, respected his own reason too much to silence its voice. Accordingly, he sought to convince his people of the futility of idol-worship with argument and proof. Once he seized the opportunity of the absence of worshipers from the temple and destroyed all the statues of the gods but that of the principal deity. When he was accused in public of this crime he was asked: "Was it you Ibrāhīm, who destroyed our gods?" He answered: "No, rather, it was the principal god who destroyed the other gods. Ask them, for they would speak, wouldn't they?"[1] Ibrāhīm's destruction of the idols came after he had long pondered the error of idol worship and searched earnestly for a worthier object of devotion.

فَلَمَّا جَنَّ عَلَيْهِ الَّيْلُ رَا كَوْكَبًا قَالَ هٰذَا رَبِّى فَلَمَّا أَفَلَ قَالَ لَآ أُحِبُّ الْآفِلِينَ ۞ فَلَمَّا رَا الْقَمَرَ بَازِغًا قَالَ هٰذَا رَبِّى فَلَمَّا أَفَلَ قَالَ لَئِنْ لَمْ يَهْدِنِى رَبِّى لَأَكُوْنَنَّ مِنَ الْقَوْمِ الضَّالِّينَ ۞ فَلَمَّا رَا الشَّمْسَ بَازِغَةً قَالَ هٰذَا رَبِّى هٰذَآ أَكْبَرُ فَلَمَّا أَفَلَتْ قَالَ يَا قَوْمِ اِنِّى بَرِىءٌ مِّمَّا تُشْرِكُوْنَ ۞ اِنِّى وَجَّهْتُ وَجْهِىَ لِلَّذِى فَطَرَ السَّمٰوٰتِ وَ الْأَرْضَ حَنِيْفًا وَّمَآ أَنَا مِنَ الْمُشْرِكِيْنَ

"When the night came, and Ibrāhīm saw the star rise, he took it to be the true God. Soon, however, the star set and Ibrāhīm was disappointed. 'How could a veritable God set and disappear?' he asked himself. He then observed the moon shining brilliantly and thought: 'That is my Lord.' But when it too set, he was all the more disappointed and thought: 'Unless God guides me truly, I shall certainly go astray.' Later on Ibrāhīm observed the sun in its brilliant and dazzling glory and he thought: 'This finally must be my Lord, for it is the greatest of all.' But then it too set and disappeared. Ibrāhīm was thus cured of the star worship common among his people. 'I shall devote myself,' he therefore resolved, 'to Him Who has created the heavens and the earth, I shall dedicate myself as a *hanīf* and not be an idol worshiper.' "[2]

Ibrahīm and Sārah in Egypt

Ibrahīm did not succeed in liberating his people from paganism. On the contrary, they punished him by throwing him into the fire. God rescued him by allowing him to run away to Palestine together with his wife, Sārah. From Palestine he moved on to Egypt, which was then ruled by the Hyksos or Amalekite kings. Sārah was a beautiful lady, and as the Hyksos kings were in the habit of taking into their households any beautiful married women they met, Ibrahīm therefore pretended that Sārah was his sister and hence unmarried so that the king might not take her away and kill him in the process. The king, however, did take her and later realized that she was married. He returned her to Ibrahīm, blamed him for his lie, and gave him a number of gifts, one of which was a slave girl by the name of Hāgar.[3] As Sārah remained barren after many years of married life, she urged her husband to go into Hāgar. After Ibrahīm did so, Hāgar soon bore him his son Isma'īl. Later on, after Isma'īl became a youth, Sārah bore a son who was called Ishaq.

Who Was the Sacrificial Son?

Historians of this period disagree on the matter of Ibrahīm's sacrifice of Isma'īl. Did the event take place before the birth of Ishaq or thereafter? Did it take place in Palestine or in the Hijāz? Jewish historians insist that the sacrificial son was Ishaq, not Isma'īl. This is not the place to analyze this issue. In his book *Qiṣaṣ al Anbiyā'*, Shaykh 'Abd al Wahhāb al Najjār concluded that the sacrificial son was Isma'īl. His evidence was drawn from the Qur'ān itself where the sacrificial son is described as being Ibrahīm's unique son, which could only be Isma'īl, and only as long as Ishaq was not yet born.[4] For with the birth of Ishaq, Ibrahīm would have no "unique" son but two, Isma'īl and Ishaq. But to accede to this evidence implies that the sacrifice should have taken place in Palestine.[5] This would equally be true in case the sacrificial son was Ishaq, for the latter remained with his mother Sārah in Palestine and never left for the Hijāz. On the other hand, the report which makes the sacrifice take place on the mountain of Minā near Makkah identifies the sacrificial son as Isma'īl. The Qur'ān did not mention the name of the sacrificial son, and hence Muslim historians disagree in this regard.

The Qur'ānic Version of the Sacrifice

The story of the sacrifice is that Ibrahīm saw in a dream God commanding him to sacrifice his son to Him. In the morning he took his son and went out to fulfill the command. "When they reached the destination Ibrahīm said to his son: 'My son, I saw in a dream God commanding me to sacrifice you. What will you say?' His son answered: 'Fulfill whatever you have been commanded; by God's will you will find me patient.' When Ibrahīm threw his son on the ground for the sacrifice and both had acquiesced to the commandment, God called out to him: 'O Ibrahīm, you have fulfilled the commandment. We shall reward you as We reward the virtuous. You have manifestly succeeded in your travail.' We ransomed him with a worthy animal to sacrifice."[6]

The Historians' Version

Some historians tell this story in more dramatic way. The beauty of some versions justifies a brief pause despite the fact that the story itself does not belong in this *aperçu* of Makkan history. It is told, for instance, that when Ibrahīm saw in his dream that he should sacrifice his son and ascertained that that was God's commandment, he asked his son to take a rope and a knife and to go ahead of him to a nearby hill in order to collect some wood for fuel. The boy complied with his father's request. Satan took the guise of a man, came to Isma'īl's mother and said: "Do you know where Ibrahīm is taking your son?" She answered: "Yes, they both went to collect some wood." Satan said: "By God, he did not take him except to sacrifice him." The mother answered, "Not at all! His father is even more loving and gentler to him than me." Satan said: "But he claims that God has commanded him to do so." The mother answered: "If God has thus commanded him then so let it be." Thus Satan lost the first round. He ran to the son as he was following his father and repeated to him the same temptations he offered to his mother. But the son answered in exactly the same way as his mother did. Satan then approached Ibrahīm and told him that what he saw in his dream was only a Satanic illusion that he may kill his son and grieve thereat the rest of his days. Ibrahīm dismissed him and cursed

him. Iblīs (Satan) returned maddened and frustrated at his failure to dissuade Ibrahīm, his wife, and his son from fulfillment
of God's command. The same story tellers also report that Ibrahīm divulged his dream to his son and asked for his opinion. They
report the son as answering: "O father, do what you are commanded to do." A still more fanciful version of the story reports
the son as saying: "O father, if you want to kill me, then bind
me tight that I may not move and splatter you with my blood and
thus reduce my own reward for the fulfillment of God's command. I know that death is hard, and I am not certain I will stay
still when it comes. Therefore sharpen your blade that you may
finish me quickly. Lay me face down rather than on my side, for
I fear that if you were to witness my face as you cut my throat
you would be moved by compassion for me and fail to complete
that which God had asked you to do. And if you see fit to return
my shirt to my mother that she may remember me therewith
and, perhaps, find some consolation, please do so.' Ibrahīm answered: 'My son, you are the best help in the fulfillment of God's
command.' As he prepared for the sacrifice, bound the child, and
laid him down, Ibrahīm was called to stop. For he had given evidence of his obedience to God's command, and the son was ransomed with a sheep which Ibrahīm found close by and which he
killed and burnt."

That is the story of the sacrifice. It is the story of submission
to God and His decree as well as of the fulfillment of His commandment.

Ibrahīm, Ismaʿīl, and Hāgar's Trip to the Valley of Makkah

Ishāq grew up in the company of his brother Ismaʿīl. The
father loved both equally, but Sārah was not pleased with this
equation of her son with the son of the slave girl Hāgar. Once,
upon seeing Ismaʿīl chastising his younger brother, she swore
that she would not live with Hāgar nor her son. Ibrahīm realized
that happiness was not possible as long as the two women lived
in the same household; hence, he took Hāgar and her son and
traveled south until they arrived to the valley of Makkah. As we
said earlier, the valley was a midway place of rest for caravans
on the road between Yaman and al Shām. The caravans came in
season, and the place was empty at all or most other times.
Ibrahīm deposited Ismaʿīl and his mother there and left them
some sustenance. Hāgar built a little hut in which she settled

with her son and whereto Ibrahīm returned when he came. When water and provisions were exhausted, Hāgar set out to look for food, but she could not find any. As the story tellers put it, she ran towards the valley seeking water and, not finding any, would run in another direction. After running to and fro seven times between Ṣafā and Marwah, she returned in despair to her son. But what surprise when she found him! Having scratched the surface of the earth with his foot, he uncovered a water fountain which sprung under his feet. Hāgar drank and gave Isma'īl to drink until they were both satisfied. She then closed in the spring that its water might not be lost in the sand. Thereafter the child and his mother lived in Makkah. Arab travelers continued to use the place as a rest stop, and in exchange for services they rendered to the travelers who came with one caravan after another, Hāgar and Isma'īl were sufficiently provided for.

Subsequently a number of tribes liked the fountain water of Zamzam sufficiently to settle nearby. Jurhum was the first such tribe to settle in Makkah. Some versions assert that Jurhum was already settled in Makkah even before Hāgar and her son arrived there. According to other reports, no tribes settled in Makkah until Zamzam had sprung forth and made life possible in this otherwise barren valley and hence, after Isma'īl's advent. Isma'īl grew up, married a girl from the tribe of Jurhum and lived with this tribe in the same area where he built the holy temple. Thereafter, the city of Makkah arose around the temple. It is also told that Ibrahīm once took leave of Sārah to visit Isma'īl and his mother. When he inquired about the house of Isma'īl and found it, he asked Isma'īl's wife, "Where is your husband?" She answered, "He went out to hunt." He then asked her whether she had any food or drink to give him. She answered in the negative. Before he turned back, Ibrahīm asked her to convey to her husband a message. "Give him my greetings," he said, "and tell him that he should change the threshold of his house." When Isma'īl's wife related to her husband his father's message, he divorced her and married a girl from the Jurhum tribe, the daughter of Muḍād ibn 'Amr. This second wife knew well how to entertain Ibrahīm when he came to visit his son a second time later. At the end of his second visit, Ibrahīm asked Isma'īl's wife to greet her husband for him and to tell him, "Now the threshold of your house is straight." Twelve sons were born to Isma'īl from this marriage with the Jurhum girl. These were the ancestors of the twelve tribes of Arabized or Northern Arabs. On their mother's side

these were related through Jurhum to the Arabizing Arabs, the
sons of Ya'rub ibn Qaḥtān. They were also related to Egypt
through their grandmother on their father's side, Hāgar, which
was a close relation indeed. Through their grandfather Ibrahīm,
they were related to 'Irāq and to Palestine, his old and new
abodes.

Discussion of the Story

Despite disagreement on details, the main theme of this story
which history had brought down to us, namely the emigration of
Ibrahīm and Isma'īl to Makkah, is backed by an almost complete
consensus on the part of the historians. The differences center on
whether, when Hāgar arrived with Isma'īl in the valley of
Makkah, the springs were already there and whether the tribe of
Jurhum had already occupied the place and had welcomed Hāgar
when Ibrahīm brought her and her son to live in their midst.
When Isma'īl grew up, he married a Jurhum girl and had several
sons from her. It was this mixture of Hebrew, Egyptian and
Arab blood that gave to Isma'īl's descendants resoluteness, courage, and all the virtues of the native Arabs, the Hebrews, and the
Egyptians combined. As for the detail regarding Hāgar's difficulty when she ran out of water, and of her running to and fro
between Ṣafā and Marwah and the way in which Zamzam sprang
forth, all these are subject to debate.

Sir William Muir, for instance, doubts the whole story of
Ibrahīm and Isma'īl's trip to Ḥijāz and denies it altogether. He
claims that it is one of the Israelitisms which the Jews had invented long before Islām in order to strike a link with the Arabs
by making them descendents of Ibrahīm, now father of all. Since
the Jews regarded themselves as descendants of Isḥaq, they
would become the cousins of the Arabs and therefore entitled to
Arab hospitality if the Arabs were declared the sons of Isḥaq's
brother, namely Isma'īl. Such a theme, if properly advocated, was
probably thought to help establish Jewish trade in the Peninsula.
In making this claim, Muir assumed that the religious situation
in Arabia was far removed from the religion of Abraham. The
former was pagan whereas Ibrahīm was a Ḥanīf and a Muslim.
For our part, we do not think that this is sufficient reason to
deny a historical truth. Our evidence for the paganism of the
Arabs is centuries later than the arrival of Ibrahīm and Isma'īl
to the scene. It cannot therefore constitute any proof that at the

time of Ibrahīm's arrival to Ḥijāz and his building of the Ka'bah with his son Isma'īl that the Arabs were pagan. Neither would Sir William's claims be corroborated had the religion of the Arabs been pagan at the time. Ibrahīm's own people, whom he tried to bring forth to monotheism without success, were also idol worshipers. Had Ibrahīm called the Arabs to monotheism, as he did his own people earlier, and not succeeded, and the Arabs remained idol worshipers, they would not have acquiesced to Ibrahīm's coming to Makkah nor in his son's settlement there. Rather, logic would here corroborate the report of history. Ibrahīm, the man who left 'Irāq to escape from his people and traveled to Palestine and to Egypt, was a man who knew how to travel and was familiar with desert crossing. The road between Palestine and Makkah was one trodden by the caravans for ages. There is, therefore, no reason to doubt a historical event which consensus has confirmed, at least in its general themes.

Sir William Muir and others who shared his view claim that it is possible that a number of the descendants of Ibrahīm and Isma'īl had moved to the Arabian Peninsula after they had settled in Palestine and that the blood relationship had developed after their arrival to Arabia. That is a fine opinion indeed! But if it is possible for the sons of Ibrahīm and Isma'īl to do such a thing, why should it not have been possible for the two men, Ibrahīm and Isma'īl personally, only a generation or two earlier? How can we deny a confirmed historical tradition? And how can we doubt an event which the Qur'ān, as well as a number of other old scriptures, has mentioned?

Ibrahīm and Isma'īl's Construction of the Ka'bah

Together Ibrahīm and Isma'īl laid down the foundations and built the holy temple. "It was the first house built for public worship in Makkah. It still stands as a blessing and guidance to mankind. In it are manifest signs; that is the house of Ibrahīm. Whoever enters it shall be secure."[7] God also says: "For We made the house a refuge and a place of security for the people. We commanded them to take the house of Ibrahīm as a place of worship and We have commanded Ibrahīm and Isma'īl to purify My house for pilgrims and men in retreat, for those who kneel and prostrate themselves in prayer. When Ibrahīm prayed, 'O Lord, make this town a place of security and give its people of Your bounty, those of them who have believed in God and in the

day of judgment,' God answered: 'Yea, even those who do not
believe will enjoy my security and bounty for a while before I
inflict upon them the punishment of fire and the sad fate they
deserve.' As Ibrahīm and Isma'īl laid the foundations and raised
the walls of the house, they prayed: 'O Lord, bless our work; for
You alone are all-hearing and all-knowing.' "⁸

Religious Development in Arabia

How did it happen that Ibrahīm built the house as a place of
refuge and security for the people so that the believers in God
alone might use it for prayer, and then it became a pantheon
full of statues for idol worship? What were the conditions of
worship after Ibrahīm and Isma'īl? In what form and with what
ritual was worship conducted in the holy house? When were
these conditions and forms superceded by paganism? In vain do
we turn the pages of history books looking for answers to these
questions. All we find therein are presumptions which their
authors think are reports of facts. The Sabeans were star worshipers, and they enjoyed great popularity and prestige in Arabia. As the reports go, the Sabeans did not always worship the
stars for their own sake. At one time it is said that they had
worshiped God alone and venerated the stars as signs of
His creation and power. Since the majority of people were neither endowed nor cultivated enough to understand the transcendent nature of the Godhead, they confused the stars with God and
took them as gods. Some of the volcanic or meteoric stones
appeared to men to have fallen from heaven and therefore to be
astral in nature. Consequently, they were taken as hierophanies
of the astral divinities and sanctified as such. Later on they were
venerated for their own sake, and then worshipped as divinities.
In fact, the Arabs venerated these stones so much that not only
did they worship the black stone in the Ka'bah, but they would
take one of the stones of the Ka'bah as a holy object in their
travels, praying to it and asking it to bless every move they
made. Thus all the veneration and worship due to the stars, or to
the creator of the stars, were now conferred upon these stones. It
was in a development similar to this that paganism was established in Arabia, that the statues were sanctified, and that sacrifices were made to them.

This is the picture which some historians give of religious
development in Arabia after Ibrahīm dedicated the Ka'bah to the

worship of God. Herodotus, father of written history, mentions the worship of al Lāt in Arabia; and Diodorus, the Sicilian, mentions the house of Makkah venerated by the Arabs. Their two witnesses point to the antiquity of paganism in the Peninsula and therefore to the fact that the religion of Ibrahīm was not always observed there.

The Arab Prophets

During these long centuries many prophets called their tribes to the worship of God alone. The Arabs gave them little hearing and continued with their paganism. Hūd was one of those prophets sent to the tribe of 'Ad which lived in the north of Ḥaḍramawt. Few tribesmen responded to his call. The majority were too proud to relinquish their old ways and they answered, "O Hūd! You brought us no sign. We cannot relinquish our gods just because you tell us to. We shall not believe."[9] Hūd kept on calling for years, but the more he called the more obstinate they became. Similarly, Ṣāliḥ arose in the tribe of Thamūd who lived in al Ḥijr between Ḥijāz and al Shām, this side of Wādī al Qurā and to the southeast of the land of Madyan, close to the Gulf of 'Aqabah. His call bore no more fruit than Hūd's. Shu'ayb arose among the people of Madyan who then lived in the Ḥijāz. He called them to the worship of God alone, but they refused to hear and they perished as the people of 'Ād and Thamūd before them. The Qur'ānic narratives told us about the stories and missions of other prophets who called men unto God alone, and of their peoples' obstinacy and pride, their continued paganism, their worship of the idols of the Ka'bah, and their pilgrimage to the Ka'bah from every corner of the Arabian Peninsula. All this is implied in God's statement, "And We inflict no punishment on anyone until We have sent them a prophet to warn them."[10]

Offices of the Ka'bah

Ever since its establishment, the Ka'bah gave rise to a number of offices such as those which were held by Qusayy ibn Kilāb when he took over the kingship of Makkah, in the middle of the fifth century c.e. His offices included *ḥijābah*, *siqāyah*, *rifādah*, *nadwah*, *liwā'* and *qiyādah*. *Ḥijābah* implied maintenance of the house and guardianship over its keys. *Siqāyah* implied the provision of fresh water—which was scarce in Makkah—as well as date wine to all the pilgrims. *Rifādah* implied the provision of food to the pilgrims. *Nadwah* implied the chairmanship of all convocations held. *Qiyādah* implied the leadership of the army at war. *Liwā'* was the flag which, hoisted on a spear, accompanied the army whenever it went out to meet the enemy and, hence, it meant a secondary command in times of war. All these offices were recognized as belonging to Makkah, indeed to the Ka'bah, to which all Arabs looked when in worship. It is more likely that not all of these offices developed at the time when the house was constructed but rather that they arose one after the other independently of the Ka'bah and its religious position, though some may have had to do with the Ka'bah by nature.

At the building of the Ka'bah, Makkah could not have consisted, even at best, of more than a few tribes of 'Amāliq and Jurhumīs. A long time must have lapsed between Ibrahīm and Isma'īl's advent to Makkah and their building of the Ka'bah on the one hand, and the development of Makkah as a town or quasiurban center on the other. Indeed, as long as any vestiges of their early nomadism lingered in the mind and customs of the Makkans, we cannot speak of Makkah as urban. Some historians would rather agree that Makkah had remained nomadic until the kingship of Quṣayy in the middle of the fifth century C.E. On the other hand, it is difficult to imagine a town like Makkah remaining nomadic while her ancient house is venerated by the whole surrounding country. It is historically certain that the guardianship of the house remained in the hands of Jurhum, Isma'īl's in-laws, for continuous generations. This implies continuous residence near the Ka'bah—a fact not possible for nomads bent on movement from pasture to pasture. Moreover, the well established fact that Makkah was the rendezvous of the caravans traveling between Yaman, Hīrah, al Shām and Najd, that it was connected to the Red Sea close by and therefrom to the trade routes of the world, further refutes the claim that Makkah was merely a nomad's campsite. We are therefore compelled to acknowledge that Makkah, which Ibrahīm called "a town" and which he prayed God to bless, had known the life of settlement many generations before Quṣayy.

Ascendency of Quraysh

After their conquest of the 'Amāliq, the tribe of Jurhum ruled Makkah until the regime of Muḍāḍ ibn 'Amr ibn al Ḥārith.

During these generations, trade had prospered so well that the tribe of Jurhum waxed fat and forgot that they were really living in a desolate place and that they ought to work very hard to keep their position. Their neglect led to the drying up of the Zamzam spring; furthermore, the tribe of Khuzā'ah had even thought of conquering Makkah and establishing their authority over its whole precinct.

Muḍāḍ's warning to his people did not stop their indulgence and carelessness. Realizing that his and his tribe's power was on the decline and would soon be lost, he dug a deep hole within the well of Zamzam in which he buried two golden gazelles and the treasure of the holy house, with the hope that he would return some day to power and reclaim the treasure. Together with the Jurhum tribe and the descendants of Isma'īl he withdrew from Makkah in favor of the tribe of Khuzā'ah, who ruled it from generation to generation until the advent of Quṣayy ibn Kilāb, the fifth grandfather of the Prophet.

Quṣayy ibn Kilāb (circa 480 C.E.)

Fāṭimah, daughter of Sa'd ibn Sayl, mother of Quṣayy, married Kilāb and gave him two sons, Zuhrah and Quṣayy. Kilāb died when Quṣayy was an infant. Fāṭimah then married Rabī'ah ibn Ḥarām who took her with him to al Shām where she gave birth to a son called Darrāj. Quṣayy grew up knowing no other father than Rabī'ah. When a quarrel broke out between Quṣayy and some members of the Rabī'ah tribe, they reproached him as they would a foreigner and betrayed the fact that they never regarded him as one of their own. Quṣayy complained to his mother and related to her the reproach he heard. Her answer was as defiant as it was proud. "O my son," she said, "your descendance is nobler than theirs, you are the son of Kilāb ibn Murrah, and your people live in the proximity of the holy house in Makkah."

This was the cause of Quṣayy's departure from al Shām and return to Makkah. His seriousness and wisdom soon won him the respect of the Makkans. At the time, the guardianship of the holy house was in the hands of a man of the Khuzā'ah tribe called Ḥulayl ibn Ḥubshiyyah, a very wise man with deep insight. Soon Quṣayy asked for and married Ḥubbā, daughter of Ḥulayl. He continued to work hard at his trade and acquired much affluence, great respect, and many children. When his father-in-law died, he committed the keys of the Ka'bah to Ḥubbā, wife of

Quṣayy. But the latter apologized and committed the keys to Abū Ghibshān, a man from Khuzā'ah. Abū Ghibshān, however, was a drunkard and one day he exchanged the keys of the Ka'bah for a jug of wine from Quṣayy. The Khuzā'ah tribe realized that it was in danger should the guardianship of the Ka'bah remain in the hands of Quṣayy whose wealth and influence were always increasing and around whom the tribe of Quraysh was now rallying. They therefore thought to dispossess him of his guardianship. Quṣayy called upon the Quraysh tribe to help him and, with the concurrence of a number of tribes from the surrounding area, he was judged the wisest and the mightiest and confirmed in his guardianship. When the tribe of Khuzā'ah had to evacuate, Quṣayy combined in his person all the offices associated with the holy house and became king over the Quraysh.

Construction of Permanent Residences in Makkah

Some historians claim that Makkah had no constructed houses other than the Ka'bah until Quṣayy became its king because neither Khuzā'ah nor Jurhum wanted to raise any other construction besides the holy house and neither one spent his life outside of the holy area in the open desert. They added that upon his assumption of the kingship of Makkah, Quṣayy commanded his people, the Quraysh tribe, to build their residences in the vicinity of the holy house. They also explained that it was Quṣayy who built the house of Nadwah where the elders of Makkah met under his chairmanship in order to run the affairs of their city, for it was their custom not to allow anything to happen without their unanimous approval. No man or woman of Makkah married except in the Nadwah and with the approval of the Quraysh elders. According to this view, it was the Quraysh that built, at the command of Quṣayy, their houses around the Ka'bah, leaving sufficient space for circumambulation of the holy house. Their residences in the vicinity were spaced so as to leave a narrow passage to the holy house between every two houses.

The Descendants of Quṣayy

Although 'Abd al Dār was the eldest of Quṣayy's children, his brother 'Abd Manāf was more famous and more respected by the people. As Quṣayy grew old and weak and became unable to carry out the duties of his position, he delegated the *ḥijābah* to 'Abd al

Dār and handed over to him the keys of the holy house. He also delegated to him the *siqāyah*, the *liwā'*, and the *rifādah*.[11] The *rifādah* implied a contribution the tribe of Quraysh used to levy from every member to help Quṣayy in the provision of food for pilgrims incapable of procuring nourishment on their own. Quṣayy was the first to impose the *rifādah* on the Quraysh tribe; and he incepted this practice after he rallied the Quraysh and dislodged the tribe of Khuzā'ah from Makkah. At the time the *rifādah* was imposed, Quṣayy said, "O people of Quraysh! You are the neighbors of God and the people of His house and temple. The pilgrim is the guest of God and visitor of His house. Of all guests that you receive during the year, the pilgrim is the most worthy of your hospitality. Provide for him food and drink during the days of pilgrimage."

The Descendants of 'Abd Manāf

'Abd al Dār discharged the new duties incumbent upon him as his father had directed. His sons did likewise after him but could not match the sons of 'Abd Manāf in honor and popular esteem. Hence, Hāshim, 'Abd Shams, al Muṭṭalib and Nawfal, the sons of 'Abd Manāf, resolved to take over these privileges from their cousins. The tribe of Quraysh stood divided into two factions, each supporting one of the contestants. The descendants of 'Abd Manāf concluded the *Ḥilf al Muṭayyibīn*, a treaty so called because the covenantors dipped their hands in perfume as they swore allegiance to its new terms. The descendants of 'Abd al Dār, for their part, entered into another treaty called *Ḥilf al Aḥlāf* [literally, the alliance of the allies—Tr.], and the stage was set for a civil war which could have dissolved the Quraysh tribe. A peace was reached, however, under which the descendants of 'Abd Manāf were granted the *siqāyah* and *rifādah*, and the descendents of 'Abd al Dār kept the *ḥijābah*, the *liwā'*, and the *nadwah*.[12] Thereafter the two parties lived in peace until the advent of Islām.

Hāshim (646 c.e.)

Hāshim was the leader of his people and a prosperous man. He was in charge of the *siqāyah* and the *rifādah*. In the discharge of his duties he called upon every member of the Quraysh to make a contribution for use in providing food for the pilgrims.

Like his grandfather Quṣayy, he argued with his contemporaries
that the pilgrims and visitors to the house of God are God's
guests and, therefore, worthy of their hospitality. He discharged
his duties well and provided for all the pilgrims during the time
of their pilgrimage in Makkah.

Makkan Affluence and Prosperity

Hāshim did for the people of Makkah more than his duty demanded. In a year of drought he was generous enough to provide
food for the whole population and turned the occasion into one
of joy. It was he who regulated and standardized the two main
caravan trips of the Makkan traders, the winter trip to Yaman,
and the summer trip to al Shām. Under his good ordering and
wise leadership Makkah prospered and its position rose throughout the Peninsula. It soon became the acknowledged capital of
Arabia. From this position of influence the descendents of 'Abd
Manāf concluded peace treaties with their neighbors. Hāshim
went in person to Byzantium and to the neighboring tribe of
Ghassān to sign a treaty of friendship and good neighborliness.
He obtained from Byzantium permission for the tribe of Quraysh
to move anywhere in the territories of al Shām in peace and
security. 'Abd Shams, on the other hand, concluded a treaty of
trade with the Negus of Abyssinia and Nawfal and al Muṭṭalib,
both a treaty of friendship with Persia and a trade treaty with
the Ḥimyarīs of Yaman. The glory of Makkah increased with its
prosperity. The Makkans became so adept in trade that nobody
could compete with them. The caravans came to Makkah from
all directions, and the goods were exported in two big convoys
in summer and winter. Surrounding Makkah all kinds of markets
were built to deal with all the attendant business. This experience
developed in the Makkans competence in business affairs as well
as adeptness in the administration of the calendar and interest
in financing.

Hāshim remained the uncontested chief of Makkah throughout his life. Nobody thought of competing with him in this
regard. His nephew, however, Umayyah ibn 'Abd Shams, did entertain such ideas but he lost and chose to live in exile in al Shām
for ten full years. On one of his trips to al Shām, Hāshim stopped
in Yathrib where he saw a woman of noble birth engaging in
business with some of her agents. That was Salmā, daughter of
'Amr of the Khazraj tribe. Hāshim fell in love with her and

inquired whether she was married. When he learned that she was a divorced woman, but a very independent person, he asked her directly to marry him. As his position and prestige were known to her, she accepted. She lived with him in Makkah for a while before she returned to Madīnah where she gave birth to a son called Shaybah, whom she kept with her in Yathrib.[13]

Al Muṭṭalib

Several years later Hāshim died on one of his trips and was buried in Gaza. His brother, al Muṭṭalib, succeeded him in his posts. Though al Muṭṭalib was younger than 'Abd Shams, he was well esteemed by the people. The Quraysh used to call him "Mr. Abundance" for his generosity and goodness. Naturally, with such competence and prestige as al Muṭṭalib enjoyed, the situation in Makkah continued to be prosperous and peaceful.

One day al Muṭṭalib thought of his nephew Shaybah. He went to Yathrib and asked Salmā to hand the child over now that he had become fully grown. On return to Makkah, al Muṭṭalib allowed the young man to precede him on his camel. The Quraysh thought that he was a servant of al Muṭṭalib and called him so, namely 'Abd al Muṭṭalib. When al Muṭṭalib heard of this he said, "Hold it, Fellow Tribesmen. This man is not my servant but my nephew, son of Hāshim, whom I brought back from Yathrib." The title 'Abd al Muṭṭalib was so popular, however, that the young man's old name, Shaybah, was forgotten.

'Abd al Muṭṭalib (495 C.E.)

When al Muṭṭalib sought to return to his nephew the wealth which Hāshim left behind, Nawfal objected and seized the wealth. 'Abd al Muṭṭalib waited until he grew and then asked for the support of his uncles in Yathrib against his uncles in Makkah. Eighty Khazraj horsemen arrived from Yathrib ready to give him the military support he needed in order to reclaim his rights. Nawfal refused to fight and returned the seized wealth. 'Abd al Muṭṭalib then was assigned the offices which Hāshim occupied, namely the *siqāyah* and the *rifādah*, after al Muṭṭalib passed away. He experienced no little difficulty in discharging the requisite duties because at that time he had only one son, al Ḥārith. As the well of Zamzam had been destroyed, water had to be brought in from a number of subsidiary wells in the outskirts of Makkah and placed in smaller reservoirs near the Ka'bah. Plurality of descendants was an asset in the execution of such a task as this but 'Abd al Muṭṭalib had only one son, and the task nearly exhausted him. Naturally, he gave the matter a good deal of thought.

The Redigging of Zamzam

The Makkans still had memories of the Zamzam well which was filled with dirt by Muḍāḍ ibn 'Amr of the Jurhum tribe a few hundred years back and wished that it could be reactivated. This matter concerned 'Abd al Muṭṭalib more than anyone else, and he gave it all his attention. Suffering under his duties, he thought so much about the matter that he even saw in his dreams a spirit calling him to re-dig the well whose waters sprang under the feet of his ancestor, Isma'īl. But no one knew where the old well stood. Finally, after much investigation, 'Abd al Muṭṭalib was inspired to try the place between the two idols, Isāf and Nā'ilah. Helped by his second son al Mughīrah, he dug at the place until water sprang forth and the two golden gazelles and swords of Muḍāḍ of the Jurhum tribe appeared. The Quraysh wanted to share his find with 'Abd al Muṭṭalib. After objecting, he finally came to an agreement with them to determine the rightful ownership of the treasure by the drawing of lots among three equal partners, namely the Ka'bah, the Quraysh, and himself. The divinatory arrows were drawn near the idol Hubal within the Ka'bah, and the result was that the Quraysh lost completely, 'Abd al Muṭṭalib won the swords, and the Ka'bah won the two gazelles. 'Abd al Muṭṭalib ordered his part, namely the swords, reforged as a door for the Ka'bah, and placed the two golden gazelles within the holy house as a decoration. Now that the Zamzam water was close by, 'Abd al Muṭṭalib performed his *siqāyah* duties with ease.

The Vow and Its Fulfillment

'Abd al Muṭṭalib realized the limitations which his lack of children imposed upon him. He vowed that should he be given ten sons to grow to maturity, and to help him in his task he would sacrifice one of them to God near the Ka'bah. 'Abd al Muṭṭalib's wish was to be fulfilled: he had ten fully grown sons. When he called them to assist him in the fulfillment of his vow, they accepted. It was agreed that the name of each one of them would be written on a divinatory arrow, that the arrows would be drawn near Hubal within the Ka'bah and that he whose name appeared on the drawn arrow would be sacrificed. It was then customary among the Arabs whenever they faced an insoluble problem to resort to divination by means of arrows at the foot of the greatest idol in the area. When the arrows were drawn it was the arrow of 'Abdullah, the youngest son of 'Abd al Muṭṭalib and the most beloved, that came out. Without hesitation 'Abd al Muṭṭalib took the young man by the hand and prepared to sacrifice him by the well of Zamzam between the idols of Isāf and Nā'ilah. 'Abd al Muṭṭalib insisted upon the sacrifice, but the whole of Quraysh insisted that 'Abdullah be spared and that some kind of indulgence be sought from the god Hubal. Finally, in answer to 'Abd al Muṭṭalib's inquiry as to what should be done to please the gods, al Mughīrah ibn 'Abdullah al Makhzūmī volunteered the answer, "Perhaps the youth can be ransomed with wealth; in that case, we shall be pleased to give up all the necessary wealth to save him." After consultation with one another, they decided to consult a divineress in Yathrib renowned for her good insight. When they came to her, she asked them to wait until the morrow; upon their return she asked, "What, in your custom, is the amount of a man's blood wit?" "Ten camels," they answered. She said, "Return then to your country and draw near your god two arrows, one with the name of the youth and the other with the term 'ten camels.' If the arrow drawn is that of the youth, then multiply the number of camels and draw again until your god is satisfied. They accepted her solution and drew the divinatory arrows which they found to converge on 'Abdullah. They kept multiplying the number of camels until the number reached one hundred. It was then that the camels' arrow was drawn. The people were satisfied and told 'Abd al Muṭṭalib, who stood nearby in terror, "Thus did your god decide, O 'Abd al Muṭṭalib." But he answered, "Not at all! I shall not be convinced that this is my god's wish until the same result comes out three times consecutively." The arrows were drawn three times, and in all three it was the camels' arrow that came out. 'Abd al Muṭṭalib then felt sure that his god was contented, and he sacrificed the one hundred camels.

In this way the books of biography have reported to us some of the customs of the Arabs and of their religious doctrines. In this way they have informed us of the Arabs' adherence to these doctrines and of their loyalty and devotion to their holy house. In confirming this custom al Ṭabarī reports that a Muslim woman had once vowed to sacrifice one of her sons. She sought the advice of 'Abdullah ibn 'Umar without much avail. She went to 'Abdullah ibn al 'Abbās who advised her to sacrifice one hundred camels after the example of 'Abd al Muṭṭalib. But when Marwān, the governor of Madīnah, knew of what she was about, he forbade her to do it, holding to the Islāmic principle that no vow is valid whose object is illegitimate.

The Year of the Elephant (570 c.e.)

The respect and esteem which Makkah and her holy house enjoyed suggested to some distant provinces in Arabia that they should construct holy houses in order to attract some of the people away from Makkah. The Ghassānīs built such a house at al Ḥīrah. Abrahah al Ashram built another in Yaman. Neither of them succeeded, however, in drawing the Arabs away from Makkah and its holy house. Indeed, Abrahah took a special care to decorate the house in Yaman and filled it with such beautiful furniture and statues that he thought that he could draw thereto not only the Arabs but the Makkans themselves. When later he found out that the Arabs were still going to the ancient house, that the inhabitants of Yaman were leaving behind the newly built house in their own territory and did not regard the pilgrimage valid except in Makkah, he came to the conclusion that there was no escape from destroying the house of Ibrahīm and Isma'īl. The viceroy of the Negus therefore prepared for war and brought a great army for that purpose from Abyssinia equipped with a great elephant on which he rode. When the Arabs heard of his war preparations, they became quite upset and feared the impending doom of Makkah, the Ka'bah, its statues, and the institution of pilgrimage. Dhū Nafar, a nobleman from Yaman, appealed to his fellow countrymen to revolt and fight Abrahah and thus prevent him from the destruction of God's house. Abrahah, however, was too strong to be fought with such tactics: Dhū Nafar as well as Nufayl ibn Ḥabīb al Khath'amī, leader of the two tribes of Shahrān and Nāhis, were taken prisoners after a brief but gallant fight. On the other hand, the people of al Tā'if, when they learned that it was not their house that he intended to destroy, cooperated with Abrahah and sent a guide with him to show him the way to Makkah.

Abrahah and the Ka'bah

Upon approaching Makkah, Abrahah sent a number of horsemen to seize whatever there was of Quraysh's animal wealth in
the outskirts. The horsemen returned with some cattle and a
hundred camels belonging to 'Abd al Muṭṭalib. The Quraysh and
other Makkans first thought of holding their ground and fighting
Abrahah, but they soon realized that his power was far superior
to theirs. Abrahah sent one of his men, Ḥunāṭah al Ḥimyarī to
inform 'Abd al Muṭṭalib, chief of Makkah, that Abrahah had
not come to make war against the Makkans but only to destroy
the house and that should the Makkans not stand in his way, he
would not fight them at all. When 'Abd al Muṭṭalib declared the
intention of Makkah not to fight Abrahah, Ḥunāṭah invited
'Abd al Muṭṭalib and his sons and some of the leaders of Makkah
to Abrahah's encampment in order to talk to Abrahah directly.
Abrahah received 'Abd al Muṭṭalib well and returned his seized
camels. But he refused to entertain any suggestion of saving the
Ka'bah from destruction as well as the Makkans' offer to pay
him one-third of the yearly crop of the Tihāmah province. The
conference therefore came to no conclusion, and 'Abd al Muṭṭalib
returned to Makkah. He immediately advised the Makkans to
evacuate the city and withdraw to the mountains and thus save
their own persons.

It was certainly a grave day on which the Makkans decided to
evacuate their town and leave it an open city for destruction by
Abrahah. 'Abd al Muṭṭalib and the leaders of the Quraysh
grasped the lock of the door of the Ka'bah and prayed to their
gods to stop this aggression against the house of God. As they
left Makkah, and Abrahah prepared to send his terrifying and
formidable army into the city to destroy the house, small-pox
spread within its ranks and began to take its toll. The epidemic
attacked the army with unheard of fury. Perhaps the microbes of the disease were carried there by the wind from the
west. Abrahah himself was not spared; and terrified by what he
saw, he ordered the army to return to Yaman. Attacked by death
and desertion, Abrahah's army dwindled to almost nothing, and,
by the time he reached San'ā', his capital in Yaman, he himself
succumbed to the disease. This phenomenon was so extraordinary
that the Makkans reckoned time with it by calling that year "The
Year of the Elephant." The Qur'ān had made this event immortal when it said,

اَلَمْ تَرَ كَيْفَ فَعَلَ رَبُّكَ بِأَصْحَابِ الْفِيلِ ۝ اَلَمْ يَجْعَلْ كَيْدَهُمْ فِي تَضْلِيلٍ ۝ وَأَرْسَلَ عَلَيْهِمْ
طَيْراً أَبَابِيلَ ۝ تَرْمِيهِمْ بِحِجَارَةٍ مِنْ سِجِّيلٍ ۝ فَجَعَلَهُمْ كَعَصْفٍ مَأْكُولٍ ۝

"Consider what your Lord had done to the people of the elephant.
Did he not undo their evil plotting? And send upon them wave
after wave of flying stones of fire? And made their ranks like a
harvested corn field trodden by herds of hungry cattle?"[14]

The Position of Makkah after the Year of the Elephant

This extraordinary event enhanced the religious position of
Makkah as well as her trade. Her people became more committed
than ever to the preservation of their exalted city and to resist
every attempt at reducing it.

Makkan Luxury

The prosperity, affluence, and luxury which Makkah provided
for its citizens, like an island in a large barren desert, confirmed
the Makkans in their parochial zeal. The Makkans loved their
wine and the revelry it brought. It helped them satisfy their
passionate search for pleasure and to find that pleasure in the
slave girls with which they traded and who invited them to ever
increasing indulgence. Their pursuit of pleasure, on the other
hand, confirmed their personal freedom and the freedom of their
city which they were prepared to protect against any aggressor
at any cost. They loved to hold their celebrations and their drinking parties right in the center of the city around the Ka'bah.
There, in the proximity of three hundred or more statues belonging to about three hundred Arab tribes, the elders of the
Quraysh and the aristocracy of Makkah held their *salons* and
told one another tales of trips across desert or fertile land, tales
of the kings of Ḥirah on the east or of Ghassān on the west,
which the caravans and the nomads brought back and forth. The
tribes carried these tales and customs throughout their areas
with great speed, efficiency, and application. Makkan pastimes
consisted of telling these stories to neighbors and friends and of
hearing others, of drinking wine, and of preparing for a big
night around the Ka'bah or in recovering from such a night.
The idols must have witnessed with their stone eyes all this
revelry around them. The revelers were certain of protection

since the idols had conferred upon the Ka'bah a halo of sanctity and peace. The protection, however, was mutual, for it was the obligation of the Makkans never to allow a scripturist,[15] *i.e.*, Christian or Jew, to enter Makkah except in the capacity of a servant and under the binding covenant that he would not speak in Makkah either of his religion or of his scripture. Consequently, there were neither Jewish nor Christian communities in Makkah, as was the case in Yathrib and Najrān. The Ka'bah was then the holy of holies of paganism and securely protected against any attack against its authorities or sanctity. Thus Makkah was as independent as the Arab tribes were, ever unyielding in its protection of that independence which the Makkans regarded as worthier than life. No tribe ever thought of rallying with another or more tribes in order to form a union with superior strength to Makkah, and none ever entertained any idea of conquering her. The tribes remained separated, leading a pastoral nomadic existence but enjoying to the full the independence, freedom, pride, and chivalry, as well as the individualism which the life of the desert implied.

The Residences of Makkah

The houses of the Makkans surrounded the Ka'bah and stood at a distance from it proportionate to the social position, descendance, and prestige these inhabitants enjoyed. The Qurayshis were the closest to the Ka'bah and the most related to it on account of the offices of *sidānah* and *siqāyah*[16] which they held. On this account no honorific title was withheld from them, and it was for the sake of these titles that wars were fought, pacts concluded, and treaties covenanted. The texts of all Makkan treaties and pacts were kept in the Ka'bah so that the gods who, undoubtedly, were taken as witnesses thereto, might punish those covenanters who violated their promises. Beyond these stood the houses of the less important tribes, and further still stood the houses of the slaves, servants and those without honor. In Makkah the Jews and Christians were slaves, as we said earlier. They were therefore allowed to live only in these far away houses on the edge of the desert. Whatever religious stories they could tell regarding Christianity or Judaism would be too far removed from the ears of the lords and nobles of Quraysh and Makkah. This distance permitted the latter to stop their ears as well as their conscience against all serious concern. Whatever they heard of Judaism or Christianity they obtained from a monastery or a hermitage recluse in the desert which lay on some road of the caravans.

Even so, the rumors circulating at the time about the possible rise of a prophet among the Arabs caused them great worry. Abū Sufyān one day strongly criticized Umayyah ibn Abū al Salṭ for repeating such Messianic stories as the monks circulated. One can imagine Abū Sufyān addressing Umayyah in some such words as these, "Those monks in the desert expect a Messiah because of their ignorance of their own religion. Surely they need a prophet to guide them thereto. As for us, we have the idols right here close by, and they do bring us close to God. We do not need any prophet, and we ought to combat any such suggestion." Fanatically committed to his native city as well as to its paganism, it was apparently impossible for Abū Sufyān to realize that the hour of guidance was just about to strike, that the prophethood of Muhammad—may God's blessing be upon him—had drawn near, and that from these pagan Arab lands a light was to shine over the whole world to illuminate it with monotheism and truth.

'Abdullah ibn 'Abd al Muttalib

'Abdullah ibn 'Abd al Muṭṭalib was a handsome young man admired by the unmarried women of his town. They were fascinated by the story of ransom and the hundred camels which the god Hubal insisted on receiving in his stead. But fate had already prepared 'Abdullah for the noblest fatherhood that history had known, just as it had prepared Āminah, daughter of Wahb, to be mother to the son of 'Abdullah. The couple were married and, a few months after their marriage, 'Abdullah passed away. None could ransom him from this later fate. Āminah survived him, gave birth to Muhammad, and joined her husband while Muhammad was still an infant.

Following is a geneological tree of the Prophet with approximate birth dates.

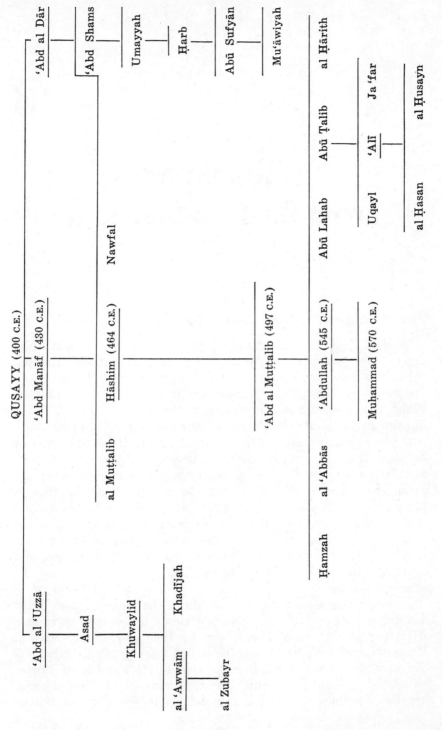

QUṢAYY (400 C.E.)

'Abd al Dār

'Abd Manāf (430 C.E.)

'Abd al 'Uzzā

'Abd Shams

Umayyah

Ḥarb

Abū Sufyān

Mu'āwiyah

Nawfal

Hāshim (464 C.E.)

al Muṭṭalib

Asad

Khuwaylid

Khadijah

al 'Awwām

al Zubayr

al Ḥārith

Abū Ṭalib

Ja'far

'Alī

Uqayl

Abū Lahab

'Abd al Muṭṭalib (497 C.E.)

'Abdullah (545 C.E.)

Muhammad (570 C.E.)

al 'Abbās

Ḥamzah

al Husayn

al Ḥasan

45

3

Muḥammad: From Birth to Marriage

The Marriage of 'Abdullah and Āminah

'Abd al Muṭṭalib was seventy years old or more when Abraha arrived in Makkah to destroy the ancient house. His son 'Abdullah was twenty-four years of age and was hence ready for marriage. His father chose for him Āminah, daughter of Wahb ibn 'Abd Manāf ibn Zuhrah, the chief of the tribe of Zuhrah as well as its eldest and noblest member. 'Abd al Muṭṭalib took his son and went with him to, the quarter of the tribe of Zuhrah. There, he sought the residence of Wahb and went in to ask for the hand of Wahb's daughter for his son. Some historians claim that 'Abd al Muṭṭalib went to the residence of Uhayb, uncle of Āminah, assuming that her father had passed away and that she was under the protection of her uncle. On the same day that 'Abdullah married Āminah, his father 'Abd al Muṭṭalib married a cousin of hers named Hālah. It was thus that the Prophet could have an uncle on his father's side, namely Ḥamzah, of the same age as he.

As was the custom in those days, 'Abdullah lived with Āminah among her relatives the first three days of the marriage. Afterwards, they moved together to the quarter of 'Abd al Muṭṭalib, and soon he was to be called on a trading trip to al Shām. When he left, Āminah was pregnant. A number of stories circulated telling of 'Abdullah's marriage with other women besides Āminah and of many women's seeking to marry

46

'Abdullah. It is not possible to ascertain the truth of such tales. What is certainly true is that 'Abdullah was a very handsome and strong young man; and it is not at all surprising that other women besides Āminah had wished to marry him. Such women would have at least temporarily given up hope once 'Abdullah's marriage to Āminah was announced. But who knows! It is not impossible that they may have waited for his return from al Shām hoping that they might still become his wives along with Āminah. 'Abdullah was absent for several months in Gaza. On his way back he stopped for a longer rest at Madīnah, where his uncles on his mother's side lived, and was preparing to join a caravan to Makkah when he fell ill. When the caravan reached Makkah his father was alerted to 'Abdullah's absence and disease. 'Abd al Muṭṭalib immediately sent his eldest son al Ḥārith to Madīnah in order to accompany 'Abdullah on the trip back to Makkah after his recovery. Upon arriving at Madīnah, however, al Ḥārith learned that 'Abdullah had died and that he had been buried in Madīnah a month after the start of that same caravan to Makkah. Al Ḥārith returned to Makkah to announce the death of 'Abdullah to his aged father and his bereaved wife Āminah. The shock was tremendous, for 'Abd al Muṭṭalib loved his son so much as to have ransomed him with a hundred camels, a ransom never equalled before.

'Abdullah left five camels, a herd of sheep, and a slave nurse, called Umm Ayman, who was to take care of the Prophet. This patrimony does not prove that 'Abdullah was wealthy, but at the same time it does not prove that he was poor. Furthermore, 'Abdullah was still a young man capable of working and of amassing a fortune. His father was still alive and none of his wealth had as yet been transferred to his sons.

The Birth of Muḥammad (570 C.E.)

There was nothing unusual about Āminah's pregnancy or delivery. As soon as she delivered her baby, she sent to 'Abd al Muṭṭalib, who was then at the Ka'bah, announcing to him the birth of a grandson. The old man was overjoyed at the news and must have remembered on this occasion his loved one 'Abdullah. He rushed to his daughter-in-law, took her newborn in his hands, went into the Ka'bah and there called him "Muḥammad." This name was not familiar among the Arabs, but it was known. He then returned the infant to his mother and awaited by her side for the arrival of wet nurses from the tribe of Banū Sa'd in order to arrange for one of them to take care of the new born, as was the practice of Makkan nobility.

Historians have disagreed about the year of Muhammad's birth. Most of them hold that it took place in "the Year of the Elephant," *i.e.* 570 C.E. Ibn 'Abbās claims that Muhammad was born on "the Day of the Elephant." Others claim that he was born fifteen years earlier. Still others claim that he was born a few days, months, or years, after "the Year of the Elephant." Some even assert that Muhammad was born thirty years and others seventy years later than "the Year of the Elephant." Historians have also differed concerning the month of Muhammad's birth although the majority of them agree that it was Rabī' al Awwal, the third month of the lunar year. It has also been claimed that he was born in Muharram, in Safar, in Rajab, or in Ramaḍān. Furthermore, historians have differed as to the day of the month on which Muhammad was born. Some claim that the birth took place on the third of Rabī' al Awwal; others, on the ninth; and others on the tenth. The majority, however, agree that Muhammad was born on the twelfth of Rabī' al Awwal, the claim of ibn Ishāq and other biographers. Moreover, historians disagreed as to the time of day at which Muhammad was born, as well as to the place of birth. Caussin de Perceval wrote in his book on the Arabs that after weighing the evidence, it is most probable that Muhammad was born in August, 570 C.E., *i.e.* "the Year of the Elephant," and that he was born in the house of his grandfather 'Abd al Muttalib in Makkah. On the seventh day after Muhammad's birth, 'Abd al Muttalib gave a banquet in honor of his grandson to which he invited a number of Quraysh tribesmen and peers. When they inquired from him why he had chosen to name the child Muhammad, thus changing the practise of using the ancestors' names, 'Abd al Muttalib answered: "I did so with the wish that my grandson would be praised by God in heaven and on earth by men."

Muhammad's Nurses

Āminah waited for the arrival of the wet nurses from the tribe of Banū Sa'd to choose one for Muhammad, as was the practise of the nobles of Makkah. This custom is still practiced today among Makkan aristocracy. They send their children to the desert on the eighth day of their birth to remain there until the age of eight or ten. Some of the tribes of the desert have a reputation as providers of excellent wet nurses, especially the tribe of Banū Sa'd. At that time, Āminah gave her infant to Thuwaybah, servant of Muḥammad's uncle Abū Lahab, who nursed him for a while as she did his uncle Ḥamzah later on, making the two brothers-in-nursing. Although Thuwaybah nursed Muḥammad but a few days, he kept for her great affection and respect as long as she lived. When she died in 7 A.H. Muḥammad remembered to inquire about her son who was also his brother-in-nursing, but found out that he had died before her.

The wet nurses of the tribe of Banū Sa'd finally arrived at Makkah to seek infants to nurse. The prospect of an orphan child did not much attract them since they hoped to be well rewarded by the father. The infants of widows, such as Muhammad, were not attractive at all. Not one of them accepted Muḥammad into her care, preferring the infants of the living and of the affluent.

Ḥalīmah, Daughter of Abū Dhu'ayb

Having spurned him at first as her colleagues had done before her, Ḥalīmah al Sa'diyyah, daughter of Abū Dhu'ayb, accepted Muḥammad into her charge because she had found no other. Thin and rather poor looking, she did not appeal to the ladies of Makkah. When her people prepared to leave Makkah for the desert, Ḥalīmah pleaded to her husband al Ḥārith ibn 'Abd al 'Uzzā, "By God it is oppressive to me to return with my friends without a new infant to nurse. Surely, I should go back to that orphan and accept him." Her husband answered, "There would be no blame if you did. Perhaps God may even bless us for your doing so." Ḥalīmah therefore took Muḥammad and carried him with her to the desert. She related that after she took him, she found all kinds of blessings. Her herd became fat and multiplied, and everything around her seemed to prosper.

In the desert Ḥalīmah nursed Muḥammad for two whole years while her daughter Shaymā' cuddled him. The purity of desert air and the hardness of desert living agreed with Muḥammad's physical disposition and contributed to his quick growth, sound formation, and discipline. At the completion of the two years, which was also the occasion of his weaning,

Halīmah took the child to his mother but brought him back with her to the desert to grow up away from Makkah and her epidemics. Biographers disagree whether Halīmah's new lease on her charge was arranged after her own or Āminah's wishes. The child lived in the desert for two more years playing freely in the vast expanse under the clear sky and growing unfettered by anything physical or spiritual.

The Story of Splitting Muhammad's Chest

It was in this period and before Muhammad reached the age of three that the following event is said to have happened. It is told that Muhammad was playing in a yard behind the encampment of the tribe with Halīmah's son when the latter ran back to his parents and said, "Two men dressed in white took my Qurayshī brother, laid him down, opened his abdomen, and turned him around." It is also reported that Halīmah said, "My husband and I ran towards the boy and found him standing up and pale. When we asked what happened to him, the boy answered, "Two men dressed in white came up to me, laid me down, opened my abdomen and took something I know not what away." The parents returned to their tent fearing that the child had become possessed. They therefore returned him to Makkah to his mother. Ibn Ishāq reported a *hadīth* issuing from the Prophet after his commission confirming this incident. But he was careful enough to warn the reader that the real reason for Muhammad's return to his mother was not the story of the two angels but, as Halīmah was to report to Muhammad's mother later on, the fact that a number of Abyssinian Christians wanted to take Muhammad away with them once they had seen him after his weaning. According to Halīmah's report, the Abyssinians had said to one another, "Let us take this child with us to our country and our king, for we know he is going to be of consequence." Halīmah could barely disengage herself from them and run away with her protégé. This story is also told by al Tabarī, but he casts suspicion on it by reporting it first at this early year of Muhammad's age as well as later, just before the Prophet's commission at the age of forty.

Orientalists and many Muslim scholars do not trust the story and find the evidence therefor spurious. The biographies agree that the two men dressed in white were seen by children hardly beyond their second year of age—which constitutes no witness at all—and that Muhammad lived with the tribe of Banū Saʿd in the desert until he was five. The claim that this event had taken place while Muḥammad was two and a half years old and that Ḥalīmah and her husband returned the child to his mother immediately thereafter, contradicts this general consensus. Consequently, some writers have even asserted that Muḥammad returned with Ḥalīmah for the third time. The Orientalist, Sir William Muir, refuses even to mention the story of the two men in white clothes. He wrote that if Ḥalīmah and her husband had become aware of something that had befallen the child, it must have been a sort of nervous breakdown which could not at all have hurt Muḥammad's healthy constitution. Others claim that Muḥammad stood in no need of any such surgery as God had prepared him at birth for receiving the divine message. Dermenghem believes that this whole story has no foundation other than the speculative interpretations of the following Qur'ānic verses:

أَلَمْ نَشْرَحْ لَكَ صَدْرَكَ ۞ وَوَضَعْنَا عَنْكَ وِزْرَكَ ۞ الَّذِيٓ أَنْقَضَ ظَهْرَكَ

"Had we not revived your spirit [literally, "opened your chest"] and dissipated your burden which was galling your back."[1]

Certainly, in these verses the Qur'ān is pointing to something purely spiritual. It means to describe a purification of the heart as preparation for receipt of the divine message and to stress Muḥammad's over-taxing burden of prophethood.

Those orientalists and Muslim thinkers who take this position *vis-à-vis* the foregoing tradition do so in consideration of the fact that the life of Muḥammad was human through and through and that in order to prove his prophethood the Prophet never had recourse to miracle-mongering as previous prophets had done. This finding is corroborated by Arab and Muslim historians who consistently assert that the life of the Arab Prophet is free of anything irrational or mysterious and who regard the contrary as inconsistent with the Qur'ānic position that God's creation is rationally analyzable, that His laws are immutable, and that the pagans are blameworthy because they do not reason.

Muḥammad in the Desert

Until the fifth year of his life Muḥammad remained with the tribe of Banū Saʿd inhaling with the pure air of the desert the spirit of personal freedom and independence. From this tribe he learned the Arabic language in its purest and most classical form. Justifiably, Muhammad used to tell his companions, "I am the most Arab among you, for I am of the tribe of Quraysh and I have been brought up among the tribe of Banū Sa'd ben Bakr."[2]

These five years exerted upon Muhammad a most beautiful and lasting influence, as Halīmah and her people remained the object of his love and admiration all the length of his life. When, following his marriage with Khadījah a drought occurred and Halīmah came to visit Muhammad, she returned with a camel loaded with water and forty heads of cattle. Whenever Halīmah visited Muhammad, he stretched out his mantle for her to sit on as a sign of the respect he felt he owed her. Shaymā', Halīmah's daughter, was taken captive by the Muslim forces along with Banū Hawāzin after the seige of Tā'if. When she was brought before Muhammad, he recognized her, treated her well, and sent her back to her people as she wished.

The young Muhammad returned to his mother after five years of desert life. It is related that when Halīmah brought the boy into Makkah, she lost him in the outskirts of the city. 'Abd al Muttalib sent his scouts to look for him and he was found with Waraqah ibn Nawfal.[3] 'Abd al Muttalib took his grandson under his protection, and made him the object of great love and affection. As lord of Quraysh and master of the whole of Makkah, the aged leader used to sit on a cushion laid out in the shade of the Ka'bah. His children would sit around that cushion, not on it, in deference to their father. But whenever Muhammad joined the group, 'Abd al Muttalib would bring him close to him and ask him to sit on the cushion. He would pat the boy's back and show off his pronounced affection for him so that Muhammad's uncles could never stop him from moving ahead of them to his grandfather's side.

Orphanhood

The grandson was to become the object of yet greater endearment to his grandfather. His mother, Āminah, took him to Madīnah in order to acquaint him with her uncles, the Banū al Najjār. She took with her on that trip Umm Ayman, the servant left behind by her husband 'Abdullah. In Madīnah, Āminah must have shown her little boy the house where his father died as well as the grave where he was buried. It was then that the boy must have first learned what it means to be an orphan. His mother must have talked much to him about his beloved father who had left her a few days after their marriage, and who had met his death among his uncles in Madīnah. After his emigration to that city the Prophet used to tell his companions about this first trip to Madīnah in his mother's company. The traditions have preserved for us a number of sayings which could have come only from a man full of love for Madīnah and full of grief for the loss of those who were buried in its graves. After a stay of a month in Yathrib, Āminah prepared to return to Makkah with her son and set out on the same two camels which carried them thither. On the road, at the village of Abwā'[4] Āminah became ill, died, and was buried. It was Umm Ayman that brought the lonely and bereaved child to Makkah, henceforth doubly confirmed in orphanhood. A few days earlier he must have shared his mother's grief as she told him of her bereavement while he was yet unborn. Now he was to see with his own eyes the loss of his mother and add to his experience of shared grief that of a grief henceforth to be borne by him alone.

The Death of ʿAbd al Muṭṭalib

The doubled orphanhood of Muḥammad increased ʿAbd al Muṭṭalib's affection for him. Nonetheless, his orphanhood cut deeply into Muḥammad's soul. Even the Qur'ān had to console the Prophet reminding him, as it were, "Did God not find you an orphan and give you shelter and protection? Did He not find you erring and guide you to the truth?"[5] It would have been somewhat easier on the orphaned boy had ʿAbd al Muṭṭalib lived longer than he did, to the ripe age of eighty when Muḥammad was still only eight years old. The boy must have felt the loss just as strongly as he had felt that of his mother. At the funeral Muḥammad cried continuously; thereafter, the memory of his grandfather was ever present to his mind despite all the care and protection which his uncle Abū Ṭālib gave him before and after his commission to prophethood. The truth is that the passing of ʿAbd al Muṭṭalib was a hard blow to the whole clan of Banū Hāshim, for none of his children had ever come to enjoy the respect and position, the power, wisdom, generosity, and influence among all Arabs as he had. ʿAbd al Muṭṭalib fed the pilgrim, gave him to drink, and came to the rescue of any Makkan in his hour of need. His children, on the other hand, never achieved that much. The poor among them were unable to give because they had little or nothing, and the rich were too stingy to match their father's generosity. Consequently, the clan of Banū Umayyah prepared to take over the leadership of Makkah, till then enjoyed by Banū Hāshim, undaunted by any opposition the latter might put forth.

Under Abu Ṭālib's Protection

The protection of Muhammad now fell to Abū Ṭālib, his uncle. Abū Ṭālib was not the eldest of the brothers. Al Ḥārith was the eldest but he was not prosperous enough to expand his household responsibilities. Al 'Abbās, on the other hand, was the richest but he was not hospitable: he undertook the *siqāyah* alone and refused to assume responsibility for the *rifādah*. Despite his poverty, Abū Ṭālib was the noblest and the most hospitable and, therefore, the most respected among the Quraysh. No wonder that the protection of Muhammad devolved upon him.

The First Trip to al Shām

Abū Ṭālib loved his nephew just as 'Abd al Muttalib had done before him. He loved him so much that he gave him precedence over his own children. The uprightness, intelligence, charity, and good disposition of Muhammad strengthened the uncle's attachment to him. Even when Muhammad was twelve years old, Abū Ṭālib did not take him along on his trade trips thinking that he was too young to bear the hardship of desert travel. It was only after Muhammad's strong insistence that Abū Ṭālib permitted the child to accompany him and join the trip to al Shām. In connection with this trip which he took at an early age, the biographers relate Muhammad's encounter with the monk Baḥīrah at Buṣrā, in the southern region of al Shām. They tell how the monk recognized in Muhammad the signs of prophethood as told in Christian books. Other traditions relate that the monk had advised Abū Ṭālib not to take his nephew too far within al Shām for fear that the Jews would recognize the signs and harm the boy.

On this trip Muhammad must have learned to appreciate the vast expanse of the desert and the brilliance of the stars shining in its clear atmosphere. He must have passed through Madyan,

Wādī al Qurā, the lands of Thamūd, and his attentive ears must have listened to the conversation of the Arabs and desert nomads about the cities and their history. On this trip, too, Muḥammad must have witnessed the luscious green gardens of al Shām which far surpassed those of Ṭā'if back at home. These gardens must have struck his imagination all the more strongly as he compared them with the barren dryness of the desert and of the mountains surrounding Makkah. It was in al Shām that he came to know of Byzantine and Christian history and heard of the Christians' scriptures and of their struggle against the fire-worshipping Persians. True, he was only at the tender age of twelve, but his great soul, intelligence, maturity, power of observation, memory and all the other qualities with which he was endowed in preparation for his prophethood enabled him at an early age to listen perceptively and to observe details. Later on he would review in memory all that he had seen or heard and he would investigate it all in solitude, asking himself, "What, of all he has seen and heard, is the truth?"

In all likelihood, Abū Ṭālib's trip to al Shām did not bring in much income. He never undertook another trip and was satisfied to remain in Makkah living within his means and taking care of his many children. Muḥammad lived with his uncle, satisfied with his lot. There, Muḥammad grew like any other child would in the city of Makkah. During the holy months he would either remain with his relatives or accompany them to the neighboring markets at 'Ukāẓ, Majannah, and Dhū al Majāz. There he would listen to the recitations of the *Mudhahhabāt* and Mu'allaqāt[6] poems and be enchanted by their eloquence, their erotic lyricism, the pride and noble lineage of their heroes, their conquests, hospitality, and magnanimity. All that the visits to these market places presented to his consciousness, he would later review, approve of, and admire or disapprove of and condemn. There, too, he would listen to the speeches of Christian and Jewish Arabs who strongly criticized the paganism of their fellow countrymen, who told about the scriptures of Jesus and Moses, and called men to what they believed to be the truth. Muḥammad would review and weigh these views, preferring them to the paganism of his people, though not quite convinced of their claims to the truth. Thus Muḥammad's circumstances exposed him at a tender age to what might prepare him for the great day, the day of the first revelation, when God called him to convey His message of truth and guidance to all mankind.

The Fijār War

Just as Muhammad learned the routes of the caravans in the
desert from his uncle Abū Ṭālib, and just as he listened to the
poets and the orators in the markets around Makkah during the
holy months, he learned how to bear arms. In the Fijār War[7]
he stood on the side of his uncle. The war was so-called because,
unlike other wars, it was fought during the holy months. Arabia
stood then under the convention that during the holy months no
tribe should undertake any hostile activity against another; the
general peace permitted the markets of 'Ukāz between Ṭā'if
and Makkah, of Majannah and Dhū al Majāz in the proximity of
'Arafāt, to be held and to prosper. On these market occasions,
men were not restricted to trade. They competed with one another in poetry and debated, and they performed a pilgrimage
to their gods in the Ka'bah. The market at 'Ukāz was the most
famous in Arabia. There, the authors of the Mu'allaqāt poems
recited their poetry. Quss exercized his oratory,[8] and Jews,
Christians and pagans spoke freely each about his faith in the
peace and security that the holy months provided.

In violation of the holiness of such months, al Barrād ibn
Qays al Kinānī stealthily attacked 'Urwah al Raḥḥāl ibn 'Utbah
al Hawāzinī and killed him. Every year at this time, al Nu'mān
ibn al Mundhir, King of Ḥīrah, used to send a caravan to 'Ukāz
to bring thither a load of musk and to take hence a load of hides,
ropes, and brocade from Yaman. Al Barrād al Kinānī offered
his services to guide the caravan as it passed through the lands
of his tribe, namely Kinānah. 'Urwah al Hawāzinī did likewise
and offered to guide the caravan through the Ḥijāz on the road
of Najd. King al Nu'mān chose 'Urwah and rejected the offer
of al Barrād. The latter, enraged with jealously, followed the
caravan, committed his crime, and ran away with the caravan
itself. Al Barrād then informed Bishr ibn Abū Ḥāzim that the
tribe of Hawāzin would avenge the murder of 'Urwah from
Quraysh because the crime took place within the area under
Quraysh jurisdiction. Indeed, members of the tribe of Hawāzin
followed members of the tribe of Quraysh and caught up with
them before the latter entered the holy sanctuary. Hawāzin,
not yet satisfied, warned that they would make war next year at
'Ukāz. This war continued to rage between the two parties for
four consecutive years. It ended in reconciliation and a peace
treaty, very much the kind of arrangement usually met with in
the desert. The tribe with the lesser number of casualties would

pay the other tribe the bloodwit of the victims making up the difference. In the arrangement between Quraysh and Hawāzin, the former paid the latter the bloodwit of twenty men. Henceforth, al Barrād became the exemplar of mischief. History has not established the age of Muḥammad during the Fijār War. Reports that he was fifteen and twenty years old have circulated. Perhaps the difference is due to the fact that the Fijār War lasted at least four years. If Muḥammad saw its beginning at the age of fifteen, he must have been close to twenty at the conclusion of the peace.

There is apparent consensus as to the kind of participation that Muḥammad had in this war. Some people claim that he was charged with collecting the arrows falling within the Makkan camp and bringing them over to his uncle for re-use against the enemy. Others claim that he himself participated in the shooting of these arrows. Since the said War lasted four years, it is not improbable that both claims are true. Years after his commission to prophethood, Muḥammad said, "I had witnessed that war with my uncle and shot a few arrows therein. How I wish I had never done so!"

The Alliance of Fuḍūl

Following the Fijār War, the Quraysh realized that their tragedy and deterioration as well as all the loss of Makkah's prestige in Arabia which they entailed ever since the death of Hishām and 'Abd al Muṭṭalib were largely due to their disagreement and internal division. They realized that once they were the unquestioned leaders of Arabia, immune to all attacks, but that every tribe was now anxious to pick a fight with them and deprive them of what was left of their prestige and authority. With this recognition, al Zubayr ibn 'Abd al Muṭṭalib called together the houses of Hāshim, Zuhrah, and Taym and entertained them at the residence of 'Abdullah ibn Jud'ān. At his request and appeal, they covenanted together, making God their witness, that they will henceforth and forever stand on the side of the victim of injustice. Muḥammad attended the conclusion of this pact, which the Arabs called the Alliance of Fuḍūl,[9] and said, "I uphold the pact concluded in my presence when ibn Jud'ān gave us a great banquet. Should it ever be invoked, I shall immediately rise to answer the call."

In the Fijār War, hostilities were waged only during a few days every year. During the rest of the year the Arabs returned

to their normal occupations. Neither losses in property nor in
life were grave enough to change the Makkans' daily routines of
trade, usury, wine, women, and other kinds of entertainment.
Was this Muhammad's daily routine as well? Or did his poverty
and dependence upon his uncle for protection force him to stay
away from the luxury and extravagance of his contemporaries?
That he kept away from these indulgences is historically certain.
That he did so not on account of his poverty is equally certain.
The debauchees of Makkah who were hardly capable of providing for themselves the immediate needs of the day could still
afford their life of turpitude. Indeed, some of the poorest among
them could outdo the nobles of Makkah and the lords of Quraysh.
Rather, the soul of Muhammad was far too possessed by his will
to learn, to discover, and to know, to incline towards any such
depravities. His having been deprived as a boy of the learning
which was the privilege of the rich made him all the more
anxious to learn on his own. His great soul whose light was later
to fill the world and whose influence was to fashion history was
so involved in its will to perfection that Muhammad could only
turn away from the recreative pursuits of his fellow Makkans.
As one already guided by the truth, Muhammad's mind was
always turning towards the light of life evident in every one
of its manifestations in the world. His constant preoccupation
was with the discovery of the underlying truth of life, the perfection of its inner meaning. Ever since he was a youth his conduct was so perfect, manly, and truthful that all the people of
Makkah agreed to call him "al Amīn", or "the truthful", "the
loyal."

Muhammad as Herdsman

Muhammad's occupation as herdsman during the years of his
youth provided him with plenty of leisure to ponder and to contemplate. He took care of his family's and neighbors' herds.
Later, he used to recall these early days with joy, and say
proudly that "God sent no prophet who was not a herdsman . . .
Moses was a herdsman; David was also a herdsman; I, too,
was commissioned to prophethood while I grazed my family's
cattle at Ajyād." The intelligent sensitive herdsman would surely
find in the vastness of the atmosphere during the day and in the
brilliance of the stars during the night fair enticement to thinking and contemplation. He would try to penetrate the skies, to
seek an explanation for the manifestations of nature around

him. If he were profound enough, his thoughts would bring him
to realize that the world around him is not quite separate from
the world within him. He would ponder the fact that he takes
the atmosphere into his lungs, that without it he would die. He
would realize that the light of the sun revives him, that that of
the moon guides him, and that he is not without relation to the
heavenly bodies of the high and immense firmament. He would
ponder the fact that these heavenly bodies are well ordered together in a precise system in which neither sun overtakes the
moon nor night overtakes the day. If the security of this herd of
animals demanded his complete and constant attention, if it
were to be safeguarded against attack by the wolf and loss in the
desert dunes, what supreme attention and what perseverence
were needed to guard the order of the universe in all its detail!
Such speculative thought can indeed divert man from preoccupation with worldly cares and passions; it can pull him
beyond their apparent persuasiveness and appeal. Thus, in all
his deeds, Muḥammad never allowed anything to detract from
his reputation, but answered to every expectation to which his
nickname "al Amīn" gave rise.

Further evidence to this effect may be found in the reports
Muḥammad made about this early period of his life. It is said
that while he was a herdsman he had a companion whom he
asked to take over his duties while he spent the night in town
in some recreation as other youths were wont to do in those
days. Before he reached his destination, however, Muḥammad's
attention was arrested by a wedding in one of the houses on the
way. He stopped there to listen to the sounds emanating from
the house and fell asleep. He came back to Makkah on another
occasion for the same purpose, and again on the way his attention was arrested by the sound of beautiful music. He sat down
on the street to listen, and again fell asleep. The temptations of
Makkah had no power over the disciplined soul of Muḥammad
whose prime concern was contemplation. This is not surprising.
Far lesser men than Muḥammad have also overcome these
temptations. He led a life far removed from vice and immorality,
and found his pleasures in immersing himself in thought and
contemplation.

The Life of Thought and Contemplation

The life of thought is satisfied with very little of the world's
wealth and pleasure. Herding cattle and goats never brings

much material return, anyway. Material return, however, did
not concern Muḥammad, for he regarded the world stoically
and avoided, often with ascetic detachment, pursuing anything
beyond the barest needs of survival. Did he not say, "We are
a people who do not eat until we become hungry, a people who
when sitting to eat would never eat their fill?" Was he not
known throughout his life to call men to a life of hardness and
himself to lead a life of stoic self-denial? Those who long after
wealth and strive hard to obtain it satisfy passions which
Muḥammad never knew. Muḥammad's greatest spiritual pleasure
was that of beholding the beauty of the universe and responding
to its invitation to ponder and to admire. Such pleasure is known
only to the very few, but it was Muḥammad's nourishment ever
since he was a young child, and it was his only consolation when
life began to try him with the unforgettably cruel misfortunes
of the death of his father, of his mother, and of his grandfather.
Spiritual and intellectual pleasures are free. Their pursuit demands no wealth but requires the moral tautness to direct one's
gaze inward, to penetrate one's very essence. Even if Muḥammad
had never been called to prophethood, his soul would never have
allowed him to waste his energy in the pursuit of wealth. He
would have been happy to remain as he was—namely, a herdsman—but he would have been a herdsman whose soul encompassed the whole universe and was in turn encompassed by that
universe as if he were the very center of it.

Khadījah

As we have said earlier, Muḥammad's uncle, Abū Ṭālib, was
poor and had many mouths to feed. It was necessary that he
find for his nephew a higher paying job than herdsmanship.
One day he heard that Khadījah, daughter of Khuwaylid, was
hiring men of the Quraysh tribe to work for her in her trade.
Khadījah was a tradeswoman of honor and great wealth. She
used to hire men to bid and compete in the market on her behalf
and rewarded them with a share of the profits. Being of the tribe
of Banū Asad and having married twice within the tribe of
Banū Makhzūm, she had become very rich. Her father Khuwaylid
and other people whom she trusted used to help her administer
her large wealth. She had turned down several noblemen of
Quraysh who asked for her hand, believing that they were after
her wealth. Bound to a life of solitude, she had given all her
energy to the development of her business. When Abū Ṭālib

learned that she was preparing a caravan to send to al Shām, he called his nephew, who was then twenty-five years of age, and said to him, "My nephew, I am a man devoid of wealth and possessions. The times have been hard on us. I have heard that Khadījah has hired a man to do her trade for a remuneration of two young camels. We shall not accept for you a remuneration as little as that. Do you wish that I talk to her in this regard?" Muḥammad answered, "Let it be as you say, my uncle." Abū Ṭālib went to Khadījah and said, "O Khadījah, would you hire Muḥammad? We have heard that you have hired a man for the remuneration of two young camels, but we would not accept for Muḥammad any less than four." Khadījah answered: "Had you asked this for an alien or a hateful man, I would have granted your request. How then can I turn you down when your request is in favor of a dear relative?" Abū Ṭālib returned to Muḥammad and told him the news, adding, "That is a true grace from God."

Muḥammad in the Employ of Khadījah

On his first trip in the employ of Khadījah, Muḥammad was accompanied by Maysarah, her slave, who was also recommended to Muḥammad by his uncle. The caravan made its way to al Shām, passing through Wādī al Zahrān, Madyan and Thamūd as well as those spots through which Muḥammad had passed once before with his uncle Abū Ṭālib when he was twelve years old. This trip must have recalled to Muḥammad the memory of his first trip in that area. It furnished more grist for his thinking and contemplating as he came to know more of the doctrines and rituals of the people of al Shām. When he arrived at Busrah, he came into contact with Syrian Christianity and talked to the monks and priests, some of whom were Nestorians. Perhaps those very priests or some others discussed with him the religion of Jesus which had by then divided itself into several sects and parties. Muḥammad's adeptness and loyalty enabled him to make great gains for Khadījah—indeed more than anyone had done before!—and his loyalty and gentleness had won for him the love and admiration of the slave, Maysarah. When the time came for them to return, Muḥammad bought on behalf of Khadījah all that she had asked him to buy of the products of al Shām.

When the caravan had returned to al Zahrān near Makkah, Maysarah said to Muḥammad, "Run to Khadījah, O Muḥammad, and bring to her the news of your success. She will reward you

well." Muhammad galloped on his camel toward the residence
of his employer and arrived there about noon. Khadījah happened to be in an upper story of her house, saw Muhammad
coming, and prepared to receive him. She listened to his report—
which he must have rendered in his very eloquent style—about
his trip, the successes he achieved in his trade, and the goods
he had imported from al Shām. She must have been well pleased
with her new employee. Later on, Maysarah arrived and reported to her about Muhammad, his gentle treatment of him,
and his loyalty to her that confirmed what she had already known
of Muhammad's virtue and superiority over the other youths of
Makkah. Shortly, despite her forty years of age and the indif-
ference with which she rejected the offers of the noblest of
Quraysh, her satisfaction with her employee was to turn into
love. She desired to marry this youth whose eloquence and looks
had made such a profound impression upon her. According to
one version, she intimated her desire to her sister, and according
to another, to her friend Nufaysah, daughter of Munyah.
Nufaysah approached Muhammad and said, "What prevents you
from getting married?" Muhammad answered, "I have no means
with which to afford it." She said, "What if you were excused
from providing such means and were called by a person of
beauty, wealth, status and honor; what would be your response?"
He answered, "Who can such a person be?" She said, "Khadījah."
Muhammad wondered, "How could that be?" He too had felt
inclined toward Khadījah but he never allowed himself to entertain the idea of marrying her. He knew of her rejection of
the noblest and wealthiest men of Quraysh. When, therefore,
Nufaysah reported to him in answer to his question, "I shall
arrange it," he hastened to declare his acceptance. Soon Khadījah
appointed the hour at which the uncles of Muhammad could
find her people at her home and thus arrange for the completion
of the marriage. It was her uncle, 'Umar ibn Asad, who gave
her away as her father Khuwaylid had died before the Fijār
War. This fact disproves the claim that Khadījah's father did
not agree to the marriage and that his daughter had given him
wine in order to extract such agreement from him.

Here a new page in the life of Muhammad begins. It is the
page of married and family life which had brought great happiness to him as well as to Khadījah. It was also a page of fatherhood in which he was to suffer the loss of children even as
Muhammad had in his childhood suffered the loss of parents.

4

From Marriage to Prophethood

Muḥammad married Khadījah and gave her a dowry of twenty young camels. He moved to her house and thus began a new chapter in the life of both. Muḥammad offered Khadījah the love of a man of twenty-five, though not the raging passion of youth which is as quickly kindled as cooled or put off. Khadījah gave him sons as well as daughters. The sons, namely al Qāsim and 'Abdullah, died in childhood to the great grief of their father. The daughters survived and constantly remained the object of Muḥammad's love and compassion just as he was the object of their love and devotion.[1]

Muḥammad's Qualities

Muḥammad was handsome of face and of medium build, and neither conspicuously tall nor inconspicuously short. He had a large head, very black thick hair, wide forehead, heavy eyebrows, and large black eyes with a slight redness on their sides and long eyelashes to add to their attractiveness. He had a fine nose, well spaced teeth, a thick beard, a long handsome neck, wide chest and shoulders, light colored skin, and thick palms and feet. He walked resolutely with firm steps. His appearance was always one of deep thought and contemplation. In his eyes there lurked the authority of a commander of men. It is no wonder that Khadījah combined love for him with obedience to his wishes or that she soon excused him from having to administer

her trade and took over its reins as she had done before
marriage in order to give him leisure to pursue a life of
contemplation.

Aided by a marriage which complemented his geneological
honor and provided amply for his needs, Muhammad spent his
days respected and loved by all the people of Makkah. His family
life, numerous offspring, along with the ample provisions he
now enjoyed, kept him from falling in public esteem. On the
other hand, Muhammad had not withdrawn from society, from
participating in the public life of Makkah as he did before. His
new status added to his prestige among his peers as well as
strengthened his already great modesty. Despite his great intelligence and outstanding ability, he listened well and attentively
to anyone who spoke to him, never turning his face away from
his interlocutor. Whosoever addressed him, Muhammad was
never satisfied to lend his ear alone but turned to him with all
his being. He spoke little, listened much, and inclined only to
serious conversation though he did not refuse to share a joke.
He always spoke the truth. Sometimes he would laugh until
one could see his molars, but his anger could never be recognized
except by perspiration between his eyebrows. His anger and
fury were always sublimated, and his magnanimity, candidness,
and loyalty knew no bounds. He loved to do the good, and was
charitable, hospitable, and friendly, as well as resolved and
strong willed. Once resolved on a course of action, he was per-
severing and knew no hesitancy. Whoever came into contact with
him was deeply impressed by all these qualities; whoever saw
him would immediately fear him; and whoever had anything to
do with him, loved him. All these qualities helped strengthen the
bond of loyalty, truthfulness, and love which united him to
Khadijah.

Reconstruction of the Ka'bah

We have said that Muhammad did not withdraw from the
people of Makkah or from participating in the public life of the
city. At the time, the Makkans were preoccupied with the rebuilding of the Ka'bah after a sudden flood had shaken its
foundation and cracked its walls. The Ka'bah had for some time
been the concern of the Quraysh. It had no ceiling and the
treasures it housed were exposed to robbery. The Makkans were
afraid, however, that a rebuilding of the Ka'bah with doors and

ceilings might bring upon them a curse. The Ka'bah was girded by a series of superstitions designed to frighten the people from ever altering anything that pertained to it. Any such change would have been regarded as forbidden innovation and anathema. When the floods cracked its walls, it was imperative to do something about it despite fear and hesitancy. Coincidentally, a ship coming from Egypt belonging to a Byzantine trader called Pachomius was washed ashore. Pachomius was a builder by trade and knew something of carpentry. When Quraysh heard of him, al Walīd ibn al Mughīrah headed a delegation of Makkans to Juddah to negotiate with him. They bought from him the ship and commissioned him to come with them to Makkah and help them in the building of the Ka'bah. Pachomius accepted. In Makkah, there resided another Coptic man who knew something of carpentry. They asked him to assist Pachomius and the work began.

Wrecking and Rebuilding the Ka'bah

To everyone of the four clans of Makkah fell the duty of wrecking and rebuilding one of the four walls of the Ka'bah. No one, however, volunteered to begin the work of wrecking for fear of punishment by its gods. Al Walīd ibn al Mughīrah, approaching his task with strong premonitions, prayed to the gods before pulling down part of the Yamanī wall assigned to his tribe. The rest waited in order to see what would befall al Walīd as a result of his deed. When the morning came and nothing had happened to him, they took courage and began their work. Like the rest, Muḥammad carried stones back and forth, and the wrecking continued until the Ka'bah was leveled. Below the walls green stones were found which the Makkans were unable to shake loose. They decided to use them as foundation on which to build the new walls. From the neighboring mountains, they carried stones of blue granite. As the walls rose from the ground and the time came to place the sacred black stone in its place in the east wall, they differed as to who would have the honor of laying it in place. Competition was so keen that it almost led to a new civil war. The descendents of 'Abd al Dār and of 'Adiyy allied themselves together and swore that none would rob them of this honor. They were so serious in their resolution that members of the clan of Banū 'Abd al Dār brought a bowl full of blood in which they dipped their hands in confirmation of their solemn

oath. For this act they were later called "the bloodmongers".
When Abū Umayyah, son of Mughīrah al Makhzūmī saw what
happened, he took advantage of his power and prestige and said
to the Makkans, "While we are all standing here, let the first
one to pass through the gate of al Ṣuffah be our arbitrator in
this dispute." The first one to pass through the gate was
Muhammad. When they beheld him they said, "There goes al
Amīn. We shall agree with his verdict." Realizing, as he listened to them, that the contenders had worked themselves up
into a passion, Muhammad thought for a moment and said,
"Bring me a robe." He took the robe they brought, spread it on
the ground, and placed the black stone on it and then said, "Let
the elders of each clan hold onto one edge of the robe." They all
complied and together carried the stone to the site of construction. There, Muhammad picked up the stone and laid it in its
place by himself. Bloodshed was thus averted and the dispute
was solved. The Quraysh completed the building of the Ka'bah,
raising its walls to a height of eighteen cubits. In order to make
it more defensible, they raised its entrance above ground level.
Inside the Ka'bah, they erected two parallel rows of three
pillars each to support the ceiling and built a stairway on its
north side leading to the roof. Hubal, the idol, was placed inside
the Ka'bah together with all the treasures whose security
concerned the Makkans.

There is disagreement about the age of Muhammad at the
time of the rebuilding of the Ka'bah and of his arbitration between the Quraysh clans concerning the black stone. While
some claimed that he was twenty-five years old, Ibn Isḥaq reported him to be thirty-five. Regardless which of the two claims
is true, the acceptance by the Quraysh of his arbitration and
verdict—as well as his taking over the stone with his own
hands and laying it down first on the robe and then in its place
in the wall—all this proves the very high prestige Muhammad
enjoyed among all Makkans as well as appreciation by his fellow
countrymen for his objectivity and candidness of purpose.

Dissolution of Authority in Makkah and Its Effects

The foregoing dispute between the clans, the alliance of "the
bloodmongers," and the recourse to arbitration by the first man
to pass through the gates of al Ṣuffah, all proved that public
power and authority in Makkah had by that time dissolved and

that none of the absolute power of Qusayy, Hāshim, or 'Abd al Muṭṭalib had passed to any Makkan. Undoubtedly, this dissolution was furthered by the power struggle between Banū Hāshim and Banū Umayyah after the death of 'Abd al Muṭṭalib. Such dissolution of public power and authority was bound to harm the city sooner or later were it not for the sanctified status of the ancient house and the awe and reverence it commanded in the hearts of all Arabs. Nonetheless, a natural consequence of political dissolution was the noticeable increase in the liberty of many to speak out their religious and other views. It was equally evident in the boldness of Jews and Christians, hitherto living in fear, publically to criticise Arab idolatry. This dissolution of public power also contributed to the gradual disappearance among large numbers of Qurayshīs of their old veneration of the idols, though their elders continued at least to appear to respect them. Anxious to safeguard the old ways, the elders held that to stabilize the situation and to prevent further deterioration of Makkan unity, idol worship in the Ka'bah might preserve for Makkah its place in the trade relations and religious life of Arabia. In fact, Makkah continued to benefit from this position of religious eminence, and its commerce continued to prosper. In the hearts of the Makkans themselves, however, Makkan prosperity could not for long impede the deterioration and final disappearance of idol worship.

Dissolution of Idol Worship

It is reported that one day the Quraysh tribe convened at a place called Nakhlah to celebrate the day of the goddess al 'Uzzā. Four Qurayshīs failed to show up and participate in this sacrament: namely, Zayd ibn 'Amr, 'Uthmān ibn al Ḥuwayrith, 'Ubayd Allah ibn Jaḥsh and Waraqah ibn Nawfal. They are reported to have addressed one another in these words, "Mark well these words! By God, the people are unworthy and surely misguided. As for us, we shall circumambulate no stone which neither hears nor sees, which is capable of neither harm nor good and on which the blood of sacrifice runs. O people, seek for yourselves a religion other than this!" Waraqah joined Christianity, and it is reported that he translated into Arabic some of the contents of the Evangels. 'Ubayd Allah ibn Jaḥsh remained a man without religion until he joined Islām and emigrated with his fellow Muslims to Abyssinia. There it is reported that he

joined Christianity and died a Christian. His wife Umm
Ḥabībah, daughter of Abū Sufyān, remained a Muslim. She
returned to Madīnah and became one of the wives of the Prophet
and a "Mother of the Faithful."[2] As for Zayd ibn 'Amr, he separated himself from his wife and from his uncle al Khaṭṭāb,
lived for a while in al Shām and 'Irāq and returned to Arabia
without ever joining either Judaism or Christianity. He also
separated himself from Makkan religion and avoided the idols.
Leaning on the walls of the Ka'bah he used to pray, "O God! If
I knew in which form you preferred to be worshipped, I would
surely worship you in that form." Finally, as for 'Uthmān ibn
al Ḥuwayrith, a relative of Khadījah, he traveled to Byzantium,
became a Christian and, for some time, achieved a position of
eminence in the imperial court. It is said that he sought to
subjugate Makkah to Byzantium and to get himself appointed as
the emperor's viceroy. The Makkans finally banished him from
Makkah. He joined the Ghassānīs in al Shām. From there he
sought to cut off the trade route of Makkah, but the Makkans
undid his schemes by sending all sorts of gifts to the Ghassānī
court. There, ibn al Ḥuwayrith died by being poisoned.

Muhammad's Sons

The years passed while Muḥammad participated in the public
life of Makkah and found in Khadījah, the loving woman who
gave him many children, the best of all woman companions. She
gave him two sons, al Qāsim and 'Abdullah—the last of whom
was nicknamed al Ṭāhir and al Ṭayyib—and four daughters,
Zaynab, Ruqayyah, Umm Kulthūm and Fāṭimah. Hardly anything
is known of al Qāsim and 'Abdullah except that they died before
the coming of Islām, while still infants. Undoubtedly their loss
caused their parents great grief and affected them deeply. As
their mother, Khadījah must have received a permanent wound
at their loss. She must have turned to her idols, inquisitively
asking why the gods did not have mercy on her, and why they
did not prevent her happiness from repeated shipwreck by the
loss of her children. Certainly, Muhammad must have shared
her grief and unhappiness. It is not difficult for us to imagine
the depth of their tragedy in an age when daughters used to
be buried alive and male descendants were sought after as the
substance of life itself—indeed more. Sufficient proof of this
grief is the fact that Muhammad could not last long without a

male heir. When he saw Zayd ibn Ḥārithah offered for sale, he asked Khadījah to buy him; no sooner was the new slave bought than Muḥammad manumitted and adopted him as a son. He was called Zayd ibn Muḥammad, lived under his protection, and became one of his best followers and companions. There was yet more grief ahead for Muhammad when his third son Ibrahīm passed away in the Islāmic period, after Islām had prohibited the burial of live daughters and declared paradise to stand under the feet of mothers. It is not surprising, therefore, that Muhammad's losses in his children should leave their deep mark upon his life and thought. He must have been quite shocked when on each of these tragic occasions, Khadījah turned to the idols of the Kaʻbah, and sacrificed to Hubal, to al Lāt, al ʻUzzā, and Manāt in the hope that these deities would intercede on her behalf and prevent the loss of her children. But Muḥammad must have then realized the vanity and futility of these hopes and efforts in his tragic bereavement and great sorrow.

Muḥammad's Daughters

Muḥammad took care to marry his daughters to good husbands. He married Zaynab, the eldest, to Abū al ʻĀṣ ibn al Rabīʻ ibn ʻAbd Shams, whose mother was Khadījah's sister, and who was an upright and successful citizen. This marriage proved a happy one despite the separation of the two spouses following Zaynab's emigration to Madīnah after Islām, as we shall see later.[3] He married Ruqayyah and Umm Kulthūm to ʻUtbah and ʻUtaybah, the sons of his uncle Abū Lahab. These marriages did not last, for soon after the advent of Islām, Abū Lahab ordered his two sons to divorce their wives. It was ʻUthmān that married both of them one after the other. Fātimah, who was still a child, did not marry ʻAlī until after Islām.

Still, Muḥammad's life during these years was one of well being, peace, and security. Were it not for the loss of his sons, it would have been a very happy one blessed with progeny and Khadījah's constant love and loyalty. During this period it was natural for Muḥammad to allow his soul to wander, his mind and imagination to contemplate and to listen to the Makkan dialogue concerning their religion, to Jews and Christians concerning theirs, as well as to the latter's critique of Makkan religion. He could afford to give these problems his time and energy and to concern himself with them far more than could

his compatriots. Endowed with such penetrating insight and
prepared for conveying the divine message to mankind and ready
for guiding their spiritual life to the true path, Muhammad
could not enjoy his peace and security while men sank in misguidance and untruth. It was necessary for such a soul as he
had to seek the truth perennially and everywhere, for only by
such seeking and soul searching would it receive that which God
was about to reveal. Despite this keen and noble obsession with
the spiritual, this natural impulsion to religion, Muhammad
never sought to become a priest nor a wise counsellor, such as
Waraqah ibn Nawfal and others were, to whom men ran for
advice. Rather he sought first to convince himself of the truth,
not to pass it on to others. Consequently, he spent long intervals
alone, completely absorbed in his thoughts and meditation, and
hardly ever given to communicating his ideas to anyone.

The Arabs' Annual Retreat

It was Arabia's custom at the time for the pious and thought-
ful to devote a period of each year to a retreat of worship,
asceticism, and prayer. They would seek an empty place far
away from their people where they could concentrate on their
prayers and genuinely seek a new level of seriousness, wisdom,
and ethical goodness through meditation. This practice was
called *tahannuth* or *tahannuf*. Therein Muhammad found the
best means of satisfying his will to thinking and meditating.
In its solitude he could find a measure of spiritual detachment
and peace that would enable his consciousness to screen the
whole universe for inspiration and to pursue his thought wherever it might lead. At the head of Mount Hirā', two miles north
of Makkah, Muhammad discovered a cave whose perfect silence
and total separation from Makkah made of it a perfect place
for retreat. In that cave Muhammad used to spend the whole
month of Ramadān. He would satisfy himself with the least provisions, carried to him from time to time by a servant, while
devoting himself uninterruptedly to his spiritual pursuits in
peace, solitude and tranquility. His devotion often caused him
to forget himself, to forget his food, and, indeed, to forget the
whole world around him. At these moments the very world and
existence must have appeared to him like a dream. Through his
mind he would turn the pages of all that he had heard and

learned, and his search could only whet his appetite for the truth.

Groping after Truth

Muḥammad did not hope to find the truth he sought in the narratives of the rabbis or the scriptures of the monks but in the very world surrounding him, in the sky and its stars, moon, and sun, and in the desert with its burning air under the brilliant sun—its impeccable purity enclosed by the light of the moon or that of the stars in the balmy night, in the sea with its countless waves, and in all that which underlies this existence and constitutes its unity of being. It was in the world that Muḥammad sought to discover the supreme truth. He sought to unite his soul to it, to penetrate it, and to grasp the secret of its being. He did not take much thought to realize that his peoples' understanding of the nature of this world, of their religiosity and devotion, was all false. Their idols were mere stones —speechless, thoughtless, and powerless. Hubal, al Lāt, and al 'Uzzā, as well as every one of these idols and statues inside or around the Ka'bah, had never created even so much as a fly and never did Makkah any good. Where was to be found the truth in this vast universe of infinite skies and stars? Is it in the brilliant stars which give men their light and warmth and sends them rain? Is it in their water, the light and warmth as sources of life to all mankind throughout the world? No! For all these are creatures like the earth itself. Is the truth then behind the sky and their stars, in the boundless space beyond? But what is space? And what is this life which is today and is gone tomorrow? What is its origin and source? Is this world and our presence therein all a mere accident? The world and its life have, however, immutable laws which cannot be the product of circumstances. Men do good and they do evil. But do they do it willingly and deliberately, or is their action a mere instinct which they are powerless to control? It was of such spiritual and psychological problems that Muḥammad thought during his solitary retreat in the cave of Ḥirā', and it was in the totality of spirit and life that he sought to discover the truth. His ideas filled his soul, his heart, his consciousness, indeed all his being. This paramount occupation diverted him from the commonplace problems of everyday. When at the end of Ramaḍān, Muḥammad

returned to Khadījah, his perturbed thoughts showed on his
face and caused Khadījah to inquire whether he was well.

In his devotions during that retreat, did Muḥammad follow
any one of the known religious schools? That is a question on
which scholars disagree. In his *Al Kāmil fi al Tārīkh,* ibn Kathīr
reported some of the current views in answer to this question.
Some claimed that Muḥammad followed the law of Noah; others,
the law of Ibrahīm; others, the law of Moses; others the law of
Jesus. Others claimed that Muḥammad had followed every known
law and observed it. Perhaps this last claim is nearer to the
truth than the others, for it agrees with what we know of
Muḥammad's constant search for answers and for ways to the
truth.

The True Vision

Whenever the year revolved and the month of Ramaḍān
arrived, Muḥammad would return to the cave of Ḥira' for meditation with a soul yet more ripe and more concerned. After years
of preoccupation with such problems, Muḥammad began to see
in his dreams visions of the truth he sought. Contrasted with
these visions, the illusory character of this life and the vanity
of its ornaments became especially apparent. He had become
perfectly convinced that his people had gone utterly astray and
that their spiritual lives had been corrupted by their idols and
the false beliefs associated with them. He was also convinced
that neither the Jews nor the Christians had anything to offer
that would save his people from their misguidance. Some truth
there certainly was in the claims of both Judaism and Christianity, but there was also a fair measure of falsehood and illusion,
of outright paganism, which could not possibly agree with the
simple absolute truth beyond all the barren dialectics and futile
controversies in which Christians as well as Jews indulged. This
simple absolute truth is God, Creator of the universe, other than
Whom there is no God. The truth is that God is Lord of the
universe, that He is the Compassionate and the Merciful, and
that men are responsible for their deeds. "Whoever will do an
atom's weight of good, will be rewarded therefor on the Day of
Judgment; and whoever does an atom's weight of evil, will likewise be punished therefor."[4] The truth is that paradise and hell
are true; that those who worship other gods than God shall
dwell in hell and suffer eternal punishment.

When Muḥammad retreated into the cave of Ḥirā' as he approached the fortieth year of his age, his soul was fully convinced of the vision of truth he had seen. His mind was cleansed of all illusion and falsehood. His soul was well disciplined by the search for truth and devotion to it. His whole being was now oriented toward the eternal truth, and his whole life was devoted to the pursuit of its path. He had prayed with all his power that God might deliver his people from their misguidance and error. In his retreat he prayed day and night and fasted long periods. He would come down from the cave for a stroll on the desert highway and then return to his retreat, always rethinking, contemplating and reconsidering. This continued for six whole months while Muḥammad was unable to tear himself away. Naturally he was scared, and intimated to his wife, Khadījah, the fear that he might even be possessed by an evil spirit. His loving and loyal wife reassured him, reminding that he was al Amīn" [*i.e.*, the faithful], that evil spirits could not approach him precisely because of his faith and strong morality. It had never occurred to either that God was preparing His chosen one by means of all these spiritual exercises for a truly great day, the day of the great news, the day of the first revelation. It did not occur to them that God was preparing His Prophet for prophethood.

The Beginning of Revelation (610 C.E.)

One day, while Muḥammad was asleep in the cave, an angel approached with a sheet in his hand. The angel said to Muḥammad, "Read." Muḥammad answered in surprise, "What shall I read?" He felt as if the angel had strangled and then released him and heard once more the command, "Read." Muḥammad's reply was, "What shall I read?" Once more he felt the angel strangling and then releasing him, and he heard him repeat the command, "Read." For the third time Muḥammad answered, "What shall I read?" fearful that this time the strangling would be stronger. The angel replied, "Read in the name of your Lord, the Creator, Who created man of a clot of blood. Read! Your Lord is most gracious. It is He who taught man by the pen that which he does not know."[5] Muḥammad recited these verses, repeating them after the angel who withdrew after they were permanently carved upon his memory.[6] Thus the earliest of the biographies reported, and so did ibn Isḥāq.

Many of the Muhaddithūn [*i.e.*, "reporters of the Prophet's traditions"—Tr.] have reported likewise. Some of them have claimed that the beginning of revelation was in the hours of wakefulness, and they mention a *hadīth* to the effect that Gabriel first said words of reassurance to assuage Muhammad's fear at his appearance. In his *Al Kāmil fī al Tārīkh*, Ibn Kathīr gave a quotation from the book, *Dalā'il al Nubuwwah* by Abū Na'īm al Isbahānī, in which the latter reported that 'Alqamah ibn Qays had said, "The first revelations come to the prophets in their sleep until their hearts are reassured. Thereafter, revelation comes any time of the day or night." To this report Abū Na'īm added, "This report comes to me from 'Alqamah ibn Qays in person. It is sound and reasonable, and it is corroborated by that which comes before and after it."

Muhammad's Fear

Stricken with panic, Muhammad arose and asked himself, "What did I see? Did possession of the devil which I feared all along come to pass?" Muhammad looked to his right and his left but saw nothing. For a while he stood there trembling with fear and stricken with awe. He feared the cave might be haunted and that he might run away still unable to explain what he saw. He walked in the area around the mountain asking himself who could have commanded him to read. Until that day in his retreat, Muhammad used to have visions of the truth dawning upon him after his meditation and filling his consciousness with great light. In these visions, Muhammad was guided to the truth, his doubts were dissolved, and the darkness which had enveloped the Quraysh in their idol worship was exposed. This light that illuminated the way in front of him was that of the truth which provided him with true guidance. It was the One and only God. But who was this who came to remind Muhammad of Him, that He had created man, and that He was the most gracious who taught man by the pen that which he does not know? Pursued by his own questioning and still trembling in fear of what he had seen and heard in the cave, Muhammad stopped in the middle of the road when the same voice called to him from above. Mesmerized in his place, Muhammad lifted his head toward heaven. He saw the angel in the form of a human giant across the sky. For a moment he sought to escape, but wherever he looked or ran, the angel stood right there before him. In his absence from the cave a messenger from Khadījah looked for him and could not find him. Filled with what he had seen, Muḥammad returned home once the angel disappeared. His state was one of extreme dread. He had literally experienced the *Mysterium Tremendum et Fascinans*.

Khadījah, the Faithful

As Muḥammad entered his house he asked Khadījah to wrap him in blankets. She could see that her husband was shivering as if struck with high fever. When he calmed down, he cast toward his wife the glance of a man in need of rescue and said, "O Khadījah, what has happened to me?" He told her of his experience and intimated to her his fear that his mind had finally betrayed him, and that he was becoming a seer or a man possessed. Khadījah was still the same angel of mercy, peace, and reassurance she had always been. As she did on earlier occasions when Muḥammad feared possession by the devil, she now stood firm by her husband and devoid of the slightest doubt. Respectfully, indeed reverently, she said to him, "Joy to my cousin! Be firm. By him who dominates Khadījah's soul I pray and hope that you will be the Prophet of this nation. By God, He will not let you down. You will be kind to your kin; your speech will all be true; you will rescue the weary; entertain the guest and help the truth to prevail."

Reassured, Muḥammad thanked Khadījah and was grateful for her faith. Exhausted, he fell asleep. This sleep was to be followed by a spiritual life of utmost strength, a life whose sublimity and beauty was to confront each and every mind. His life was to be dedicated purely to God, to truth, and to humanity. He was being commissioned to convey to man the message of His lord. He was to carry out his charge not by force, but by argument yet more gentle, sound and more convincing than any man has known. Despite every unbeliever, the light of God and His guidance will yet fill the world.

5

From the Beginning of Revelation to the Conversion of 'Umar

Muḥammad lapsed into perfect sleep while Khadījah's eyes, full of compassion and hope, were pinned on him. She withdrew from his room pensive and restless at what she had just heard. She looked to the morrow hoping that her husband would become the Prophet of this Arab nation long lost in error. She wished her husband could bring his people to the religion of truth and blaze for them the path of goodness and virtue. But she was very apprehensive of that morrow, fearful for the good of her loving and faithful husband. She reviewed in her mind the events he had reported to her, and imagined the beautiful angel appearing to her husband across the sky after conveying to him the words of His Lord. She tried to imagine the angel perched in the sky so that, following Muḥammad's description, wherever one looked one could not lose sight of him, and she recalled the holy words which Muḥammad recited to her after they had been carved on his memory. As she reviewed all this she may have at one moment smiled with hope and conviction and later frowned with fear for what might have befallen her husband. She could not bear her solitude long, and the alternation of sweet hope and bitter fear overpowered her. She therefore thought to divulge what she knew to someone sure of insight and wisdom who could give her some advice and good counsel.

The Conversation of Waraqah and Khadījah

Khadījah ran to her cousin Waraqah ibn Nawfal who, as we
saw earlier, had already become a Christian and had translated
part of the Evangel into Arabic. When she finished telling him
what Muḥammad had seen and heard and of her compassionate
and hopeful response to her husband, Waraqah broke into these
words: "Holy, Holy! By Him who dominates Waraqah's soul, if
your report is true, O Khadījah, this must be the great spirit
that spoke to Moses. Muḥammad must be the Prophet of this
nation. Tell him that he must be firm." Khadījah returned home
and found Muḥammad still asleep. For a while, she stared at him
lovingly, faithfully, and hopefully. Suddenly she noticed that he
was shivering, breathing deeply and perspiring. As he opened
his eyes, he heard the angel say, "O you who lie wrapped in your
mantle. Arise and warn. Glorify your Lord. Purify yourself.
Shun uncleanliness. Give not in order to have more in return.
For the sake of your Lord endure patiently."[1] Seeing him in this
state, Khadījah pleaded that he return to his bed and resume
his rest. But Muḥammad sprang to his feet and said to her, "The
time of slumber and rest is past, O Khadījah. Gabriel has commanded me to warn men and to call them to God and to His
worship. But whom shall I call? And who will listen to me?"
Khadījah tried to appease and reassure him, to encourage him
with predictions of success. She told him what she had heard
from Waraqah and declared to him her *Islām, i.e.,* her faith in his
prophethood.

It was natural for Khadījah to be the first one to believe in
Muḥammad. For many long years she had known him to be the
examplar of truthfulness, fidelity, honesty, charity, and compassion. In his many retreats during the last few years, she had
noticed how he had been constantly preoccupied with the search
for the truth, with the truth alone; how he had sought that truth
with his heart, mind, and spirit beyond the idolatrous superstitions of the people and their sacrifices, and beyond the deities
that are capable of neither good nor evil but which the people
venerated without avail. She had witnessed his great doubt and
utter perplexity on his return from the cave of Ḥirā' after the
first revelation. She asked him to tell her when the angel would
come. When he did she seized Muḥammad and placed him on her
left leg, then on her right leg, then in her lap, always asking him
whether he was still seeing the angel and Muḥammad answering

in the affirmative. She then uncovered herself and threw off her
clothes and asked Muḥammad whether he still saw the angel,
but the angel then disappeared. At this her doubt that the appearance was that of the devil rather than of the angel was
dissolved once and for all.

Waraqah and Muhammad

One day Muḥammad went to the Kaʻbah for circumambulation.
He was met by Waraqah ibn Nawfal, who asked him about himself. Muḥammad related the events as they had happened. When
he finished, Waraqah said, "By Him Who dominates my soul I
swear that you are the Prophet of this nation. The great spirit
that has come to Moses has now come to you. You will be denied
and you will be hurt. You will be abused and you will be pursued.
If I should ever live to see that day I shall surely help the cause
of God. God knows that I will." Waraqah then approached
Muḥammad, kissed his forehead and went away. Muḥammad
realized the faithfulness of Waraqah, and at the same time felt
the burden weighing on his shoulder. Waraqah's warning that
the struggle ahead would be hard only confirmed Muḥammad's
fears that the Quraysh were so attached to their false beliefs
that they would fight to death for them. How could he fight
them when they were his very people, his nearest relatives?

Surely the Makkans were mistaken. Just as surely, it was
to the truth that Muḥammad was now calling them. He was
calling them to transcend themselves, to commune with the
God Who created them as well as their parents, and to worship Him alone in purity and faith. He called them to bring
themselves near to God with good works, to give the neighbor and the wayfarer his due, and to reject the worship of those
idols which they had taken as gods who overlooked their vices
and immorality, their usury and robbery of orphans. But in doing
all this, Muḥammad was calling men whose minds and hearts
were petrified and hardened beyond the stones to which their idol
worship oriented them. Muḥammad called men to consider the
sky and the earth and all therein which God created, to perceive
all this in its sublimity and gravity and grasp the laws by which
heaven and earth exist. Muḥammad called men to rise, through
their worship of the sole Creator of all existence, beyond all
that is mean and unworthy, to treat the misguided lovingly and
to help him achieve proper guidance, to bring charity and goodness to every orphan, to the weak, the oppressed, and the poor.

Yes, to all this did God command Muḥammad to call men. But these obstinate souls, these coarse hearts, had committed themselves to remain forever loyal to the religion of the ancestors. Around this religion they had built trade relations which gave Makkah its eminence and centrality as a center of pilgrimage. Would the Makkans abjure the religion of their ancestors and expose their city to loss of prestige, a loss which would surely follow if all idol worship were to stop? Even if such a renunciation were possible, how could their hearts be purified of their chronic passion for every pleasure? How could they be lifted above the animal satisfaction of these passions? Muḥammad called men to rise above their passions and above their idols. But what if they didn't respond to his call and refused to believe in him? What would he do?

Subsiding of the Revelations

Muḥammad expected the revelations to guide his path from day to day, but they subsided. Gabriel did not appear for some time, and all around him there was nothing but silence. Muḥammad fell into solitude, separated from himself as well as from the people. His old fears recurred. It is told that even Khadījah said to him, "Does it not seem that your Lord is displeased with you?" Dismayed and frightened, he returned to the mountain and the cave of Ḥirā'. There, he prayed for God fervently, seeking assiduously to reach Him. Particularly, he wanted to ask God about the cause of this divine displeasure. Khadījah did not dread these days any less than Muḥammad, nor was she any less fearful. Often Muḥammad wished to die, but he would again feel the call and the command of his Lord which dispelled such ideas. It was also told that he once thought of throwing himself down from the top of Mount Ḥirā' or Mount Abū Qubays, thinking what good was this life if his greatest hope therein was to be frustrated and destroyed? Torn between these fears on one hand and despair on the other, revelation came to him after a long interval. The word of God was as clear as it was reassuring:

وَالضُّحَىٰ ۞ وَالَّيْلِ إِذَا سَجَىٰ ۞ مَا وَدَّعَكَ رَبُّكَ وَمَا قَلَىٰ ۞ وَلَلْآخِرَةُ خَيْرٌ لَّكَ مِنَ الْأُولَىٰ ۞ وَ
لَسَوْفَ يُعْطِيكَ رَبُّكَ فَتَرْضَىٰ ۞ أَلَمْ يَجِدْكَ يَتِيمًا فَآوَىٰ ۞ وَوَجَدَكَ ضَآلًّا فَهَدَىٰ ۞ وَوَجَدَكَ
عَآئِلًا فَأَغْنَىٰ ۞ فَأَمَّا الْيَتِيمَ فَلَا تَقْهَرْ ۞ وَأَمَّا السَّآئِلَ فَلَا تَنْهَرْ ۞ وَأَمَّا بِنِعْمَةِ رَبِّكَ فَحَدِّثْ ۞

"By the forenoon, and by the night as it spreads its wings
over the world in peace, your Lord has not forsaken you; nor
is He displeased with you. Surely, the end shall be better for
you than the beginning. Your Lord will soon give you of His
bounty and you will be well pleased. Did He not find you an
orphan and give you shelter? Did He not find you erring and
guide you to the truth? Did He not find you in want and provide
for you? Do not, therefore, oppress the orphan nor turn away
whosoever seeks your help. And the bounty of your Lord, always
proclaim."[2]

The Call to Truth Alone

Oh, what divine majesty, what peace of mind, what joy of
heart and exaltation to the soul! Muḥammad's fears dissolved
and his dread was dissipated. He was overjoyed with this fresh
evidence of his Lord's blessing and fell down in worship to God
and praise of Him. There was no more reason to fear, as
Khadījah had done, that God was displeased with him, and there
was no cause for his dread. God had now taken him under His
protection and removed from him every doubt and fear. Henceforth there was to be no thought of suicide but only of a life
dedicated to calling men unto God and unto God alone. To the
Almighty God on High shall all men bend their brows. To Him
shall all that is in heaven and earth prostrate themselves. He
alone is the True, and all that they worship besides him is false.
To Him alone the heart should turn, on Him alone the soul should
depend, and in Him alone the spirit should find its confirmation.
The other realm is better for man than this realm. In the other
realm, the soul becomes aware of all being as well as the unity
of being; and in this unity space and time disappear and the
needs and considerations of this realm are forgotten. It is in the
other realm that the forenoon with its brilliant and dazzling
sun, the night with its widespread darkness, the heavens and
the stars, and the earth and the mountains all become one; and
the spirit which enters into awareness of this unity is happy and
felicitous. That is the life which is the objective of this life.
And that is the truth which illuminated with its light the soul
of Muḥammad. When revelation subsided for a while, it was this
truth which inspired him anew to solicit and think of his Lord
and to call men unto Him. The calling of men unto God demands
the purification of oneself, the shunning of evil, and the bearing

with patience all the harm and injury with which the caller may meet. It demands that he illumine the path of true knowledge for the benefit of ignorant mankind, that he never rebuke the inquisitive, and that he never reject the man in need or oppress the orphan. Sufficient unto him must be the fact that God had chosen him to convey His message to mankind. Let this message then be the permanent subject of his conversation. Sufficient unto him must be the fact that God had found him an orphan and given him shelter under the protection of his grandfather, 'Abd al Muṭṭalib, and his uncle, Abū Ṭālib. Sufficient unto him must be the fact that God had found him in want and provided for him through his trustworthiness, and had shown him His favor by granting to him Khadījah, the companion of his youth, of his solitude and retreat, of his prophetic mission, and of love and kindness. Sufficient unto him must be the fact that God had found him erring and had guided him to the truth through His message. All this must be sufficient unto him. Let him now call to the truth and exert himself as heartily as he could. Such was the command of God to His Prophet whom He had chosen, whom He had not forsaken, and with whom He was not displeased.

Ṣalāt [Islāmic Worship]

God taught His prophet how to worship. In turn Muḥammad taught Khadījah, and both worshipped together. Besides their own daughters, 'Alī ibn Abū Ṭālib, who was still a boy, lived with them in the same house. 'Alī's residence with Muhammad dated from the time that Makkah suffered from economic depression. Since Abū Ṭālib had a very large family, Muḥammad approached his uncle al 'Abbās, who was the richest member of the Banū Hāshim clan, saying, "Your brother Abū Ṭālib has a very large family, and he is in a state of want as a result of this depression. Let us together lighten his burden and take into our homes some of his children." Al 'Abbās agreed and took into his care Ja'far, and Muḥammad took 'Alī. One day while Muḥammad and Khadījah were worshipping together, 'Alī entered their room suddenly and found them kneeling and prostrating themselves and reciting together some of the Qur'ānic revelations. Surprised at this behavior, the youth stood still at the door until the pair finished their prayer. To his question, "To whom did you prostrate yourselves?" Muhammad answered, "We

have prostrated ourselves to God Who has sent me a prophet
and Who has commanded me to call men unto Him." Muhammad
then invited his nephew to worship God alone without associates,
and to enter into the religion that He had revealed to His Prophet.
He asked him to repudiate the idols, like al Lāt and al 'Uzzā, and
recited to him something from the Qur'ān. 'Alī was overwhelmed.
The beauty and sublimity of the verses he heard gripped him.
He pleaded for time to consult his father. After a tempestuous
night, 'Alī rushed to Muhammad and Khadījah and declared to
them his conversion without consulting his father. The youth
said, "God created me without consulting Abū Tālib, my father.
Why should I now consult him in order to worship God?" 'Alī
was then the first youth to enter Islām. He was followed by Zayd
ibn Hārithah, Muhammad's client.[3] Islām remained limited to one
house. Besides Muhammad himself, the converts of the new faith
were his wife, his cousin, and his client. The problem of how to
call Quraysh to the new faith continued to press for a solution.
Considering how attached the Makkans were to the religion of
their ancestors and to their idols, and how fiercely they resisted
any innovation, there was no easy solution in sight.

The Conversion of Abū Bakr

Abū Bakr ibn Abū Quhāfah al Taymī was a very close friend to
Muhammad. He trusted Muhammad, whom he knew to be worthy
of this trust, and whose truthfulness was, as far as Abū Bakr
was concerned, beyond doubt. Outside Muhammad's own household, Abū Bakr was the first man to be called to the worship
of God alone and to the repudiation of idols. He was the first
outsider to whom Muhammad confided the vision he had seen and
the revelations he had heard. Abū Bakr did not hesitate to respond favorably to the call of Muhammad and to believe therein.
But what soul would hesitate to leave idol worship for the worship of God alone if it were open at all to the voice of truth?
What soul would prefer the worship of stones to the worship
of God if it were endowed with any kind of nobility and transcendent awareness? What soul would resist self-purification,
giving of one's bounty and doing good to the orphan, if it had
any degree of innate purity and goodness? Abū Bakr broadcast
his conversion and new faith in God and in His Prophet among
his companions. He was "a good man and a noble character,
friendly to his people, and amiable and gentle. He enjoyed the

noblest lineage in Quraysh and was the most knowledgeable of its clans and geneologies and its past and present history. Better than any other member of the tribe, he knew its strengths and weaknesses. By profession he was a trader, well known and honest. His people loved him and respected him for his knowledge, his honesty and his entertaining conversation."[4] Abū Bakr began to call unto Islām those of his people whom he trusted, and a number of them were converted. 'Uthmān ibn 'Affān, 'Abd al Raḥman ibn 'Awf, Ṭalhah ibn 'Ubayd Allah, Sa'd ibn Abū Waqqās, and al Zubayr ibn al 'Awwām were the first to respond favorably to his cause. Thereafter Abū 'Ubaydah ibn al Jarrāḥ was converted as well as a number of other Makkans. Whenever a man converted to Islām, he would seek the Prophet and declare his Islām to him and receive from him his instruction. Fearful of arousing the enmity and antagonism of Quraysh for their departure from idol worship, the new Muslims used to hide the fact of their conversion. They would go to the outskirts of Makkah in order to hold their prayers. For three years while Islām continued to spread among the Makkans, the Muslims continued to hide. In the meantime, the Qur'ān was continually being revealed to Muḥammad and this fortified the Muslims in their faith and confirmed them in it.

The personal example of Muhammad was the best support for the spread of his cause. He was merciful and charitable, humble yet manly, sweet of word yet just, giving to each his due yet full of compassion and sympathy for the weak, the orphan, the deprived, and the oppressed. In his nightwatch and prayer, in his chanting the Qur'ān revealed to him, in his constant scrutinizing of the heavens and of the earth, he looked for the meaning of their existence and that of everything they contain; in his permanent orientation toward God alone, in his search for the meaning of existence and quintessence of life, deep within his own soul, he provided such an example for his followers that they became ever more convinced of their faith and ever more anxious to adhere to its precepts. The new Muslims did so notwithstanding the fact that they were repudiating the religion and practice of their ancestors as well as exposing themselves to injury by those who believed otherwise. Many noblemen and tradesmen from Makkah believed in Muḥammad, but all were already known for their purity, honesty, kindness, and mercy. In addition, Muslim ranks included many converts from the weak, deprived, and oppressed classes of Makkah. The cause of God and His Prophet spread as men and women entered the faith wave after wave.

The Muslims and Quraysh

People talked about Muḥammad and his message. The obdurate and hard-hearted among the Makkans did not pay much attention to him, thinking that his cause would not go beyond what they had known of the causes of Quss, Umayyah, Waraqah, and others among the wise men and priests. They were certain men will eventually return to the religion of their ancestors, and that victory would finally belong to Hubal, al Lāt, al 'Uzzā, Isāf, and Nā'ilah. But they forgot that candid faith is invincible and that the truth must someday prevail.

Muḥammad's Nearest Relatives

Three years after the revelation began, God commanded the Prophet to proclaim Islām openly and to bring His revelation to the public. The following verses were revealed: "Warn, O Muḥammad, your nearest relatives. Extend your gentle protection to all those believers who follow in your footsteps and obey you. As for those who disobey, proclaim your repudiation of their doings. . . . Proclaim what you are commanded and turn away from the associationists."[5]

Muḥammad invited his kinsmen to a banquet in his home at which he tried to talk to them about Islām and to call them unto God. His uncle, Abū Lahab, interrupted his speech and asked the guests to stand up and leave. Muḥammad invited them again on the morrow. After they had eaten he said, "I do not know of any man in Arab history who served his people better than I have served you. I have brought you the best of this world as well as of the next. My Lord has commanded me to call you unto Him. Who of you then would stand by me on this matter"? To this appeal, his kinsmen were unsympathetic and prepared to leave." 'Alī, however, though only a boy, arose and said, "Prophet of God: I shall be your helper. Whosoever opposes you, I shall fight as mortal enemy." The Banū Hāshim smiled at this; others laughed loudly. All present looked once at 'Alī, once at Abū Ṭālib, his father, and left full of ridicule for what they beheld.

After addressing his kinsmen, Muḥammad now directed his call to the Makkans as a whole. One day he climbed to the top of al Ṣafā and called, "O People of Quraysh!" Hearing his call, the Quraysh assembled around him and asked what was the matter. Muḥammad answered, "Tell me, O Men of Quraysh, if I were to tell you that I see a cavalry on the other side of the mountain, would you believe me?" They answered, "Indeed, for we trust you, and we have never known you to tell a lie." Muḥammad said, "Know then that I am a warner and that I warn you of a severe punishment. O Banū 'Abd al Muṭṭalib! O Banū 'Abd Manāf! O Banū Zuhrah! O Banū Taym! O Banū Makhzūm! O Banū Asad! God has commanded me to warn you, my nearest kinsmen, that I can guarantee to you no good on earth or in heaven unless you witness that there is no God but God." Abū Lahab, fat but quick of temper as he was, arose and said, "Woe to you on this day! Did you assemble us for this?"

Severely shocked, Muḥammad looked toward his uncle for a moment. Soon the following verses were revealed: "Accursed be the hands of Abū Lahab and accursed may he be. Neither his property nor his wealth will save him. He shall burn in the flames of hell."[6]

Islām and Freedom

Neither the rancor of Abū Lahab nor the antagonism of other opponents in Quraysh prevented the spread of the Islāmic call among the people of Makkah. Hardly a day passed without some new person joining the faith. Those inclined toward asceticism accepted Islām more readily, as neither trade nor vested interest could prejudice their consideration of the call. Such men had observed that Muḥammad depended upon Khadījah's wealth, but that he never allowed wealth to influence his religious judgment. The material considerations were always rejected wherever they ran counter to the dictates of love, compassion, friendship, and forgiveness. Indeed, revelation itself commanded that the will to wealth is a curse upon the spirit. Did it not say, "The pursuit of wealth has exhausted all your energies and pre-occupied your life to the very end? But you will surely come to know—and you will surely come to know it well!—that your wealth will not avail a thing. Had you known it with certainty,

you would have known of hell and you would have convinced
yourselves of it. But it is on the Day of Judgment that you will
be 'questioned concerning the moral worth of your deeds."[7]
What is better than that to which Muhammad calls? He calls to
freedom, to absolute and limitless freedom, to that freedom which
is as dear to the Arab as his very life. Does he not liberate men
from the bondage which the worship of other gods besides
God imposes? Has he not destroyed all the obstacles that have
once stood between man and God? Neither Hubal, al Lāt, nor al
'Uzzā, neither the fire of the Zoroastrians nor the sun of the
Egyptians, neither the astral bodies of the star worshippers,
the apostles of Christ as princes of the church, nor any other
human, angel or genii could stand between man and God. Before
God and before Him alone is man responsible for his good
and evil works. Man's works alone are his intercessor. On
earth man's conscience alone is the final judge of his deeds,
as it is its sole subject. Upon its everyday verdicts depends the
last judgment of the person. What liberty is wider than this
liberty to which Muhammad called men? Did Abū Lahab and
his companions call to anything like it? Do they not call men
to remain enslaved under superstitions so great that the light
of truth and guidance can hardly penetrate and reach through
them?

The Poets of Quraysh

Abū Lahab and Abū Sufyān, noblemen of Quraysh and lords
of its commerce and entertainment, began to feel the threat
which the call of Muhammad presented. They therefore decided
to begin by ridiculing him and belying his prophethood. Their
first act was to tempt their poet friends to attack Muhammad
in their poetry. It was then that Abū Sufyān ibn al Hārith· 'Amr
ibn al 'Ās, and 'Abdullah ibn al Zib'arī launched their vituper-
ative attacks in verse. A number of Muslim poets undertook to
answer these attacks in kind, despite the fact that Muhammad
hardly needed their efforts. Besides the poets, others advanced
and asked Muhammad to perform some miracles with which to
prove his prophethood. They challenged him to do as much as
Moses or Jesus had done. They asked, "Why don't you change
Mount Safā and Mount Marwah into gold? Why don't you
cause the book of which you speak so much to fall down from
heaven already written? Why don't you cause Gabriel to appear

to all of us and speak to us as he spoke to you? Why don't you resurrect the dead and remove these mountains which bound and enclose the city of Makkah? Why don't you cause a water fountain to spring whose water is sweeter than that of Zamzam, knowing how badly your town needs the additional water supply?" The unbelievers did not stop at these demands for miracles. In ridicule, they asked, "Why doesn't your God inform you of the market prices of the future in order to help you and us in the trade of the morrow?" Whether serious or in ridicule, all these questions and demands were answered once and for all by revelation. God commanded Muḥammad, "Say: 'I have no power whatever to bring advantage or avoid disadvantage. What God wills, that will happen. If it were given me to tell the future I would have used such knowledge to my own advantage. But I am only a man sent to warn you, and a messenger to convey a divine message that you may believe."[8]

Indeed: Muḥammad was only a warner and a messenger. How could they demand of him that which reason denies while he demanded of them only that which reason commends—nay, dictates and imposes? How could they demand of him that which no morality can tolerate, whereas he called them to goodness and genuine virtue? How could they ask him to perform miracles when the Book that was being revealed to him, which was his guide to the truth, was the end of all miracles? How could they ask him to prove his prophethood with miracles that they might then see whether or not they would follow him, while their so-called gods were dead and cold, utterly devoid of power to do anything, whether miracle or nonmiracle? How could they ask him to prove himself with miracles when they worshipped their stone and wooden gods without ever asking them to prove their divinity? If they had only once asked their gods to prove their divinity, they would have seen through their wood and stone and convinced themselves that they were no gods at all but dead, immobile, and unable to defend themselves against anyone.

Muḥammad's Attack against the Idols

Muḥammad did take the initiative of attacking their gods. Hitherto he had not mentioned them at all. Now, he attacked them directly. To the Quraysh this was so serious that it aroused deep hatred. This man had become a threatening problem to them demanding definite solution. Until then they had not taken him seriously but had ridiculed him. When they assembled in Dār al Nadwah or around the Ka'bah and its idols and happened to mention him, they would speak lightly of him and ridicule his cause. Now that he had directly attacked their gods, ridiculed their worship as well as their ancestors', severely condemned Hubal, al Lāt, al 'Uzzā and all other idols, the matter called for something more than ridicule. It called for a fight-plan and serious thinking of how to combat and counter-attack. If this man were to succeed in converting the people of Makkah and in turning them against their old worship, what would happen to Makkan trade? What would remain of Makkah's religious eminence? These and like thoughts were ominous and called for the most careful strategy.

Abū Ṭālib, Muhammad's uncle, had not joined the faith, but he continued to protect his nephew and let everyone know of his preparation to fight for him. Led by Abū Sufyān ibn Harb, some noblemen of Quraysh went to Abū Ṭālib and addressed him in these words: "O Abū Ṭālib, your nephew has blasphemed our gods, attacked our religion, ridiculed our ideals and condemned our fathers for unbelief. Either you stop him or you relinquish your protection of him. Our faith which he attacks is equally your faith. Why don't you let us take care of him for you?" Abū Ṭālib talked to them gently and discharged them. Muhammad continued his preaching and intensified his missionary activity. His followers multiplied. Once more Quraysh plotted against him. They went to Abū Ṭālib and brought with them 'Umārah ibn al Walīd ibn al Mughīrah, the most handsome youth in Quraysh. They asked Abū Ṭālib to adopt 'Umārah as his son and to let them handle Muhammad. Once more they were turned down. As Muhammad continued his missionary activities, they continued to plot. Finally, they went to Abū Ṭālib for a third time saying, "O Abū Ṭālib, you are an honorable elder among us. We have asked you to stop your nephew but you have not. By God, we cannot permit him to insult our fathers, to ridicule our ideals, and to castigate our gods. Either you stop him or we shall fight both you and him until one of us perishes in the process." To alienate them and to arouse their enmity was too much for Abū Ṭālib, and yet he was neither prepared to join the faith of his nephew nor to betray him. What would he do? He called Muhammad and told him what had happened and pleaded with him: "Save me as well as yourself, and do not cause me to carry a burden I cannot bear."

The Logic of History

For a while Muḥammad stood motionless in his place. It was a moment in which the history of being itself stopped without knowing which course to take. Whichever word this one man was about to say, would be a judgment of manкind. Should the world continue to wallow in its darkness? Should Zoroastrianism triumph over a corrupt and lifeless Christianity? Should paganism be allowed to raise its superstitious, rotten head? Or should he, Muḥammad, proclaim to this world the unity of God, enlightening it with the light of truth, liberating the minds of men from the bondage of superstition, and raising the souls foɪ communion with the Supernal Plenum? There was his uncle—weakened by the people's opposition, unable to help or protect—indeed, likely to betray him. And there were the Muslims, few and weak, unable to wage war or to resist a strong and well equipped army such as Quraysh had. There was none to lend him support in this hour of dire need. Only the truth which he proclaimed and of which he was the advocate could console or rescue him. Nothing was left to count upon except his own faith and conviction of that truth. That alone was his whole force. Well, let it be. The other realm is better than this one. Let him then discharge his duty and convey his message. It is better to die faithful to the truth than to betray it or stammer in its cause. Refreshened and energized by the strength and determination of new resolution, he turned to his uncle and said, "O uncle! By God Almighty I swear, even if they should put the sun in my right hand and the moon in my left that I abjure this cause, I shall not do so until God has vindicated it or caused me to perish in the process."

How great is the truth! And how sublime is faith in the truth! The old man was shaken to his depths when he heard the answer of Muḥammad. It was his turn to stand motionless and speechless in front of this holy power and great will which had just spoken on behalf of a life above life. Choked with emotion at his uncle's request as well as at his own certainty of the course he was to follow, Muḥammad got up to leave. For but a moment Abū Ṭālib hesitated between the enmity of his people and the

cause of his nephew. Immediately, he called Muhammad back.
"Go forth, my nephew," he said, "and say what you will. By
the same God I swear I shall never betray you to your enemies."

Banū Hāshim Protects Muḥammad against Quraysh

Abū Ṭālib communicated his resolution to Banū Hāshim and
Banū al Muṭṭalib and spoke to them about his nephew with
great admiration and deep appreciation of the sublimity of
Muhammad's position. He asked them all to protect Muhammad
against the Quraysh. All of them pledged to do so except Abū
Lahab, who declared openly his enmity to him and his withdrawal
to the opposite camp. Undoubtedly, the tribal bond they shared
with Muhammad and their traditional enmity with Banū Umayyah influenced their decision to stand by Muhammad. Tribal
solidarity and politics, however, do not completely explain their
new opposition to all Quraysh in a matter so grave as to require
them to repudiate the faith and beliefs inherited from the fathers.
The attitude of Muhammad toward them, his firm conviction, his
calling them in kindness to the worship of God alone, and their
awareness that among the tribes of Arabia there were certainly
other religions besides their own—all these factors caused them
to realize that to their nephew and fellow tribesman belonged
the right to speak out his views, just as Umayyah ibn Abū al
Salt and Waraqah ibn Nawfal and others had done before him.
If Muhammad were saying the truth—and they did not think
that that was the case—truth will certainly prevail, and they
stand to share in the glory of its victory. If, on the other hand,
Muhammad was not telling the truth, then people would pass
his claim by as they had other claims before. In this case it
would not destroy their traditions, and there was, therefore,
no reason why they should betray him to his enemies and allow
them to kill him.

Persecution of the Muslims by Quraysh

From whatever harm might come from Quraysh Muhammad
took refuge behind his people. From the worries he generated
within himself he took refuge in the person of Khadījah. With
her faith and great love she was for him a refreshing source
of joy. She supported him against every symptom of weakness

or despondency generated by the harm his enemies had inflicted against him or against his followers. In fact, ever since Muḥammad made public cause of his revelations, Quraysh knew no peace, and the tranquility of earlier days vanished. Instigated by the Quraysh, every clan and tribe began to attack its Muslim members to dissuade them from their faith. One unbeliever threw his Abyssinian slave, Bilāl, onto the sand under the burning sun, laid a heavy stone on his chest and left him there to die, for no reason except his insistence upon Islām. Bearing himself gallantly under this torture, Bilāl kept on repeating, "God is one, God is one." Abū Bakr saw him, bought him from his master and set him free. Indeed, Abū Bakr bought many of the slaves and clients who were being thus tortured by the unbelievers. Among these there was even a slave woman whom Abū Bakr had bought from 'Umar ibn al Khaṭṭāb before the latter's conversion. One woman is known to have been tortured to death because of her attachment to Islām and her refusal to return to the old faith. Muslims of pure Arab blood were beaten and subjected to all sorts of maltreatment and contemptuous humiliation. Even Muḥammad did not escape, despite the protection of Banū Hāshim and Banū al Muṭṭalib. Umm Jamīl, Abū Lahab's wife, used to throw the refuse from her house onto Muḥammad's door. All Muḥammad could do was simply to remove it. While Muḥammad was praying near the Ka'bah, Abū Lahab threw on him the entrails of a goat sacrificed to one of the gods; and Muḥammad could only go to his daughter Fāṭimah for her to clean him and wash the dirt off his clothes. This abuse was all in addition to the terrible vituperation and vile calumnies the unbelievers directed against the Muslims on every occasion and in every quarter. Such persecution continued for a long time, but it only confirmed the Muslims in their faith and challenged them to sacrifice everything for the sake of their convictions.

Muslim Patience

This period of Muḥammad's life is one of the noblest and greatest pages of human history. Neither he nor his followers sought wealth or reputation, power or sovereignty. Rather, they were seekers after the truth and believers therein. To those who did harm him, Muḥammad prayed for guidance, for liberation from the yoke of vile paganism and from its immorality and villainy. It was for this noble spiritual objective that Muḥammad suffered persecution. The poets insulted him; the tribe plotted against him, threw stones at his house, threatened his folks and followers, and came close to killing him near the Ka'bah. The more they persecuted, the more patience and resolve Muḥammad showed in his mission. The believers repeated and were encouraged by Muḥammad's pledge that he would not abjure this cause even if given both sun and moon. Great sacrifices became small, and death itself became a welcome alternative. One must appreciate the strength of these men's faith and the depth of their commitment at a time when the new religion was not even complete and the Qur'ān was not yet fully revealed. No doubt Muḥammad's gentleness, good character, truthfulness, resoluteness, strength of will, and conviction were contributing factors. But there were other factors besides.

Muḥammad lived in a free country very much like a republic. As far as social eminence and nobility of lineage, he ranked among the highest and best. Muḥammad did not have much wealth, but he had all he needed, and so did Banū Hāshim. To them belonged the *sidānah* of the Ka'bah and the *siqāyah* and all that they wished by way of religious titles. Therefore, Muḥammad stood in no need of money, prestige, political power, or religious eminence. In this respect, Muḥammad was quite different from the prophets that preceded him. Moses, for instance, was born in Egypt when Pharaoh was worshipped by its people as God. It was he who called to them, "I am your supreme God."[9] The priesthood assisted Pharaoh in tyrannizing over the people and in exploiting them. The revolution that Moses led by command of his Lord was a revolution against the political as well as the religious order. Did Moses not seek to reduce Pharaoh to the equal of the most ordinary peasant in front of God, even though that peasant was of the meanest class who drew their water from the Nile with the *shadoof?* Pharaoh's divinity, Moses thought, as well as the social order on which it stood, must all be destroyed. The revolution must first be political. Consequently, from the very beginning the Mosaic call was met by Pharaoh with all-out war, and miracles were necessary that the Mosaic call might be believed by the rank and file. When, for instance, Moses threw his stick on the ground, it became a living serpent devouring what Pharaoh's magicians had created. These miracles, however, turned out to be futile, for Moses had to flee from his country of birth. His flight was assisted by another miracle, that of the splitting of the waters of the sea. As for Jesus, he was born in Nazareth, in Palestine, a province under the yoke of Roman colonialism. He called men to patience in their suffering of injustice, to forgiveness after repentence and to forms of love and mercy which the rulers regarded as tantamount to rebellion against their tyranny. The miracles of resurrecting the dead, healing the sick, and all that Jesus did with the support of the Holy Spirit were necessary for the success of his cause. In their essence, the doctrines of Jesus and Muḥammad were built on the same premises and led to the same conclusions, with differences in detail not relevant for our present discussion. The point is that these various factors, especially the political among them gave to the call of Jesus the orientation it took. As for Muḥammad, since his circumstances were what we have just seen, his message was spiritual and rational. At every stage of its development, it rested on a foundation of truth, goodness, and beauty for their own sakes. Because of its distance from any political struggle, Muḥammad's message did not disturb the republican regime of Makkah in the least, nor was it disturbed thereby.

The Call of Muḥammad and Modern Scientific Inquiry

The reader may be surprised by our emphasis on the similarity of Muḥammad's teaching to the methods of modern science. The scientific method demands that were one to undertake an investigation, he should suspend his personal views, beliefs and doctrines. It demands that he begin his study by observation, classification, comparison, experimentation, and then draw his conclusions from these scientific observations as premises. A conclusion reached through this method is scientific and, by the same token, it remains susceptible to further scrutiny and investigation. It remains valid as long as further scientific study has not disproved any one of the premises on which it is based. This scientific method is the highest human achievement in the cause of free thought. And yet this very method is none other than that of Muḥammad, the very foundation of his cause. How did his followers become convinced of it? They repudiated all their previous beliefs and began to concentrate their thoughts on what lay before them. But what was before them? What were the facts of religious life in Arabia? Every one of the Arab tribes had its own idols; but which one was true and which false? Besides, within Arabia as well as in the surrounding countries, there were Christians, Jews, Sabeans, Zoroastrian fire-worshippers, and others who worshipped the sun. Whose faith was true and whose false?

The Essence of Muḥammad's Call

Suppose we lay all this aside and completely avoid its influence upon our minds and hearts. Suppose we cut ourselves loose from every view and every doctrine we have previously entertained. And suppose we observe and consider. The first truth to stand out is that every being is somehow connected with all other beings. In the case of man, the clans, the tribes, and nations are obviously interconnected. Man is also connected with the animals and the world of things. This earth of ours is connected with the sun, the moon, and all the heavenly bodies.

Necessary and immutable laws regulate and govern all these interconnections. Neither may the sun overtake the moon nor the night overtake the day. If any one being in the universe were to alter or change these laws, the cosmos itself would change and would no more be what it is. If the sun, for instance, failed to provide the earth with light and heat and thus violate the laws by which nature has been running for millions of years, the earth and the sky would not be what they are. As long as this does not happen it is not possible for the totality of the cosmos to hold itself together except by a moving spirit, a spirit from which it has arisen and has developed and to which it must return. This spirit alone is that to which man should be subject. Everything else in this universe is subject to that spirit just as man is. Man, the cosmos, space, and time are therefore a unity; and this spirit is the origin and substance of this unity. To this spirit alone therefore belongs worship. To this spirit alone all minds and hearts should be oriented. Everywhere in this universe we should be able by reason and meditation to discover this spirit's eternal laws. Hence, whatever men worship besides God—be it idols, kings, Pharaohs, fire, or sun—is a falsehood and an illusion unworthy of man, of human reason, of the human capacity to discover the laws of God through examination of the creation with which God has endowed man.

That is the essence of the message of Muḥammad as the early Muslims knew it. It was conveyed to them by Muḥammad as a revelation cast into such sublime form that it is still regarded as a miracle. This revelation has combined the truth of content with the perfection of form. Upon contact with it, the souls of the Muslims became ennobled, and their hearts were moved to seek communion with the noble spirit of Muḥammad. Muḥammad led them to the realization that good works constitute the road of felicity and that men shall be rewarded for their works on the day they complete in piety their duties in this world, *i.e.* when every soul shall receive its due. "And whosoever does an atom's weight of good shall be rewarded therefor, and whosoever does an atom's weight of evil shall be punished therefor."[10]

What great and ennobling respect for human reason! What sweeping destruction of all the impediments that stand in the way of human reason! Sufficient is it to man to understand this for him to appreciate it, to believe in it, and to realize what it demands of him to rise to the highest level of humanity. As long as one takes his stand on the side of reason, every sacrifice demanded by such heights seems easy.

The Conversion of Ḥamzah

The majestic stand of Muḥammad and of his followers convinced Banū Hāshim and Banū al Muttalib to strengthen their protection of him. Once, on encountering Muḥammad on the road, Abū Jahl insulted him and abused his new religion. Muḥammad did not answer him and walked away. Ḥamzah, Muḥammad's uncle and brother-in-nursing, still followed the religion of Quraysh and was very strong and fear-inspiring. He was an addicted hunter who would circumambulate the Ka'bah every time he returned from a hunting trip and before he entered his home. As he entered the city on the day that Abū Jahl insulted Muḥammad and learned of what had happened to his nephew, he became furious, and went straight to the Ka'bah. Upon entering the Mosque, he did not greet anyoe as he used to do. Rather, he went straight to Abū Jahl and hit him very hard with his bow. Some members of Banū Makhzūm rose to the help of Abū Jahl, but Abū Jahl pushed them aside. He acknowledged that he had insulted Muḥammad and then decided that the dispute had better be cut short rather than allowed to spread. Ḥamzah then declared his conversion to Islām, took the oath of allegiance to Muḥammad and promised to sacrifice everything for the sake of God.

Delegation of 'Utbah ibn Rabī'ah

Undaunted by any harm or injury that befell them, their faith unshaken, the Muslims kept on increasing in numbers and strength. They proclaimed their faith loudly and performed their prayers publicly—all to the alarm of Quraysh, who were at a loss what to do next. For a moment they thought that they could get rid of Muḥammad by satisfying what they took to be his personal ambitions. Obviously they forgot the greatness of the Islāmic call, the purity of its spiritual essence, and its noble transcendence of any political partisanship. 'Utbah ibn Rabī'ah, one of the distinguished leaders of Arabia, convinced the Quraysh at one of their community meetings to delegate him to approach Muḥammad with a number of alternative offerings of which, he thought, Muḥammad would surely accept one. He therefore went to Muḥammad and said, "O Nephew, you certainly enjoy among us great eminence and noble lineage, and you have brought about a great issue and divided your people. Listen to me for I am about to make several offers to you, certain as I am that one of them will prove satisfactory to you. If by bringing about the conflict you did, you have sought to achieve some wealth, know that we are prepared to give you of our wealth until you become the richest man among us. If, on the other hand, you desired honor and power, we would make you our chief and endow you with such power that nothing could be done without your consent. Even if you wanted to be a king, we should not hesitate to crown you king over us. Finally, if you are unable to cure yourself of the visions that you have been seeing, we shall be happy to seek for you at our expense all the medical service possible until your health is perfectly restored." When he finished, Muḥammad recited to him, the *surah* "al Sajdah."[11] 'Utbah listened attentively to the divine recitation. Facing him was a man devoid of all ambition for wealth, prestige, honor, power, or sovereignty. Neither was he sick. Facing him was indeed a man telling the truth, calling to the good, answering him with arguments yet more soundly and sublimely expressed than any he had ever heard. When Muḥammad finished, 'Utbah returned to Quraysh spellbound by the beauty and sublimity of what he had seen and heard and by the greatness of this man and his eloquence. The Quraysh were obviously not happy with this turn, nor did they agree with 'Utbah's opinion that they should leave Muḥammad for all the Arabs together to deal with; they would thereby reap a harvest of pride in the event that Muḥammad wins, or enjoy an effortless victory in the event he loses. In fact, Quraysh resumed their attacks upon Muḥammad and his followers, intensified their aggression, and inflicted upon his companions all sorts of injuries from which Muḥammad was saved only through the protection of Abū Ṭālib, Banū Hāshim, and Banū al Muṭṭalib.

Emigration to Abyssinia

Makkan persecution of the Muslims increased in intensity. Many Muslims now became so subject to torture and murder that Muḥammad instructed them to disperse throughout the world. When they asked where they should go, he advised them to escape to Abyssinia, the Christian kingdom—where "a king rules without injustice, a land of truthfulness—until God leads us to a way out of our difficulty." Fearful of Makkan persecution and desirous of worshipping God in peace and freedom, a number of Muslims emigrated to Abyssinia at Muḥammad's advice. The first group to emigrate included eleven men and four women. After secretly leaving Makkah, they arrived in Abyssinia where they lived under the protection of the Negus until they heard that the Muslims in Makkah had become secure against Quraysh's attacks, as we shall see a little later. When upon return they found the Quraysh's persecution stronger than it ever was before, they emigrated once more to Abyssinia, this time about eighty men strong, not counting women and children. This larger group of Muslims lived in Abyssinia until after the Prophet's emigration to Yathrib. Their emigration to Abyssinia is usually referred to as "the first emigration in Islām."

Quraysh's Delegation to the Negus

It is perfectly appropriate for the biographer of Muḥammad to ask whether the purpose of this emigration undertaken by the Muslims at the advice and command of Muḥammad was merely to escape from the pagans of Makkah and their persecution and harm. Or was it dictated by an Islāmic political strategy by which Muḥammad sought to realize a higher objective? These questions are indeed proper when we consider that the whole history of the Arab Prophet confirms ever more clearly that he was a profound and far-sighted statesman in addition to being the carrier of the divine message and a man of unrivaled discipline and magnanimity. What makes this matter especially questionable is the report that the Makkans were so upset at this exodus of the Muslims to Abyssinia that they immediately sent a delegation to the Negus carrying precious gifts in order to bring about the emigrants' extradition and return to Makkah. Abyssinia, as well as its Negus, were all Christians and, therefore, there was no fear that they might follow the religion of Muhammad. Did the Makkans then fear that the Negus' protection of the Muslims might provide support for the cause of Muhammad's religion within Arabia? Or did they think that the Muslim emigrants would one day return greater in numbers, wealth, and power in order to wage a retaliatory war against them?

The two ambassadors, 'Amr ibn al 'Āṣ and 'Abdullah ibn Abū Rabī'ah, presented to the Negus and his patriarch their precious gifts and asked for permission to have the Muslim emigrants extradited and sent back to Makkah. They said to the Negus, "O King! A number of ignoble plebeians from Makkah have taken refuge in your county. They have apostasized from the religion of their people and have not joined your religion. They follow a new religion, known neither to us nor to you, which they created. The leading noblemen of Makkah, who are their parents, uncles, and relatives, have sent us to you to ask for their return. Their elders at home are better judges of the differences between them" The two ambassadors had already obtained the approval of the patriarch for extradition without prior reference of the matter to the Negus. Apparently, the Makkan gifts to the patriarch were instrumental in obtaining this summary decision.. The Negus, however, refused to concur in the judgment of his patriarch until he had had a chance to hear the refugees plead their own case. He sent after them and asked, "What is this new religion which caused you to separate yourselves from your people, a religion which is different from mine as well as from any other of the known religions?"

The Muslims' Answer to the Ambassadors' Claims

Ja'far ibn Abū Ṭālib rose and said in answer, "O King! We were in a state of ignorance and immorality, worshipping idols, eating carrion, committing all sorts of iniquity. We honored no relative and assisted no neighbor. The strong among us exploited the weak. Then God sent us a prophet, one of our own people, whose lineage, truthfulness, loyalty, and purity were well known to us. He called us to worship God alone and to repudiate all the stones and idols which we and our ancestors used to worship. He commanded us always to tell the truth, to remain true to trust and promise, to assist the relative, to be good neighbors, to abstain from blood and things forbidden, and to avoid fornication, perjury, and false witness. He commanded us not to rob the wealth of the orphan or falsely to accuse the married woman. He ordered us to worship God alone and never to associate any other being with Him, to hold prayers, to fast, and to pay the *zakāt* (the five pillars of Islām were here enumerated and explained). We believed in him and what he brought to us from God and followed him in what he enjoined and forbade. Our people, however, tried to sway us away from our religion and persecuted us and inflicted upon us great suffering that we might re-enter into the immoral practices of old. As they vanquished and berated us unjustly and made life intolerable for us in Makkah, we chose you and your country and came thither to live under your protection in justice and peace." Thereupon the Negus asked, "Will you show me some of the revelation which your Prophet claims to have come to him from God?" Ja'far answered, "Yes!" and recited to the Negus the *surah* of Mary from its beginning until the following verses:

فَأَشَارَتْ إِلَيْهِ قَالُوا كَيْفَ نُكَلِّمُ مَنْ كَانَ فِي الْمَهْدِ صَبِيًّا ۞ قَالَ إِنِّي عَبْدُ اللَّهِ آتَانِيَ الْكِتَابَ وَجَعَلَنِي نَبِيًّا ۞ وَجَعَلَنِي مُبَارَكًا أَيْنَ مَا كُنْتُ وَأَوْصَانِي بِالصَّلَاةِ وَالزَّكَاةِ مَا دُمْتُ حَيًّا ۞ وَبَرًّا بِوَالِدَتِي وَلَمْ يَجْعَلْنِي جَبَّارًا شَقِيًّا ۞ وَالسَّلَامُ عَلَيَّ يَوْمَ وُلِدْتُ وَيَوْمَ أَمُوتُ وَيَوْمَ أُبْعَثُ حَيًّا

"Mary, therefore, pointed to the child as her only answer. Her people asked, 'How can we inquire of an infant in the cradle?' At this, Jesus spoke, 'I am the servant of God to whom He has given the Book and whom He has blessed and commissioned with prophethood; whom He has enjoined with holding the prayer and giving the *zakāt* as long as he lives. My mother is innocent and I am neither unjust nor evil. Peace be upon me on the day I was born, on the day I shall die, and on the day I shall be resurrected."[12]

Answers of the Negus and the Patriarchs

When the patriarchs heard this statement confirming as it did the message of the Evangel, they were pleasantly surprised and said: "These words must have sprung from the same fountainhead from which the words of our master Jesus Christ have sprung." The Negus then said, "What you have just recited and that which was revealed to Moses must have both issued from the same source. Go forth into my kingdom; I shall not extradite you at all." On the following day, 'Amr ibn al 'Āṣ returned to the Negus and pleaded, "There is another side to the Muslims' new religion in which they judge Jesus, Son of Mary, in totally different but condemnable terms." The Negus sent after the Muslims, brought them back into his presence and asked them to tell him more about Jesus. The same Ja'far ibn Abū Ṭālib answered for them, "Our judgment of Jesus is exactly the same as that which was revealed to our Prophet; namely, that Jesus is the servant of God, His Prophet, His spirit, His command given unto Mary, the innocent virgin." The Negus drew a line on the floor with his cane and said with great joy, "Between your religion and ours there is really no more difference than this line." Thus the Negus was convinced, after hearing the two parties, that the Muslims not only acknowledged Jesus and Christianity as true religion but worshipped the same God as well. The Muslims found under his protection the peace and tranquility they sought, and lived in his country until they found cause to return while Muhammad was still in Makkah. Apparently they had been misinformed that Quraysh's antagonism to the Muslims had subsided. When they discovered that the Makkans were still persecuting Muhammad and his followers, they returned to Abyssinia, this time eighty strong besides women and children. The question remains, however, whether these two emigrations were merely for escape from injury or were, at least in the foresight of Muhammad alone, devised for a political motive which the historian ought to investigate and clarify.

The Muslims and Abyssinian Christianity

The historian may certainly ask why Muhammad trusted that his companions and followers would go to a country whose religion was Christianity, a scriptural religion, and whose prophet was Jesus, whom Islām acknowledged as prophet and in whose message it concurred, without fearing that they might be exposed to abjuring their faith even though in favor of one different from that of Quraysh. How did he trust that his followers would remain faithful and loyal when Abyssinia was a far more fertile and affluent country than that of Quraysh? One of the Muslims that emigrated to Abyssinia did, in fact convert to Christianity, thus establishing that the danger was real. It was natural for Muḥammad to have felt such fears, especially since Muḥammad, himself, was still weak and his old followers were still in great doubt as to his ability to protect them or to come to their rescue. Assuming, therefore, Muḥammad's great intelligence and foresight, his charity, kindness and compassion, it is most likely that such fears must have stirred within his soul. But he felt absolutely secure in this regard. Islām was on that day, as it was to remain throughout the Prophet's life, absolutely pure and unspoiled by internal doubts, divisions, and deviations. On the other hand, Abyssinian Christianity, like the Christianity of Najrān, al Ḥīrah, and al Shām, was mixed up with devious doctrines brought into the faith by the apotheosizers of Mary, the apotheosizers of Jesus, and the opponents of both. The Muslims, drawing directly from the pure fountainhead of prophetic revelation, could not possibly stand in any danger of being swayed by any such confusion.

The Spirit in Islām

In actual fact, most religions did not survive for a number of generations without becoming polluted by some kind of idolatry. Even if it were not of the same ignoble kind prevalent in early days in the Arabian Peninsula, it was still some form of idolatry. Islām is diametrically opposed to idolatry in any form or kind. From the earliest days of church history Christianity has accorded to the priesthood a special status in the religion itself; Islām has never given such position to anyone. On the contrary, Islām both condemned the priesthood and transcended it. Then as now, Islām has remained precisely the religion which enables the human soul to rise to the greatest heights. It has not tolerated any link between man and God except a person's own piety and good works and his wishing for his fellow men that which he wishes for himself. Nothing—neither idols nor priesthood, diviners nor officiators—could prevent the human

soul from rising to a consciousness of unity with ultimate reality
and to a unity of good will and good works, and, thereby, from
winning its great reward with God. The human soul! That
spirit which is from God! That spirit which is connected to
eternal time! That spirit, which as long as it does the good, is
not separated from God by anything whatever and is subject
to no being whatever other than God. The rich, the mighty,
and the evil can all lay hold upon the body. They can torture
it and prevent it from realizing its passions and pleasures. They
can even destroy it and rob it of its life. But they can never
reach the soul as long as that person wants the soul to rise
above matter, above power, and above time to link itself with
ultimate, total reality! Only on the Day of Judgment will the
human soul receive the punishment or reward that is its due.
On that Day no father may take the place of his son, and no son
may replace his father. On that Day neither the wealth of the
rich, the strength of the mighty, nor the argument of the
eloquent will avail them. Good works will be the only witness
and the only defense for or against their author. On that Day,
all being—its eternal past as well as its eternal future—will
stand as one integral unit. On that Day none will be done an
injustice, and none will receive aught except his due.

How could Muhammad fear that his companions would abjure
the spiritual meaning and values which he had so well inculcated
upon their hearts? Why should he fear that they might be
diverted from this conviction and faith when his example was
ever present to them in his own person, so beloved of them
that they cherished him more than themselves, their families
and people? How could there be any chance of their deviation
from the faith when Muhammad's resolution not to abjure the
cause even if they should place the sun in his right hand and
the moon in his left hand is a living reality, ever present to
their minds? How could they abjure their faith when the spirit
of Muhammad filled their being with the light of conviction,
wisdom, justice, goodness, truth, and beauty; when their character and ethos had been molded by Muhammad's humility,
charity, loving kindness, and compassion? Muhammad felt at
ease toward the emigration of his companions to Abyssinia. The
religious freedom and security the emigrants enjoyed under the
Negus had caused the Quraysh no little embarrassment. That
the Muslims were free among total strangers but persecuted by
their own relatives, despite the closest bonds of family and tribe,

must have been an annoying spectacle for Quraysh. It must have hurt their tribal pride to see their fellow tribesmen enjoy security and peace after having been subjected to all kinds of injustice and injury. After the victims had suffered much despair and helplessness, they began to see in suffering and patience, although this view runs counter to the logic of Islām, a very rapprochement to God, an attunement of themselves to His mercy.

The Conversion of 'Umar ibn al Khaṭṭāb

At that time, 'Umar ibn al Khaṭṭāb was a mature man of thirty to thirty-five years of age. Physically he was well built and strong of muscle. Temperamentally he was capable of strong passion. He loved wine and amusement, and despite his very harshness of character, he was gentle and compassionate toward his people. As for the Muslims, he was one of their strongest opponents, a merciless aggressor upon their peace, security and religion. Their emigration to Abyssinia and the Negus's protection of them caused him no little resentment. His pride as a national of Makkah was wounded by the fact that a foreign king and country were protecting Makkans who can find neither security nor peace in their own homes. Muḥammad was meeting one day with his own companions in a house in al Ṣafā quarter of Makkah. Among those present were his uncle Ḥamzah, his cousin, 'Alī ibn Abū Ṭālib, Abū Bakr ibn Abū Quḥāfah, and other Muslims. 'Umar learned of their meeting and went there resolved to kill Muḥammad and thus relieve the Quraysh of its burden, restore its ravaged unity, and re-establish respect for the gods that Muḥammad had castigated. On the road to Makkah he was met by Nu'aym ibn 'Abdullah. Upon learning what 'Umar was about, Nu'aym said, "By God, you have deceived yourself, O 'Umar! Do you think that Banū 'Abd Manāf would let you run around alive once you had killed their son Muḥammad? Why don't you return to your own house and at least set it straight?" When 'Umar learned that Fāṭimah, his sister, and her husband, Sa'īd ibn Zayd, had already been converted to Islām, he turned around and went straight to their house. Upon entering the house without knocking, he found them listening to a third person reciting the Qur'ān. They, too, having heard him approach, had hid their visitor and put away the manuscript of the Qur'ān from which they were reading. 'Umar asked, "What is this cantillation that I have heard as I walked in?" The pair denied hearing anything.

Flying into a rage, 'Umar told them that he knew that they had foresworn their faith and entered into that of Muḥammad. He chastised them and delivered a strong blow to his brother-in-law, Sa'īd. Fāṭimah rose to protect her husband. As she came between the two men, 'Umar hit her on the head and caused her to bleed. At this, the pair lost their fear entirely and said together, "Yes, indeed! We have become Muslims. Do what you will!" At this surge of courage, as well as upon seeing the blood of his sister flow, 'Umar was moved. After calming down a little, he asked his sister to let him see the manuscript which she and her husband had been reading together. After she surrendered the manuscript to him, he read it and his face changed to an expression of regret for what he had just done. As for what he had just read, he was deeply shaken by its beauty, its majesty, the nobility of its call, and the magnanimity of its message. In short, 'Umar's good side got the better of him. He left the house of his sister, his heart mellow and his soul reassured by the new certainty which he had just discovered. He went straight to al Ṣafā, where Muḥammad was meeting with his companions, sought permission to enter, and declared his conversion to Islām in front of the Prophet. The Muslims acclaimed his conversion and found therein, as they did in the conversion of Ḥamzah, new security for the community as a whole.

The conversion of 'Umar divided the Quraysh further. It reduced their power and caused them to reconsider their strategy. In fact, it increased Muslim power so greatly and so significantly that both they and the Quraysh had to change their positions *vis-à-vis* each other. Moreover, it triggered a whole line of events in inspiring new levels of sacrifices and stirring new forces which, together, led to the emigration of Muḥammad and to the inception of the political side of his career.

Courtyard of Qarawiyyin Mosque, Fez, Morocco.

6

The Story of
the Goddesses

The Emigrants Return from Abyssinia

The emigrants resided in Abyssinia three months during which 'Umar ibn al Khattāb converted to Islām. In their exile, they heard that upon 'Umar's conversion the Quraysh had stopped their persecution of Muḥammad and his followers. According to one report a number of them had returned to Makkah, according to another, all. On reaching Makkah they realized that the Quraysh had resumed persecution of the Muslims with stronger hatred and renewed vigor. Unable to resist, a number of them returned to Abyssinia while others entered Makkah under the cover of night and hid themselves away. It is also reported that those who returned took with them a number of new converts to Abyssinia where they were to stay until after the emigration to Madīnah and the establishment of Muslim political power.

We may ask what incited the Muslims of Abyssinia to return to Makkah three months after their emigration. It is at this stage that the story of the goddesses is told by ibn Sa'd in his *Al Ṭabaqāt al Kubrā,* by al Ṭabarī in his *Tārīkh al Rusul wa al Mulūk,* as well as by a number of Muslim exegetes and biographers. This story arrested the attention of the western Orientalists who took it as true and repeated it *ad nauseam.* This story tells that realizing how alienated the Quraysh had become and how intensely they had persecuted his companions, Muḥammad expressed the wish that a revelation might come that would reconcile his people rather than further alienate them. When, one day, he was sitting with the Quraysh in one of their club houses around the Ka'bah, he recited to them *sūrah* "al Najm." After reading the verses, "Would you consider al Lāt and al 'Uzzā? as well as Manāt, the third goddess?"[1] he continued the recitation with the statement, "They are the goddesses on high. Their intercession is worthy of being sought." He then proceeded with his reading of the *sūrah* as we know it. When he finished he prostrated himself, and all the Quraysh likewise followed him. At this moment, the Quraysh proclaimed its satisfaction with what the Prophet had read and said, "We have always known that God creates and gives life, gives food, and resuscitates. But our gods intercede for us with Him. Now that you have allowed for them a place in your new religion, we are all with you." Thus the difference between Muhammad and the Quraysh was dissolved. When the news of this reconciliation reached Abyssinia, the Muslims there decided to return to their beloved country and people. As they reached the approaches of Makkah, they met some Kinānah tribesmen who informed them that Muhammad allowed the gods a good position in his religion, reconciled the Quraysh, and was now followed by everyone. The story then relates how Muhammad reverted by blaspheming those gods and the Quraysh reverted to persecution. It further adds that the returnees stopped to consider what their next course should be. They longed so much to see their relatives and next of kin that they went ahead and entered Makkah.

Other versions of the same story give detailed descriptions of Muhammad's attitude toward the gods of Quraysh. They claimed that Quraysh's plea that if he but grant their gods a share in his religion the Makkans would all support him, troubled the Prophet. They relate how Muhammad one evening reviewed *sūrah* "al Najm" with Gabriel when the latter made a timely appearance. When he arrived at the sentence in question, Gabriel asked where it came from. Muhammad answered, "I must have attributed to God that which He did not say." God then revealed the following verses: "They have almost succeeded in inducing you, under promise of their friendship, to attribute to Us, against Our command, that which We did not reveal to you. Had We not confirmed you in your faith, you might have been tempted and hence fallen under the inescapable punishment."[2] Thereafter, Muhammad returned to his condemnation of the gods, and Quraysh returned to their persecution.

Incoherence of the Story

Such is the story of the goddesses reported by more than one biographer, pointed to by more than one exegete of the Qur'ān, and singled out and repeated by a number of western Orientalists. It is a story whose incoherence is evident upon the least scrutiny. It contradicts the infallibility of every prophet in conveying the message of his Lord. All the more wonder, therefore, that some Muslim scholars have accepted it as true. Ibn Isḥāq, for his part, did not hesitate at all to declare it a fabrication by the *zindīqs*.[3] Those who were taken in by it rationalized it further with the verse, "Every prophet We sent before you was such that whenever he pressed for revelation to come, Satan would hasten to inspire him with something satisfying his wish and thus necessitate God's abrogation of it if scripture is to be kept absolutely pure and true. God is all-wise and all-knowing. That which Satan had given is a lure for those who are sick of mind and hard of heart. Surely the unjust are deep in error."[4] Some explain the word *"tamannā"* in the foregoing verse as meaning "to read;" others give it the usual meaning of "to press wishfully." Muslim and Western scholars who accept the story explain that the Prophet suffered heavily from the persecution the unbelievers directed at his companions. They tell how the unbelievers killed some Muslims, exposed others to burning by the sun while pinned down to the ground with heavy stones (as was the case with Bilāl), and how these sufferings pressured Muḥammad to permit his companions to migrate to Abyssinia. They underscore Quraysh's alienation and the psychological effect of their boycott upon the Prophet. Since Muḥammad was very anxious to convert them to Islām and to save them from idol worship, they claim that his thinking of reconciling them by adding a few verses to *sūrah* "al Najm" is not farfetched. Finally, they allege that Muḥammad's jubilation was all too natural when, coming to the end of his recitation and prostrating himself, the Quraysh joined in, showing their preparation to follow him now that he had given a share to their gods with God.

To these tales of some books of biography and exegesis, Sir William Muir adds what he thinks is a final and conclusive proof. He says that the emigrants to Abyssinia had hardly spent three months there during which the Negus had tolerated as well as protected them when they decided to return to Makkah. Had they not heard news of a reconciliation between Muḥammad

and Quraysh nothing would have caused them to return so soon.
But, reasons Muir, how could there be reconciliation between
Muhammad and Quraysh without a determined effort to that
effect on the part of Muhammad? In Makkah, the Muslims had
then been far fewer and weaker than the Quraysh. They were
still incapable of protecting themselves against the injuries
which the Quraysh had been inflicting upon them. Why, then,
should the Quraysh have taken the initiative in such reconciliation?

Refutation of These Arguments

These are the arguments on which stands the claim for veracity
of the story of the goddesses. They are all false, incapable of
standing any scrutiny or analysis. Let us begin with the argument of the Orientalist Muir. The Muslims who returned from
Abyssinia did so for two reasons. First, 'Umar ibn al Khattāb
was converted to Islām shortly after their emigration. With
him, he brought to the Muslim camp the same boldness, determination, and the tribal standing with which he had been
fighting the Muslims before. He never concealed his conversion
nor did he ever shun the Quraysh opponents. On the contrary,
he proclaimed his conversion publicly and challenged the Quraysh
openly. He did not approve the Muslim's concealment of themselves, their secret movement from one end of Makkah to the
other, and their holding of prayers at a safe distance from any
Quraysh attack. 'Umar began to fight the Quraysh as soon as he
entered the faith of Islām, constantly pressed his way close
to the Ka'bah, and performed his prayer there in company with
whatever Muslims that decided to join him. It was at this new
challenging turn of events that the Quraysh came to the realization that any further injury inflicted upon Muhammad or
his companions would henceforth create a civil war of which
nobody knew the consequences. By this time, a great number
of men from the various clans of Quraysh had joined Islām.
To kill any one of these would necessarily imply the rise to war
not only of his fellow Muslims but of all the clans of which
the various Muslims or allies were members, even though the
rest of the clan or the tribe were still of a different religion.
After the conversion of 'Umar and the entry of so many members
of other clans into the faith, it became impossible to fight
Muhammad in the same way as before. Such a course could easily

expose the whole of Quraysh to terrible peril. It was necessary to find a new way which did not incur such risks, and until such way was found, the Quraysh thought it advantageous to enter into an armistice with Muhammad and the Muslims. It was this news which reached the emigrants in Makkah and prompted them to return home.

Two Revolutions in Abyssinia

The emigrants would have hesitated to return to Makkah were it not for another reason. A revolution broke out against the Negus in which his personal faith as well as his protection of the Muslims were under attack. For their part, the Muslims had prayed and wished that God would give the Negus victory over his enemies. But they could not participate in such a conflict since they were foreigners who arrived there too recently. When, at the same time, they heard of the news of an armistice between Muhammad and Quraysh favorable to the Muslims and protecting them from injury, they decided to escape from the Abyssinian revolution and return home. That is exactly what all or some of them did. They hardly reached Makkah, however, when Quraysh decided upon a course of action against the Muslims and entered into a pact with their allies to boycott Banū Hāshim completely in order to prevent any intermarriage with them and to stop any purchase by or sale to them. As soon as this new alliance was concluded, open war broke out again. The returning Muslims sought immediately to re-emigrate and take with them all those who could manage to go. These were to meet greater difficulties as the Quraysh sought to impede their move. What caused the Muslims to return from Abyssinia, therefore, was not, as Orientalist Muir claims, the reconciliation of Muhammad with Quraysh. Rather, it was the armistice to which the Quraysh was compelled to resort following the conversion of 'Umar and his bold support of the religion of God with his tribal relations. The so-called reconciliation, therefore, constitutes no evidence for the story of the goddesses.

Inverted Evidence of the Qur'ānic Text

As for the argument of some biographers and exegetes that the verses, "They had almost succeeded in inducing you . . ."[5] and "Every prophet We sent before you was such that, whenever he

pressed for revelation . . ."⁶ constitute evidence for the story of
the goddesses, it is yet more incoherent than that of Sir Muir. It
is sufficient to remember that the first group of verses include
the statement, "Had We not confirmed you in your faith, you
might have been tempted." This group shows that even if Satan
had actually hastened to inspire Muḥammad with something
satisfying his wish and thus induced him to favor the unbelievers,
God had confirmed the Prophet in his faith and prevented him
from falling to the temptation. Had Muḥammad really fallen,
God would have inflicted upon him inescapable punishment. The
point is, precisely, that he did not fall. Hence, these verses prove
the opposite of what these advocates assume them to prove.
The story of the goddesses asserts that Muḥammad did indeed
incline toward the Quraysh, that the Quraysh had indeed induced
him to add to the divine word, and that he indeed did attribute
to God that which God had not said. The text, on the other
hand, tells us the exact opposite, namely that God confirmed
him in his faith and that he did not add to the divine word.
Moreover, we should well bear in mind the fact that the books
of exegesis and the books dealing with the causes and circumstances of revelation—regardless of whether or not they subscribe to the story in question—affirm that these verses had
been revealed at a time other than that during which the story
of the goddesses had presumably taken place. To resort to the
story of the goddesses in order to disprove the infallibility of
the prophets in their conveyance of divine messages not only
runs counter to the whole history of Muḥammad but constitutes
a fallacy of incoherent reasoning and, hence, a futile and perverse
argument.

As for "Every prophet We sent before you . . . ," these verses
are utterly devoid of relation to the story of the goddesses.
Moreover, they clearly affirm that God will abrogate all that
the devil may bring forth, that Satan's work is only a lure
to those who are sick of mind and hard of heart, and that God,
the all-wise and all-knowing, would keep His scripture absolutely
pure and true.

Fallacious Reasoning of the Claim

Let us now turn to a critical and scientific analysis of the
story. The first evidence which imputes suspicion to the story
is the fact that it has been reported in many forms and versions.

First there is the report that the fabricated verses consist of the following words: "*Tilka al gharānīq al 'ulā; wa inna shafā- 'atahunna laturtajā.*" Others reported them as consisting of, "*al gharāniqah al 'ulā: inna shafā'atahum turtajā.*" Still others reported that they consist of the following words, "*Inna shafā- 'atahunna turtajā*" without mentioning the word "*al gharānīq*" or "*al gharāniqah*" at all. According to a fourth version, they were supposed to consist of the words: "*Innahā lahiya al gharānīq al 'ulā.*" A fifth version reads, "*Wa innahunna lahunna al gharānīq al 'ulā wa inna shafā'atahunna lahiya allatī turtajā.*" The collections of Ḥadīth have given us still more varied versions. The multiplicity of the versions proves that the report itself is fabricated, that it had been fabricated by the *zindīqs*—as ibn Isḥāq had said earlier—and that the forgers had sought thereby to spread doubt into the message of Muhammad and to attack his candidness in conveying the message of his Lord.

The Story's Violence to the Contextual Flow of Sūrah "al Najm"

Another proof of the falsity of the story, stronger and more conclusive than the foregoing, is the fact that the contextual flow of *sūrah* "al Najm" does not allow at all the inclusion of such verses as the story claims. The *sūrah* reads:

لَقَدْ رَأَىٰ مِنْ آيَاتِ رَبِّهِ الْكُبْرَىٰ ۞ أَفَرَأَيْتُمُ اللَّاتَ وَالْعُزَّىٰ ۞ وَمَنَاةَ الثَّالِثَةَ الْأُخْرَىٰ ۞ أَلَكُمُ الذَّكَرُ وَلَهُ الْأُنثَىٰ ۞ تِلْكَ إِذًا قِسْمَةٌ ضِيزَىٰ ۞ إِنْ هِيَ إِلَّا أَسْمَاءٌ سَمَّيْتُمُوهَا أَنتُمْ وَآبَاؤُكُم مَّا أَنزَلَ اللَّهُ بِهَا مِن سُلْطَانٍ إِن يَتَّبِعُونَ إِلَّا الظَّنَّ وَمَا تَهْوَى الْأَنفُسُ وَلَقَدْ جَاءَهُم مِّن رَّبِّهِمُ الْهُدَىٰ ۞

"He has witnessed many of the great signs of his lord. Would you consider the case of al Lāt, al 'Uzzā, and of Manāt, the third goddess? Would you then ascribe to God the females and to yourselves the males? Wouldn't that be a wretched ascription? All these are nothing but names, mere names which you and your ancestors had coined. Men are so prone to follow opinion! They credulously fall for the product of their own wishful thinking. But true guidance has indeed come from the Lord."

The logical and literary flow of these verses is crystal-clear. *Al Lāt* and *al 'Uzzā* are mere names devoid of substance given by the past and present unbelievers to works of their own creation. There is no deity such as the words name. The context does not

allow any such addition as is here claimed. If, assuming such
addition, the text were now to read: "Would you consider the
case of al Lāt, al 'Uzzā, and of Manāt, the third goddess? These
are the goddesses on high. Their intercession is to be sought.
Would you then ascribe to God the females and to yourselves
the males? Wouldn't that be a wretched ascription?" its corruption and outright self-contradiction become obvious. The
text would have praised al Lāt, al 'Uzzā, and Manāt as well as
condemned them within the space of four consecutive verses.
Such a text cannot proceed from any rational being. The contextual background in which the addition is supposed to have
been made furnishes unquestionable and final evidence that the
story of the goddesses was a forgery. The forgers were probably
the *zindīqs;* and the credulous whose minds are not naturally
repulsed by the irrational and the incoherent, accepted the forgery and passed it as true.

The Linguistic Evidence

There is yet another argument advanced by the late Shaykh
Muhammad 'Abduh. It consists of the fact that the Arabs have
nowhere described their gods in such terms as "al gharānīq."
Neither in their poetry nor in their speeches or traditions do
we find their gods or goodesses described in such terms. Rather,
the word *"al ghurnūq"* or *"al gharnīq"* was the name of a black
or white water bird, sometimes given figuratively to the handsome blond youth. The fact is indubitable that the Arabs never
looked upon their gods in this manner.

The Story Contradicts the Fact of Muhammad's Candidness

There is yet one more final argument against the story of
the goddesses that is based upon the nature of Muhammad's
personal life. Ever since his childhood and throughout his adoles-
cence, adulthood and maturity, he was never known to lie. So
truthful was he that he had been nicknamed "al Amīn" before
he reached his twenty-fifth year of age. His truthfulness was
unquestioned by anyone. He himself once addressed the Quraysh
after his commission to prophethood: "Suppose I were to tell
you that an enemy cavalry was advancing on the other side of
this mountain, would you believe me?" His enemies themselves

answered: "Yes, indeed! As far as we are concerned, you are innocent, for we have never found you to lie at all." How can we believe that such a man who had been known to be truthful in his relations with his fellow men from childhood to maturity, would be any less candid in his relation to God? How could such constant truthfulness allow him to lie and ascribe to his God that which He had not said? How could we believe that such a man did so in fear of the people and defiance of Almighty God? That is utterly impossible. Its impossibility is evident to all those who have studied these great, strong and distinguished souls of the prophets and religious leaders known for their dedication to the truth *pereat mundus*. How can we reconcile such an allegation with Muḥammad's great declaration to his uncle that he will not adjure this cause even if his foes should put the sun in his right hand and the moon in his left? How can we accept such a claim when it imputes to the Prophet the heinous charge of attributing to God that which God had not said, of violating the very foundation of the religion he was commissioned to proclaim and teach to mankind?

Furthermore, we may ask, when, according to the story, did Muḥammad turn to praise the gods of Quraysh? Ten years or so after his commission to prophethood, is the reply. But, then that is also after ten years of patient sufference of all kinds of injury and harm, all kinds of sacrifices, after God had reinforced Islām with the conversion of Ḥamzah and 'Umar, and, in short, after the Muslims had begun to feel themselves a significant power in Makkah and the news of their existence and exploits had begun to spread throughout Arabia, indeed to Abyssinia and other corners of the globe. Such a claim is not only uninformed, it is positively silly. The forgers of this story themselves must have realized its inadmissibility and sought to conceal its falsehood with the claim, "Muḥammad hardly heard Quraysh's words of reconciliation once he granted to their gods the honor of interceding with God, when his compromise appeared to him objectionable and he felt compelled to repent and to review the text of revelation with the angel Gabriel when he visited him that same evening." This concealment, however, exposes the forgery rather than hides it. As long as the compromise appeared objectionable to Muḥammad no later than he had "heard Quraysh's words of reconciliation," would he have not paused to reconsider it immediately and on the spot?

How natural it would have been then for him instantly to
recite the true version of the text! We may, therefore, conclude
that this story of the goddesses is a fabrication and a forgery,
authored by the enemies of Islām after the first century of
the Hijrah.

Attack upon Tawḥīd[8]

The forgers must have been extremely bold to have attempted
their forgery in the most essential principal of Islām as a whole:
namely, in the principle of *tawḥīd*, where Muhammad had been
sent right from the very beginning to make proclamations to
all mankind in which he has never accepted any compromise
whatever; he was never swayed by anything the Quraysh had
offered him whether by way of wealth or royal power. These
offers had come, it must be remembered, at a time when Muhammad had very few followers within Makkah. Later persecution by the Quraysh of his companions did not succeed in
swaying Muhammad away from the call of his God or away
from his mission. The *zindīqs'* strategy to work their forgery
around the first principle of the faith, where Muhammad was
known to be the most adamant, only points to their own in-
consequence. Acceptance of the forgery by the credulous only
points to their naiveté in the most conspicuous of cases.

The story of the goddesses, therefore, is absolutely devoid of
foundation. It is utterly unrelated to the return of the Muslims
from Abyssinia. As we said earlier, the latter returned after
the conversion of 'Umar, the strengthening of Islām with the
same tribal solidarity with which he used to fight Islām hitherto,
and the compulsion of Quraysh to enter into an armistice with
the Muslims. Moreover, the Muslims' return from Abyssinia was
partly due to the revolution which had broken out in that
country and to their consequent fear of losing the Negus's
protection. When the Quraysh learned of the Muslims' return,
their fears reached a new level of intensity with the increase of
Muhammad's followers within the city, and, therefore, they
sought a new strategy. Their search for a new strategy was
concluded with the signing of a pact in which they and their
allied clans and tribes resolved to boycott the Banū Hāshim
in order to prevent any intermarriage with them, to stop all
commercial relations and finally, to seek to kill Muhammad if
they could only find the means.

7

The Malevolent
Conduct of Quraysh

The conversion of 'Umar to Islām reduced the power of Quraysh significantly in that 'Umar brought with him to the faith the tribal loyalties with which he had fought Islām earlier. He did not hide himself or conceal his Islām. On the contrary he proclaimed it to all the people and fought them for not joining him. He did not at all approve of the Muslims' hiding themselves or holding prayers in the outskirts of Makkah far beyond the Quraysh's reach. He continued to struggle against the Quraysh until he could pray near the Ka'bah where his fellow Muslims joined him. Henceforth, Quraysh became certain that no injury inflicted upon Muḥammad or his companions would stop men from entering the religion of God since they could now rely upon the tribal protection of 'Umar, Ḥamzah, the Negus of Abyssinia, or others capable of protecting them. The Quraysh then sought a new strategy, and agreed among themselves to a written pact in which they resolved to boycott Banū Hāshim and Banū 'Abd al Muṭṭalib completely, prevent any intermarriage with them, and stop all commercial relations. The written pact itself was hung inside the Ka'bah, as was then the practice, for record and sanctification. They thought that this negative policy of boycott, isolation, and starvation would be more effective than the previous policy of harm and injury, though the latter was never stopped. The Quraysh blockaded the Muslims as well as the Banū Hāshim and Banū 'Abd al

Muttalib for two or three years during which time they hoped that these tribes would renounce Muhammad and thus cause him to fall under the hand of Quraysh. They had hoped that such a measure would isolate Muhammad and remove all danger from his mission.

The new strategy of Quraysh served only to strengthen Muhammad's faith in God and his followers' determination to protect his person and God's religion against attack. It did not prevent the spreading of Islām, not only within the bounds of Makkah but outside of it as well. Muhammad's mission became widely known among the Arabs of the Peninsula, and the new religion became the subject of conversation everywhere. This growth, in turn, increased the fury and determination of Quraysh to oppose and fight the man who abandoned and blasphemed her gods and to prevent the spread of his cause among the Arab tribes. Loyalty of these tribes was indispensible for Makkan commerce and trade relations with other people.

The Arm of Propaganda

It is nearly impossible for us to imagine the intensity and extent of the efforts which Quraysh spent in its struggle against Muhammad, or its perseverence during many long years in that struggle. The Quraysh threatened Muhammad and his relatives, especially his uncles. It ridiculed him and his message, and it insulted him as well as his followers. It commissioned its poets to revile him with their sharpest wits and to direct their most caustic sting against his preaching. It inflicted injury and harm on his person and on the persons of his followers. It offered him bribes of money, of royalty and power, of all that which satisfies the most fastidious among men. It not only banished and dispersed his followers from their own country but injured them in their trade and commerce while impoverishing them. It warned him and his followers that war with all its tragedies would fall upon them. As a last resort, it began a boycott of them designed to starve them. All this notwithstanding, Muhammad continued to call men with kind and gentle argument unto the God of truth who sent him as a prophet and a warner. Would Quraysh lay down its arms and believe the man whom it had always known to be truthful and honest? Or would they, under the illusion that they could still win, resort to new means of hostility to save the divine status of their idols and the hallowed position of Makkah as their museum?

No! The time had not yet come for the Quraysh to submit and to convert to the new faith. Rather, they were more apprehensive than ever when the religion began to spread outside of Makkah within the Arab tribes. They had still another weapon which, though they had used it right from the very beginning, was yet capable of more power and damage. That was propaganda, or mental warfare, with all it implies by way of debate, counter-argument, spreading of false rumors, ridicule of the opponent's point of view, and positive apologetics in favor of their own view. The development of this weapon was not to be limited to Makkah but would apply to the whole countryside, to the whole desert, and to the tribes of the Peninsula. Threat, bribery, aggression, and gangsterism allayed the need for propaganda within Makkah. There was a great need for it, however, among the thousands who came into Makkah every year for trade or pilgrimage, and among the attendants of the markets of 'Ukāẓ, Majannah, and Dhū al Majāz, who later arrived at the Ka'bah for thanksgiving and worship near the Ka'bah idols. Therefore, it was expedient for the Quraysh, the moment the lines of battle against Muḥammad were clearly drawn, to plan and organize its propaganda forces. It had all the more reason to do so since Muḥammad himself had always taken the initiative of approaching the pilgrim and addressing him on the subject of restricting worship to God alone without associates. The idea of such initiative did not occur to Muḥammad until years after his commission to prophethood. At the beginning, revelation had commanded him to warn his nearest relatives. It was only after he had warned Quraysh and those who wanted to convert had converted that his revelation commanded him now to address his warning to the Arabs as a whole. He was later to be commanded to address his call to all mankind.

The Charge of Magical Eloquence

As Muḥammad began to approach the pilgrims coming from various corners of Arabia with his call to God, a number of Quraysh leaders met with al Walīd ibn al Mughīrah to consult for a possible strategy. What would they say regarding Muḥammad to the Arabs coming for pilgrimage? Their answers to this question should be universally the same; otherwise they would constitute arguments in favor of Muḥammad's claims. Some suggested that they should claim that Muḥammad was a diviner. Al Walīd rejected this suggestion on the grounds that

what Muḥammad recited was unlike the secret formulae of
common diviners. Others suggested that they should claim that
Muḥammad was possessed or mad. Al Walīd again rejected this
view on the grounds that the symptoms of madness or possession
were not apparent in Muḥammad. Still others suggested that
they should claim that Muḥammad was a magician, but al Walīd
again rejected this view on the grounds that Muḥammad did
not practice the common tricks of magicians. After some discussion, al Walīd suggested that they should tell the non-Makkan
Arab pilgrim that Muḥammad was a magician whose craft was
eloquence—that by means of eloquent words he was capable of
dividing the man against his father, his brother, his spouse
and his own tribe. Al Walīd advised that they could produce
evidence for such nefarious eloquence by pointing to the division
which befell Makkah after Muḥammad began to practice his
craft. Any consideration of the present division, internal struggle,
and internecine fighting raging among the Makkans who were
once the exemplars of tribal solidarity and social unity would
convince the observer that Muḥammad's influence had brought
the worst. During the pilgrimage season the Quraysh made a
special effort to warn every visitor to Makkah against ever
lending his ear to Muḥammad for fear that he would be mesmerized by his magic eloquence and then suffer in turn the
same evils that had befallen Makkah and thus bring about a
general war in Arabia detrimental to all.

Al Naḍr ibn al Ḥārith

A mental warfare of such order could not be expected to withstand or counteract Muḥammad's so-called magic eloquence all
alone. If genuine truth were to come on the wings of this
so-called magic eloquence, what would prevent the people from
accepting it? Is the acknowledgment of the distinction of the
antagonist and the acknowledgment of the inferiority of the
protagonist ever successful as a propaganda weapon? There must
needs be other fronts on which to attack Muḥammad in addition
to this proposed mental warfare. Let the Quraysh seek this
second front with al Naḍr ibn al Ḥārith. The said al Naḍr was
one of the sophisticated geniuses of Quraysh. He had studied
at al Ḥīrah the history, religion, wisdom, theories of good and
evil, cosmology, and other literature of the Persians. Whenever
Muḥammad finished preaching his faith in an assembly calling
men to God, and warning them of the consequences on the Day

of Judgment—taking the bygone peoples and civilizations as examples of such divine punishment for failure to worship God— al Naḍr would rise and tell his fellow Makkans about Persia and its religion. He would conclude by asking the assembly, "Why is Muḥammad's speech better than mine? Does he not draw from the tales of antiquity just as I do?" The Quraysh used to memorize al Nadr's speeches and statements and circulate them around and outside Makkah as counter–measures to the claims of Muḥammad and his message.

Jabr, the Christian

Muḥammad used to tarry at the shop of a Christian youth called Jabr whenever he passed by the Marwah quarter of Makkah. The Quraysh took advantage of the fact and began to spread the rumor that this Christian Jabr had taught Muḥammad all that he knew and that if anyone were expected to apostatize from the religion of his ancestors, the Christian should be the first one to do so. As this rumor spread, revelation itself answered the claim in the verse: "We know they claim that the Qur'ān is taught to him by another man. But the man whom they suspect is Persian of tongue, whereas the tongue of this Qur'ān is pure and clear Arabic."[1]

Al Ṭufayl ibn ʿAmr al Dawsī

With this and like feats of propaganda the Quraysh sought to fight Muḥammad in hope of achieving by these means more than they did by means of injury and harm to his person and followers. The clear and simple might of truth, however, shone brilliantly in Muḥammad's preaching. While the struggle between the two forces continued, Islām spread more and more widely among the Arabs. When al Ṭufayl ibn ʿAmr al Dawsī, a nobleman of great poetic talent, arrived in Makkah, he was immediately approached by the Quraysh and warned against Muḥammad and his magical eloquence. They admonished him that Muḥammad's craft might well divide him and his people and that his tribe might well suffer the same evil as had befallen Makkah. They asked him not to visit Muḥammad or hear him if he wanted to avoid the evil. Al Ṭufayl, however, went one day to the Kaʿbah and there heard a little of the preaching of Muḥammad and liked it. He then thought, "Woe to me! Am I, the intelligent poet, the mature man, to fear that I may not distinguish between the

genuinely beautiful and the really ugly in human discourse?
Shouldn't I go to Muhammad, hear all that he has to say and
apply my own judgment? If I should find it good, why shouldn't
I accept it? And if I find it evil, surely I shall avoid it." He
followed Muhammad one day to his house and there told him
exactly what he thought and what he had decided. Muhammad
welcomed him, presented to him the new religion, and recited
for him the Qur'ān. Al Ṭufayl was immediately converted, recited
the confession of truth, and returned to his people a missionary
for Islām. He was responsible for the conversion of many, though
not all, of his tribesmen. For many years, he continued his
missionary activity and succeeded in converting the greater
number of them. He and they joined themselves to the forces of
Muhammad after the conquest of Makkah once the political
structure of the Islāmic community began to crystallize.

Al Ṭufayl ibn 'Amr al Dawsī is only one of many examples.
The idol worshippers were not the only ones responding favorably to the message of Muhammad. While Muhammad was still
in Makkah, twenty Christian men arrived, sent by their own
people on a fact-finding mission concerning the new faith. They
sat with Muhammad and asked him all kinds of questions and
listened to him. They, too, were converted on the spot, believed
in Muhammad and in the revelation. This conversion aroused
great anger and resentment among the Quraysh. Indeed the latter
addressed the new converts in these words: "Wretched fact-
finding mission that you are! Your fellow religionists sent you
here in order to investigate the man and bring them the factual
news concerning him. But you have hardly sat down with him
before you apostatized from your religion and believed him in
everything he said." In vain did the Quraysh try to dissuade
the Christian delegation from following Muhammad and converting to his faith. On the contrary, the Quraysh's attack against
their sincerity had strengthened their faith in God and added
to their monotheistic convictions since, before they heard
Muhammad, they were already Christian and hence submissive
to God.

Abū Sufyān, Abū Jahl, and al Akhnas

The struggle against Muhammad reached even greater proportions. The most antagonistic of the Quraysh began to ask
themselves: "Is it true that this man is really calling unto the
religion of truth? That what he promises us and threatens us

with in the hereafter is true?" Abū Sufyān, Abū Jahl and al Akhnas ibn Sharīq went out one night to hear Muhammad preach in his own house without any one of them knowing what the other was about. Unobserved by his colleagues, each one of them took his place in some corner and spent the night listening to Muhammad preach, then pray and recite the Qur'ān in the still of night, cantillating its holy verses with his beautiful voice. As dawn arrived and the three auditors repaired to their houses, they met one another on the road. Each one of them knew what the others were about and blamed the others for such behavior. Arguing that this would be a blow to the morale of the rank and file of the Quraysh if they ever knew of it, they mutually promised one another never to do it again. When the following night came, however, and the hours of yesterday struck, each one of them felt as if he were being carried to the house of Muhammad without being able to stop himself. An irresistible power was drawing them to spend another night of listening to Muhammad's prayer, preaching, and cantillation of the divine verses. Again they met one another at dawn on their way back and blamed one another anew. Even this repeated violation of their mutual threat and promise did not prevent them from going to the same place the third night. It was only after the third violation that they realized their weakness and the strong attraction they felt toward the voice of Muhammad, his faith, and Qur'ānic recitation. They pledged solemnly never to return again, but what they had heard from Muhammad during the three previous nights left such a deep impression upon their souls that it disturbed their inner peace and reduced their spirit of resistance. Naturally, they were quite apprehensive that, being leaders of their people, their inner disturbance would some day be discovered by their followers and sap the morale of the whole community.

"He Frowned and Turned Away"

What prevented these men from following Muhammad? He had not asked of them either reward or power or kingship. Rather, Muhammad was a very modest man, full of love for his people, anxious to do good to them and to guide them in the true path. He was both strongly self-critical and fearful of bringing the least harm to the weak or the oppressed. In suffering the injuries inflicted upon him by others and forgiving their authors, he found peace and tranquility of conscience. Evidence

of this personal characteristic of Muḥammad may be found in
the story of ibn Umm Maktūm. Muḥammad was once involved
in serious conversation with al Walīd ibn al Mughīrah, one
of the leading aristocrats of Quraysh, whom he hoped he would
convert to Islām. Ibn Umm Maktūm, the blind, stopped by and
asked Muḥammad to recite some Qur'ānic verses for him. Preoccupied with his conversation, Muḥammad did not answer. Ibn
Umm Maktūm insisted until he interrupted the conversation
of the two men, to the severe annoyance of Muḥammad. The
conversation thus abruptly ended, Muḥammad frowned, gave
an angry look to the blind man and moved on without satisfying
his request. When Muḥammad came to himself, he began to
criticize himself for this maltreatment of the blind man, and
soon the following verses were revealed to him: "He frowned
and turned aside when the blind man approached him. Perhaps,
the blind man may have sought to purify himself, to remember
the words of God and to benefit therefrom. But to him who is
disdainfully indifferent, you [Muḥammad] pay great attention,
though you are not responsible if he should never become purified.
But he who came to you exerting himself and striving in fear
and reverence, him you neglected. No! No! The whole matter
is a reminder. So let him who so desires, be reminded of
it. The Qur'ān is inscribed in honored sheets, exalted and purified, and written by hands noble and virtuous."[2] If such was
Muḥammad's character, what did in fact prevent the Quraysh
from following him and from helping him in his cause, especially
as their hearts had mellowed, as the years had caused them to
forget the obsolete traditions to which they had lethargically
attached themselves, and as they saw in Muḥammad's message
true majesty and perfection?

The Will to Perfection

But is it true that time makes men forget their obsolete past
and lethargic conservatism? Perhaps so, but only among those
who are endowed with superior intelligence and a will to perfection. Such people spend their lives trying out and testing
the truth which they have taken to be such in order to keep it
free of admixture, superstition, and error. The minds and hearts
of such people are cauldrons forever boiling, accepting every
new idea in order but to boil it down, purify it, and separate
its good from its evil as well as its beauty from its ugliness.
Such souls seek the truth in everything, everywhere, and from

every source. In every nation and age, such people are few; they are the chosen and the distinguished. Such men always find themselves on the other side of any contest with the rich, the established, and the powerful. The latter are forever apprehensive of anything new lest it may adversely affect their wealth, prestige, or power and, generally speaking, they do not know any other facts besides those of concrete everyday living. Everything is true, in their opinion, if it leads to an increase in the substance of this very life, and false if it implies the slightest doubt regarding that substance. For the capitalist, virtue is good if it increases the substance, evil if it dissipates it. Religion itself, is indeed true only if it serves his passions and desires, and false if it denies or fails to satisfy them.

The man of political power and the man of social prestige stand here on a par with the capitalist. In their enmity to everything new and fearful, they mobilize the masses on whom their wealth, social prestige, or power depend against the innovator. This mobilization of the masses is carried out under an appeal to save the sanctity of the old order which may very well have become corrupt, obsolete, and spiritless. They present the old order they seek to save in great monuments of stone designed to delude the innocent rank and file. They pretend that the great spirit and value which moulded those monuments still lives therein with all its majesty and grandeur. The masses usually respond to their appeal with enthusiasm, for they are above all concerned with their daily bread; it is not easy for them to realize that any truth cannot remain for long imprisoned within the walls of any temple or monument, however beautiful or majestic it may be. It is hard for them to understand that it is of the nature of truth to be free, to invade the souls of men and to nourish them without discrimination between nobleman and slave; that no matter how hardily a system may defend itself against the truth and how closely it may be protected, the truth is always bound to win. How then could those Quraysh leaders who were seeking to listen to the Qur'ān in secret, believe in its call when it proclaimed the wrath of God against the very practices which they were doing? How could they believe in a religion which did not differentiate between the blind pauper and the great capitalist except as regards the purity of their own souls? How could they believe in the call of Islām unto all men that "the greatest of you with God is the most pious and virtuous?"[3] If, therefore, Abū Sufyān and his colleagues remained true to the religion of their ancestors, it was

not due to their faith in its truth-value. Rather, it was due
to their zeal to preserve the old order that not only protected
them but also enabled them to achieve their position of wealth,
social prestige, and power.

Jealousy and Competition

In addition to this anxiety and despair, jealousy and competition did their work to prevent the Quraysh from following
the Prophet. Umayyah ibn Abū al Ṣalt was one of those who
predicted the rise of a prophet among the Arabs; indeed, he hoped
that he himself was such a prophet. He was full of resentment
and jealousy when revelation came to Muḥammad rather than
to him; he could not, despite his own superiority over Muḥammad as far as poetical composition is concerned, follow a person
whom he believed was his competitor. When Muḥammad heard
the poetry of Ummayyah, he exclaimed: "What a man is Ummayyah! His poetry believes, but his heart does not." Likewise,
al Walīd ibn al Mughīrah said: "It is incomprehensible to me
that revelations would come to Muḥammad and not to me
while I am the greatest elder and master of Quraysh. Neither
do I understand that revelation would not come to Abū Mas'ūd
'Amr ibn 'Umayr al Thaqafī, the elder and master of Thaqīf."
It was in reference to such commonplace sentiments that the
Qur'ān says: "They said: would that this Qur'ān be revealed
to one of the great men in one of the two cities. Would they
thus divide the mercy of your Lord? It is We who do so, as
We do divide their livelihood among them in the world."[4]
After Abū Sufyān, Abū Jahl, and al Akhnas had listened for
three consecutive nights to Muḥammad's recitation of the
Qur'ān, as we have reported earlier, al Akhnas visited Abū
Jahl in his home and asked, "O Abū al Ḥakam, what do you
think of what we heard from Muḥammad?" Abū Jahl answered,
"What did you hear? Our house and the house of Banū 'Abd
Manāf have been competing for the honor: They have given
the people to eat and so did we; they have carried the water
to the pilgrims and so did we; they have assumed other burdens
and so did we, they have given and so did we. Whenever we and
they mount on our horses it always looks as if we are in a race.
Now they are saying, among us is a prophet to whom revelation
comes straight from heaven! When, if ever, will we achieve
such a feat? Now, by God, we shall never believe in their prophet:
we shall never accept what he says as true."

In these Bedouin souls of Muḥammad's contemporaries, jealously and competition were deeply rooted, and it would be a great mistake to overlook them. We should remember that such passions are not unique to the Arabs but are shared by all men. To neutralize their effects or get rid of them demands long and arduous self-discipline, a radical self-transformation that raises reason far above passion and ennobles one's spirit and heart to the degree of acknowledging the ţruth whithersoever it may come from, be he enemy or friend. It also demands believing that the possession of the truth is more precious than all the wealth of Midas, the glory of Alexander, or the power of Caesar. Such nobility and magnaminity of soul is hardly ever reached except by those whose hearts God Himself guides. Commonplace men are usually blinded by the wealth and pleasure of the world and by the present moment in which alone they spent their lives. Obviously, they are unable to rise to such spiritual height. In pursuit of quick satisfaction during the fleeting present, they struggle, fight, and kill one another. For its sake, nothing seems to prevent any of them from striking his teeth and claws into the very neck of truth, goodness and virtue, and from trampling to death the noblest and highest values. Seeing Muḥammad's followers increasing in numbers and strength day by day, the Arabs of Quraysh were horrified by the idea that the truth which Muḥammad proclaimed would one day achieve victory and power over them, over their allies and beyond, and over all the Arabs of the Peninsula. Heads shall roll rather than allow such a thing to happen, they thought. Counter-propaganda and mental warfare, boycott, blockade, injury and harm, persecution—all these and the vials of wrath shall be poured over Muḥammad and his followers.

Fear of Resurrection and the Day of Judgment

A third reason prevented the Quraysh from following Muḥammad, namely, the terror of the resurrection on the Day of Judgment with its punishment of hell. They were a people immersed in recreation and the pursuit of pleasure; trade and usury were their means to its attainment. Those of them who could afford to indulge in these pursuits did not see in them anything immoral and felt no imperative to avoid them. Through their idol worship they thought that their evil deeds and sins could all be atoned for and forgiven. It was sufficient for a man to strike a few arrows at the foot of the statue of Hubal for

him to think that anything he was about to undertake was
blessed if not commanded by the god. It was sufficient to sacrifice
something to these idols for him to have his sins and guilt
wiped out and forgotten. Therefore, to kill, to rob, to commit
adultery, to indulge in unbecoming speech and indecency were
all proper and permissible as long as one was capable of bribing
those gods and placating them with sacrifices.

On the other hand, Muḥammad was proclaiming that the Lord
was standing in wait for them, that they will be resurrected on
the day of judgment, and that their works will be their only credit.
Moreover, he did so with verses of such tremendous power that
they shook men's hearts to the foundation and threw their consciousness into horror and panic. The Qur'ān proclaimed: "But
when the deafening cry is heard, when man would flee from his
brother, from his father and mother, his wife and children, everyone will have enough to concern himself with his own destiny. On
that day some faces will be bright, joyous and gay. Others will
be dark and gloomy. The latter are the unbelievers, the wicked."[5]
It proclaimed that the deafening cry would come—"the day
when heaven will be like molten copper, when mountains will be
like flakes of wool, when no friend will be able to concern himself for his friends. Beholding the fate which is to be theirs,
the condemned will wish to ransom themselves with their own
children, their wives and brothers, their tribes that gave them
protection, even the whole of mankind if such could save them
from the impending doom. No indeed! There shall be a flame
of fire, burning and dismembering, grasping without relief
him who turned his back to the call of God, who played deaf to
the moral imperative, who hoarded wealth and withheld it from
the needy. . . ."[6]

يَوْمَئِذٍ تُعْرَضُونَ لَا تَخْفَى مِنكُمْ خَافِيَةٌ ۞ فَأَمَّا مَنْ أُوتِيَ كِتَابَهُ بِيَمِينِهِ فَيَقُولُ هَاؤُمُ اقْرَؤُوا كِتَابِيَهْ ۞
إِنِّي ظَنَنتُ أَنِّي مُلَاقٍ حِسَابِيَهْ ۞ فَهُوَ فِي عِيشَةٍ رَّاضِيَةٍ ۞ فِي جَنَّةٍ عَالِيَةٍ ۞ قُطُوفُهَا دَانِيَةٌ ۞
كُلُوا وَاشْرَبُوا هَنِيئًا بِمَا أَسْلَفْتُمْ فِي الْأَيَّامِ الْخَالِيَةِ ۞ وَأَمَّا مَنْ أُوتِيَ كِتَابَهُ بِشِمَالِهِ فَيَقُولُ
يَا لَيْتَنِي لَمْ أُوتَ كِتَابِيَهْ ۞ وَلَمْ أَدْرِ مَا حِسَابِيَهْ ۞ يَا لَيْتَهَا كَانَتِ الْقَاضِيَةَ ۞ مَا أَغْنَى عَنِّي مَالِيَهْ ۞
هَلَكَ عَنِّي سُلْطَانِيَهْ ۞ خُذُوهُ فَغُلُّوهُ ۞ ثُمَّ الْجَحِيمَ صَلُّوهُ ۞ ثُمَّ فِي سِلْسِلَةٍ ذَرْعُهَا سَبْعُونَ
ذِرَاعًا فَاسْلُكُوهُ ۞ إِنَّهُ كَانَ لَا يُؤْمِنُ بِاللَّهِ الْعَظِيمِ ۞ وَلَا يَحُضُّ عَلَى طَعَامِ الْمِسْكِينِ ۞ فَلَيْسَ لَهُ
الْيَوْمَ هَاهُنَا حَمِيمٌ ۞ وَلَا طَعَامٌ إِلَّا مِنْ غِسْلِينٍ ۞ لَا يَأْكُلُهُ إِلَّا الْخَاطِئُونَ

"On that day you will be presented before God; none of your secrets will be hidden. Then, he who has received his record with his right hand will say: 'Come, read my record. I had rightly thought that I was to meet my reckoning.' Such a man will lead a blessed life in a lofty garden whose fruits are ripe and within reach. When he is brought therein he will be told: 'Eat and drink joyfully for in the days gone by, you have done the good deeds.' As for him who is given his record in his left hand he will say: 'Would I that I had never been given my record; that I never knew of my reckoning. Oh, would that death had made an end of me! My wealth is of no avail, and my power has come to nought.' To him God will say: 'Seize him and fetter him. Broil him in the fire. Then bind him in a chain seventy cubits long. For he did not believe in Almighty God, nor did he urge the feeding of the hungry. Today, he shall have no loyal friends and no food except what is foul, which none eat except his fellow sinners.'"[7]

After this I may ask the reader: Have you read this well? Did you ponder every word of it? Have you fully understood its meaning? Are you not petrified and panic stricken? But that is only a portion of Muḥammad's warning to his people. You read these verses today and remember that you have read them many times over before. Concurrently with your reading, you will remember the Qur'ān's description of hell. "On that day, We shall ask hell, 'Are you full?' And hell will answer: 'Give me more!' . . . Whenever their skins wear out, We shall give them new skins that they may continue to suffer the punishment."[8] You can well imagine then the horror which must have struck Quraysh, especially the rich among them wallowing in the protection of their gods and idols whenever Muḥammad warned them of the imminent punishment. It would then become easy for you to appreciate the degree of their enthusiasm in belying Muḥammad, opposing him, and urging the people to fight him. Previous to the Prophet's preaching, the Arabs had no idea of the Day of Judgment or of the resurrection, and they did not believe what they heard thereof from non-Arabs. None of them thought that he would be reckoned with after death for what he had done in this world. Whatever concern they had for the future was limited to this world. They feared disease, loss of wealth and children, of power and social prestige. This life, to them, was all there is to life. Their energies were exhausted in the amassing of the means with which to enjoy this life and to keep it safe from misfortune. The future was utterly opaque. Whenever their consciences were disturbed by a premonition of evil following upon their misdeeds, they had recourse to divination by arrows, pebbles, or bird-chasing in order to dissipate the fear or confirm it. If confirmed they would sacrifice to their idols and thereby avoid the imminent misfortune.

As for reckoning after death, resurrection, and the Day of Judgment—paradise for the virtuous and hell for the unjust— all this completely escaped them despite the fact that they had heard of it in connection with the religion of the Jews and of the Christians. Nonetheless, they never heard of it described with such emphatic, frightening, indeed horrifying, terms and seriousness such as Muhammad's revelation had brought to them. What they had heard of before Muhammad never succeeded in pressing home to them the recognition that their continued life of pleasure, pursuit of wealth, exploitation of the weak, robbery of the orphan, neglect of the poor, and excess in usury, would surely incur eternal punishment. They had no idea of impending suffering in the depth of hell, and when they heard of it described in these terms, it was natural for them to be seized with panic. How strongly they must have felt when they realized, though they did not openly admit it, that the other world with its reward and punishment is truly there, waiting for them only one step beyond this life which was soon to end in death!

Quraysh and Paradise

As for God's promise to the virtuous of a paradise as large as heaven and earth, where there is neither evil word nor deed but only peace and blessedness, the Quraysh were quite suspicious. They doubted paradise all the more because of their attachment to this world and their anxiousness to enjoy its blessings right here and now. They were too impatient to wait for the Day of Judgment though they did not believe in any such day at all.

The Struggle of Good and Evil

One may indeed wonder how the Arabs locked their minds against any idea of the other world and its reckoning when the struggle of good and evil in this world has been raging eternally without let-up or peace. Thousands of years before Muhammad, the ancient Egyptians provided their dead with their needs for the other world. In the coffins, they enclosed *The Book of the Dead,* which was full of psalms, invocations, and other prayers, and in their graves they painted pictures of judgment and scenes of repentance and punishment. The Indians, too, conceived of the other world in terms of Nirvana and transmigration of souls. A soul, they held, may suffer for thousands and millions of years before it is guided to the truth, purified, and rehabilitated to the good life at the end of which is Nirvana. Likewise, the Zoroastrians of Persia recognized the struggle of good and evil, and their gods were gods of light and darkness. So, too, did the Mosaic and the Christian religions, both of which describe a life of eternity dependent upon God's pleasure or wrath. Did the Arabs not know any of all this, though they were a people of trade in continual contact through their voyages with all the adherents of these religions? How could the case be otherwise? Why did they not have similar notions of their own when, as people of the desert, they were closer to infinity and eternity, to a conception of the spiritual existence induced by the heat of noon and the darkness of night, to good and evil spirits, which they had already conceived of as residing within the statues which interceded for them with God? Undoubtedly, they must have had an idea of the existence of the other world, but since they were a people of trade, they were more realistic and hence appreciative of that which they could see and touch. They were one and all *bon vivants* and, hence, all the more determined to deny punishment or reward in the hereafter. They thought that what man needs in this world is precisely the consequence of his deed whether good or evil. Further consequences of his deeds in the other world were therefore superfluous. That is why most of the revelations of Muḥammad which warned, threatened, and made promises concerning the other world were revealed in Makkah at the beginning of Muḥammad's commission. This revelation answered the need for saving those among whom Muḥammad was sent. It was natural that Muḥammad draw their attention as strongly as he could to their error and misguidance and that he call them to rise above idol worship to the worship of the One Almighty God.

For the Sake of Salvation

In the course of bringing spiritual salvation to his people and to all mankind, Muḥammad and his followers suffered great harm. They were subjected to many travails of body and spirit, to emigration, to alienation from peers and relatives, and they bore these sacrifices with gallantry and patience. It was as if the more his people harmed Muḥammad, the stronger became his love for them and the greater his desire and care to bring about their salvation. Resurrection and the day of judgment were the supreme ideas to which they were to give their attention if they were to be saved from their idolatry and evil deeds. Consequently, in the first years of Muḥammad's prophethood, revelation constantly repeated divine threats and warnings that the Makkans might open their eyes and recognize the veracity of resurrection and the Day of Judgment. It was this constant assault by revelation which, in final analysis, had inflamed the terrible war between Muḥammad and Makkah whose rage did not subside until God had given victory to Islām, His religion, over the religions of man.

8

From the Violation of the Boycott to al Isrā'

Calling the Tribes to Islām during the Holy Months

The pact into which the clans of Quraysh had entered for boycotting Muḥammad and blockading the Muslims continued to be observed for three consecutive years. During this time Muḥammad and his family and companions fortified themselves against attack in one of the hills within Makkah. In their isolation, however, they suffered all kinds of privations; often they could not find enough food to satisfy their hunger. It was not possible either for Muḥammad or the Muslims to mix with other people or to talk to them except during the holy months, when the Arabs would come to Makkah on pilgrimage and all hostilities would cease. In those months, no killing, persecution, aggression or vengence was permitted. Muḥammad used to approach the Arabs and call them unto the religion of God and warn them of His imminent punishment as well as announce to them the blessings of paradise. The pilgrims knew what Muḥammad had suffered in the cause of his mission, and this stirred their sympathy and compassion for him as well as their sensitivity to his call. Indeed, this boycott imposed by Quraysh, and Muḥammad's patient bearing of it for the sake of his cause, won for him and his cause many hearts. Not all men were as hard of feeling as Abū Jahl and Abū Lahab.

131

Blockade of the Muslims

The long duration of the blockade and, consequently, the great sufferings inflicted upon the Muslims by the Quraysh, caused a number of Makkans to realize the hardness and injustice to which their very brethren, in-laws, and cousins, had been subjected. Were it not for the few who compassionately furnished the Muslims food, the latter would have surely starved. Hishām ibn 'Amr was the most compassionate to the Muslims in their tragedy. He used to load his camel with food and other supplies, take it during the night and pass by the entrance to the quarter where the Muslims were isolated. He would detach the reins of the camel and let it go free, whipping it on the sides so that the camel would enter into the quarter and be seized by the Muslims. The more Muhammad and his companions suffered, the more disturbed a number of Qurayshīs became. Unable to withhold his compassion, Hishām ibn 'Amr went to Zuhayr ibn Abū Umayyah, whose mother was 'Ātikah, daughter of 'Abd al Muttalib. He said, "O Zuhayr, how could you eat and wear new clothes and marry and enjoy life when your uncles are locked up and isolated, unable to buy or purchase anything, to give or to take anyone in marriage? By God I swear that if the Muslims were the uncles of Abū al Hakam ibn Hishām and you had asked him to boycott them as he asked you to boycott the Muslims, he would have never fulfilled your request." Together the two men agreed to revoke the pact of the boycott and sought to convince others to do likewise, although secretly. Al Mut'am ibn 'Adiyy, Abū al Bakhtarī ibn Hishām, and Zam'ah ibn al Aswad agreed to denounce the pact of boycott and to work together for its repudiation.

One day after circumambulating the Ka'bah seven times, Zuhayr ibn Abū Umayyah addressed the Makkans: "O People of Makkah, would you that we eat food and enjoy ourselves while the Banū Hāshim are dying one after another unable to buy or acquire anything? By God, I shall not sit still until this unjust pact of the boycott is revoked." Upon hearing this, Abū Jahl immediately rose and said to Zuhayr, "You are a liar. The pact is sacred and inviolable." At this, Zam'ah, Abū al Bakhtarī, al Mut'am, as well as Hishām ibn 'Amr, rose from their places to argue against Abū Jahl and to confirm Zuhayr in his request. At this show of strength, Abū Jahl realized that a previous agreement must have been reached between these men and that direct opposition to them might not prove advantageous. He therefore withdrew. Al Muṭ'am rose to tear up the pact hanging on the wall of the Ka'bah only to find that insects had already devoured most of it except the opening words "In the name of God." At this, Muḥammad and his companions were permitted to come out of their isolation and circulate in Makkah, to buy and to sell as usual, although the antagonism and hostility remained as they were, and each party continued to look forward to a day when it could overcome the other.

Infallibility of Muḥammad in Conveying the Revelation

Some biographers claimed that the unbelievers who brought about the revocation of the boycott pact went to Muḥammad and asked him to make some gesture of reconciliation toward the Quraysh in order to strengthen them in their attempts and to put a stop to further harm. They asked him to agree to give their gods a place, at least to grant them occasional recognition with the fingers of his hand as the Makkans were accustomed to do. The same biographers claim that Muḥammad inclined toward doing some of this in gratitude for the good deeds just done to him. They even allege that he said to himself: "What blame is there if I do such a thing? God knows that I am innocent!" Other biographers report that the same men who helped revoke the pact of boycott went one evening to Muḥammad, talked to him all night, and praised him so much and endeared themselves to him, calling him "Our Master, Our Master," until he was moved to answer some of their demands. The first version was reported by Sa'īd ibn Jubayr; and the second by Qatādah. In both versions, it is reported that God protected Muḥammad against their subversion and revealed to him the following verse: "They have almost succeeded in inducing you, under promise of their friendship, to attribute to Us, against Our command, that which We did not reveal to you. Had We not confirmed you in your faith, you might have been tempted and hence fallen under the inescapable punishment."[1]

It should be remembered that these verses were claimed to have been revealed in connection with the forged story of the goddesses which we have investigated earlier; the present reporters attribute it to the story of the revocation of the boycott pact. The same verses have also been claimed by ibn 'Abbās, as reported by 'Atā', to have been revealed in connection with

another story. That is the story of the delegation of Thaqīf
who came to Muhammad to ask him to declare their valley holy
just as Makkah had declared her trees and birds and animals
holy. It is claimed that the Prophet—may God's peace be upon
him—hesitated until these verses were revealed. Whatever the
historical circumstances which occasioned the revelation of these
verses, the verses themselves bespeak the greatness of Muhammad
as well as his candidness. The same aspects of Muhammad's
personality are equally in evidence in the verses we have reported
from *Sūrah* 80. Indeed, they are supported by the history of
Muhammad's life as a whole. Muhammad had repeatedly told
the people that he was only a man, that as a man God had
revealed to him certain messages for their guidance, and that
without God's special protection in this regard he was as fallible
as anyone. Muhammad did in fact err when he frowned in the
face of ibn Umm Maktūm and sent him away. He almost erred
as reported above in the verses from the *sūrah* "al Isrā'" as
well as in the foregoing verses which tell of his inclination
away from that which had been revealed to him and of the
people's invitation to Muhammad to invent a revelation. But
revelation did, in fact, come to Muhammad and condemned what
he did in connection with the blind beggar, his near succumbing
to Quraysh's temptation. Muhammad, however, reported all
these revelations to the Quraysh people with equal truthfulness
and candidness. Neither self-esteem nor pride nor any other
human feeling prevented him from conveying the revelation,
whether it was for or against him. The truth and the truth alone
was the essence of his message. He declared the truth even
if it were against himself. We are accustomed to expect the
great man to bear resolutely and patiently whatever harm he
might be exposed to on account of his conviction, but we hardly
ever expect the great man to acknowledge that he almost succumbed to his temptations. Such temptations are usually not
talked about, and most great men are contented to reckon with
themselves strongly only in secret. He was therefore greater than
the great, for his soul enabled him to rise to the height where
it would acknowledge the truth even regarding its own struggle
and proclaim it to the public. Such greatness that is greater
than the great belongs exclusively to the prophets. It demands
of the prophet the very utmost in truthfulness and candidness
in the conveyance of the message of truth that comes from
God alone.

Death of Abū Ṭālib and Khadījah

After the repudiation of the boycott pact, Muḥammad and his companions emerged from their quarters. Muḥammad immediately resumed his call to the Quraysh and to the tribes that used to come to Makkah during the holy months. Despite the spreading of his fame among the Arab tribes and the number of his followers, neither he nor they were quite yet safe from injury, and nothing he could do would have guaranteed such safety. A few months later two tragedies were to add to his troubles. First, the death of Abū Ṭālib, his protector, and then that of Khadījah, his wife. Abū Ṭālib died at about the age of eighty. When Quraysh knew of his approaching end, they feared that the conflict with the Muslims would reach a new height now that their leadership would pass into the less temperate hands of Ḥamzah and 'Umar, well known for their hardness and determined hostility. The leaders of Quraysh went up to Abū Ṭālib and addressed him as he lay on his deathbed: "O Abū Ṭālib, we hold for you great respect and we appreciate your counsel and wisdom. Now that you are about to leave us, and, knowing the conflict that has arisen between us and your nephew, do please call him and ask him to give us assurance as we are wont to give you for him, that he will leave us alone and we will leave him alone, that he will leave us to practice our religion and we shall leave him to practice his." Muḥammad and his companions came to the meeting in his uncle's house. After he was told about their purpose he said: "Yes, indeed! All I want from you is this one word of assurance which, if given, will bring you mastery of all Arabia as well as Persia, namely . . ." "Speak out," interrupted Abū Jahl, "by your father we shall give it to you! Not one word but ten." Muḥammad continued: "Namely, that you witness with me that there is no God but God and repudiate all that you worship besides Him." Some of them said to Muḥammad: "Do you want to make all the gods one?" Turning to one another, the men of Quraysh said: "By God, this man is not going to give you any word of assurance such as you require." The leaders of Quraysh left Abū Ṭālib's house without satisfaction, and Abū Ṭālib died a few days later, the situation between him and the Quraysh being more hostile than ever before.

Later on, Khadījah, who supported Muḥammad with her love and goodness, her purity, gentleness and strong faith, passed away. At her death, Muḥammad lost an angel of mercy who reassured and reconciled him whenever he felt crushed under the burdens of his cause. Henceforth, Muḥammad was forever to miss the believing eyes of Khadījah and her reassuring smile, just as he had lost in Abū Ṭālib his protection and refuge from his enemies. How deeply these tragedies must have cut into Muḥammad's heart! Surely they were strong enough to shake the most determined soul, to bring doubt and despair to the most resolute, and to leave behind the greatest degree of emptiness and despondence.

Increase of Quraysh's Hostility

Soon thereafter, the Quraysh were to increase their attacks against Muḥammad. An example of the least of such injuries was the covering of Muḥammad's head with soil thrown at him by one of the plebeians of Quraysh. Muḥammad withdrew to his home where his daughter, Fāṭimah, moved to tears by the sight of her father, washed his head for him. It is certainly painful to us to hear our children cry, and more so to hear our daughters cry. Indeed, every tear dropped from a daughter's eye is a ball of fire fallen upon our hearts, causing us to cry in pain. The daughter's sob and painful murmur fall heavily upon the father's heart, and Fāṭimah's cries must have choked a compassionate father such as Muḥammad. However, what was he to do to reassure a person who had just lost her mother and who is now appalled by the insults heaped upon her father? Nothing but to orient himself all the more to God, and to proclaim his conviction that God would give him final victory. He said to his daughter: "Do not cry, O Fāṭimah! Your father has God for protector." Often Muḥammad would be heard saying: "By God. Quraysh never harmed me so much as after the death of Abū Ṭālib."

Muḥammad's Excursion to Ṭā'if (628 c.e.)

The Quraysh doubled and redoubled their injuries to Muḥummad and his followers until Muḥammad could bear it no longer. Alone, and without telling anyone, he undertook a trip to the city of Ṭā'if where he solicited the support of the tribe of Thaqīf after calling them to Islām. When they refused, he asked them not to spread the news of their refusal to his enemies that they might not rejoice at his failure. The tribe of Thaqīf, however, not only repudiated Muḥammad's call but sent their servants to insult him and throw him out of their city. He ran away from them and took shelter near a wall which belonged to 'Utbah and Shaybah, sons of Rabī'ah. There, he sat under a vine pondering his defeat, within sight of the sons of Rabī'ah. He raised his hands to heaven and prayed with noticeable pain: "O God, please consider my weakness, my shortage of means, and the little esteem that people have of me. Oh, most Merciful God, You are the Lord of the oppressed, and You are my Lord. To whom would You leave my fate? To a stranger who insults me? Or to an enemy who dominates me? Would I that You have no wrath against me! Your pleasure alone is my objective. Under the light of Your faith which illuminates all darkness and on which this world and the other depend, I take my refuge. I pray that I may not become the object of Your wrath and anger. To You alone belongs the right to blame and to chastise until Your pleasure is met. There is neither power nor strength except in You."

'Addās, the Christian

For some time, the sons of Rabī'ah watched Muḥammad until a feeling of compassion and sympathy for him began to stir within them. They sent their christian servant, 'Addās by name, with a bunch of grapes. Before Muḥammad partook of the grapes, he said: "In the name of God." 'Addās was surprised and said, "That is not what the natives of this country usually say." Muḥammad then asked him about his religion and his country of origin, and when he learned that he was a Christian from Nineveh, he said, "Are you then from the City of the Righteous Jonah, son of Mathew?" Still more surprised, 'Addās asked, "What do you know about Jonah, son of Matthew?" Muḥammad answered, "That was my brother; he was a true prophet and so am I." Moved with emotion, 'Addās covered Muḥammad with kisses. The two sons of Rabī'ah were surprised at what they saw although they remained unmoved by Muḥam-

mad's religious claims. When their servant returned to them
they counseled him: "O 'Addās, do not allow this man to convert you from your faith. Your faith is better for you than
his."

Muhammad Offers Himself to the Tribes

The news of the injuries inflicted upon Muhammad lightened
the hostility of the tribe of Thaqīf, but it never succeeded in
moving them to follow him. The Quraysh knew about this expedition and increased their injuries. Nothing, however, could
dissuade Muhammad from continuing his call. At every season,
whenever the tribes of Arabia came to Makkah, he offered
himself and his cause to them, informed them that he was a
commissioned prophet, and asked them to believe in him. His
uncle 'Abd al 'Uzzā, son of 'Abd al Muttalib, otherwise known
as Abū Lahab, would not let him; he would follow Muhammad
everywhere he went to dissuade the people from listening to
him. Muhammad, for his part, did not only preach his religion
to the tribes in the pilgrimage season in Makkah, but sought
those tribes in their own quarters. He visited the tribe of Kindah
and the tribe of Kalb, of Banū Hanīfah, Banū 'Āmir ibn Sa'sa'ah,
each in its own province. None of them responded favorably to
him, and they all repudiated his call—sometimes with insults,
as did the tribe of Banū Hanīfah. The tribe of Banū 'Āmir felt
more ambitious and imagined that they could assume a position
of leadership should the cause of Muhammad triumph. But when
Muhammad told them, "The matter belongs wholly to God; He
places leadership wheresoever He wishes," they turned away
and repudiated his call like the rest.

Did all these tribes repudiate Muhammad's call for the same
reasons for which Quraysh did before them? We have seen the
disappointment of the tribe of Banū 'Amir upon the frustration
of their ambition of leadership and power. As for the tribe of
Thaqīf, they had a different opinion. In addition to the cool
atmosphere and vineyards which made it a summer resort, the
city of Tā'if was the center of worship of al Lāt, for it was in
its midst that the idol stood and on its account the city had
become a place of pilgrimage. Should the tribe of Thaqīf follow
Muhammad, the goddess al Lāt would lose her place of worship,

the city its pilgrimage site, and ensuing hostility with Quraysh would soon cut off all summer visits by the Makkans. Every tribe had thus its own reason, economic or other, for which it refused to accept Islām besides the personal attachment to the religion of the fathers and the worship of old idols.

Muḥammad's Engagement to 'Ā'ishah

The rejection of Muḥammad by the tribes increased his isolation, as the doubled and redoubled injuries of the Quraysh increased Muḥammad's pain and grief. The period of mourning for Khadījah passed, and Muḥammad thought of marrying again in the hope of finding consolation in a new companion. He also thought that marriage might even furnish a new occasion for strengthening the bond of brotherhood and commitment between himself and the earlier converts to Islām. He therefore asked Abū Bakr for the hand of his daughter, 'Ā'ishah. Since she was still too young to marry, the engagement was announced, but the marriage was postponed for three more years until 'Ā'ishah reached the age of eleven. In the meantime, Muḥammad married Sawdah, the widow of one of the Muslim companions who emigrated to Abysinnia but died upon his return to Makkah. In both these instances, it is hoped that the reader will have a glimpse of the principle regulating Muḥammad's later domestic life which we shall discuss in a forthcoming chapter.

Al Isrā' (621 c.e.)

It was during this period that *al Isrā'* and *al Mi'rāj* had taken place.[2] On the night of *al Isrā'*. Muḥammad was staying in the house of his cousin, Hind, daughter of Abū Ṭālib, who was also called Umm Hāni'. Hind related that "The Prophet of God spent the night in my quarters. He recited his night prayers and went to sleep. Just before dawn, the Prophet of God awoke us and we all prayed the dawn prayer together. When the prayer was through, he said, "O Umm Hāni', I prayed with you the night prayer in this place; then I went to Jerusalem and I prayed there, and as you see, I have just finished praying with you the dawn prayer.' I answered, 'O Prophet of God, do not

tell this to the people for they will belie you and harm you.'
He said, 'By God I shall tell them.' "

Was al Isrā' in Body or in Soul?

Those who claim that al Isrā' and al Mi'rāj of Muhammad—
may God's peace be upon him—had taken place in soul rather
than in body refer to this report of Umm Hāni'. They also
refer to another report by 'Ā'ishah which says, "The body of
the Prophet of God—may God's peace and blessing be upon him—
was never missed from his bed. Rather, God caused him to
travel in soul alone." Whenever Mu'āwiyah ibn Abū Sufyān
was asked about al Isrā' of the Prophet, he used to answer, "It
was a true vision from God." Those who share such a view
confirm their claim with the Qur'ānic verse, "The vision which
We have shown you is but a trial to the people."[3] According
to the other view, al Isrā' from Makkah to Jerusalem took place
in body. In confirmation of this, they mention that Muhammad
had related what he saw in the desert on the way hither and
add that his ascension to heaven was in soul. Others hold that
both al Isrā' and al Mi'rāj were in body. As a result of this great
controversy, thousands of books have been written on the subject. We have a view of this matter which we shall give shortly,
a view that somebody else may have held before us. Before we
proceed, however, we shall give the story of al Isrā' and al Mi'rāj
as it was reported in the biography books.

Al Isrā' as Given in Literature

The Orientalist Dermenghem has reported the following eloquent story culled from a number of biography books. We shall
quote it as he related it:

"In the middle of a solemn, quiet night when even the night-
birds and the rambling beasts were quiet, when the streams
had stopped murmuring and no breezes played, Mahomet
was awakened by a voice crying: 'Sleeper, awake!' And
before him stood the Angel Gabriel with radiant forehead,
countenance white as snow, blond hair floating, in garments
sewn with pearls and embroidered in gold. Manifold wings
of every colour stood out quivering from his body.
"He led a fantastical steed, Boraq ('Lightning'), with a

human head and two eagles' wings; it approached Mahomet, allowed him to mount and was off like an arrow over the mountains of Mecca and the sands of the desert toward the North . . . The Angel accompanied them on this prodigious flight. On the summit of Mt. Sinai, where God had spoken to Moses, Gabriel stopped Mahomet for prayer, and again at Bethlehem where Jesus was born, before resuming their course in the air. Mysterious voices attempted to detain the Prophet, who was so wrapped up in his mission that he felt God alone had the right to stop his steed. When they reached Jerusalem Mahomet tethered Boraq and prayed on the ruins of the Temple of Solomon with Abraham, Moses, and Jesus. Seeing an endless ladder appear upon Jacob's rock, the Prophet was enabled to mount rapidly to the heavens.

"The first heaven was of pure silver and the stars suspended from its vault by chains of gold; in each one an angel lay awake to prevent the demons from climbing into the holy dwelling places and the spirits from listening indiscreetly to celestial secrets. There, Mahomet greeted Adam. And in the six other heavens the Prophet met Noah, Aaron, Moses, Abraham, David, Solomon, Idris (Enoch), Yahya (John the Baptist) and Jesus. He saw the Angel of Death, Azrail, so huge that his eyes were separated by 70,000 marching days. He commanded 100,000 battalions and passed his time in writing in an immense book the names of those dying or being born. He saw the Angel of Tears who wept for the sins of the world; the Angel of Vengeance with brazen face, covered with warts, who presides over the elements of fire and sits on a throne of flames; and another immense angel made up half of snow and half of fire surrounded by a heavenly choir continually crying: 'O God, Thou hast united snow and fire, united all Thy servants in obedience to Thy Laws.' In the seventh heaven where the souls of the just resided was an angel larger than the entire world, with 70,000 heads; each head had 70,000 mouths, each mouth had 70,000 tongues and each tongue spoke in 70,000 different idioms singing endlessly the praises of the Most High.

"While contemplating this extraordinary being, Mahomet was carried to the top of the Lote-Tree of Heaven flowering at the right of God's invisible throne and shading myriads

of angelic spirits. Then after having crossed in a twinkling
of an eye the widest seas, regions of dazzling light and
deepest darkness, traversed millions of clouds of hyacinths,
of gauze, of shadows, of fire, of air, of water, of void, each
one separated by 500 marching years, he then passed more
clouds—of beauty, of perfection, of supremacy, of im-
mensity, of unity, behind which were 70,000 choirs of angels
bowed down and motionless in complete silence. The earth
began to heave and he felt himself carried into the light
of his Lord, where he was transfixed, paralysed. From here
heaven and earth together appeared as if imperceptible to
him, as if melted into nothingness and reduced to the size
of a grain of mustard-seed in the middle of a field. And
this is how Mahomet admits having been before the Throne
of the Lord of the World.

"He was in the presence of the Throne 'at a distance of
two bows' length or yet nearer' (Koran, liii), beholding God
with his soul's eyes and seeing things which the tongue
cannot express, surpassing all human understanding. The
Almighty placed one hand on Mahomet's breast and the
other on his shoulder—to the very marrow of his bones he
felt an icy chill, followed by an inexpressible feeling of
calm and ecstatic annihilation.

"After a conversation whose ineffability is not honored by
too precise tradition, the Prophet received the command
from God that all believers must say fifty prayers each day.
Upon coming down from heaven Mahomet met Moses, who
spoke with him on this subject:

" 'How do you hope to make your followers say fifty
prayers each day? I had experience with mankind before
you. I tried everything with the children of Israel that it
was possible to try. Take my word, return to our Lord and
ask for a reduction.'

"Mahomet returned, and the number of prayers was
reduced to forty. Moses thought that this was still too many
and made his successor go back to God a number of times.
In the end God exacted not more than five prayers.

"Gabriel then took the Prophet to paradise where the
faithful rejoice after their resurrection—an immense garden
with silver soil, gravel of pearls, mountains of amber, filled
with golden palaces and precious stones.

"Finally, after returning by the luminous ladder to the earth, Mahomet untethered Boraq, mounted the saddle and rode into Jerusalem on the winged steed."[4]

Ibn Hishām's Report about al Isrā'

Such is the report of the orientalist Dermenghem concerning the story of *al Isrā'* and *al Mi'rāj*. Every item he reported may be readily found, perhaps with greater or lesser detail, in many of the biographies. An example of the fertility of the reporters' imagination may be read in ibn Hishām's biography. Reporting on Muhammad's conversation with Adam in the first heaven, ibn Hishām wrote: "Then I saw men with lips like those of camels. In their hands were balls of fire which they thrusted into their mouths and collected from their extremities to thrust into their mouths again. I asked, 'Who are these, O Gabriel?' He said: 'These are men who robbed the orphans.' I then saw men with large bellies, the likes of which I have never seen before even on the road to the house of Pharaoh where the greatest punishment is meted out to the greatest sinners. These are trodden upon by men who when brought to the fire run like maddened camels. Those whom they tread upon remain immobile, unable to move from their place. I asked, 'Who are those, O Gabriel?' He answered, 'Those are the usurers.' I then saw men sitting at a table loaded with delicious and fat meat as well as spoilt and stinking meat. They were eating of the latter and leaving the former untouched. I asked, 'Who are these, O Gabriel?' He answered, 'These are men who left their own women whom God had permitted them to enjoy and ran after other women illegitimately.' I then saw women hanging from their breasts and asked, 'Who are these, O Gabriel?' He answered, 'These are women who fathered on their husbands children not their own.' ... He then took me into Paradise where I saw a beautiful damsel with luscious lips. As I was attracted by her I asked her, 'To whom do you belong?' She answered: 'To Zayd ibn Hārithah.' The prophet of God—may God's peace and blessing be upon him—announced this glad tiding to Zayd ibn Hārithah."

Whether in ibn Hishām's or in other biographies of the Prophet or in the books of Qur'ānic exegesis, the reader will find many details besides the above-mentioned. It is certainly the historian's right to question how closely these reports have been scrutinized

and investigated by their collectors, with the view to finding
out how much of them may be truly ascribed to the Prophet
and how much was the invention of the fancy of the Ṣūfīs and
others. Although there is no room here to undertake such
investigation, nor to decide the issue of whether or not al Isrā'
or al Mi'rāj were both in body or in soul or the one in body
and the other in soul, there is still no doubt that every one of
these views has reasons which their advocates claim to be
legitimate. There is no a priori reason why one may not adhere
to one of these views rather than another. Whoever wishes to
hold the view that al Isrā' and al Mi'rāj were in soul and not
in body, could turn to the evidence of the reports we have
already cited as well as to the Qur'ānic emphasis that

قُلْ اِنَّمَاۤ اَنَا بَشَرٌ مِّثْلُكُمْ يُوحَىٰۤ اِلَیَّ اَنَّمَاۤ اِلٰهُكُمْ اِلٰهٌ وَّاحِدٌ ۚ فَمَنْ كَانَ يَرْجُوا لِقَآءَ رَبِّهِ فَلْيَعْمَلْ عَمَلًا
صَالِحًا وَّلَا يُشْرِكْ بِعِبَادَةِ رَبِّهٖۤ اَحَدًا

"I am but a human like you unto whom a revelation is given that
your God is one God;"[5] that the book of God is the sole "miracle"
of Muḥammad; and that "God does not forgive any association
of aught with Him but He forgives to whomsoever He wishes
anything else."[6]

Whoever holds a view of al Isrā and al Mi'rāj such as this is
perhaps better entitled to inquire about the meaning of these
ideas. And that is precisely the issue to which, perhaps for the
first time ever, we want to address ourselves in the following
sections.

Al Isrā' and the Unity of Being

As phenomena in the spiritual life of Muḥammad, al Isrā'
and al Mi'rāj carry great and noble meanings that are greater
than the foregoing descriptions have suggested—much of which
being the product of pure imagination. In the moment of al Isrā'
and al Mi'rāj, Muḥammad grasped the unity of being in all its
totality and perfection. In that moment, neither space nor time
could prevent his consciousness from encompassing all being;
whereas our consciousness, determined by weaker perceptive and
rational faculties, is incapable of transcending the limitations
of space and time. In that moment, all frontiers fell before

Muḥammad's insight; and all being was, as it were, gathered in his soul. In that moment, he came to know totality from beginning to end and represented this totality as the self-realization of the forces of goodness, truth, and beauty in their struggle against and conquest of evil, untruth, and fraud. All this happened to Muḥammad by God's grace.

No one is capable of such transcendent vision except by means of superhuman power. If any of the followers of Muḥammad were unable to match him in his struggle to rise to or to achieve such vision and perception, there should be neither blame nor surprise. Men's degrees of endowment differ, and their vision of the truth is always determined by these limitations which our ordinary powers are unable to transcend. There is perhaps an analogy between Muḥammad's understanding of the universe at that moment and that of any other person who has risen to the highest level of consciousness possible for man. It is that of the story of the blind men who, upon being brought into contact with the elephant, were asked to identify it. It will be remembered that the first thought it was a long rope because he had touched its tail; the second, a thick tree because he had touched its leg; the third, a spear because he had touched its ivory; and the fourth, a moving round tube because he had touched its trunk. These views are to the unimpaired view of the elephant as the understanding of most of us to that of Muḥammad, implied in *al Isrā'* and *al Miʿrāj*, of the unity and totality of being. In Muḥammad's vision, the finitude of space and time disappeared, and he beheld the universe all "gathered up" and present. Men capable of such great moments of consciousness see the details of space-time and problems of worldly living as mathematical atoms appended to the person without ever affecting him. None of them affect in the least the life of his body, the beat of his heart, the illumination of his soul, the enlightenment of his consciousness, nor his vibration with energy and life. For by existing, such a person enters into communion with all existence and all life, as it were, *ipso facto*.

A spiritual *Isrā'* and *Miʿrāj* cannot be different in its meanings of beauty, majesty, and transcendence than a bodily one.[7] In itself, the story is a very strong figurization of the spiritual unity of all being. Muḥammad's detour for a stop on Mount Sinai where God spoke to Moses face to face, at Bethlehem where Jesus was born, and the spiritual meeting of Muḥammad, Jesus, Moses and Abraham in the moment of prayer is another very strong figurization of the unity of religious experience and life, a unity constitutive of the world as it tends to value and perfection.

Al Isrā' and Modern Science

In our modern age, science confirms the possibility of a spiritual Isrā' and Mi'rāj. Where there is a meeting of genuine forces, that which shines forth is genuine reality; just as a meeting of the same forces of nature configured by the genius of Marconi, produced the real effect of lighting a light in distant Australia by means of an electric radiation directed at it on the waves of space from his ship in Venice. In this age of ours, science has confirmed the possibility of prestidigitation, of broadcast of sound through space by means of the radio, as well as of pictures and writing, all of which was considered too fanciful even for the imagination. The forces latent in nature are still being discovered by science, and every new day brings a new surprise. Strong and powerful spirits such as Muhammad's are perfectly capable of being carried in one night from Makkah to Jerusalem and of being shown God's signs. That is not opposed to reason, especially when the moral of it is the figurization of divine truths, of extraordinary meanings of beauty and transcendence, and of the unity of spirit and world so clearly achieved in the consciousness of Muhammad. Though extraordinary and unique to Muhammad, the experience is certainly possible for man upon removal of the illusions of this world, penetration of ultimate reality, and relation of oneself and the world thereto.

Doubt of Quraysh and Apostasy of Some Muslims

The Arabs of Makkah, however, were incapable of understanding such meanings. Therefore, as soon as Muhammad related his Isrā', they could not progress beyond the question of the possibility or otherwise of instantaneous bodily transportation to Jerusalem. Even those who followed Muhammad and believed in him were troubled by doubt. Some said, "This is clear and decisive. By God, camels run continually for a whole month to reach al Shām and another whole month to return. Would Muhammad achieve such a feat in one night?" Many of the Muslims apostatized. Those who were troubled by doubt went to Abū Bakr and related to him Muhammad's claim. Abū Bakr answered, "Surely you are telling me lies." They said, "There is Muḥammad in the mosque telling the people of his trip." Abū Bakr answered, "By God, if Muḥammad himself has said so, then it is true. He tells us that the word of God comes to him directly from heaven to earth in an hour of night or day and we believe him. Isn't this a greater miracle than what you are doubting today?" Abū Bakr came to the Prophet and listened to him describing Jerusalem and its mosque. When he finished, Abū Bakr said, "You said the truth, O Prophet of God." From that day on Muḥammad called Abū Bakr *"al Ṣiddīq."*[8]

Al Isrā' in Body

Those who claim that *al Isrā'* took place in body explain, in support of their view, that when the Prophet proclaimed the news, Muslims and non-Muslims asked him for proof. Muḥammad described to them a caravan of camels he had encountered on the road to Jerusalem. He related how he led the leaders of that caravan to one of their beasts which had gone astray in the desert, how he drank from a water jar carried on the back of one of those camels, and how he lowered the lid of the jar after he drank from it. They related that the Quraysh had inquired about that caravan and that the reports of the caravan leaders confirmed Muḥammad's claim and description. On the other hand, those who believe that *al Isrā'* took place in spirit do not find such reports unbelievable now that science in our own days has confirmed the possibility of hypnotism and of the hypnotized one to report about events far removed from him. For a spirit holding in unity and presence the spiritual life of the universe *in toto,* for one so endowed with vision and power so as to penetrate the secret of all life from eternity to eternity, such a feat is not at all surprising.

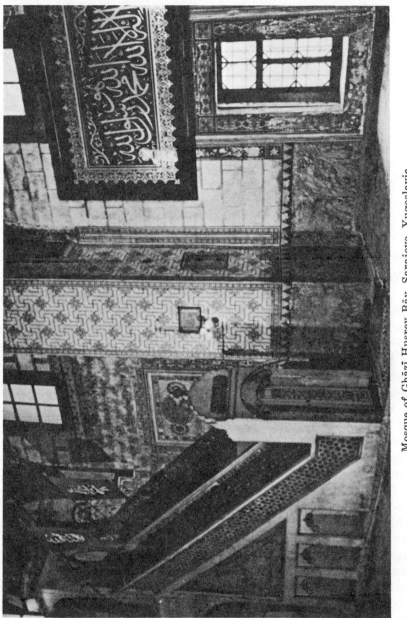

Mosque of Ghāzī Husrev Bāy, Sarajevo, Yugoslavia.

9

The Two Covenants
of al 'Aqabah

Muslim Weakness after al Isrā'

Quraysh did not understand the meanings behind *al Isrā'*. Neither did many of the Muslims who themselves apostatized in consequence, as we saw earlier. Encouraged by this relapse, Quraysh intensified its attacks against Muḥammad and his followers until they could cope with it no more. Muḥammad's hope of enlisting the tribes into his ranks was dissipated after his rejection by Thaqīf at al Ṭā'if, as well as by the tribes of Kindah, Kalb, Banū 'Āmir and Banū Ḥanīfah at their annual pilgrimage in Makkah. After all these experiences, Muḥammad nearly gave up hope of converting any more men from Quraysh. Realizing the isolation imposed upon Muḥammad and the irreconcilable opposition of Quraysh to his cause, the other tribes of the Peninsula, especially those surrounding or having business relations with Makkah, became all the more reluctant to receive his calls. Despite his reliance upon Ḥamzah and 'Umar, and his confidence that Quraysh could not harm him any more than they had already done on account of the tribal loyalties and alliances involved, Muḥammad realized that the spread of God's call, limited as it were to a small number of weak people, exposed to the danger of apostasy or extermination, had come to a halt unless some victory from God was forthcoming. Days passed while Muḥammad's increasing isolation kept pace with Quraysh's ever-growing enmity.

Muḥammad's Fastness

Did this isolation of Muhammad weaken his determination or impair his morale? No! Rather, it strengthened his faith in the truth which had come to him from his Lord. Such travails would have discouraged any person of ordinary spirit; but the noble, the truly gifted, they can only be stimulated to higher levels of conviction, of resolution, and self-exertion. Rather than being shaken, Muḥammad and his companions continued to have the strongest faith that God would raise His religion above all religions and bring victory to them in the process. The storms of hatred raging around them did not shake the faith. Muḥammad spent his year in Makkah unconcerned that his and Khadījah's wealth was being rapidly exhausted to the point that poverty and want were imminent. Only the victory which he was absolutely certain God soon would grant him occupied his thought. When the season of pilgrimage came again and men from all over the Arabian Peninsula gathered in Makkah, he renewed his call to the revealed truth, undaunted by any violent rejection with which these tribes might meet his call. The plebeians of Makkah renewed their attacks against his person whenever he preached in public, but their injuries did not reduce Muḥammad's self assurance. He knew that it was Almighty God who sent him a messenger of the truth, that there could be no doubt but that God would confirm His truth and give it victory. He knew that God had asked him always to present his revelations to men with arguments yet more sound and gentle, counseling "and then, your enemy will become your very warm friend."[1] He knew too well that God has asked him to be gentle to men that they might remember and fear. It was in this certainty, therefore, that Muhammad received the attacks of the Quraysh and bore patiently their injuries and harm. All along, he knew that God is always with the patient.

The First Signs of Victory in Yathrib

Muḥammad did not have to wait more than a few years before the first signs of victory began to loom on the horizon, in the direction of Yathrib. Muḥammad was related to Yathrib in ways other than trade. He had relatives in Yathrib. Moreover, in Yathrib was his father's grave. In Yathrib lived Banū al Najjār, uncle of his ancestor 'Abd al Muṭṭalib, and hence his

relative. To that grave, Āminah, the loyal wife, as well as 'Abd
al Muṭṭalib, the father who lost his son at the very height of his
youth and power used to come for yearly visits. Muḥammad himself accompanied his mother to Yathrib when he was six years
old and visited his father's grave with her. On their way back
to Makkah, his mother, Āminah, fell ill and died and was buried
at al Abwā' midway between Yathrib and Makkah. It was no
surprise to Muḥammad that the first sign of victory came from
a town to which he was so closely associated, a town which stood
in the direction of al Aqṣā Mosque in Jerusalem, toward which
he prayed and where stood the shrines of his two predecessors,
Moses and Jesus. No wonder that circumstances prepared the
town of Yathrib for this great destiny that Muḥammad might
achieve victory therein and that it might become the capital
from which Islām was to conquer and to spread over the world.

Al Aws, al Khazraj, and the Jews

For this illustrious career, the town of Yathrib was better
fitted than any other. Both al Aws and al Khazraj were idolaters
sharing their town with the Jews whom they hated and often
fought, and were hated and fought by them. History relates
that the Christians of al Shām who then belonged to the dominant church in the East Roman Empire hated the Jews very
strongly, regarding them as the crucifiers and torturers of Jesus.
These Christians had raided Yathrib in the past for the express
purpose of killing its Jewish citizens. When they could not succeed, they sought the assistance of al Aws and al Khazraj in
order to draw the Jews of Madīnah into their trap. Such a
plan was responsible for the death of many a Jew and deprived
the Jewish community of its dominion and power within the
city. It also raised al Aws and al Khazraj to a position of power
greater than that which trade relations with the Byzantines
had hitherto established for them. History further relates that
once more the Madinese tried to destroy Jewish power in their
city in order to extend their possessions and influence, and that
they had succeeded. The surviving Jews hated al Aws and al
Khazraj deeply. Enmity was hence deeply rooted in the hearts
of both. However, the followers of Moses were quick to realize
that they neither had the power nor the numbers needed to

meet force with force, and that continuation of such adventures would in the end result in their own extermination should al Aws and al Khazraj ever find allies among their own co-religionists in Arabia. Hence they changed their tactics and, instead of victory in battle, they sought to divide and separate al Aws from al Kharzaj and cause the two tribes to hate and fight each other. In this they succeeded far better, for the two tribes were soon at each other's throats. Through the continuing hostility of the two Arab tribes, the Jews secured their position, increased their trade and wealth, and re-established the dominion, possession, and prestige which they had once enjoyed.

The Jews' Spiritual Influences

Besides this competition for power and dominion, there is a sphere in which the Jews exerted greater influence upon al Aws and al Khazraj than they had over any other tribe of Arabia. That is the realm of the spirit. As adherents of a mono-theistic faith, the Jews had been castigating their idolatrous neighbors for worshipping at the feet of idols which they took to be intercessors for them with God. The Jews had been threat-ening them with the prediction that soon a prophet would arise among the Arabs who would destroy them and ally himself to the Jews. Nonetheless, they did not succeed in judaizing the Arabs for two reasons: the first was that perpetual enmity be-tween Christianity and Judaism did not allow the Jews to enter-tain any hope of political dominion in Yathrib. To realize for themselves a measure of security and prosperity through trade was the highest desideratum to which they would aspire. The second was that the Jews had thought of themselves as God's chosen people and objected that any other people might share with them such favored position. They do not missionarize their faith, for they do not wish for it to include other than their own people, the children of Israel. This notwithstanding, neigh-borliness and trade between Arab and Jew enabled al Aws and al Khazraj to become more familiar with and more prepared for spiritual and religious discussion than other tribes. The evidence of this preparation is in the fact that nowhere had the Arabs responded to Muhammad's spiritual call with the same understanding and enthusiasm.

Suwayd ibn al Ṣāmit

Suwayd ibn al Ṣāmit was one of the noblest men of Yathrib. His people called him "the perfect" for his bravery, his eloquent poetry, his great honor, and his noble lineage. During this period Suwayd, who came to Makkah for pilgrimage, was approached by Muḥammad, who called him unto God and Islām. Suwayd said, "Perhaps what you have, Muḥammad, is like that which I have." Muḥammad answered, "What is it that you have?" He answered, "The wisdom of Luqmān." Muḥammad asked him to explain this wisdom, and after hearing him, he said: "Your words are good, but those which I have are even better. For they are a Qur'ān revealed by God to me as light and guidance." He read to him the Qur'ān and called him to Islām. Suwayd was pleased with what he heard, and said: "That is indeed good." When he left Muḥammad, he was in deep thought; there are reports that when al Khazraj killed him he had already become a Muslim.

Iyās ibn Muʿādh

Suwayd ibn al Ṣāmit was not the only example of the spiritual influence of the Jews upon the Arabs of Yathrib. The Jews had not only instigated the enmity of al Aws for al Khazraj and vice versa, but fanned its flames as well. This enmity caused each of the two hostile tribes to seek alliances with other tribes to consolidate its power. It was in search of an alliance from the Quraysh against al Khazraj that Abū al Ḥaysar Anas ibn Rāfiʿ came to Makkah with a number of men from Banū ʿAbd al Ashhal, including Iyās ibn Muʿādh. After Muḥammad heard of their arrival, he visited with them for a while, calling them unto Islām and reading to them the Qur'ān. When he finished, Iyās ibn Muʿādh, still young and of tender age, rose and said: "O my people, this is by God far better than your religion." The delegation returned to Yathrib with one convert to Islām, namely Iyās. Apparently, they were too busy to listen attentively to Muḥammad's preaching and too preoccupied with their war preparations. Upon the return of Abū al Ḥaysar and his delegation from Makkah, al Aws engaged them in the war of Buʿāth where both parties suffered grave losses. Nonetheless, the words of Muḥammad—may God's peace be upon him—left such a deep impression upon them that both al Aws and al Khazraj came to see in Muḥammad a prophet, a messenger of God, and a worthy spiritual leader.

The Battle of Bu'āth

Al Aws fought the battle of Bu'āth against al Khazraj in which both tribes gave full vent to their chronic enmity and hostility. So fierce did the battle rage that each party was seriously considering exterminating the enemy and finishing with the affair once and for all if it could only achieve victory. Abū Usayd was the general not only of the legions of al Aws but of their hate and resentment as well. In the first round of battle, al Aws lost and they ran toward the desert for their lives. Al Khazraj, who accused them of cowardice, began to sing in verse of their unmanliness and poltroonery. When Abū Usayd heard this, he plunged his own spear in his leg, fell from his horse and shouted, "Woe! Woe! By God I shall not move from this spot until they kill me. If you my people must forsake me, go ahead and run." Moved by this sacrifice of their own leader, al Aws returned to the battle with such enthusiasm and resoluteness—indeed despair—that they inflicted a terrible defeat upon al Khazraj. Pressing forth against their enemy, they burnt their houses as well as their orchards until stopped by Sa'd ibn Mu'ādh al Ashhalī. Indeed Abū Usayd had intended to wipe out the Khazraj tribe completely, house by house, tree by tree, and person by person, until not one of them remained alive. Abū Qays ibn al Aslat, however, stood in his way and begged him to save al Khazraj saying, "They are your co-religionists; it would still behoove you to keep them alive. They would be better neighbors for you than the foxes and beasts of prey of the desert."

Islāmic Beginnings in Yathrib

After that day, the Jews recaptured their position of dominance in Yathrib. Both conqueror and vanquished realized the tragedy of what they had done, and they pondered their fate with gravity. Together they looked forward toward appointing a king to manage their affairs, a choice to fall upon 'Abdullah ibn Muḥammad, of the vanquished al Khazraj, on account of his wisdom and sound opinions. The situation, evolved too rapidly, however, to allow a realization of this dream. A group of al Khazraj made a pilgrimage to Makkah where, they were met by Muḥammad and asked about their affairs. The Prophet knew they were clients of the Jews. In order to keep their clients in check, the Jews used to threaten them that a new prophet was about to appear whom they would follow and bring to any of their enemies that dared oppose them the total destruction which was meted out to the ancient tribes of 'Ad and Iram. When the Prophet talked to this group and called them unto God, they looked to one another and said, "By God, this is the Prophet by whom the Jews had threatened us. Let us acclaim him before they do." They responded favorably to Muḥammad's call, were converted, and said, "We have left our people, al Aws and al Khazraj, who are alienated from one another and are full of hatred for one another. Would to God that they might meet you and unite under your leadership! Should this ever become the case, you will be the strongest man in Arabia." The group included in their numbers two men from Banū al Najjār, the uncles of 'Abd al Muṭṭalib, and the grandfather of Muḥammad who had protected him ever since his birth; the latter returned to Madīnah and reported to their people their conversion to the new faith. The relatives received the news with joy and enthusiasm, for now they could boast of a religion that made them monotheists like the Jews—indeed more excellent than they. Soon, there was no house in al Aws or al Khazraj in which the name of Muḥammad—God's peace by upon him—was not mentioned with reverence and awe.

The First Covenant of 'Aqabah

As the year passed and the holy months and the pilgrimage season returned, twelve men from Yathrib set out for Makkah. They met the Prophet at al 'Aqabah and entered with him into an alliance known as "the first covenant of al 'Aqabah." In this covenant they agreed to adhere to the absolute unity of God, neither to steal nor to commit adultery, neither to kill their children nor knowingly to commit any evil, and not to fail to obey God in His commandment of any good. They were satisfied that, in case they succeeded in living the life of virtue and obedience, their reward would be paradise; otherwise, their judgment belonged to God, His being the power to punish as well as to forgive. On their return to Yathrib, Muḥammad sent with them Mus'ab ib 'Umayr to teach them the Qur'ān and the precepts of Islām. After this covenant, Islām spread in

Yathrib. Muṣ'ab resided with the Muslims of al Aws and al Khazraj and taught them the religion of God and the revelation of truth while their numbers increased with new converts every day. When the holy months returned, Muṣ'ab traveled to Makkah and reported to Muḥammad the progress of the Muslims at Madīnah in solidarity and power and informed the Prophet that a greater number of them, surpassing their predecessors in faith, would be arriving this season to perform the pilgrimage.

Muḥammad Thinks of Emigration

Muḥammad pondered the news which Muṣ'ab had brought for a long time. He thought of his followers in Yathrib who were increasing in number and power and who were progressing without let or hindrance from either Jews or others, unlike their colleagues in Makkah who suffered from Quraysh at every turn. He thought of Yathrib, the city of greater prosperity than Makkah on account of its large fields, its orchards and vineyards. It must have occurred to him to ask whether it might not be better that the Makkan Muslims emigrate to Yathrib, live with their co-religionists, and enjoy the security they missed so much at Makkah. In all likelihood, he pondered the observation which a member of the first group of converts from Yathrib once made, namely, that should al Aws and al Khazraj unite under him, he would be the strongest man in the country. Was it not better, now that God had united them under him, that he, too, should consider to emigrate to Yathrib? Muhammad did not want to return the injuries of Quraysh since he knew he was still weaker than they. As for his allies, Banū Hāshim and Banū al Muṭṭalib, it is one thing for them to come to his rescue as a sufferer of their injustice, but a totally different matter for them to support him in a war of aggression against the Quraysh. He also pondered the fact that Banū Hāshim and Banū al Muṭṭalib were not really capable of protecting all the Muslims in such an open war with Quraysh. It is true that religious conviction is man's strongest and most precious possession, for which he is prepared to sacrifice wealth, peace, freedom and life itself. It is equally true that the nature of religious conviction is such that physical injury inflames as well as strengthens it. Nonetheless, it is also true that persistence of injury, suffering, and sacrifice rob the believer of the possibility of the peaceful contemplation and precise vision necessary for the nourishment of faith and the deepening of man's awareness of ultimate reality. Previously,

Muḥammad had commanded his followers to emigrate to Christian Abyssinia because of its sound faith and just rule. There was all the more reason now to permit them to emigrate to Yathrib, to strengthen and be strengthened by their fellow Muslims in order to achieve a measure of peace and security against the evil designs of the enemy. There was all the more reason to ask them to do so in order to give them the chance to contemplate the religious truths, to cultivate their understanding, and to preach their faith to their fellow men. Islām had ruled out coercion and propagated itself through gentleness, persuasion, and conviction by argument alone.

The Second Covenant of 'Aqabah

The year 622 C.E. saw a great number of pilgrims, seventy-three men and two women, from Yathrib. When Muḥammad learned of their arrival, he thought of concluding another pact with them which would not be limited to the preaching of Islām in the way followed during the last thirteen years. Beyond the preaching of gentleness and forbearance and sacrifice under attack, the times and their present dangers called for an alliance by which the Muslims would help one another to prevent as well as to repel injury and aggression. Secretly Muḥammad contacted the leaders of the group and learned of their good preparation for a task such as this. They agreed to meet at al 'Aqabah during the night on the second day following the pilgrimage. The Muslims of Yathrib kept this appointment secret and did not inform the unbelievers among their own tribe. When the time came, they went to their rendezvous with the Prophet, stealing themselves away under the cover of night. When they reached al 'Aqabah, men and women ascended the mountain and there awaited the arrival of the Prophet.

Muḥammad arrived with his uncle al 'Abbās ibn 'Abd al Muṭṭalib. Al 'Abbās, who had not yet converted to Islām, knew from his nephew that this meeting was to conclude an alliance which might incite Quraysh to a war of aggression as much as it was designed to achieve peace and security. Muḥammad had informed his uncle that together with some members of Banū al Muṭṭalib and Banū Hāshim he had agreed with the new group from Yathrib that they would protect him personally. Anxious to strengthen his nephew and people against a war whose losses might fall heavily upon Banū Hāshim and Banū al Muṭṭalib, al 'Abbās sought to make sure that among this group from

Yathrib he would find real helpers and allies. Consequently, he was the first one to open the discussion. He said, "O men from Khazraj, Muḥammad's eminence and prestige among us are known to you. We have protected him even against those of his own people who think as highly of him as we do. Among us, he stands strong and secure. But he insists on joining your party. If you find yourselves capable of fulfilling toward him what you have promised, then you may proceed. But if you would betray him and send him over to his enemies once he has joined your party, you had better now say so and leave him alone." After hearing this speech of al 'Abbās, the men from Yathrib said, "We have heard what you said, O 'Abbās," and turning to the Prophet, they continued, "O Prophet of God, speak out and choose for yourself and your Lord what you desire."

Muḥammad, after reciting some verses from the Qur'ān, preached his faith in God in moving terms. He then said to the men from Yathrib, "I covenant with you on the condition that you will protect me against all, just as you would protect your women and children." Al Barā' ibn Ma'rūr, who was chief of his people and their elder, had entered into Islām after the first covenant of al 'Aqabah. Since then he had been fulfilling all that Islām required of him, except that he directed himself toward the Ka'bah whenever he prayed. Muḥammad and all the Muslims were in the practice of turning their faces toward al Aqsā mosque in Jerusalem. His disagreement with his people on the subject of the *qiblah* was brought to the attention of the Prophet upon their arrival to Makkah. The Prophet enjoined al Barā' not to turn his face toward the Ka'bah during prayer. Nonetheless, it was the same al Barā' who first stretched forth his hand to covenant with the Prophet when the latter asked for the protection that the people of Yathrib were wont to give their women and children.

Discussion before Conclusion of the Covenant

Al Barā' said, "We have covenanted with you, O Prophet of God. By God, we are men of many wars; we are men of the sword, having inherited it from father unto son." Before al Barā' finished his words, Abū al Haytham ibn al Tayyihān said, "O Prophet of God, there are pacts between us and some Jews which we are going to denounce. Should your cause succeed later on among your own tribe, would you return to them and leave us alone?" Muḥammad smiled and said, "No! Rather, your blood

is my blood and your destruction is my destruction. You are of
me and I am of you. I shall fight whomsoever you fight and
make peace with whomsoever you will make peace." The people
were about to rise and give covenant to Muḥammad when al
'Abbās ibn 'Ubādah interrupted and said, "O men of Khazraj!
Are you fully aware of what you are about to covenant with
this man? You are about to covenant with him to make war
against all sorts of men without discrimination. If you have
any fear that, should you lose your wealth and should your
leaders fall by the sword, you might betray Muḥammad, say
so now and withdraw from this covenant. For if you do not
and then betray your oath, you will have lost this world as
well as the next. But if you feel certain that you can stand by
him and fulfill this oath, notwithstanding the loss of your property and the murder of your dear ones, then go ahead and
covenant with him. He is, by God, the best gain in this world
and in the next."

All the people present answered together, "We take him
despite all threats to property, wealth and life. Tell us, O
Prophet of God, what will be our reward'if we remain true
to this oath?" With his usual self-reliance Muhammad answered,
"Paradise." They stretched out their hands to him, and he to
them, and the covenant was concluded. Thereafter, the Prophet
said, "Elect among yourselves twelve representative who will be
responsible to me regarding your behavior and conduct." After
they elected nine from al Khazraj and three from al Aws, the
Prophet addressed them in the following words: "You are the
guarantors of your people, just as the disciples were guarantors
of theirs before Jesus, Son of Mary. I, for my part, am the
guarantor of my people." Such was their second covenant which
included the words, "We have covenanted to listen and to obey
in health and in sickness, in fortune and misfortune, to tell the
truth wherever we might be and, at all times, to fear none
in the cause of God."

The Covenant

All this had taken place in the middle of the night atop one
of the hills of al 'Aqabah in perfect isolation from the surrounding world. Only God, the covenantors felt certain, knew what
they were about. No sooner had they terminated their meeting,
however, than they heard a crier warning the Quraysh in the
following words, "Muḥammad and the apostates have covenanted

to make war against you." The case of this, however, was unique. He had heard a little bit about the matter as he traveled to al 'Aqabah and, being a Qurayshī and idolator, he thought of spoiling the arrangement of Muḥammad and of frightening the Muslims by pretending everything the Muslims did was known to their enemies. Al Khazraj and al Aws, however, stood firm by their covenant. Indeed, al 'Abbās ibn 'Ubādah told Muḥammad immediately after he heard the crier, "By God, who has sent you with the truth, if you order us to pounce upon Minā tomorrow morning with our swords, we shall do so." Muḥammad answered, "God has not commanded us to fight. Return to your quarters." The covenanters returned to their quarters and slept until the morning.

Quraysh and the Covenant of al 'Aqabah

The morrow had hardly come when the Quraysh, learning of the new pact, was disturbed by it. The Quraysh leaders went to al Khazraj in their own quarters and blamed them for what they had just done. The Quraysh reiterated that they sought no war against them and asked them why they had covenanted with Muḥammad to fight them on his side. The unbelievers of al Khazraj denied that any of this had taken place. The Muslims, on the other hand, kept silent and were saved from embarrassment when the Quraysh believed the claim of their co-religionists. Thus the news was neither confirmed nor denied, and the Quraysh allowed the matter to stand until new evidence could be brought forth. The people of Yathrib returned to their city before the Quraysh had reached any certainty about what had happened. When later the Quraysh did learn the truth, they ran after the people of Yathrib who had exited the day before but could catch up with none except Sa'd ibn 'Ubādah. They took him to Makkah in chains and tortured him until Jubayr ibn Mut'am ibn 'Adiyy and al Ḥārith ibn Umayyah ransomed him as their agent in Yathrib when they passed by there on their way to al Shām.

Tension between the Two Parties

Neither in its fear of them nor in its attempt to catch up with the people of Yathrib, who covenanted with Muḥammad to fight against them, did the tribe of Quraysh overestimate the danger. For thirteen long years they had known and observed

Muḥammad. They had exerted enough effort in their war against
Muḥammad to exhaust their own as well as Muḥammad's energies. The Quraysh knew Muḥammad to be a very strong and
tenacious man who held only to his God and the message He
had entrusted to him. The Quraysh knew him as an unwavering
man who feared neither harm nor death. For a moment it seemed
to the Quraysh that after all the injuries they inflicted upon
him, after blockading him within Makkah, and frightening the
tribesmen enough to keep them from joining him, Muḥammad's
cause was about to fall. They predicted that Muḥammad's activity
would henceforth be restricted to his followers alone and that
these would soon fall apart under the constant pressures of
Quraysh to seek reconciliation. The new covenant brought a new
determinant into the situation and gave Muhammad and his
followers some hope of victory. It at least strengthened their
freedom to conduct their missionary activity and renew their
attack upon the idols of the Ka'bah and their worship. But who
could predict what the situation would turn out to be throughout
the Arabian Peninsula after Yathrib had come to the rescue
of Muḥammad and both its tribes of al Aws and al Khazraj
were united under his leadership? The Quraysh were rightly apprehensive of the future since the covenant of al 'Aqabah
rendered the Muslims safe against attack and gave them freedom
to practice their new faith, to preach it to the others, and to
welcome the new converts under their protection. Quraysh
thought, therefore, that unless this movement was uprooted and
destroyed completely, the future would continue to be threatening
and the victory of Muḥammad would be a most disturbing
possibility.

The Quraysh thought very hard how it could counter-attack
Muḥammad and outmaneuver him in order to destroy this latent
power. He, too, gave the same problem no less thought than
did the Quraysh. He looked upon the covenant as a gate which
God had unlocked before him in order to bring power and
glory to His religion, to God's truthful words. The war between
him and the Quraysh had then reached a new level of tension
by becoming a matter of life and death for both parties.
Muḥammad trusted, however, that victory belonged to the truthful. He decided to rally his people to trust in God, in utter
disregard to Quraysh and its plotting. He therefore must march
forward, but with wisdom, precision, and sure step. The new
situation called for the greatest possible statesmanship and the
ablest generalship in time of battle.

The Muslims' Emigration to Yathrib

Subsequently, Muḥammad commanded his companions to follow *al Anṣār*[2] in Yathrib. He ordered them to exit from Makkah in very small groups so that they would not give cause to Quraysh to suspect or attack them. The Muslims began their exodus individually or in small groups. When the Quraysh realized what they were about, it began to return those whom it could catch to Makkah to suffer punishment and torture. This Makkan counter-measure was carried out with such zeal and determination that man and wife were separated whenever a pair wanted to exit from Makkah. Those who disobeyed were locked up in jail. But the Quraysh could not do more, fearful as they were of alienating the tribes by killing their Muslim members and thereby adding to their list of enemies. The Muslims, nonetheless, continued to exit from Makkah and to emigrate to Yathrib. Muḥammad remained where he was, nobody knowing whether he, too, was planning to emigrate or not. None suspected him. Previously, he had permitted his companions to emigrate to Abyssinia without going there himself; he had stayed behind and continued to call the Makkans to Islām. Indeed, even Abū Bakr asked the Prophet for permission to emigrate to Yathrib. The Prophet advised, "Do not hurry; perhaps God may yet give you a companion for your trip." No more was said regarding this matter.

The Quraysh and the Prophet's Emigration

All this notwithstanding, the Quraysh were quite apprehensive lest the Prophet himself emigrate to Yathrib. The Muslims in that city had become so numerous that the dominion of the city was almost theirs. The *Muhajirūn*,[3] who were arriving at Yathrib in numbers, consolidated and increased Muslim power. Should Muḥammad himself go there, the Quraysh feared that under his wise and farsighted leadership and persistence, the people of Yathrib might even seek to attack Makkah or, at least, to cut off their trade route to al Shām. If this should ever become a real possibility, the Muslims would avenge the boycott and isolation of the Muslims in kind by cutting off the Makkan trade routes.

On the other hand, even if the Quraysh were to succeed in keeping Muḥammad in Makkah and thus prevent him from joining his companions, the Quraysh were still exposed to the danger of the people of Yathrib's attacking them in defense of their Prophet. Hence, the Quraysh decided that there was really no alternative but to kill Muhammad and get rid of this persistent trouble once and for all. But in case they did succeed in killing him, Banū Hāshim and Banū al Muttalib would surely seek to avenge his blood, and the civil war which they feared so much would break out within Makkah and bring a greater danger than that which they feared might come from the side of Yathrib. In al Nadwah, their community house, the Quraysh gathered in order to find a means and solution. One of them suggested, "Let us catch Muhammad and lock him up in jail. Then, wait to see happen to him that which has happened to other possessed people and poets like Zuhayr, al Nābighah, and others." This view found no supporters. Another suggested, "Let us carry him out of our country and banish him and then forget about him altogether." This, too, found no supporters because the Quraysh feared that Muhammad might then join his followers in Yathrib and lead them against Makkah—a frightful possibility, indeed. Finally, they concluded that the best solution is that each one of their clans delegate a strong youth and arm him with a sharp sword so that all these delegates can kill Muhammad together in one stroke; therefore, responsibility for his death would be equally divided among all, thus making vengeance on the part of Banū 'Abd Manāf virtually impossible. The clan of Muhammad would then be forced to accept his bloodwit, and the Quraysh would put an end to this instigator who had rent its unity and sapped its power. The Quraysh thought well of this counsel and carefully chose their executioners. They expected that the story of Muhammad was soon to come to a close, that his cause would soon be buried and forgotten, and that those who had migrated to Yathrib would soon return to their tribe, their former religion and gods, and that Quraysh would resume the unity and leadership which it had almost lost.

Al Hijrah or the Prophet's Emigration

The Command to Emigrate

Muḥammad discovered that the Quraysh had plotted to kill him rather than to allow him to emigrate to Madīnah where he might entrench the forces of Islām for a resolute stand against Makkah and from where he might cut off its trade with al Shām. No one doubted that Muḥammad would henceforth seize any opportunity to carry out his plan for emigration. But no one knew of any plans he might have had; not even Abū Bakr, who had been commanded to keep two beasts alert and ready ever since he asked the Prophet for permission to emigrate and the Prophet advised him to wait. Muḥammad remained in Makkah until he learned of the Quraysh's plot to assassinate him, and until none but the fewest Muslims were still left there with him. He waited for the command of his Lord for emigration. When, finally, that command did come, he went to the house of Abū Bakr and informed him of the permission God had granted. He asked Abū Bakr to accompany him on the trip.

'Alī in the Prophet's Bed

Here begins one of the greatest adventures history has known in the cause of truth and religious conviction. It is one of the noblest and most beautiful. Abū Bakr had chosen his two beasts and given them to 'Abdullah ibn Urayqit to graze until the time when they would be needed. When the two men planned to leave Makkah they were absolutely certain that Quraysh would follow them in their trail in order to seize them and bring them back. Hence, Muhammad decided to surprise his enemies by leaving under circumstances and at a time hardly conceivable to them. The young men whom the Quraysh had prepared for performing the assassination had blockaded his house during the night in fear that he might run away. On the night of the Hijrah, Muhammad confided his plan to 'Alī ibn Abū Ṭālib and asked him to cover himself with the Prophet's green mantle from Hadramawt and to sleep in the Prophet's bed. He further asked him to tarry in Makkah until he had returned all things left with Muhammad to their rightful owners. The Quraysh men waiting to kill the Prophet felt reassured whenever, looking through a hole in the door, they saw somebody sleeping in the Prophet's bed. Just before dawn, Muhammad left without being noticed, picked up Abū Bakr at the latter's house and from there they proceeded through a back door south-ward toward the cave of Thawr. The southerly direction of their flight was inconceivable to everyone.

Nobody knew of their hiding place in the cave except 'Abdullah, son of Abū Bakr, his two sisters, 'Ā'ishah and Asmā', and their servant 'Āmir ibn Fuhayrah. 'Abdullah spent his day in Makkah listening to what the Quraysh said and plotted about Muhammad and then reported it to the pair at their hideout under cover of night. 'Āmir grazed the sheep of Abū Bakr and passed by the cave in the evening in order to give them some milk and meat. Upon 'Abdullah's return from the cave, 'Āmir would follow him with all his sheep and then conceal any trace of his steps. For three long days, the pair remained in the cave and the Quraysh persistently looked for them without avail. For the Quraysh it was absolutely necessary to find Muhammad and to prevent his emigration to Yathrib. Meanwhile, Muhammad spent most of his time praying to God and invoking his blessings, and Abū Bakr continually sought to find out whether they were being discovered and to look after their security.

The young men of Quraysh who were chosen to kill Muhammad continued their search and came close to the cave fully armed and ready for the kill. When they found a shepherd in the vicinity, they asked him about Muhammad and Abū Bakr. He answered, "Perhaps they are within the cave, although I have not seen anyone go in or out." When he heard the shepherd's answer, Abū Bakr trembled with fear and expected the Quraysh to break into the cave any moment. He withdrew into a corner

and, trusting in God, remained motionless. Some members of the
Quraysh party climbed up to the cave, and the foremost among
them turned round as soon as he saw the cave entrance. His
companions asked him, "Why have you not gone into the cave?"
He answered, "Its entrance is covered with cobwebs, and there is
a pair of wild pigeons on the threshold. Obviously, no one could
have gone in without disturbing the pigeons and destroying
the cobwebs." At that moment, Muḥammad prayed while Abū
Bakr continued to shake with fear. To Abū Bakr, who pressed
ever closer to Muḥammad, the latter whispered, "Do not grieve;
God is with us." According to some Ḥadīth books, it is reported
that when the Quraysh party arrived at the cave entrance, Abū
Bakr exclaimed: "If any one of them looks at his feet he will
find us," and that the Prophet had answered, "O Abū Bakr,
how can you fear for two men whose constant companion is
God Himself?" The Quraysh men were further convinced that
the cave was empty when they saw the entrance to the cave
covered—indeed blocked—with branches growing from a tree
nearby. They then agreed to leave and called one another for
their return to Makkah. Only then did the two refugees within
the cave feel reassured. Abū Bakr's faith in God and His Prophet
became stronger, and Muḥammad prayed: "Praise be to God!
God is greater than all!"

The Miracle of the Cave

The cobwebs, the two wild pigeons, and the tree and its
branches—these are the miracles which the biography books
relate concerning the hiding in the cave of Thawr. The miracle
is that none of these things were there when the Prophet and
his companion entered the cave, and that thereafter, the spider
hurried to weave its cobwebs, the two pigeons to build their nest
and to lay their eggs, and the tree to grow its branches around
the door. In this connection the orientalist Dermenghem wrote,
"These three things are the only miracles recorded in authentic
Mussulman history: the web of a spider, the love of a dove, the
sprouting of a flower—three miracles accomplished daily on
God's earth."[1]

Some Biographers Omit the Story

This miracle received no mention in Ibn Hishām's biography.
His version of the story of the cave ran as follows: "They

[Muḥammad and Abū Bakr] went to the cave of Thawr, on
the south side of Makkah. Abū Bakr ordered his son 'Abdullah
to stay in Makkah during the day, listen to the news of the
Quraysh and bring them knowledge thereof in the evening. He
ordered his servant, 'Āmir ibn Fuhayrah, to continue to graze
his sheep and to come by the cave at night. Asmā', daughter
of Abū Bakr, brought them provisions of food in the evening,
also. The Prophet of God—may God's peace and blessing be
upon him—stayed in the cave three days. The Quraysh had
announced a prize of one hundred camels to whosoever would
bring back Muḥammad to Makkah. 'Abdullah, son of Abū Bakr,
used to spend his day in Makkah listening well to the plotting
and gossip of the Quraysh, and when visiting the pair in the
evening, related the news to them. 'Āmir ibn Fuhayrah, servant
of Abū Bakr, used to graze the flock of sheep around Makkah
and, in the evening, passed by the cave and gave milk and meat
to the pair. When 'Abdullah, son of Abū Bakr, returned home
to Makkah, he was followed by 'Āmir ibn Fuhayrah and his
sheep in order to cover over his footprints. Three days later,
when the interest of the Quraysh in this search had subsided,
the man whom Abū Bakr had appointed to graze the two camels
for the trip came with the three camels, two for Muḥammad and
Abū Bakr, and a third for himself. . . ." That is all that Ibn
Hishām says concerning the story of the cave.

In the same connection, the following verses of the Qur'ān
were revealed:

وَ اِذْ يَمْكُرُ بِكَ الَّذِينَ كَفَرُوا لِيُثْبِتُوكَ اَوْ يَقْتُلُوكَ اَوْ يُخْرِجُوكَ وَ يَمْكُرُونَ وَ يَمْكُرُ اللّٰهُ
وَاللّٰهُ خَيْرُ الْمَاكِرِينَ ۞ . . . اِلَّا تَنْصُرُوهُ فَقَدْ نَصَرَهُ اللّٰهُ اِذْ اَخْرَجَهُ الَّذِينَ كَفَرُوا ثَانِيَ
اثْنَيْنِ اِذْ هُمَا فِى الْغَارِ اِذْ يَقُولُ لِصَاحِبِهِ لَا تَحْزَنْ اِنَّ اللّٰهَ مَعَنَا فَاَنْزَلَ اللّٰهُ سَكِينَتَهُ
عَلَيْهِ وَ اَيَّدَهُ بِجُنُودٍ لَمْ تَرَوْهَا وَجَعَلَ كَلِمَةَ الَّذِينَ كَفَرُوا السُّفْلَىٰ وَكَلِمَةُ اللّٰهِ هِيَ
الْعُلْيَا وَاللّٰهُ عَزِيزٌ حَكِيمٌ ۞

"When the unbelievers plotted to imprison you, to kill you
or to banish you, God planned on your behalf, and He is the
best of planners. . . If you [the people] do not help Muḥammad,
then know that God Will. For God helped him when the un-

believers drove him out, and he and his companion hid in the cave. At that time, the Prophet said to his companion, 'Grieve not for God is with us.' It was then that God sent down his peace upon him and assisted him with hosts invisible that the word of God might be supreme and that of the unbelievers might be repudiated. God is almighty and all-wise."[2]

The Trip to Yathrib

On the third day, when they felt certain that the Quraysh had called off the hunt for them in the vicinity, Muḥammad and Abū Bakr commanded their servant to bring them their camels for escape. The servant managed to bring a third camel for himself. Asmā', daughter of Abū Bakr, brought them provisions. As they mounted, they could not find ropes with which to tie their provisions of food and water. Asmā' cut her robe in two and used one half of it for the purpose while covering herself with the other half. For this reason she was called "the woman with the two half-robes." Their provisions taken care of, the three men went forth. Abū Bakr carried five thousand Dirhims,[3] which was all that was left of his wealth. Lest the Quraysh should find them, they cautiously took an untrodden path toward their destination. Their servant and guide, 'Abdullah ibn Urayqit, from the tribe of Banū al Du'il, headed south of Makkah and then to the mountain range of Tihāmat close by the shore of the Red Sea. From there he took an unknown path northward parallel to the shore but far removed from it. His purpose was always to remain off the beaten track. All night and most of the day the riders pressed forth unaffected by fatigue or hardship, for every hardship was preferable—indeed easy by comparison—to what the Quraysh was prepared to do to destroy them and their cause! Muḥammad never doubted that God would come to his help, but God had also commanded man not to expose himself to open risks. God had counselled that He would assist man only as long as man helped himself and his brother. The two men were successful in their hiding in the cave. However, the Quraysh's announcement of an hundred camel prize to whoever would bring them back or furnish information which would lead to their capture was sufficient to mobilize the wealth-seeking Makkans for the search, even if it was a criminal one. Still, the Arabs of Quraysh had additional motivation to conduct such a search, for they regarded Muḥammad as their enemy *par excellence;* and they were so revengeful and passionate in their hate that no consideration could stop them from exploiting the weak and injuring the harmless. Therefore, they redoubled their attentiveness and renewed their vigor for the search.

The Story of Surāqah

Their intuition did not fail them. A man soon arrived at Makkah to report that on his way he met three riders whom he thought were Muhammad and his companions. Upon hearing this report, Surāqah ibn Mālik ibn Ju'shum immediately said, "Those are the sons of so and so." His purpose was to lead his companions into disregarding the report so that he might capture Muhammad single-handed and win the prize of the hundred camels. A moment later, he returned home, loaded himself with arms, and ordered his servant to take his horse to the outskirts of the city so that no one would see him go. There, he arrayed himself for battle, mounted his horse, and galloped toward the spot where Muhammad was reported to have been seen. Muhammad and his two companions had at that time repaired to a tree to rest a little under its shade, to eat a meal and to replenish their energies.

The time was close to evening. Muhammad and Abū Bakr began to ready their beasts to resume their ride. Surāqah was still as far from them as the eye could see. Exhausted with fatigue from all its galloping, Surāqah's horse fell twice on the way. When the travelers came into his sight, and he realized he could now capture or kill them, Surāqah forgot that his horse had fallen twice already. He spurred it once more and hurried it toward them. The horse fell to the ground with its rider. At this turn, Surāqah felt very apprehensive that the gods were against the execution of his scheme and that he might be exposing himself to grave danger should he spur his horse forward for the fourth time. After stopping, he called to the travelers: "I am Surāqah ibn Ju'shum. Wait for me so that I may talk to you. By God, I shall do you neither harm or injury." When he arrived, he asked Muhammad to write him a note with which to prove his present encounter. At the Prophet's command, Abū Bakr wrote a note to this effect which Surāqah took and returned home. Made contrite by his unfortunate venture, he spread the news that the riders were not Muhammad and his party at all!

The Hardships of the Road

Muḥammad and his two companions set forth toward Yathrib across mountains, hills, and deserts whose sands were glowing with heat. Since they were off the beaten track, they found hardly anything with which to alleviate the hardships of sun and thirst. Furthermore, they were ever apprehensive that the Quraysh or some other people might surprise and overtake them. Their only consolation was their patient trust in God and the truth revealed to His Prophet. For seven consecutive days they travelled, lying low during the heat of day and moving with great haste under cover of night. In the stillness of night and the brilliance of its stars lay their only security and assurance. When they reached the quarters of the tribe of Banū Sahm, where elder chieftain Buraydah came over to greet them, their fears lessened, and for the first time, their hearts palpitated with the hope and assurance of victory. They had almost reached their destination.

Awaiting the Prophet in Yathrib

During Muḥammad's long and exhaustive trip, the news reached his companions in Yathrib that he had emigrated from Makkah in order to join them. Aware of the enmity of the Quraysh and of their attempts to follow and to seize the Prophet, the Muslims waited anxiously for his arrival and looked very much forward to hearing the details of his escape. Many of them had never seen the Prophet before although they had heard a great deal about his eloquence and resolution. Naturally, they were quite anxious to meet him. We can imagine the enthusiasm of these men when we know that a number of notables from Yathrib had followed Muḥammad even though they had never seen him before. Their knowledge of him depended on his companions who had spoken to them of their love for him and who had been staunchly carrying his message about.

The Spread of Islām in Yathrib

Sa‘d ibn Zurārah and Mus‘ab ibn ‘Umayr once sat in one of the courtyards of Banū Ẓafar listening to the speech of those who entered into Islām. Their news had reached Sa‘d ibn Mu‘ādh and Usayd ibn Ḥuḍayr, chieftains of their tribes. Sa‘d said to

Usayd, as one chieftain to another, "Go out to these two men
who came here to subvert the weaklings among us. Chastise
them and forbid them to come here again. You can do this better
than I because Sa'd ibn Zurārah is a cousin of mine and I cannot
be harsh enough to him." Usayd went out to seek the two men.
Mus'ab said, "Will you not sit down and listen to us? If you
hear something worthwhile, accept it. If, on the other hand,
you hear something unworthy, you may put a quick end to it."
Usayd replied, "You are fair." He stuck his spear into the ground
and sat down listening to Mus'ab's preaching of Islām. No
sooner had Mus'ab finished than Usayd was converted to Islām.
When he returned, his fellow chieftain, Sa'd, was annoyed at
this and sought out the two men in person. They offered him
the same choice, and he, too, was converted. Following upon
this, Sa'd went to his people and said, "Oh, Banū 'Abd al
Ashhal, what do you think of me?" They answered, "You are our
chieftain, our dearest relative, our wise leader and righteous
representative." He said, "Then I shall forbid myself to speak
to any of your men and women until you believe in God and
in His prophet." Banū 'Abd al Ashhal then entered into the
faith *en bloc*.

Islām had spread so widely in Yathrib and the Muslims had
gathered so much strength before the emigration of the Prophet
that some Muslim youths were encouraged to attack the idols
of the unbelievers. Apparently Islām had enjoyed a strength
that the Muslims of Makkah had never dreamt of before. 'Amr
ibn al Jamūh had a wooden idol which he called Manāt and which
he kept in his house according to the custom of the nobility, for
he was one of the noblemen of Banū Salamah. When the
youths of his tribe joined Islām, they raided his house at night
and, without his knowledge, would steal away the idol and
place it in the refuse dump outside the city. In the morning,
'Amr would miss his statue and look for it. When he found it,
he would cleanse, purify, and return it to its place. All along,
he would curse and threaten the offenders in the strongest terms.
The youth of Banū Salamah continued their attacks upon this
idol until one day 'Amr hung his sword on the shoulder of
the statue and said to it, "If there is any power in you, there's
my sword, defend yourself." The following morning, however,
he found the idol robbed of its sword and tied to a dead dog
inside an empty pit. At that moment, his people talked to him
and showed him how unworthy of man is idolatry. He was
convinced and entered Islām.

With all these successes which Islām had been scoring in
Yathrib, the people of Yathrib looked forward quite eagerly
to the arrival of Muḥammad when they heard of his emigration.
For many days before his arrival, they went out to the outskirts
of their city at dawn to spend the morning seeking signs of
the Prophet's arrival.

The month was July and the days were hot. Muḥammad
reached Qubā', two leagues from Madīnah,[4] and stayed there
four days with Abū Bakr being constantly with him. During this
interval, he founded a mosque and before he left for Madīnah,
'Alī ibn Abū Ṭālib had joined his party. 'Alī had returned the
trusts left with Muḥammad which Muḥammad had asked him
to return to their rightful owners, and he came to Yathrib on
foot, walking during the night and hiding during the day. He
had been on the road for two whole weeks in order to join the
Prophet and his fellow Muslims in Madīnah.

Muḥammad's Entry into Madīnah

One day, as the Muslims waited the arrival of Muḥammad, a
Jew of Yathrib announced to them, "O People of Qaylah, your
man has finally arrived." It was a Friday, and Muḥammad performed his prayer in Madīnah at the mosque situated in the
valley of Rānūqna. The Muslims of Yathrib arrived there from
all quarters in order to see the man whom they had not seen,
but whom they loved with all their minds and hearts, in whose
message they had believed, and whose name they had mentioned
many times in their daily prayers. A number of notables invited
the Prophet to stay in their houses and to enjoy the comforts,
security, and protection of their quarters. As Muḥammad apologized, he rode his camel, which he allowed to go free, toward
the city. As it ran forth surrounded by the Muslims who opened
the way for it, the people of Yathrib, whether Jews or unbelievers,
looked with surprise on the new agitation and vitality that had
suddenly seized their city. They looked at this great visitor who
was equally acclaimed by al Aws and al Khazraj, who had until
recently been death enemies of each other. No one among them
apparently grasped the new direction which history was taking
at that auspicious moment, nor the great destiny at work to
make their city immortal. The Prophet's camel continued to
run until it stopped at a yard belonging to two orphans of Banū
al Najjār. There, the camel lay down and the Prophet dismounted. Upon inquiring who the owner of the yard was, he

learned from Mu'ādh ibn 'Afrā' that it belonged to Sahl and Suhayl, sons of 'Amr, of whom he was the guardian. He asked the Prophet to build a mosque there and made a promise to satisfy the two orphans. Muḥammad accepted the request by building his mosque as well as his living quarters there.

A map of
Al Madīnah al Munawwarah and vicinity
appears on the following two pages.

al Ghābah

al Jurf

Mt. Thawr

Zughābah

Mt. Uhud

orchards

ʿAyn al Shuh
al Darīḥ

Rūmah Well

Mt. Ḥabashah

ruins

Yathrib
Jabal ʿAynayn
Mt. Salaʿ
al Mas
Mosque
al

Mosque
of Two
Qiblahs

Fatḥ
Mosque

ʿAli

Road to U
Road to
Well
Well of
Ḥāʾ...

al
Ḥaram

Palace of
Saʿīd ibn al ʿĀs

al ʿArṣah al Ṣughrā al ʿArṣah al Kubrā

Wādī al ʿAqīq

al Khandaq

Wādī al Wabrah

Ḥarrah al Wabrah

al Manākhah

al Tahāwlah

Jammāʾ ʿAqīl

Road to
Yanbuʿ

Well of
Suqyā

Palaces of al ʿAqīq

old
grave

Jammāʾ Umm Khālid

Road to Qubāʾ

Al

Wādī Batḥ

Jammāʾ Tudārūʾ

Wādī Rānūnāʾ

al Jumʿah
Mosque

Well of Arīs

Well of ʿUrwah

Mosque

Aṭum al Dahyān

ʿAyn al Azraq

Qubāʾ

House of

House of

Dams

Dhū al Ḥulayfah

Mt. ʿAsīr

al Ḥ

AL MADĪNAH
AL MUNAWWARAH

AND VICINITY

North ↑

½

Qanāt

^^^^^ Banū Hārithah
^^^^^ ^ Camp
^^^^^
^^^^^

al 'Arīd

al Bahīr
Mosque

Ayyūb

Banū Mu'āwiyah
Camp
^^^^ ^^^
^^^ ^^^

Harrah Wāqim

Safiyyah
ajd Road   Al Ijābah
            Mosque

^^^^^ ^^^
^^^^^ ^ Banū 'Abd
^^^^^^ ^ al Ashhal Camp
^^^ ^^

ān

Banū Zafar Mosque

^^^^^^ ^^^
^^^^^^^ Banū Zafar Camp
^^^^^^

Wādī Mahzūr

Well of Ghars ⊙   ^^^^^ Banū Qurayzah Camp
                   ^^^^^

Wādī Qurbān   al 'Awālī

al Faḍīkh Mosque

Mudhaynīb

haythamah   ^^^^^^ Banū al Naḍīr Camp
              ^^^ ^
al Hadm   ^^ ^
           Fortress of
           Ka'b ibn al Ashraf

KEY

mountain	⌐⌐⌐⌐⌐
valley	=====
forest	⊙⊙⊙
orchards	ｒｒｒｒ
date palms	ϯϯ
ditch	⋯⋯⋯
dam	═══
campsite	^^^
house	▣
spring ('ayn)	•
well	⊙
grave	⌷
mosque	⌂

1   Thaniyyah al Wadā'
2   Mt. al Mustandir
3   Saqīfah Banū Sā'idah
4   Thaniyyah 'Ath'ath
5   Dar al Diyāfah
6   Al Sāhah Quarter
7   Al 'Aynī Road
8   Sūq al Hadrah
9   Al Suqyā Mosque
10 Al Ghumāmah Mosque
11 Gate of al Shām
12 Gate of al Jum'ah
13 Gate of al 'Awālī
14 Gate of al Qubā'
15 Gate of al 'Anbariyyah
16 Well of Dharwān

Beginning of the Yathrib Period

Explanation of the City's Welcome

Having heard the news of his emigration, of Quraysh's plot
to kill him, and of his travel in mid-summer on an untrodden
path ridden with hardships—across rocky mountains and valleys
aglow with fire under the torrid sun—individuals and groups
of men and women went out to welcome Muḥammad to their
city. Excited by their own curiosity after the spread of the
news of Muḥammad's mission throughout the Arabian Peninsula,
the people of Yathrib went out to see and meet the author of
this call to renounce the holy faith and sacred beliefs of their
ancestors. More importantly, they went out to meet Muḥammad
and to welcome him because his intention was henceforth to
live with them in their own city. Every clan and tribe of Yathrib
well knew what political, social, and other advantages it stood
to gain should it succeed in convincing the new guest to reside
in its midst. Indeed, they went out to take a look at this man
that they might confirm their intuition concerning him. Hence,
neither the unbelievers of Yathrib nor its Jews were any less
enthusiastic than the Muslims, whether Muhājirūn or Ansār.
That is why they came from all sides to walk in his procession
although each was naturally moved by different feelings. As
Muḥammad allowed his camel to run loose, they followed him
in a disorderly manner; it was as if he had intended it that
way in order to give each one of them a chance to come closer

to him to take a nearer glimpse of his face. It was as if everyone had come out in order to gather in one moment of consciousness all that he had heard about and all that he could
see of the person to whom he had given the grand oath of
allegiance at al 'Aqabah where he pledged to lay down his life
when necessary in fighting any man whatever that stood in the
way of the faith. It was, furthermore, as if everyone wanted
to see the man who taught the unity of God based upon a scientific
investigation of the cosmos and an objective search for the
truth: a doctrine for the sake of which he had abandoned his
native town, its people, and borne their enmity and harm for
some thirteen consecutive years.

Building of the Prophet's Mosque

We have seen that the Prophet's camel stopped in the courtyard of Sahl and Suhayl. The Prophet bought the land in order
to build his mosque there. While the mosque was being erected,
he stayed in the house of Abū Ayyūb Khālid ibn Zayd al Ansārī.
In the construction of the mosque, Muḥammad worked with his
own hands as did the Muslims, whether Muhājirūn or Ansār.
When the mosque was completed, they built on one side of it
living quarters for the Prophet. These operations did not over-
tax anyone, for the two structures were utterly simple and
economical. The mosque consisted of a vast courtyard whose
four walls were built out of bricks and mud. A part of it was
covered with a ceiling made from date trunks and leaves.
Another part was devoted to shelter the poor who had no home
at all. The mosque was not lit during the night except for an
hour at the time of the night prayer. At that time some straw
was burned for light. Thus it continued to be for nine years,
after which lamps were attached to the tree trunks on which
stood the ceiling. The living quarters of the Prophet were no
more luxurious than the mosque although they had to be more
closed in order to give a measure of privacy.

Upon completion of the building, Muḥammad left the house
of Abū Ayyūb and moved into the new quarters. He began to
think of this new life which he had just initiated and the wide
gate it opened for his mission. The various tribes and clans
of this city were already competing with one another; and they
differed among themselves in ways and for reasons unknown to
any Makkan. Yet it was equally obvious that they all longed

for peace and freedom from the differences and hostilities which had torn them apart in the past. Moreover, they were ambitious for and willing to build a peaceful future capable of greater prestige and prosperity than Makkah had ever enjoyed. That is not to say that these matters concerned Muḥammad in the least. Rather, his concern, whether immediate or ultimate, was the conveyance of the message God had entrusted to him. The people of Makkah had resisted that message with every weapon they knew, and their hostility prevented its light from shining in the hearts of most men. The injury and harm the Quraysh were wont to inflict upon anyone who ventured into the new faith was sufficient to prevent conversion of those who were not yet convinced of its truth and value. Hence it was a cardinal need that Muslims as well as others feel certain that whoever followed the new guidance and entered into the religion of God was absolutely secure against attack. This precaution was necessary in order to confirm the believers in their faith and to enable the weak, the fearful, and the hesitant to enter into the faith with confidence. This consideration preoccupied Muḥammad as he moved to the security of his new home in Yathrib. In the years to follow, it constituted the cornerstone of his policy. All biographies have emphasized this orientation of Muḥammad's policies. At the time, he thought of neither property, nor wealth, nor trade, but only of realizing the security of his followers and their right to worship as they pleased on an equal footing with men of other faiths. It was absolutely necessary that the Muslim, the Jew, and the Christian have an equal opportunity in their exercise of religious freedom as well as in their freedom to hold different opinions and to preach their own faiths. Only such freedom can guarantee victory for the truth and progress of the world toward perfection in the higher unity of mankind. Every war against this freedom furthers the cause of falsehood. Every limitation of it gives power to the forces of darkness to cut off the light shining within the soul calling man to unity with mankind and the world to an eternal bond of harmony and love instead of alienation, war, and extinction.

Muḥammad's Aversion to War

Ever since the Hijrah, revelation persistently confirmed this orientation of Muḥammad and caused him strongly to incline toward peace, away from fighting, hostility or war. It made him regard fighting as the last resort in defense of this freedom and this faith. When, at the cry of the Qurayshī spy, the people of Yathrib who pledged to him their allegiance at the second al 'Aqabah meeting proclaimed, "By God who sent you as a messenger of the truth, if you wish us to pounce on the quarter of Minā tomorrow morning with swords drawn, not one of us will stay behind," did Muhammad not respond: "God has not commanded us to fight"? Did not the first verse granting such authority say: "Permission to fight is granted to those who are being fought, for they suffer injustice, and God is certainly capable of coming to their assistance"?[1] Was not this verse immediately followed by the revelation,

$$ وَقَاتِلُوهُمْ حَتَّى لَا تَكُونَ فِتْنَةٌ وَّ يَكُونَ الدِّيْنُ كُلُّهُ لِلَّهِ ۚ $$

"And fight them until all persecution has stopped and religion has become all God's"?[2]

Muhammad's thought was then guided by one final objective, namely, the guarantee of freedom of religion and thought. It was for the sake of this freedom alone that fighting was permitted. It was in its defense that repulsion of the aggressor was allowed, that no one might be persecuted on account of his faith and that no injustice might befall anyone because of his faith or opinion.

The Thinking of Yathrib

While Muhammad was occupied by this line of thought and pondered over the measures necessary for guaranteeing this freedom, the people of Yathrib entertained different ideas. Each clan and party followed a line of thought peculiar to itself. The Muslims were either Muhājirūn or Ansār; the unbelievers belonged to either al Aws or al Khazraj and were committed to a long history of mutual hostility, as we have shown earlier. There were also the Jews, of whom the Banū Qaynuqā' lived within the city, the Banū Qurayzah in the suburb of Fadak, the Banū al Nadīr, nearby, and those of Khaybar toward the north. As for the Muslims, Muhammad feared that, despite the strongest ties with which the new religion had bound them together, the old hatred and prejudice might some day break out anew between them. The unbelievers, from al Aws or al Khazraj, were exhausted by the previous wars; they found themselves situated, in the new configuration of society, between the Jews and the Muslims. The unbelievers' strategy concentrated on dividing Jew and Muslim and pulling them farther apart. The Jews, for their part, gave Muḥammad a good welcome in the hope of winning him over to their side. Their strategy demanded that they make use of the new unity of the Peninsula which he could help forge to bolster their opposition to Christendom. For to avenge their banishment from Palestine, the land of promise, and their national home, was the guiding concern of the Jews who saw themselves as God's chosen people. Each group followed its own train of thought and began to seek the means to realize its objective.

Muslim Brotherhood

At this time a new stage, unlike any other prophet before him, began in the career of Muḥammad. Here began the political stage in which Muḥammad showed such great wisdom, insight, and statesmanship as would arrest attention first in surprise and then in awe and reverence. Muḥammad's great concern was to bring to his new home town a political and organizational unity hitherto unknown to Ḥijāz, though not to ancient Yaman. He consulted with Abū Bakr and 'Umar, his two viziers, as he used to call them. Naturally, the first idea to occur to him was that of reorganizing Muslim ranks so as to consolidate their unity and to wipe out every possibility of a resurgence of division and hostility. In the realization of this objective, he asked the Muslims to fraternize with one another for the sake of God and to bind themselves together in pairs. He explained how he and 'Alī ibn Abū Ṭālib were brothers, how his uncle Ḥamzah and his client, Zayd, were also brothers, as were likewise Abū Bakr and Khārijah ibn Zayd, and 'Umar ibn al Khaṭṭāb and 'Itbān ibn Mālik al Khazrajī. Despite the Muhājirūn's rapid increase in number, following the emigration of the Prophet, everyone of them was now bound to a member of al Ansār group in a bond of mutual assistance. The Prophet's proclamation in this regard transformed that bond into one of blood and real fraternity. A new, genuine brotherhood arose which forged the Muslim ranks into an indivisible unity.

The Traders

Al Ansār showed their Muhājirūn brethren great hospitality which the latter had first accepted with joy. For when they emigrated from Makkah, they had left behind all their property, wealth, and goods and entered Madīnah devoid of the means with which to find their food. Only 'Uthmān ibn 'Affān was able to carry with him enough of his wealth to be prosperous in his new residence. The others had hardly been able to carry much or little that was of use to them. Even Ḥamzah, the Prophet's uncle, had one day to ask the Prophet to give him some food to eat. 'Abd al Rahman ibn 'Awf and Sa'd ibn al Rabī' were bonded together in brotherhood. The former had nothing. The latter offered to split his wealth with him. 'Abd al Rahman refused and asked that he be shown the market place. There he began to sell cheese and butter and in short time achieved a measure of affluence fair enough to enable him to ask the hand of a Madīnese woman as well as to send caravans in trade. Many other Muhājirūn followed the example of 'Abd al Rahman; for, the Makkans, it should be remembered, were quite adept in trade. Indeed, they were so expert at it that it was said of them that they could by trade change the sand of the desert into gold.

The Harvest

Those who could not engage in trade such as Abū Bakr, 'Umar, 'Alī ibn Abū Ṭālib and others, took to farming on the land owned by al Ansār under the system of sharecropping. Another group of truly helpless people, with a past full of suffering and hardship, put their hand to menial jobs, preferring hard labor to living as parasites on the earnings of others. Despite their meager earnings, they found consolation in the new peace and security of their own persons and of their faith. There was yet another group of emigrants so poor and helpless that they could not find even a place to sleep. To these, Muhammad permitted the use of the covered part of the mosque during the night. That is why they were called "Ahl al Ṣuffah," "suffah," meaning the covered area of the mosque. To these, Muhammad assigned a ration from the wealth of the more affluent Muslims, whether Ansar or Muhājirūn.

Muḥammad's Friendliness to the Jews

By this new brotherhood, Muḥammad achieved an operational Muslim unity. Politically, it was a very wise move destined to show Muḥammad's sound judgment and foresight. We shall better appreciate its wisdom when we learn of the attempts to divide al Aws against al Khazraj, and al Ansār against al Muhājirūn. The politically greater achievement of Muḥammad was his realization of a unity for the city of Yathrib as a whole, his construction of a political structure in which the Jews entered freely into an alliance of mutual cooperation with the Muslims. We have already seen how the Jews gave Muḥammad a good welcome in the hope of winning him as an ally. He, too, returned their greeting with like gestures and sought to consolidate his relations with them. He visited their chiefs and cultivated the friendship of their nobles. He bound himself to them in a bond of friendship on the grounds that they were scripturists and monotheists. So much had Muḥammad defended the Jews that the fact that he fasted with them on the days they fasted and prayed toward Jerusalem as they did increased his personal and religious esteem among them. Everything seemed as if the future could only strengthen this Muslim-Jewish friendship and produce further co-operation and closeness between them. Similarly, Muḥammad's own conduct, his great humility, compassion, and faithfulness, and his outgoing charity and goodness to the poor, oppressed and deprived, as well as the prestige and influence which these qualities had won for him among all the people of Yathrib—all these enabled him to conclude the pact of friendship, alliance, and cooperation in the safeguarding of religious freedom throughout the city. In our opinion, this covenant is one of the greatest political documents which history has known. Such an accomplishment by Muḥammad at this stage of his career had never been reached by any prophet. Jesus, Moses, and all the prophets that preceded them never went beyond the preaching of their religious messages through words and miracles. All of them had left their legacy to men of power and political authority who came after them; it was the latter who put their powers at the service of those messages and fought, with arms where necessary, for the freedom of the people to believe. Christianity spread at the hands of the disciples of Jesus and after his time, but only in extremely limited

measure. The disciples as well as their followers were persecuted
until one of the kings of the world favored this religion, adopted
it, and put his royal power behind its missionary effort.[3] All
other religions in the East and the West have had nearly the same
history, but not the religion of Muhammad. God willed that
Islām be spread by Muhammad, and that the truth be vindicated
by his hand. He willed Muhammad to be prophet, statesman,
fighter, and conqueror, all for the sake of God and the truth
with which he was commissioned as prophet. In all these aspects
of his career Muhammad was great, the exemplar of human
perfection, the *typos* of every realized value.

The covenant of Madīnah concluded between Muhājirūn and
Ansār on one side and Jews on the other, was dictated by
Muhammad. It was the instrument of their alliance which confirmed the Jews in both their religion and position in society,
and determined their rights as well as their duties. Following
is the text of this important document:

"In the name of God, the compassionate, the merciful.
This is a covenant given by Muhammad to the believers and
Muslims of Quraysh, Yathrib, and those who followed them,
joined them, and fought with them. They constitute one
Ummah to the exclusion of all other men. As was their
custom, the Muhājirūn from Quraysh are bound together
and shall ransom their prisoners in kindness and justice
as believers do. Following their own custom, Banū 'Awf
are bound together as they have been before. Every clan
of them shall ransom its prisoners with the kindness and
justice common among believers. [The text here repeats
the same prescription concerning every clan of the Ansār
and every house including Banū al Hārith, Banū Sā'idah,
Banū Jusham, Banū al Najjār, Banū 'Amr ibn 'Awf and
Banū al Nabīt.] The believers shall leave none of their
members in destitution without giving him in kindness what
he needs by way of ransom or bloodwit. No believer shall
take as an ally a freedman of another Muslim without the
permission of his previous master. All pious believers shall
rise as one man against whosoever rebels or seeks to commit
injustice, aggression, sin, or spread mutual enmity between
the believers, even though he may be one of their sons.
No believer shall slay a believer in retaliation for an unbeliever; neither shall he assist an unbeliever against a

believer. Just as God's bond is one and indivisible, all
believers shall stand behind the commitment of the least
of them. All believers are bonded one to another to the
exclusion of other men. Any Jew who follows us is entitled
to our assistance and the same rights as any one of us,
without injustice or partisanship. This *Pax Islamica* is one
and indivisible. No believer shall enter into a separate peace
without all other believers whenever there is fighting in
the cause of God, but will do so only on the basis of equality
and justice to all others. In every military expedition we
undertake our members shall be accompanied by others
committed to the same objective. All believers shall avenge
the blood of one another whenever any one of them falls
fighting in the cause of God. The pious believers follow
the best and most upright guidance. No unbeliever shall
be allowed to place under his protection against the interest
of a believer, any wealth or person belonging to Quraysh.
Whoever is convicted of killing a believer deliberately but
without righteous cause, shall be liable to the relatives of
the killed. Until the latter are satisfied, the killer shall be
subject to retaliation by each and every believer. The killer
shall have no rights whatever until this right of the believers
is satisfied. Whoever has entered into this covenant and
believed in God and in the last day shall never protect
or give shelter to a convict or a criminal; whoever does
so shall be cursed by God and upon him shall the divine
wrath fall on the day of judgment. Neither repentence nor
ransom shall be acceptable from him. No object of contention
among you may not be referred to God and to Muḥammad—
may God's peace and blessing be upon him—for judgment.
As the Jews fight on the side of the believers, they shall
spend of their wealth on equal par with the believers. The
Jews of Banū Aws are an *ummah* alongside the believers.
The Jews have their religion and the Muslims theirs. Both
enjoy the security of their own populace and clients except
the unjust and the criminal among them. The unjust or the
criminal destroys only himself and his family. The Jews
of Banū al Najjār, Banū al Ḥārith, Banū Sā'idah, Banū
Jusham, Banū al Aws, Banū Tha'labah, Jafnah, and Banū
al Shutaybah—to all the same rights and privileges apply
as to the Jews of Banū Aws. The clients of the tribe of
Tha'labah enjoy the same rights and duties as the members

of the tribe themselves. Likewise, the clients of the Jews, as the Jews themselves. None of the foregoing shall go out to war except with the permission of Muḥammad—may God's peace and blessing be upon him—though none may be prevented from taking revenge for a wound inflicted upon him. Whoever murders anyone will have murdered himself and the members of his family, unless it be the case of a man suffering a wrong, for God will accept his action. The Jews shall bear their public expenses and so will the Muslims. Each shall assist the other against any violator of this covenant. Their relationship shall be one of mutual advice and consultation, and mutual assistance and charity rather than harm and aggression. However, no man is liable to a crime committed by his ally. Assistance is due to the party suffering an injustice, not to one perpetrating it. Since the Jews fight on the side of the believers they shall spend their wealth on a par with them. The town of Yathrib shall constitute a sanctuary for the parties of this covenant. Their neighbors shall be treated as themselves as long as they perpetrate no crime and commit no harm. No woman may be taken under protection without the consent of her family. Whatever difference or dispute between the parties to this covenant remains unsolved shall be referred to God and to Muḥammad, the Prophet of God— may God's peace and blessing be upon him. God is the guarantor of the piety and goodness that is embodied in this covenant. Neither the Quraysh nor their allies shall be given any protection. The people of this covenant shall come to the assistance of one another against whoever attacks Yathrib. If they are called to cease hostilities and to enter into a peace, they shall be bound to do so in the interest of peace. If, on the other hand, they call upon the Muslims to cease hostilities and to enter into a peace, the Muslims shall be bound to do so and maintain the peace except when the war is against their religion. To every smaller group belongs the share which is their due as members of the larger group which is party to this covenant. The Jews of al Aws, as well as their clients, are entitled to the same rights as this covenant has granted to its parties together with the goodness and charity of the latter. Charity and goodness are clearly distinguishable from crime and injury, and there is no responsibility except for one's own deeds.

God is the guarantor of the truth and good will of this covenant. This covenant shall constitute no protection for the unjust or the criminal. Whoever goes out to fight as well as whoever stays at home shall be safe and secure in this city unless he has perpetrated an injustice or committed a crime. God grants His protection to whosoever acts in piety, charity and goodness."

New Horizons in Political Life

The foregoing political document, which Muḥammad wrote down fourteen centuries ago, establishes the freedom of faith and opinion, the invioliability of the city, human life, and property, and the forbiddance of crime. It certainly constitutes a breakthrough in the political and civil life of the world of that time. For that age was one in which exploitation, tyranny, and corruption were well established. Though the Jews of Banū Qurayẓah, Banū al Nadīr, and Banū Qaynuqā' did not sign this covenant at its conclusion, they did enter later on into like pacts with the Prophet. Thus Madīnah and all the territories surrounding it became inviolate to their peoples who were now bound to rise to their defense and protection together. These peoples were now bound to guarantee one another in the implementation of the covenant, in the establishment of the rights arising therefrom, and in the provision of freedom it has called for.

The Prophet's Marriage to 'Ā'ishah

Muḥammad was satisfied with the result of his negotiations. The Muslims felt secure in their religion and began to practice its duties and precepts as individuals and groups in public, without fear of attack or harm from any source. At this time Muḥammad married 'Ā'ishah, daughter of Abū Bakr, who was then ten or eleven years old. She was a beautiful, delicate, and amiable young girl, emerging out of childhood and blossoming into full womanhood. Although she was fully grown, she was still quite attracted by amusement and play. She had a room of her own near that of Sawdah alongside the mosque. In Muḥammad, she found not only a sympathetic and loving husband but also a compassionate father who was not at all offended by her inclination to play games and amuse herself with trifles. On the contrary, she was for him a source of relaxation from the continuous tension imposed upon him by his great burden to which the government of Yathrib had just been added.

Adhān or the Call to Prayer

It was during this interval in which the Muslims felt secure in their religion that the duties of *zakāt,* fasting, and legal sanctions of Islām were imposed and its dominion was firmly established in Yathrib. Ever since Muḥammad arrived in Madīnah, whenever the time of prayer came, the people assembled around the Prophet without call. It occurred to him to have the Muslims called for prayer by means of a horn, following the style of the Jews, but he found the idea unbecoming. He had also thought of using the clapper, in the manner of the Christians. After consulting 'Umar and a number of Muslims, according to one report, and by the command of God, according to another, he changed his idea to the *adhān* and commanded 'Abdullah ibn Zayd ibn Tha'labah: "Get up with Bilāl and dictate the call to prayer to him, but let him deliver it forth for he has a more beautiful voice than yours." A woman of Banū al Najjār owned a house next door to the mosque which was higher than the latter. Bilāl used to ascend to the roof of that house and deliver the call to prayer from there. Thus the people of Yathrib all began to hear the call to prayer many times a day beginning at dawn. The Islāmic call to prayer was equally a call to Islām sung beautifully by a beautiful voice and carried on the waves of the air unto all corners of the horizon. It was a call which penetrated the ear of life itself. It said, "God is greater. God is greater. I witness that there is no God but God. I witness that Muḥammad is the Prophet of God. Rise to prayer. Rise to felicity. God is greater. God is greater. There is no God but God." Henceforth, the Muslims' fears were dissipated and they felt secure. Yathrib became Madīnah al Nabiy or "the City of the Prophet." While the non-Muslim inhabitants began to fear Muslim power—knowing well that it stemmed from the depth of hearts which had tasted sacrifice and persecution for the sake of faith, the Muslims collected the fruits of their patience and enjoyed their religious freedom. There peace and freedom were now made constitutional by the Islāmic principles that no man has any authority over any other, that religion belongs to God alone, that service is to Him alone, that before Him all men are absolutely equal, and that nothing differentiates them except their works and intentions. In Madīnah, the atmosphere was finally cleared of all impediments, and Muḥammad openly proclaimed his teachings. The theater was ready and the stage was set for Muḥammad to constitute by his conduct the ideal exemplification and embodiment of these teachings and principles, and for his laying down the foundation stone of Islāmic civilization.

Brotherhood: Foundation of Islāmic Civilization

The rock bottom foundation of Islāmic civilization is human brotherhood, a brotherhood under which man does not become truly human until he has loved for his brother what he loves for himself and implemented this love by deeds of goodness and mercy without weakness or servility. A man once asked Muḥammad, "Which Islam is better?" Muḥammad answered, "That you give food to the needy and that you greet those whom you know as well as those whom you don't." He opened the first sermon he delivered in Madīnah with the statement, "Whoever can protect his face from the fire even with a basket of dates, let him do so; and whoever does not find even that much, then let him do so with a good word, for the good word brings a reward ten times greater than itself." In his second sermon he said, "Worship God and do not associate any being with Him. Fear and revere Him as He ought to be feared and revered. Be true unto Him by saying always the best than can be said. Love one another in the spirit of God. God is displeased whenever His covenant is violated." By this and like exhortations, Muḥammad used to counsel his companions and preach to the people in his mosque, leaning against one of the date trunks supporting the ceiling. Later on, he ordered a pulpit of three steps to be made for him, the first to stand upon when delivering a sermon and the second to sit down upon.

Muslim Brotherhood

The brotherhood which Muḥammad made the cornerstone of Islāmic civilization did not rest on his preachings alone. It was embodied in its highest perfection in his deeds and concrete example. True, he was the Prophet of God, but he consistently refused to adopt any of the appearances of power, authority, kingship, or temporal sovereignty. He emphatically repeated to his companions, "Do not praise me as the Christians have praised the son of Mary, for I am but the servant of God. Rather, call me the servant of God and His Prophet." Once, he arrived at a gathering of his companions leaning on a stick and they all rose up in respect for him. He said, "Do not stand up for me as the Persians do in aggrandizement of one another." Whenever he joined his companions, he always sat at the edge of the space they occupied. He used to joke and mix with them, to talk to them about their own affairs, to pamper and coddle their children, and to answer the call of freeman, slave, maid servant and destitute alike. He used to visit the sick in the farthest district of Madīnah, to take the initiative in greeting whomever he met, and to stretch his hand in welcome to his visitors. No man came to visit Muḥammad and found him in prayer but he shortened his prayer, attended to his visitor and returned to his prayer after the visitor had left. He was the most charitable of people, always smiling in the face of everyone except when revelation came to him or when he delivered a speech or a sermon. In his home, he felt no superiority over the members of his family. He washed his own robe and mended it by his own hand. He milked his own goat, repaired his own sandals, attended to himself and to his camel, ate with his servant, and fulfilled the request of the weak, the oppressed and the destitute. Whenever he found somebody in need, however lowly or plebeian, he preferred to attend to him first rather than to himself or to his family. That is why he never saved anything for the morrow, and when he died his shield was in possession of a Jewish pawnbroker as lien for a loan made to Muḥammad to spend on his family. He was exceedingly modest and extremely loyal. When a deputation from the Negus of Abyssinia arrived to see him, he rose to serve them. His companions sought to stop him, but he said to them: "The Abyssinians were kind to our companions when they went to their country; I would like to treat them likewise and reward them." He was so loyal to Khadījah that whenever she was mentioned he gave her the best of praises so that 'Ā'ishah used to say, "I have never been jealous of a woman as I have been of Khadījah for all that I have heard the Prophet praise her." Once when a woman came to him, he rose to greet her, spoke to her gently, and attended to her pleas; people asked him who she was. He answered, "She used to befriend us in the days of Khadījah; loyalty to one's friends is of the faith." Indeed, he was so compassionate and gentle that he did not mind his grandsons' playing with him during his prayer. Once, he even prayed while Umāmah, his granddaughter through Zaynab, sat on his shoulders and had to be put down when he prostrated himself.

Muḥammad's Kindness to Animals

His kindness and mercy, on which he founded the new Islāmic civilization, were not limited to man alone but extended to animals. Muḥammad used to rise and open the door for a cat seeking to enter. He attended with his own hands to a sick rooster and rubbed down his own horse with his own sleeve. When 'Ā'ishah rode on an obstinate camel and began to pull him hardly, he said to her, "Softly and gently please." Thus his kindness and mercy embraced all that ever came in touch with him—every creature that sought to stand near his person.

The Brotherhood of Justice and Mercy

Muḥammad's mercy did not proceed from weakness or servility, nor was it ever vitiated by pride, haughtiness, or the expectation of gratitude. It was done purely for the sake of God. Hence, nothing was excluded from it. This kindness differentiates the foundation of the civilization of Islām from all other civilizations. Islām puts justice side by side with kindness and judges that kindness is not kindness without justice.

فَمَنِ اعْتَدَى عَلَيْكُمْ فَاعْتَدُوا عَلَيْهِ بِمِثْلِ مَا اعْتَدَى عَلَيْكُمْ

"Whoever commits an aggression against you, return to him his aggression in like manner."[4]

وَلَكُمْ فِي الْقِصَاصِ حَيَوةٌ يَا أُولِي الْأَلْبَابِ

"In punishment a whole life lies implicit, O you who have minds to reason with!"[5]

Kindness is felicitous and the good deeds that issue from it are praiseworthy only when the motivation is internal, the will is free, and the purpose is the seeking of God's sake alone. Kindness should proceed from a strong soul that has known no submission to anything but God, has not succumbed to weakness, does not go to extremes in the name of piety, and knows no fear or contrition except on account for a misdeed it has done or a crime it has committed. As long as the soul is under alien dominion, it can never be strong; it can never be strong, either, if it stands under the dominion of its own passions and desires. Muḥammad and his companions emigrated from Makkah precisely in rebellion against the dominion of Quraysh who attempted to weaken their souls by means of dominion and the injuries it perpetrates. On the other hand, the soul is said to be under the dominion of passions and desires whenever the body's demands take precedence over those of the spirit, when passion vanquishes reason, when external life exerts any power over internal life—in short, when the soul does not know that it has no need of either passion or desire and is really their final master.

Muḥammad's Power to Surmount Life

Muḥammad provided the highest example of the power to overcome life. He achieved such a degree of mastery over life that he did not hesitate to give all that he had whenever he wanted to give. A contemporary of Muḥammad once said of him, "Muḥammad gives as if he has no fear of want at all." In order not to allow anything to exercise any power over him but rather to enable himself to determine it, Muḥammad led a very ascetic life. Despite his strong desire to know the secrets of life and understand its structure, he was quite contemptuous of its joys and attractions. He slept in a bed of palm fibers; he never ate his fill; he never ate barley bread on two consecutive days, gruel being his main daily meal together with dates. Neither he nor his family had ever had enough *tharīd*.[6] He felt the pangs of hunger more than once, and learned to press a stone against his stomach as a means to silence those pangs. This remarkable restraint, however, did not prevent his enjoying the delicacies of God's bounty if such were available, and he was known to love to eat leg of lamb, squash, honey, and other sweets.

In his dress he was as ascetic as he was in his food. His wife once gave him a new robe because he was in need of one. One of his companions asked him for something with which to shroud a dead relative, and Muḥammad gave him the new robe he had just received. His wardrobe consisted of shirts and robes made out of wool, cotton, or linen. But on special occasions he had no objection to wearing a luxurious robe from Yaman should it be called for. He used to wear a simple sandal, and he did not wear slippers until the Negus of Abyssinia sent him some together with other clothes.

Muḥammad's denial of the world and its luxuries was not pursued for its own sake. Nor was it a duty imposed by religion. The Qur'ān said: "Eat of the delicacies of God's providing," and "Do seek the other world in what God has given you of this, but do not give up your share of this world. Do good, as God has done good to you."[7] In the traditions of the early Muslims it is said, "Work for this world as if your life in it is eternal; work for the other world as if you were to die tomorrow." Certainly Muḥammad sought to give mankind the highest possible example of a mastery of life absolutely free of weakness, in which no goods, wealth, or power dedicated to another being beside God could have any effect. When brotherhood is based upon such a power over life and its attractions issue into such exemplary deeds as Muḥammad had done, it is pure, candid, and has no other object whatever besides the lofty fraternalism of man and man. In it, justice dovetails with mercy, and the subject is not determined except by his own free and deliberate judgment. Islām places both mercy and forgiveness side by side with justice. It insists that if they are to be themselves at all, mercy and forgiveness must issue from power. Only then will their purpose be the genuine good of the neighbor and his reconstruction.

The Sunnah of Muḥammad

The foundation for a new civilization which Muḥammad laid down was expressed very succinctly in a report by 'Alī ibn Abū Ṭālib. He asked the Prophet of God concerning his Sunnah, and the latter replied: "Wisdom is my capital, reason the force of my religion, love my foundation, longing my vehicle, the remembrance of God my constant pleasure, trust my treasure, mourning my companion, knowledge my arm, patience my robe, contentment my booty, poverty my pride, asceticism my profession, conviction my strength, truthfulness my intercessor, obedience my argument, holy war my ethics, prayer my supreme pleasure."

Beginning of Jewish Fears

Muḥammad's teachings, example, and leadership had the deepest effect upon the people. Large numbers of men joined the ranks of Islām and their conversion consolidated and increased Muslim power in Madīnah. It was at this stage that the Jews began to rethink their position *vis-à-vis* Muḥammad and his companions. They had concluded a pact with him and were still ambitiously hoping to win him over to their side in order to increase their power against the Christians. Muḥammad, however, was becoming more powerful than both Christians and Jews, and his command was growing in effect and application. Muḥammad had even begun thinking of Quraysh, of their banishment of him and the Muhājirūn from Makkah, and of their forced conversion of some Muslims to the old idolatry. It was at this time that the Jews asked themselves whether they should let his call, spiritual power, and authority continue to spread while remaining satisfied with the security they enjoyed under his protection and the increased trade and wealth which his peace had brought to their city. Perhaps they might have done so had they felt certain that his religion was not going to spread in their midst and their own men would not abjure the exclusivism of Jewish prophethood and the people of Israel to convert to Islām. A great number of their priesthood and a learned rabbi, 'Abdullah ibn Salām, approached the Prophet and announced to him his conversion as well as that of his own household. 'Abdullah himself feared the calumny of the Jews and their defamation of him should they learn of his conversion. He therefore asked the Prophet to inquire of them about him, before any of the Jews had learned of his conversion. The Jews answered Muḥammad, " 'Abdullah ibn Salām is our master, son of our master, our priest, and learned rabbi." When, however, 'Abdullah went back to them as a Muslim and called them to Islām, they attacked him and spread in the Jewish quarters of Madīnah all sorts of calumnies against him. This was the event which triggered their suspicions of Muḥammad and their denial of Muḥammad's prophethood. Those members of al Aws and al Khazraj tribes who never entered Islām or who did so in hypocrisy or for an ulterior purpose were quick to rally around the Jews once their opposition to Muḥammad and to Islām began to crystallize.

The War of Words between Muḥammad and the Jews

A war of words between Muḥammad and the Jews, which proved to be greater and more sinister than that which raged between Muḥammad and Quraysh, followed ibn Salām's conversion. Unlike the hostility with Quraysh, the new war in Yathrib witnessed the connivance of treason, deception, and scriptural knowledge for the attack against Muḥammad, his message, and his companions, whether Muhājirūn or Ansār. The Jews sent some of their rabbis to feign conversion to Islām in order to enter Muslim ranks and councils. While showing all piety, these rabbis were commissioned to disseminate doubt and suspicion of Muḥammad among his own people. They asked Muḥammad questions which they thought might shake the Muslims' conviction and arouse doubt in the message Muḥammad was teaching. A number of hypocrites from al Aws and al Khazraj tribes joined Islām for the same purpose. Both Jews and unbelievers, however, reached such levels of deception that they denied either Torah or God in order to ask Muḥammad, "If God created creation, who then created God?" Muḥammad used to answer them with the divine verses: "Say, 'God is One, the Eternal. He was not born, nor did He give birth to anyone. None is like unto Him.' "[8] The Muslims soon detected their purpose and uncovered their attempts. When some of them plotting in secrecy in one of the mosque's corners were discovered one day by the Muslims, Muḥammad had to command that they be expelled from the mosque. However, their efforts to split Muslim ranks continued. A Jewish leader called Shās ibn Qays passed one day by a group of al Aws and al Khazraj tribesmen enjoying one another's company in good harmony. He remembered how they were once divided and warring against each other, and thought that should the Banū Qaylah[9] remain united in this territory the Jews would not be able to live in peace for long. He therefore instructed a young Jew who frequented their sessions to seek an opportunity to arouse memories of the Day of Buʻāth when al Aws vanquished al Khazraj. The youth did

speak and recalled the memory of that war and succeeded in
arousing the old pride and hatred of the two tribes, convincing
some that a return to that *dies nefastus* was possible as well as
desirable. When Muḥammad learned of this, he hurried with
his companions and reminded the divisive elements how Islām
had sweetened their hearts and made of them mutually loving
brethren. Muḥammad continued to talk to them, emphasizing
their Islāmic unity and brotherhood until their tears ran down
in emotion and they embraced one another.

The war of words between Muḥammad and the Jews increased
in intensity. The evidence therefor is what the Qur'ān has to say
about it. The first eighty-one verses of *Sūrah* "al Nisā'," mention
the people of the book, their denial of their own scripture, and
condemns their unbelief and denial in strong terms:

وَلَقَدْ اتَيْنَا مُوسَى الْكِتَبَ وَقَفَّيْنَا مِنْ بَعْدِهِ بِالرُّسُلِ وَ اتَيْنَا عِيسَى ابْنَ مَرْيَمَ الْبَيِّنَتِ وَاَيَّدْنَهُ بِرُوحِ
الْقُدُسِ اَفَكُلَّمَا جَاءَكُمْ رَسُولٌ بِمَا لاَ تَهْوَى اَنْفُسُكُمُ اسْتَكْبَرْتُمْ فَفَرِيقًا كَذَّبْتُمْ وَفَرِيقًا تَقْتُلُونَ ۝
وَقَالُوا قُلُوبُنَا غُلْفٌ بَلْ لَعَنَهُمُ اللّٰهُ بِكُفْرِهِمْ فَقَلِيلاً مَا يُؤْمِنُونَ ۝ وَلَمَّا جَاءَهُمْ كِتَبٌ مِنْ عِنْدِ اللّٰهِ
مُصَدِّقٌ لِمَا مَعَهُمْ وَكَانُوا مِنْ قَبْلُ يَسْتَفْتِحُونَ عَلَى الَّذِينَ كَفَرُوا فَلَمَّا جَاءَهُمْ مَا عَرَفُوا كَفَرُوا بِهِ فَلَعْنَةُ
اللّٰهِ عَلَى الْكَفِرِينَ

"Verily, We revealed to Moses the scripture and called after
him messengers to follow in his footsteps. To Jesus, Son of
Mary, We gave manifest signs and We strengthened him with
the spirit of holiness. 'Will you then, O Jews, every time a
prophet comes to you with what you yourselves do not like
take to false pride and arrogantly belie some and kill others?'
They rationalize and seek to excuse themselves by admitting
to dimness of vision. God, however, curses them for their dis-
belief. Little are they convinced of the truth! And when the
book which came from God and which confirmed their own
scripture was brought to them and invoked for their benefit
they denied it. Hitherto they were boasting of such revelation
and deriding the unbelievers for never receiving any. Now that
the same truth which they had known beforehand has come to
the believers from God they reject it. God's wrath will surely fall
upon the unbelievers."[10]

The Story of Finḥāṣ

Sometimes, controversy and argument between Jews and Muslims reached such a level of intensity that the participants attacked each other. In order to appreciate how provocative the Jews were in their war of words against the Muslims, suffice it to remember the story of Finḥāṣ. The gentleness, patience, and *largeur de coeur* of Abū Bakr are proverbial. And yet he too could and did lose his temper. He once talked to Finḥāṣ calling the latter unto Islām. Finḥāṣ answered, "By God, O Abū Bakr, we do not need God. Rather, it is He who needs us. It is not I who pray to Him, it is He who prays to us. We are self-sufficient and He is not. If God were self-sufficient, He would not borrow our wealth as your Prophet claims. If He were truly not in need of us, He would not have prohibited usury to you and allowed it to us." Finḥāṣ was actually referring to the Qur'ānic verse which said: "Will you then lend God a good loan which He will repay to you many times over?"[11] At this point in the conversation, Abū Bakr lost his patience and struck Finḥāṣ on the face saying, "By God, were it not for the covenant between your people and mine, I would have struck your head off, O enemy of God." The said Finḥāṣ took his complaint to the Prophet and denied his blasphemy. It was then that this verse was revealed: "God has heard those who said, 'He is poor and we are rich.' On the day of judgment, God will remember this as well as their murder of the prophets. Then will he say: "Taste the punishments of hell."[12]

Not satisfied with their attempt to divide the Muhājirūn and Ansār, al Aws and al Khazraj, in order to dissuade the Muslims from their religion and return them to idolatry—without ever seeking to convert them to Judaism—the Jews even tried to trap Muhammad himself. A number of their rabbis, elders, and noblemen went to him one day and said: "You know who we are and you know well our prestige with our people. You know that if we should follow you, the Jews would do likewise. Would you then not help us against our people by giving a verdict in our favor when we bring to you our litigation with them to arbitrate? If you do, we shall then follow you and believe in you. At this the following divine words were revealed: "Judge between them by that which God has revealed, and do not follow their desires. Take care lest they sway you away from

some of the revelations made to you. If they turn away from
you, know that God is punishing them for some of their misdeeds. Most of them are immoral. What? Do they seek judgment
on the basis of the idolatrous principles of pre-Islām? Is not
God's judgment preferable? But they are people devoid of
certain knowledge."[13]

Orientation to the Ka'bah in Prayer

By this time, the Jews had lost their patience and began
to plot against Muḥammad. They sought to get him to leave
Madīnah as the Quraysh had succeeded in causing him and
his companions to leave Makkah. Their method, however, was
different. They said to Muḥammad that each and every prophet
hitherto had gone to Jerusalem and there established his
residence. They challenged him by asserting that if he were
a true prophet, he would only do as his predecessors had done
in considering Madīnah only as an intermediate station between
Makkah and the city where al Aqṣā Mosque stood. Muḥammad,
however, did not have to think hard to realize that they were
plotting against him. It was then, seventeen months after his
emigration from Makkah, that God commanded him to orient
himself in prayer toward the holy mosque, the house of Ibrahīm
and Isma'īl. It was then that the verse was revealed: "We see
your yearning for a direction to take in prayer. Let us then
guide you to a direction that you will accept. Orient yourself
in prayer toward the holy mosque of Makkah, and wherever
you may be, turn your face toward it."[14] The Jews condemned
Muḥammad for this and sought to trap him once more. They
went to him pleading that they would all enter into his faith
if he would but return to Jerusalem, his old direction in prayer.
In this connection, God revealed the following verses:

سَيَقُولُ السُّفَهَاءُ مِنَ النَّاسِ مَا وَلَّهُمْ عَنْ قِبْلَتِهِمُ الَّتِى كَانُوا عَلَيْهَا قُلْ لِلَّهِ الْمَشْرِقُ وَ
الْمَغْرِبُ يَهْدِى مَنْ يَشَاءُ اِلَى صِرَاطٍ مُسْتَقِيمٍ ۞ وَكَذٰلِكَ جَعَلْنَاكُمْ اُمَّةً وَسَطًا لِتَكُونُوا
شُهَدَاءَ عَلَى النَّاسِ وَيَكُونَ الرَّسُولُ عَلَيْكُمْ شَهِيدًا وَمَا جَعَلْنَا الْقِبْلَةَ الَّتِى كُنْتَ عَلَيْهَا اِلَّا لِنَعْلَمَ مَنْ
يَتَّبِعُ الرَّسُولَ مِمَّنْ يَنْقَلِبُ عَلَى عَقِبَيْهِ وَاِنْ كَانَتْ لَكَبِيرَةً اِلَّا عَلَى الَّذِينَ هَدَى اللَّهُ

"Some foolish people will ask, 'What caused them to change their
old orientation?' Say: 'To God belongs the East as well as the

West. He guides unto His straight path whomsoever he wills."
Thus We have caused you to be a nation following the course
of the golden mean, witnessing unto mankind and witnessed
to by the Prophet. The whole question of the orientation in
prayer was intended by us to sift the true believers from the
apostates and deceptors. To change orientation is a big travail
only to those who have missed the divine guidance."[15]

The Christian Delegation from Najrān

While the war of words was raging between Muḥammad and
the Jews in full intensity, a delegation from the Christians of
Najrān consisting of sixty riders arrived in Madīnah. Among
them were some of the nobles, learned men, and religious leaders
of the tribe whom the emperors of Byzantium had been protecting, encouraging, financing, and assisting in the building
of churches. Perhaps this delegation arrived in Madīnah after
they learned of the conflict between Muḥammad and the Jews
with the hope of adding fuel to the fire so that neighboring
Christendom, whether in al Shām or in Yaman, might relax
and feel safe from Jewish plots and Arab aggression. The three
scriptural religions thus confronted one another in Madīnah.
The delegation entered with the Prophet into public debate and
these were soon joined by the Jews, thus resulting in a tripartite
dialogue between Judaism, Christianity and Islām. The Jews
were obstinately denying the prophethood of Jesus as well as
of Muḥammad, as we have seen earlier, and pretending that
Ezra was the son of God. The Christians were defending trinitarianism and the divinity of Jesus. Muḥammad was calling
men to recognize the unity of God and the spiritual unity of
mankind. Most Jews and Christians asked Muḥammad which
prophets he believed in. He answered: "We believe in God, in
what has been revealed to us, to Ibrahīm, Ismaʻīl, Isḥaq, Yaʻqūb,
and his children. We believe in what has been revealed to Moses,
to Jesus, as well as in all the revelations which the prophets
have received from their Lord. We do not differentiate between
them. And we have submitted ourselves to God."[16] Muḥammad
criticized both Jews and Christians in very strong terms for
their compromise of the monotheistic faith that God is one,
for tampering with the words of God in their scriptures, and
for interpreting them in ways violating the understanding of
the prophets whose prophethood they themselves acknowledged.

He criticized them for asserting that the revelation of Jesus, Moses, and their predecessors in prophethood differed in many essential matters from his own revelation. In support of this, Muḥammad argued that what those prophets had received from God was the same eternal truth as that revealed to him. Being the truth, its light shines forth clear and distinct, and its content is majestic and simple to any researcher submitting to none but God and to anyone capable of seeing the world as a connected and integrated unity rather than as ephemeral intimations of desire, passion, and ulterior motives. Being the truth, it must be readily recognized by the man liberated from blind submission to old wives' tales or to the sanctified legends of the fathers and ancestors. By nature, such truth must be open and possible for everyone to perceive.

Congress on the Three Religions

This was a truly great congress which the city of Yathrib had witnessed. In it, the three religions which today dominate the world and determine its destiny had met, and they did so for the greatest idea and the noblest purpose. It had neither political nor economic aims, but stood beyond the materialistic objectives which our present world is anxiously, yet so vainly trying to realize. The objective of the congress was purely spiritual. Whereas in the case of Christianity and Judaism the spiritual objective was backed or motivated by political, capitalistic, and worldly ambitions, Muḥammad's spiritual purpose was pure and advocated for the sake of humanity as a whole. It was God that gave this purpose of Muḥammad's its form, and this same form was proclaimed not only to the Jews but to the Christians and all mankind. Muḥammad was commanded to address the delegates of both faiths,

قُلْ يَا أَهْلَ الْكِتَبِ تَعَالَوْا إِلَى كَلِمَةٍ سَوَآءٍ بَيْنَنَا وَبَيْنَكُمْ أَلَّا نَعْبُدَ إِلَّا اللَّهَ وَلَا نُشْرِكَ بِهِ شَيْئًا وَلَا يَتَّخِذَ بَعْضُنَا بَعْضًا أَرْبَابًا مِّن دُونِ اللَّهِ فَإِن تَوَلَّوْا فَقُولُوا اشْهَدُوا بِأَنَّا مُسْلِمُونَ ۞

"Say, 'O People of the Book, come now to a fair principle common to both of us, that we do not worship aught but God, that we do not associate aught with Him and that we do not take one another as lords besides God.' But if they turn away, then say, 'Bear witness that we are Muslims.' "[17]

Withdrawal of the Christian Delegation

What can Jews, Christians, or any other people say of this call to worship none but God, to associate none with Him and never to take one another as lords besides God? The spirit which is sincere and truthful, which is endowed with reason and candid emotion cannot but believe in this call and in it alone. But human life is not entirely dominated by such noble dispositions. There is yet the materialistic consideration. Man is indeed weak; and it is this inclination to material gain which causes him to subject himself to the dominion of another man for material advantage. Man suffers terribly from false pride, his considerateness, self-respect and reason are destroyed thereby. It was this materialistic ambition for wealth, worldly prestige and social eminence that caused Abū Ḥārithah, the most learned of the people of Najrān, to tell a friend of his that he was perfectly convinced of the truth of which Muḥammad was teaching. When that friend asked him why he did not then convert to Islām, he answered: "I cannot do so on account of what my people have done to me. They have honored, financed, and respected me; and they insist on differing from him. Should I follow him, they would take away from me all this that I now have."

It was to this message that Muḥammad summoned Jews and Christians alike. Muslim relationships with the former were already under the governance of the Covenant of Madīnah. Those of the latter depended upon the Christians' response to Muḥammad's invitation. Though they did not join Islām at this time, the Christians resolved neither to oppose Muḥammad nor the missionary activity of his followers. Appreciating the perfect justice of Muḥammad's new order, they asked him to appoint for them a Muslim to act as judge in their own disputes at home. Muḥammad sent with them Abū 'Ubaydah ibn al Jarrāḥ, who was vested with the proper judicial authority.

Rethinking the Problem of Quraysh and Makkah

Muḥammad continued to consolidate the civilization for which his teaching and example provided the foundation. Together with his Muhājirūn companions, he thought over the problem of Quraysh, which had vexed them ever since their emigration.

The Muslims were moved by many considerations. In Makkah stood the Ka'bah, the house of Ibrahīm, pilgrimage center to them as well as to all the Arabs. Until their exile, they had performed this sacred duty in season, every year. In Makkah too many of their friends, relatives, and loved ones had stayed behind and were still practicing the old idolatry. In Makkah, their wealth, worldly goods, trade, and properties were still under the jurisdiction of the Quraysh. Madīnah itself was struck with epidemic diseases which attacked the Muslims and inflicted upon them great suffering; indeed, the very trip to Madīnah on foot and without provisions had so worn them out that they entered the city on their first arrival already diseased and exhausted. This hard journey had naturally increased their longing for their hometown. Moreover, they did not leave Makkah of their own accord but under compulsion and full of resentment for their overlords who threatened them with all kinds of punishments and sanctions. It was not in their nature to suffer such injustices or to submit to such tyranny for long without thinking of avenging themselves. Besides these determinants, there was the natural motivation of longing to return to one's homeland, to one's home where one was born and grew up. There was the natural longing for the land, the plain, and the mountains, the water and the vegetation, all of which had constituted their earliest associations, friendships, and love. The land in which he grows and to which he returns at the end of his life has a special appeal for man. It determines his heart and his emotion and moves him to defend it with all his power and wealth as well as to exert all possible effort—indeed his life —for its guardianship and well being. It is to the land from which we came out, as it were, that we want to return and be buried in at death. This natural feeling added a degree of intensity to the other emotions. Indeed, the Muhājirūn could never forget Makkah nor stop thinking about the problem of their relation with the Quraysh. From the very nature of the case, and after thirteen long years of persecution and cònflict in which they held their ground firmly, the Muslims could not possibly entertain any ideas of withdrawal or giving up. The religion itself to which they had converted and for the sake of which they had emigrated did not approve of weakness, despair, servile submission, or the patient bearing of injustice. Although it was strongly opposed to aggression and condemned it in no uncertain terms, and although it called for and promoted fraternity and brotherhood, it demanded that man rise up to the defense of his person, of his dignity, of the freedom of religion, and the freedom of homeland. It was for this defense and purpose that Muḥammad concluded with the Muslims of Yathrib the great covenant of al 'Aqabah. Now the question posed itself: how may the Muhājirūn fulfill this duty imposed upon them for the sake of God, His holy house, and their beloved homeland, Makkah? Toward the realization of this objective will the policy of Muḥammad and of the Muslims now turn. This objective was to preoccupy them all until the conquest of Makkah had been achieved, and the religion of God, and the truth which it proclaimed, had become supreme.

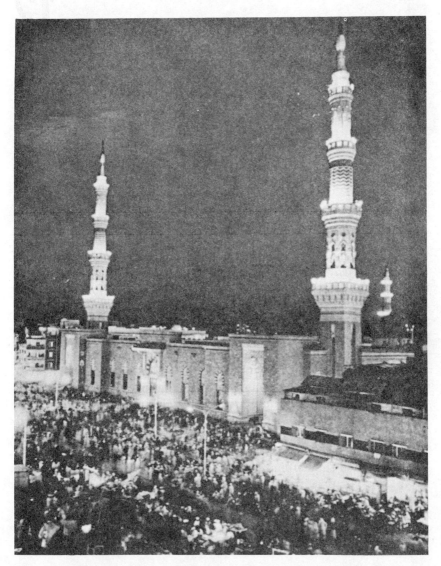

The Mosque of the Prophet in Madīnah, Saudi Arabia.

The First Raids and Skirmishes

Muslim Policy in Madīnah

The Muslims were all well settled in Madīnah only months after the Hijrah. Their longing for Makkah increased with every new day, as they thought of their loved ones whom they had left behind, of their property and wealth which they had forsaken, and of the injuries which the Quraysh had inflicted upon them in the past. What they would now do was for them a constant question. The majority of historians think that the Muslims, led by Muḥammad, thought of avenging themselves on the Quraysh and of declaring war against them. Some even claim that the Muslims had thought of declaring this war ever since they arrived in Madīnah, and that if they had not opened hostilities at that time it was because they were preoccupied with the business of settling down and organizing their own lives. They reasoned that Muḥammad had concluded the great covenant of al 'Aqabah precisely in order to wage war against all opponents and that it was natural for his and his companions' attention first to fall upon the Quraysh—a fact proven by Quraysh's own mobilization upon hearing of the conclusion of the said pact.

The First Raids

This general hypothesis of the historians is supposedly proved by events which took place eight months after the Hijrah of

Muḥammad. The Prophet then sent his uncle Ḥamzah ibn 'Abd al Muṭṭalib with forty riders from the Muhājirūn, rather than the Anṣār, to the seacoast near al 'Is where Abū Jahl ibn Hishām was camping with three hundred Makkan riders. Ḥamzah was just about to enter into battle with the Quraysh force when Majdiy ibn 'Amr al Juhanī, who was in peaceful relation with both parties, interfered to separate them before the battle had begun. At the same time, Muḥammad sent 'Ubaydah ibn al Hārith with sixty riders from the Muhājirūn to go to a well in the valley of Rābigh in Ḥijāz where they met more than two hundred riders led by Abū Sufyān. The Muslim forces withdrew without engaging the enemy, except for the report that Sa'd ibn Abū Waqqās shot one single arrow, later to be called, 'the first arrow shot in the cause of Islām.' It is also reported that Muḥammad had sent Sa'd ibn Abū Waqqāṣ to lead a number of Muhājirūn riders (eight according to one version and twenty according to another) into the Ḥijāz, but he returned without engaging the enemy.

Raids Led by the Prophet

As further evidence to all the foregoing it is said that the Prophet himself had undertaken the leadership of the raids on al Abwā' twelve months after the Hijrah and appointed Sa'd ibn 'Ubādah as his vice-regent in Madīnah during his absence. In their search for the Quraysh as well as the Banū Ḍamrah, the Muslims reached Waddān. They did not meet any man from Quraysh on that expedition, but they did succeed in winning Banū Ḍamrah as allies. A month later, Muḥammad led a force of two hundred riders from both the Muhājirūn and Ansār camps with Buwāṭ as their objective, where a caravan of 1,500 camels accompanied by one hundred riders under the leadership of Umayyah ibn Khalaf was reported to be passing. No engagement took place because the caravan had taken an untrodden, unknown route. Two or three months after Muḥammad's return from Buwāṭ by way of Raḍwā, he appointed Abū Salamah ibn 'Abd al Asad to take his place in Madīnah while he and more than two hundred Muslim riders went on an expedition to 'Ushayrah in the district of Yanbu'. There he spent the whole month of First Jumādā and a few days of Second Jumādā of the second year A.H. (October 623 C.E.) waiting for a Quraysh caravan headed by Abū Sufyān to pass, without success, for it

had already gone earlier. During his stay in the area, he concluded
a pact of friendship with the tribe of Banū Mudlaj and their
allies from Banū Damrah. He had hardly spent ten days in
Madīnah after his return when Kurz ibn Jābir al Fihrī, an ally
of Quraysh, raided the camels and cattle of Madīnah. The Prophet
immediately led a force after him, appointing Zayd ibn Hārithah
as his representative during his absence. The force marched
until it reached a valley called Safawān in the district of Badr
and again missed their objective, the said Kurz ibn Jābir al
Fihrī. It is to this raid that biographers refer as the first
raid of Badr.

The Historians' View of the First Raid

Does not all this constitute evidence that the Muhājirūn as
well as Muhammad sought first of all to avenge themselves
on the Quraysh and to open hostilities against them? There is
full evidence, according to these historians, that for these
expeditions and raids the Muslims had two objectives: first to
seize the caravans of the Quraysh, on their way to or from al
Shām during the summer, in order to take possession of the
goods which they carried; second to cut off the Quraysh caravan
routes to al Shām. This latter goal was to be achieved by concluding covenants and pacts with the various tribes settled along
these routes. Thus, it would be all the easier and safer for the
Muhājirūn to attack these caravans without fear of detection
or attack from the local inhabitants, and the caravans themselves
would then be at the total mercy of the Muslims. The raids
which the Prophet sent out under the leadership of Hamzah,
'Ubaydah ibn al Hārith, and Sa'd ibn Abū Waqqās, as well as
the pacts of friendship and peace which he concluded with
Banū Damrah, Banū Mudlaj, and others, confirmed this second
objective and proved that the Muslims had definitely aimed at
cutting the road to al Shām for the Quraysh and Makkah.

Our View of These Raids

That by means of these raids, begun six months after their
settlement in Madīnah and undertaken by the Muhājirūn alone,
the Muslims sought to wage war against Quraysh and to attack
its caravans is an opinion which cannot be accepted without
hesitation and scrutiny. The expedition of Hamzah did not
consist of more than thirty men, that of 'Ubaydah, sixty, that

of Sa'd eight, according to one version, and twenty according to another. The number of fighters assigned by the Quraysh to the protection of their caravan was in each case many times the number of riders the Muslims had sent out. Moreover, ever since Muhammad emigrated to Madīnah and began to forge a chain of alliances around the city, the Quraysh multiplied the number of escorts for their caravans and improved their weapons. Whatever the personal courage of Hamzah, 'Ubaydah, and Sa'd among the leaders of those expeditionary forces of the Muhājirūn, their military equipment was not such as would encourage them to make war. They were satisfied with threatening the Quraysh rather than engaging them in battle. The only exception to this was the single arrow shot by Sa'd, as reported above.

Exposure of Quraysh's Trade to Danger

The caravans of Quraysh were protected by escorts of the people of Makkah who were related to many Muhājirūn as members of the same tribe, the same house and clan, and often the same family. It was not easy, therefore, for them to decide to enter into an engagement in which members of the same tribe, clan, and family would kill one another and then expose to retaliation all their fellow tribesmen on each side, in fact to expose the whole of Makkah and Madīnah at once to the *lex talionis* of the desert. Hardly any change affected the inability and unwillingness of Muslims and others to launch a civil war which both parties had ably struggled to avert for thirteen long years, from the commission of Muhammad to prophethood to the day of his emigration to Madīnah. The Muslims knew too well that the covenant of al 'Aqabah was a defensive one which both al Aws and al Khazraj had undertaken to protect Muhammad. These tribes of Madīnah have never agreed either with Muhammad nor with anyone else to commit aggression on anyone. It is not possible, therefore, to accept the view of the earliest historians, who did not begin to write the history of the Prophet until two centuries or so after his death, that the first raids and expeditions had actually been intended for fighting. Hence, we must understand these events in a more reasonable way to harmonize with what we know to have been the policy of the Muslims in this early period of Madīnah, and to be consistent with the Prophet's policy of common understanding, mutual friendship, and co-operation to obtain religious freedom for all.

It is more likely, therefore, that these early expeditions had only psychic objectives, and were meant to press home to the Quraysh the realization that their own interest demanded that they come into some kind of understanding with the Muslims. The Muslims were, after all, their own people, compelled to migrate from their own city to escape the persecution so far inflicted. Rather than to bring war and hostility, these expeditions were intended to put an end to the old hostility, to guarantee to the Muslims the freedom they sought for calling men to their religion, and to ensure for Makkah the security it needed for its caravans to al Shām. This trade, in which both Makkah and Ṭā'if were involved and which Makkah used to carry on with the south as well as with the north, had built up large interests and businesses. Some caravans consisted of two thousand camels or more, and carried a load whose value amounted to fifty thousand Dīnārs.[1] According to the estimates of the Orientalist, Sprenger, the annual exports of Makkah amounted to 250,000 Dīnārs or 160,000 gold pounds. If the Quraysh could be made to realize that this precious trade and wealth were exposed to danger by their own sons who had migrated to Madīnah, perhaps they might be inclined to reach an understanding with the Muslims in order to grant them the freedom to preach their faith, visit Makkah, and perform the pilgrimage, which was all they really sought. Such an understanding was not possible, however, unless the Quraysh were brought to realize that their emigrant sons were capable of impeding that trade and inflicting some material harm. To my mind, this explains the return of Ḥamzah and his riders without battle after their encounter with Abū Jahl ibn Hishām on the seacoast when Majdiy ibn 'Amr al Juhanī intervened between him and the Quraysh. It also explains the fact of the small numbers of riders which the Muslims sent on these expeditions in the direction of the trade routes of Makkah. Otherwise, it would be unreasonable that the Muslims go out to war in such small numbers. This also explains Muḥammad's alliances of peace which he concluded with the tribes settled along the routes of these caravans while Quraysh persisted in its hostility toward the Muhājirūn. Apparently, Muḥammad had hoped that the news of these alliances would reach the Quraysh and cause them to reconsider their position and, perhaps, open the road to some understanding.

Al Anṣār and Offensive Attack

The foregoing hypothesis is corroborated by a very reliable tradition to the effect that when the Prophet—may God's blessing be upon him—went with his men to Buwāṭ and to al 'Ushayrah, a great number of Anṣār from Madīnah accompanied him. These Anṣār had covenanted with him for his protection, not in order to launch any offensive attack against anyone. This point will become clear when we study the great battle of Badr. There, Muḥammad hesitated whether or not to permit the fighting to take place until the people of Madīnah had clearly agreed to join that specific sortie. Although the Anṣār saw no violation of their covenant with Muḥammad if the latter entered into other covenants of peace and friendship, they were not thereby committed to join him in a war against Makkah which no Arab morality or custom would approve. The effect of the alliances which Muḥammad concluded with the tribes settled along the trade route was surely that of endangering Makkan trade. But how far removed is such an attempt from declaring and entering into a full scale war! We may conclude, therefore, that the views that Ḥamzah, 'Ubaydah ibn al Ḥārith, and Sa'd ibn Abū Waqqāṣ were sent to fight the Quraysh, and that their expeditions should be called military raids, are unsound and unacceptable. Likewise, the view that Muḥammad had gone to al Abwā, Buwāṭ, and al 'Ushayrah for purposes of war is refuted by the considerations we have just given. The fact that such a view is held by the historians of Muḥammad does not constitute a sound argument because the said historians did not write until toward the end of the second century A.H. Furthermore, the said historians were looking at these events as they occurred after the great battle of Badr. Hence, they looked upon them as preliminary skirmishes preceding that great battle and leading toward it. It was a natural mistake for them to add these sorties to the list of battles the Muslims fought during the Prophet's lifetime.

Nature of the Madīnese

A large number of Orientalists have perceived these facts and realized their opposition to the said claim, although they did not expressly say so in their works. We are moved to accredit them with this realization despite their following the Muslim historians in their general attribution to Muḥammad and the

Muhājirūn of the intention to make war against Makkah from the first days of residence in Madīnah. They point out that these early expeditions were, rather, intended as raids on the caravans to rob their goods, and they argue that this kind of robbery was embedded in the nature of the people of the desert and that the Madīnese were attracted by prospective booty to co-operate in violation of their pledge at al 'Aqabah. This is spurious reasoning, of course, and to be rejected outright. The people of Madīnah were not people of the desert living on robbery and raids. Rather, like the people of Makkah, they had other sources of income and were motivated the same way as all settled people who live on agriculture and trade. Such people do not make war except for an extraordinary and stirring purpose. On the other hand, the Muhājirūn were entitled to seize Quraysh goods in retaliation for the goods which the Quraysh had seized from them. But they did not have recourse to such action before the battle of Badr. This was not, therefore, the reason for those expeditions. Besides, fighting had not yet been permitted in Islām. Neither Muhammad nor his companions could have indulged in it for the nomadic purpose erroneously explained by the Orientalists. Fighting was permitted in Islām, and carried out by Muhammad and his companions, in order to stop their being persecuted for their faith and to have all the freedom they needed to call men to it. Later, when we see the details and the proofs of this, it will become clear that in all these alliances Muhammad's purpose was the consolidation of the defense of Madīnah. The objective was to remove Madīnah beyond any design the Quraysh might have against its Muslim inhabitants. Muhammad could not have forgotten that the Makkans once sought to extradite the Muslims from Abyssinia. At that time, Muhammad did not see any objection at all to entering into a treaty of peace with Quraysh. Such a treaty would have stopped persecution, given him the freedom to call unto the new faith, and to witness for God unto all men.

Threat to the Jews

Perhaps, too, by these expeditions and armed sorties, Muhammad sought to warn the Jews of Madīnah and the neighboring area. We have already seen how, upon Muhammad's arrival at

Madīnah, the Jews hoped to bring him into alliance with them
and how, after befriending him and pledging to honor his freedom to practice and preach the new religion, they had begun to
oppose and plot against him. In fact, no sooner had Muḥammad
settled down and the prospects of Islām had begun to improve,
than the Jews, for their part, began their undeclared war against
him. Their opposition and hostility were never open. Above all,
they feared lest any harm might befall their trade; and, although
they had fanned and fueled the fires of civil war in the past,
they adeptly avoided every possible involvement. Henceforth,
their covenant with Muḥammad at least prevented them from
any such open involvement; and they recoursed to every hidden
way to instigate enmity and hostility between the Muhājirūn
and Ansār so as to revive the old hatreds between al Aws and
al Khazraj by reminding them of the day of Buʻāth in reciting
the war poetry which had been composed on that occasion.

Jewish Plots

The Muslims realized what the Jews were about, for the latter
were neither gentle nor discrete. Their instigation was always
overdone. The Muslims accused those who entered into the
Covenant of Madīnah of hypocrisy, and classified them with the
munāfiqūn.[2] Some Jews were once violently expelled from the
mosque, and were later isolated and boycotted. After failing to
convince them of the truth of Islām, the Prophet—may God's
blessing be upon him—let them alone. But to let them alone
religiously did not mean that they should be allowed to instigate
the Muslims to a civil internecine war. Politically speaking,
it was not enough to warn them and to warn the Muslims of
their instigation. It was necessary to impress them with the
fact that the Muslims were sufficiently strong to stamp out any
such war as the Jews were instigating as well as to uproot
its causes. A good way for pressing this realization upon them
was the sending out of Muslim forces on military expeditions in
all directions on condition that such sorties entail no actual fighting and no military setback. This account seems to be factual,
for men like Ḥamzah, whom we know to have been quick to
fly into a rage, turned around in front of the enemy without
engagement. The appearance of an honored friend asking for
peace is not enough to separate two parties either of which is
bent upon fighting. Rather, non-engagement was a deliberate

and carefully laid out plan. Its specific purpose was on one side to threaten and warn the Jews, and, on the other, to seek an understanding with the Quraysh to let the religious call take its course freely, without impediment or recourse to war or fighting.

Islām and Fighting

This peaceful show of strength by Islām does not at all mean that Islām, at that time, forbade fighting in defense of personal life and of religion, or to put a stop to persecution. Indeed, Islām did not. Rather, it imposed such defense as a sacred duty. What it did really mean at that time, as it does today or will ever do, was to condemn any war of aggression. "Do not commit any aggression," God commands. He counsels, "God does not love the aggressors."[3] If, at that time, the Muhājirūn felt justified in seizing the property of the Quraysh in retaliation for the latter's confiscation of their property when they emigrated, they certainly realized that to protect the Muslims against apostasy from their faith was a greater duty in the eyes of God and His Prophet. The latter was the main purpose for the sake of which God had permitted the Muslims to fight at all.

'Abdullah ibn Jaḥsh's Expedition

The proof of the foregoing contention may be found in the expedition of 'Abdullah ibn Jaḥsh al Asadī, who was sent by the Prophet of God at the head of a number of Muhājirūn in the month of Rajab of the second year A.H. The Prophet gave him a document and asked him not to look at it until two days after the start of his journey. He was then supposed to follow its instructions without forcing any of his companions to comply with them. Two days after he started off, 'Abdullah, having unsealed the document, read the following instructions: "As soon as you have read this document, proceed to Nakhlah between Makkah and Ṭā'if, and there seek to learn for us the news of the Quraysh and their movements." When his companions learned that they were under no compulsion to go along with him, they all decided to do so except for Sa'd ibn Abū Waqqāṣ al Zuhrī and 'Utbah ibn Ghazwān, who preferred to look, on their own, for some of their camels which the Quraysh had seized. 'Abdullah and his companions proceeded as instructed. At Nakhlah, they saw a donkey caravan carrying trade goods for the Quraysh which were guarded by 'Amr ibn al Ḥadramī. The date was the end of the month of Rajab. Remembering the old persecutions of the Quraysh and the latter's seizure of their wealth and property, 'Abdullah ibn Jaḥsh, after consulting with his Muhājirūn companions, said: "Surely, if you allow the caravan to pass through tonight unmolested, they will reach the holy territory tomorrow and will thereby become forbidden to you. And yet, if you kill them today, you will have killed them in the holy month when killing is forbidden." The hesitant Muslims were afraid to attack the caravan; but, encouraging one another, they agreed to kill whomever they could and to seize the goods in his possession. One of them shot an arrow at 'Amr ibn al Ḥadramī and killed him. The Muslims captured two men from the Quraysh.

Sedition Greater Than Murder

'Abdullah ibn Jaḥsh arrived in Madīnah together with the two Quraysh captives and the donkey caravan loaded completely with goods. He had already earmarked one-fifth of the booty to the Prophet. But when the Prophet saw them, he said: "I have not instructed you to fight during the holy months." He stopped the caravan in its place as well as the two captives and refused to take any part of the booty. He castigated 'Abdullah ibn Jaḥsh and his companions and, later on, they were further scolded and punished by their fellow Muslims for what they had done. The Quraysh seized the opportunity to spread the propaganda everywhere that Muḥammad and his companions had violated the sanctity of the holy month by having killed, robbed and captured. The Muslims of Makkah answered that the event had taken place not in the holy months but during the following month of Sha'bān. The Jews immediately joined the chorus of Quraysh propaganda with the hope of engaging the Muslims in a war with the Quraysh over a case in which the Muslims were apparently in the wrong according to Arabian custom. It was then that God revealed the judgment:

يَسْئَلُونَكَ عَنِ الشَّهْرِ الْحَرَامِ قِتَالٍ فِيهِ قُلْ قِتَالٌ فِيهِ كَبِيرٌ وَصَدٌّ عَنْ سَبِيلِ اللهِ وَكُفْرٌ

بِهِ وَالْمَسْجِدِ الْحَرَامِ وَإِخْرَاجُ أَهْلِهِ مِنْهُ أَكْبَرُ عِنْدَ اللهِ وَالْفِتْنَةُ أَكْبَرُ مِنَ الْقَتْلِ وَلَا

يَزَالُونَ يُقَاتِلُونَكُمْ حَتَّى يَرُدُّوكُمْ عَنْ دِينِكُمْ إِنِ اسْتَطَاعُوا

"They ask you concerning the holy month whether or not fighting is permitted therein. Answer: 'to fight therein is a grave
misdeed. But to impede men from following the cause of God, to
deny God, to violate the sanctity of the holy mosque, to expel
its people from its precincts is with God a greater wrong than
fighting in the holy month. Moreover, to divide the community of
Muslims against itself is greater yet. Your enemies continue to
fight you by all these means in order to compel you to abjure
your religion."[4]

This revelation brought the Muslims relief, and the Prophet
accepted his share of the booty. When the Quraysh sought to
ransom the two captives, the Prophet answered: "We shall not
accept your ransom for the two captives unless you return our
two men whom you have captured, namely Sa'd ibn Abū Waqqās
and 'Utbah ibn Ghazwān. If you kill them we shall likewise kill
your two men." Sa'd and 'Utbah were returned and the two
Quraysh captives were released. One of them, al Ḥakam ibn
Kaysān, was immediately converted to Islām and spent the rest of
his life in Madīnah. The other returned to Makkah where he
remained to the end.

It is well worth our while to pause here for further consideration of the evidence which this expedition of 'Abdullah ibn
Jaḥsh and the Qur'ānic verse, which was revealed in that connection, furnish for our generalization concerning the political
theory of Islām. The event occurs as it were at the very cross-
roads of the development of Islāmic policy. In kind, it is new.
It points to a spirit strong in its nobility, human in its strength,
a spirit which orders the material, moral, and spiritual aspects
of life very strictly while enhancing man's quest of perfection.
The Qur'ān answered the question of the idolaters concerning
whether or not fighting is permissible in the holy months and
approved their view that it is a grave misdeed. But it also
warned against something yet greater in its evil and immorality: that is to impede men from following the path of God
and to deny Him, to stop men from entering the holy mosque,
to expel the worshipers therefrom, or to sway and lure man
away from his religion by promise, threat, bribery, and persecution. All these are greater misdeeds than fighting during
the holy months or any months. The Quraysh and the idolaters
who blamed the Muslims for killing during the holy months
were themselves still fighting the Muslims by these means
in order to compel them to renounce their religion. If the Quraysh

and the idolators perpetrated all these misdeeds together, the victims of their misdeeds cannot be blamed for fighting during the holy months. Rather, the real misdeed is that of perpetrating these evils during the holy month against the innocent and the peaceful.

The Qur'ān and Fighting

Fitnah, or sedition, is a greater crime than murder. It is a right, nay a duty, of whosoever witnesses it, whether perpetrated against an individual or a whole community, to take up arms and fight for the sake of God and thus put an immediate end to it. It is here that the Orientalists and the missionaries raise their eyebrows and voices, shouting: "Do you see? Here is Muḥammad agreeing that his religion actually calls to war, to *jihād* in the cause of God, that is, to compel man by the sword to enter into Islām. Isn't this precisely what is meant by fanaticism? Now contrast this with Christianity, which denies fighting and condemns war, which calls for peace and advocates tolerance, which binds men in bonds of brotherhood in God and in Christ. . . ." In arguing this point I do not wish to mention the statement of the New Testament, "I have not come to send peace but a sword. . . ."[5] Nor do I want to analyze the meanings implicit in such statements. The Muslims understand the religion of Jesus only as interpreted by the Qur'ān. Rather, I want to begin by refuting the claim that Muḥammad's religion calls for fighting and coercion of men into Islām. That is a false accusation denied by the Qur'ānic judgment:

لَاۤ اِكْرَاهَ فِى الدِّيْنِ قَدْ تَّبَيَّنَ الرُّشْدُ مِنَ الْغَيِّ

"There is no compulsion in religion—the truth is now distinct from error;" as well as by the command, "Fight in the cause of God those who fight you, but do not commit any aggression. God does not love the aggressor."[6]

The same directives are contained in a number of other verses.

War in the Cause of God

Jihād, or war for the sake of God, is clearly defined in the verses which we have mentioned and which were revealed in connection with the expedition of 'Abdullah ibn Jaḥsh. Its definite meaning is to fight those who sway the Muslim away from his religion and prevent him from walking in the path of God. This fight is waged solely for the freedom to call men unto God and unto His religion. To use a modern expression consonant with the usage of the present age, we may say that war in Islām is permitted—nay, it is rather a duty—when undertaken in defense of freedom of thought and opinion. All weapons used by the aggressors may be used against them. If somebody seeks to sway a man from conviction or opinion, and he effectively uses propaganda and logic without physical coercion, persecution, discrimination, or use of illicit means such as bribery, no man may stop him except by answering his argument and analyzing and exposing his logic. However, if he resorts to armed force to prevent a man from holding a certain opinion, then it becomes necessary to answer his armed power with equal armed power wherever practical. Man has no dignity if his convictions have none. Convictions are far more precious than wealth, position, power or life itself. To those who appreciate the meaning of humanity, convictions are far more precious than the material life which man shares with the animals. If man's humanity consists of no more than eating and drinking, growing and struggling for survival, he is one with the animals. Man's spiritual and moral convictions constitute the moral bond which unites him to his fellow-men, the spiritual link between him and God. The life of conviction is man's great distinction from the animal kingdom. By it, man wills for his brother that which he wills for himself; by it, he inclines to share his wealth with the poor, the destitute, and the miserable, though such sharing may imply some deprivation to his near relatives; by it, man enters into communion with the universe to perform that which enables the universe to realize the perfection which God has prescribed and established for it.

Should conviction take possession of a man and should another man attempt to make him renounce it under conditions in which self-protection or defense are impossible, such a man would do what the Muslims did before their emigration from Madīnah, namely, to bear patiently all injury, persecution, and injustice. Neither hunger nor deprivation of any kind would cause him to succumb to ignoble desires; patient forbearance was precisely what the Muslims practiced in Makkah as well as what the early Christians had practiced. But those who suffer in patience for the sake of their convictions are not the majority of mankind nor the plebians among them. They are, however, the select and chosen few whom God has endowed with such moral strength that they are capable of standing up against any injury or injustice, however great. It was precisely this kind of conviction which the New Testament has associated with the judgment that whoever is endowed therewith "shall say unto this mountain, remove hence to yonder place, and it shall remove."[7] But if it is possible for man to defend himself against aggression with the same arms as the aggressor, to fight the man who blocks the path of God by use of his own means, then it is his duty to do so. Otherwise, one would be weak of faith and doubtful in conviction. That is what Muḥammad and his companions did after they had achieved a measure of security for themselves in Madīnah. That is equally what the Christians did after they had achieved power in Rome and Byzantium, after the conversion of the Roman emperors.

Christianity and Fighting

The missionaries say, "But the spirit of Christianity condemns fighting altogether." I do not wish to pause here for investigating the truth, or lack of it, of such a claim. The history of Christianity, however, is a legitimate witness in this matter and so is the history of Islām. From the dawn of Christianity until today every country of the world has been soaked with blood in the name of Jesus Christ. The Romans and the Byzantines of old as well as the European peoples of modern times are guilty of shedding blood in religious causes. The Crusades were launched and their fires fanned by Christians, not by Muslims. For hundreds of years, one army after another rolled out of Europe in the direction of the Muslim Orient to fight, to destroy, and to shed blood. In every case, the popes who claimed to be the vicars of Jesus Christ, blessed and encouraged these armies and hurried them to Jerusalem and other destinations. Were all these popes heretics? Was their Christianity spurious? Or was every one of them a pretender, an ignoramus, unaware that Christianity absolutely condemns fighting? The missionaries rejoin, "Those were the Middle Ages, ages of darkness, unfit as evidence against Christianity." If this is an argument on which they pin some hope, let us then turn to the twentieth century in which we now live and which they call "the century of the highest human civilization." This century has indeed seen the same darkness as did the Middle Ages. Lord Allenby, representing the allied forces of England, France, Italy, Rumania, and America, stopped in Jerusalem in 1918 after his conquest of that city toward the end of the first World War and said: "Today the Crusades have come to an end."

The Saints in Islām and Christianity

If in every age and period, there have been Christian saints who have condemned fighting and who rose to the pinnacles of human brotherhood—indeed, of brotherhood among all elements of the universe—so there were among the Muslims saints who have reached these very pinnacles and related themselves to all existence and being in a bond of brotherhood, love, and illumination and who realized within their souls the very unity of being. These saints, however, whether Muslim or Christian, do not represent human life in its constant development and struggle toward perfection. Rather they represent the highest example of the realization of that perfection. The general run of men, however, seek to understand and realize such perfection, but neither their reason nor their imagination succeeds in doing so with any amount of precision or completeness. Their attempts to realize it are understandable as preliminaries and trials. One thousand three hundred and fifty-seven years have so far passed since the emigration of the Arab Prophet from Makkah to Madīnah. Throughout these years men have increased their capacities to fight, improved their devilish art of war, and made its weapons more destructive than ever. However, disarmament and the cessation of war are still words of mere propaganda spread before the eyes of the credulous in war after war, each more devastating than the preceding. These noble ideals have hardly been more than propaganda claims made by people thus far incapable—and who knows, perhaps never capable—of realizing any such desiderata, of bringing true peace into the world, a peace of brotherhood and justice instead of an armed peace which is only a preliminary to another war.

Islām, the Natural Religion

The religion of Islām is not one of illusion and fantasy. Neither is it a religion which addresses only the individual as such and urges him to rise to perfection. Rather, Islām is the natural religion, the religion which naturally belongs to all men, individuals as well as groups. It is the religion of truth, of freedom, and of order. As long as it is also the nature of man to fight and to make war, to discipline that nature and to limit this inclination within the narrowest frontier is all that is possible for men to bear and abide by; it is all that humanity can hope to achieve in its struggle toward goodness and perfection. By far the best disciplining of this inclination to war is to limit it to pure defense of one's person, one's faith, one's freedom of opinion, and one's freedom to preach. The greatest wisdom is to regulate the making of war so that all the rights and dignities of man may be respected and observed to the utmost. And this is precisely what Islām has sought to do, as we have seen and as we shall have occasion to see later. That is precisely what the Qur'ān has commanded, as we have seen, and shall have occasion to see in the sequel.

13

The Great Battle
of Badr

The expedition of 'Abdullah ibn Jahsh constitued the cross-roads of Islāmic policy. It was the occasion when Wāqid ibn 'Abdullah al Tamīmī shot an arrow at 'Amr ibn al Ḥaḍramī and killed him, thus shedding blood by a Muslim hand for the first time. It was in regard to this sortie that the Qur'ānic verses constituting the Islāmic position on war and fighting were revealed. And it was in consequence of this revelation that fighting was permitted, but only against those who seek to compel the Muslims to renounce their religion and who stand in the way of calling men unto God. The same expedition constituted also the crossroads of Muslim policy toward Quraysh, for it now opened the door for the two parties to compete in military power and strength as they had done formerly in word and idea. It was after that expedition that the Muslims began to think seriously of extracting their goods from Quraysh by force and conquest. The Quraysh saw in this an opportunity to stir up the whole peninsula against Muḥammad and his companions, and therefore accused them of the most heinous crime in the eyes of all Arabs, namely the desecration of the holy months. In the resultant situation, Muḥammad became convinced that there was no more hope of reaching any kind of agreement with them. Toward the beginning of autumn of the second year A.H., Abū Sufyān led a great caravan toward al Shām. It was this trade which the Muslims had previously threatened when the Prophet—may God's peace and blessing be upon him—joined the expedition to al 'Ushayrah in person. When the Muslims reached that locality, the caravan of Abū Sufyān had passed two days earlier. The Muslims decided to withdraw and wait for the caravan's return. When that time came and the caravan was supposedly in the vicinity of Madīnah, Muḥammad sent Ṭalhah ibn 'Ubaydullah and Sa'īd ibn Zayd to reconnoitre its whereabouts. The two men ran in the direction of the usual trade route and arrived at the campsite of Kashd al Juhaniy in al Ḥawrā'. There, they hid until the caravan passed. They returned quickly to Madīnah in order to give Muḥammad the information he asked for.

The Muslims Mobilize for Badr

Muḥammad did not await the return of his two messengers from al Ḥawrā'. He had already heard that the caravan in question was a very large one and that practically all the Makkans were involved in the trade it carried since all Makkan capitalists had already bought a share in it. The goods the caravan carried were estimated at 50,000 dinars. Muḥammad feared that if he were to await the news of his two messengers, the caravan would pass him by on its return to Makkah as it had passed him by on its northward trip to Syria earlier. Consequently, he called the Muslims together and addressed them in the following words: "Yonder is the caravan of Quraysh. Mobilize your forces and seek to capture it. Perhaps God may give it to you as booty." Some Muslims responded and others did not. Some non-Muslims were anxious to join, but Muḥammad prevented them from doing so until they had believed in God and his Prophet.

Abū Sufyān's Messenger to Quraysh

On the other side, Abū Sufyān had also heard of Muḥammad's sortie to intercept his caravan on its way north to al Shām, and he was equally apprehensive that the Muslims would again attempt to do so on his return. He therefore sought to learn of their movements as assiduously as the Muslims sought to learn of his. He was especially apprehensive of the return trip because his trade, so far, had been particularly successful. The same al Juhaniy who played host to Muḥammad's messengers at al Ḥawrā' was asked by Abū Sufyān concerning the Muslims.

Al Juhaniy did not tell the truth to Abū Sufyān; but this did not matter inasmuch as Abū Sufyān already knew as much about the Muslims as the Muslims knew about him. He feared a catastrophe because his caravan had but thirty or forty men to guard it. Anticipating danger, he decided to send Damdam ibn 'Amr al Ghifārī in haste to Quraysh with the message that Muhammad and his companions had set out to intercept the caravan and to appeal to them to send men for escort. As instructed by Abū Sufyān, just before he entered Makkah, Damdam cut off the ears of his camel, broke its nose, turned its saddle sideways, tore his own robe in front and in back, and entered the city standing on the back of his camel shouting: "O People of Quraysh, your wealth and trade are being lost. Abū Sufyān and the caravan are being intercepted by Muhammad and his companions. Perhaps you may still catch them. Help! Help!" As soon as he heard the news, Abū Jahl called upon all Makkans to join in the rescue operation. He, a man of acid temper, eloquent speech, and strong insight, could inflame any audience. The Quraysh, however, were not in need of eloquent speeches to rise against Muhammad. Every one of them had a share in the trade this caravan carried.

Old Enmity of Quraysh and Kinānah

At the time, a group of Makkans felt that Quraysh had been too unjust toward its Muslim members for having compelled them to emigrate first to Abyssinia and then to Madīnah. This group, hesitant to answer the call of Abū Jahl, simply hoped that the caravan would not be destroyed. This same group remembered that the Quraysh and Kinānah tribes were quite alienated from each other and were only waiting for an opportunity to avenge themselves against each other. They feared that should the Quraysh all go out to meet Muhammad and protect their caravan, the Banū Bakr of Kinānah might seize the opportunity to attack them from behind. This cautious judgment would nearly have carried the day against the appeal of Abū Jahl were it not for the arrival upon the scene of Mālik ibn Ju'shum al Mudlijī, a nobleman and leader of Banū Kinānah. He said, addressing the Makkans: "I deliver myself to you as a surety that Kinānah will not pounce upon you in your hour of need." With this, the group supporting Abu Jahl and 'Āmir ibn al Hadramī for general mobilization and war against

Muḥammad and his companions, succeeded in convincing the Makkans in favor of war. No reason remained for any Makkan capable of fighting to stay behind, or for the incapable to equip and send somebody in his stead. None of the noblemen of the Quraysh stayed behind except Abū Lahab, who sent in his stead al 'Ās ibn Hishām ibn al Mughīrah in compensation for some four thousand dirhams the latter owed him which he was not able to pay back. 'Umayyah ibn Khalaf, a very old and obese man, decided to stay behind. He was visited in the mosque by 'Uqbah ibn Abū Mu'ayṭ and Abū Jahl. The first carried an incense burner; the second, instruments of beautification for women. 'Uqbah placed the incense burner in Umayyah's hands and said, "O Abū 'Alī, fill your atmosphere with incense for you are a woman." Abū Jahl handed over the instruments of beautification and said, "O Abū 'Alī, beautify yourself for you are only a woman." At this, Umayyah rose and said, "Buy for me the best and strongest camel in Makkah." He rode it and joined the force. Because of this and like tactics, no man capable of bearing arms remained behind.

The Path of the Muslim Army

The Prophet—may God's blessing be upon him—had started off from Madīnah with his companions on the eighth day of Ramaḍān in the second year A.H. He had appointed 'Amr ibn Maktūm to lead the prayer in Madīnah, and Abū Lubābah, whom he called back from al Rawḥā', to govern Madīnah in his place during his absence. The Muslim force was preceded by two black flags, and their camels counted seventy. Since three or four men were assigned to one camel, each one rode for only a brief while. Muḥammad's share in riding was like that of his companions. He, 'Alī ibn Abū Ṭālib, and Marthad ibn Marthad al Ghanawī had one camel assigned to them. Abū Bakr, 'Umar, and 'Abd al Raḥman ibn 'Awf shared another. The total number of men on this expedition amounted to three hundred and five. Eighty-three of them were Muhājirūn, sixty-one belonged to al Aws, and the rest to al Khazraj. Their pace was swift because they feared Abū Sufyān would pass them by if they tarried. They arrived to a place called 'Irq al Ẓubiah where they found a Bedouin whom they asked concerning the caravan but could not learn anything from him. They continued on their march until they arrived at a valley called Dhafirān where they encamped.

It was at this moment that the news reached them that the Quraysh had come out in force to meet them and protect the caravan. This news radically changed the situation. It was no more a question of intercepting Abū Sufyān, his caravan, and the thirty or forty escorts who were no match for Muḥammad and his companions. The whole of Makkah, led by its nobles and elders, was out to protect its trade. If the Muslims were to catch up with Abū Sufyān, overcome his men and take away his camels and all they carried, would the Quraysh not follow and catch up with them, stirred up by this new attack of the Muslims and encouraged by their great numbers and armaments? Would they not catch up with the Muslims and fight them to the finish? On the other hand, if Muḥammad were to return without victory, would not both the Quraysh and the Jews of Madīnah realize his weakness and seek to take advantage of it? Would he then not have to compromise and, perhaps, suffer a Jewish tyranny in Madīnah such as the Quraysh tyranny he had suffered in Makkah? In such eventuality, how could the revelation of truth and the religion of God ever become successful or achieve victory?

Muḥammad consulted the members of his expedition concerning the news just received. After Abū Bakr and ʻUmar presented their views, al Miqdād ibn ʻAmr stood up and said: "O Prophet of God, press forward toward that which God has shown you. We are with you. By God, we shall never say to you, as the Jews had said to Moses, 'Go alone with your Lord and fight with Him for us, while we remain here and await your return.' Rather, we say, 'Go forth, you and your Lord to fight, for we are fighting with you.' " Al Miqdād's speech was followed by silence. The Prophet said: "Speak out, O men, and give me your counsel." He was especially anxious to hear al Ansār's view who, on the day of al ʻAqabah, pledged to protect him as they would their children and women but not to permit any aggression with him outside their own area. When al Ansār realized that he was waiting for them to speak, Saʻd ibn Muʻādh, their leader, rose and addressed Muḥammad: "Does it seem, O Prophet of God, that you are seeking to hear our view?" The Prophet answered, "Indeed." Saʻd said, "We have believed in you, and we have witnessed that what you have brought to us is the truth. We have covenanted with you to hear and to obey. Go ahead with whatever you decide, for we are with you. By Him who sent you as a prophet, if you lead us toward the sea, we shall enter into it with you and not one of us will stay behind.

We do not fear that you cause us to face our enemy tomorrow. We shall hold fast to our ground and stand firm or press forward toward the enemy in solid ranks. We hope that God will show you such of our deeds as you may not be disappointed therein but may be proud of. Lead us forth with God's blessing." Sa'd had hardly finished his words when Muhammad's face radiated with joy and his eyes shone with energy. He said: "Go forward and be optimistic; for God had promised me one of the two— either the caravan or the Makkan army. By God, it is as though I see the enemy lying prostrate in the field." When the force arrived at Dhafirān, Muhammad advanced on his camel alone and, reaching an old bedouin settler in the area who did not know him, asked about Quraysh, as well as about Muhammad and his companions, and learned that the caravan of Quraysh was indeed close by.

Reconnaissance and Espionage

When Muhammad returned to his party, he sent 'Alī ibn Abū Tālib, al Zubayr ibn al 'Awwām, and Sa'd ibn Abū Waqqās with a number of other companions to the well of Badr to seek out fresh news. The little group returned with two boys who, upon interrogation by Muhammad, revealed that the Quraysh army stood behind the hill on the further side. When they could not answer his questions regarding the strength of the Quraysh army, Muhammad asked how many animals they killed for food every day. The boys answered, "Nine on one day and ten on the other." The Prophet concluded from this that their number must be between nine hundred and one thousand. He also learned from the two boys that the leaders of Quraysh were all present. Turning to his own companions he said, "There is Makkah confronting you with all its sons in one body." It was therefore absolutely necessary, he thought, that Muslims mobilize all efforts, harden their hearts and wills, and prepare themselves for a battle so fierce that none would emerge victorious from it except those whose hearts were completely possessed by faith in God alone.

Escape of the Caravan and Abū Sufyān

As 'Alī and his companions came back from Badr with the two youths and some information about Quraysh, two other Muslims went in a slightly different direction to seek news of the caravan. They came to a sandhill not too far from the springs of Badr. There they took a jug and went down to the spring to get some water. While they were there they overheard two maid servants involved in an argument in which the one was asking the other to pay back her debt to her; the latter answered that either on the next day or the day after the caravan would come for whom she would work, and she would earn enough to pay her back. The two men returned to Muḥammad and reported what they heard. As the caravan approached the area, Abū Sufyān marched ahead reconnoitering the territory, apparently fearful that Muḥammad might have preceded him to the place. When he arrived at the spring, he met Majdī ibn 'Amr, whom he asked whether anyone had been seen in the vicinity. Majdī answered that he had not seen anyone except two idlers who stopped at the nearby sand dune, and pointed to the spot where the two Muslims stopped in order to get the water. Abū Sufyān came to the spot and found some refuse of their two camels. As he examined it, he found it contained grains which he recognized as coming from crops known to be grown and used in Madīnah. He returned quickly to his caravan and altered its course. By leading it toward the sea coast with great speed, he managed to escape.

The morrow arrived while the Muslims were still awaiting the arrival of the caravan. The news now reached them that the caravan had passed them by on a different route and that the Quraysh army were still in the vicinity close by. With this news, whatever hope for booty some of them may have entertained collapsed. The Prophet discussed with his companions whether or not they should now return to Madīnah and not force a showdown with the Quraysh army. In this connection, the following verses of the Qur'ān were revealed: "Now that God has promised that one of 'the two' shall fall to you, you wish that it would be the one devoid of strength or resistance. But, rather than easy booty, God wishes that the truth become supreme, that justice be done, and that the unbelievers be scattered."[1]

Prospects of Battle

For their part, the Quraysh asked themselves the same question. What need do they have to fight now that their caravan had escaped? Was it not better for them to return to their homes

and to let the Muslims return to theirs empty handed? These
were the thoughts of Abū Sufyān, who sent word to the Quraysh
to this effect. He told them, "You have prepared for war and
come out in strength in order to protect your caravan, your
men, and your goods. God has saved all these. Return, then,
home." Some men agreed. Abū Jahl thought otherwise. To Abū
Sufyān's message, he responded, "By God, we shall not return
home until we have come to Badr, spent three nights in eating
good food, drinking wine, and reveling, that all Arabs may hear
of our sortie, our strength, and continue to fear us." The locality
of Badr was the center of a seasonal gathering in that part of
Arabia. For the Quraysh to withdraw soon after the escape
of their caravan might be interpreted as fear of Muḥammad
and his companions. This event would increase Muḥammad's
power and encourage the spread of his cause. Such would especially be the case as the expedition of 'Abdullah ibn Jaḥsh, the
killing of ibn al Ḥaḍramī, the capture of two Qurayshīs, and
Quraysh's loss of the caravan were all common knowledge
throughout the desert.

The Muslims Camp at Badr

There was some hesitation in the camp of Quraysh, whether to
follow Abū Jahl or return home. Banū Zuhrah, under the leadership of al Akhnas ibn Sharīq, listened to Abū Sufyān's counsel
and returned home; but they were alone. All the rest followed
Abū Jahl in deciding to encamp as if in preparation for war
and to consult with one another later on. They set up camp on
the farthest side behind a sand dune which they took as center.
The Muslims, on the other hand, having now missed the booty,
decided together to stand firm should the enemy engage them.
They hurried to the springs of Badr while a rain which fell upon
them from heaven helped their quick advance to that place.
When they reached the first water well, Muḥammad dismounted
with the intention of camping there. Cognizant of the area, al
Ḥubāb ibn al Mundhir ibn al Jamūḥ approached the Prophet
and said: "O Prophet of God, is this spot where you have dismounted a place to which God has guided you and, therefore,
may we neither step beyond it nor stay far behind it? Or is this
simply a question of ordinary war strategy, of measures and
moves and counter measures and moves?" Muḥammad answered,
"It is indeed the latter, just as you said." Al Ḥubāb then said,

"O Prophet of God, this is not a good place to be. We should move forward until we reach the well closest to the enemy. There we would bring a trough to it to fill with water and then fill the well with sand. We would fight the enemy; and when we withdraw we would be able to drink, whereas they would not." Muḥammad, immediately agreeing, rose to go forward with his force. He sent a reminder to all his companions that he is but a man like them, that all decisions have to be taken by all of them in consultation with one another, that he will not decide anything without them finally, and that he stands in great need of their good counsel.

Building a Booth for the Prophet

When they completed the building of the trough, Saʻd ibn Muʻādh addressed the Prophet thus: "O Prophet of God, let us build a booth for you to stay in, and let us prepare for you some mounts before we engage our enemy. If God gives us the strength and we are victorious, that would be fine and well. If otherwise, you would then ride these mounts, join the rear ranks of our forces and return home. Many Muslims have stayed in Madīnah who do not love you any less than we do. No one had expected that our expedition would turn out to be one of war. Had they realized this, they would not have let you go out without them. On your return to Madīnah, they would be there to protect you, counsel you and fight with you." Muḥammad thanked Saʻd and prayed for him. The booth was readied for the Prophet and preparations were made for his return in case of defeat so that he would not fall into the hands of his enemies as a captive.

The True Faith of the Muslims

We must pause here to appreciate with wonder the faithfulness of the Muslims, their great love for Muḥammad, and their absolute conviction of the truth of his prophethood. They knew too well that Quraysh far exceeded them in number; in fact, their enemy had three times as many fighters as they. Nonetheless, they decided to stand firm in the cause and to fight. After they saw their booty escape, whatever motivation they had for material gain must now be discounted. All this notwithstanding, by siding with the Prophet they confirmed his prophethood and strengthened his ranks. They were not sure of victory, though they wished for it; and they were afraid of defeat. Nonetheless, they thought of protecting the Prophet and arranged lest he should fall a captive in the hands of his enemies. They planned for him to return to Madīnah and join the Muslims behind. What stand is more wonderful than this! What faith guarantees victory as this faith of theirs!

Ḥamzah Kills Ibn 'Abd al Asad

The Quraysh arranged and readied themselves for battle. Their spies had informed them that the Muslims were three hundred strong or a little more, that they had neither provisions nor a hiding place, and that their only protection was their swords, determined as they were to kill before falling. As the cream of Quraysh forces had joined this expedition, the wise among them feared that should a number of these fall by Muslim hands, Makkah would soon lose its position of leadership. However, they coud not speak out for fear that Abū Jahl would accuse them of cowardice. Nonetheless, 'Utbah ibn Rabī'ah did. "O men of Quraysh," he advised his peers, "we will surely not achieve anything by meeting Muḥammad and his companions in battle. If we should defeat them, every one of us would recognize in their dead a cousin, an uncle, or a relative from his own clan and tribe. Return to your homes and leave Muḥammad alone among the tribes. Should they kill him and defeat him, your purpose would have been met. Should it turn out to be otherwise, you will not have to suffer the consequences." But when Abū Jahl heard these words of 'Utbah, he raged in anger, sent after 'Āmir ibn al Ḥadramī, and said to him: "Your ally is shamelessly courting men to return to Makkah now that you have beheld your enemy with your own eye. There is your enemy, on whom you ought to avenge yourself. Rise and avenge the slaying of your brother." 'Āmir stood up and yelled, "Woe! 'Amr shall be avenged! To battle! To battle!" With this, the last chance of peace was shattered. Al Aswad ibn 'Abd al Asad al Makhzūmī, springing out of the ranks of the Quraysh toward the Muslims, sought to destroy the trough which they had just built. Ḥamzah ibn 'Abd al Muṭṭalib struck him with his sword. The blow cut off his leg, and the victim fell on his back with his leg bleeding profusely. Immediately Ḥamzah struck him again and killed him. Nothing draws the swords out of mens' sheaths faster than the

sight of blood. Nothing stirs the will to kill more than the
sight of a friend slain by an enemy hand in front of his
own people.

Engagement of the Two Armies

As soon as al Aswad fell, 'Utbah ibn Rabī'ah, flanked by his
brother Shaybah on one side and his son al Walīd ibn 'Utbah
on the other, sprang forth and challenged the Muslims to duel.
A number of youths from Madīnah went out to meet them.
When Shaybah recognized them, he said: "We have not come
to fight you. Rather we want to fight our own tribesmen." The
Quraysh crier called forth: "O Muhammad, send out our own
peers of our own tribe to fight us." At this, Hamzah ibn 'Abd al
Muttalib, 'Alī ibn Abū Tālib, and 'Ubaydah ibn al Hārith advanced forth. A duel was fought in which Hamzah killed Shaybah,
and 'Alī killed al Walīd. Then both of them came to assist
'Ubaydah who had not yet finished off 'Utbah. When the Quraysh
army saw this, they advanced in force and the two armies
collided. It was the morning of Friday, seventeenth of Ramadān,
2 A.H.

Muhammad's Prayer and Invocation

Muhammad led the Muslims and organized their ranks. As he
looked over the Quraysh army and compared them with his
thin ranks and poor equipment, he felt quite apprehensive. He
returned to his booth with Abū Bakr, strongly moved by fear
and pity for the career of Islām should the Muslims lose on
this day. Turning his face to Makkah and his whole soul to God,
he began to pray, calling on God to give him victory. He prayed
to God for a very long while, and was heard repeating the following words: "O God, here is Quraysh with all her tribe seeking
to belie your Prophet. O God, give us the assistance which You
promised. O God, if this little army perishes, when will You
be worshiped again?" Muhammad prayed with hands raised to
heaven. His mantle fell off and Abū Bakr had to pick it up
and put it back on his shoulders. Abū Bakr said to him: "O
Prophet of God, enough calling on God; He will surely give you
what He promised. Muhammad continued to pray, pouring out
his whole soul in pious invocation to God to help him in this

hour of precipitous danger. After near collapse, he came back
to himself and told of a vision he saw of God's victory. With
radiant face, he went out to meet his men and incited them
to put their faith in God and enter the battle without fear.
He assured them one by one: "By Him who controls Muḥammad's
soul, not one of you today fights and falls but God will enter
him into His paradise."

Muslim Morale

Out of Muḥammad's strong soul a stronger power than God
might have imparted on any other occasion spread among the
Muslim ranks, fortifying their will and determination and
making each and every one of them the equivalent of two—nay
ten—men in strength. We can easily imagine the effect of this
sudden reinforcement of Muslim morale upon their personalities
when the cause is as morally justified as theirs has been. The
feeling of patriotism with which modernity is familiar is certainly one such supporting moral justification in modern wars.
The soldier who exposes himself to all kinds of danger in the
belief that he is defending his fatherland walks into battle with
superior morale; the greater his love for and faith in his fatherland, the more frightful the risks he stands prepared to take.
Consequently, nations inculcate upon their young at a very tender
age the love of the fatherland and the will to sacrifice for its
sake. Conviction of the fatherland's right to justice, freedom,
and the higher human values reinforce the soul; and this, in
turn, doubles the material power issuing from the person. Those
who remember the allied propaganda against the Germans during
World War II will recall that the allies saturated the atmosphere
with their claim that they were fighting a war for the sake of
freedom and justice, and were laying down their lives in a
last war against the militaristic state of Germany precisely in
order to usher in an age of peace and security and light. This
allied propaganda not only doubled the strength of their soldiers
but provided them as well with a warm welcome freely given
by most peoples of the world. But what patriotism and what
cause of peace and security dare compare with what Muḥammad
was calling for! For Muḥammad, it was a matter of one's
communion with ultimate reality, of union with all being in a
bond giving man determining power in the universe, and of

blazing for him the path of goodness, blessedness and perfection.
Yes, indeed: What kind of patriotism or cause of peace dares
to stand beside the communion with God which puts to an end
the persecution of the believers for their faith in Him and
removes the hindrances of idolatry and associationism from the
path of God? If patriotism increases the power of the soul by
as much power as corresponds with the value of fatherland,
and if the love of peace for mankind increases the power of
the soul by as much power as corresponds with the value of
the whole of mankind, how great must have been the power of
the soul when it was reinforced by faith in total being as well
as in the Creator of total being? Surely it makes that soul
capable of moving mountains, of determining the heavenly bodies,
of exerting its power and influence supremely over all men endowed with less faith? Moral power doubles and redoubles
material power. When, before the battle, this strength was not at
its highest because of division within Muslim ranks, Muslim material power suffered in consequence. But the situation changed,
and their power increased tremendously under the inspiration
of Muhammad. And it was this new resurgence of power by
this means that compensated the Muslims for their small number
and poor equipment. It was in connection with this spiritual
phenomenon that the two Qur'ānic verses were revealed:

يَا أَيُّهَا النَّبِيُّ حَرِّضِ الْمُؤْمِنِينَ عَلَى الْقِتَالِ إِنْ يَكُنْ مِنْكُمْ عِشْرُونَ صَابِرُونَ يَغْلِبُوا
مِائَتَيْنِ وَإِنْ يَكُنْ مِنْكُمْ مِائَةٌ يَغْلِبُوا أَلْفًا مِنَ الَّذِينَ كَفَرُوا بِأَنَّهُمْ قَوْمٌ لَا يَفْقَهُونَ
أَلْآنَ خَفَّفَ اللهُ عَنْكُمْ وَعَلِمَ أَنَّ فِيكُمْ ضَعْفًا فَإِنْ يَكُنْ مِنْكُمْ مِائَةٌ صَابِرَةٌ يَغْلِبُوا
مِائَتَيْنِ وَإِنْ يَكُنْ مِنْكُمْ أَلْفٌ يَغْلِبُوا أَلْفَيْنِ بِإِذْنِ اللهِ وَاللهُ مَعَ الصَّابِرِينَ

" 'O Prophet, urge the believers to fight.' If there be twenty
steadfast men they will overcome two hundred. And if there be
a hundred, they will overcome a thousand unbelievers. These
are a people devoid of knowledge, faith, or conviction. For the
present, God has lightened your burden. He knows that there
is weakness in you. So if there be a hundred steadfast men
among you, they will overcome two hundred; and if there be a
thousand, they will overcome two thousand by God's permission.
God is surely with those who are steadfast."[2]

Bilāl Kills Umayyah ibn Khalaf

At Muḥammad's urging and inspiration, his standing in their midst and inciting them against the enemy, and his announcement that paradise belongs to the men of valor who plunge fearlessly into the ranks of the enemy, the Muslims doubled and redoubled their strength. Before entering battle, they resolved to direct their attention to the leaders and nobles of the Quraysh. They planned to seek them and to kill them first, remembering the persecution and travails they suffered at their hands in Makkah, especially the blocking of the road to God and to the holy mosque. Bilāl saw Umayyah ibn Khalaf and his son on the field surrounded by a number of Muslims who had recognized him and sought to take him as captive. This Umayyah was Bilāl's previous master who used to torture him by forcing him down to the ground where he placed a large rock on his chest, letting him burn under the torrid sun in order to force him to abjure Islām. Bilāl survived all these travails in certainty of his faith while repeating continuously, "God is one! God is one!" When his eyes fell upon Umayyah in the field, he shouted, "Umayyah, the head of idolatry! Death to me if he escapes!" and charged furiously toward him. The Muslims surrounding Umayyah sought to prevent Bilāl from reaching him. Bilāl called to them at high voice: "O Helpers of God! The head of idolatry is Umayyah ibn Khalaf. Death to me if he escapes!" He charged again toward Umayyah and killed him. Mu'ādh ibn 'Amr ibn al Jamūh killed Abū Jahl ibn Hishām. Ḥamzah, 'Alī and other Muslim heroes penetrated deeply into enemy lines, forgetting themselves, their small numbers, and their being surrounded by their enemies. Muslims hurled themselves into the *mêlée*. The dust rose, the battle raged at its hottest and wildest, and the heads of the Quraysh flew off their bodies. Possessed by their faith and chanting, "God is one! God is one!" the Muslims exerted tremendous power and pressed ever forward. It was as if space and time had lost their meaning, and God's angels were hovering above to encourage and draw them ever forward. They were so great that even their arms brandishing their swords in the air and striking the necks of their enemies seemed as if they moved not by ordinary human power but by the supernatural power of God Himself. Muḥammad was in the midst of the battlefield fighting as well as observing his companions. At one moment he took dirt in his hand and threw it in the face of an advancing party of Quraysh, commanding his companions to stand firm. The Muslims stood their ground and forced the superior enemy to withdraw. It did not matter to the Muslim that he was surrounded by his enemies. His soul was filled with the breath of God; this divine spirit made him ever-firm and gave him the very power with which he wielded his arms. It was of this battle that God said: "Your lord revealed to the angels that He is with you and commanded them to give firmness to those that believe. He announced that He will cast terror into the hearts of those who disbelieve. God commands: 'Smite your enemies; strike off their heads and forearms . . . You killed them not when you did, but it was God who killed them; and you threw not when you did throw your arrows but it was God who threw them.'"[3] When the Prophet saw that God had fulfilled His promise and given the Muslims victory, he returned to his booth. The Quraysh were not only withdrawing but running away, and the Muslims were pressing after them to capture those of them whom they did not kill on the battlefield.

The Muslims Spare the Just

This was the great battle of Badr that established Muslim power throughout the Arabian Penninsula and began the movement of Arab unity under the leadership of Islām. It was the beginning of a large Islāmic empire which gave the world a civilization which has so far played and will ever play a very important role in the history of the universe. It may surprise some readers to learn that as he urged his companions to fight the enemy and scatter their forces, Muḥammad asked them not to kill Banū Hāshim and some other leaders of the Quraysh despite the fact that they were all arrayed in battle on the other side. In so doing, he was not seeking any advantage for his tribe or relatives. Muḥammad was too noble to be moved by such con-siderations. Rather he wanted to reward Banū Hāshim for their protection of him and of his cause during thirteen long years between his commission to prophethood and emigration. It should be remembered that his uncle, al 'Abbās, was the one who concluded the covenant of al 'Aqabah. He also remembered other members of the Quraysh besides the Banū Hāshim, who once sought to revoke the boycott pact which emprisoned the

One of the Gates of Al Ḥaram al Sharīf,
Makkah al Mukarramah, Saudi Arabia.

Muslims in one of the districts of Makkah with little or no
food supplies. Muḥammad considered a good deed as worthy of
regard—of a gesture equal to it in charity and good will—
despite the idolatry of its author. Thus, he interceded with the
Muslims at the hour of battle on behalf of those Makkans who
did the good deeds. Some of them, however, refused Muḥammad's
good will move and kind gesture. Such was the case of Abū al
Bakhtarī, who was responsible for the rescinding of the boycott
pact but who fought and was killed in battle.

People of the Grave

The people of Makkah ran away from the field despondent,
dejected, and mourning their dead. They would hardly catch
sight of their companions when their eyes would fall down in
shame for what had happened. The Muslims remained at Badr
until the end of the day. They collected the dead of the Quraysh
and buried them on the spot. Muḥammad and his companions
spent that night on the battlefield burying the dead, collecting
the booty and keeping their eyes on the captives. As the night
drew on, Muḥammad sat down to think both of this victory,
which God had just given the Muslims despite their small number,
and the terrible defeat He had inflicted upon an enemy devoid
of a sound faith capable of fusing their large numbers into one
strong will. He pondered the matter over many long hours of
the night. He was even heard addressing the dead in their new
graves: "O people of the grave"! he murmured, "O ʿUtbah ibn
Rabīʿah! O Shaybah ibn Rabīʿah! O Umayyah ibn Khalaf! O
Abū Jahl ibn Hishām!" After calling by name the fallen one
by one, he addressed them in these words: "Have you really
found that which your Lord had promised you? I have found
what my Lord had promised me. But have you? The Muslims
who overheard him asked, "Are you calling the dead?" and the
Prophet answered, "They hear me no less than you do, except
that they are unable to answer me." The Prophet of God looked
Abū Ḥudhayfah ibn ʿUtbah straight in the face and realized
that he was pale. He asked him, "O Abū Ḥudhayfah, are you
despondent over the sad fate your father met today?" Abū
Ḥudhayfah answered, "No, by God, O Prophet of God! I have
not censured my father or bemoaned his fate. I have known him
to be a wise and good man, and I had hoped that his wisdom
and virtue would one day lead him to Islām. When I saw what

befell him, I remembered his idolatry despite all the hope I had entertained for him. Thus I am only sorry for him." The Prophet of God spoke to him gently and prayed for him.

Muslim Differences Concerning Booty

When the morning came and it was time for the Muslims to return to Madīnah, they began to consider the disposition of the booty. Those who collected it claimed it as their own. Those who ran after the enemy and captured the captives said: "By God, we deserve it more than they; for without us it would not have been realized." Those who were guarding Muhammad and protecting him against a resurgence of the enemy forces, said: "Neither one of you deserve the booty. We surely could have killed the enemy and taken possession of his goods, but we preferred to protect the Prophet of God and, therefore, we stayed behind near him while you went out capturing and collecting it." At this Muhammad commanded every Muslim to return every piece of the booty he had taken and to keep all the booty together until he had reached judgment regarding it, or God had revealed the way it should be disposed of.

Equal Division of the Booty

Muhammad sent to Madīnah 'Abdullah ibn Rawāhah and Zayd ibn Hārithah to bring news of the victory to the people of Madīnah. He and his companions returned to Madīnah accompanied by the captives and carrying the booty of war. He had appointed 'Abdullah ibn Ka'b as the guardian of it. After reaching the valley of al Safrā', Muhammad camped on a hill and there began to divide the booty among the Muslims in equal parts. Some historians claim that Muhammad had divided the booty after he had appropriated one-fifth of it in accordance with the Qur'ānic command: "And know that whatever you take as spoils in war, a fifth thereof shall go to God, His Prophet, the kindred, the orphans, the needy, and the wayfarer. If you believe in God and in what We send down to Our servant and the day of decision [the day of Badr] when the two armies met, you will accept this division. God has power over all things."[4] Most biographers, especially the earlier among them, believed that this verse was revealed after the battle of Badr as well as after Muhammad's division of its booty. They hold that Muḥammad had divided the booty in equal parts, giving to the fighter with a horse twice the amount he gave to the fighter on foot, and allowing the share of the Muslims who were killed at Badr to go to their heirs. They also hold that Muḥammad had assigned a share to the Muslims who were left behind in Madīnah on assignment to work for the Muslim cause there during the absence of the army in Badr, or who had remained in Madīnah for good reason. Muḥammad divided the booty justly. Not only did he include in his division the soldier but also everyone who worked for the cause and helped achieve this victory, whether on the battlefield or far from it.

Execution of Two Captives

While the Muslims were on their way back to Madīnah, two of the captives were executed, al Naḍr ibn al Ḥārith and ʿUqbah ibn Abū Muʿayṭ. Neither Muḥammad nor his companions had until that moment any law regarding the captives regulating their execution, ransom, or enslavement. Al Naḍr and ʿUqbah were terribly hard on the Muslims in Makkah and had inflicted upon them all the harm and injury they could. Al Naḍr was executed when the captives were arrayed in front of the Prophet near the locality called al Uthayl. As the Prophet looked at al Naḍr, the latter trembled and called to his neighbor: "Muḥammad is surely going to kill me. He had looked at me with eyes in which I saw the judgment of death." His neighbor rejoined: "You are a coward." Al Naḍr approached Musʿab ibn ʿUmayr, the closest of the captives to Muḥammad and asked him: "Please approach your relative concerning me. Let him allow me to be one of his companions. If you do not, I am certain he is going to kill me today." Musʿab replied, "You used to speak all kinds of calumnies against the Book of God and His Prophet; you also used to persecute and harm his companions." Al Naḍr said, "Had Quraysh taken you captive, I would have never allowed them to kill you as long as I was alive"; to which Musʿab replied, "By God I do not believe you; I am not like you; Islām has severed my relations with you." Al Naḍr was the captive of al Miqdād who expected to receive a great ransom from the captive's family. When al Miqdād heard the conversation regarding the execution of al Naḍr, he said: "Al Naḍr is my captive. Hands off!" At this the Prophet—may God's blessing be upon him—said: "Strike his neck. O God, give al

Miqdād plenty of Your bounty instead." 'Alī ibn Abū Ṭālib executed the Prophet's order with the sword. As the party arrived at 'Irq al Ẓubyah, the Prophet ordered the execution of 'Uqbah ibn Abū Mu'ayt. When 'Uqbah pleaded, "Who will take care of my children, O Muḥammad?" Muḥammad answered, "The fire." According to one version, it was 'Ali ibn Abū Ṭālib who executed him; according to another, it was 'Āṣim ibn Thābit.

News of the Victory in Madīnah

Before the Prophet and the Muslims reached Madīnah, the two messengers, Zayd ibn Ḥārithah and 'Abdullah ibn Ka'b, had arrived and entered the city from different directions. 'Abdullah galloped through the city on his horse and Zayd ibn Ḥārithah followed him riding on al Qaswā', Muḥammad's she-camel. Both were calling al Ansār and announcing to them the victory, mentioning the names of the fallen idolators. The Muslims, pleased to hear the news, went out of their houses and gathered in the streets acclaiming this great victory. As for the Jews and the idolators of Madīnah, they were saddened by this turn of events. Indeed, they even tried to convince themselves as well as the Muslims in Madīnah that it was not true. They proclaimed at the top of their voices: "Muḥammad was killed, and his companions were defeated. There is his she-camel which we all know. Had he achieved victory, his she-camel would have stayed there. Zayd said otherwise because he lost his mind out of terror in the course of fighting." The Muslims, however, quickly confirmed the news and went on with their celebration. Only the death of Ruqayyah, daughter of the Prophet, which had occurred on that day, marred their joy. As his daughter was sick on the day Muḥammad left for Badr, he ordered her husband, 'Uthmān ibn 'Affān, to stay behind and take care of her. When the idolators and munāfiqūn realized that the news of victory was true, they felt that their position was degenerating into one of weakness and isolation. A Jewish leader said, "Death for us is better on this day than life. What kind of life can we have now that the noblest of men, their lords and kings—the Makkan guardians of security and peace—are dead or vanquished?"

The Captives of Badr

The Muslims entered Madīnah without the captives who were to follow the next day. When they did, Sawdah, daughter of

Zam'ah and wife of the Prophet, was returning from a morning
visit to the relatives of the two sons of 'Afrā'. She saw Abū
Yazīd Suhayl ibn 'Amr, one of the captives, whose hand was
bound to his neck. Unable to control her indignation at the sight,
she approached him and said, "O Abū Yazīd! Did you give
yourself up, and surrender voluntarily? Woe! The pity that you
had not fallen nobly and met a heroic death on the battlefield!"
Muḥammad called her away and said to her, "O Sawdah, are
you inciting the man against God and against His Prophet?"
She answered, "O Prophet of God, by Him who sent you a
Prophet of the truth, I could not control myself when I saw
Abū Yazīd with his hand tied to his neck and felt impelled to
say what I said." Muḥammad distributed the captives among
his companions and said to them, "Treat them well." The
question of what to do with them, to kill them or to accept
ransom for them, continued to trouble him. Many of them are
strong warriors; their hearts are now filled with hatred following their defeat and shameful captivity. If he were to accept
ransom for them, surely they would wage another war against
him. And yet, if he were to kill them would he not incite their
people in Quraysh to further acts of violence? To a new height
of enmity which might be avoided if he were to accept their
ransom?

Abū Bakr and 'Umar's Views Regarding the Captives

Muḥammad submitted the matter to the Muslims and sought
their advice. He wanted them to share freely in the decision.
The Muslims, for their part, discovered that the captives desired
to live and, therefore, that a great amount of wealth could
be reaped from them as ransom. The captives sent word to
Abū Bakr knowing that he was the nearest to the Quraysh and
the most merciful and compassionate of the Muslims as well as
the closest adviser and friend of Muḥammad. They said to Abū
Bakr: "O Abū Bakr, among us are fathers, brothers, uncles, and
cousins of the Muslims. The most distant of us is still a relative.
Approach your friend on our behalf and ask him to forgive
us or to allow us to be ransomed. Abū Bakr promised them
to do his best. At the same time, they feared that ibn al Khattāb
would counsel against Abū Bakr's pleas; therefore, they sent
after him to ask as they did Abū Bakr. 'Umar ibn Khattāb
looked at them in anger and did not answer. The two approached
Muḥammad and each presented his point of view. Abū Bakr

appealed to Muhammad's gentleness and stirred his compassion.
He pleaded, "O Prophet of God, you are dearer than my father
and my mother. Your captives consist of men who are parents,
sons, cousins, uncles and brothers of your own people. The
most removed of them is still a member of your clan and a
blood relative. Be good to them and forgive them. God will
forgive you and be good to you. Otherwise allow them to be
ransomed and take from them that which would increase the
Muslims in power. Perhaps, by such action, God will soften
their hearts toward Islām." Muhammad listened without answering. 'Umar, coming after Abū Bakr, sat in his place and
pleaded: "O Prophet of God, these are the enemies of God. They
have belied you, fought you, and banished you. Strike their
necks. They are the leaders of idolatry and misguidance. By
this course God will consolidate Islām and bring low the
idolators." Again Muhammad did not answer. Later, Abū Bakr
returned to Muhammad and sought once more to stir his compassion by reminding him of the captives' relation and hoping
for their conversion to Islām in case they were allowed to live.
'Umar, too, the exemplar of stern justice, returned to Muhammad to plead once more still unmoved as ever by any feelings
of leniency or mercy. When both Abū Bakr and 'Umar said all
they had to say, Muhammad withdrew to his room to ponder
the matter alone. When he came out, he found the Muslims
divided between Abū Bakr's view and 'Umar's. He consulted
them again, characterizing both Abū Bakr and 'Umar for their
benefit. Abū Bakr, Muhammad said, was like Michael, a carrier
of God's pleasure and foregiveness. Compared with the prophets
he is like Ibrahīm who was sweeter to his people than honey
itself. Ibrahīm's people had condemned him to the fire and threw
him into it, but all he could say to them was, "Fie on you and
on that which you worship instead of God! Would you not use
your reason? . . . Whoever follows me is surely of me, but
whoever disobeys me, God is merciful and forgiving."[5] Abū Bakr
is like Jesus when the latter said: "If You punish them they
are only Your servants; and if You forgive them, You are the
All-wise and Almighty."[6] 'Umar, on the other hand, is like
Gabriel among the angels. He is the carrier of God's wrath and
condemnation of His enemies. Among the prophets he is like
Noah when the latter said: "O God, spare not one of the
unbelievers;" or like Moses when he said: "O God, destroy their
wealth and confirm them in their error that they may not believe
until they receive the painful punishment."[7] Then turning to

the Muslims, the Prophet said: "You have families to support. Do not therefore let any of these captives escape before you receive a ransom from him. Otherwise, strike off his neck." As the Muslims consulted with one another, one of the captives, a poet by profession, and Abū 'Izzat 'Amr ibn 'Abdullah ibn 'Umayr al Jumahī by name, stepped forward toward the Prophet and said: "I have five daughters whom I must support. Do give me to them as your charity, O Muḥammad. For my part I pledge to you that I shall never fight you nor will I ever criticize you." The Prophet forgave him and sent him back to his family without ransom. He was the only captive thus liberated. But he violated his pledge and fought again against the Muslims in the battle of Uḥud, a year later. There he was taken captive, and, this time, executed. After a while, the Muslims reached a consensus to accept ransom for the captives. The following verse of the Qur'ān was revealed on this occasion:

مَا كَانَ لِنَبِيٍّ اَنْ يَكُوْنَ لَهُ اَسْرَى حَتّى يُثْخِنَ فِى الْاَرْضِ تُرِيْدُوْنَ عَرَضَ الدُّنْيَا وَ
اللهُ يُرِيْدُ الْاٰخِرَةَ ، وَ اللهُ عَزِيْزٌ حَكِيْمٌ ۞

"It does not behoove a prophet to hold captives; nor to tyrannize in the world. You seek the advantages of this world whereas God wishes you to seek the advantages of the other. God is almighty and all-wise."[8]

Orientalists' Controversy

A number of Orientalists pause at this affair of the captives of Badr and especially at the execution of al Naḍr and 'Uqbah. They argue: Doesn't this prove the thirst of this new religion for blood? Without such thirst, the two captives would not have been executed. It would have been more charitable and nobler for the Muslims after they won the battle to return the captives and to be satisfied with the booty they acquired. The Orientalists' argument is designed to stir mercy and compassion simply in order to provide means for condemning Islām and its Prophet. But such emotions were utterly out of place on the day of Badr, and much more so a thousand or more years after that battle. The incoherence of the argument is evident upon comparison of the execution of al Naḍr and 'Uqbah with what happens today and will always happen as long as western civilization rules the world under the banner of Christianity. Is their execution com-

parable in any possible manner to what the Christian imperialists
do when they put down the uprisings of their colonies against
their rule? Is it equivalent to any part, however, infinitesimal,
of the slaughter that took place in the first or second World War?
Is it at all comparable to the events of the French Revolution,
or the many other revolutions which have taken place among the
Christian nations of Europe?

Revolution against Idolatry

There is no doubt that the whole matter between Muhammad
and his companions was one of a strong revolution led by
Muhammad against idolatry and its adherents. It was a revolution that started in Makkah where Muhammad and his companions were subjected to all kinds of suffering for thirteen
long years. Thereafter, the Muslims emigrated to Madīnah and
there organized themselves and built up their strength under
revolutionary principles dominating the scene in both their camp
and the Quraysh's. The Muslims' emigration to Madīnah, the
peace they had concluded with the Jews, all the skirmishes preceding the battle of Badr as well as the battle of Badr itself—
all these were steps in the general plan of revolution, but not its
guiding principles. They constitute the policy line decided by
the leader of this revolution and his companions as instruments
in the realization of principles which the Prophet had received
from God. The policy of a revolution should not be confused with
its principles. The plan followed cannot be identified with the
purpose for which it was drawn. Since Islām made human
brotherhood the foundation of its civilization, it had to seek that
civilization by following whatever means are necessary, including
violence.

The Slaughter of St. Bartholomew's Day

What the Muslims did with the captives of Badr was an
instance of sublime mercy and charity when compared with
what happened in the revolutions praised by the western peoples
as embodiments of justice and mercy. What happened to the
captives of Badr was really nothing compared to the many
slaughters carried out in the name of Christianity such as that
which occurred on St. Bartholomew's Day in France. This
slaughter is really a curse in the history of Christianity un-
matched by anything in the whole history of Islām. It was a

slaughter planned deliberately during the night. The Catholics rose the next morning to slaughter systematically the Protestants of Paris and France with deception, wantonness, and the lowliest and worst kind of cruelty. If the Muslims had killed two of the fifty captives for the cruel suffering they had previously inflicted upon the Muslims during thirteen years in Makkah, it was an act of further mercy and benefit which occasioned the revelation of the already quoted verse: "It does not behoove a Prophet to hold captives; nor to tyrannize in the world. You seek the advantages of this world, while God wishes you to seek the advantages of the other. God is almighty and all-wise."[9]

Warning to Makkah

While the Muslims were celebrating the victory God had granted to them, al Ḥaysumān ibn 'Abdullah al Khuzā'ī was making his way toward Makkah. He was the first one to reach the city to announce to its people the defeat of the Quraysh and the fall of its leaders and nobles. Makkah was so shaken by the news that it hardly believed what it heard. Al Ḥaysumān, however, was not angry but insisted on the veracity of his news and shared their grief. When the Makkans finally realized what had happened, they were so shocked that they fell to the ground. Indeed, Abū Lahab was immediately seized by a fever and died seven days later. The Quraysh, consulting together on the course of action to follow, agreed not to mourn their dead lest Muḥammad and his companions be pleased at their suffering. They also decided not to seek to ransom their captives lest Muḥammad and his companions increase their demands. A number of days passed while the Quraysh bore their tragedy silently. But an occasion soon presented itself. Mikraz ibn Ḥafs arrived seeking to ransom Suhayl ibn 'Amr. 'Umar ibn al Khaṭṭāb hated to see Suhayl return home unharmed. He therefore asked Muḥammad: "O Prophet of God, let me pull out Suhayl's front teeth so that he would never be able to exercise his oratory against you." Without hesitation, Muḥammad gave this supremely noble answer: "I shall not mutilate anyone under any circumstance. God would mutilate me though I am His Prophet."

Ransom and Conversion of Abū al 'Aṣī ibn al Rabī'

Zaynab, daughter of the Prophet, sent out to ransom her husband Abū al 'Aṣī ibn al Rabī'. Included in the wealth she

sent for the ransom was a necklace that once belonged to
Khadījah, the Prophet's wife, which the latter had given to her
daughter on the day of her wedding to Abū al 'Āsī. When the
Prophet saw the necklace, he remembered his former wife and
was deeply moved. He said to his companions: "If you find fit
to send her captive back to her and to return to her what she
paid, do so." The Prophet had also agreed with the captive,
Abū al 'Āsī, that he would divorce his wife Zaynab now that
Islām had separated the two spouses. Muhammad sent Zayd ibn
Hārithah and another companion to escort Zaynab to Madīnah.
Soon, however, Abū al 'Āsī left Makkah on a trade trip to al
Shām. When he passed by the vicinity of Madīnah, a Muslim
patrol discovered and confiscated his caravan. While in Madīnah
he managed to reach his wife Zaynab under the shadow of night
and begged her to intervene on his behalf. She did and his goods
were returned to him. He ran back to Makkah with his goods
and there returned to each his due. He asked all his creditors
to speak out in case they had any claim against him. When none
spoke out and everyone thanked him for his loyalty, he announced
to his fellow Makkans: "I witness that there is no God but
God, and that Muhammad is His servant and prophet. By God,
I have not refrained from joining Islām earlier except out of
fear of suspicion that I have run away with your goods. Now
that everyone has received his due and my reputation is safe,
I declare my conversion." He returned to Madīnah, and the
Prophet permitted his wife Zaynab to return to him. The Quraysh
continued to ransom their captives with varying amounts running from 1000 to 4000 dirhims per person. As for those prisoners
who were too poor to afford a ransom, Muhammad granted them
their liberty as a gift.

Quraysh Mourns Her Dead

Having ransomed her captives, Quraysh still felt the wounds
of her tragedy. Makkah could find no reason to make peace with
Muhammad, and the memory of defeat at his hand remained
alive for a long time to come. For one whole month, the women
of Quraysh mourned their dead. They shaved off their hair,
whipped themselves, and cried when a dead man's camel or
mare was paraded in the streets. Only Hind, daughter of 'Utbah
and wife of Abū Sufyān, did not cry in public at all. She
was once asked by other Quraysh women about this mastery

of nerve: "Would you not publicly mourn your father, your brother, your uncle, and your other fallen relatives?" She answered: "Were I to mourn them publicly, the news will reach Muḥammad and his companions and the women of Banū al Khazraj who will all be pleased at my misfortune. No, by God, I shall not mourn them publicly until I have avenged them. Fat and perfume shall be forbidden to me until we have defeated the enemy. By God, if crying would take away sadness from my heart I would have cried. But I know that sadness will not leave me until I have seen with my own eye vengeance taken on the murderers of my dear ones." True to her vow, Hind never touched fat or perfume, nor came close to her husband's bed until the battle of Uḥud; and she spared no moment or occasion to incite her fellow Makkans to war. As for her husband, Abū Sufyān, he vowed never to wash himself until he had defeated Muḥammad.

14

Between Badr and Uḥud

The Effect of Badr in Madīnah (January, 624 C.E.)

We have just taken note of the deep effect that the Battle of Badr had upon Makkah. Above all, this effect included the will of the Quraysh to seek revenge against Muḥammad and the Muslims at the first opportunity. The effect of this battle in Madīnah was, however, much more obvious and more closely connected with the survival of Muḥammad and his fellows. The Jews, associationists, and hypocrites felt Muslim power increase after Badr. They realized that this alien who came to them less than two years ago as an escaping emigrant from Makkah had increased his power and influence almost to the point of dominating not only the Muslims but their city as a whole. As we have had occasion to see, the Jews had begun to complain even before Badr that they had had many skirmishes with the Muslims and that were it not for the Covenant of Madīnah, the explosion would have come sooner. Consequently, soon after the Muslims' victorious return, the non-Muslims of Madīnah began to meet clandestinely and to encourage the composition and recitation of divisive poetry. It was as if the battlefield had moved from Makkah to Madīnah and the dispute from religion to politics. It was not Muḥammad's call to God that was being fought; rather, it was his political power, his worldly influence, and his success which incited these parties not only to plot against him but even to think of assassinating him. None of this, of course, was beyond Muḥammad's ken. All the happenings within his city, including the rumors, reached him in constant flow. Simmering in hatred and anger against each other, Muslims and Jews lay in wait for one another.

Muslims Kill Abū 'Afk and 'Aṣmā'

Before the victory of Badr the Muslims used to fear the Madīnese non-Muslims, for they were still too weak to return any aggression inflicted upon them. But when they returned victorious from Badr, Sālim ibn 'Umayr took upon himself the job of getting rid of Abū 'Afk, a tribesman of Banū 'Amr ibn 'Awf. The latter was a poet who composed verses disparaging Muḥammad and the Muslims and inciting his own tribe to rise against them. Even after Badr, Abū 'Afk still composed and disseminated abusive verse. Sālim attacked Abū 'Afk in his sleep in his own yard and killed him. Likewise, 'Asmā', daughter of Marwān, of the tribe of Banū Umayyah ibn Zayd, used to insult Islām and the Prophet by encouraging bad feeling against the Muslims. The Battle of Badr did not make her reconsider. One day, 'Umayr ibn 'Awf attacked her during the night while she was surrounded by her children, one of whom she was nursing. 'Umayr was weak of sight and had to grope for her. After removing the child from his victim, he killed her; he then proceeded to the Prophet and informed him of what he had done. When her relatives returned from the funeral, they asked him whether he had killed her. "Indeed so," said 'Umayr, "You may fight me if you wish. By Him Who dominates my soul, if you should deny that she composed her abusive poetry, I would fight you until either you or I fall." It was this courage of 'Umayr that caused the Banū Khuṭmah, the tribe of 'Asmā''s husband, to turn to Islām. Having converted to Islām but fearing persecution at the hand of their fellow tribesmen, some of them had hidden their convertion. Henceforth, they no longer did so.

Murder of Ka'b ibn al Ashraf

It is sufficient to add to these two examples the murder of Ka'b ibn al Ashraf. When learning of the fall of the noblemen of Makkah, he exclaimed, "Those were the nobles of Arabia, the kings of mankind. By God, if Muḥammad has vanquished these people, the interior of the earth is a better dwelling than the top of it." Having assured himself of the news of defeat, he traveled to Makkah to incite its people against Muḥammad, to recite war poetry, and to mourn the victims. Furthermore, it was he who falsely accused the Muslim women upon return to Madīnah. The reader is perhaps aware of Arab custom and ethic in this regard, and can appreciate the Muslims' anxiety over such false accusations directed against their women's honor. Indeed, they were so incensed and irritated by him that, after unanimously agreeing to kill him, they authorized Abū Nā'ilah to seek his company and win his confidence. Abū Nā'ilah said to Ka'b, "The advent of Muḥammad was a misfortune to all of us. The tribes have become our enemies and fought against us; our roads are cut off, our families separated and dispersed, and our lives exhausted." With this and similar remarks, Abū Nā'ilah won Ka'b's confidence and asked him to lend some money to himself and his friends, pledging to pawn his and their armor. Ka'b agreed and asked the Muslims to return. They came to his house in the outskirts of Madīnah after dark. Abū Nā'ilah called out to him. Despite his wife's warning, Ka'b went out to meet his new friend. The two men walked in the night and were later joined by the companions of Abū Nā'ilah, whom Ka'b never suspected. Together they walked for a whole hour and covered a long distance, conversing and complaining about the hardships Muḥammad had brought upon their community, thus reassuring Ka'b of their sincerity. From time to time Abū Nā'ilah would touch the hair of Ka'b and exclaim, "I have never smelled such perfume in my life!" Then, after gaining Ka'b's complete trust, Abū Nā'ilah seized him by the hair, pulled him down to the ground, and said to his companions, "Kill the enemy of God!" They struck him with their swords.

Jewish Fears and Aggression

The murder of Ka'b increased the fears of the Jews to the point that not one of them felt secure. Nonetheless, they continued to attack Muḥammad and the Muslims and incite the people to war. A desert woman came one day to the Jews' market in the quarter of Banū Qaynuqā' seeking to remodel some jewelry at one of their shops. They persistently asked her to remove her veil, but the woman refused. Passing behind her without her knowledge, one of them tacked her robe with a pin to the wall. When the woman got up to leave, the robe was pulled down and her nakedness exposed. The Jews laughed and the woman cried. Seeing what happened, a Muslim passerby jumped upon the shopkeeper and killed him on the spot. The Jews gathered around the Muslim and likewise killed him. The Muslims' relatives called for help against the Jews and a general fight between them and the Banū Qaynuqā' erupted. Muḥammad first asked the Jews to stop their attacks and keep the covenant of mutual peace and security or suffer the kind of treatment meted out to the Quraysh. They ridiculed his request saying: "O Muḥammad! Fall not under the illusion that you are invincible. The people with whom you have fought were inexperienced. By God, if you were to turn your arm against us, you will find us adept in the arts of war." After this, little option was left to the Muslims but to fight the Jews. Otherwise, Islām would suffer political deterioration, and the Muslims would become the ridicule of Quraysh when they had just succeeded in making the Quraysh the ridicule of Arabia.

Blockade of Banū Qaynuqā'

For fifteen consecutive days, the Muslims blockaded Banū Qaynuqā' within their quarters, preventing any exit or entry. The Jews had no alternative but to surrender and yield themselves to Muḥammad's judgment. After consulting the Muslim leaders, Muḥammad decided to kill his captives. 'Abdullah ibn Ubayy ibn Salūl, allied to both Jews and Muslims, asked Muḥammad to be merciful toward his allies. When the Prophet declined, 'Abdullah repeated his request, and the Prophet declined again. 'Abdullah then seized the Prophet by his shield and would not let him go. At this, the Prophet seemed rather angry and said with a loud voice, "Leave me; hands off!" Ibn Ubayy replied, "No, by God, I shall not let you go until you give mercy to my *protégés*. Three hundred armed and four hundred unarmed men have so far protected me against every sort of people. Would you kill them all at once? By God, I will never agree to such a judgment, for I fear the turns of fortune." 'Abdulla was still a man of great power, having command of the associationists of the Aws and Khazraj tribes, although this power had largely waned with the growth of Muslim power. His insistence caused the Prophet to regain his good temper and patience, especially since 'Ubādah ibn al Ṣāmit had joined ibn Ubayy in making the same plea. He therefore decided to stretch his hand to 'Abdullah,

to all his *protégés*, whether associationists or Jews, and to grant
them all his mercy and benevolence. He decreed only that the
Banū Qaynuqa' should evacuate Madīnah in punishment for their
misdeeds. Once more, ibn Ubayy tried to plead with Muhammad
on behalf of his *protégés* that they be allowed to remain in
Madīnah. One of the Muslims, however, prevented ibn Ubayy
from reaching the Prophet and forced him to remove himself.
The tribesmen of Banū Qaynuqā' then announced that "By God,
we shall not remain in a city where ibn Ubayy is pushed by force
and we are unable to protect him." 'Ubādah subsequently led
them in the surrender of their arms and jewel-making machinery
and in the exodus from Madīnah. They went to Wādī al Qurā
where they tarried a while and then proceeded northward until
they reached Adhri'āt near the frontier of al Shām, where they
settled. Perhaps they went there because they wanted to be nearer
the Land of Promise that attracted the Jews then as it still does
today.

Political Unity in Madīnah

Jewish power in Madīnah was considerably reduced after the
expulsion of Banū Qaynuqā', for most of the Jews who called
themselves Madīnese lived far from Madīnah, in Khaybar and
Umm al Qurā. It was this political objective at which Muhammad
had aimed, and it reveals most clearly his political wisdom and
foresight. It was the first of a number of political consequences
of Muhammad's strategy. Nothing could be more harmful to the
unity of a state than internal division. And if internal strife
is inevitable, it is equally inevitable that one faction will finally
establish its authority and dominion over all the others. Some
historians have criticized the conduct of the Muslims toward
the Jews. They claim that the incident of the Muslim woman
at the jeweler's shop was relatively easy to settle as long as
each party had already paid with the loss of one of its members.
In answer to this claim, we may say that the victimization of
the Jew and the Muslim did not efface the insult which the
Muslims suffered at the hands of the Jews in the person of
that woman. We may also argue that among the Arabs, more
than among any other people, such an insult produces far greater
commotion and, according to custom, would have easily caused
continual war between two tribes for many long years. Examples

of such incidents and the wars which followed them are legion in Arab history. Besides this consideration, however, there is yet a stronger one. The incident at the jeweler's shop was to the blockade of Banū Qaynuqā' and their expulsion from Madīnah as the murder of the Austrian heir-apparent in Serajevo in 1914 was to World War I, which enveloped the whole of Europe. The incident was only the spark which inflamed Muslims and Jews and caused them to explode. The fact was that the presence of Muslims, Jews, associationists and *munāfiqūn* in one city with all their disparate ideals and customs made that city a political volcano replete with explosive power. The blockade of Banū Qaynuqā' and their expulsion were a prologue to the coming explosion.

The Campaign of Al Sawīq

After the expulsion of Banū Qaynuqā', the non-Muslims of Madīnah naturally withdrew from public life and the city appeared peaceful and quiet. The peace lasted one whole month and would have lasted longer were it not for Abū Sufyān who, unable to bear the memory of Makkan defeat at Badr, resolved to venture again outside of Makkah. He sought to reimpress the Arabs of the Peninsula with the notion that Quraysh was still strong, dominant and capable of attack and war. He mobilized two hundred Makkans (forty according to other versions) and led them out in secret in the direction of Madīnah. Upon arrival in the vicinity of Madīnah, they attacked at night a locality called al 'Urayd. Only one Madīnese and his client were in the locality at the time. They were killed and their house and orchard destroyed. Abū Sufyān thought his vow to attack Muḥammad had now been fulfilled, and he and his associates therefore left the scene quickly, fearing pursuit by the Prophet or his men. The Muslims did in fact pursue Abū Sufyān as far as Qarqarat al Kudr. In order to hasten their flight, Abū Sufyān and his party every now and then threw away some of their provisions of wheat and barley flour. While the Muslims followed their trail, they picked up these provisions; they soon realized, however, that the Makkans had escaped, and they decided to return home. By this raid Abū Sufyān had sought to console Quraysh after its defeat at Badr and to recapture its lost pride. In fact, his scheme turned against him and his flight in face of his pursuers brought further shame to Quraysh. Because of *al sawīq* (*i.e.*, the flour), which the men of Quraysh dropped on their path, this expedition was given the name "Al Sawīq Campaign."

Threat to the Shore Route of al Shām

The news of this event spread throughout the Arabian Peninsula. The distant tribes remained safe in their distance and concerned themselves but little with the affairs of those Muslims who, until the recent Battle of Badr, were nothing more than a weakly group of refugees in Madīnah. Even though the Muslims had resisted Quraysh successfully, expelled Banū Qaynuqāʻ from Madīnah, humbled ʻAbdullah ibn Ubayy, frightened Abū Sufyān away, and broke the traditional pattern of power distribution in the desert, it was only the tribes close to Madīnah which realized what threat this whole movement of Muḥammad posed. Only they were aware of the serious consequences of the contest for power between the Quraysh of Makkah and the Muslims of Madīnah. The shore route to al Shām was Makkah's well trodden path of trade that brought significant economic advantages to these tribes. Muḥammad had entered into threatening alliances with a number of tribes flanking the shore route and thereby exposed Makkah's commerce to serious danger. The tribes which lived on this commerce feared that Quraysh might now choose another route. Before the Hijrah of Muḥammad and his companions to Yathrib, indeed before Muslim victory at Badr, these tribes had felt relatively safe and secure. Now they pondered the future and the threat to their prosperity. If Makkan trade were to take another route, how would they sustain themselves in their arid and barren lands?

The Tribes' Fear of the Muslims

The Battle of Badr struck fear into the hearts of these tribes. Their leaders considered whether or not to strike against Madīnah now, before the situation got utterly out of hand. Soon enough, it came to the ear of Muḥammad that an army of Ghatafān and Sulaym tribesmen were marching in the direction of Madīnah; in turn, he led an expedition of Muslim fighters to Qarqarat al Kudr to meet them. When the Muslim force arrived, they found camel traces but no men. Muḥammad sent a number of his companions to reconnoiter the upper levels of the valley.

While waiting for them to return, he met a young boy by the name of Yasār and asked him about the whereabouts of the enemy. The boy answered that they had gone to the spring at the higher extremity of the valley. The Muslims seized the camels they found in the area without battle and divided the booty as the Qur'ān demanded, one-fifth going to Muḥammad. It was reported that their booty amounted to five hundred camels of which the Prophet took one-fifth and distributed the rest equally among his companions, each one getting two camels. Later on, it reached the ear of Muḥammad that Tha'labah and Muḥārib tribesmen had gathered at Dhū Amarr with aggressive designs. The Prophet immediately led an expedition of four hundred and fifty fighters to search out the enemy in their own grounds but without meeting them. He did, however, come across a man from Tha'labah whom he questioned regarding the whereabouts of the enemy. This man warned the Prophet that, should they hear of his advance, they would run away to the mountain heights; and he offered his services as a guide. The enemy soon heard of Muḥammad's approach and retreated to the mountains. Later learning that a great force of Banū Sulaym tribesmen from Baḥrān were advancing on Madīnah, the Prophet went out in haste with a Muslim force of three hundred to meet them. A day's distance from Baḥrān, the Muslims came across a man from Banū Sulaym who reported, upon questioning by the Prophet, that the tribesmen had dispersed and returned home. All these tribesmen were stricken with panic and fear for their future. They plotted against the Muslims and oft went out in force to fight them. But no sooner did they hear of Muḥammad's sortie with his companions to meet them, than they would lose heart and run away.

The Jews' Fear of Muḥammad

It was during these times that Ka'b ibn al Ashraf was killed. This event instilled in the Jews such fear that none of them dared leave his house. Muḥammad's blockade and expulsion of Banū Qaynuqā' intensified these fears.

They then came to Muḥammad pleading their cause and accusing the Muslims of having killed Ka'b deliberately, in spite of his personal innocence. Muḥammad answered, "The man whom you claim to be innocent has indeed harmed us deeply and composed libelous poetry against us. Had he remained quiet like his

co-religionists, nothing would have befallen him." After long
discussion of the matter, Muḥammad invited the Jews to enter
with him into a new covenant agreeable to both and which both
·vould henceforth respect. But this covenant did not allay fears.
Their plotting against Muḥammad continued as later events
were to make evident.

The 'Irāq Route to al Shām

How was Quraysh to conduct her trade now that Muḥammad
had cut off its route? Makkah, it must be remembered, lived on
trade. Without trade, its whole economy was bound to founder.
By cutting her trade route as he did, Muḥammad had practically
imposed a blockade on her which would soon destroy her place
and influence in Arabia. It is reported that Ṣafwān ibn Umayyah
advised the Quraysh at this stage that "Muḥammad and his
companions have spoiled our trade. What shall we do with him
and his companions if they do not remove themselves from the
coastal area? The Muslims befriended the tribes who inhabited
the coastal regions and most of these have even joined their
party. What shall we do with ourselves? To live in Makkah
devoid of trade is tantamount to eating up our capital funds and
then starving. Our whole life in the city, therefore, depends upon
our summer trade with al Shām and our winter trade with
Abyssinia." To this al Aswad ibn 'Abd al Muttalib replied that
the Makkans ought to abandon the coastal route to al Shām and
henceforth take the eastern route passing through al 'Irāq. To
help satisfy this requirement, al Aswad suggested to Ṣafwān
that he should appoint Furāt ibn Ḥayyān, a tribesman of Banū
Bakr ibn Wā'il, to show him the new route he should take. Furāt
explained to them that the eastern route was safe because none
of Muhammad's companions ever approached it, but that it was
an empty, waterless desert. The desert did not frighten Ṣafwān
because the season was winter and the need for water relatively
small. He gathered merchandise amounting to one hundred thousand Dirhams and prepared to start off toward al Shām. Nu'aym
ibn Mas'ūd al Ashja'ī, who was in Makkah at the time, learned
of the preparation of this caravan. Upon returning to Madīnah
he reported this news to Muḥammad. The Prophet sent Zayd
ibn Ḥārithah with a hundred riders to intercept the caravan
at the oasis of al Qardah in the center of Najd. The Makkans
ran away at the encounter, leaving behind the caravan which the

Muslims took away as booty. Upon Zayd's return to Madīnah, Muḥammad took one-fifth of the booty and divided the rest among his men. Furāt ibn Ḥayyān, the guide of the caravan, accepted Islām and thereby saved himself.

Muḥammad's Marriage to Ḥafṣah

Did all these successes convince Muḥammad that his position was really secure? Did his present victories delude him about the dangers of the future? Did the fear of Makkah and the various booty he had seized from Quraysh persuade him that the word of God and His Prophet was really safe and secure? Did his faith in God's timely help and providence cause him to let things take care of themselves on the grounds that divine government is supreme? Certainly not. Although time and space belong to God, yet the world runs according to unalterable laws innate to human nature and everywhere the same. Quraysh, for instance, enjoyed mastery over Arabia. It was not possible to expect her to give it up without a fight. Therefore, the fate of the caravan of Ṣafwān ibn Umayyah succeeded only in increasing their eagerness to avenge themselves and to double their preparation for the day of vindication. Neither could this escape Muḥammad's vision, foresight, or wise planning. It was necessary therefore, in anticipation of hostilities, for him to seek to strengthen his relationship with his fellow Muslims. However closely Islām had knitted the wills of its adherents and however strong the resultant social fabric, Muḥammad must have deemed further consolidation and unity desirable. For him to link himself to them in familial bonds was regarded by Muḥammad as well as by his companions as meeting this noble objective. Thus he married Ḥafṣah, daughter of 'Umar ibn al Khaṭṭāb, just as formerly he had married 'Ā'ishah, daughter of Abū Bakr. The former was the widow of Khunays, an early convert to Islām, who died seven months previously. The Prophet's marriage to Ḥafṣah increased ibn al Khaṭṭāb's attachment to him. In the same spirit, Muḥammad gave his daughter Fāṭimah in marriage to 'Alī, his cousin, though the latter had loved Muḥammad perhaps more than anyone else and had remained loyal to him ever since he was a child. When the Prophet's daughter, Ruqayyah, passed away, Muḥammad gave 'Uthmān ibn 'Affān, her bereaved husband, his other daughter, Umm Kulthūm. Thus he united in a bond of family and blood Abū Bakr, 'Umar, 'Uthmān,

and 'Alī, the four strongest personalities of his community. By
this and similar action, Muḥammad guaranteed the solidarity
of Muslim ranks. He assured them that the booty they seized
in their conquests would be theirs. He encouraged them to go
to war by combining in a single objective service to God and
fighting for His sake with the desire to make up their lost possessions in Makkah with captured Makkan booty. Muḥammad, by
following the news of Quraysh very closely throughout this
period, always kept himself abreast of her preparations for
war. It was common knowledge that Quraysh was preparing for
her day of revenge and for the reopening of the coastal trade
route to al Shām. She was preparing for a war to preserve her
commercial and religious position without which it was impossible for her to exist.

15

The Campaign of Uḥud

Quraysh's Preparations for Revenge

Ever since the Battle of Badr, Quraysh had not been at ease. The debacle of its al Sawīq campaign and the recent loss of its caravan on the route of al 'Irāq to the Muslims under the command of Zayd ibn Ḥārithah had intensified its resentment and bent its mind upon the avenging of Badr. The tribesmen of Quraysh, lords, notables, and noblemen of Makkah, could not forget their fallen brethren. How could they do so while Makkah women were still mourning their sons, brothers, fathers, husbands, and other relatives? Ever since Abū Sufyān ibn Ḥarb reached Makkah with the caravan that had caused the confrontation at Badr, he, together with those who participated in the battle and other notables of Quraysh, such as Jubayr ibn Muṭ'im, Ṣafwān ibn Umayyah, 'Ikrimah ibn Abū Jahl, al Ḥārith ibn Hishām, Ḥuwayṭib ibn 'Abd al 'Uzzā and others, agreed to deposit the whole caravan in the community house of Makkah (Dār al Nadwah) for public auction so that the proceeds might be used in preparing an army to fight Muḥammad. Their plans called for equipping a great strong army and inciting the tribes to join in this war of revenge. They had already incited Abū 'Azzah, the poet, a captive of Badr who was forgiven by the Prophet, to defect to their side. Likewise, they invited their Abyssinian clients to join ranks with them. The women of Quraysh, for their part, insisted on accompanying the army in order to

253

witness and to enjoy the revenge. In deliberating whether or
not to permit them to do so, some argued that for the women
to march alongside the men and sing the songs of war would
remind the soldiers of their fallen relatives and further arouse
them to fight. Those who argued in this vein were truly desperate,
for they were unwilling to return to their homes without either
avenging themselves or perishing in the process. Others thought
otherwise. Some said, "O Men of Quraysh, it is not wise to expose
your women to your enemies. Since it is not absolutely impossible
that you may have to run away for your lives, shame would
then befall your women." As the people deliberated, Hind,
daughter of 'Utbah and wife of Abū Sufyān said: "Indeed! We
shall accompany the army and watch the fighting. None may
stand in our way or force us back to our homes as happened
at al Juḥfah[1] on that *dies nefastus* when our beloved ones fell in
battle. And on the Day of Badr, had the women been there to
witness the soldiers run away from the battle front, this would
never have happened." Hind thus attributed the defeat at Badr
to the absence of women to arouse their men to sufficient self-
exertion in battle. Her little speech sealed the argument, and
the Quraysh began its march against Muḥammad together with
the women who were now led by the most resentful woman of all,
Hind, who suffered at Badr the loss of two dearest relatives, her
father and brother. The Makkan army started off in solemn
procession from Dār al Nadwah in three divisions. Only a
hundred men were from Thaqīf whereas all the others were
Makkans and Arab or Abyssinian clients of Makkah equipped
with great amounts of armour, two hundred horses, and three
thousand camels. They also counted seven hundred men clad
in heavy armour.

The Makkans' March against Madīnah

While all these preparations were taking place with the consent
and enthusiasm of everyone, al 'Abbās ibn 'Abd al Muṭṭalib, the
Prophet's uncle, watched from a distance and pondered. Despite
his loyalty to the faith of his fathers and the religion of his
people, he was moved in his feeling toward Muḥammad by a
sense of admiration complemented by a feeling of tribal solidarity
within him. He recalled how well Muḥammad had treated him
on the Day of Badr. It was the same sort of admiration and
tribal solidarity which had previously moved him to conclude

the Great Covenant of al 'Aqabah with al Aws and al Khazraj
tribes of Madīnah, for the purpose of guaranteeing the same
safeguard and protection to Muḥammad, his nephew, as those
which belonged to Madīnese women and children. At the time, he
warned those tribes that were they ever to falter in providing
such protection to his nephew, they should withdraw and give
up Muḥammad's protection to his own people. The same kind
of feeling stirred within him when he saw Quraysh's ubiquitous
enthusiasm against Muḥammad and when he witnessed this
great army marching forward toward Madīnah. He wrote a letter
describing the whole preparation, military equipment, and
number of Makkan soldiers and gave it to a man from Ghifār
whom he trusted to deliver to the Prophet in time. Soon, the
Quraysh army reached al Abwā' where Āminah, daughter of
Wahb and mother of Muḥammad, was buried. Some Makkans
thought of digging up her grave. However, their leaders stopped
them, fearful lest they set a precedent among the Arabs, and
recalling that the Muslims too could retaliate with the Makkans'
own dead buried in their vicinities. Upon arrival at the locality
of al 'Aqīq, the Makkan army camped at the foot of Mount
Uḥud, five miles from Madīnah.

Al 'Abbās's Message to the Prophet

The man from Ghifār, carrying the letter of al 'Abbās ibn 'Abd
al Muttalib, arrived at Madīnah and found that Muḥammad was
at Qubā'. There he proceeded; and, upon meeting Muḥammad at
the door of the mosque when he was just about to leave, handed
over the letter to him. The message was read for Muḥammad
by Ubayy ibn Ka'b who was then asked to keep its contents
secret. Muḥammad proceeded to Madīnah and called upon Sa'd
ibn al Rabī' at his home, told him the content of the message,
and asked him to keep it secret. Sa'd's wife, however, who was
at home at the time overheard the conversation and the matter
could no longer remain secret. Muḥammad then sent Anas and
Mu'nis, the two sons of Faḍālah, to reconnoiter the movements
of Quraysh. They found out that the army had approached
Madīnah and let its horses and camels loose to graze in the
plantations surrounding the city. Muḥammad then sent another
scout, al Ḥubāb ibn al Mundhir ibn al Jamūḥ. When enough
information had reached him to confirm the news his uncle had
sent, Muḥammad became gravely concerned and perplexed.

Salamah ibn Salāmah reported thereafter that the Quraysh cavalry was coming closer and closer to Madīnah and that they were about to enter the city. He rushed to his people and warned them of the imminent danger. All the inhabitants of Madīnah were apprehensive due to the descriptions of the might and equipment of the enemy. Their Muslim leaders even saw fit to guard the person of the Prophet with their own swords throughout the night. Sentries were posted at all corners of the city. When morning came, the Prophet called upon all Muslims, whether sincere or insincere,[2] for a public consultation on the fate of the city and the means by which they should meet the enemy.

Varying Opinions on Madīnah's Defense

The Prophet—May God's blessing be upon him!—suggested that the Muslims should hold fast to Madīnah, reinforce themselves therein, and keep out the Quraysh. Should the enemy decide to attack, the Muslims would fight from within and, knowing their own ground, should be better able to repulse the enemy. 'Abdullah ibn Ubayy ibn Salūl agreed with the Prophet and added: "Prophet of God, in the past we always fought our enemies in Madīnah by placing our women and children safely in the upper stories of the houses and building walls connecting one house with another on the perimeter of the city, thus making the town a single fortress. When the enemy advanced on us, the women and children would hit them with stones with which they had been amply provided while we would meet them with our swords in the streets. Our city, O Prophet of God, has never been violated by an enemy because none has ever entered it without meeting defeat. On the other hand, we have never met an enemy outside our city without loss to ourselves. Please listen to me in this matter and follow this wise plan which I inherited from the greatest leaders and wise men of Madīnah who have gone before."

The Prophet as well as the prominent among the Prophet's companions, whether Muhājirūn or Ansār, agreed with this view. However, the young Muslims who had not participated in Badr, as well as others who had witnessed Badr but became thereafter convinced that Muslim power was invincible, desired to go out of Madīnah and meet the enemy wherever he might be. They were disturbed by the idea that unless they spoke to this effect, they might be suspected of cowardice. They argued that since the enemy was not too far from Madīnah, the Muslims would be stronger than at Badr when they fought many miles away from their people and land. An advocate of this view said: "I hate to see the Quraysh return to Makkah saying that they have locked up Muḥammad in the houses and buildings of Yathrib and have prevented him and his companions from going out. Such talk would undoubtedly incite the Quraysh to further acts of aggression. Now that they have entered our very orchards and plantations, shown off their numbers and strength, and incited the Arab tribes and Abyssinian clients to follow them, how could we allow them to blockade us in our own homes and let them return without injury? Should we do that, they would surely return to raid our frontiers, to blockade us again, and to cut off our roads to the outside world." A number of other speakers spoke in favor of going out to meet the enemy, arguing that in case God gave them victory they would have met their objective. This would be a substantiation of the promise which God made to His Prophet. On the other hand, should they be defeated and die, they would have fallen as martyrs and would have won Paradise.

Call to Bravery and Martyrdom

This bold talk about bravery and martyrdom moved every Muslim heart and incited the community as a whole to spring to its feet in enthusiasm over a prospect of fighting in God's cause. With their eyes on Muḥammad, their hearts filled with faith in God, in His Prophet, Book, and Judgment, the image of their victory over this aggressive force standing out to attack them dissipated every other idea. They began to imagine themselves marching deep within enemy ranks, cutting them down with their swords and seizing their booty. The picture of paradise hovering before their eyes as martyrs in God's cause was just as the Qur'an had described it. It was a garden replete with everything desirable and beautiful where they would be reunited with the martyrs of Badr who preceded them, therein to dwell eternally, and "where there is neither gossip nor accusation and where every conversation is a talk of peace."[3] At this juncture, Khaythamah Abū Saʻd ibn Khaythamah said: "Perhaps, God will give us victory over them, or our turn will be one of martyrdom. Despite my great desire to be at Badr, it was not my fortune to go, but my son's. God was pleased to grant him his martyrdom. Last night, I saw him in a dream calling to me, 'Hurry up, Father, and join us in Paradise, for here I have truly found everything that God had promised me.' By God, Prophet, of God, I now long to join my son in Paradise. I am advanced in years and my hair has turned gray. Surely do I yearn to meet my Lord." Overwhelmed by this and similar speeches, the Muslims present inclined toward going out to meet the enemy. Muḥammad nonetheless advised against it, as if apprehensive of what it was to bring. But everybody insisted, and he had to agree with them. Community consensus and decision had always been his system of worldly government, and he departed from it only in case of a direct revelation to the contrary.

Discipline and Mutual Consultation

The day was a Friday. Muḥammad led the prayer and informed the congregation that their victory depended on their patience and careful preparation for war. After the mid-afternoon prayers, he returned home with Abū Bakr and 'Umar, who helped him put on his armour and handed to him his sword. In the meantime, the people were waiting outside and arguing with one another. Usayd ibn Ḥuḍayr and Sa'd ibn Mu'ādh, who had argued in favor of remaining in Madīnah, addressed the people in these words: "You must have noticed that the Prophet was of the opinion that we should remain in Madīnah and meet our enemy here. In saying what you did, you dissuaded him from this position against his will. Had you not better delegate the matter to him entirely, follow his verdict, and obey him?" The protagonists of the opposite view were suddenly struck by the idea that they might have opposed the Prophet in a matter in which God might have guided him. When he came out of his house wearing his armour and carrying his sword, they came to him pleading that they did not mean to disagree with him. They declared themselves prepared to abide by his and God's judgment whatever that may be. Muḥammad answered: "I have previously called you to follow such a course but you resisted. The Prophet is not one to put away his armour and sword once he puts them on until God's judgment is rendered between him and his enemies. Obey me henceforth. Victory will be yours provided you bear yourselves in patience." Thus, besides the

principle of consensus, Muḥammad placed order at the foundation
of government. Once the community has made up its mind
after due deliberation, it should not alter it in haste, but endeavor resolutely to see through. It is then the responsibility of
its executive to see to it that the course followed does indeed
accomplish the objective sought.

The Muslims' March

Muḥammad set out at the head of his force in the direction
of Uḥud. His first stop was at a locality called al Shaykhān where
he met a group of people unknown to him and who, upon inquiry,
turned out to be the Jewish allies of ibn Ubayy. The Prophet
ruled that unbelievers may not be taken as allies against unbelievers unless they become Muslims. The Jewish column therefore was commanded to return to Madīnah. The friends of ibn
Ubayy began to whisper in his ear that Muḥammad had slighted
him by disregarding the ancestral wisdom which he had put at
the disposal of Muḥammad but which the latter had rejected in
favor of the childish views of the Muslims. Soon ibn Ubayy
became convinced that the Muslims were following the wrong
course and returned with his own men to Madīnah. The sincere
believers who remained with the Prophet numbered seven hundred as against the three thousand Makkan fighters of the
Quraysh tribe.

Ordering the Ranks for Battle

The Muslim force reached Uḥud toward the morning. They
crossed the valleys and ascended over dunes. Muḥammad ordered
his companions in rows and placed fifty archers on the side
of the mountain. Fearing that the enemy might surprise the
Muslims from the rear, he ordered the archers to protect that
side under all circumstances. Specifically, he commanded them
never to leave their place regardless of whether the Muslims
plunged into the enemy camp and won, or fell in their places at
the hand of the enemy. Should the enemy cavalry charge, it was
the duty of the archers to repel that charge with arrows. He
commanded everyone not to begin the fight except on his command, but he ordered the archers to attack the enemy on sight
and before he reached Muslim ranks.

Quraysh Women

Quraysh, too, ordered its forces in rows, placing Khālid ibn al Walīd on the right and 'Ikrimah ibn Abū Jahl on the left. They gave the command to 'Abd al Uzzā Ṭalḥah ibn Abū Ṭalḥah. The women were running back and forth between the lines of the fighters striking their drums and tamburines and, led by Hind, daughter of 'Utbah and wife of Abū Sufyān, sang:

"Ho Ho, Sons of 'Abd al Dār!
Ho Ho, Guardians of the land!
Strike down your enemies!
Advance forward and we shall embrace you!
Advance forward and we shall spread the carpets for you!
Turn your backs and we shall avoid you!
Turn your backs and we shall never come to you!"

Abū Dujānah and His Death-Scarf

Thus the two parties were poised for battle and the leaders aroused their own men to fight, the Quraysh by summoning the memory of Badr and its victims, the Muslims by remembering God and the promise of His victory. Muḥammad raised his sword in front of his companions and invited them to come forward to get it provided they could fulfill one condition. A number of them rushed to him but were sent back. Abū Dujānah Simāk ibn Kharashah, brother of Banū Sā'idah, rose and asked, "What is the provision, O Prophet of God?" The Prophet answered, "That you continue to strike the enemy with it until it breaks." Abū Dujānah was a very brave man who had a red scarf which, as everybody knew, signaled that he was bent on fighting until victory or death. As he drew this scarf and wrapped it around his head, the Prophet gave him the sword. He took it and started to dance in joy between two rows of fighters, as he was wont to do before entering into battle. When Muḥammad saw him perform this dance, he said that "Such would be hateful to God except under the circumstances."

Abū 'Āmir, slave of 'Amr ibn Ṣayfī al Awsī, was the first to start the hostilities. Previously, he had moved from Madīnah to Makkah in order to arouse the Quraysh to fight Muḥammad. He had not witnessed the Battle of Badr. Anxious not to miss this time, he came to Uḥud with a retinue of soldiers consisting of fifteen al Aws tribesmen and a number of slaves from Makkah. Once he claimed that he could persuade his fellow tribesmen who converted to Islām to fight with Quraysh against Muḥammad. Putting this large claim to the test, he called to them and announced his identity. But his tribesmen replied with curses and damnations. Infuriated at the result, he approached Muslim ranks and started to fight. To the left, 'Ikrimah ibn Abū Jahl with a company of slaves attempted to penetrate Muslim lines at the flank. The Muslims met them with stones and caused them to withdraw. At this moment, Ḥamzah ibn 'Abd al Muṭṭalib gave the war cry, "Die! Die!" and sprang forward into the thick of the Quraysh lines. Ṭalḥah ibn Abū Ṭalḥah, carrier of the Makkan flag, sprang forward asking the Muslims to duel with him. 'Alī ibn Abū Ṭālib advanced forth to fight with him. The encounter was soon over as 'Alī struck his enemy a single fatal stroke. Exalted, the Prophet and the Muslims yelled, "God is Great," and advanced for the general charge. Abū Dujānah, with the Prophet's sword in hand and its head wrapped in the "scarf of death," as he called it, killed everyone with whom he fought. He saw one Makkan fighting a Muslim with his fingernails. As he prepared to deal with him, he discovered that it was a woman and that it was Hind, daughter of 'Utbah. He immediately withdrew and saved the Prophet's sword from ever touching a woman's blood.

The Martyrdom of Ḥamzah

The Quraysh forces advanced ferociously, and the general *mêlée* between the disproportionately balanced forces began. The larger army was motivated by resentment and a consuming will to vengeance; the smaller by its faith in God and His religion and the will to defend its homeland as well as its interests. Those who sought revenge surpassed them in number and equipment. They were heartened and cheered by the women, each of whom promised one soldier or another her most precious possessions if he could only avenge for her previous loss of her father or brother, husband, or relative. Ḥamzah ibn 'Abd al Muttalib was one of the greatest and most courageous of Arab heroes. At Badr, it was he who killed 'Utbah, father of Hind, as well as her brother and a number of other close relatives of hers. True to his reputation, Ḥamzah distinguished himself in battle on the

Day of Uhud. He killed Arṭāt ibn 'Abd Shuraḥbīl, Sibā' ibn 'Abd al 'Uzzā al Ghubshānī, and a number of others. His sword seemed invincible. Hind had promised Wahshī, the Abyssinian client of Jubayr, a great amount of wealth should he succeed in killing Hamzah. To encourage him further, Jubayr ibn Muṭ'am, his master whose uncle was also killed at Badr, promised Wahshī his freedom if he succeeded. The story following was later told by Wahshī: "I set out among others, planning to fight with my javelin as all Abyssinians do, for I hardly ever miss my objective with it. When the great encounter took place, I looked around for Hamzah and caught him with my eyes. I saw him right in the middle of the *mêlée*, standing out as clearly as a black camel in the herd and felling everybody around him with his sword. I swung my javelin and, making sure it was well balanced, I threw it at him and it fell right on him hitting him in the abdomen and piercing him through. I left my javelin and its victim pinned down under it until he died. Later on I came to him and pulled my javelin away and returned then to the camp and fought no longer. I had killed him in order to win my liberty, and that I had now achieved. When I returned to Makkah, my manumission was officially recognized."

Those in the Muslim camp fell into two categories: The sincere Muslims and the *munāfiqūn*. The prototype of the latter was Quzmān, who joined Islām but never really believed in it. When the Muslim army left Madīnah, Quzmān refused to march. The next morning the women of Banū Zafar began to shame him for his cowardice. "O Quzmān," they said to him, "have you lost your sense of shame or have you become a woman to stay behind while all the men are out fighting?" Incensed, Quzmān went to his home, put on his armour, bow, arrows and sword, and set out to join the Prophet's army. He was known to be a brave soul. When he arrived on the scene, he found the Prophet ordering the ranks of the Muslim soldiers. He went straight through to the first row and was the first to throw himself into the battle. He shot his arrows and pierced many an enemy's chest. Toward the end of the day, he was still determined to fall fighting, and he continued to fight until he did. He killed seven of the enemy in one short hour in addition to all the others whom he had killed with his arrows. Passing by him and finding him about to die, Abū al Ghaydāq congratulated him on his achievement of martyrdom. Quzmān answered, "O Abū 'Āmir, I have not really fought for the faith. I have fought only in order to prevent Quraysh

from invading our territory and violating our homes and properties. By God, I fought only in order to protect my people and my
land. Without those I would never have done it."

The other group were the true believers. They were not over
seven hundred strong and they faced three thousand of the enemy.
What has so far been said concerning the deeds of Ḥamzah and
Abū Dujānah reveals an idea of the power of Muslim morale.
This was a power before which the soldiers of Quraysh reeled
like worms, despite all the courage and heroism for which they
were famous throughout Arabia. Their flag was carried so
proudly that none would allow it to lay fallen; and as soon as it
fell, another soldier would raise it anew. When 'Alī ibn Abū Ṭālib
killed its carrier, Ṭalḥah ibn Abū Ṭalḥah, it was immediately
raised again by 'Uthmān ibn Abū Ṭalḥah. And when 'Uthmān
fell at the hands of Ḥamzah, it was raised again by Abū Sa'd ibn
Abū Ṭalḥah. At the moment he raised the Makkan flag he
shouted at the Muslims, "Do you pretend that your martyrs are
in paradise and ours in hell? By God, you lie! If anyone of you
truly believes such a story, let him come forward and fight with
me." His challenge attracted 'Alī[4] who killed him on the spot.
The Banū 'Abd al Dār kept on carrying the Makkan flag until
they lost nine men. The last of them was Ṣu'āb, the Abyssinian
slave of Banū 'Abd al Dār, whose right hand carrying the flag was
struck by the aforementioned Quzmān. Ṣu'āb seized the flag and
raised it high with the left arm. Quzmān struck it with his sword
again. Having lost both arms, Ṣu'āb now seized the flag and
pressed it to his chest with whatever was left of his arms and
even bent his back to support it while saying "O Banū 'Abd al
Dār, have I not done my duty?" Either Quzmān or Sa'd ibn
Abū Waqqāṣ killed him. When all the party in charge of the
Makkan flag were decimated, the Makkan associationists realized
their defeat and began to run for their lives. Even their women
were now exposed, and the statue which they had brought with
them on camel back to bless them had now fallen to the ground
and was broken.

Muslim Victory on the Morning of Uḥud

Actually, the victory the Muslims achieved on that morning
was a genuine war miracle. Some may attribute it to the sound
judgment of Muḥammad in placing the archers on the mountain
side so that they could hit the enemy cavalry before they could

reach the Muslim lines while at the same time protecting the rear of all Muslim forces. Muḥammad's good judgment is undoubtedly true. But it is equally true that when six hundred Muslims threw themselves against an enemy force five times greater than theirs, they could not possibly have done so and achieved such bravery unless their deeds sprang from their candid faith in the righteousness of their own cause. Whoever believes in the cause of truth is not bothered by the material preponderance of any power, however great, and his will would not be shaken even if all the forces of evil rallied against him. Sincere faith in God Almighty is the greatest power, the greatest idea. It is invincible. As long as its subject remains sincere and loyal to it, there is no doubt that sincere faith must obtain all it wills. Therefore, Quraysh was shattered and defeated with all its three thousand fighters by the six hundred Muslims. That is why the women of Quraysh were about to be taken captive. When the Muslims followed up their enemies far from the battlefield, those who remained fell upon the large booty left behind. Indeed, many Muslims were thus drawn away from pursuing the defeated enemy.

The Muslims' Preoccupation with Booty

The archers whom Muḥammad had commanded not to leave the mountainside even to rescue the Prophet and his companions from what might seem to them to be certain death watched the battle from their height, and saw the defeated enemy running away and the pursuing Muslims seizing the booty. This whetted their appetites. For a moment, they argued with one another in seeking to convince themselves that no purpose would be served by keeping their position now that God had defeated their enemy. As they watched their fellow Muslims gather the booty, they strongly felt like joining them. When a wiser voice reminded them that the Prophet had commanded them not to leave their position even for rescuing the Muslims from certain death, they rationalized that he had not intended for them to remain in their positions that long, certainly not after the defeat of the enemy. 'Abdullah ibn Jubayr advised them not to violate the Prophet's commandment whatever the circumstances. The majority did not heed his advice, however, but descended to the plain. Ten men only kept their ground. This provided Khālid ibn al Walīd, Commander of the Makkan cavalry, the golden opportunity to attack and seize the mountainside where the archers were. He eliminated the remainder of the Muslim archers and occupied the mountainside. The other Muslims were not aware of what was happening, preoccupied as they were in gathering everything of value on the field. After he occupied the mountainside, ibn al Walīd signaled to the Quraysh to attack again and he advanced upon the Muslims from the rear. The defeated Makkans rallied to his call, turned about and resumed the fighting. The Muslims dropped the booty they carried, drew their swords and defended themselves. But their victory was lost. Their ranks were disorderly and their unity was in shreds. Quraysh took a heavy toll of Muslim lives. Earlier, the Muslims were fighting by the command of God and out of their faith in Him and in victory; now they fought in order to save their own lives from certain death and humiliation. Earlier, the Muslims were fighting in a united and orderly manner, under a strong and resolute leadership; now they fought without order or leadership. So great was the disorder that some may have struck their own fellows. Finally, when somebody raised the cry that Muḥammad was killed, chaos reined supreme, Muslim morale plunged to the bottom and Muslim soldiers fought sporadically and purposelessly. This chaos was responsible for their killing of Ḥusayl ibn Jābir Abū Ḥudhayfah by mistake, as everyone sought to save his own skin by taking flight except such men as 'Alī ibn Abū Ṭālib whom God had guided and protected.

The Prophet's Injury

When the Quraysh heard of the fall of Muḥammad, their forces fell upon Muslim ranks with renewed vigor. Every one of them was seeking to hit Muḥammad, even if dead, that he might have the honor and pride of having participated in his downfall. The Muslims who stood close to the Prophet protected him and drew a close circle around him. Their faith had come back to them and they now stood their ground anxious to lay down their lives in order to save their Prophet. The fact is that one of the stones thrown by the Quraysh had hit the Prophet and caused him to fall to the ground, with a cut lip, a wounded face, and a broken tooth. The stone that hit the Prophet was thrown by 'Utbah ibn Abū Waqqāṣ. It landed with such force that it pushed two links of Muḥammad's helmet chain into his wound. Muḥammad attempted to stand up behind a shield of his companions, but he fell again, this time in a hole which Abū 'Āmir had dug as a trap

for the Muslims. 'Alī ibn Abū Ṭālib ran to Muhammad and gave
him his hand and, together with Ṭalḥah ibn 'Ubaydullah, lifted
him again to his feet. He and his companions then began to retreat toward the mountain of Uḥud while fighting their pursuing
enemies.

Desperate Defense of the Prophet's Person

In a moment, however, a number of other Muslims joined the
circle of the Prophet, and these were so determined and desperate in their defense that they formed an impregnable barrier
between the Prophet and the enemy. Umm 'Amārah al Ansāriy-
yah, the Madīnese, had been on the battlefield since the morning
to give water to the Muslim fighters to drink. When the Muslims
suffered defeat, she threw down her water jug, drew her sword,
and joined the other fighters around the Prophet for his protection. She shot a number of arrows until she herself was wounded.
Abū Dujānah placed himself as a shield before the Prophet and
even exposed his back to the falling arrows lest they should hit
the Prophet. Sa'd ibn Abū Waqqās shot arrows which Muhammad passed to him while lending him encouragement. A little
earlier, Muhammad himself was using his bow and shot at the
enemy until the string of his bow broke. Those who thought that
Muhammad had perished, including Abū Bakr and 'Umar, went
toward the mountain and sat down. When Anas ibn al Nadr inquired why they were giving up so soon, and was told that the
Prophet of God had been killed, he retorted: "And what would
you do with yourselves and your lives after Muhammad died?
Rise, and die like he did." He turned, charged against the enemy,
and fought gallantly. He kept on fighting despite his wounds
and did not give up until he was hit seventy times. His body was
so torn up with wounds that only his sister could identify it by
means of his fingers alone.

The Prophet's Escape

Quraysh took the news of Muhammad's death with exhilaration
and joy, and Abū Sufyān began a search for his body on the
battlefield. The Muslims around Muhammad did not deny the
news of his death in obedience to Muhammad's own commandment
designed to prevent any new onslaught by the Quraysh against
him. Ka'b ibn Mālik, however, came close to the circle and, bend-

ing himself over Abū Dujānah, noticed that the Prophet was there and still alive. He proclaimed at the top of his voice: "O Believers, be glad, for the Prophet of God is here and still alive." The Prophet, however, asked him to keep quiet. The Muslims then reinforced the protective circle around the Prophet and moved with him farther up toward the mountain; they were led by Abū Bakr, 'Umar, 'Alī ibn Abū Ṭālib, al Zubayr ibn al 'Awwām and others. The cry of Ka'b brought about a different effect upon the Quraysh. Most of the latter did not believe it but regarded it as an enemy trick designed to rally the Muslims to fight again. A few Makkans ran toward the Muslims shouting, "Where is Muhammad? Death to me if he lives!" The Prophet hurled the javelin of al Ḥārith ibn al Ṣimmah at the oncoming party. It hit the leader, threw him off his horse, and killed him. When the Muslims reached the entrance to the valley on the other side, 'Alī filled his shield with water, washed Muhammad's face and poured some water on his head. Abū 'Ubaydah ibn al Jarrāḥ pulled out the two links of chain from Muhammad's wound, and his two front teeth fell off in the process. While this was taking place, Khālid ibn al Walīd pursued the Muslims on the hillside with a small force of Makkan cavalry. But they were repelled by 'Umar ibn al Khaṭṭāb and a number of the Prophet's companions. The Muslims continued their retreat. So great was their exhaustion that when it was noon, the Prophet led the prayer seated, suffering as he was from his wounds, and the Muslims prayed behind him seated also.

Mutilation of the Muslim Dead

Quraysh was intoxicated with her victory and deemed her vengeance for Badr fully taken. The occasion gave Abū Sufyān such cause for pride that he said, "A great day was won against the day of Badr. Next year will see the same." His wife Hind, daughter of 'Utbah, was not satisfied with this victory. Nor was she satisfied with the death of Ḥamzah ibn 'Abd al Muttalib. With her women companions she ran toward the battlefield and began the mutilation of the Muslim dead. She cut off a number of noses and ears in order to make a string and a necklace of them. She then cut the body of Ḥamzah open and pulled out his liver which she began to chew. These ugly deeds of hers and of her women companions were so unbecoming that even Abū Sufyān, her husband, denounced her. He said to one of the

Muslims: "Your dead were indeed mutilated; but I swear by God that I have never approved of such deeds. How can I be accused of commanding them?"

Muhammad's Mourning of Ḥamzah

The Quraysh returned to Makkah after burying their dead. The Muslims returned to the battlefield to bury theirs, and Muhammad sought out the body of his uncle, Ḥamzah. When he saw that his body was mutilated, Muhammad felt profoundly sad and vowed that he would never allow such a hateful thing to happen again and that he would someday avenge these evil deeds. It was on this occasion that the revelation was made:

وَإِنْ عَاقَبْتُمْ فَعَاقِبُوا بِمِثْلِ مَا عُوقِبْتُمْ بِهِ وَلَئِنْ صَبَرْتُمْ لَهُوَ خَيْرٌ لِّلصَّابِرِينَ ۞ وَاصْبِرْ وَمَا صَبْرُكَ إِلَّا بِاللَّهِ وَلَا تَحْزَنْ عَلَيْهِمْ وَلَا تَكُ فِي ضَيْقٍ مِّمَّا يَمْكُرُونَ ۞

"And if you punish, inflict the same punishment as has been meted out to you. But if you bear patiently, it is certainly better for you. Do bear then patiently; for the reward of your patience is with God. Do not feel sad nor give way to anger because of their plotting."[5]

The Prophet of God then pardoned, bore patiently, and laid down an absolute prohibition against mutilation. Ḥamzah was given burial on the spot where he lay, Muhammad conducting the funerary prayer and Ḥamzah's sister, Ṣafiyyah, daughter of 'Abd al Muṭṭalib, participating. All prayed for God to show them His mercy. The Prophet then commanded burial for all the dead, which numbered seventy; and, when this was completed, he led his party back to Madīnah. The Muslims were quite sad and solemn for having encountered such defeat after their victory, and such humiliation after their splendid accomplishment. They fully realized that it was the archers' disobedience of Muhammad as well as the Muslims' preoccupation with booty that had exposed them to this sad turn of events.

Need for Recapturing the Lost Prestige

The Prophet went home and thought deeply. The Jews, the munāfiqūn, and the associationists of Madīnah were elated at the news of the setback. Muslim power in Madīnah had been such that none could effectively oppose it. Now it stood ready to be shaken. 'Abdullah ibn Ubayy ibn Salūl did not participate in the Battle of Uhud because Muhammad as well as the Muslims did not wish to listen to his advice. Moreover, Muhammad declared himself angry against 'Abdullah's clients, the Jews. Were this setback at Uhud the last judgment on the Muslims *vis-à-vis* the Quraysh, the fate of Muhammad and his companions would have been easily disposed of by the tribesmen of the Peninsula, and their political power in Yathrib would have crumbled. The Muslims would have become objects of universal derision. In such circumstances, the associationists and pagans would surely have been emboldened to attack the religion of God, and that would have been the greatest tragedy. It was necessary, therefore, to direct some strike against the enemy in order to offset the defeat of Uhud and to recapture Muslim morale as well as to instill fear in the hearts of the Jews and the *munāfiqūn*. Such a measure was necessary if the political power of Muhammad and his companions in Yathrib was to regain its strength.

Resumption of Fighting on the Morrow

On the morrow, which fell on Sunday the 16th of Shawwāl, the *mu'adhdhin* of the Prophet called upon the Muslims to regroup and pursue the enemy. Only those who had participated in the previous day's battle were, however, allowed to proceed. When the Muslims set out toward the Makkan force, Abū Sufyān immediately learned that his enemies had returned from Madīnah with new reinforcements. Muhammad reached Hamrā' al Asad while Abū Sufyān and his companions were still at al Rawhā'. Since he passed by both camps, Ma'bad al Khuzā'ī, who was still an associationist, was asked by Abū Sufyān about Muhammad and his forces. He replied that "Muhammad and his companions are coming after you with such a large army that I have never seen the like of it. Those who were not present yesterday are all with him today shouting with anger and seeking revenge." Abū Sufyān, on the other hand, though he wanted to run away from any more confrontations with Muhammad, pondered the consequences of such a flight. Would not the Arabs say of Quraysh in such an eventuality what he himself would have liked to say of Muhammad and his companions? But then, were he to return to Muhammad and the Muslims defeat them this time, would not the Quraysh be destroyed once and for all?

He therefore made recourse to a trick. With some riders of 'Abd al Qays proceeding to Madīnah, he sent a message to Muḥammad that the Quraysh had decided to pursue the Muslims in order to finish them off. When this message reached Muḥammad at Ḥamrā' al Asad, his will and determination remained constant and his decision unchanged. The whole Muslim force, which remained in place for three days and three nights, made large bonfires during the night in order to show the world that they were there to stay. Finally, disagreeing with Abū Sufyān, the Quraysh preferred to save the memory of their victory of Uḥud and to return to Makkah. Thereafter, Muḥammad returned to Madīnah with more confidence in Muslim power, though the insincere believers began to raise their heads in derision of the Muslims and asked: "If the battle of Badr was a sign from God proving the veracity of Muḥammad's prophethood, what was the sign of the battle of Uḥud?"[6]

16

The Effects of Uḥud

Muḥammad's Policy after Uḥud

After Uḥud, Abū Sufyān returned to Makkah preceded by the news of his victory. He arrived home exalted and overjoyed for having removed from Quraysh the stain of defeat at Badr. As soon as he entered the city and before setting foot in his residence, he went to the Ka'bah where he offered thanksgiving and prayers to its high god Hubal. He then shaved his sideburns and returned to his residence feeling that the vow he had made not to touch his wife until he had defeated Muḥammad had now been fulfilled. The Muslims, on the other hand, despite the fact that they spent three whole days in the open, challenging their enemy to return and engage them without avail, were derided by the Madīnese. Nobody mentioned the Muslim victory in the first round of battle. Evidently, Madīnah was simply not favorable to the Muslims, Muḥammad's great political power notwithstanding. The Prophet—May God's peace and blessing be upon him—felt this hostility strongly, not only from Madīnah but also from all the surrounding Arab tribes who only a few days earlier feared and respected Muslim power. The Battle of Uḥud had enabled the non-Muslim elements of Madīnah and its surroundings to dare to stand in the face of Muḥammad and even to oppose him. Hence Muḥammad took especial care to keep himself abreast of developments within and without the city, and he prepared himself for recapturing and reestablishing Muslim power and reputation.

271

The Campaign of Abū Salamah ibn 'Abd al Asad

The first news of enemy movement that came to Muḥammad's ear told that Ṭulayḥah and Salamah, sons of Khuwaylid and leaders of Banū Asad, were inciting their tribesmen and clients to attack Madīnah and to seek Muḥammad in his own house. They were also inciting them to raid the city outskirts to seize the cattle of the Muslims. Apparently, they were emboldened by the consideration that Muḥammad and his companions were still shaken by defeat and that their power was on the decline. As soon as the Prophet heard of this, however, he sent forth Abū Salamah ibn 'Abd al Asad at the head of an expeditionary force of one hundred and fifty fighters including Abū 'Ubaydah ibn al Jarrāḥ, Sa'd ibn Abū Waqqās, and Usayd ibn Ḥuḍayr. He ordered the force to march by night along untrodden paths, to lie still by day, and to surprise the enemy wherever possible. Abū Salamah followed the instructions of the Prophet and found his enemy unprepared. Shortly before dawn, he talked to his men, inspiring them to holy war, and they attacked. The enemy ran away in defeat. The Muslims pursued them and returned after having stripped them of all their possessions. They divided the booty among themselves after saving one fifth of it for God, His Prophet, the poor, and the wayfarer; then they returned to Madīnah victorious. Their accomplishment restored some of the Muslim prestige which had been lost at Uḥud. Abū Salamah, however, did not live long after this raid, for his wound at Uḥud had not been completely cured. His participation in this raid, during which he reopened the wound, finally brought about his death.

The Campaign of 'Abdullah ibn Unays

Later Muḥammad learned that Khālid ibn Sufyān ibn Nubayḥ al Hudhalī was either at Nakhlah or 'Uranah arousing the people and inciting them to raid Madīnah. He commanded 'Abdullah ibn Unays to travel to Madīnah in order to reconnoiter for him. After going forth, 'Abdullah found Khālid in the company of women. When asked by Khālid about his identity, 'Abdullah answered, "I am an Arab tribesman who has heard of you and of the army you are raising to fight Muḥammad and I have come to you to join your ranks." Khālid did not hide the fact that he was actually raising an army in order to attack Madīnah. In a moment of separation from his men, and in the company of his women, 'Abdullah asked Khālid to walk with him a little while in order to discuss certain affairs. When they were at a safe distance, he fell on him with his sword and killed him. Khālid's women were the only witnesses and they began to cry and mourn for him. 'Abdullah returned home and informed the Prophet of his exploits. This singlehanded campaign had the effect of silencing the Banū Liḥyān branch of the Hudhayl tribe for some time. But the Banū Liḥyān began to think of ways and means to avenge the murder of their leader.

The Battle of al Rajī' (625 C.E.)

About this time, a group of tribesmen living in the district of Muḥammad came to him saying, "There are some Muslims among us. Please send with us some of your companions to teach us the law of Islām and to recite the Qur'ān." Muḥammad was in the habit of sending his companions upon request to such areas and tribes in order to perform such religious functions and to call men to the true faith and guidance as well as to find new political allies. It will be recalled that Muḥammad sent such companions to Madīnah after the great covenant of 'Aqabah. In fulfillment of this new request, Muḥammad sent six of his notable companions. When they were all camping at a well belonging to the tribe of Hudhayl in the Ḥijāz at a place called al Rajī', their host betrayed them to the Hudhayl tribe. The six Muslims arose to find that they were surrounded by enemies with drawn swords. They drew their swords too and prepared for battle. But the Hudhayl tribesmen said, "It is not our intention to kill you but to sell you as captives to the people of Makkah. Lay down your swords and we solemnly promise that we shall not kill you." The Muslims looked to one another and decided that a humiliating captivity in Makkah was far worse than loss of life. Rejecting the promise of Hudhayl, they began to fight knowing that they were outnumbered. Hudhayl killed three of them and overpowered the other three. They tied their hands and drove them toward Makkah. 'Abdullah ibn Ṭālib managed to pull his hands free and seized his sword to fight his captors. But they overwhelmed and killed him. The other two captives were brought to Makkah and sold by the Hudhayl. Zayd ibn al Dathinah was purchased by Ṣafwān ibn Umayyah in order to

be killed in revenge for his father, Umayyah ibn Khalaf. The
captive was given over to Ṣafwān's servant Nasṭās for execution.
Abū Sufyān questioned the captive: "Tell me, O Zayd, would
you not prefer that Muḥammad were here in your place to receive
this last punishment while you were at home with your people?"
Zayd answered, "No! By God, I certainly prefer that Muḥammad
be where he is, safe from all harm. That is more preferable to me
than reunion with my people." Stupefied, Abū Sufyān rejoined,
"Never have I seen anyone more beloved by his companions than
Muḥammad." Nasṭās executed the order of his master and killed
Zayd, the man who remained true to his religion and Prophet.
As for Khubayb, he was kept in jail until such time as they
would crucify him. In his last hour, he asked to be allowed to pray,
and they let him. After completion of his prayer, he exclaimed:
"By God, were I not afraid that you might think I was not ready
to die, I would have prolonged my prayer." They lifted him to the
cross and tied him to it. With great passion, he prayed to God:
"O God, reduce their numbers, rout, and disperse them, do not let
any one of them escape." There was such a ring in his voice that
his executioners were seized with panic and fell to the ground
as if his curse had really struck them. Like Zayd before him,
Khubayb died a martyr, true to his Creator, and loyal to His
religion and Prophet. It would have been possible for these two
pure souls to save themselves from death if they had apostatized.
But their conviction of God, of His Spirit, of the Day of Judgment—the Day on which every soul will receive its due, and no
vicarious substitutes will be allowed—caused them to see death
as a fitting finale for the life of faith. Undoubtedly, they must
have believed that their innocent lives now being laid down on
Makkan soil would one day arouse their Muslim brethren to conquer that city, destroy its idols, and purify it from paganism and
associationism. They were certain that someday the Ka'bah
should rightly be sanctified as the House of God ought to be and
that someday its walls would reverberate with none but the name
of God alone.

The western Orientalists do not note this event as they do the
execution of the two captives of Badr by the Muslims. None of
them has even condemned this treacherous execution of two innocent Muslims who participated in no war but who were dragged
stealthily into the enemy camp while they were teaching the very
men who were planning their murder or sale to their enemies.
None of them had thought to condemn the Quraysh despite the

fact that its behavior in this case was nothing short of cowardice and cold-blooded murder. The rules of the most primitive justice would have required of those western Orientalists who condemned the Muslims' execution of the two Badr captives that they condemn, *a fortiori*, this treason of Quraysh and of the men who sold her the two captives after killing their four colleagues. Neither did Quraysh capture them in an honest fight. It bought them from people who tricked them into their camp by inviting them to be the teachers of truth, to instruct, and to enlighten them in matters of the faith.

Muḥammad and the Muslim community were saddened by the news of the martyrdom of their six colleagues as a result of the treachery of Hudhayl. Ḥassān ibn Thābit, the Muslim poet, composed a poem in their memory in which Khubayb and Zayd were objects of the warmest compassion and mourning. The event gave Muḥammad reason to ponder and to fear deterioration of Muslim prestige in case such events were to recur. Nothing, of course, is more harmful to one's prestige than to be slighted by the larger community. As he was engaged in these thoughts, he was approached by Abū Barā' 'Āmir ibn Mālik, to whom Muḥammad offered the faith of Islām. Abū Barā' turned down the offer of Muḥammad, but he did not show any enmity to the new faith. On the contrary, he asked Muḥammad to send some of his companions to the people of Najd in order to preach Islām to them. "Perhaps," he said, "they may respond favorably and enter the faith." Muḥammad feared that any such companions whom he might send to Najd might be subject to treacherous attack as had befallen Khubayb and his companions on the part of the Hudhayl tribe. Unmoved, he therefore rejected Abū Barā's request. Abū Barā' said, "I shall be their guardian and protector. Send them over, therefore, and let them preach the faith." Abū Barā' was a notable with large influence among his people. No one had reason to fear when Abū Barā' had extended his personal protection to him. With this consideration, Muḥammad sent al Mundhir ibn 'Amr, brother of Banū Sā'idah, together with other men chosen from the foremost Muslim ranks.

The Battle of Bi'r Ma'ūnah

Delegates and escorts proceeded together until they reached the well of Ma'ūnah, at the frontier between Banū 'Āmir and Banū Sulaym. From there, they sent Ḥarām ibn Milḥān to 'Āmir

ibn al Tufayl with Muhammad's message. 'Āmir, not even bothering to read Muhammad's letter, killed its carrier forthwith. He
then called on the tribesmen of Banū 'Āmir to kill all the Muslims.
When his tribesmen refused to violate the protection already
extended by Abū Barā', 'Āmir summoned other tribes to do the
job. A number of these responded to his call, gave fight to the
Muslims, surrounded them completely, and killed them. Not one
Muslim survived this battle except Ka'b ibn Zayd and 'Āmr ibn
Umayyah. The former was left wounded in the field on the assumption that he was dead, and the latter was set free by 'Āmir
ibn al Tufayl as atonement for a vow involving a man's life which
his mother owed. On his way home, 'Āmir met two men on the
road whom he mistook as part of the enemy hosts which killed
his companions. He waited until they had gone to sleep and then
sprang upon them and killed them. When he reached Madīnah,
he gave the Prophet a full report of what he did and what had
happened. It then turned out that the two men whom he killed
were clients of 'Āmir and *protégés* of Abū Barā', with whom the
Prophet had entered into a covenant of good neighborliness. The
Prophet therefore commanded him to pay their bloodwits.

The fall of the Muslim martyrs at the well of Ma'ūnah deeply
grieved Muhammad. He blamed Abū Barā' for this loss since he
was the author of the request which Muhammad had satisfied,
but only with apprehension and after much hesitation. Abū
Barā' for his part, was extremely wrathful against 'Āmir ibn al
Tufayl for violating his protective covenant with the Muslims;
and sent his own son, al Rajī', to kill 'Āmir in vengeance for
the violated honor. Mourning his colleagues for one whole month,
Muhammad asked God fervently at every morning prayer to enable him to avenge their death. All the Muslims were deeply
affected by this tragedy that had befallen their brethren in
religion, though they believed that the martyrs were all in
Paradise.

The Jews and Munāfiqūn of Madīnah

The Jews and the *munāfiqūn* of Madīnah found in the tragedies
of Al Rajī' and Bi'r Ma'ūnah occasion to remember the victory
of Quraysh at Uhud and to forget the Muslim victory over Banū
Asad. In consequence, the prestige of the Prophet and his companions declined, and grave concern was directed to the Muslims'
political fortune. With proper foresight, Muhammad realized

that this deterioration of Muslim prestige in Madīnah had exposed the whole cause to the greatest danger. Nothing would so
inspire the tribes to dig their claws into Madīnah as the suspicion
that an attack upon the Muslims would immediately bring about
civil war within their city. Muḥammad also observed that both
the Jews and the *munāfiqūn* were plotting against him. He
therefore decided to force them into betraying their intentions.
As the Jews of Banū al Nadīr were the allies of Banū 'Āmir,
Muḥammad went to them near Qubā', together with ten of his
prominent companions—including Abū Bakr, 'Umar, and 'Alī—
and asked them to cooperate in furnishing the bloodwit money
for the two victims whom 'Āmr ibn Umayyah had killed by mistake, not knowing of their convenant with the Muslims.

Jewish Plots against Muḥammad

When Muḥammad submitted his request to them, they pretended acquiescence to his demand. But it was also noticeable that
while some of them were showing signs of reconciliation, others
were plotting at a safe distance. They whispered to one another
in presence of the Muslims, and the Prophet overheard them
mentioning the murder by the Muslims of Ka'b ibn al Ashraf.
When one of them, 'Amr ibn Jaḥsh ibn Ka'b, entered the house
on whose wall Muḥammad was leaning, in a suspicious and
stealthy manner, Muḥammad could no more contain his doubts
which their talk and hush-hush conversation made gradually
more certain. He rose and withdrew from their midst, leaving
behind his companions and giving the impression that he was
soon to return. The Jews knew that he was leaving for good and
addressed his companions incoherently and hesitantly. They realized that if they were to kill his men, Muḥammad would surely
take a bitter revenge. But if they let them go, the Jewish plot
against Muḥammad would not be betrayed, and at any rate they
could count on the Muslims to continue to honor their part of the
covenant. They therefore tried to convince their Muslim guests
of their good intentions and to counteract any suspicions that
their guests may have entertained. Soon, the companions began
to complain that the Prophet had not returned and that they had
better leave and look for him. They met a man on the way who
assured them that Muḥammad had safely returned to the mosque.
When they joined him, the Prophet told them of his suspicions
and of the Jewish plot to kill him. They then realized the mean-

ing of Jewish behavior and understood their moves at the recent interview. They became convinced of the Prophet's penetrating insight, which seemed all the more convincing when joined to the evidence of their own observations.

Warning to Banū al Naḍīr

Commanding Muḥammad ibn Maslamah, the Prophet said: "Go to the Jews of Banū al Nadīr and tell them that I have sent you to them with the command that they should leave this country. Tell them that by plotting to kill me, they have violated the covenant which I gave them. Tell them also that I give them ten days to evacuate after which any Jew seen in this area will be killed." When they heard of this command, Banū al Nadīr lost hope. In vain they looked for means to change the verdict. Seeking to sway the Prophet's messenger to their own side, they said: "O Muḥammad ibn Maslamah, we did not expect that such command be conveyed by an old ally of ours like you, a man from al Aws tribe which is our ally against the Khazraj." Ibn Maslamah replied, "The times have changed and so have the affiliations."

Instigation to Defy the Prophet

The Jews spent a number of days preparing for war. In the meantime, 'Abdullah ibn Ubayy sent to them two messengers with the message that they should not depart from their land and property, that they should remain in their fortresses, and that soon he himself would be coming to their assistance with two thousand Jewish and Arab fighters prepared to defend them to the death. Banū al Nadīr pondered over the message of Ibn Ubayy and wondered how he could have felt so certain of victory. They recalled that the same man had previously promised help to Banū Qaynuqā', just as he was doing today, but betrayed them when his help was needed by running for his life. They considered that since Banū Qurayẓah had contracted a peace with Muḥammad, they would not be prepared to come to their rescue. Hence, they inclined toward removing themselves to Khaybar or a nearer place, considering that they could still come to Yathrib to harvest their crops and return to their fortresses at Khaybar with no appreciable loss. Ḥuyayy ibn Akhṭab, their leader, finally resolved against this view. "No," he said "I shall send to Muḥammad telling him that we shall not leave our homes and properties and that we refuse to comply with his orders. As for us, all we have to do is to consolidate our fortresses, to fill up our granaries, to barricade our streets, to supply ourselves with stones, and to get ready. We have enough food reserves to keep us for a full year and our water supply never runs dry. At any rate, Muḥammad will not blockade us for as long a time as a year." The ten days therefore passed and no Jew left Madīnah.

Blockade of Banū al Naḍīr

The Muslims took up arms and began to fight the Jews. For twenty days and nights the battle raged. Whenever a Jew showed up on the public street or outside of his quarters, the Muslims would engage him in battle. But the Jews would withdraw quickly and often would even destroy their own property or houses before withdrawal to deeper lines. Subsequently, Muḥammad ordered his companions to cut down the date trees and to burn them in order to reduce the Jews' will to stay in Madīnah to protect and enjoy their properties. The Jews were angry and argued, "O Muḥammad, how could you, who always forbade corruption and injustice and castigated their perpetrators, command the destruction of our date orchards?" On this occasion the following verse was revealed: "Whatever tree you have cut down or left standing, you have done so with God's permission that the unjust may be overwhelmed."[1] The Jews waited in vain for military assistance to come from the side of ibn Ubayy or from that of some other Arab tribes, and they dreaded the fate which awaited them in case they prolonged the hostilities. In despair and with hearts trembling with fear, they asked Muḥammad to guarantee their lives and properties and to give them safe passage. Muḥammad agreed, permitting each one to take with him three camel loads of whatever property of goods they wanted to take away. Ḥuyayy ibn Akhṭab, their leader, led this exodus; the emigrants settled either at Khaybar or at Adhri'āt in al Shām. They left behind them large amounts of booty consisting of food, fifty pieces of armour, three hundred and forty swords, and large areas of land. This prize was greater than anything the Muslims had so far seized. These properties were not divided among the Muslims as war booty. They were all considered as a trust which the Prophet of God divided among the early emigrants, after putting away some for the purposes of the poor and deprived. Thus the necessary economic support of the Muhājirūn by al Ansār was alleviated for the first time, the Muhājirūn having now acquired as much wealth as their hosts. None of the Ansār received any of this new wealth except Abū Dujānah and Sahl ibn Hunayf. When they pleaded to Muhammad that they were really in need, Muhammad gave them as liberally as the Muhājirūn. All the Jews of Banū al Nadīr left Madīnah except two who converted to Islām and kept their property.

It is by no means easy to appreciate the true significance of the Muslim victory and of the forced evacuation of Banū al Nadīr from Madīnah. The Prophet's apprehension of what their presence in Madīnah might lead to by way of civil strife, of emboldening the *munāfiqūn* to plot against the Muslims whenever the latter suffered a set-back, and of the actual threat of civil war in case of outside attack—all these weighed heavily in the Prophet's consideration. On the occasion of the evacuation of Banū al Nadīr, the whole *Sūrah* of "al Hashr" was revealed. In it God said: "Would you not see the *munāfiqūn,* how they falsely promise their brethren—the faithless among the People of the Book—to join them in evacuation if that were imposed, to refuse obedience to anyone against them, and to come to their rescue in case of war? God knows that they lie. The People of the Book are forced to evacuate; yet, the *munāfiqūn* would not leave with them, and should the former be fought, they would not come to their assistance but would run away without giving rescue. Indeed, they fear you more than they fear God, little that they think or know."[2]

The *Sūrah* continues with a discussion of faith and its power over the human soul and asserts that only recognition of God gives the human soul value and dignity such as no other recognition of any power can give. The Qur'ān said:

$$هُوَ اللهُ الَّذِى لَا إِلٰهَ إِلَّا هُوَ عٰلِمُ الْغَيْبِ وَالشَّهَادَةِ هُوَ الرَّحْمٰنُ الرَّحِيْمُ ۚ هُوَ اللهُ$$
$$الَّذِى لَا إِلٰهَ إِلَّا هُوَ اَلْمَلِكُ الْقُدُّوسُ السَّلٰمُ الْمُؤْمِنُ الْمُهَيْمِنُ الْعَزِيْزُ الْجَبَّارُ الْمُتَكَبِّرُ$$
$$سُبْحٰنَ اللهِ عَمَّا يُشْرِكُوْنَ ۚ هُوَ اللهُ الْخَالِقُ الْبَارِئُ الْمُصَوِّرُ لَهُ الْاَسْمَآءُ الْحُسْنٰى يُسَبِّحُ لَهُ مَا فِى$$
$$التَّمٰوٰتِ وَالْاَرْضِ وَهُوَ الْعَزِيْزُ الْحَكِيْمُ$$

"God is the Being besides Whom there is no other God. He knows that which no man knows and He is the Merciful, the Compassionate. God is the Being besides Whom there is no other God.

He is the King, the Holy, the Peace-giver, the Securer, the Dominant, the Mighty, the Great, the Unchallengeable. Praised be He above everything they associate with Him. God is the Creator, the Fashioner, the Form-giver. To Him belong the noble names. To Him everything on earth and in heaven gives praise. He is the Omnipotent, the Wise."[3]

The Prophet's Secretary

Until the exit of Banū al Nadīr from Madīnah, the Prophet's secretary was a Jew. He had chosen him for his capacity to write letters in Hebrew and Syriac, as well as Arabic. After the evacuation of the Jews from Madīnah, the Prophet no longer trusted a non-Muslim to write his letters. He therefore commanded Zayd ibn Thābit, a Madīnese youth, to learn the two languages and appointed him his secretary for all affairs. The same Zayd ibn Thābit collected the Qur'ān during the caliphate of Abū Bakr, supervised the collection of the Qur'ān when the readings of it varied during the caliphate of 'Uthmān, and finally established the text known as "the recension of 'Uthmān," after which all other texts were destroyed.

The city of Madīnah recovered its peace after the evacuation of Banū al Nadīr. The Muslims no more feared the *munāfiqūn*, and the Muhājirūn were quite satisfied with the new lands they had acquired. On the other hand, al Ansār were equally happy that there was no further need to support the Muhājirūn. The period was generally one of peace and tranquillity as well as prosperity for both Muhājirūn and Ansār. This continued until the following year when, on the occasion of the memory of Uḥud, Muḥammad remembered the promise of Abū Sufyān to fight the Muslims again a year thence to the day. Muḥammad also recalled that Abū Sufyān had challenged to meet him once more at Badr, on the Day of Badr, a year later. The year was one of drought and Abū Sufyān wished to postpone the encounter for another year. Nonetheless, he sent Nu'aym to Madīnah to inform the Muslims that Quraysh had rallied a tremendous army such as the Arabs had never seen before, that Makkah was planning to fight them and destroy them once and for all and inflict upon them unheard of misery and destruction. The Muslims first reacted with apprehension and fear and were more eager to remain in Madīnah than go out to meet their enemy at Badr. Muḥammad was indignant. He castigated their cowardice and

warned them that he was going to Badr even if he had to do
so alone.

The Would-be Encounter at Badr

After this show of anger on the part of the Prophet, it was
not surprising that all hesitation and all fear on the part of the
Muslims dissolved and that they picked up their arms in order
to run to Badr. The Prophet appointed ‘Abdullah ibn ‘Abdullah
ibn Ubayy ibn Salūl to govern Madīnah in his absence. The
Muslims arrived at Badr and waited there for the Quraysh army
to come forth. Quraysh, on the other hand, sent two thousand
fighters under the leadership of Abū Sufyān. Abū Sufyān, however, was not enthusiastic about the whole affair, and he decided
to return to Makkah two days after he left. He advised his
people that since they could not do well in war outside of Makkah
except in a fertile and prosperous year, and since that year was
one of drought and poverty, it was better for them to return
home and not to fight Muḥammad. He returned to Makkah and
the army returned with him while Muḥammad awaited them eight
long days in their encampment at Badr. While waiting for their
enemy to appear, the Muslims began a little trade and they made
large gains for which they thanked God. It was on the occasion
of this would-be encounter that the following Qur’ānic verses
were revealed:

الَّذِينَ قَالُوا لِإِخْوَانِهِمْ وَقَعَدُوا لَوْ أَطَاعُونَا مَا قُتِلُوا قُلْ فَادْرَءُوا عَنْ أَنْفُسِكُمُ الْمَوْتَ إِنْ
كُنْتُمْ صَادِقِينَ ۝ وَلَا تَحْسَبَنَّ الَّذِينَ قُتِلُوا فِي سَبِيلِ اللَّهِ أَمْوَاتًا بَلْ أَحْيَاءٌ عِنْدَ رَبِّهِمْ
يُرْزَقُونَ ۝ فَرِحِينَ بِمَا آتَاهُمُ اللَّهُ مِنْ فَضْلِهِ وَيَسْتَبْشِرُونَ بِالَّذِينَ لَمْ يَلْحَقُوا بِهِمْ مِنْ
خَلْفِهِمْ أَلَّا خَوْفٌ عَلَيْهِمْ وَلَا هُمْ يَحْزَنُونَ ۝ يَسْتَبْشِرُونَ بِنِعْمَةٍ مِنَ اللَّهِ وَفَضْلٍ وَ
أَنَّ اللَّهَ لَا يُضِيعُ أَجْرَ الْمُؤْمِنِينَ ۝ الَّذِينَ اسْتَجَابُوا لِلَّهِ وَالرَّسُولِ مِنْ بَعْدِ مَا أَصَابَهُمُ
الْقَرْحُ لِلَّذِينَ أَحْسَنُوا مِنْهُمْ وَاتَّقَوْا أَجْرٌ عَظِيمٌ ۝ الَّذِينَ قَالَ لَهُمُ النَّاسُ إِنَّ النَّاسَ قَدْ
جَمَعُوا لَكُمْ فَاخْشَوْهُمْ فَزَادَهُمْ إِيمَانًا وَقَالُوا حَسْبُنَا اللَّهُ وَنِعْمَ الْوَكِيلُ ۝ فَانْقَلَبُوا بِنِعْمَةٍ مِنَ اللَّهِ وَ
فَضْلٍ لَمْ يَمْسَسْهُمْ سُوءٌ وَاتَّبَعُوا رِضْوَانَ اللَّهِ وَاللَّهُ ذُو فَضْلٍ عَظِيمٍ ۝ إِنَّمَا ذَلِكُمُ
الشَّيْطَانُ يُخَوِّفُ أَوْلِيَاءَهُ فَلَا تَخَافُوهُمْ وَخَافُونِ إِنْ كُنْتُمْ مُؤْمِنِينَ ۝

"To those who did not go to war but remained behind
complaining, 'Had they only listened to us and not gone
out to war they would not have been killed,' [Allah says,]
'If you are truthful in your allegation, will you not seek to
avoid death altogether and become immortal? Think not
that those who have laid down their lives for the sake of
God are dead. Rather, they are alive, in presence of their
Lord, and they receive His gifts. They are happy with what
God had given them of His bounty and they are awaiting
with joy the arrival of those who were not as fortunate but
who have neither reason to grieve nor to sorrow. They are
jubilant with God's bounty and grace, for God never suffers
the reward of the believers to be lost. On the other hand,
those who responded to God's call and the Prophet's even
after they had been wounded in previous battles, and to
those of them who have done well and have been pious, will
fall the great reward. As to those whom the enemy wished
to frighten by reports of the rallying of great armies, but
whose faith grew stronger at the challenge and who said,
"Sufficient for us is God, for He is the most excellent Guardian," to them God will show His favor and grant His bounty.
No evil has befallen them, only God's blessing and bene-
diction. God is the Lord of great bounty. It is Satan, rather,
that instills fear in his friends and associates. Do not fear
your enemies, therefore, but fear Me if you are true believers.' "[4]

This would-be encounter at Badr erased completely every trace
of Uḥud. Quraysh had no alternative but to wait another whole
year, enduring in the meantime an opprobrium no less great than
that of her first defeat at Badr.

Campaign of Dhāt al Riqāʻ

Fully satisfied with the implicit victory God had sent to him,
Muḥammad returned to Madīnah. He was content that the
Muslims recaptured their prestige, but he kept constant vigilance
lest the enemy should cheat him once more. In the meantime, the
news reached him that a group from Ghatafān in Najd were
rallying an army to fight him. He planned to surprise them
before they could complete their preparations. Gathering a force
of four hundred, he led his men to Dhāt al Riqāʻ where the Banū

Muhārib and Banū Tha'labah of Ghaṭafān had rallied. The
Muslims took the initiative of surprise attack, and the enemy ran
away leaving behind their women, equipment, and property. Of
these the Muslims carried what they could and returned to
Madīnah. Taking care lest the enemy launch a surprise attack
against them in turn, the Muslims established night and day
sentries, and Muhammad would only allow short prayers to be
held. While some of them prayed, the others would face the enemy
fully prepared for defense. The enemy, however, never showed
his face; and the Prophet returned to Madīnah fifteen days after
they had left it, jubilant and victorious.

Campaign of Dawmat al Jandal

A little later, the Prophet led another campaign to Dawmat al
Jandal. This is an oasis on the frontier between al Ḥijāz and al
Shām, midway between the Red Sea and the Persian Gulf. There
again, Muhammad could not find the tribes whom he had come
to punish for their attack upon the caravans. For as soon as
any heard that he was on his way, they would run, unmindful
of what the Muslims might carry away of their property as
booty. The geographic location of Dawmat al Jandal shows the
ample extent of Muhammad and his companions' political influence and military sway. In fact, the Arabian Peninsula shook
under their feet. The foregoing accounts give equally clear evidence of Muslim endurance, of their disregard for excessive heat,
for the desolateness of the countryside and shortage of water.
These reports testify to the Muslims' readiness to lay down their
lives for the cause of God and to the determination of their
faith in Him as One.

After all these exploits and campaigns, it was time for Muhammad to settle down in Madīnah for a few months before Quraysh
would trouble him again in fulfilment of Abū Sufyān's resolution
to make annual battle with the Muslims. In the meantime, the
Prophet had plenty to do to complete the organization of the
nascent Islāmic society and to order and structure its various
elements on the basis of revelation, *i.e.*, of what may be safely
deduced from revealed truths. Muhammad elaborated a complete
system of rules for the guidance of man, state and society, which
his companions canonized after his death and which still stands
viable for all ages.

17

The Prophet's Wives

The Zaynab Affair and the Orientalists

In the interval in which the events of the last two chapters took place, Muḥammad married Zaynab, daughter of Khuzaymah, Umm Salamah daughter of Umayyah ibn al Mughīrah, and Zaynab, daughter of Jahsh, after she had been divorced by Zayd ibn Ḥārithah. The last named is the same Zayd who was adopted by Muḥammad and set free after he was bought by Yasār for Khadījah. It is here that the Orientalists offer their highest condemnation, in chorus with the Christian missionaries. Glowing with vindictiveness, they say,

"Muḥammad who in Makkah called men to asceticism and contentment, to monotheism and abstinence from the pleasures of this life, has now become a man of lust whose appetite every woman could whet. He is not satisfied with three women whom he has so far taken into marriage but has now taken the three additional wives just mentioned. Indeed, he was to marry three more yet in addition to Rayḥānah. Nor was he to be satisfied by marrying the widow. He fell in love with Zaynab, daughter of Jahsh, while she was the wife of Zayd ibn Ḥārithah, his own client. Once, when he passed by the house of Zayd in the latter's absence, he was met by Zaynab wearing clothes which exposed her beauty. Muḥammad's heart was inflamed. It is

285

reported that when his eyes fell upon her, he exclaimed, 'Praise be to God who changes the hearts of men!' and that he repeated this expression at the time of his departure from her home. Zaynab heard him say this and noticed desire in his eye. Proudly, she reported what happened to her husband. Zayd immediately went to see the Prophet and offered to divorce his wife. Muḥammad answered, 'Hold to your wife and fear God.' Thereafter, Zaynab was no longer a docile wife and Zayd had to divorce her. Muḥammad did not marry her immediately despite his love for her. He waited until an express revelation came which permitted him to do so. Addressing Muḥammad, God said: 'You said to Zayd, to whom God gave of His bounty and you gave of yours, "Hold fast to your wife and fear God." Would you hide, O Muḥammad, that which God was going to bring to light? Would you fear the gossip of the people? Isn't God more worthy of being feared? After a term of married life with her husband, We permitted you to marry her so that it may hence be legitimate and morally blameless for a believer to marry the wife of his adopted son provided that wife had already been divorced. That is God's commandment which must be fulfilled.'[1] Thereupon, Muḥammad married this woman and satisfied his desire and lust. Now, what kind of Prophet is this? How could he permit himself that which he forbade to others? How can he violate the law which he himself had said had come to him from heaven? How would he amass this harem which calls to mind the behavior of the old lustful and pleasure seeking kings rather than the righteous reforming prophets? How could such a prophet fall prey to lust and desire in the case of Zaynab that he would force his adopted son to divorce her only so that he might marry her thereafter? That was definitely taboo in pre-Islāmic Arabia, and the Prophet of Islām lifted this taboo in order to satisfy his own lust and fulfill his own desire."

Thus appears the Western Orientalists' claim.

The Orientalists' Portrait of Zaynab

Western Orientalists and missionaries pause in order to give full vent to their resentment and imagination. In this chapter of Muhammad's biography, some of them take inordinate pain to paint a sensual portrait of Zaynab. They relate that when Muhammad saw her, she was half-naked, that her fine black hair was covering half her body, and that every curve of her body was full of desire and passion. Others relate that when Muhammad opened the door of the house of Zayd the breeze played with the curtains of the room of Zaynab, thus permitting Muhammad to catch a glimpse of her stretched out on her mattress in a nightgown. They then tell their readers that this view of her stormed the heart of Muhammad who was extremely passionate in his love and desire for women. They relate that Muhammad had hidden his secret desire, though he could hardly bear to conceal it for long! This and many like pictures have been painted arduously by Orientalists and missionaries and may be read in the works of Muir, Dermenghem, Washington Irving, Lammens, and others. It cannot be denied that these stories are based upon reports in fanciful Muslim biographies and Hadīth books. But these books are questionable. And it is extremely regrettable that our authors have used them without scrutiny. It is inexcusable that these scholars had built "Castles in Spain" regarding Muhammad's relations with women, castles which they thought were sufficiently justified by the fact that Muhammad married a plurality of wives, probably nine, or even more according to some versions.

Great Men and the Law

It is possible to refute all these claims with one argument. If supposed to be true, they constitute no flaw in the prophethood of Muhammad, in his own greatness or that of his message. The rules which are law to the people at large do not apply to the great. *A fortiori*, they have no application on prophets, the messengers of God. Did not Moses—May God's peace be upon him—kill the gentile whom he noticed was fighting with one of his compatriots? That was murder, forbidden by God, and there was no war or hostility to justify it. It was a clear violation of the law. Nonetheless, this did not impair Moses' prophethood, his greatness, or his status with God. The case of Jesus violates the law even more flagrantly than either Moses or Muhammad or for that matter any other prophet. For his case is not one of a unique exemplification of power or desire but a persistent violation of natural law from birth to death. First, the spirit of

God appeared to Mary, his mother, in the likeness of a handsome man to give her a fair son. Second she herself was surprised and said, "How can I have a son when no man ever touched me and I have never lost my chastity?" The messenger replied that God wished her son to be a sign to mankind. Thirdly, when she gave birth to her son she said: "I wish I was dead, given to oblivion, and lost before this." Her son, however, called unto her, "Do not grieve, for God has made rivers to issue under your feet." Fourthly, when she brought her son to her people, and they accused her of adultery, Jesus answered them from the cradle: "I am the servant of God . . . etc." However the Jews may have denied the facts of this story, and however they may have attributed Jesus' paternity to Joseph, the carpenter— a claim believed today to be true by such rationalists as Renan— the greatness and prophethood of Jesus constitute a miracle, and a miracle is precisely a breech of natural law, the cosmic pattern, and the rules of creation. It is surprising that Christians and missionaries call men to believe such breaches of the cosmic pattern in the case of Jesus and yet blame Muhammad for much less. Muhammad's violation was not one of a cosmic law but one of a social law, which is permissible to every great man. Such status above the social laws of the community is usually accorded to all kings and heads of states. Constitutional law usually grants to such persons immunity which shields them from the pursuing hand of the law.

Incoherence of the Orientalists' Account

It is possible for us to give such an answer and to thereby refute all these Orientalists' claims, the arguments of the missionaries and of those who follow in their tracks. But if we did so we would be doing a great injustice to history itself as well as to the true greatness of Muhammad and the magnanimity of his message. For the fact is that Muhammad was not a man given to passion and desire as the Orientalists and missionaries have pictured him. He did not marry his wives for lust, desire, or love. If some Muslim writers in certain periods of history have allowed themselves to attribute such things to the Prophet and thereby to present with good intent an argument to the enemies of Islām, that is because their conservatism caused them to adopt a materialistic view of things. In such a manner they pictured

Muḥammad as superlative in everything including the lusts of this world. But the picture they drew was clearly false. The history of Muḥammad denies it outright, and the logic of Muḥammad's life is utterly inconsistent with it.

As Husband of Khadījah

Muḥammad married Khadījah when he was twenty-three years old, i.e. at the height of his youth, the fullness of manhood, and the apex of power and handsomeness. He remained true and loyal to Khadījah for twenty-eight years until he was over fifty years old. This had been the case at a time when polygamy was normal among the Arabs. Moreover, since no male offspring of Khadījah survived, Muḥammad had all necessary justification to marry another woman considering that newborn daughters were customarily buried alive and male offspring alone were regarded as rightful heirs. Before Muḥammad became a prophet he had lived seventeen years of married life, and thereafter eleven more years without ever thinking of marriage with any other woman. Throughout his married life with Khadījah as well as during his celibate years, Muḥammad was never known to be one susceptible to womanly attractions at a time when women wore no veils and showed their beauty and ornaments publicly—the evidence of which is implicit in Islām's prohibition of the same later on. It is unnatural, therefore, now that Muḥammad had passed the fifty year mark, for him to suffer such a transformation as would make him fall suddenly in love with Zaynab, daughter of Jaḥsh, while he was already married to five other women, among whom was 'Ā'ishah whom he loved dearly and constantly. It is therefore unnatural that such a man would have given Zaynab, daughter of Jahsh, any thought at all, and certainly unlikely that she had occupied his thought night and day, as the Orientalists claim. It is certainly unnatural that Muḥammad, now past fifty years old, would collect in the short span of five years more than seven wives, and two years later to increase the number to nine simply on account of sexual desire. Such a claim, first made by Muslim authors and then uncritically imitated by the Western Orientalists, is absurd. It is inconsistent with the natural predilection of the commonplace, not to speak of the great, whose work has transformed the world, altered the course of history, and still plays a role in retransforming the world and reorienting historical development toward radically new goals. This claim is irrational and does not correspond with the facts. It is contrary to nature to assume that the same man who caused Khadījah to bear all her children before he reached fifty, and caused Māriyah to conceive Ibrahīm while he was sixty, could cause none of his numerous wives to bear any children when they were all still young enough and capable of doing so. Nor were they barren, since each of them had borne children before her marriage to Muhammad. This fact, true of each of the nine women, would, defy explanation if the Orientalist and missionary claim is true. We must add to this consideration the fact that Muhammad, a man like other men, was certainly anxious to obtain a male offspring. His prophetic status had made him father to all Muslims at once from a purely spiritual point of view. But that does not deny the human urge to fatherhood.

Muhammad's Marriage to Sawdah

History and the logic of its events furnish an unquestionable refutation of the Orientalist and missionary claim regarding the Prophet's wives. As we have seen earlier, Muhammad did not share his bed with any other woman besides Khadījah for twenty-eight years. When she finally passed away, he married Sawdah, daughter of Zam'ah, widow of Sakrān ibn 'Amr ibn 'Abd Shams. No one ever described Sawdah as a beautiful woman, and no one has ever reported that she possessed any wealth or social position which might have given a material reason for any one to marry her. Rather, Sawdah was a wife of one of the early converts of Islām who suffered much harm for the sake of the faith and who migrated to Abyssinia following the instructions of the Prophet in order to find a measure of safety. Sawdah had embraced Islām with her husband and migrated with him. She suffered as he did and bore Makkan oppression as patiently as her husband did. If Muhammad married her thereafter in order to provide for her and to raise her position to that of a "Mother of Believers,"[2] he certainly did a most worthy and appreciable deed.

'Ā'ishah and Hafsah were daughters of his two viziers, Abū Bakr and 'Umar, respectively. It was this relation of their fathers to Muhammad which caused the latter to cement his relationship

with them by blood. That is why he married their two daughters;
that is why he gave in marriage his two daughters to 'Uthmān
and 'Alī. If it is true that Muḥammad did in fact love 'Ā'ishah,
it must have been a love which arose after marriage, surely
neither before nor at the time of marriage. He had asked her
hand from her father while she was only nine years old, and
did not marry her until two years later. It is contrary to logic
to claim that he could have fallen in love with her while she
was at this tender age. Further evidence on this point is the
report of 'Umar that Muḥammad's marriage to his daughter
was not based on love. His report ran as follows: "In pre-
Islāmic times, we did not attach any importance to women; but
we changed radically after God revealed what He did and
assigned to them the rights He did. Once, my wife tried to
change my mind about something and suggested that I do
otherwise. When I asked her to let my business alone, she
answered, 'How strange of you, O Son of al Khaṭṭāb! You forbid
me to criticize you while your daughter is permitted to criticize
the Prophet of God himself—May God's peace and blessing be
upon him—and to do so so well that he would spend the whole
day angry.' When I heard this I immediately went to my
daughter Ḥafsah and inquired whether this was true. Ḥafsah
confirmed her mother's report. I was stupefied. I warned her
that God's punishment as well as the wrath of the Prophet would
fall upon her if she persisted. I told her that she should not
count either on her beauty or on the Prophet's love for her,
for I knew too well that the Prophet of God did not love her
and that were it not for my sake, he would have even divorced
her." There is then ample evidence that Muḥammad did not
marry either 'Ā'ishah or Ḥafsah out of any love or desire but
in order to consolidate the ties of mutual brotherhood within
the new Islāmic community, and especially between himself and
his two viziers. There is equally clear evidence that the Prophet
married Sawdah in order to teach the Muslim fighters that
should they fall martyrs in the cause of God, they would not
leave their women and children without support but that the
community would take care of them.

Another conclusive proof of this sense of social concern is
the case of Muḥammad's marriages to Zaynab, daughter of Khuzaymah, and Umm Salamah. The former was the wife of 'Ubaydah
ibn al Ḥārith ibn al Muṭṭalib who fell at the Battle of Badr. Surely

she was not beautiful, but she was so kind and gentle that she acquired the nickname of "mother of the destitute." She was past her prime in age and lived only one or two years after her marriage to Muḥammad. Besides Khadījah she was the only wife of the Prophet who died before him. As for Umm Salamah, she was the wife of Abū Salamah for whom she bore many children. It has already been mentioned that Abū Salamah was wounded at Uḥud, that he seemed to be recovering from his wound when the Prophet assigned to him the duty of fighting Banū Asad whom he defeated and whose wealth he seized. It was during the second campaign of Abū Salamah that his wound reopened, and it caused his death a few days later. The Prophet visited him in his last days and remained constantly by his bedside praying for him until he died. Four months after his death, when the Prophet asked the hand of Umm Salamah, she apologized by using the large number of her children and her old age as an excuse. But the Prophet insisted until she accepted and he assumed the duty of caring for and bringing up her offspring. Would then the missionaries and the Western Orientalists claim that Umm Salamah was a woman of rare beauty and that this is why Muḥammad had married her? If Muḥammad was indeed looking for beauty, there were scores of virgin daughters of both Muhājirūn and Ansār far surpassing his women in beauty, in youth, in position and wealth, in vitality, for him to choose from and to take in marriage. He did not have to choose those women who would bring to him large liabilities of mouths to feed and old people to take care of. The fact is that Muḥammad married Umm Salamah because of this noble motivation of his, the same reason for which he married Zaynab, daughter of Khuzaymah. It was this same reason which caused the Muslims to love their Prophet all the more and honor him as the Prophet of God and to see in him a father to the destitute and the deprived and the weak and the poor as well as to everyone who had lost his father as a martyr in the cause of God.

Historical Analysis and Its Results

What does true historical analysis conclude from all this? It concludes that Muḥammad stood for monogamy and counseled its observance. This is the substance of the example of his married life with Khadījah, as well as that of the Qur'ānic commandments,

فَانْكِحُوا مَا طَابَ لَكُمْ مِنَ النِّسَاءِ مَثْنَى وَثُلَثَ وَرُبَعَ فَإِنْ خِفْتُمْ اَلَّا تَعْدِلُوا فَوَاحِدَةً اَوْ مَا مَلَكَتْ اَيْمَانُكُمْ

"Marry such women as seem becoming to you, two, three, or four. But if you fear that you may not be just, then marry only one, or your slaves"[3]; and,

وَلَنْ تَسْتَطِيعُوا اَنْ تَعْدِلُوا بَيْنَ النِّسَاءِ وَلَوْ حَرَصْتُمْ فَلَا تَمِيلُوا كُلَّ الْمَيْلِ فَتَذَرُوهَا كَالْمُعَلَّقَةِ

"You will not be able to do justice to more than one wife however much you may try. And if you must marry another wife, do not incline excessively to one and leave the other like a thing suspended."[4]

These verses were revealed toward the end of the eighth year of the Hijrah after the Prophet had married all his wives. The purpose of these verses is to limit the number of wives to four whereas, until their revelation, there was no limit to the number of wives a Muslim could marry. This historical fact repudiates the claim that Muḥammad has allowed himself that which he had forbidden to the people. Furthermore, these verses were revealed in order to stress the superiority of monogamy over polygamy. The Qur'ān commanded the limiting of one's self to one wife out of fear of the possibility of injustice and conviction that justice to more than one wife is not within the limits of men's capability. The revelation, however, realized that in the exceptional circumstances of a people, it is quite possible that there might be a need for more than one wife; but it has limited polygamy to four and conditioned its practice to capacity for fairness and justice on the part of the husband. Muḥammad called the Muslims to realize these values by exemplifying them in his own life in a period in which Muslims made battle and fell as martyrs on every occasion. But could anyone in truth decide once and for all that monogamy is the absolute commandment in all conditions and circumstances? What would be the effect of such a law when wars and epidemics and revolution cut down thousands and millions of men in a brief while? Would then monogamy still be better than polygamy when restricted to the exceptional circumstances? Can the people of Europe in this age following World War I assert categorically that monogamy is the law of life of their own citizens, even if they may say it is the law in the books? Are not the social and economic disturbances which the world witnessed in Europe following the War the direct result of this imbalance between the two sexes, of their inability to bring about harmony and prosperity in their marital relations, and hence of their insistence to seek that harmony outside the marriage bond? It is not my intention to decide the issue here. But I leave the matter to the reader to ponder. I do wish to repeat, however, that the happiness of the family and that of the community can best be served by the limitation which monogamy imposes. That is so, however, if and only if the life of the community itself is normal.

The Story of Zaynab, Daughter of Jahsh

As for the story of Zaynab, daughter of Jahsh, the chroniclers, Orientalists, and missionaries have mixed it with such products of vivid imagination that they have made of it a story of love and passion. Critical history, on the other hand, concludes that it is one of the truly great facets of Muhammad's personality. It proves beyond question that Muhammad was the perfect example of faith and conviction, for it is an instantiation of the principle that the faith of man is complete only when he truly loves for his brother that which he loves for himself. Muhammad had made himself always the exemplar of his own legislation, especially of such laws as were intended to replace the tradition and customs of pre-Islāmic Arabia. He was the examplar of the new system which God revealed through him as a mercy and guidance to mankind. For a repudiation of the whole story of Zaynab as reported by these chroniclers or Orientalists and missionaries, it is sufficient to realize that the said woman was the daughter of Umaymah and grand-daughter of 'Abd al Muṭṭalib the uncle of the Prophet of God—May God's peace and blessing be upon him. It is sufficient to remember that this woman was brought up in sight of Muhammad and under his care, and on this account was regarded by him as a daughter or a young sister; that he knew too well whether she was beautiful or not before she ever married Zayd; that he saw her and followed her growth from childhood to maturity and youth; and that it was he who asked her hand for Zayd, his adopted son. Once the

reader knows these historical data, then all the fictitious elements and tales spun about him, namely, that he passed by her
house in the absence of her husband and was struck by her
beauty; that he opened the door of her house and, as the breezes
played with the curtains of her room, he saw her stretched in
her nightgown like a real "Madame Recamier," that his heart
was so struck by her beauty that he instantly forgot Sawdah,
'Ā'ishah, Ḥafsah, Zaynab, daughter of Khuzaymah and Umm
Salamah, his wives—not to mention the memory of Khadījah of
whom 'Ā'ishah used to say that she had never felt jealous of
any woman except Khadījah on account of the memory he kept
of her—all these tales must dissolve. If any grain of them was
true, Muḥammad would have taken her in marriage himself at
first, rather than give her in marriage to Zayd. This historical
relationship between Zaynab and Muḥammad rules out as utterly
fictitious and groundless all the stories which have been attributed
to Zaynab's attractiveness.

History, however, has more yet to tell. It proves that Muḥammad asked for the hand of his own cousin Zaynab for his adopted
son Zayd. Her brother, 'Abdullah ibn Jaḥsh, refused to let his
sister, the Hāshimī and Qurayshī noble girl that she was, and
the first cousin of the Prophet in addition, become the wife of a
slave whom Khadījah had bought and whom Muḥammad had
set free. Such a union was regarded by him as well as by the
Arabs in general as a thing of great shame. For the daughters
of the aristocracy to marry their slaves, even though their slaves
had become free, was plainly unthinkable. But Muḥammad sought
to wipe out these racial and class distinctions between men. He
sought to educate the whole world to the truth that no Arab
is superior to any non-Arab unless it be in virtue and piety.
For it was God who said,

$$ اِنَّ اَكْرَمَكُمْ عِنْدَ اللهِ اَتْقَكُمْ $$

"Highest in God's view is the most virtuous."[5]
Muḥammad did not choose to force this noble principle upon a
woman outside his own tribe and clan. Let it then be Zaynab, he
thought, his very cousin, that will carry the first burden of this
flagrant violation of Arabian custom. Let her be the destroyer
of these pagan traditions. Let her cause herself, and therewith
the whole tribe and religion of Muḥammad, to endure all the
criticisms that such an act would engender. And let Zayd, his

own adopted son, be the person of lesser lineage to marry the noble Makkan aristocrat. On the other hand, Arab custom and tradition demanded that the adopted son inherit from his adopted father, like the latter's legitimate children. And since this custom too was the object of Muhammad's attack, his choice of Zayd as the spearpoint of the first reform, would actually make of him—if he were prepared to give up the inheritance to which Arabian custom gave him title—the spearhead of another Islāmic legislation prohibiting inheritance to any but the blood heirs and relatives of the deceased. Thus, Muhammad insisted that Zaynab agree to marry Zayd and that her brother 'Abdullah ibn Jahsh accept Zayd as a brother-in-law. Indeed, this furnished the occasion for the revelation that "No believer, whether man or woman, has freedom to choose otherwise than as God and His Prophet have resolved in any given case. To do so is to disobey God and His Prophet, to err and fall into manifest misguidance."[6]

Once the foregoing verse was revealed, neither 'Abdullah nor his sister Zaynab had any alternative but to acquiesce in the Prophet's order. The Prophet helped Zayd furnish a dowry for his bride-to-be and the marriage took place. After the wedding, the husband found in his wife a woman very hard to manage and to live with. Her pride continued to know no bounds. Indeed, she continued to deride Zayd, to boast of her lineage in his presence and to look down on him because of his having once been a slave. Zayd complained about her to the Prophet more than once and even consulted with him in the matter of divorcing her. All along, the Prophet would counsel him in these terms: "Hold fast to your wife and fear God." Zayd's home life, however, did not improve and, unable to bear her false pride any longer, Zayd divorced her.

Adoption in Islām

The All-Wise Legislator willed to undo the Arab practice of adopting children and passing onto them the adopter's genealogy and name, his investment of them with all the rights of the legitimate son including that of inheritance and the prohibition of marriage on grounds of consanguinity. The divine Legislator willed to give the adopted son only the right of a client and co-religionist. In this sense, the verse was revealed that: "God did not make your adopted son as your own sons. To declare them so is your empty claim. God's word is righteous and constitutes the true guidance."[7] It follows from this revelation that the adopter may marry the ex-wife of his adopted son and vice-versa. But how is such provision to be implemented? Who, among the Arabs, could implement this legislation and thereby openly repudiate the ancient traditions? Even Muḥammad himself, despite his tremendous willpower and profound understanding of the wisdom implicit in the divine command, found himself disinclined to implement this judgment by marrying Zaynab after Zayd had divorced her. Indeed, the criticisms of the commonplace and the vituperations with which he was indicted in the public eye for breaking down such well established custom did, for a time, influence Muḥammad's judgment and affected his decision. It was at this stage that the following divine criticism was addressed to Muḥammad: "Would you hide, O Muḥammad, within yourself that which God was going to bring to light anyway? Would you fear the gossip of the people? Isn't God more worthy of being feared?"[8] The truth is, however, that Muḥammad was the exemplar of obedience to God; his life was the implementation of that which he was entrusted to convey to mankind. The outcome, therefore, was that Muḥammad would not give any weight at all to the gossip of the people if he were to marry the ex-wife of his adopted son, since the fear of social condemnation is nothing comparable to that of condemnation by God, of disobedience to divine commandment. Thus, Muḥammad married Zaynab in order to provide a good example of what the All-Wise Legislator was seeking to establish by way of rights and privileges for adoption. In this regard, God said: "After a term of married life with her husband, We permitted you to marry her so that it may hence be legitimate and morally blameless for a believer to marry the wife of his adopted son provided that wife has already been divorced. That is God's commandment which must be fulfilled."[9]

Return to the Orientalists' Views

Such is the evidence critical history furnishes in the case of Zaynab, daughter of Jahsh, and of her marriage to Muḥammad. She was his first cousin whom he knew well long before Zayd ever married her. It was he who asked for her hand on Zayd's behalf. Muḥammad often saw Zaynab even after her marriage to Zayd, for the veil was not then known. It was also the custom, on account of Zaynab's blood relation to Muḥammad and Zayd's relation as adopted son, that the couple would refer

to the Prophet any complaint each may have against the other.
As Zayd was not happy in his marriage with her, it was natural
that both of them would seek advice and judgment in their
domestic disputes. All these provisions of the divine law have
been revealed, and they have been instanced in the case of
Zayd and Zaynab's marriage and divorce, and of Zaynab's later
marriage to Muḥammad. These provisions had one purpose,
namely the raising of the manumitted slave to the full status of
freedom, and the repudiation of all the rights of masters, protectors, and adoptive parents in clear and unequivocal terms.
There is hence no ground for these fictitious stories woven by
Orientalists and missionaries and repeated by Muir, Irving,
Sprenger, Weil, Dermenghem, Lammens and other biographers
of Muḥammad. Their so-called scholarship is a scandalous piece
of missionarizing. It is a masquerade of science. Their traditional
antagonism to Islām, going back to the Crusades, has simply
taken possession of their conscience, dictating and determining
all that they write on the subject. It is this fundamental prejudice which vitiates their writing. Their "history" is a crime
against history itself, for they choose to see, to note, and to
report only the most scurrilous and fictitious reports to satisfy
this end. Even if, though impossible, their claims were true,
we would still refute them with the simple argument that the
great stand above the law; that Moses, Jesus, Jonah, and others
before Muḥammad have likewise risen above the laws of nature
as well as of society, some in their birth, others in their lives.
None of this has affected their greatness. Muḥammad, moreover,
legislated for man and society by means of his Lord's revelation.
He executed those laws equally by his Lord's command. His life
constitutes the highest ideal, the perfect example, and the
concrete instance of his Lord's command. Would those missionaries have Muḥammad divorce his wives in order not to exceed
the limit of four prescribed by Islāmic law after Muḥammad?
Wouldn't they then subject him to more severe criticism? But
Muḥammad's treatment of his wives was just and noble. We
have seen in the above-mentioned tradition of 'Umar ibn al
Khaṭṭāb some evidence thereto, and we shall see more yet in
the sequel. Evidently, Muḥammad not only honored woman more
than did any other man, but he raised her to the status which
truly belongs to her—an accomplishment of which Muḥammad
alone has so far been capable.

18

The Campaigns of
al Khandaq and
Banu Qurayzah

Muḥammad's Caution and Arab Instinct

After the forced evacuation of Banū al Naḍīr from Madīnah, and the events of the "second Badr," the campaigns of Ghatafān and Dawmat al Jandal, it was high time the Muslims felt a measure of security within their city. Hence, they applied themselves to the task of organizing their own internal affairs. Their constant preoccupation with security and war had largely prevented their engagement in agriculture or commerce. Nonetheless, their state of privation and need was largely ameliorated by the booty they acquired through these campaigns. Though Muhammad felt relatively secure, he was always cautious lest the enemy strike without notice. He therefore had to maintain eyes, ears, and channels of communication throughout the Arabian Peninsula in order to learn of all the news of the tribes so that the Muslims might have time to prepare for defense in case of emergency. It is easy for us to appreciate the need for all these precautions after hearing of the treacherous attacks of Quraysh and other tribes against the Muslims. The Arabian Peninsula of those days was covered with autonomous little republics, each of which extended over the territory inhabited or used by its various clans, and depended for its security on an intricate system of inter-tribal customs, pacts, and traditions, which we do not usually expect to find in the organizations of

299

states in modern times. Since Muḥammad himself was an Arab
and understood the will to retaliate innate in Arab character,
he took extreme care to guard the Muslim community from all
sides. Quraysh, the Jews of Banū Qaynuqāʻ and Banū al Naḍīr,
the tribes of Ghatafān and Hudhayl as well as those living in
the vicinity of al Shām, were all lying in wait for Muḥammad
and his companions. Each one of these groups awaited the
opportunity to avenge itself on this man who had divided the
Arabs in their religion, and, though emigrating from Makkah
devoid of power or ally, had acquired, within the last five years
by virtue of his great faith, such prestige and power as to make
him a real threat to the strongest cities and tribes of Arabia.

Jewish Enmity

The Jews were perhaps the most cognizant of Muḥammad's
teachings and the most apprehensive of the success of his message. They knew too well what consequences to them would be
implied in the victory of Islām. In Arabia, having distinguished
themselves through their monotheistic teachings, they competed
with the Christians and were hoping soon to wrest all power
from them throughout Arabia. They were right in their expectation inasmuch as the Semitic soul was by nature more inclined
toward monotheism than to Christian trinitarianism. As if to spoil
that promise and dash those hopes, Muḥammad, the pure Arab
and pure Semite, was calling men to the monotheistic truth
with strong and emphatic words which penetrate to the nethermost depths of consciousness. His revelation overwhelmed and
intoxicated the soul. It caused man to transcend himself. Furthermore, Muḥammad achieved such political and worldly power
that he had forced the evacuation of Banū Qaynuqāʻ from
Madīnah, and the Banū al Naḍīr from their lands. Would they
then leave him alone and return to their previous abodes in al
Shām and in the promised land of Jerusalem, or would they
confront him here in Arabia by rallying the Arab tribes to
seek revenge from him?

Jewish Preference of Paganism to Islām

It was the latter idea that finally gripped Banū al Naḍīr. In
pursuit of it, their leaders Ḥuyayy ibn Akhṭab, Sallām ibn Abū

al Ḥuqayq, Kinānah ibn al Ḥuqayq, together with Hawdhah ibn
Qays and Abū 'Ammār, both of the tribe of Banū Wā'il, went to
Makkah for consultation with the Quraysh leaders. When Ḥuyayy
was asked about his tribe, he told the Quraysh that he had left
them between Khaybar and Madīnah awaiting the arrival of the
Makkans that they might join them in battle against Muḥammad
and his companions. When the Makkans inquired about Banū
Qurayẓah, he answered that they had remained within Madīnah
in order to plot against Muḥammad and to spring against his men
from behind once the Makkans launched their attack. The Quraysh
hesitated. They knew only too well that in the last analysis, there
was no difference between them and Muḥammad except in this
matter of his new faith; and even in it, they were not quite certain
that Muḥammad was entirely wrong since his worldly power had
been on the increase every day. The Quraysh therefore asked
the Jews to tell them, since they were the first People of the
Book and held the keys of knowledge in the matters in which
the Quraysh disagreed with Muḥammad, whether or not Muḥammad's religion was better than Makkan religion. The Jews
answered by giving preference to Makkan religion over Islām
and to Makkan rights over Muḥammad's. It was to this that the
Qur'ān referred when it said, "Would you consider those who
were given part of the scripture, that they believe in evil and
injustice and commend to the unbelievers their own unbelief
as guidance superior to the true faith of those who believed?
Such men are accursed of God. And whosoever God curses, will
never prevail. Nor will anyone ever come to his rescue."[1] This
attitude of the Jews toward Quraysh and their favoring of the
latter's paganism over the monotheism of Muḥammad was the
subject of a severe rebuke by Dr. Israel Wolfenson, who wrote
in his *The Jews in Arabia:* "It was the duty of the Jews
not to allow themselves to get involved in such a scandalous
mistake. They should have never declared to the leaders of
Quraysh that the worship of idols was better than Islāmic
monotheism even if this were to imply frustration of their re-
quests. The Jews, who have for centuries raised the banner of
monotheism in the world among the pagan nations, who have
remained true to the monotheistic traditions of the fathers,
and who have suffered throughout history the greatest misfortunes, murders, and persecutions for the sake of their faith
in the One God should, in loyalty to this tradition, have sacrificed

every interest—nay their very lives—to bring about the downfall of paganism. Furthermore, by allying themselves with the
pagans they were in fact fighting themselves and contradicting
the teachings of the Torah which commands them to avoid,
repudiate—indeed to fight—the pagans."

The Jews' Rallying of the Arab Tribes

This brazen self-contradiction, this favoring of paganism over
monotheism and the encouragement of pagan forces to rise
against the monotheistic forces—all this was not enough for
Ḥuyayy ibn Akhṭab and the Jewish leaders who accompanied
him on his trip to Makkah. After securing a definite date from
the Makkans for the attack against Muḥammad, the same leaders
went to the Ghatafān clan of Qays Ghaylān, to the tribes of
Banū Murrah, Banū Fazārah, Ashja', Sulaym, Banū Sa'd, Asad,
and all those who had fought with the Muslims to instigate a
general mobilization on the side of Quraysh for a revengeful war
on Muḥammad. In order to placate these tribes, the Jews
commended and praised their pagan practices and prophesied
that victory would certainly belong to paganism. All these parties
which the Jews had rallied against Muḥammad marched against
Madīnah. The Quraysh sent an expeditionary force of four
thousand infantrymen, a cavalry of three hundred, and a camel-
corps of one thousand five hundred. This huge army was led
by Abū Sufyān in person. The flag of Makkah and, hence, the
leadership of battle was assigned to 'Uthmān ibn Ṭalḥah, whose
father had been killed carrying that same flag in the Battle of
Uḥud. The Banū Fazārah tribe sent a large number of infantrymen and a camel corps of one thousand under the leadership
of 'Uyaynah ibn Ḥisn ibn Ḥudhayfah. The tribes of Ashja' and
Murrah supplied four hundred soldiers each, under the leadership of al Ḥārith ibn 'Awf and Mis'ar ibn Rukhaylah respectively.
Sulaym, the tribe which engaged the Muslims at the battle of
the well of Ma'ūnah, sent seven hundred soldiers. To this
tremendous number, the tribes of Banū Sa'd and Banū Asad
added more soldiers and more cavalry until the total number
reached ten thousand or more. This whole army moved in the
direction of Madīnah under the general leadership of Abū Sufyān.
After they had reached the outskirts of Madīnah and encamped,
the leadership of the army as a whole really revolved among
the leaders of the various tribes.

The Muslims' Panic

When news of this tremendous mobilization reached Muhammad and the Muslims in Madīnah, it struck them all with panic. The mobilization of the whole of Arabia against them instilled fear in their hearts as they faced the prospect of being not only defeated but wiped out. The gravity of the situation was evident in the fact that the army the Arab tribes had now raised surpassed in number and equipment anything the Peninsula had ever seen before. If the Quraysh had won a victory over the Muslims at Uhud singlehanded, what was likely to be the outcome of a battle in which the enemy's force was many times greater in number and equipment? What would they do against such an overwhelming preponderance of men, horses, camels, arms, and ammunitions? Obviously, there was no defense open to them except self-fortification within the walls of Yathrib, the invincible city, as 'Abdullah ibn Ubayy had previously described it. But would such fortification stand in face of such overwhelming power? Salmān al Fārisī, who knew far more of the techniques of warfare than was common in the Peninsula, advised the digging of a dry moat around Madīnah and the fortification of its buildings within. The Muslims hurried to implement this counsel. The moat was dug and the Prophet—May God's peace and blessing be upon him—worked with his hands alongside his companions lifting the dirt, encouraging the Muslim workers, and exhorting everyone to multiply his effort. All the Muslims picked up their digging utensils, their picks and shovels, and borrowed more tools from the Qurayẓah Jews who remained true to their covenant with Muhammad. With tremendous effort and exertion, the whole moat was dug in six days. At the same time, the walls of the buildings on the perimeter of the city facing the enemy were also reinforced, their inhabitants were evacuated and the buildings were reserved for military use. The women and children were removed to the interior and placed within fortified walls. Rocks were gathered and placed on the inner side of the moat for use as possible projectiles against the enemy if the need arose.

Quraysh in Front of the Dry Moat

The Quraysh and their allies arrived at Uhud hoping to meet the Muslim forces there. Disappointed in this, they proceeded to Madīnah where, to their surprise, they found an impassable ditch surrounding the whole city. They never expected this kind of defense, and their anger and resentment became so strong that they accused the Muslims of cowardice for taking refuge behind such an unusual trick of war. Their army encamped in the plain called Rūmah, and the forces of Ghatafān and its allies encamped in the plain called Dhanab Naqamā. Muhammad amassed three thousand Muslims on the side of Sal' mountain in Madīnah. Only the ditch separated him from the enemy. There the Muslim army built a number of tents to prepare itself for the long siege, and Muhammad had his own red tent erected for his use. The Quraysh and the Arab tribes realized the impossibility of crossing the moat and were, therefore, forced to restrict their military activity to the exchange of javelins for a number of days.

Soon, Abū Sufyān and his colleagues became convinced that they were going to have to lay siege to Yathrib for a very long time before they could storm it. The season was winter, the cold unbearable, and wind and storm continually threatened heavy rain. It was possible for the people of Makkah and Ghatafān to protect themselves from the storm only if they were in the shelter of their own cities. But here, the tents which they had put up before Yathrib provided little or no protection. They had joined the expedition in search of easy victory, expecting the whole affair to last a day or two, as did the Battle of Uhud. They expected to return quickly home, there to celebrate with songs of victory while dividing all kinds of wealth and booty. How could the army of Ghatafān return empty handed when the sole reason for its participating in this war was the Jewish promise that in case of victory a whole year's crop of the orchards of Khaybar would be theirs as a free gift? Now, they realized that victory was not going to be easy, for it was going to cost at least the trouble of spending the whole wintry season, and this alone counterbalanced all the fruits and crops of the orchards. As for Quraysh, they were eager to avenge themselves for the previous defeats. But it was becoming amply clear that victory was impossible as long as Muhammad controlled the other side of the ditch while the Banū Qurayzah supplied Madīnah with enough food provisions to enable them to hold to their fortress for months and even years. No wonder, then, that some of the allies of Makkah began to think of returning home. Their leaders realized, however, that the remobilization of such an overwhelming force would not be easy to accomplish once they were demobilized and allowed to disperse. Led by Ḥuyayy ibn Akhṭab, the Jews had been capable of mobilizing these tribes as they sought to avenge themselves on Muḥammad for all the injuries he had inflicted upon them as well as upon the Banū Qaynuqāʻ. If this opportunity were to escape, would it ever return again? If Muḥammad were to gain an easy victory by the withdrawal of the Makkans and their allies, would he then not turn against the Jews?

Jewish Fear of Makkan Withdrawal

Ḥuyayy ibn Akhṭab weighed all these considerations. He realized that there was no escape from using the very last trump card he had. He told his allies that he would convince the Banū Qurayẓah to violate their covenant with the Muslims in order to join his camp, and that Muslim supplies would then be cut off and a road to the interior of Yathrib would lie open. Quraysh and Ghaṭafān were quite pleased with the news. Pursuing this scheme, Ḥuyayy went to the quarter of Banū Qurayẓah and asked to see Kaʻb ibn Asad, their leader, whose door was slammed shut in his face. Apparently, Banū Qurayẓah knew too well that treason might bring some advantages in case of Muslim defeat but that it would provide cause for extermination in case of Muslim victory. Ḥuyayy, however, insistently kept knocking at the door until the gate was opened and he was let in. He asked Kaʻb to listen to his warning that he had come with the greatest army ever assembled in Arabia, the armies of Quraysh, Ghaṭafān, and all their leaders and noblemen. He pleaded that all these allies and leaders had pledged not to leave the place until Muḥammad and his companions were utterly destroyed. Kaʻb hesitated, remembering Muḥammad's loyalty to his covenant. He feared the evil consequences a sad turn of events might bring. Ḥuyayy determinedly continued to reiterate the sufferings which the Jews had borne at the hand of Muḥammad and which they would have to bear in case the war did not succeed. At last Kaʻb weakened and began to lend his ear. Ḥuyayy described the forces of the Makkan allies, their equipment and number, and reasoned that only the ditch prevented the forces from assaulting the Muslims and finishing them off in a brief hour. To Kaʻb's question as to what would be the fate of the Banū Qurayẓah in case the Makkans and their allies were to withdraw, Ḥuyayy

answered that he. and his party of Jews would then join the
Banū Qurayẓah in their own quarter and share with them
whatever fate might bring. At this, Ka'b's Jewish feeling stirred,
moving him to yield to Ḥuyayy, to accept his demands, to
repudiate his covenant with Muḥammad and the Muslims, and
to join the ranks of their enemies.

The Prophet's Warning to Banū Qurayẓah

The news of this betrayal by the Banū Qurayẓah reached
Muḥammad and his companions and shook them greatly. Sa'd
ibn Mu'ādh, leader of al Aws, and Sa'd ibn 'Ubādah, leader of
al Khazraj, together with 'Abdullah ibn Rawāḥah and Khawwāt
ibn Jubayr, were ordered by Muḥammad to ascertain the news
and report back to him. They were instructed not to announce
their findings in case the news was true, for fear it might
adversely affect the army's morale. The delegates came to the
Jewish quarter and found the situation worse than it had been
reported. They sought by argument to bring the Jews back to
honoring their covenant with Muḥammad. But Ka'b impertinently required that the Muslims return the Jews of Banū al
Naḍīr back to their quarters in Madīnah. Sa'd ibn Mu'ādh,
with whose tribe the Banū Qurayẓah were closely allied, sought
to convince Ka'b that the fate of Banū al Naḍīr or something
worse might befall them in case they persisted in this treason.
Giving full vent to their resentment, the Jews began to insult
the Prophet—May God's peace be upon him. Ka'b said: "And
who is this so-called Prophet of God? There is neither covenant
nor peace between us and him." The conversation was quickly
ended, and the Muslims left the scene hastily to prevent the possible outbreak of open fighting.

Morale of the Makkans and Their Allies

Muḥammad's delegates returned and reported to him what
they had seen and heard. Muslim leaders were gravely apprehensive. They feared that the side of Qurayẓah would now open
for the Makkans and their allies, that the latter would enter
the city and rout them. Their fear was not imaginary but quite
real. As was expected of them, Banū Qurayẓah immediately cut
off all supplies to the Muslims. On the Makkan side, there was
rejoicing when Ḥuyayy ibn Akhṭab reported the treason of

Banū Qurayẓah, and their rallying to Quraysh and Ghaṭafān. The morale of the Makkan forces took a sharp rise as they began to prepare for the day of battle. The Banū Qurayẓah had actually requested the Makkans, first, to wait ten days before invading Madīnah so that they might prepare themselves; and second, to keep constant pressure upon the Muslims and thus prevent any Muslim attack upon them before their military preparations were complete. That was exactly what happened. The enemy divided itself into three main brigades. The first, led by Ibn al A'war al Sulamī, was to assault the Muslims from across the valley. The second, led by 'Uyaynah ibn Ḥisn, was to attack from the flank. Finally, the third under the command of Abū Sufyān was to launch its attack across the ditch. It was with reference to this deployment of enemy forces that the Qur'ān said:

اِذْ جَآءُوْكُمْ مِنْ فَوْقِكُمْ وَمِنْ اَسْفَلَ مِنْكُمْ وَاِذْ زَاغَتِ الْاَبْصَارُ وَبَلَغَتِ الْقُلُوبُ الْحَنَاجِرَ وَتَظُنُّوْنَ بِاللهِ الظُّنُوْنَا ۞ هُنَالِكَ ابْتُلِيَ الْمُؤْمِنُوْنَ وَزُلْزِلُوْا زِلْزَالًا شَدِيْدًا ۞ وَاِذْ يَقُوْلُ الْمُنٰفِقُوْنَ وَالَّذِيْنَ فِيْ قُلُوْبِهِمْ مَّرَضٌ مَّا وَعَدَنَا اللهُ وَرَسُوْلُهٗ اِلَّا غُرُوْرًا ۞ وَاِذْ قَالَتْ طَّآئِفَةٌ مِّنْهُمْ يٰٓاَهْلَ يَثْرِبَ لَا مُقَامَ لَكُمْ فَارْجِعُوْا ۚ وَيَسْتَاْذِنُ فَرِيْقٌ مِّنْهُمُ النَّبِيَّ يَقُوْلُوْنَ اِنَّ بُيُوْتَنَا عَوْرَةٌ ۚ وَمَا هِيَ بِعَوْرَةٍ ۚ اِنْ يُّرِيْدُوْنَ اِلَّا فِرَارًا ۞

"When they attacked you from above and from below, when your eyes knew no more where to turn and your hearts were ready to give up and you entertained all sorts of thoughts about God, then the believers were truly shaken and faced disaster. Then did the false pretenders and the disheartened doubt that what God had promised them and His Prophet was all in vain. Then did a group of them counsel the people of Madīnah against war and suggested withdrawal while another group sought the Prophet's permission to withdraw on the ground that their houses were exposed whereas their houses were neither exposed nor in danger, but the suppliants only sought to flee."[2]

It was only too human for the people of Yathrib to grumble with fear and panic. They were disappointed at this turn of events. Whereas Muḥammad had promised them the wealth and treasures of Chosroes and Caesar, they now felt as afraid to venture outside the confines of their own city as did those who were disheartened at the prospects of the war. Did they not see death advancing upon them, shining in the brilliance of the swords which were being brandished by the Quraysh and Ghaṭafān tribesmen? Did they not have reason to be disheartened when their immediate neighbors, the Banū Qurayẓah, threatened to attack them treacherously from within and to enable their enemies to infiltrate behind their lines? Would it not have been better for them, they pondered, to have utterly destroyed the Banū al Nadīr rather than allow them to emigrate and take their possessions with them? Had the Muslims finished them then, Ḥuyayy and his companions would not have now instigated this general Arab war. Certainly, this was a moment of great apprehension and danger. Surely this was a terrible and fateful day. Its disposal was in the hand of the Almighty alone.

Engagement of the Forces

The Makkans and their allies were encouraged and their morale was uplifted by the news of the new alliance. Some Quraysh horsemen, including 'Amr ibn 'Abd Wudd, 'Ikrimah ibn Abū Jahl, and Ḍirār ibn al Khaṭṭāb sought to advance across the ditch. After finding a point where the ditch was narrow, they succeeded in entering it and took position on its inner side near Sal'. 'Alī ibn Abū Ṭālib and other Muslims proceeded to meet them and to seal the breach through which they advanced. 'Amr ibn 'Abd Wudd challenged the Muslims to a duel. When 'Alī ibn Abū Ṭālib answered his call, 'Amr replied: "Why, O Cousin! By God, I do not wish to kill you." 'Alī answered, "But I do." The duel started, and no sooner had it got under way than 'Alī killed 'Amr and the companions of the latter ran for their lives. They jumped over the ditch thinking only of the death which was following them. Nawfal ibn 'Abdullah ibn al Mughīrah sought to jump over the ditch shortly after sunset on that same day. But the ditch was too wide and both horse and rider fell into it to their death. Abū Sufyān then demanded one hundred camels as bloodwit. The Prophet rejected the demand, however, and condemned Nawfal as an aggressor whose death was unworthy of bloodwit.

The Makkans and their allies now launched a tactical war of nerves against the Muslims in order to destroy their spirit. In order to frighten the Muslims, tribesmen of Banū Qurayẓah began to descend from their fortifications and occupy the houses closer to the Muslim quarters. Ṣafiyyah, daughter of 'Abd al Muṭṭalib, was at Fāri', the fortress of Ḥassān ibn Thābit, which was also full of women and children. A Jew approached their house and started to circumscribe it, inspecting its sides and fortifications. Ṣafiyyah asked old Ḥassān to go out and kill the Jew because he was obviously reconnoitering the fort preliminary to storming it. At the time the Prophet and his companions were busy with other matters, and Ṣafiyyah felt that the danger should be eliminated at once by herself, if not by Ḥassān. When Ḥassān declined to do as she requested, she seized a solid bar, went to the Jew, and beat him with it until she killed him. When she returned, she asked Ḥassān to go down and to dispossess the Jew of what he had. She apologized, saying that she would have finished the job herself had the victim not been a man. Nonetheless, Ḥassān refused to budge.

Dividing the Enemies against Themselves

While the people of Madīnah suffered from fear and threat, Muḥammad concentrated his thoughts on finding means of saving the community. Certainly no purpose would be fulfilled by forcing a confrontation with the enemy. The only alternative left for him was to attempt a ruse. He therefore sent a messenger to Ghaṭafān with the promise of one third of the total crop of Madīnah if they withdrew and went home. Actually, Ghaṭafān was beginning to show signs of exhaustion and disapproval of this long siege for which they were not prepared. They had joined in this venture simply in order to appease Ḥuyyay ibn Akhtab and his other Jewish companions. On the other hand, the Prophet sent Nu'aym ibn Mas'ūd to the Banū Qurayẓah, their old friend from pre-Islāmic days whose conversion to Islām was not yet known to them, with the message that they should not join the ranks of the Makkans and fight with them unless and until the latter would give them a concrete guarantee that they would not be left alone to the mercy of Muḥammad should the tide of battle turn against them. Nu'aym had been a very good friend of the Banū Qurayẓah for a long time before his conversion, and they therefore had no reason to doubt him. He reminded them of this friendship and warned them that their rallying to the side of Quraysh and

Ghaṭafān against Muḥammad was liable to bring disaster,
especially since neither Quraysh nor Ghaṭafān were likely to
continue the siege for long. In that eventuality, nothing would
prevent Muḥammad from inflicting upon them great harm. This
made such good sense that the Banū Qurayẓah were dissuaded
from their treacherous course. Nu'aym then proceeded to the
Quraysh camp and there intimated to their leaders that the
Banū Qurayẓah had repented their violation of the covenant
with Muḥammad and that they were seeking to appease and
befriend him anew by plotting to give up the noblemen of
Quraysh that Muḥammad might execute them. Furthermore,
he counseled them not to send their men to the Banū Qurayẓah
for fear that the latter might seize them and give them up to
Muḥammad. Nu'aym then proceeded to Ghaṭafān and there
repeated the same offer and warning. His ruse worked, and the
leaders of Quraysh and Ghaṭafān began to probe each other
on the matter. When Abū Sufyān sent to Ka'b, leader of Banū
Qurayẓah, asking him to advance against the Muslims on the
morrow and promising to follow up their advance with an
advance of their own by Makkan forces, his messenger was
turned back with the message that since the next day was a
Saturday the Jews would neither fight nor work. Angry at their
disobedience, Abū Sufyān believed the words of Nu'aym. He
sent word to them that they had better hold their Sabbath on
another day as fighting Muḥammad had become extremely
necessary and the need for engaging him immediate. Abū Sufyān
also warned that unless they joined the Makkans in battle on
Saturday he would declare his pact with them null and void
and, indeed, subject them to the brunt of Makkan attack. When
the Banū Qurayẓah heard this message of Abū Sufyān, they
reiterated their resolution not to violate the Sabbath, reminding
the messenger of divine wrath against its desecration. Moreover,
they demanded guarantees for their future security. Their
response dissipated any lingering doubts in Abū Sufyān's mind
regarding Nu'aym's report. Discussing the problem with the
leaders of Ghaṭafān, he discovered, much to his great dismay,
that they deliberately hesitated to start the fight because of
the Prophet's promise to them of one-third of the crops of
Madīnah. Evidently, the Muslims' maneuver worked, much as it
was objected to at the time by Sa'd ibn Mu'ādh, the leaders of
al Aws and al Khazraj tribes, and other elderly consultants of
the Prophet.

The Anger of Nature

On that same night a very strong wind blew and an extremely heavy rain fell. Thunder deafened the ears and the lightning was blinding. The storm was so wild that it swept the tents of the enemy off the ground and brought havoc to their camp. It struck fear into their hearts, and they believed that the Muslims were seizing this opportunity to launch their attack. Ṭulayhah ibn Khuwaylid was the first to rise and openly to suggest to the Makkans and their allies to flee for their lives. He claimed that these evil omens signaled the start of Muḥammad's attack. Abū Sufyān followed him with the same counsel. "O people of Quraysh," he said, "Surely this is no place for you. The date trees around are uprooted and our work camels have perished. The Banū Qurayẓah have abandoned us and cooperated with our enemies; the storm has taken its toll. All these things have brought terrible disadvantage to us. Let us move away from here. I shall be the first to give up." The armies prepared to withdraw, and each man carried as little as his camel, horse, or shoulders could bear and began to move while the storm continued to rage. The withdrawal was led by Quraysh, followed by Ghaṭafān and their allies. When the morning came, there was not one of them to be seen in the area. The Muslims returned to their homes in Madīnah with the Prophet and gave praise and thanks to God for their escape from the travails of war.

The Campaign against Banū Qurayẓah

Muḥammad pondered the general situation of the cause of Islām. God had seen fit to remove the outside enemy, but the Banū Qurayẓah remain in the midst of Madīnah. Surely they were capable of repeating their treason in another season. Were it not for the internal division and sudden withdrawal of the Makkans and their allies, the Banū Qurayẓah would have attacked Madīnah and helped in the routing of the Muslims. Did not the common saying counsel, "Do not cut off the tail of the viper and allow it to go free?" The Banū Qurayẓah, therefore, must be completely destroyed. The Prophet—May God's peace and blessing be upon him—ordered a *mu'adhdhin* to proclaim: "No pious Muslim will hold the mid-afternoon prayer except in the quarter of Banū Qurayẓah," and a general invasion began. He appointed 'Alī commander of the operation. Despite their exhaustion after the long siege, the Muslims advanced fully confident of the result. It is true that the Banū Qurayẓah had fortified houses like those of Banū al Naḍīr. But if these were sufficient for defending them from Makkan attack, they were futile against the Muslims who were already in possession of the lands surrounding the Banū Qurayẓah. Upon arrival at the Banū Qurayẓah quarters, the Muslims found Ḥuyayy ibn Akhṭab al Naḍīrī bitterly reviling Muḥammad, refuting his message and attacking the honor of his women. It was as though the Banū Qurayẓah had a notion of what was coming to them now that the Makkans and their allies had withdrawn. When the Prophet arrived at the scene, he was met by 'Alī, who asked him not to approach the Jewish camp. Upon enquiry, Muḥammad heard the Jews reviling him, and he said: "Miserable wretches that you are, didn't God Himself put you to shame and send His curse upon you?" In the meantime, the Muslims continued to pour into the area, and soon thereafter Muḥammad ordered the siege to begin.

The siege lasted twenty-five days and nights during which only a few javelins, arrows, and stones were shot between the two combatants. The Banū Qurayẓah did not dare leave their quarters a single time. When, exhausted, they realized that their fortifications were not going to avail them, and that they must sooner or later fall into Muslim hands, they sent word to the Prophet asking for Abū Lubābah, an al Aws tribesman and former ally, to negotiate with them. As he arrived, he was met by women and children in tears whose sight touched his heart. The Jews asked whether he counseled acquiescence to Muḥammad's judgment. He answered, "By all means!" And, passing his hand over his throat, he said: "Otherwise, it will be a general carnage." Some biographers report that Abū Lubābah later regretted having given them this counsel. After he left, Ka'b ibn Asad, their leader, suggested that they follow Muḥammad and convert to his faith, thereby securing themselves, their children, properties, and wealth from any harm. But the majority refused, promising not to abandon the Torah or exchange it for anything else. Ka'b then suggested that they kill their own women and children and go out to meet the Muslims with drawn swords free of any apprehension for their loved ones, and to fight Muḥammad to the bitter end. His idea was that should they lose, there would be neither family nor children for which to worry, but if they should win, Muslim women and children would all become theirs. Once more, the Banū Qurayẓah said "No." They argued that life without their families was not worth the effort. Finally, Ka'b said that there remained no alternative for them but to acquiesce in Muḥammad's disposal of their case. After consulting one another, they decided that their fate would not be worse than that of Banū al Naḍīr, that their friends and former allies from al Aws tribe would give them some protection and that if they were to remove themselves to Adhri'āt in al Shām, Muḥammad would have no objection to letting them go.

Arbitration of Sa'd ibn Mu'ādh

Banū Qurayẓah sent word to Muḥammad proposing to evacuate their territory and remove themselves to Adhri'āt, but Muḥammad rejected their proposal and insisted on their abiding by his judgment. They sent to al Aws pleading that they should help them as al Khazraj had helped their client Jews before them. A group of al Aws tribesmen sought Muḥammad and pleaded with him to accept from their allies a similar arrangement to that which he accepted from the allies of al Khazraj. Muḥammad asked, "O men of al Aws, would you be happy if we allowed one of your men to arbitrate the case?" When they agreed, he asked them to nominate whomsoever they wished. This was communicated to the Jews, and the latter, unmindful of the fate that was lying in store for them, nominated Sa'd ibn Mu'ādh. Sa'd was a reputable man of al Aws tribe, respected for his sound judgment. Previously, Sa'd was the first one to approach the Jews, to warn them adequately, even to predict to them that they might have to face Muḥammad one day. He had witnessed the Jews cursing Muḥammad and the Muslims. After his nomination and acceptance as arbitrator, Sa'd sought guarantees from the two parties that they would abide by his judgment. After these guarantees were secured, he commanded that Banū Qurayẓah come out of their fortress and surrender their armour. Sa'd then pronounced his verdict that the fighting men be put to the sword, that their wealth be confiscated as war booty, and that the women and the children be taken as captives. When Muḥammad heard the verdict, he said: "By Him Who dominates my soul, God is pleased with your judgment, O Sa'd; and so are the believers. You have surely done your duty." He then proceeded to Madīnah where he commanded a large grave to be dug for the Jewish fighters brought in to be killed and buried. The Banū Qurayzah did not expect such a harsh judgment from Sa'd ibn Mu'ādh, their former ally. They thought that he would plead on their behalf as 'Abdullah ibn Ubayy had done in the case of Banū Qaynuqā'. It must have occurred to Sa'd that if the Makkans and their allies had achieved victory through the treachery of Banū Qurayzah, the Muslims would surely have been subjected to the same fate of being killed and mutilated. He therefore imposed upon them the fate to which they sought to subject the Muslims. That the Jews showed great patience in the midst of tragedy is recorded for us in the story of Ḥuyayy ibn Akhtab when he was brought for execution. The Prophet said to him, "Had not God put you to shame, O Ḥuyayy?" Ḥuyayy answered, "Every man is going to taste of death. I have an appointed hour which has now come. I do not blame myself for arousing your emnity." He then turned toward the people present and said, "O Men, it is all right to suffer God's decree. This tragic fate has been decreed by God for Banū Isrā'īl." Al Zubayr ibn Bātā al Quraziyy, another Jew, had done a favor to Thābit ibn Qays on the day of Bu'āth when he let him free after capturing him. Thābit wanted to reciprocate the good deed on this occasion and asked the Prophet to grant him the favor of al Zubayr's life. The Prophet approved Thābit's request. When this came to the knowledge of al Zubayr, he pleaded that being an old man condemned to live in separation from his family and children, he had no use for life. Thābit then begged the Prophet of God to grant him also the life of Zubayr's wife and children, and the sparing of his property that al Zubayr might live in happiness. The Prophet again granted his request. After al Zubayr heard of his family's salvation, he inquired about Ka'b ibn Asad, Ḥuyayy ibn Akhtab, 'Azzāl ibn Samaw'al, and other leaders of the Banū Qurayzah. When he was told that they had all been killed, he asked to be dispatched with them, pleading: "I ask you, O Thābit, to dispatch me with my people, for life without them is not worth living, and I shall have no patience until I have rejoined my loved ones." Thus, he was killed at his own demand. The Muslims were always opposed to killing any women or children. On that day, however, a Jewish woman was executed because she had killed a Muslim by dropping a millstone on his head. It was of this woman that 'Ā'ishah used to say: "By God, I shall never cease to wonder how serenely that woman met her death." On that day, four Jews converted to Islām and were saved from death.

Ḥuyayy's Responsibility for the Tragedy

We have seen how the lives of Banū Qurayẓah were dependent upon Ḥuyayy ibn al Akhtab, though the lives of both were terminated at the same time. It was he who violated the covenant that he, himself, had entered into with Muḥammad when the latter forced Banū al Naḍīr's evacuation from Madīnah without killing a single person. Also, it was he who so incited the Quraysh, Ghaṭafān, and the other Arab tribes to fight Muḥammad that he became the very embodiment of Jewish-Muslim enmity. It was he who indoctrinated the Jews with the idea that they should have no peace unless Muḥammad and the Muslims were utterly destroyed. Likewise, it was he who inspired Banū Qurayẓah to violate their covenant with Muḥammad and to repudiate their neutrality in the struggle needlessly and at such terrible cost. Finally, it was he who came to the Banū Qurayẓah after the withdrawal of the Makkans and aroused them to engage the Muslims in a hopeless fight that was doomed before it started. Had the Banū Qurayẓah acquiesced in the judgment of Muḥammad from the first day, and acknowledged their mistake in violating their previous covenant, their lives would have been saved. Unfortunately, Ḥuyayy's soul was possessed by a consuming Jewish enmity to the Muslims. He imparted such a measure of this enmity to the Banū Qurayẓah that their own ally, Saʿd ibn Muʿādh, believed that even if they were forgiven, they would soon rally the tribes again to fight the Muslims anew. Such was their obsession with hatred of Muḥammad and the Muslims that the Jews believed no life was worth living as long as the Muslim power was not broken and the Muslims were not subjugated or killed. However harsh the verdict which the arbitrator had reached in this regard, it was dictated by self-defense, as the arbitrator had become convinced that the presence or destruction of the Jews was a question of life and death for the Muslims as well.

The Spoils of War

The Prophet divided the properties, women, and children of Banū Qurayẓah among the Muslims after he had separated one-

fifth for public purposes. Each man of the cavalry received two
shares, one for himself and one for his horse. On that day,
the Muslim force included thirty-six cavalrymen. Sa'd ibn Zayd
al Anṣārī sent a number of Banū Qurayẓah captives to Najd
where he exchanged them for horses and armour in order to
increase Muslim military power.

Rayhānah, a captive woman of Banū Qurayẓah, fell to the
share of Muhammad, who offered her Islām. But she refused obstinately. Muhammad even offered to marry her, but she preferred to remain his captive. It was her strong attachment to her
religion and people which must have prevented her from joining
Islām as well as from marrying the Prophet. Her hatred for the
Muslims and for their Prophet must have continued. No one
had spoken of her beauty as they spoke of Zaynab, daughter
of Jahsh, though a slight mention of this could be found in
the chronicles. There was some disagreement as to whether
she, upon entering the quarters of the Prophet, was asked to
wear a veil as the protocol of the Prophet's house demanded,
or whether she remained like most other women of the Peninsula
without a veil. One thing, however, is certain: namely, she
remained in the quarters of Muhammad until her death.

This expedition of the Makkans and their allies with its
resultant destruction of the Banū Qurayẓah enabled the Muslims
to establish themselves as Madīnah's absolute masters. The power
of the *munāfiqūn* was finally broken, and all Arab tribes admired
Muslim power, dominion, and the new prestige of Muhammad
as sovereign of Madīnah. The Islāmic message, however, was
not meant for Madīnah alone but for the whole of mankind.
The Prophet and his companions still faced the task of preparing
for the greater task ahead, namely bringing the word of God
to the wide world, calling all men to the true faith and making
that faith secure against all enemies. That is precisely what
awaited them, and what we shall study in the sequel.

19

From the Two
Campaigns to the
Treaty of Ḥudaybiyah

Organization of the Arab Community

After the Battle of the Ditch and the destruction of Banū
Qurayẓah, the situation in Madīnah stabilized in favor of
Muḥammad and the Muslims. The Arab tribes so feared the
Muslims that many Qurayshīs began to think that it might
have been better for their tribe to have made peace with Muḥammad, especially since he himself was a Quraysh tribesman
and the Muhājirūn were all among its leaders and noblemen.
The Muslims felt quite secure after they had destroyed Jewish
power within and outside Madīnah once and for all. For six
months, they remained in Madīnah during which their commerce
prospered and they enjoyed a spell of peace and comfort. At
the same time, the message of Muhammad crystallized in the
minds of his followers, and they learned better to appreciate
his teachings and observe his precepts. The Muslims followed
their Prophet in reorganizing and remodeling the Arab community. Departing from tradition and reshaping society according to model principles were necessary steps in the making of
that new society that Islām sought to establish in the world.
In pre-Islāmic days, the only social system known to the Arabs
was that which their own customs had sanctified. In the matters
of family and its organization, of marriage and its laws and
divorce, and of the mutual relations of parents and children—
in all these human relations—pre-Islāmic Arabia had not gone

317

beyond the elementary dictates of its hard topography; namely, extreme *laissez-faire* on the one hand and extreme conservatism reaching to slavery and oppression on the other. Islām was therefore called upon to organize a nascent society which as yet had developed no traditions and looked with disdain on its heritage of social customs. Muslim society had great ambitions, however, for it looked forward to becoming within a short time the nucleus of a great civilization ready for a destiny of absorption of the Persian, Roman, and Egyptian civilizations. Islām was to give this nascent civilization its character and gradually to impress it with its own ethos and brand until, some day, God might find it proper to say of it:

$$\text{ٱلْيَوْمَ أَكْمَلْتُ لَكُمْ دِينَكُمْ وَأَتْمَمْتُ عَلَيْكُمْ نِعْمَتِي وَرَضِيتُ لَكُمُ ٱلْإِسْلَامَ دِينًا}$$

"Today I have completed for you your religion; my bounty and grace have been conferred upon you conclusively; and I am pleased that your religion shall henceforth be Islām."[1]

Relations between Men and Women

Whatever the nomadic nature of Arabian civilization had been before Islām, and regardless of whether or not such cities as Makkah and Madīnah had enjoyed a level of civilization unknown to the desert, relations between men and women had never extended much beyond the sexual. According to the witness of the Qur'ān, as well as of the traditions of that age, such relations were determined only by considerations of class or tribe, and were quite primitive in every other respect. The women used to show themselves off not only to their husbands but to any other men they pleased. They used to go out into the open country singly or in groups and meet with men and youths without hindrance or sense of shame. They exchanged with men glances of passion and expressions of love and desire. This was done with such blasé frankness and lack of shame that Hind, wife of Abū Sufyān, had no scruples whatever about singing on such a public and grave occasion as the Day of Uhud:

"Advance forward and we shall embrace you!
Advance forward and we shall spread the carpets for you!

Turn your backs and we shall avoid you!
Turn your backs and we shall never come to you."

Arab Eroticism

Among a number of tribes, adultery was not at all regarded as
a serious crime. Flirting and courting were common practices.
Despite the prominent position of Abū Sufyān and his society,
the chroniclers tell, concerning his wife, a great many tales of
love and passion with other men without implying any stain
on her reputation. Whenever a woman gave birth to an illegitimate child, she felt no restraint about proclaiming the identities of all the men with whom she had had love affairs so
that her child might be attributed to the man whom he most
resembled. Likewise, there was no limit to the number of wives
a man could take or to the number of his women slaves and
concubines. Men were completely free to do as they pleased,
and women were perfectly free to give birth as they pleased.
The whole domain of man-woman relations had no seriousness
or gravity except where a scandal was uncovered which brought
about disputes, fighting, or libel between one clan and another
within the larger tribe. Only on such occasions did the flirta-
tions, courtings, and adulterous rendezvous become reasons for
shame, vituperation, or war. When hostility broke out between
one house and another, men and women alike felt free to
claim and accuse as they wished. The Arab's imagination is by
nature strong. Living as he does under the vault of heaven
and moving constantly in search of pasture or trade, and being
constantly forced into the excesses, exaggerations, and even
lies which the life of trade usually entails, the Arab is given
to the exercise of his imagination and cultivates it at all times
whether for good or for ill, for peace or for war. Should a
man, for instance, pour out his imagination in the most senti-
mental and affected forms when addressing his sweetheart in
private, one would think that was normal. But when the same
man readily and publicly pours out that same imagination, in
the event of war against his sweetheart's tribe or in personal
disaffection for her, by describing her neck, breast, waist, hips,
and all other aspects of her feminine form, we must conclude
that that imagination knows little more of the woman than her
sex, feminine form, and adeptness at making love. Despite
the decisive blow which Islām had directed at this excessive

cultivation of the imagination, much of it was embedded in the
Arab psychic character described in the poetry of 'Umar ibn
Abū Rabī'ah. Indeed, Arabic love poetry has hardly ever been
free of this trait; a measure of it can still be found in the
modern poetry of our own day.

Woman in Other Civilizations

The foregoing account may have struck the reader who is
full of admiration for the Arabs and their civilization, including
the Arabs of pre-Islām, as somewhat exaggerated. Such a reader
is certainly excused for so thinking, for he must be comparing
the picture we have given with the actualities of the present
age, intermingled as they certainly are with the ideal relations
between man and woman, parents and children. Such com-
parisons, however, are false and lead the investigator astray.
If the comparison is to be fruitful, one should undertake to
contrast Arab society as we have described it in the seventh
century C.E. with other societies of the same period. I do not
think it is an exaggeration to say that Arab society, despite all
its aberrations, was far superior to the societies of Asia and
Europe. We do not have enough information to speak with
authority on Chinese or Indian society of that age. But we do
know that Europe was wallowing in such darkness that its family
structure stood little higher than the most primitive levels of
human organization. The *Imperium Romanum,* possessor of the
law, master of the world, and the sole competitor of the Persian
Empire, regarded woman as far more inferior to man than
she was in the Arabian desert. In Roman law, woman was
regarded as a piece of movable property, owned by a man and
disposable by him in any way he wished. The Roman male
citizen exercised the right of life and death over his women,
and did so by law. The law enabled the Roman citizen to treat
his women as he would his slaves, making no distinction between
them. It regarded a woman as the property of her father, then
of her husband, and finally of her son. The right of property
exercised over her person was complete, just as complete as
the right of property over animals, things, and slaves. Moreover,
woman was looked upon as a source of desire. Like an animal,
she was not expected to have any control over her sex life.
Because morality did not apply to her, it was necessary to fabricate the western artificial framework of absolute chastity in

order to instil a sense of ethics in man-woman relations. This necessary though artificial framework furnished the womanly ideal of that society for several centuries afterwards. It will be recalled that Jesus—May God's peace be upon him—was quite compassionate toward women, and that when his disciples expressed surprise at his fair treatment of Mary Magdalene, he proclaimed: "He that is without sin among you, let him first cast a stone at her."[2] Despite this charitable attitude toward women on the part of Christianity, Christian Europe continued to deride woman and to hold her in the greatest contempt very much as pagan Europe had done before. Europe did not only regard the relation of man to woman merely as a relation of male and female. It coalesced with this relationship that of owner to owned, master to slave, and the honorable to the dishonorable and contemptible. These attitudes have so determined the mind of Europe so long that for centuries the Europeans have asked whether woman has a soul; whether she is a morally responsible being; whether she is to render account on the Day of Judgment; or whether, like an animal, she is devoid of soul, subject to neither judgment nor responsibility, and entitled to no place at all in the kingdom of God.

Muḥammad and Social Reconstruction

Led by divine revelation, Muḥammad recognized that there can be no social reconstruction of society without the cooperation of all its men and women members in mutually helping, loving, and sympathizing with one another. He realized that no society is viable where women do not enjoy rights as well as duties, where these rights and duties are not exercised in cooperation, reciprocal love and respect, and where men are nonetheless the leaders. To realize these conditions in Arab society quickly and by force of authority was not an easy affair. However strong the faith of Muḥammad's Arab followers, to take them slowly forward without exposing them to undue hardships was surer to succeed than otherwise. Slow progress intensifies the faith of the adherents and wins more converts, whereas forced progress creates dissension and weakens the faith of many. The same was true of every social reconstruction God prescribed for the Muslims. Indeed, the same progressive reconstruction characterized the religious duties of Islām, namely prayer, fasting, *zakāt*, abstaining from gambling, eating pork, and the like.

Muḥammad began to teach social reconstruction and to define the rights and duties of men and women to one another by talking about exemplary instances occurring between himself and his wives which all Muslims could witness. The veil was not imposed upon the wives of the Prophet until shortly before the Campaign of al Khandaq, and the limitation of polygamy to four was not imposed until after that Campaign, indeed a whole year thereafter. It would be interesting to see how the Prophet anchored the relationships of man and woman to sound foundations and how he prepared his followers for the equality of men and women under Islām. Islām wanted its women to have the same rights even as they have duties. But it wanted these rights and duties to be exercised in an atmosphere of mutual love, fairness, and compassion, and its men to enjoy the position of leadership.

Islām Forbids Fornication

As we saw earlier, the relationship between man and woman among the Muslims of the period, as among all Arabs, was limited to that of male to female. Fornication, exposure of the woman's flesh and ornaments in a way inviting molestation by men and arousing in them sexual desire, dominated the relationship. There was little or no room for any relationships expressing human spirituality, or for any communion between man and woman in their service to God. The presence of Jews and munāfiqūn in Madīnah and their hostility to the new faith caused many of their men to molest the Muslim women and led, as in the case of Banū Qaynuqā', to serious harm and injury to Muslim women. A great many unnecessary problems resulted from this situation. Had the Muslim women not exposed themselves outside their homes, thus inviting fornication, their identities would not have been known to the public and they would not have been harmed. Had this been the case, the Muslims would have avoided all these problems and could have made a fair start toward realizing the equality which Islām sought to realize between the sexes. This ideal might have been realized even without hardship to Muslim men and women. It was in this spirit that the Qur'ān announced:

> "Those who harm the believers unjustly, whether men or women, do great wrong. O Prophet, command your women, your daughters, and the women of the believers to lengthen

their garbs that they may not be harmed. God is merciful and compassionate. If the *munāfiqūn*, those who are ill of heart or cause agitation in the city do not stop their evil work, We shall give you mastery over them and the power to terminate forthwith their residence in your midst. They shall be accursed wherever they go, seized, and put to the sword. That is the pattern of God, already realized in earlier history and immutable for ever and ever."[3]

With this simple introduction, the Muslims were taught the necessity of outgrowing the customs of their predecessors. The Islāmic legislation aimed at reorganizing society on a foundation of pure family life, free of intrusion from the outside. To reach this purpose, Islām declared adultery a grave sin. In consequence, the Muslims learned to appreciate the evil inherent in a woman's fornication and entanglement outside her family. The Qur'ān said,

قُلْ لِّلْمُؤْمِنِينَ يَغُضُّوا مِنْ أَبْصَارِهِمْ وَيَحْفَظُوا فُرُوجَهُمْ ذَلِكَ أَزْكَى لَهُمْ إِنَّ اللَّهَ خَبِيرٌ بِمَا يَصْنَعُونَ وَقُلْ لِّلْمُؤْمِنَاتِ يَغْضُضْنَ مِنْ أَبْصَارِهِنَّ وَيَحْفَظْنَ فُرُوجَهُنَّ وَلَا يُبْدِينَ زِينَتَهُنَّ إِلَّا مَا ظَهَرَ مِنْهَا وَلْيَضْرِبْنَ بِخُمُرِهِنَّ عَلَى جُيُوبِهِنَّ وَلَا يُبْدِينَ زِينَتَهُنَّ إِلَّا لِبُعُولَتِهِنَّ أَوْ آبَائِهِنَّ أَوْ آبَاءِ بُعُولَتِهِنَّ أَوْ أَبْنَائِهِنَّ أَوْ أَبْنَاءِ بُعُولَتِهِنَّ أَوْ إِخْوَانِهِنَّ أَوْ بَنِي إِخْوَانِهِنَّ أَوْ بَنِي أَخَوَاتِهِنَّ أَوْ نِسَائِهِنَّ أَوْ مَا مَلَكَتْ أَيْمَانُهُنَّ أَوِ التَّابِعِينَ غَيْرِ أُولِي الْإِرْبَةِ مِنَ الرِّجَالِ أَوِ الطِّفْلِ الَّذِينَ لَمْ يَظْهَرُوا عَلَى عَوْرَاتِ النِّسَاءِ وَلَا يَضْرِبْنَ بِأَرْجُلِهِنَّ لِيُعْلَمَ مَا يُخْفِينَ مِنْ زِينَتِهِنَّ وَتُوبُوا إِلَى اللَّهِ جَمِيعًا أَيُّهَ الْمُؤْمِنُونَ لَعَلَّكُمْ تُفْلِحُونَ

"Command the believers to lower their eyes and to live a life of chastity. That is better for them, for God knows what they do. Command the women believers also to lower their eyes, to live the life of chastity, not to show off their beauty and ornaments except what must be shown in the course of daily life. Command them to cover themselves up, not to show their beauty and ornamentation except to their husbands, their fathers, the fathers of their husbands, their sons or the sons of their husbands, their brothers or the sons of their brothers, the sons of their sisters, their women-slaves or eunuchs, or immature children. Command them not to stamp their feet in order to show off their hidden ornaments. O Believers, repent to God that you may achieve felicity."[4]

Thus Islām worked toward the transformation of man-woman relations into one in which sex is possible only when legitimate, and illegitimate sexual relationships are condemned as evil. In all other matters of human life, the relationships of men to women and vice versa are based on a foundation of absolute equality. Everybody is a servant of God, and everybody is mutually responsible for promoting virtue and the fear of God. If anyone stirred the sexual passion in other people, he would be guilty and obliged to repent and atone to God.

All this, however, was not sufficient to transform Arab character and wean it away from its original customs. Unlike the repudiation of associationism, the tranformation of character could not be brought about with speed. This was only natural, for once a material has been given a certain form, it is not easy to transform that material except slowly and progressively. Even so, the desired change cannot be too radical. Human life is such that inherited custom and local traditions knead and mold it into a definite pattern. If this pattern is to bring change, it must be done slowly by degrees. Moreover, no such gradual change may be undertaken unless man transforms his inner self. It is possible for man to change one aspect of himself by removing the hindrances abetting such change in that aspect. That is precisely what Islām did with the Muslims when it converted them to the unitization of God, to faith in Him, in His Prophet, and in the Day of Judgment. But many other aspects of Arab character, especially the material or social aspects, were not so radically transformed but remained nearer to what they had been before Islām. Arab laziness and love of conversation with women, traits kneaded into their character by life in the desert, were chronically resistant to change.

The Prophet's Home and His Wives

In spite of the aforementioned rectification by the new religion of the relationships between the sexes, the Muslims did not depart radically from their previous customs. Often, one of them would enter the Prophet's house and stay there for a long time enjoying conversation with the Prophet or with his wives. But the Prophet had no time to spend on listening to each of his visitors, nor could he tolerate them to converse with his wives and broadcast their gossip. Seeking to free the Prophet from these minor cares, God revealed the following verses:

"O Men who believe, do not enter the house of the Prophet without permission. Do not wait there until meal time, but eat if food is served. Enter therein if you are invited; but once fed, disperse and do not tarry. Such gossiping in his presence harms the Prophet, who is shy to ask you to leave. But God is not shy of saying the truth. And if you ask the wives of the Prophet for something, then talk to them from behind a curtain. That is purer and more seemly for you and for them. It behooves you not to hurt the Prophet of God nor to marry his wives after him. If you do, your deed will be a great crime in God's eye."[5]

While this verse was addressed to the believers, the following was addressed to the Prophet's wives:

"O Wives of the Prophet, you are distinguished only as long as you are righteous. Do not, therefore, be soft or tempting in speech lest the ill-hearted fall to temptation. Be always gentle and good. Maintain your homes with dignity and do not show off yourselves as pre-Islāmic women were wont to do. Observe prayer, pay the *zakāt*, and obey God and His Prophet. God only wishes to keep you pure and to remove from you all uncleanliness and temptation."[6]

Social Foundations of Muslim Brotherhood

On this foundation Islām sought to construct the social order of the human community. Its core was the new relationship between man and woman. By its means Islām sought to remove the unchallenged dominion sex had hitherto exercised over this relationship. Its aim was to direct the community to a higher life where man might enjoy the pleasures of this world without corrosion of his moral fabric, and to lead man to a spiritual relationship with all creatures transcending agriculture, industry, trade, and the other preoccupations of life—the relationship implicit in the life of faith which makes man the partner of angels. Other means which Islām employed for that same purpose were fasting, prayer, and zakāt—by virtue of what each commands against adultery, injustice and evil doing and by virtue of what each enjoins by way of self-purification, submission to God alone, fraternity between the believers, and communion between man and all that is.

The Campaign of Banū Liḥyān

The slow reorganization of society in preparation for the great transformation for which Islām was preparing humanity did not prevent Quraysh and the tribes from lying in wait for Muḥammad. Nor did it prevent Muḥammad from taking the requisite precaution and being always on the alert, ready to strike terror in the hearts of his enemies should the need arise. A case in point was the campaign of Banū Liḥyān. Six months after the destruction of Banū Qurayẓah, it came to Muḥammad's notice that the Banū Liḥyān were marching from a locality near Makkah. Immediately, he remembered the case of Khubayb ibn 'Adiy and his companions, who were murdered by Banū Liḥyān at the well of al Rajī' two years ago, and sought to avenge them. However, he did not announce his purpose for fear that the enemy might be alerted and take refuge. He therefore announced that he wanted to go to al Shām and, after mobilizing his forces, he led them toward the north. When he felt secure that neither the Quraysh nor their neighbors were aware of his intentions, he turned to Makkah and proceeded in its direction full haste until he reached the camping grounds of the tribe of Banū Liḥyān at 'Urān. Some people, however, had noticed his change of direction, and eventually the Banū Liḥyān were informed of his plan. They took refuge in the heights of the surrounding mountains, gathering with them their cattle and property. The Prophet, therefore, could not reach them. He sent Abū Bakr and a hundred cavalrymen in hot pursuit until they reached a place not far from Makkah called 'Usfān. He himself returned to Madīnah on a day that was remembered for the hardship to the traveller which its extreme heat presented, as the following tradition clearly states: "We returned and, by God's leave, we repent to God and praise Him. We take shelter and refuge in God from the travail of travel, the sadness of tragedy, and the realization of loss in relatives and property."

The Campaign of Dhū Qarad

A few days after Muḥammad returned to Madīnah, a group led by 'Uyaynah ibn Ḥiṣn raided the outskirts of the city, seized the camels grazing in the area, killed their shepherd, and carried off his wife. Apparently, he thought that the Muslims would not realize what had happened in time to catch up with him. Salamah ibn 'Amr ibn al Akwa' al Aslamī, however, who happened to be going that way to the forest with bow and arrows, beheld the raiders running away with their booty as they passed through the place called Thaniyyah al Wadā' near al Sal'. He followed them, shot arrows at them and called for help throughout the pursuit. His call was soon heard by the Prophet who alerted the people of Madīnah, and Muslim cavalrymen came out from every direction. Muḥammad ordered them to pursue the raiders immediately, and he followed a little later with another force until he arrived at the mountain of Dhū Qarad. 'Uyaynah and his companions pressed ever faster toward Ghatafān where they could find protection from its tribesmen and escape from the Muslims. The Madīnese cavalry overtook the enemy's rear, seized the stolen camels, and liberated the captive woman. Some companions were prepared to press the pursuit further and avenge the Muslims against 'Uyaynah. The Prophet advised against this course, knowing that 'Uyaynah and his companions had already reached the tribe of Ghatafān and had fallen under their protection. The Muslims therefore returned to Madīnah bringing with them the liberated woman and the camels. While in captivity and driving her own camel, the Muslim woman vowed that should that camel ever bring her back home, she would sacrifice it to God. When she informed the Prophet of her vow in Madīnah, the Prophet answered: "What a terrible reward you propose to the camel which served you and carried you to freedom! That is clearly an evil act, and no vow to perform an evil is valid."

The Campaign of Banū al Muṣṭaliq

Muḥammad remained in Madīnah for about two months, until the campaign of Banū al Mustaliq at al Muraysi', which has arrested the attention of every biographer of the Arab Prophet and every historian. The importance of this campaign lies not in its military significance, but rather, in the internal division which it almost caused within the Muslim community, and which the Prophet settled resolutely. Another important aspect of this campaign is its connection with the Prophet's marriage to Juwayriyyah, daughter of al Ḥārith. A third aspect is its connection with the malignant slander of 'Ā'ishah who, though hardly seventeen years of age, was able to repulse these falsehoods by her strong faith and sublime character.

The news reached Muḥammad that the Banū al Muṣṭaliq, a clan of Khuzā'ah tribe, were mobilizing for war in the vicinity of Makkah and inciting the Arab tribes around them to assassinate Muḥammad. Their leader was al Ḥārith ibn Abū Ḍirār. Acting quickly in seizing the initiative, Muḥammad hastened to strike and take them by surprise as was his custom. The two divisions of al Muhājirūn and al Anṣār which rallied to his immediate call were led by Abū Bakr and Sa'd ibn 'Ubādah, respectively. The Muslims encamped near a well called al Muraysi', not far from the encampment of their enemies. The allies of Banū al Muṣṭaliq ran away upon hearing the news of the advancing Muslim army, with the result that the Banū al Muṣṭaliq themselves were quickly encircled. In the short engagement which followed, the Muslims lost one man, Hishām ibn al Khaṭṭab by name, who was killed accidentally by a fellow Muslim. After losing ten men, the Banū al Muṣṭaliq realized that they had better surrender to the Muslim forces. They were all made captives and their cattle confiscated.

The Plot of 'Abdullah ibn Ubayy

'Umar ibn al Khaṭṭab had a servant charged with taking care of his horse. After the Campaign of Banū al Muṣṭaliq was over, this servant crowded out one of the al Khazraj tribesmen from the proximity of the well. As they quarreled together the man from Khazraj called on al Anṣār for help; the other called for help from al Muhājirūn. 'Abdullah ibn Ubayy, who had accompanied the Muslim forces on this expedition in order to secure some booty, arose when he heard the call and, venting his old hatred of al Muhājirūn as well as of Muḥammad, said to al Anṣār:

"Indeed, al Muhājirūn have not only crowded us here but even in our own homes. The case of our hospitality to them has been nothing short of the common saying, 'Feed your beast and one day it will devour you.' Surely when we return to Madīnah, the stronger party shall force the evacuation of the weaker. Such is the fate that you have incurred with your own hands. You have allowed the Muslims to occupy your lands; you have willingly shared your wealth and crops with them. By God, if you could only deny them these privileges, they would have to leave you alone and seek somebody else's help."

The news of this speech of 'Abdullah ibn Ubayy was soon reported to the Prophet of God. Muḥammad, satisfied that operations against the enemy had all been completed, was visiting with 'Umar ibn al Khaṭṭāb at the time. When the latter heard the report, 'Umar suggested that Bilāl be sent out to kill him instantly. With his usual foresight, patience, experience, and sense of leadership, the Prophet declined 'Umar's suggestion, saying: "O 'Umar, what would the people think if they heard that Muḥammad had begun to kill his own companions?"

Nonetheless, the Prophet calculated that unless he took some resolute action, the situation might worsen. He therefore commanded his people to start off on their return to Madīnah despite the inappropriateness of the hour. Ibn Ubayy in turn heard what had been reported to the Prophet, and he ran to him to deny the report and to explain that he had never entertained such ideas. This action did not affect Muḥammad's resolution to command the return. He traveled with his people continuously throughout the whole day and night and most of the second morning until they could bear the desert sun no longer. As soon as the people dismounted or sat down, they were so exhausted that they fell asleep. Their exhaustion caused them to forget the affair of Ibn Ubayy; and after they had rested, they hurried to Madīnah carrying the captives and booty from Banū al Musṭaliq. One of those captives was Juwayriyyah, daughter of al Ḥārith ibn Abū Dirār, the leader of the vanquished tribe.

Ibn Ubayy's Resentment of the Prophet

After his return to Madīnah with the victorious Muslims, Ibn Ubayy could not reconcile himself to their success, and his resentment of Muḥammad and the Muslims stirred with unabated vigor. His hatred continued despite his apparent adherence to the faith and his emphatic claim that what was reported to the Prophet at al Muraysi' was false. It was on this occasion that

the *Sūrah* "al Munāfiqūn" was revealed in which we read the
following verses:

هُمُ الَّذِينَ يَقُولُونَ لَاتُنْفِقُوا عَلَى مَنْ عِنْدَ رَسُولِ اللهِ حَتَّى يَنْفَضُّوا ۗ وَ لِلهِ خَزَآئِنُ
السَّمٰوٰتِ وَالْاَرْضِ وَ لٰكِنَّ الْمُنٰفِقِينَ لَا يَفْقَهُونَ ۘ يَقُولُونَ لَئِنْ رَّجَعْنَآ اِلَى الْمَدِينَةِ
لَيُخْرِجَنَّ الْاَعَزُّ مِنْهَا الْاَذَلَّ ۗ وَ لِلهِ الْعِزَّةُ وَ لِرَسُولِهِ وَ لِلْمُؤْمِنِينَ وَ لٰكِنَّ الْمُنٰفِقِينَ
لَا يَعْلَمُونَ ۚ

"It is the *munāfiqūn* who counsel against spending anything for
the benefit of the Muhājirūn so that the latter may get out of
Madīnah. But it is to God that all the treasures of heaven and
earth belong. The *munāfiqūn* are simply ignorant. They threaten
that when the Muslims return to Madīnah, the stronger will force
the evacuation of the weaker. But they do not know that might
belongs to God, to his Prophet, and to the believers."[7]

Some people believed that the revelation of these verses was a verdict of death passed on Ibn Ubayy and that Muḥammad would
soon command his execution. Upon learning of this revelation,
'Abdullah, son of 'Abdullah ibn Ubayy, who was a true and loyal
Muslim, ran to the Prophet and said: "O Prophet of God, I have
heard that you are seeking to kill 'Abdullah ibn Ubayy because of
reports which have reached you about him. If this is true, I ask
that you command me to do the execution, and I promise to bring
to you his head forthwith. By God, it is known that nobody supported al Khazraj tribe as my father did. Should anyone else besides me kill him, I will have to suffer myself to see the murderer
of my father go about without avenging him. But I cannot bear
such a torture, and the results may be that I will kill the murderer
of my father, thereby killing a believer and incurring eternal punishment for myself in hell." Such were the words of 'Abdullah ibn
Ubayy's son to Muḥammad. It is hardly possible to appreciate the
struggle within 'Abdullah's soul of filial loyalty, genuine faith,
tribal chivalry, concern for the preservation of peace, and the pre-
vention of blood feuds among the Muslims. Though he realized
that his father was going to be killed, he did not plead to save the
condemned life. He believed that the Prophet does what he is
commanded by his Lord, and was absolutely certain of his

father's treason. But his filial loyalty, personal dignity, and Arab chivalry demanded that he avenge the death of his father. Hence, he was prepared to undertake the killing of his own father, however such a deed might rend his heart and expose his conscience to ruinous self-reproach. He found consolation for his tragedy in his own faith in the Prophet and in Islām. This faith convinced him that if he were to follow the voice of Arab chivalry and filial piety and kill the executioner of his father, he would incur eternal punishment. His was a sublime struggle between faith, emotion, and moral character; and his tragedy was beyond comparison. After hearing his plea, the Prophet answered: "We shall not kill your father. We shall be kind to him, and we shall appreciate his friendship as long as he wishes to extend it to us."

The sublimity and greatness of forgiveness! Muḥammad was touched and he stretched forth a kindly hand toward the one who had incited the people of Madīnah to rise against the Prophet and his companions. His gentleness and pardon were to have far greater effect than punishment. After this episode, whenever an occasion arose for the Muslims to criticize 'Abdullah ibn Ubayy, they used to remind him that his very life was a gift Muḥammad had made to him. One day, when the Prophet was conversing with 'Umar on the affairs of the Muslim community, the criticism ibn Ubayy was meeting from his peers was mentioned. Muḥammad asked 'Umar: "Had I commanded him to be killed the day you advised me to do so, many men would have never entered Islām. These same men, were I to command them today to kill him they would do so without hesitation." 'Umar apologized and acknowledged the Prophet's superior judgment.

'Ā'ishah at the Campaign of Banū al Muṣṭaliq

All the foregoing took place after the Muslims had returned to Madīnah with their fruits of victory. Something else had happened on that expedition which was far removed from military affairs and concerning which there was little talk at first. The Prophet was in the habit of drawing lots among his wives whenever he went on an expedition, and would take in his company that wife whose lot happened to be drawn. On the occasion of the campaign of Banū al Muṣṭaliq, it was the lot of 'Ā'ishah that was drawn. 'Ā'ishah was petite, slim and light; her presence inside the palanquin in which she rode was hardly noticeable by the men who would lift it for placement on camelback. As the Prophet and his expeditionary force were returning to Madīnah after their long and exhaustive journey, they camped not far from Madīnah in order to spend the night and recover their energies. At dawn or before, Muḥammad gave the sign to resume the travel. 'Ā'ishah had stepped out of the Prophet's tent while her palanquin was placed at the entrance of it that she might ride therein and travel be resumed. On her way back she realized that she had lost her necklace. She quickly retraced her own footsteps, looking for the lost necklace. It took her a long time to find it. She had had very little sleep the previous day, and it is possible that she might have fallen asleep in her search for the necklace. At any rate, by the time she returned to her tent, she discovered that her servants had disappeared with the palanquin and that the whole company had vanished into the desert. Apparently thinking that 'Ā'ishah was inside for there was hardly any difference in its overall weight, the servants attached it to the camel's back and proceeded unaware that the "Mother of the Believers" was left behind. 'Ā'ishah looked around herself, and though not finding anyone, she did not panic; for she believed that her people would soon discover her absence and would return to seek her. She judged that it would be better for her to stay where she was rather than to strike out in the desert on her own and risk getting lost. Unafraid, she wrapped herself in her mantle and laid down waiting for her people to discover her. While she waited, Ṣafwān ibn al Mu'aṭṭal al Salamī, who had been out of camp on an errand in the desert, returned to camp to find that he had missed his companions who were already on their way to Madīnah. When he came close to 'Ā'ishah and discovered that she was indeed the wife of the Prophet, he stood back surprised and angry that she had been left behind. He asked her why she had been left behind and, receiving no reply, he brought her his camel and invited her to ride on it. 'Ā'ishah rode on the camel and Ṣafwān rushed toward Madīnah as fast as he could, hoping to join the Muslims before their entry into the city. The Muslims, however, were traveling at a very fast pace, purposely commanded by the Prophet of God in order to keep them exhausted and unable, as it were, to bring to a head the old hatreds between the various Muslim factions which 'Abdullah ibn Ubayy had been fomenting. Ṣafwān arrived at Madīnah in full daylight; 'Ā'ishah was riding on his camel. When he reached the Prophet's house, 'Ā'ishah dismounted and entered her home.

No one present ever entertained any suspicion of unusual behavior on anybody's part, and the Prophet himself never suspected either the daughter of Abū Bakr, or Ṣafwān, the loyal Muslim and pious believer, of the slightest misdemeanor.

Considering that 'Ā'ishah entered Madīnah during the day and in front of everybody, and that her return was soon after the return of the Muslim forces, nobody could entertain any suspicion as to her behavior. She entered Madīnah bearing her usual pride and unperturbed by any feeling of guilt. The whole city went about its business as usual, and the Muslims occupied themselves with dividing the captives and booty which they had seized from the Banū al Mustaliq. Their life in Madīnah was actually becoming more prosperous as their faith gave them more power over their enemies. Their faith had reinforced their wills and had encouraged them to think lightly of death, whether in the cause of God and of His religion, or in defence of religious freedom which they had earned after such a long and hard struggle against their own fellow tribesmen.

Muḥammad's Marriage to Juwayriyyah

Juwayriyyah, daughter of al Ḥārith, was one of the captives of the Banū al Mustaliq. She was a noble and attractive woman and her lot fell to a man of al Ansār. She sought to ransom herself but her captor, knowing that she was the daughter of the leader of the Banū al Muṣṭaliq, demanded a very high price which he thought her people were capable of paying. Afraid of him and his ambition, Juwayriyyah sought the Prophet in the house of 'Ā'ishah and, announcing her identity as the daughter of al Ḥārith ibn Abū Ḍirār, chief of the Banū al Mustaliq, she asked for the Prophet's assistance in ransoming herself from captivity. After listening to her story, the Prophet thought of a better fate for her. He suggested that he ransom and marry her as well. Juwayriyyah accepted his proposal. When the news reached the people, everyone who held a captive of the Banū al Mustaliq granted that particular captive his or her freedom in deference to the new status the new captives had acquired as the in-laws of the Prophet. 'Ā'ishah had said of her: "I know of no woman who brought as much good to her people as Juwayriyyah."

Such is the story according to one version. Another version tells that al Ḥārith ibn Abū Ḍirār came to the Prophet to ransom his daughter, and that after talking to the Prophet, he believed

334 THE LIFE OF MUHAMMAD

in him and declared his conversion. The same version tells that Juwayriyyah followed her father and was converted to Islām, whereupon the Prophet asked for her hand and offered her a dowry of four hundred dirhams. A third version tells that her father was not agreeable to her marriage to the Prophet and that a relative of hers intervened and gave her to the Prophet against the will of her father. Muḥammad did in fact marry Juwayriyyah and built for her a room adjoining his other quarters by the mosque. By this, Juwayriyyah became one of the "Mothers of the Believers." While still busy in the aftermath of the wedding, some people began to whisper about 'Ā'ishah's delayed return to the camp mounted on the camel of Ṣafwān. Ṣafwān was a young and handsome man. Zaynab, daughter of Jaḥsh, had a sister called Ḥamnah who knew too well that 'Ā'ishah was preferred by Muḥammad to her own sister. It was this Ḥamnah who began to broadcast gossip about 'Ā'ishah. In Ḥassān ibn Thābit she found a helper and in 'Alī ibn Abū Ṭālib, an audience. 'Abdullah ibn Ubayy found her gossip of inestimable value in dividing the community and satisfying his hatred. He therefore spread the news in the market places. Al Aws tribesmen defended 'Ā'ishah' however, for they knew she was an example of nobility, chastity and purity. This story and the gossip to which it gave rise almost led to civil war.

'Ā'ishah's Illness

When the gossip finally reached the ear of Muḥammad, he felt deeply hurt. He could not believe 'Ā'ishah would violate her marriage vows. Such indictment was impossible. 'Ā'ishah was pride and purity personified. She enjoyed such fervent love and strong affection from her husband that the mere thought of accusing her was the greatest crime. Yes indeed! But then, woe to women! Who can ever understand them or reach with certainty to their inner core? 'Ā'ishah was still a child. For, how could she lose her necklace and then retrace her steps looking for it in the middle of the night? And why didn't she say anything about her loss when she came to the camp? These and other questions bothered the Prophet; he did not know what to believe and what not to believe.

As for 'Ā'ishah, nobody dared inform her of the people's gossip. She noticed that her husband was unusually laconic and unfriendly to her, a departure from his usual tenderness and preoccupation with her. She fell severely ill and was attended by her mother. But when Muḥammad visited her, he hardly said any more than, "How are you?" Indeed, noticing this coolness on the part of the Prophet, 'Ā'ishah asked whether or not Juwayriyyah had now taken her place in his heart. These strained relations being too much for her patience, she one day asked her husband's permission to move to her parent's quarters where her mother could take care of her. After permission was granted, she moved to her parent's house all the more alarmed at this new expression of unconcern. She remained bedridden for over twenty days, and no knowledge of the gossip spreading around her was ever brought to her notice. The people continued to gossip and annoyed the Prophet so much that he found himself obliged to mention the matter in one of his speeches. "O Men," he said, "why are some of you staining the reputation of my family by accusing them falsely? By God, the members of my family have always been good. Why are you staining the reputation of one of my companions whom I know to be good and who has never entered my house except in my company?" Usayd ibn Ḥuḍayr rose and said, "O Prophet of God, if the false accusers are our own fellows of al Aws tribe, we promise that we shall put a quick stop to them. But if they are of the tribe of al Khazraj, then command us and we shall obey. By God, to whichever tribe they belong, they are worthy of having their heads struck off." Saʻd ibn 'Ubādah commented on Usayd's proposition that the latter had made it because he knew too well that the false accusers belonged to al Khazraj tribe. A spirit of civil dispute and strife hovered over the whole community that took the Prophet's wisdom and sound judgment to dissipate.

The Gossip and 'Ā'ishah

The gossip finally reached 'Ā'ishah through a woman of al Muhājirūn. When she learned of it she almost collapsed in alarm. She cried so hard that she felt as if she were falling apart. Despondent and dejected, she went to her mother and blamed her with broken voice. "May God forgive you, O Mother," she said. "People talk as they do and you do not inform me of it?" Realizing her anguished state, her mother sought to alleviate her pains and said, "O, my daughter, relax and take things lightly. Surely, hardly ever has a beautiful woman such as you, more loved by her husband than his other wives, not been slandered and gossiped about by those wives." 'Ā'ishah, however, was not consoled by this. It began to dawn upon her that the Prophet's coolness and disaffection which had recently replaced his gentleness and affection must have been the result of this gossip and of the suspicion which it has caused. But what could she do now? Would she openly discuss the matter with him? Would he believe her if she swore to him that she was innocent? Or would she acquiesce in the false accusations and seek to offset them by her faith and pleading? Would she show him the same cold shoulder which he had shown her? But he is the Prophet of God, and he has loved her more than any of his other wives. It is surely not his fault that the people have gossiped about her delay in returning to the camp and her return to Madīnah with Safwān. Would to God that she could discover some way of convincing Muhammad of the truth so that the real facts might be made clear once and for all and that Muhammad would return to his old love and gentle treatment of her!

The Revolt of 'Ā'ishah

Muhammad was not in a better position. The gossip of the marketplace had hurt him so much that he was forced to consult on the matter with his personal friends. He proceeded to the house of Abū Bakr and there called 'Alī and Usāmah ibn Zayd to join him. Usāmah denied all that had been attributed to 'Ā'ishah as falsehood and lies. He claimed that the people had no more knowledge of any inclination to disloyalty on the part of 'Ā'ishah than he had. On the contrary, they knew as much about her loyalty and innocence. As for 'Alī, he answered, "O Prophet, women are many. Perhaps you might get some information out of the servant of 'Ā'ishah, loyal as we all know her to be to you." The servant was called in and 'Alī immediately seized her and struck her painfully and repeatedly as he commanded her to tell the truth to the Prophet of God. The servant, however, continued to deny all the gossip and assert that she knew nothing but good as far as 'Ā'ishah was concerned. Finally, Muhammad had no alternative but to put that question directly to his wife, asking that she confess and tell him the truth. He went into her room and, in the presence of her parents and another woman of al Ansār, he found her and that woman crying together. As he entered the room, 'Ā'ishah could see the suspicious look on his face and this cut most deeply into her heart. The man whom she loved and adored, the man in whom she believed and for whom she was prepared to lay down her life, loved her no more. On the contrary, he suspected her. As she composed herself, she listened to him say: "O 'Ā'ishah, you have heard what the people are saying about you. Fear God. If you have done an evil such as they say you did, repent to God for God accepts the repentence of His servants." No sooner had he finished than 'Ā'ishah sprang to her feet, her tears completely vanished, her blood rushing to her face. She glanced at her father and mother hoping that they would speak out for her. But when they remained silent, her rebellious spirit could hold her tongue no longer. She shouted to the top of her voice addressing her parents: "Don't you answer? Won't you speak out?" Despondently, her parents replied that they had nothing to say. At that moment 'Ā'ishah broke out in tears, and this seemed to temper the fire of the storm raging within her. Her tears drying again, she turned suddenly to the Prophet and said: "By God, I will not repent to God because I do not have anything to repent for. If I were to agree with what the people are saying, God knows that I am innocent and that I would be admitting that which is not true. And yet if I persist in my denial, you do not seem to believe me." After a pause, she said: "Rather, I shall say to myself as did the father of Joseph of his lying sons: 'Patience and more patience. God is my refuge against what you describe.' "

Revelation of 'Ā'ishah's Innocence

Silence reigned for a while; nobody could describe it as long or short. Muḥammad had not moved from his spot when revelation came to him accompanied by the usual convulsion. He was stretched out in his clothes and a pillow was placed under his head. 'Ā'ishah later reported, "Thinking that something ominous was about to happen, everyone in the room was frightened except me, for I did not fear a thing, knowing that I was innocent and that God would not be unjust to me. As for my parents, when the Prophet recovered from his convulsion, they looked pale enough to die before the gossip was proven true." After Muḥammad recovered, he sat up and began to wipe his forehead where beads of perspiration had gathered. He said, "Glad tidings! O 'Ā'ishah, God has sent down proof of your innocence." 'Ā'ishah exclaimed, "May God be praised." Immediately Muḥam-

mad went to the mosque and there read to the Muslims the
verses which had just been revealed to him.

> "Those who brought forth this lie and spread it are some
> of you. However, do not regard this, O Muhammad, as
> an evil. You may yet draw good therefrom. Everyone of
> those who spread the lie shall have his share of due punish-
> ment. As for him who has taken the chief part in that gossip,
> his will be the greatest punishment. . . . When you heard
> the great lie, you thought that it was unbecoming of you
> to listen or to respond to it, and you condemned it saying,
> 'Holy God, that is a great calamity!' God admonishes you
> never to do such a thing if you are believers. He, the
> Omnipotent, the All-Wise, shows forth His signs to you.
> Those who like to see immorality spread among the believers
> will receive a painful punishment in this world as well
> as in the next. God knows and you do not."[8]

It was on this occasion that the punishment for false accusation
of adultery was promulgated through the revelation of the
following verse:

وَالَّذِينَ يَرْمُونَ الْمُحْصَنَاتِ ثُمَّ لَمْ يَأْتُوا بِأَرْبَعَةِ شُهَدَاءَ فَاجْلِدُوهُمْ ثَمَانِينَ جَلْدَةً وَّ

لَا تَقْبَلُوا لَهُمْ شَهَادَةً أَبَدًا ۚ وَأُولَٰئِكَ هُمُ الْفَاسِقُونَ ۙ

"Those who falsely accuse chaste women of adultery and do not
bring forth four witnesses to this effect shall be flogged with
eighty stripes and their witness shall never be admitted as evidence in any matter. Those are the decadent, the immoral."[9] In
pursuit of this Qur'ānic injunction, Mistah ibn Athāthah, Hassān
ibn Thābit, and Hamnah, daughter of Jahsh, who had spread the
false accusation of 'Ā'ishah in the marketplace were flogged
eighty stripes each, and 'Ā'ishah returned to her rightful place
in the house as well as in the heart of Muhammad.

Commenting on this event in the life of the Prophet, Sir
William Muir concluded: "The whole career and life of 'Ā'ishah
before that event as well as after it furnishes unquestionable
evidence that she was sincere and innocent. There should therefore be no hesitancy in rejecting every report of malconduct

imputed to her." Despite his grave misdemeanor, Ḥassān ibn Thābit repented, made amends with Muḥammad and was able to win back the latter's friendship. On the other hand, Muḥammad himself asked Abū Bakr not to deny Misṭaḥ ibn Athāthah the kindness which he used to extend to him. Henceforth, the whole event was forgotten in Madīnah. 'Ā'ishah's health improved rapidly, and, after returning to her quarters in the Prophet's residence, she recaptured her favorite position with him and with all the Muslims. Thus, the Prophet was able to devote all his energies to his message, to the administration of policy, and to preparing himself for the events leading to the Treaty of Ḥudaybiyah that would bring to the Muslims new and certain victories.

20

The Treaty of
Ḥudaybiyah

Six years had passed since the emigration of the Prophet and his companions from Makkah to Madīnah. During that time, they were constantly occupied with war and conflict, now with the Quraysh, now with the Jews. All along, Islām was gaining converts as well as power. From the first year of the Hijrah, Muḥammad changed his orientation in prayer from al Aqsā Mosque to the Mosque of Makkah. The Muslims turned toward the house of God which Ibrahim had built in Makkah and which was renewed and reconstructed during Muḥammad's youth. The reader will remember that it was Muḥammad who lifted and placed the Black Stone in its position in the wall of that house, long before he could have ever thought that he was to become the recipient of a revelation from God on High.

Proscription of the Sanctuary to Muslim Entry

For hundreds of years, this Mosque had been the center toward which the Arabs turned in their worship and to which they went in pilgrimage during the holy month of every year. Everybody entering the area of the Mosque was to be safe and secure. The most hostile enemies met on its grounds without anyone ever drawing his sword or shedding the blood of his enemy. Ever since Muḥammad had emigrated with the Muslims to Madīnah, the Quraysh resolved to prevent them from entering the Mosque. This prohibition applied only to the Muslims among all the Arabs of the Peninsula. To this effect, God said in the Qur'ānic verses revealed during the first year of the Hijrah:

$$يَسْأَلُونَكَ عَنِ الشَّهْرِ الْحَرَامِ قِتَالٍ فِيهِ قُلْ قِتَالٌ فِيهِ كَبِيرٌ وَصَدٌّ عَنْ سَبِيلِ اللهِ وَكُفْرٌ بِهِ وَالْمَسْجِدِ الْحَرَامِ وَإِخْرَاجُ أَهْلِهِ مِنْهُ أَكْبَرُ عِنْدَ اللهِ$$

"They challenge you regarding the sacred month, that there should be no fighting whatsoever during its whole course. Answer, that fighting in the holy month is a great transgression. But to hinder men in their pursuit of God's path, to be blasphemous to Him and to the Holy Mosque, to force the worshippers out of the Mosque—all these are greater transgressions in the eye of God."[1]

Likewise, the following verse was revealed after the Battle of Badr: "And why should they not be punished by God when they prevent men from entering the Holy Mosque for worship? Surely, they are not its guardians. The guardians of the Holy Mosque are only the pious and righteous. But most of them are utterly ignorant. As for their worship in the House of God, it is nothing but whistling and clapping and garbling. They should then be punished for their ungodliness. The unbelievers spend of their wealth for the purpose of hindering men from the path of God. Their expenditure is wasted and will bring about their own ruin. For it is to Hell that they shall finally be assigned."[2] During these six years many other verses were revealed centering on the Mosque of Makkah which God had declared to be a place of repentance and of security for mankind. But the Quraysh never saw in Muḥammad and his companions who turned their backs on the idols of that house—namely, Hubal, Isāf, Nā'ilah and the others—anything but men who ought to be fought and combatted and denied the privilege of pilgrimage to the Ka'bah until they repented and returned to the gods of their ancestors.

Muslim Yearning for Makkah

During the whole time the Muslims were kept from fulfilling their religious duty, they suffered deeply. The Muhājirūn especially felt this privation more strongly as it was combined with banishment from their own hometown and people. All the Muslims, however, were convinced that God would soon give victory to His Prophet and to them and would raise Islām high above all other religions. They firmly believed that the day would soon come when God would unlock for them the gates of Makkah that they might perform their pilgrimage to the ancient house and thus fulfill the duty which God had imposed upon all men. If so far the years had passed one after another with frequent campaigns and battles, beginning with Badr, Uḥud, the Ditch and others, so too the day of victory which they believed to be necessary must soon come. How strong was their longing for this day! And how intensely did Muḥammad himself share their very faith in the proximity of that day of victory!

The Arabs and the Ka'bah

The truth is that the Quraysh had done a great injustice to Muḥammad and his companions by forbidding them to visit the Ka'bah and to perform the duties of pilgrimage and *'umrah*.[3] The ancient sanctuary of Makkah was not a property of the Quraysh but of all the Arabs together. The Quraysh enjoyed only the services attached to the Ka'bah such as the *sidānah*, *siqāyah*, and other functions pertinent to the sanctuary or to the care for its visitors. The fact that one tribe worshiped one idol rather than another never permitted the Quraysh to forbid any tribe from visiting the Ka'bah, from circumambulating it, or from filling any religious duties or acts of worship demanded by the tribe's loyalty to that god. If Muḥammad came to call men to repudiate idol worship, to purify themselves from paganism and associationism, to raise themselves to the worship of God alone, devoid of associates, to conduct themselves for the sake of God in a manner free of all moral flaws, to elevate their spirit to consciousness of the unity of being and the unity of God, and if the new faith imposed on its adherents the duty of pilgrimage and *'umrah* to the sanctuary of Makkah, it would be sheer aggression and injustice to prevent the followers of that faith from fulfilling their religious duty. The Quraysh, however, feared that were Muḥammad and his Makkan companions to visit Makkah, they might persuade the majority to follow them, especially since they were related to the Makkans with bonds of blood and family and had been separated from them long enough to arouse in them the strongest longing. Such a development would start a civil war in Makkah which the Quraysh wanted to avoid. Moreover, Makkan leaders and noblemen had not forgotten that Muḥammad and his companions had destroyed their faith, cut off their trade route to al Shām, and antagonized them so deeply that no common loyalty to the sanctuary and no common feeling that it belonged to God and to all the Arabs could compose their differences. The Quraysh could not be convinced that their relationship to the house was merely one of taking care of it and of its visitors.

The Muslims and the Ka'bah

Six whole years had passed since the Hijrah, during which the Muslims longed to visit the Ka'bah and perform the pilgrimage and *'umrah*. One day, while they congregated in the mosque in the morning, the Prophet informed them of a vision he had seen that they should enter the holy sanctuary of Makkah secure, shaven, and unarmed, and without fear for their safety. As soon as the Muslims heard of the news, they praised God for His grace and spread the tidings all over Madīnah. No one, however, could imagine how this was going to be accomplished. Would they fight and enter Makkah after battle? Would they force the evacuation of Quraysh and pull down its guardianship of the Ka'bah? Or would Quraysh open the road to them in humiliation and acquiescence?

Muhammad's Proclamation Concerning Pilgrimage

No! There was to be neither war nor fighting. Muḥammad proclaimed to the people that pilgrimage to Makkah would take place in the holy month of Dhū al Qi'dah. He had sent his messengers to the tribes, whether Muslim or otherwise, inviting them to participate with the Muslims in a visit to the sanctuary of God in security and peace. Apparently, he sought to make the group performing the pilgrimage the largest possible. His objective was to let the whole Peninsula know that this expedition of his during the holy month was intended purely for pilgrimage and not for conquest, as well as to proclaim the fact that Islām had imposed pilgrimage to Makkah just as pre-Islāmic Arab religion had done and, finally, that he had actually invited even the Arabs who were not Muslims to join in the performance of this sacred duty. If, despite all this, the Quraysh insisted on fighting him during the holy month and preventing him from the performance of a duty commonly held by all Arabs regardless of their personal faith, the Quraysh would surely find themselves isolated and condemned by all. In that eventuality, the Quraysh would find the Arabs unwilling to help them in fighting the Muslims. In the eyes of all the tribes, the Quraysh would have indicted themselves. They would have to appear as stopping men from visiting the sanctuary, as combating the religion of Isma'īl and of his father, Ibrahīm. By this means, the Muslims would guarantee that the Arab tribes would not rally against them under Makkan leadership as they did hitherto in the campaign of the Ditch, and their religion would itself gain some credit among the tribes who had not yet been converted to it. What would the Quraysh say to a people who came to their doors armless except for their undrawn swords, and in a state of ritualistic purity, accompanied by the cattle which they planned to sacrifice near the Ka'bah and whose every care was simply to circumambulate the House, the duty common to all the tribes of the Peninsula?

Muhammad publicly proclaimed that the pilgrimage had started and asked the tribes, including the non-Muslim, to accompany him on that holy mission. Some of the tribes rejected his invitation and others accepted. His procession set forth on the first of Dhū al Qi'dah, one of the holy months; and it included al Muhājirūn, al Ansār, and a number of other tribes. He led the procession riding on his she-camel, al Qaswā'. Their total number was about one thousand four hundred men. They took with them seventy camels and donned the garb demanded by the ritual of 'umrah that the people might know that this was no military campaign but a pilgrimage to the holy sanctuary and a fulfillment of religious duty. When he reached Dhū al Hulayfah, the pilgrims shaved their heads, purified themselves as the ritual demanded, and isolated their sacrificial cattle by placing them to their left. The sacrificial cattle included the camels of Abū Jahl which were seized in the Battle of Badr. No man in the whole group carried any arms except the undrawn sword usually worn by all travelers. Umm Salamah, the wife of the Prophet, accompanied him on this trip.

Quraysh and Muslim Pilgrimage

When the Quraysh learned that Muhammad and his companions were approaching Makkah for purposes of pilgrimage, they were filled with fear and pondered whether or not Muhammad was now playing a war game against them in order to enter Makkah after they and their allies had failed to enter Madīnah. Their fear was not dissipated when they learned that the pilgrims had actually donned the ritual garb demanded by *'umrah,* nor by Muslim proclamation across the Peninsula that they were coming solely to fulfill a religious duty approved and accepted by all the Arabs. None of this prevented them from resolving to stop Muḥammad from entering Makkah at whatever cost. Quickly, they mobilized an army, including a cavalry force of two hundred. They gave the command to Khālid ibn al Walīd and 'Ikrimah ibn Abū Jahl. This army advanced to Dhū Ṭuwā and took up position to prevent the Muslims' religious march to Makkah.

Encounter

Muḥammad and the Muslims continued their march. At 'Usfān, they met a tribesman of Banū Ka'b whom the Prophet questioned regarding the Quraysh. The man answered: "They heard about your march; so they marched too. But they wore their tiger skins, their traditional war apparel, pledging that they will never let you enter Makkah. Their general, Khālid ibn al Walīd, set up camp for his cavalry at Karā' al Ghamīm." Upon learning this, Muḥammad said: "Woe to Quraysh! Their hostility is undoing them. Why should they object to letting me settle this affair with all the tribes without intervention? If the Arab tribes destroy me, that will be the realization of their objective. If, on the other hand, God gives me victory, then they can enter into Islām with dignity; and if they resist, they can then fight with good cause. What does the Quraysh think? By God, I shall continue to serve that for which God has commissioned me until the divine message has become supreme or I lose my neck in the process." Pondering over the issue, he thought that, whereas he did not come thither as a conquerer but as a Muslim pilgrim seeking the sanctuary as a religious duty, he might be compelled to fight and perhaps lose unless he should take the precaution of arming his people. Should he lose in such an engagement, the Quraysh would parade their victory throughout the Peninsula and thus deal a tragic blow to the Muslim position. Indeed, it is perhaps for that reason that the Quraysh delegated the command of their army to Khālid ibn al Walīd and 'Ikrimah, their most illustrious generals, that they might attain this very objective, knowing that Muhammad was not prepared to fight on this occasion.

Muhammad's Caution to Safeguard the Peace

While Muhammad pondered these issues, Makkan cavalry was looming on the horizon. The presence of the enemy prepared for war showed the Muslims that it was impossible for them to reach their objective without going through these lines and engaging in a battle in which the Quraysh had come prepared to repulse the threat to their dignity, honor, and homeland. Such would have been a battle undesired and uncalled for by Muhammad and forced upon him. The Muslims were not afraid of battle. With the high morale they enjoyed, their swords alone would be sufficient to stop this new aggression of the Makkans. But if they did fight the Makkans, the peaceful purpose of the whole affair would not be realized. On the contrary, the Quraysh would use such fighting as proof of Muhammad's guilt before the tribes. Muhammad was too farsighted to allow such a course to be followed. He therefore asked his party to find someone who could show them a road to Makkah other than the main one which was blocked by the Quraysh. Apparently, he was still of the same mind as before he started out from Madīnah. A man was found to lead the procession by a different route which was yet more desolate and full of hardships. That road led them to a valley at the end of which a turn by al Murār brought them to the locality of al Ḥudaybiyah, south of Makkah. When the Quraysh discovered the movement of Muhammad and his companions, they returned quickly to Makkah in order to defend it against what they thought to be a Muslim invasion from the south. Upon arrival at the plain of al Ḥudaybiyah, al Qaswā', she-camel of the Prophet, stopped. The Muslims thought the she-camel was exhausted; but the Prophet explained that it was stopped by the same power which stopped the elephant from entering Makkah. He continued, "If only the Quraysh would ask us for guarantees of Muslim intentions based upon our blood relationship to them, we should be happy to give them the same." He then called upon the Muslims to encamp. When they complained that the place was waterless, he sent a man with a stick to one of the wells of the area and asked him to verify the existence of water. When the man plunged his stick into the bottom of the well, water sprang up; the people felt reassured, and they put up camp.

Quraysh's Delegates to the Muslims

The Muslims encamped and the Quraysh observed their moves. The Makkans had resolved to prevent the Muslims by force from entering their city. To them, this was a clear and final commitment. The Muslims, on the other hand, did not know whether or not they were heading for an all-out war with the Quraysh which would decide the matter between them once and for all. Undoubtedly, some people on both sides preferred a settlement by the sword. The Muslims who approved of this course thought their victory would bring about a final destruction of the Quraysh. The Quraysh's reputation throughout the Peninsula as well as their *sidānah* and *siqāyah* functions in pilgrimage—indeed, their pride and religious distinction—would be eliminated. The two camps were poised seeking an answer. Muhammad did not change his original plan to perform the *'umrah* in peace and to avoid war unless attacked. In case of attack, there would be no escape from recourse to the sword. As for the Quraysh, while hesitant, they decided to send some delegates to the Muslim camp, partly to reconnoiter Muslim strength and partly to dissuade Muḥammad from executing his plan. For this purpose, Budayl ibn Warqā' arrived at the Muslim camp, together with some tribesmen from Khuzā'ah. Inquiry into Muḥammad's objectives convinced them that he did not come to fight but to honor the sanctuary and pay to it the homage due. The delegation returned to the Quraysh and counseled that the Muslims be permitted to fulfill their religious wish. The Quraysh, however, remained unconvinced. Indeed, they accused their own delegates of conniving with Muḥammad. They argued that even though Muḥammad might not have come to make war, he should not be allowed to enter Makkah against their will and with such preponderant numbers. Otherwise, the Quraysh would become the mockery of Arabia. In order to make sure that their first delegates told them the truth, the Quraysh sent another delegation which returned with exactly the same reports, which the Quraysh now believed. The Quraysh were depending for their war against Muhammad upon their Aḥābīsh allies.[4] They thought of sending the Aḥābīsh leader to talk to Muḥammad with the hope that the two leaders would misunderstand each other and the Quraysh ally would become increasingly committed to fight on Makkah's side against Muḥammad. Al Ḥulays, as the leader of the Aḥābīsh was called, went to the Muslim camp to see for himself. When the Prophet saw him

arriving, he ordered the sacrificial cattle paraded in front of him
as material proof of Muslim intention to perform the pilgrimage
and to honor the sanctuary. Al Ḥulays saw the seventy sacrificial
camels shaved and readied for sacrifice and was moved by the
view of this display of Arab religiosity. He soon became convinced
that the Quraysh were doing an injustice to those people who had
come neither for war nor for hostility. Without bothering to meet
Muḥammad and converse with him, he returned to Makkah and
told the Quraysh of his opinion. Full of resentment, the Quraysh
slighted al Ḥulays as a bedouin and neglected his advice as that
of one uninstructed. Al Ḥulays was naturally angered, and he
threatened them that he had not allied himself with them in order
to stop pilgrims from performing their religious duties. He even
threatened that unless they allowed Muḥammad and his party
into the sanctuary, he would remove himself and his tribe from
Makkah. The Quraysh feared the consequences of such a move and
begged him to give them time to reconsider.

The Delegation of 'Urwah ibn Mas'ūd al Thaqafī

The Quraysh then thought of sending somebody whom they
could trust and whose judgment stood beyond suspicion. They
approached 'Urwah ibn Mas'ūd al Thaqafī and apologized to
him for having slighted the delegate whom they had sent before
him to negotiate with Muḥammad. When they assured him of
their respect and pledged their compliance with his advice, he
agreed to meet with Muḥammad. He proposed to the latter that
since Makkah was his own hometown whose honor it was his
duty to safeguard, it would be opprobrious for him to prefer the
commonplace people he brought with him to the noblemen of
Quraysh who were none other than his own people. 'Urwah
stressed the point that such opprobrium would attach to Muḥammad as well as to the Quraysh even though the two had
been at war with each other. On hearing this, Abū Bakr objected
loudly to 'Urwah's request that the Prophet of God separate
himself from the people. While talking to Muḥammad, 'Urwah
touched Muḥammad's beard in supplication, and al Mughīrah
ibn Shu'bah, standing on the side of the Prophet, struck the
hand of 'Urwah every time it was stretched toward Muḥammad's
beard despite the fact that 'Urwah had ransomed al Mughīrah
by paying the bloodwit of the thirteen men whom all Mughīrah
had killed prior to his conversion to Islām. Accordingly, 'Urwah

returned to Makkah after convincing himself that Muḥammad had not come to wage war but to honor the holy sanctuary in fulfillment of a divine imperative. Upon return to the Quraysh, he said to them: "O Men of Quraysh, I have visited Chosroes, Caesar, and the Negus in their respective courts. By God, I have never seen a king attaching himself to his people as Muḥammad does. His companions love him and honor him and revere him so much that they carefully lift every hair that falls off his body, and they save the water with which he performs his ablutions. They will never allow any hand to fall on him. Judge then accordingly."

Muḥammad's Delegation to Quraysh

In this way, negotiations between Muḥammad and the Quraysh lasted a long time. Muḥammad wondered whether or not the delegates of Quraysh had enough courage and initiative to convince the Quraysh with the facts which they had noted. He therefore sent a delegate from his own camp to inform the Quraysh of the Muslim view. The Makkans slew the camel of Muḥammad's delegate and were about to kill him when the Aḥābīsh intervened and let him go free. This conduct of the Makkans only confirmed their hostile spirit and, consequently, the Muslims began to lose patience and think of fighting their way through. While still considering what to do, some plebeians from Makkah went out under the cover of night to throw stones at the tents of the Muslims. The latter sent out forty or fifty men who encircled the attackers, captured them and brought them to the Prophet for judgment. To the surprise of everyone, Muḥammad forgave the attackers and allowed them to go free in accordance with his general plan for peace and in deference to the holy month in which no blood was to be shed in al Ḥudaybiyah, an area falling within the holy ground of Makkah. The Quraysh for their part were stupefied by this conduct of Muhammad and lost every argument they had that Muḥammad wanted war. It had become absolutely certain that any attack on the part of the Quraysh against Muḥammad would be regarded by all Arabs as a sneaking, treacherous act of aggression which Muḥammad would be perfectly entitled to repel with all power at his disposal.

The Prophet of God—May God's blessing be upon him—tested the patience of the Quraysh once more by sending a delegate from his camp to negotiate with them. He called 'Umar ibn al Khaṭṭāb for the job of conveying his message to the noblemen of Quraysh. 'Umar, however, pleaded with the Prophet of God that since none of his people, the Banu 'Adiyy ibn Ka'b, were left in Quraysh, he would be unprotected prey for them to pounce upon in revenge for his many offenses against them. He counselled the Prophet to send another man, 'Uthmān ibn 'Affān, who was far more protected among the Quraysh than he. The Prophet called 'Uthmān ibn 'Affān, his son-in-law, and sent him to Abū Sufyān and the noblemen of Quraysh. 'Uthmān proceeded to Makkah, and on its outskirts was met by Abān ibn Sa'id who extended to him his protection for the duration of time that it would take him to convey his message. 'Uthmān approached the noblemen of Quraysh and handed over the Prophet's message. They suggested to him that he might circumambulate the sanctuary if he wished. But he declined, saying, "I shall never do so until the Prophet of God had done so himself." He continued to insist that the Muslims had come to Makkah simply in order to visit the holy shrine and to glorify it and to perform the religious duty of pilgrimage. He pointed out that the Muslims had brought with them their sacrificial animals and pleaded that if they were allowed to sacrifice them, they would return in peace. The Quraysh pleaded that they had already sworn defiantly that Muḥammad would not be allowed to enter Makkah this year. The negotiations lasted a long time during which 'Uthmān was forced to stay in Makkah. Soon the Muslims began to suspect that he had been treacherously put to death. Perhaps during this time the noblemen of Quraysh were busy conversing with 'Uthmān in an attempt to find a common form in which their pledge not to allow Muḥammad to enter Makkah this year, and the Muslim's desire to visit the Holy House and to fulfill their religious duty, could be composed. Perhaps, too, they appreciated 'Uthmān's frankness and sincerity and were seriously engaged in discussing with him how best to reorganize the relations with Muḥammad in the future.

The Covenant of al Riḍwān

Whatever the reason, 'Uthmān's failure to return quickly caused the Muslims at Ḥudaybiyah no little anxiety. They began to give vent to their imagination by picturing the Quraysh treacherously attacking them in the holy month despite the sanctity of the occasion and of the purpose for which they came. They feared that the Quraysh would violate the religious conscience of all Arabia with impudence, even within the holy sanctuary or on the holy grounds of Makkah. With tension rising in the Muslim camp, and everybody reaching for his sword, Muḥammad assured them that he would not allow them to return without challenging their enemies. He called his companions to him under a large tree in the middle of that valley, and there they covenanted with him to fight to the last man. Their faith was certain, their conviction was strong, and their will was determined to avenge the blood of 'Uthmān whom they thought the Quraysh had murdered in Makkah. This covenant was called the Covenant of al Ridwān; and in its regard, the following verse was revealed: "God is pleased with the believers who have covenanted with you under the tree. God knows what is in their hearts and, therefore, He has granted them His peace and will soon give them great victory."[5] When the Muslims concluded their covenant, Muḥammad—May God's peace and blessing be upon him—pledged the same covenant on behalf of 'Uthmān, and the latter was regarded as if he were present. Thereupon, swords shook in their scabbards and the Muslims realized that war was now inevitable. Everybody looked forward to the day of victory or martyrdom with a mind convinced and satisfied, and a heart reassured and at peace. While in this state, the news reached them that 'Uthmān had not been murdered, and soon the man himself returned safe and sound. The Covenant of al Ridwān, however, like the great Covenant of al 'Aqabah, remained a great landmark in Muslim history. Muḥammad was particularly pleased with this covenant for the evidence it furnished of the strength of the bonds which tied him and his companions together, and for the readiness of the Muslims to face the greatest dangers without fear. For whoever is willing to face death will find that death itself shies away from him, life itself surrenders to him, and victory is always his own to reach.

The Quraysh's Response

Upon return, 'Uthmān conveyed to Muḥammad the message of the Quraysh. They entertained no more doubt that the Muslims had come to Makkah for anything but the religious purpose of pilgrimage to the Holy House, and they realized that they had no right to prevent any Arab from performing his pilgrimage or 'umrah during the holy month. Nonetheless, they had mobilized their army under the leadership of Khālid ibn al Walīd to prevent Muhammad and his companions from entering Makkah, and some skirmishes had taken place between the two parties. After all this had happened, to let Muhammad enter Makkah would allow the tribes to conclude that the Quraysh had been defeated and, as a result, their position in the Peninsula would suffer greatly. Therefore, the Quraysh argued, they must insist on maintaining this decision of theirs in order to preserve their reputation and prestige. They invited Muhammad to think out with them both his and their position that together they might find an outlet from this difficulty. By themselves they saw no escape from a war which they would have to wage whether they wanted to or not. Rather, they wished they might not have to fight during the holy months because of their religious sanctity and out of fear that should those months be violated, then the tribes would never feel secure that they would not be violated again in the future. The result of a present conflict would be that the security of passage to Makkah and to its market, of the religious rites and of the prosperity of the Makkans and Arabs alike would all go aground.

Negotiations

Another round of negotiations between the two parties followed. The Quraysh sent Suhayl ibn 'Amr to reconcile Muhammad and to ask him to return for the same purpose the following year. They argued that in such an arrangement the tribes would not claim that Muhammad had entered Makkah in defiance of the Quraysh. Suhayl began his negotiations with the Prophet, and these lasted a long time during which they were interrupted and resumed again by both parties, anxious as they were for the negotiations to succeed. In the Muslim camp the Muslims listened in on these negotiations and often lost patience at their involvement and length, the obstinacy with which Suhayl refused to make any concessions, and the leniency with which the Prophet made his. Were it not for the absolute confidence the Muslims had in their Prophet, they would have never accepted the terms reached by those negotiations. They would have fought with the Makkans and either entered Makkah victorious or perished in the process. Even such a great man as 'Umar ibn al Khaṭṭāb lost patience and said to Abū Bakr, "O Abū Bakr, isn't Muḥammad the Prophet of God and aren't we Muslims?" Abū Bakr answered in the affirmative. 'Umar then said, "Why then should we give in to the unbelievers in a matter vital to our faith?" Abū Bakr replied, "O 'Umar, do not trespass one inch where you ought not to go. Remember that I witness that our leader is the Prophet of God." Angrily, 'Umar acquiesced by replying: "I, too, witness that our leader is the Prophet of God."

Conclusion of the Treaty *(March,* 628 C.E.*)*

'Umar turned to Muḥammad and complained to him with the same anger and resentment, but could not alter the Prophet's determination and patience. Their talk was concluded with the Prophet's statement that he was the servant of God and His Prophet and that he would not deviate from the divine commandment nor entertain any doubt of divine support. So patient was Muḥammad in these negotiations that many Muslims remembered anecdotes which speak most eloquently to this effect. It is reported, for instance, that Muḥammad called 'Alī ibn Abū Ṭālib and said to him: "Write, 'In the name of God, the Merciful, the Compassionate.'" Suhayl, the non-Muslim delegate of Quraysh interrupted. "Stop," he said, "I do not know either 'the Merciful' or 'the Compassionate.' Write, 'In your name, O God.'" The Prophet of God instructed 'Alī to write accordingly and continued: "Write, 'Following is the text of a pact reached by Muḥammad, the Prophet of God and Suhayl ibn 'Amr.'" Suhayl again interrupted. "Stop it. If I accepted you as a Prophet of God I would not have been hostile to you. You should write only your name and the name of your father." The Prophet of God instructed 'Alī to write accordingly, referring to himself as Muḥammad ibn 'Abdullah. The text of the treaty was redacted and agreed upon. In the opinion of most biographers, the treaty specified that the peace was to last for ten years. According to al Wāqidī, the peace was stipulated for only two years. The pact also specified that any person from Quraysh emigrating to Muḥammad's camp without permission from his guardian would have to be returned to Makkah, whereas any Muslim emigrating from Muḥammad's camp to Makkah would not have to be returned. It also specified that any tribe was free to ally itself to Muḥammad without incurring any guilt or censure from Quraysh, and likewise, any tribe seeking an alliance with Quraysh could do so without let or hindrance from the Muslims. The pact stipulated that Muhammad and his companions would leave the area of Makkah that year without fulfilling their religious function but that they might return the next year, enter the city and stay therein three days for this purpose while carrying no more than swords in their scabbards.

Promulgation of the Treaty

As soon as this pact was solemnly concluded by the parties concerned, the tribe of Khuzā'ah entered into an alliance with Muhammad and that of Banū Bakr with Quraysh. Soon after, Abū Jandal ibn Suhayl ibn 'Amr left Makkah forever and came to the Muslim camp seeking to join the Muslims. When Suhayl, the delegate of Quraysh to the Muslim camp, saw his son change loyalties in his presence, he struck him in the face and pulled him by the hair to return to the Quraysh. Abū Jandal was calling upon the Muslims to save him from the fate of being returned to the unbelievers who would persecute him for his faith. This greatly increased the Muslims' resentment and their dissatisfaction with the pact the Prophet had just concluded with Suhayl. But Muhammad spoke to Abū Jandal. "O Abū Jandal," he said, "have patience and be disciplined; for God will soon provide for you and your other persecuted colleagues a way out of your suffering. We have entered with the Quraysh into a treaty of peace and we have exchanged with them a solemn pledge that none will cheat the other." Abū Jandal returned to Quraysh in compliance with the demand of this treaty and Suhayl returned to Makkah. Muhammad, too, was disconcerted with the resentment and dissatisfaction of the Muslims around him. After reciting his prayers he felt reassured, sought his sacrificial animal, and slaughtered it. Then, he sat down and shaved his head, thus declaring the 'umrah, or lesser pilgrimage, complete. His soul was satisfied and his heart full of contentment, as if the peace of God had come upon him. When the people saw what he did and observed the peace of soul shining through his face, they began to slaughter their animals and to shave off their hair. Some of them shaved off their hair completely and others only in part. Muhammad said, "God Bless those who shaved their heads." The people asked him about those who only cut their hair short, and Muhammad repeated his blessing for the benefit of those who *shaved* their heads. After the people asked him three times and he repeated the same blessing three times, he was asked: "Why, O Prophet of God, do you exclude those who cut off their hair short from your blessing?" He answered, "Because the shavers did not doubt, whereas the others did."[6]

The Treaty of Ḥudaybiyah: A Genuine Victory

Nothing remained for the Muslims to do except to return to Madīnah and there await the arrival of the coming season for another trip to Makkah. Most of them accepted this idea grudgingly, and consoled themselves purely on the grounds that the unwelcome compliance therewith was only the command of the Prophet himself. They were not accustomed to acquiesce in a defeat or to surrender without a fight. Moreover, in their faith in God and in the timely assistance that God would grant to His Prophet, his religion and themselves, they could entertain no shadow of a doubt of their ability to storm Makkah if only Muḥammad had commanded it. They stayed in al Ḥudaybiyah a few days questioning one another regarding the wisdom of this pact which the Prophet had concluded. Some of them were inclined to doubt its wisdom. But they bore in patience and then returned home. On their way home between Makkah and Madīnah, the *sūrah* "al Fatḥ" was revealed to the Prophet, and he recited it to his companions.

$$\text{اِنَّا فَتَحْنَا لَكَ فَتْحًا مُبِينًا لِّيَغْفِرَ لَكَ اللهُ مَا تَقَدَّمَ مِنْ ذَنْبِكَ وَمَا تَأَخَّرَ وَيُتِمَّ نِعْمَتَهُ عَلَيْكَ وَ}$$
$$\text{يَهْدِيَكَ صِرَاطًا مُّسْتَقِيمًا}$$

"We have granted to you a clear victory that God may forgive you your past and future shortcomings, grant you His blessings, and guide you to the straight path."[7]

There was hence no reason to doubt that the Ḥudaybiyah Treaty was a victory for the Muslims. History has shown that this pact was the product of profound political wisdom and farsightedness and that it brought about consequences of great advantage to Islām and indeed to Arabia as a whole. It was the first time that Quraysh acknowledged that Muḥammad was an equal rather than a mere rebel and runaway tribesman. It was the first time that Makkah acknowledged the Islāmic state that was rising in Ara-

bia. Makkan acquiescence in the right of the Muslims to visit the
sanctuary and to perform the pilgrimage was equally a recognition on her part that Islām was an established and approved religion in the Peninsula. Furthermore, the peace of the following
two or ten years gave the Muslims the peace and security they
needed on their southern flank without fear of an invasion from
Quraysh. The peace also contributed to the spread of Islām. Even
Quraysh, the most determined enemy of Islām and its greatest
antagonist, had by this pact come to recognize Islām and its community, and to acquiesce in that in which it had never acquiesced
before. Indeed, Islām spread after this treaty more widely and
quickly than it had ever spread before. While those who accompanied Muhammad to Hudaybiyah counted one thousand and four
hundred, those who accompanied him on his conquest of Makkah
two years later counted well over ten thousand. The greatest objection to those who doubted the wisdom of the Hudaybiyah pact
was directed to the provision that any Quraysh member joining
the Muslims without the permission of his guardian would have
to be returned to Quraysh, and that any apostate from Islām
would not have to be returned to Madīnah. Muhammad's opinion
in this matter centered on the consideration that the apostate
from Islām who seeks the shelter of Quraysh is not really worthy
of readmission to the Muslim community; that for the convert
who wished to join that community but who was not allowed
to at present, God would soon find an outlet. Events have confirmed this judgment of Muhammad far more quickly than his
companions anticipated, and given evidence that Islām had actually drawn great advantages. Indeed, the treaty even made it possible two months later for Muhammad to begin to address himself
to the kings and chiefs of foreign states and invite them to join
Islām.

The Story of Abū Baṣīr

Events succeeded one another very rapidly, all of which
confirmed Muhammad's judgment and wisdom. Abū Basīr became a Muslim and escaped from Makkah to Madīnah. Obviously,
the provisions of the Hudaybiyah Treaty applied to him and
demanded his return to the Quraysh, for he had not obtained
the permission of his master. Azhar ibn 'Awf and al Akhnas
ibn Sharīq wrote to the Prophet to this effect and sent their
letter with a tribesman of Banū 'Āmir and a slave of theirs.

When the demand was made, the Prophet called Abu Baṣīr and said to him: "We have covenanted with the Quraysh to honor the Treaty of Ḥudaybiyah which you well know. In our religion, we are not permitted to cheat. You should therefore return to your people. God will grant to you and to the other persecuted Muslims a means of emancipation in His good time." Abū Baṣīr objected to the Prophet that the unbelievers would force him to apostatize. The Prophet, however, repeated the same judgment to him. Abū Baṣīr had, therefore, to give himself up to the two messengers and accompany them back to Makkah. Once they arrived at Dhū al Ḥulayfah, Abū Baṣīr asked the Banū 'Āmir tribesman to show him his sword, and as soon as he laid his hand upon it, he struck the tribesman with it and killed him. The Makkan slave ran toward Madīnah and into the Prophet's presence with obvious signs of fear and panic on his face. When interrogated, the slave told the Prophet that Abū Baṣīr had killed his master. Soon, Abū Baṣīr himself arrived brandishing his sword and addressing Muḥammad: "O Prophet of God, you have fulfilled your duty under the Treaty and God has relieved you of your obligation, for you have in fact surrendered me to my people as the treaty prescribed. But I was not willing to allow myself to be persecuted, enticed away, or forced to abjure my religion." The Prophet did not hide his admiration for him and wished that he had many companions. Later on, Abū Baṣīr went to al 'Is on the sea coast, on the road which the Quraysh followed to al Shām and which the Treaty of Ḥudaybiyah prescribed to keep open for Makkan trade. When his story and that of Muḥammad's admiration of him reached Makkah, the Muslims still residing there were elated, and about seventy of them ran away to al 'Is to follow him as their chief. Abū Baṣīr and his companions began to cut off the trade route on their own initiative, killing any unbeliever they caught and seizing any camels belonging to Quraysh. Only then did it dawn on the Quraysh what a loss they had incurred by insisting as they did on keeping their Muslim members or slaves in forced residence in Makkah. They realized that the man who is truly committed to Islām was a greater handicap to them than the loss of him altogether to the Muslim camp. Such a man would escape at the first opportunity without entering into the camp of Muḥammad and, hence, without becoming an outlaw under the prescriptions of the Ḥudaybiyah Treaty. He would then wage a terrible war against the Makkans in which the Makkans had everything to lose and nothing to gain. Remembering too well that Muḥammad had cut off the caravan road after his emigration to Madīnah, the Quraysh feared that Abu Basīr would do likewise. They therefore wrote to the Prophet asking him, in violation of the Ḥudaybiyah Treaty, to accept their fugitives into his camp in order to keep the caravan route open. In the consequent negotiation, the Quraysh relinquished the privilege emphasized by Suhayl ibn 'Amr so strongly, namely, that the Muslims of Quraysh who escape therefrom without approval of their masters or guardians be returned to Quraysh. Thus, the concession criticized by 'Umar ibn al Khaṭṭāb and for the sake of which he revolted against Abū Bakr was dropped by request of the Quraysh. Muḥammad then invited all the Muslims to enter Madīnah, and the caravan route to al Shām became once more secure.

Muslim Women Emigrants

As for the Muslim women of Quraysh who escaped to Madīnah, Muḥammad had a different opinion. Umm Kulthūm, daughter of 'Uqbah ibn abu Mu'ayṭ, escaped from Makkah to Madīnah after the Ḥudaybiyah Treaty, and her two brothers 'Umarah and al Walīd came to the Prophet demanding her return under terms of the Treaty. The Prophet refused, judging that the treaty did not apply to women and that if women called for assistance and shelter, their request could not be turned down. Furthermore, when a woman becomes a Muslim, she is no more legally tied to her husband who is an unbeliever. Dissolution of the bond of marriage is then automatic. On this point, the revelation is clear: "O Men who believe, if the women believers come to you for shelter, examine them, remembering that God knows the nature of their faith better than anyone. If you find them to be true believers, do not return them to the polytheists to whom they are no longer legitimate. Return to them that which they have spent and marry them if you wish; for there is no blame upon you if you do so, provided you give them their dowries. Do not hold to your matrimonial ties with women unbelievers, but ask them to return what you have spent and return to them what they have spent and separate yourselves from each other. That is the judgment of God and He wishes to see it observed among you. God is All-Knowing and All-Wise."[8] Thus events confirmed Muḥammad's wisdom, foresight, and deep political insight. History has indeed proved that the Treaty of al Ḥudaybiyah actually laid down a very important foundation for Islām's political career as well as for its spread throughout the world. That is the meaning of the clear victory God had promised.

Relations between Quraysh and Muḥammad became quite peaceful and settled after the Treaty of al Ḥudaybiyah. Both parties felt secure. The Quraysh embarked on enlarging trade, hoping to recapture the losses which had resulted from the war with the Muslims in which the road to al Shām was cut. As for Muḥammad, he embarked on a wider policy of mission, seeking to bring his message to all men in all corners of the earth and to lay down the foundations for the happiness and success of the Muslims throughout the Peninsula now that their security was guaranteed. Both these considerations enabled him to send his messengers to the kings in the surrounding empires and, especially after the Battle of Khaybar, to expel the Jews from the Arabian Peninsula altogether.

21

The Campaign of Khaybar and Missions to Kings

Muḥammad and the Muslims returned from al Ḥudaybiyah to Madīnah three weeks after the signing of the treaty with Quraysh and the agreement that they would not enter Makkah that year but the following year. Many of them returned with wounded pride. They continued to feel dejected and despondent until *sūrah* "al Fatḥ,"[1] revealed on the road to Madīnah, alleviated their despondency. While in Ḥudaybiyah as well as after the return to Madīnah, Muḥammad thought about what he should do to strengthen the faith of his companions and to spread the message of Islām. He thought of sending messengers to Heraclius, Chosroes, the Archbishop of Alexandria, the Negus of Abyssinia, King al Ḥārith of Ghassān, and the satrap of Chosroes in Yaman. He also pondered the necessity of eliminating Jewish influence in the Arabian Peninsula once and for all.

Crystallization of the Islāmic Call

In fact, the Islāmic message had by this time reached a high level of crystallization and comprehensiveness. The time was ripe for its dissemination among mankind. Besides the doctrine of the unity of God and its implications for worship and ethics, the Islāmic message developed so widely as to include within its purview all aspects of social activity and human relations. These it sought to regulate and infuse with its ethos and spirit. It attached such importance to man's social relations that it put its precepts for social behavior on a level with the doctrine of the unity of God. The system of principles Islām elaborated came nearer than any other to enable man to attain perfection and to realize the absolute, or the highest ideals in space-time. Hence, a large number of specific proscriptions were revealed during this period to regulate man's social relationships.

The Proscription of Alcohol

Biographers of the Prophet have disagreed regarding the time of the prohibition of alcohol. Some assert that it took place in the fourth year A.H. Most of them; however, agree that it took place in the same year as the Ḥudaybiyah pact. The purpose of the prohibition of alcohol was purely a social one, unrelated to the unity of God as a purely theological doctrine. The evidence for this is the fact that the Qur'ān remained silent on this problem for a period of approximately twenty years after Muḥammad's commission to prophethood. Throughout this period, the Muslims continued to use alcohol. Further evidence to this effect comes from the fact that the prohibition itself was not categorically laid down all at once, but was revealed progressively and at intervals. There was a series of prohibitions, each prescribing a limitative measure of use. Total abstinence was not demanded until near the end of the Madīnese period of the revelation. It is told that 'Umar ibn al Khaṭṭāb inquired about the drinking of wine and prayed for God to show the Muslims His will in this regard, and that it was in this connection that the verse was revealed saying, "When they ask you about drinking wine and gambling, answer that they constitute great evil as well as advantage to the people but that their evil is greater than their good."[2] Despite the indication this verse gave, the Muslims who were in the habit of drinking did not stop. Some of them in a state of drunkenness would pray without knowing what they were reciting. Again 'Umar prayed God to show more of His will in this matter. The common Arabic saying, "Alcohol causes the loss of both mind and money," is attributed by tradition to him. Later, another step toward prohibition was taken with the following revelation: "O Men who believe, do not hold the prayers while you are in a state of drunkenness. Recover yourselves first until you become fully conscious of what you are about to recite."[3] From that day on, the town crier of the Prophet proclaimed at the times of prayer: "Let no drunken

man come to prayer." Despite this new limitation upon alcohol,
'Umar continued to pray to God to send down yet clearer
revelation concerning it. Personally, 'Umar was quite opposed
to alcohol because the Arabs often drank to the point of losing
decorum, pulling one another's beards and hitting one another.
It so happened that at a banquet which included Muhājirūn
and Anṣār, a member of the former group boasted of his peoples'
superiority over the latter group. A member of al Ansār, equally
intoxicated, wounded the former in the nose by hitting him with
a skull bone. Under the influence of liquor, the two groups
quarrelled, fought, and generated all kinds of hatred toward one
another until they almost destroyed their previous harmony
and mutual esteem. On this occasion, God said in a special
revelation:

يَٰٓأَيُّهَا ٱلَّذِينَ ءَامَنُوٓا۟ إِنَّمَا ٱلْخَمْرُ وَٱلْمَيْسِرُ وَٱلْأَنصَابُ وَٱلْأَزْلَٰمُ رِجْسٌ مِّنْ عَمَلِ ٱلشَّيْطَٰنِ
فَٱجْتَنِبُوهُ لَعَلَّكُمْ تُفْلِحُونَ ۝ إِنَّمَا يُرِيدُ ٱلشَّيْطَٰنُ أَن يُوقِعَ بَيْنَكُمُ ٱلْعَدَٰوَةَ وَٱلْبَغْضَآءَ فِى
ٱلْخَمْرِ وَٱلْمَيْسِرِ وَيَصُدَّكُمْ عَن ذِكْرِ ٱللَّهِ وَعَنِ ٱلصَّلَوٰةِ فَهَلْ أَنتُم مُّنتَهُونَ ۝

"O men who believe, alcohol, gambling, idols, and divination arrows are an abominition of Satan's handiwork. Avoid them, therefore, that you may be felicitous. Satan wishes to infuse enmity
and hatred among you through alcohol and gambling. He wishes
to keep you intoxicated that you may not remember God, and
hence fail to hold prayer. Will you not listen and stop being his
tools?"[4]

On the day this revelation was made and the prohibition of alcohol
was instituted, Anas, the wine seller and server, spilled all the
alcohol in his possession. Other men who were not pleased by the
new legislation asked: "Could alcohol be a real abomination even
though it was consumed by some of the martyrs of Uḥud and
Badr?" In response to them, the following verse was revealed:
"Those who believed and did the good may not be blamed for what
they consumed, inasmuch as they feared God, believed, and did
good works. For God loves the virtuous."[5]
    By commanding mercy and compassion, the doing of good
works, disciplining the soul and character by means of worship,
and eliminating false pride by means of kneeling and prostration

in prayer, Islām became the natural perfection of all previous religions, the religion to which all men are called.

The Persian and Byzantine Empires

Heraclius and Chosroes were at the time the chiefs of the Roman and Persian empires, the greatest states of the age and the makers and arbiters of world policy and world destiny. Between them war was continual, as we have had occasion to see. The Persians were at first victorious and conquered Palestine and Egypt. They governed Jerusalem from where they moved away the cross of Christ. Later, the arm of destiny moved, and it was the Roman flag that flew over Egypt, Syria, and Palestine. Heraclius recovered the cross and put it back in its original place after a pilgrimage to Jerusalem on foot in fulfilment of a vow he had taken before victory. One can easily appreciate the position of the two empires if one remembers the tremendous fear which their very names inspired in any person who fell within their reach. Men were so awed by the two empires that no state or community could think of opposing them, and every man kept on good terms with their authorities and representatives as essential to survival. Since the world of the time was one divided between the spheres of influence of these two giants, it was natural for the Arabian Peninsula to fall within the one or the other. 'Irāq was under Persia while Egypt and al Shām were under the influence of Rome. Ḥijāz and the entire remainder of the Arabian Peninsula were divided between the two. Whatever prosperity the Arabs enjoyed depended wholly upon trade between Yaman and al Shām. It was absolutely essential, therefore, that the Arabs enjoy the friendship of Khosrau as well as of Heraclius if their trade was to be successful. The Arab population consisted of tribes, sometimes mutually hostile, sometimes peaceful, but never related to one another by a bond constituting a political structure capable of counteracting the influence of either of the two great powers. It was hence amazing that Muḥammad would think of sending his messengers to the two great kings, as well as to Ghassān and Yaman, to Egypt and Abyssinia, and to call them all to his religion without fear of the consequences of such deeds for the Arabian Peninsula as a whole, or without fear that Roman and Persian influence in Arabia might actually be transformed into a solid yoke of subjugation.

The Prophet's Delegates

Muhammad, however, did not hesitate to call all these men to the religion of truth. One day, addressing his companions, Muhammad said: "O men, God has sent me to be a Prophet of mercy to all mankind. Do not, therefore, disagree and divide as the disciples of Jesus, son of Mary, did after him." When his companions asked him to explain, he replied: "Jesus had called his disciples to the same truth to which I have called you. Those of them whom he sent to places close by accepted and observed the truth that Jesus had conveyed; those whom he sent to faraway places did not like that truth and could not accept it." Muhammad mentioned to them that he was planning to send messengers to Heraclius, the Archbishop of Alexandria; to al Harith of Ghassan, King of al Hirah; to al Harith of Himyar, King of Yaman; and to the Negus of Abyssinia, calling them all to Islam. The companions approved and made for him a seal out of silver which read "Muhammad, the Prophet of God." Muhammad sent letters to these chiefs, an example of which is the message sent to Heraclius. It read as follows: "In the name of God, the Merciful, the Compassionate. From Muhammad ibn 'Abdullah to Heraclius, Emperor of Byzantium. Peace be upon the rightly guided. I call you to the religion of Islam. If you convert, you will be saved and God will double your reward. If you do not convert, responsibility for the salvation of your subjects rests with you.[6] 'O People of the Book, come now to a fair principle, common to both of us, namely, that we worship only God, that we do not associate aught with Him and that we do not take one another as lords besides God. But if they refuse, then say, "Take note that we are Muslims." ' " The Prophet gave this message to Dihyah ibn Khalifah al Kalbi and asked him to convey it to Heraclius. He dictated a similar letter to Chosroes and asked 'Abdullah ibn Hudhafah al Sahmi to convey it to him. Another letter addressed to the Negus was handed to 'Umar ibn Umayyah al Damri. A letter to the Archbishop of Alexandria was handed to Hatib ibn abu Balta'ah; to the King of Yamanah, to Salit ibn 'Amr; to the King of Bahrayn, to al 'Ala' ibn al Hadrami; to al Harith of Ghassan, King of the Approaches of al Sham, to Shuja' ibn Wahb al Asadi; to al Harith of Himyar, King of Yaman, to Ibn Umayyah al Makhzumi. All these men went out each to the destination assigned to him by the Prophet. Most historians affirm that they started their journeys in various directions at the same time. Some, however, assert that they were sent at different intervals.

Persia and Byzantium

That Muḥammad sent such missions to the kings of the world is truly surprising. More surprising still is the fact that within barely thirty years of the time he sent those missions, the kingdoms of these kings were conquered by the Muslims and most of their inhabitants converted to Islām. The surprise, however, is dissipated when one remembers that the two great empires disputing the leadership of the world and dividing it between their two civilizations were really disputing only the material possessions of the world. In both of them, spiritual power had long been decaying. Persia, for its part, was divided between paganism and Zoroastrianism. The Christianity of Byzantium, on the other hand, was rife with dispute and controversy between various sects. There was no single conviction, neither faith nor world view, to inspire the hearts and satisfy the minds of the people. Rather, religion had become a series of rites and superstitions by which the Church was exercising its control and exploitation of the masses of mankind. As for the new call of Muḥammad, it was purely spiritual, raising man to the highest levels of his humanity. Wherever matter contends with spirit, wherever care for the present contends with the hope for eternity, matter and concern for the present are sure to lose.

Furthermore, despite their greatness, both Persia and Byzantium had lost the power of initiative, creativity, and culture-building. In thought, feeling and action, the two empires had declined to the level of ancestor-imitation where every novelty was looked upon as misguidance and abomination. But human society, like individual men and all living organisms, must renew itself every day. Either it remains youthful renewing itself, recreating, reconstructing, and always adding to its life, or it reaches old age and, being incapable of recreation and reconstruction, spends its own life-capital. Its ensuing history is a continuing reduction and downfall toward a tragic end. Any human society which has thus fallen is susceptible to renewal and recreation by another society youthful enough to instill new life into anything it touches. Such a new element, full of life power and youth and growing in close proximity to Persia and Byzantium was Muḥammad. His mission was so new and vigorous that it breathed new life into the masses of mankind whose spirit had been destroyed internally by the vacuitous rites and superstitions of the decaying societies in the great empires. The fire of the new faith which illumined the soul of the Prophet and the indomitable power of his soul explain the fact of his calling the kings of the earth to Islām, the religion of truth and perfection, the religion of God—May He be revered! The great kings were called to the religion which liberated the mind to reason and the heart to see for itself. Islām was the religion which gave man, whether in the life of worship or in the ordering of society, general principles which harmonized the powers of spirit and matter and made possible the highest levels of life on earth. Where such harmony prevails, there is neither weakness nor false pride. After going through all the stages of necessary development, human society can reach the highest possible level of existence designed for it.

Elimination of Jewish Influence in Arabia

But would Muḥammad send his missions to the foreign kings while his own domain was threatened by the treacherous Jews who were still living to the north of Madīnah? It is true that the Treaty of Ḥudaybiyah had secured his southern flank, especially from Quraysh. But what about the north, where both Heraclius and Chosroes might attack Madīnah in cooperation with the Jews of Khaybar who were anxious for an opportunity to take revenge upon Muḥammad? It would be relatively easy for either emperor to remind the Jews of the fate of their coreligionists, the Banū Qurayẓah, Banū al Naḍīr, and Banū Qaynuqāʿ, who had previously been expelled from their dwellings after blockade, fighting, and war, and to incite them to new ventures against Muḥammad. For their enmity and bitterness surpassed that of Quraysh. They were more attached to their religion, more intelligent, and more learned. On the other hand, it was not possible to reconcile them with a peace treaty like that of Ḥudaybiyah since the covenant of Madīnah had been violated by them much to their own detriment. Were help to come to them from the side of Byzantium, their natural inclination to rise again against Muḥammad could not be contained. Hence, it was thought necessary to put a final end to their influence in the Arabian Peninsula, and to do so quickly without giving them

the time to forge any new alliances with Ghaṭafān or any of
other tribe hostile to Muḥammad.

And such Muḥammad did. He had hardly spent fifteen days
after his return from al Ḥudaybiyah—a month according to
another version—when he commanded the people to prepare for
the campaign of Khaybar, restricting the call to arms to those
who had accompanied him to al Ḥudaybiyah. His purpose was
to leave behind all those interested in booty, and to go out with
the truly loyal followers who sought service for the sake of God.
The Muslims marched forth one thousand and six hundred strong,
including a cavalry of one hundred. They were confident of God's
assistance and victory, and recalled *sūrah* "al Fatḥ" which was
revealed shortly after the signing of the Ḥudaybiyah treaty:
"When you go forth and booty lies ahead of you, those who
remained behind and did not participate in the previous campaign
will ask to accompany you that they might share in the spoils.
Thus they seek to change the decrees of God. Say to them, 'It is
not given to you to accompany us, for that is the decree of God
which has been given.' They will accuse you of jealousy and
envy, but their understanding is meager and their intelligence
is dim."[7]

The March against Khaybar

Muḥammad and his men crossed the distance between Khaybar
and Madīnah in three days. Khaybar did not learn of their move
until the Muslims' forces stood in front of their fortifications.
In the morning, when the Khaybar workmen went out of their
homes to go to their plantations, they saw the Muslim army
for the first time and ran away shouting to one another, "There
is Muḥammad and his army." When Muḥammad heard them,
he said: "Khaybar is doomed; whenever we enter the enemy's
land, the fate of that enemy is sealed."

Jewish Reaction

Nonetheless, the Jews of Khaybar did in fact anticipate
Muḥammad's move and thought of ways and means of escape.
Some leaders advised Khaybar to form a block with the Jews
of Wādī al Qurā and Taymā' and to take the initiative in
attacking Madīnah first. This group saw no point in depending

upon Arab tribes. Other leaders advised that it was more
salutary for them to enter into a new pact with the Prophet
in order to mitigate Muslim hatred and hostility, especially among
al Ansār. This suggestion was particularly appealing after the
experience in Madīnah, when Ḥuyayy ibn Akhṭab and his party
had instigated the Arab tribes to attack Madīnah and sack its
fortification in the Campaign of al Khandaq. The truth is, however, that neither Jews nor Muslims were ready for any conciliation, especially since the Muslims had killed Sallām ibn Abū
al Ḥuqayq and al Yasīr ibn Razzām, two Khaybar chieftains,
before venturing out on their present expedition against Khaybar.
As a consequence, the Jews were constantly in touch with the
tribe of Ghaṭafān and sent to them for help as soon as they
discovered Muḥammad's army in their domain. Historians differ
regarding Ghaṭafān's answer to Khaybar's call, whether they
actually did come to Khaybar's rescue or whether the Muslim
army prevented any such assistance from reaching Khaybar.

The Two Armies

Regardless of whether Ghaṭafān had actually helped the Jews
or not, it soon renounced its attachment to them and became
neutral as early as Muḥammad promised it a share in the spoils
of war. The campaign of Khaybar was one of the greatest. The
masses of Jews living in Khaybar were the strongest, the
richest, and the best equipped for war of all the peoples of
Arabia. The Muslims, for their part, were certain that as long
as the Jews held any power in the Peninsula, the two religions
would have to compete with each other endlessly. That is why
they advanced so resolutely and fought so valiantly. The Quraysh
as well as the whole Arabian Peninsula watched the campaign
and awaited its results. Some Quraysh tribesmen wagered with
one another concerning its outcome; many believed that the
tables would now be turned against the Muslims, knowing how
fortified were the dwellings, how impregnable the city stood
perched over rocks and mountains, and how experienced its
people were in the arts of war.

The Muslims' Blockade

The Muslims, on the other hand, brought to Khaybar all the
equipment and preparation they could muster. After consulting

one another and listening to Sallām ibn Miskham, their chief, the Jews decided to assemble their wealth and children in the fortified quarters of al Waṭīḥ and al Sulālim, to place their ammunition at Naʻīm, and to deploy their fighting men at Naṭāt where Sallām ibn Mishkam would lead them in battle to the bitter end. The two armies met at Naṭāt and fought each other strongly. The encounter, however, was not decisive. There were fifty wounded among the Muslims on the first day and probably many more than this among the Jews. When Sallām ibn Mishkam was killed, al Ḥārith ibn Abū Zaynab took over the leadership of the Jewish forces. Charging from the fortress of Naʻīm, the new leader attacked the Muslim army at the flank, but he was soon repulsed by Banū al Khazraj, who were deployed in that area. As a result of this engagement, the Muslims tightened their encirclement of Khaybar. Realizing that this was their last stand in Arabia, the Jews fought desperately. As the days went by, the Prophet sent Abū Bakr with a contingent and a flag to the fortress of Naʻīm; but he was not able to conquer it despite heavy fighting. The Prophet then sent ʻUmar ibn al Khaṭṭāb on the following day, but he fared no better than Abū Bakr. On the third day, the Prophet called ʻAlī ibn Abū Ṭālib and, blessing him, commanded him to storm the fortress. ʻAlī led his force and fought valiantly. In the engagement, he lost his armor and, shielding himself with a portal he had seized, he continued to fight until the fortress was stormed by his troops. The same portal was used by ʻAlī as a little bridge to enable the Muslim soldiers to enter the houses within the fortress. The fortress of Naʻīm fell after the Jewish leader, al Ḥārith ibn Abū Zaynab, was killed in battle. Evidently, both Jews and Muslims were determined to fight it out to the end.

Having stormed the fortress of Naʻīm, the Muslims then directed their attention to the fortress of al Qamūs which they stormed after equally strenuous fighting. Provisions were becoming rather scarce within the Muslim army, and many began to approach Muḥammad personally to ask him for something with which to stave off their hunger. Unable to find provisions, Muḥammad permitted them to eat horse meat. Later on, a Muslim soldier noticed a herd of goats entering one of the fortifications of the Jews, launched an immediate attack, and seized two animals which were immediately killed and consumed. Not until after they had conquered the fortress of al Ṣaʻb ibn Muʻādh was their shortage relieved. For within that fortress, they found large stores of food that enabled them to continue the blockade of other fortresses. Throughout this campaign, the Jews would not give up a single inch of territory without putting up a heroic struggle for it. Whenever they retreated, it was only before preponderant Muslim forces. At one stage in the campaign, Marhab came out of one of the fortresses fully covered with his military attire and singing the following verses: "Khaybar knows that I am Marḥab, that I am an experienced hero fully prepared for war. I deal blows to my enemies and I strike them. Even the lions I face with drawn sword. The ground I hold is unassailable. Even the most experienced in war dares not approach it." Muḥammad asked his companions, "Who will rise to meet him?" Muḥammad ibn Maslamah rose and said, "Send me, O Prophet of God. For I am the angry bereaved who lost his brother yesterday." The Prophet permitted him and he sprang to meet Marhab. The pair fought valiantly and, at one stage, Marḥab almost killed the Muslim. Ibn Maslamah, however, intercepted the falling sword with his shield which bent under its weight and was cut so that the sword could not be pulled out and disengaged. Muḥammad ibn Maslamah seized the opportunity and gave Marḥab a fatal blow. This war between Muslim and Jew was a hard and savage struggle, and the fortifications of the Jews made it even more so.

Jewish Despair and Collapse

The Muslims then directed their attention to the fortress of al Zubayr and surrounded it for a long time, waging a number of harsh attacks without being able to storm it. At one stage, they seized the water supply of the fortress and stopped its flow. The Jews were forced to come out and engage the Muslims in battle but, faced with preponderant Muslim forces, they fled. Their fortresses fell one after another into Muslim hands, the last of them being those of al Watīh and al Sulālim in the al Katībah area. Only then did the Jews become truly desperate, and they begged for peace. The Prophet had already seized most of their possessions at the fortresses of al Shaqq, Naṭāt, and al Katībah. In the circumstances, they had only their own skins to seek to save. Muḥammad accepted their plea and permitted them to stay on their land whose title now passed to him by right of conquest. The terms of their surrender provided that they would be given half their crops in compensation for their labor.

The Jews of Khaybar were thus treated differently from those of Banū Qaynuqāʻ and Banū al Nadīr who were forced to evacuate their lands altogether. With the fall of Khaybar, Jewish power no more threatened Islām or the Muslims. Moreover, Khaybar had large areas of orchards and groves of date trees whose maintenance needed an experienced labor force. Although al Ansār, the Muslims of Madīnah, were agriculturalists, they were needed back home to tend their own gardens and orchards. The Prophet also needed his men for the purpose of war and could not afford to demobilize his army for the sake of agriculture. The Jews of Khaybar were hence allowed to continue to work their own groves after their political dominion had been destroyed. Despite Muhammad's sharecropping arrangement, the agricultural economy of Khaybar retrogressed after the destruction of Jewish political power. 'Abdullah ibn Rawāhah, Muhammad's deputy for the division of the Khaybar crops, dealt justly with the Jews, following in this regard the instructions of the Prophet himself. So honorable was his conduct that he returned to them copies of the Torah seized by the Muslims in the course of the hostilities. This is in direct contrast to the manner in which the Romans treated the Jews when they conquered Jerusalem and burned all the sacred writings they found in the temple and trampled them under foot. It is also far from the Christian persecution of the Jews in Spain where every Torah seized was put to the torch.

As the Jews of Khaybar pleaded for peace while the Muslims blockaded al Watīh and al Sulālim at Khaybar, the Prophet sent a message to the Jews of Fadak asking them to surrender their properties and wealth or accept his terms. The people of Fadak were so panic-stricken at the news of Khaybar that they agreed to give up half their wealth without fighting. The wealth of Khaybar was to be distributed among the members of the Muslim armed forces according to rule because they had fought to secure it. The wealth of Fadak, on the other hand, fell to Muhammad,[8] as no Muslims and no fighting were involved in its acquisition.

The Prophet prepared to return to Madīnah by way of Wādī al Qurā where the Jews of that area prepared to fight the Muslims. Some fighting did indeed take place, but the Jews realized the futility of their resistance and pleaded for peace as Khaybar and Fadak had done before. As for the Jews of Taymā', they accepted to pay the *jizyah* without fighting. Thus, all the Jews of the Peninsula submitted to the authority of the Prophet and their political influence was brought to an end. The northern flank of Muslim power, namely the whole area north of Madīnah, was now as secure as the south had become through the Treaty of al Ḥudaybiyah. With the collapse of Jewish political power, Muslim hatred of the Jews mellowed, and this was especially true of the Ansār of Madīnah who even closed their eyes when a number of Jews returned to Madīnah to resume their normal trades and professions. Indeed, the Prophet himself sympathized with such Jewish returnees and joined with them in mourning 'Abdullah ibn Ubayy by presenting condolences to his son. Moreover, the Prophet took especial care to instruct Mu'ādh ibn Jabal not to sway the Jews from their religion but to allow them to practice it as they had done before. He did not impose any *jizyah* on the Jews of al Baḥrayn despite the conservatism of the latter and their attachment to the faith of their forefathers. The Prophet also reconciled the Jews of Banu Ghāziyah and Banū 'Arīd and offered them his covenant and protection provided they agree to pay *jizyah*. On the whole, the Jews of the Peninsula lost their political power and fell under that of the Muslims. So much had their prestige deteriorated, however, that they soon found themselves having to emigrate from a land which once felt their influence. According to some versions, this Jewish emigration took place during the lifetime of the Prophet; according to others, shortly after his death.

Jewish acquiescence in their fate under the dominion of Islām did not take place at one and the same time or immediately after their military defeat, for they were exceedingly resentful and full of hatred for their Muslim fellows. Zaynab, daughter of al Ḥārith, and wife of Sallām ibn Mishkam, cooked a goat and presented it to Muḥammad after the peace treaty with Khaybar and Jewish-Muslim relations returned to normal. Muḥammad sat down at the table with his companions to eat of this Jewish prepared food. Taking the first mouthful, he realized that the taste was strange. Bishr ibn al Barā' likewise had the same realization and could hardly swallow the first mouthful. As he threw his away, the Prophet said: "I have a premonition that this dish is poisoned." He then called Zaynab and questioned her, and she confessed. In defense of herself, she said to the Prophet: "You know what has befallen my people at your hand, and you can appreciate my resentment and hatred. In pondering the whole event, I arrived at the conclusion that if you, the source of all the evil, were a king like other kings, then to put an end to your life would bring peace to me and my people. If, on the other hand, you are a true prophet, then surely you would find out that the food was poisoned and you would not eat." The one mouthful which Bishr ate was fatal to him. The chroniclers disagree regarding the fate of Zaynab. Most of them agree that the Prophet appreciated her defense, forgave her, and sympathized with her loss of father and husband. Others relate that she was killed in revenge for the life of Bishr.

Muḥammad's Marriage to Ṣafiyyah

This treacherous deed of Zaynab adversely affected the attitudes of the Muslims. It destroyed whatever confidence they still had in the Jews. Indeed, it confirmed their presentiment that there could be no peace with the Jews as long as they were not finally destroyed. Ṣafiyyah, daughter of Ḥuyayy ibn Akhtab of Banū al Naḍīr, was one of the captives the Muslims had seized inside the fortresses of Khaybar. Her husband, Kinānah ibn al Rabī', was known by the Muslims to have been the guardian of all the wealth of Banū al Nadīr. When the Prophet had asked Kinānah about his treasure, the latter solemnly declared that he did not know where it was hidden. Muḥammad threatened him that in case the treasure was found hidden in his place he would be put to death. Kinānah agreed. One day when Kinānah was seen moving about an uninhabited house in the outskirts, his movement was reported to the Prophet. After the Prophet ordered the inside of the house be dug out, part of the treasure was revealed. Kinānah was killed as a result. When a companion learned of Ṣafiyyah's captivity, he approached the Prophet with the suggestion that, since she was the lady of Banū Qurayẓah and Banū al Naḍīr, she was fit to become the wife of the Prophet alone. The Prophet granted her her freedom and then married her, following the example of the great conquerors who married the daughters and wives of the kings whom they had conquered, partly in order to alleviate their tragedy and partly to preserve their dignity. Abū Ayyūb Khālid al Anṣārī, however, feared that Ṣafiyyah's tragic loss of father, husband,

and people might incite her to avenge herself against the Prophet. He therefore spent the night near Muḥammad's tent where the wedding had taken place, with sword drawn. When the morning came and the Prophet saw him in that state, he asked him for an explanation. Abū Ayyūb answered that he feared for the Prophet that this woman, who until very recently had been a non-Muslim, might attack him. The truth, however, was otherwise. Safiyyah remained loyal to Muḥammad throughout his life. In his last illness, when the Prophet was surrounded by his wives, Ṣafiyyah came forward and said: "O Prophet of God, I surely wish that that from which you suffer might be in me rather than in you." Muḥammad's wives winked at one another and the Prophet, observing their reaction, said: "Go on and wink at one another! By God, I know that Ṣafiyyah is truthful and loyal." Ṣafiyyah, who survived Muḥammad, lived until the time of the caliphate of Mu'āwiyah. She was buried at al Baqī'.

Delegation to Heraclius

Whatever happened to the messengers whom Muḥammad sent to Heraclius, Chosroes, the Negus, and other kings and men of power surrounding Arabia? Did they go forth before the Campaign of Khaybar, or did they participate in that Campaign until Muslim victory had been achieved and traveled thereafter? Historians differ so widely in this respect that it is very difficult to reach a conclusion. We are inclined to think that they did not all go forth at the same time, that some of them began their travel before the campaign of Khaybar and others thereafter. More than one chronicler has asserted that Diḥyah ibn Khalīfah al Kalbī participated in the operations at Khaybar. Yet it was he who was commissioned by the Prophet to go to Heraclius. The Prophet's messenger met Heraclius at the time of the latter's victorious return from the war with Persia and his recapture of the cross which had been taken by the Persians when they occupied Jerusalem. The vow which Heraclius had made, namely, to perform a pilgrimage to Jerusalem on foot and return the cross to its original place, could now be fulfilled. It was on this pilgrimage of Heraclius, specifically when the imperial procession had reached the city of Ḥimṣ⁹ that the message of Muḥammad was received. Whether Muḥammad's letter was handed to the Emperor by one of the latter's employees after Diḥyah surrendered it to the Byzantine governor of Boṣrā, or whether the group of Muslims headed by Diḥyah was granted a court audience at which Diḥyah submitted the Prophet's letter in person, is not known for certain. At any rate, it is known that the Prophet's letter did reach Heraclius, and that the Emperor was not irritated by it. Instead of sending an army to conquer Arabia, Heraclius did in fact send a gentle letter in reply to Muḥammad's message. It was this gentle response to Muḥammad's message that a number of historians mistook as meaning that Heraclius had joined the ranks of Islām.

At the same time, al Ḥārith of Ghassān sent to Heraclius a message to the effect that he had just received a letter from Muḥammad, a message which Heraclius thought was similar to what he himself had received from the same source calling him to Islām. Al Ḥārith applied for permission to send an expeditionary force against this new "pretender." Heraclius saw otherwise and instructed al Ḥārith to come to Jerusalem and attend with him the ceremonies at which the cross would be reinstated. Heraclius was apparently more interested in the pomp and circumstance of those ceremonies than in the call of a new religion. He could not imagine that only a few years would pass before Jerusalem, as well as the whole of al Shām, would fall under Islāmic dominion; that the Islāmic capital would move to Damascus; that the struggle between the Islāmic state and the Byzantine Empire would not subside until the Muslims had conquered Constantinople in 1453 and converted its great church[10] into a mosque in which the name of that Prophet would be inscribed in honor; and that that same church would remain a mosque for many centuries until the Muslim Turks would change it into a museum of Byzantine art in modern times. Such was to be the influence of this Prophet whose message Heraclius did not think sufficiently worthy to deserve attention.

Delegation to Chosroes

As soon as the message of Muḥammad was read out to Chosroes, the Emperor of Persia, he went into a rage, destroyed the letter, and dictated an order to his satrap in Yaman commanding him to send forth to the capital the head of his Prophet-pretender in al Ḥijāz. Perhaps he was moved to such a decision out of a need for self-assertion following his defeat by Heraclius. When the Prophet heard of Chosroes's response, he cursed him

as well as his empire. Bāzān, the satrap of Yaman, sent his
messengers in search of Muhammad, in compliance with the
command of his emperor. In the meanwhile, however, Chosroes
passed away, and his son, Cyrus, ascended the throne. Knowing
the news of the accession, the Prophet informed the messengers
of Bāzān and asked them to carry his call to Islām to Bāzān
rather than carry out Bāzān's instructions. The people of Yaman
had learned of the defeat of Persia and realized that Persian
dominion was on the decline and would soon pass away. They
had heard, also, of the victories Muhammad had scored over
Quraysh and of his total destruction of Jewish power and
dominion. When Bāzān's messengers returned and told their
master of Muhammad's response, he immediately converted to
Islām and accepted Muhammad's appointment as governor of
Yaman. But what would Muhammad require of Bāzān, as long
as enemy Makkah separated the two? Since he did not have
much to fear, but rather everything to gain because Persian
dominion was on the wane, and because the new power rising on
the horizon of the Peninsula could, in fact, demand of him no
price in return, Bāzān preferred to enter into friendly relations
with Muhammad. Possibly, Bāzān did not quite appreciate the
fact that his joining the ranks of Islām gave the latter a very
viable *point d'appui* in the south corner of the Peninsula, as
events were to show two years later.

Delegation to the Archbishop of Egypt

The Coptic Archbishop of Egypt answered in a radically
different way from his superior Heraclius, or from Chosroes.
He informed Muhammad of his belief that a Prophet was indeed
to appear in the world, but in al Shām. He accorded to Muhammad's messenger a good reception and sent with him a gift
to the Prophet consisting of two slave girls, a white mule, a
donkey, some money, and a variety of Egyptian products. The
two slave girls were Māriyyah, whom Muhammad took in
marriage and who gave birth to Ibrāhīm, and Sīrīn, who was
given in marriage to Hassān ibn Thābit. The mule was given by
the Prophet the name of Duldul, for its unique whiteness of
skin which the Arabian Peninsula had never seen before. The
donkey was called 'Ufayr or Ya'fūr. The Archbishop explained
that he did not convert to Islām because of his fear of discharge

by his superior, and that were he not a man of authority and power, he would have been rightly guided to the true faith.

Delegation to Abyssinia

It was natural that the answer of the Negus of Abyssinia was favorable, for his country had always been on good terms with the Muslims. Indeed, some historians assert that the Negus was converted to Islām—a claim which the Orientalists suspect very strongly. The Prophet sent to the Negus a second letter asking him to send back the Muslims who had been living in Abyssinia under his protection. The Negus provided these Muslims with two ships that carried them to the shore of Arabia. They were led by Ja'far ibn Abū Ṭālib, and the group included Umm Ḥabibah, Ramlah, daughter of Abū Sufyān and wife of 'Abdullah ibn Jaḥsh who went to Abyssinia as a Muslim, converted to Christianity and died there a Christian. Following her return from Abyssinia, the same Umm Ḥabibah became one of the wives of the Prophet, a "Mother of the Believers." Some historians asserted that the Prophet married her in order to forge a blood relation with the house of Abū Sufyān and to confirm thereby the Treaty of al Ḥudaybiyah. Other historians saw in the marriage of Umm Ḥabibah to Muḥammad an attempt on the part of the latter to punish and annoy Abū Sufyān who was still a pagan.

Explanation to the Kings' Replies

Finally, as for the princes of Arab tribes and regions, it should be recorded that the Amīr of Yaman and 'Umān sent the Prophet a very antagonistic answer. The Amīr of al Baḥrayn sent a favorable reply and became a Muslim. The Amīr of al Yamāmah declared his preparation to enter into Islām if his chair and office could be secured. The Prophet cursed him for laying down conditions to his conversion, and the historians assert that the man lived but one year after the event.

The reader might well pause to consider the preponderant friendliness and appreciation which most of the kings and princes showed in response to Muḥammad's call. None of Muḥammad's messengers was killed or imprisoned. Every one of them returned to Madīnah with the response with which he had been entrusted.

Some of these messages were coarse and harsh, but most of them were gentle and sweet. Two questions naturally arise: Why did all these kings receive the new religion without seeking to destroy the man who called them to it, and why did they not unite to destroy him? The answer to these questions lies in the fact that the world of those days was, like the world of today, one in which matter had come to dominate everything, affluence and luxury had become the *summum bonum*, and nations fought and destroyed one another for the sake of power and in satisfaction of the ambitions of its king and ruling circles, or in order to increase their affluence and luxury. In such a world, faith deteriorates to mere ritual, and men perform these rituals without believing any of the truths which the rituals were meant to express. In such kingdoms, the masses seldom care but to belong to such regimes as will provide them with *panem et circencis*, with wealth and luxury. Under such circumstances, a religion is adhered to only in proportion to the material advantage its practice promises. When such advantage is not in sight, the masses of people quickly lose their attachment, and their power of resistance to another religion evaporates. That is why as soon as these masses heard the voice of the new religion with its strength and simplicity, its call to equality before the one God, the only Being worthy of worship and prayer, and the only One capable of giving true good to man, they began to thirst after the new faith and the spiritual satisfactions it provides. Verily, a ray of God's blessing dissipates the fury of all the kings of the earth combined! The fear of His wrath shakes the human soul to its very depths even though the kings of the earth might have smothered that soul in blessings and favors. The hope of God's forgiveness moves every man deprived of grace to repent, to believe and to do good works. When the people heard that the author of this new call was capable of vanquishing the enemies who persecuted him and who inflicted upon him and his followers all sorts of injustice and suffering, it was not surprising that they stretched out their necks and lent their ears to see him and hear him. For them to witness Muhammad's victory over all the material forces assembled against him and to see his power grow despite his original weakness, poverty, and deprivation, for them to see this Prophet achieve that which no one else had ever dreamt of achieving—be it in his own town or throughout the Arabian Peninsula—all this was enough to incite them to examine this faith and to want to belong to it. Were it not for their fear of the immediate consequences, most of them would not have kept themselves separated from the truth. Hence, the majority of the sovereigns answered with a consideration and sympathy which reinforced the Muslims' faith and conviction.

Muslim Return from Abyssinia

Muḥammad returned from Khaybar, and Ja'far and the Muslims returned from Abyssinia. The messengers of Muḥammad returned from those lands whither Muḥammad had sent them. All of them met again and were reunited in Madīnah. Inspiring each of them was the longing to go to Makkah in the following year and to do so in security, with shaven heads or short hair, and to perform their pilgrimage without fear. Muḥammad was so pleased to be reunited with Ja'far that he said he could not tell which was the greater: victory over Khaybar or reunion with Ja'far. It was in this period that, according to a certain report, a Jew called Labīd charmed Muḥammad and put him under a spell. The report is self-contradictory and highly questionable. The claim that Muḥammad did anything at any time without consciousness or under a spell is a sheer fabrication and hence devoid of truth.

The Muslims were safe in Madīnah where they led a prosperous and affluent life. During this period they thought neither of war nor of fighting despite the fact that they had to send some expeditionary forces to punish those who aggressed upon their lands or seized any of their property. As the year[11] came to a close, in the month of Dhū al Qi'dah, the Prophet set out with two thousand men to perform the lesser pilgrimage, in accordance with the provisions of the Ḥudaybiyah Treaty, and to satisfy the Muslim longing to visit the holy sanctuary and to perform the holy ritual.

22

The 'Umrah or Lesser Pilgrimage

The Muslims' March to Makkah

A full year had passed since the Treaty of al Ḥudaybiyah. Muḥammad and his companions were accordingly free to enter Makkah and to visit the Ka'bah under the terms of that treaty. The Prophet, therefore, proclaimed to the people that they might now prepare themselves to go to Makkah for performance of the lesser pilgrimage. It is easy to appreciate the enthusiasm of the Muslims in response to Muḥammad's call. Many among them, the Muhājirūn, were emigrants from Makkah who had left their hometown seven years ago. Others, the Ansār, conducted wide trade with Makkah and felt great love and loyalty to the holy sanctuary which they longed to visit. Those who responded to Muḥammad's call exceeded two thousand in number. Hence, there were six hundred or more than in the previous year. In compliance with the terms of the Ḥudaybiyah Treaty, none of them carried any arms except his sword which he kept in its scabbard. Muḥammad feared treachery. He therefore equipped a hundred cavalrymen and assigned them to Muḥammad ibn Maslamah. He instructed them to reconnoiter the fields ahead of the procession of Muslims but not to tread on the holy ground surrounding Makkah. His order was that they should turn to a nearby valley as soon as they reached the canyon of al Zahrān. The Muslims herded before them the sacrificial animals; the entire procession was led by Muḥammad riding his she-camel, al Qaṣwā'. They set out from Madīnah in the direction of Makkah moved by the strongest emotion to circumambulate the House of God and to see the places where they were born. Each longed to visit the house and quarter where he had grown up and played as a child. They were quite anxious to visit their old friends whom they had had no opportunity to see during those long years, and, in short, to breathe the air of their dear homeland. The non-Makkan Muslims were equally anxious to see and touch this blessed holy city which had brought out the Prophet of God and in which the revelation of God was first heard. One can imagine this great procession of Muslims numbering over two thousand, pushing forward toward Makkah with their hearts practically leaping out of their breasts in exaltation and reverence. At every opportunity, a pilgrim would tell his companion what he knew of Makkah and would recall nostalgically the days of his childhood or youth in that city. He would tell about his friends that were still there and the wealth and property which he had abandoned for the sake of God when he left it. One can imagine this unique procession animated by faith, indeed bursting with religious enthusiasm, pulling forward toward the universally revered sanctuary. The reader may well imagine the jubilation of this procession of men who for the last seven years had been prevented from performing this sacred duty but who were now certain they could enter Makkah in peace, with shaven head or cut hair, for an opportunity to re-express their loyalty to God.

The Quraysh Evacuate the City

The Quraysh learned of the arrival of Muḥammad and his companions, and they evacuated the whole town as the treaty demanded. They removed themselves with their families to the hills surrounding Makkah where they erected tents for this purpose. Those who could not afford tents spent the time in the shade of trees. From the mountains of Abū Qubays and Ḥirā' as well as from every mound or hill surrounding Makkah, the Makkans looked down upon their city which appeared to be invaded by this "refugee" and his companions. The Muslims entered the city without resistance, indeed without meeting any Makkans at all, and they poured into the sanctuary. They entered from the north led by Muḥammad on the back of al Qaṣwā' whose reins were held by 'Abdullah ibn Rawāhah. The Prophet

was surrounded by his elder companions, and behind him followed the rank and file of Muslims, whether mounted or on
foot. When the Holy house came into view, every Muslim tongue
was loosened with a single call: "At Your command, O Lord!
At Your command, O Lord!" Their hearts and souls were totally
turned to God, the Lord of Majesty.

Circumambulation of the Sacred House

In surrounding the Prophet the multitudes expressed their
hope and reverence to the man whom God had sent to convey
His guidance and true religion and whom He promised to vindicate against the adherents of all other religions. In truth, it
must have been a unique and truly great spectacle, defying
history itself. Upon witnessing it, even those most obstinate in
their paganism or hostility to Islām were softened and even
attracted to the new faith. Such a spectacle simply mesmerized
the Makkans. The voice of the Muslims calling, "At your
command, O Lord!" rocked the horizon as well as their ears
and hearts. When the Prophet reached the Ka'bah he wrapped
his mantle under his right arm, baring his shoulder and praying,
"O God, have mercy on anyone performing this rite today and
showing the enemy a side of his spiritual strength!" He then
stopped near the black stone to begin circumambulation of the
House. Followed by his companions and going at a trotting pace,
Muhammad circumambulated the holy shrine three times, paus-
ing whenever he reached the black stone at each turn. The
Muslims, all two thousand of them, followed Muhammad in
every move while the Quraysh were looking upon them from the
height of Abū Qubays. Undoubtedly, the Quraysh were stupefied
by what they saw. Every notion they previously entertained of
the Muslims' weakness, exhaustion, and moral bankruptcy was
shattered. In the enthusiasm of the moment, 'Abdullah ibn
Rawāhah wanted to challenge the Quraysh by shouting a war
cry at them. But he was stopped by 'Umar. The Prophet then
advised him to recite the following prayer instead: "There is
no God but God alone. He is always true to His word. He it is
Who gave victory to His servant, Who reinforced His army, Who
defeated all the allies assembled against His people." Ibn
Rawāhah recited this prayer at the top of his voice, and the
Muslims, in repeating these words after him rocked the horizons

thereby and inspired terror in the hearts of all the spectators of this ritual.

The Muslims' Sojourn in Makkah

When the Muslims completed their circumambulation of the Ka'bah, Muḥammad led them toward al Ṣafā and al Marwah.[1] There, he covered the distance between the two hills seven times mounted on his camel, just as the Arabs used to do, and then proceeded to slaughter the sacrificial animals at al Marwah. He then shaved his head and thereby completed the duty of the *'umrah* or lesser pilgrimage. On the morrow, Muḥammad entered into the Ka'bah and there remained until noon. Despite the fact that the Ka'bah was still full of idols, Bilāl ascended to its top, gave the call to the noon prayer and, led by the Prophet, the two thousand Muslims held the noon prayer around the Holy House. It should be remembered that for seven years the Muslims had been prevented from performing their religious functions in the sanctuary. The Muslims remained in Makkah three whole days as the Treaty of Ḥudaybiyah prescribed, and during these days, not a Makkan remained in town or came to it. The Muslims roamed throught the city without suffering any harm or being obstructed by anyone. The Muhājirūn among them visited their old houses, showing them to their Madīnese companions, the Anṣār, and generally behaving as if they were the real hosts to them. Everyone, by complying with every function Islām prescribed for the day, deepened his Islāmic awareness and effaced every trace of pre-Islāmic vanity. The Muslims were charitable to one another, the strong among them helping the weak, the rich giving to the poor, and the Prophet moving among them as a loving and beloved father, meeting the smile of the one, reconciling the other, and teaching the truth to all. The Quraysh and all other Makkans, looking down from their tents on the mountains, pondered the behavior of the Muslims. They observed that the Muslims were extremely good to one another, that they displayed exemplary nobility and morality, never touching intoxicating drink, neither doing evil nor allowing food, drink, or treasure ever to tempt them. They could not be seen disobeying God's commandments even once. What effect did such a spectacle have on the Makkans? What could they think of this new religion which raised man to the

greatest heights of spirituality and virtue possible? It is easy
for the reader to appreciate the awe and admiration for Islām
all this inspired. Only a few months later, Muhammad returned
at the head of an army of ten thousand Muslims; but Makkah
opened its gates without a struggle.

Muhammad's Marriage to Maymūnah

Umm al Fadl, the wife of al 'Abbās ibn 'Abd al Muttalib, the
uncle of the Prophet, had been asked by her sister Maymūnah
to be her agent in seeking a husband. Maymūnah was twenty-six
years old, and she was the aunt of Khālid ibn al Walīd. Umm
al Fadl delegated her function to her husband al 'Abbās. When
Maymūnah saw the Muslims performing the 'umrah, she was
attracted to Islām and permitted al 'Abbās to talk to Muhammad,
his nephew, on the subject of marrying her. Muhammad agreed
and offered her four hundred Dirhams in dowry. In the meantime, the three days prescribed by the pact of al Hudaybiyah
had passed. Muhammad sought to make of his marriage to
Maymūnah an occasion to consolidate the mutual understanding
between him and the Quraysh which the Hudaybiyah Treaty had
brought about. When Suhayl ibn 'Amr and Huwaytib ibn 'Abd
al 'Uzzā, delegates of the Quraysh, came to Muhammad and asked
him to leave the city because the time allowed by the treaty had
expired, Muhammad asked them that his marriage be performed
in Makkah, and invited Quraysh to attend both the ceremony
and the banquet which the Muslims would prepare for the
occasion. Muhammad issued this invitation to them knowing
very well the powerful reconciliatory effect his performance of
the pilgrimage ritual had had on the hearts of the Quraysh.
The Prophet sought to further this feeling by having them
participate in a joyous occasion, one which would undoubtedly
furnish the Makkans with further evidence of Muhammad's
sincerity and love of peace. He had hoped that if he could talk
to them leisurely and in an atmosphere such as a wedding ceremony and banquet would provide, he could further allay their
fears and, perhaps, Makkah would then open its gate and heart
freely to its Muslim children. That was precisely what Suhayl
and Huwaytib feared in Muhammad's invitation. Hence, they
answered: "No, we do not need your food. Please evacuate our
city forthwith." Muhammad did not hesitate to comply with
their request because it complied with the terms of the Treaty,

and he called his men to prepare for withdrawal to Madīnah. He led the exodus of the Muslims out of Makkah, leaving behind him his client Abū Rāfi' to take care of Maymūnah and to accompany her on her trip northwards. Maymūnah joined the Muslim group at Sarif outside of Makkah, where Muḥammad married her. Maymūnah hence became a "Mother of the Believers," and the last wife of the Prophet. She survived him by fifty years, and before she died she asked to be buried at the site of her wedding. Muḥammad took under his care the two sisters of Maymūnah, namely Salmā, widow of his uncle Ḥamzah, and 'Imārah al Bikr, who never married.

Conversion of Khālid ibn al Walīd and Others

The Muslims returned to their residence in Madīnah. Muḥammad did not doubt that the pilgrimage which he and his companions had just performed had made the greatest possible favorable effect upon the Quraysh and all the Makkans. The subsequent days proved Muḥammad's expectations. Indeed, as soon as the Muslims had left Makkah, Khālid ibn al Walīd, the greatest soldier of the Quraysh and the hero of the Battle of Uḥud, said to his fellow Makkans: "It has become absolutely clear to any person with the least intelligence that Muḥammad is neither a poet possessed nor a magician inspired. His words are truly the words of God, of the Lord of the Universe. It follows then that every man with common sense ought to follow him." 'Ikrimah ibn Abū Jahl was alarmed when he heard Khālid say this and said to him in reply: "O Khālid, you have been brainwashed." Khālid answered, "Neither brainwashed nor intoxicated, but simply Islāmized." 'Ikrimah said: "By God, if any man in Quraysh ought not to say what you have just said, it is you." Khālid asked, "Why?" and 'Ikrimah answered: "Because Muḥammad stained your father's honor when he wounded him and when he killed your uncle and his son in the Battle of Badr. By God, I will never allow myself to be Islāmized, nor will I ever allow myself to say such words as you did. Don't you see that the Quraysh are all ready to fight Muḥammad?" To this Khālid replied: "All you say is ignorant, tribalistic, and shows only the prejudices of pre-Islām. But now I am a Muslim and the whole truth lies clear before my eyes." Khālid sent to the Prophet his own mares together with a message that he had accepted Islām and acknowledged Muḥammad as the Prophet of God.

When Abū Sufyān learned of the conversion of Khālid, he sent for him enquiring whether or not it was true. When Khālid answered in the affirmative, Abū Sufyān flew into a rage and said: "By al Lāt and al 'Uzzā, if I were certain I heard you right, I would kill you before I kill Muḥammad." To which Khālid replied, "By God it is the truth, and you have heard right. Let the consequences be what they may!" Abū Sufyān rushed toward him but was stopped by 'Ikrimah who witnessed the conversation. The latter said to Abū Sufyān: "Slowly! By God I, too, would have said exactly what Khālid has just said, and would have joined his faith, had I not feared the crumbling of the Quraysh. Now, you seek to kill Khālid because of a view he has just adopted while the whole of Quraysh has invested him with leadership. I fear that hardly a season will pass before the whole of Makkah will follow their leader in his new faith." Khālid left Makkah and came to Madīnah where he joined the ranks of the Muslims.

After Khālid, 'Amr ibn al 'Āṣ and 'Uthmān ibn Ṭalḥah, the guardian of the Ka'bah, converted to Islām. Many Makkans followed them after hearing of their conversion to the religion of truth. With their entry, the power of Islām grew considerably and the conquest of Makkah by Muḥammad became a future certainty.

Illuminated Qur'ān dated from the late eighteenth century, Maghribī script. Museum of Dar Batha, Fez, Morocco.

23

The Campaign of Mu'tah

Skirmishes before the Campaign

Knowing that time was on his side, Muḥammad was in no hurry to conquer Makkah. The Treaty of Ḥudaybiyah was hardly more than a year old, and nothing had happened to warrant its abrogation. Being a man of his word who never failed to honor a promise, Muḥammad was satisfied to return to Madīnah and wait for his time in peace. During the few months that followed his return, a few skirmishes took place. He sent five men to Banū Sulaym for the sole purpose of teaching them Islām, and he endured their cold-blooded murder by their hosts. Only their leader managed to escape, and he did so purely accidentally. He also sent fifteen men to Dhāt al Ṭalḥ on the outskirts of al Shām in order to call its people to Islām. There, too, the messengers of Muḥammad and missionaries of the faith were put to death in cold blood. The Prophet also sent some of his men to the Banū al Layth which they successfully raided, bringing back both captives and booty. He also sent a force to punish the Banū Murrah for their previous treachery. Al Shām and the whole northern district were of particular concern to the Prophet, especially since he had already secured the south through the Treaty of Ḥudaybiyah and the conversion of the governor of Yaman. The Prophet looked upon the north as the gateway to the spread of Islām beyond the frontiers of the Arabian Peninsula. Al Shām and the adjoining territories were the first object of his mission beyond Arabia. Consequently, only a few months

after his return to Madīnah he readied an army of three thousand
fighters, some of whom had previously fought at Mu'tah, for
possible deployment in the north. According to other versions,
the number of the men involved was one or two hundred thousand.

Causes of the Campaign

Historians differ in explaining the expedition against Mu'tah.
Some give the murder of Muḥammad's companions at Dhāt al
Ṭalh as the cause. Others relate that the Prophet had sent
a messenger to the Byzantine governor of Busrā, that this messenger was killed by a tribesman of Ghassān in the name of
Heraclius, and that Muḥammad sent this force as a punitive
expedition against that governor and the empire he represented.

Just as the Treaty of Ḥudaybiyah was the forerunner of the
pilgrimage, and this in turn of the conquest of Makkah, so
was the campaign against Mu'tah an introduction to Tabūk, and
this, in turn, to the conquest of al Shām which took place shortly
after the Prophet's death. It is immaterial whether or not the
cause which led to the conquest of Mu'tah was the murder of
the Prophet's messenger to the governor of Busrā or that of
the fifteen missionaries he had sent to Dhāt al Ṭalh. The fact
is that the Prophet—May God's peace and blessing be upon him
—called up in the month of Jumādā I of the year 8 A.H. (629 C.E.),
three thousand of his best men and appointed Zayd ibn Ḥarithah
as their leader. In the event of Zayd's fall, Ja'far ibn Abū Ṭālib
was to assume command of the army. In the event of Ja'far's
death, 'Abdullah ibn Rawāḥah was to take his place. Khālid
ibn al Walīd, the recent convert from Makkah, volunteered to
join this expedition in order to prove his loyalty to the new
faith. The people of Madīnah bid the army farewell, and Muhammad saw them off at the outskirts of the city. He commanded
them not to kill any women, children, or invalids, and not to
destroy either houses or trees. Together with his companions,
he prayed for them: "May God be with you! May He shield
you with His protection, and may He bring you back to us
safe, sound, and victorious." Most of the leaders of this army
thought to surprise their enemy, as the Prophet had done on
previous occasions, and thus to achieve a quick victory and
return home with the spoils of war. They advanced till they
reached Ma'ān in the territory of al Shām without knowing
what lay ahead of them.

Byzantine Mobilization

However, the news of their march preceded them. Shuraḥbīl, Heraclius's commissioner in al Shām, mobilized all the tribes around him and sent word to Heraclius asking for more Greek and Arab armies. Some historians assert that Heraclius himself came over with his armies and camped in Ma'āb [Moab], in al Balqā', with one hundred thousand Byzantine soldiers. They also relate that another hundred thousand men joined his main force from Lakhm, Judham, al Qayn, Bahrā', and Baliyy. It is also related that Theodorus, Heraclius's brother, rather than Heraclius himself, was the leader of this army. While the Muslims were at Ma'ān, they heard of this mobilization, and for two days and nights they did not know what to do. One of them advised that a message be sent to the Prophet—May God's peace and blessing be upon him—informing him of the force of the enemy and asking him for more men or for other orders. This counsel was about to receive unanimous approval when 'Abdullah ibn Rawāḥah, who was as proud and chivalrous as he was eloquent in poetry, rose and said: "O people! By God, that which you fear might happen to you is precisely why you came here— namely, martyrdom. We Muslims do not fight either with numbers, physical strength, or material equipment. Our only power lies in this religion which God has been gracious enough to give to us. Rise to battle and march forward! One of the two greatest blessings must befall you: either victory or martyrdom." The bravery of this eloquent poet was contagious, and soon the whole army reverberated with the same war cry. Everybody approved of ibn Rawāḥah's counsel. They marched forward toward al Balqā' and a village called Mashārif, where the Byzantine armies were encamped. When the enemy attacked, the Muslims withdrew to the village of Mu'tah which presented to them strategic advantages, and they fortified their position. It was there that the battle was fought by three thousand Muslims against some one or two hundred thousand of the enemy.

Fall of the Martyrs

The majesty of religious conviction! The sublimity of the strength of faith! Zayd ibn Ḥārithah raised the banner of the Prophet and marched forward toward the enemy. He plunged deep into their ranks fully certain of the death that awaited

him. But to die under such conditions is precisely to fall a martyr
in the cause of God. Martyrdom is not one whit lesser a blessed
fate than victory. Zayd fought desperately until he was torn
apart by enemy arrows. Ja'far ibn Abū Tālib, then a brave man
of thirty-three, picked up the Prophet's banner and fought
valiantly until his horse was completely surrounded by enemy
soldiers. When his horse fell under him, he pressed ever forward
on foot to cut the enemy ranks down with the sword. He was carrying the banner in his right hand. When it was cut off, he picked
up the banner with his left; and when he lost his left hand, he
kept the banner high by pressing 'it between his legs until he
died. It is related that a Byzantine soldier struck him with his
sword and cut him in two. At the death of Ja'far, Ibn Rawāhah
seized the Prophet's banner, mounted on his mare but hesitated
to advance toward the enemy's lines. His mind being braver
than his will, he composed the following verses to encourage
himself: "O Soul, I have sworn that you will fight in battle
deliberately, or that I shall force you to fight. When people
assemble and shout the war cry, why do you not advance with
them? Or do you hate to enter Paradise?" Aroused by his own
eloquence, he drew his sword, plunged into the thick of battle
and fought valiantly until he died.

The three commanders, Zayd, Ja'far, and ibn Rawāhah, all
fell as martyrs in the cause of God in the first engagement. When
the Prophet learned of their death, he was extremely sad. He
said of them that they were lifted to Paradise on thrones of
pure gold, just as men see in their dreams. He pointed out that
in his vision of the three martyrs, he noticed the throne of
'Abdullah ibn Rawāhah hovering in the heights and not rising
as rapidly as the other two; upon enquiry he was told that the
other two advanced straight forward whereas 'Abdullah hesitated. What sound advice and good counsel the Prophet meant
to give! Surely, he meant to impress upon the Muslims that the
believer should not hesitate or fear to die in the cause of God,
but rather he should carry his life on his palm ever ready
to lay it down when he marches forward in the cause of God
and homeland. He should firmly realize that his fate is either
to succeed and realize that cause or to fall martyr and give the
supreme example to posterity. In martyrdom lies a final and
lasting memory that one has deemed the value of life to be
wholly in that for which the sacrifice had taken place; that

tenacity to life in humiliation and subjection is indeed a betrayal and destruction of life. To hold the contrary is, in fact, to lose the right to be counted among the living. Likewise, the man who exposes himself to the danger of death but does so for a mean cause; or saves his life from the danger of death when God, the Lord of Majesty, calls upon him to lay down that life in the cause of truth, has already met his death—but in ignominy. If the slight hesitation of ibn Rawāḥah merited for him a place inferior to that of Zayd and Ja'far despite the fact that he still fought and laid down his life as a martyr; if, in short, he was unworthy of the reward of those who plunge into the thick of battle and fly to martyrdom with joy, what would be the fate of one who retraced his steps and withdrew altogether in order to save his life or to attain the advantage of wealth or glory? His is surely the fate of a miserable insect, no matter how great his glory among the multitudes, or how abundant his wealth. Is the human soul capable of any joy greater than that which sacrifice for the sake of conviction brings? Is man capable of any nobler fate than that of martyrdom in the cause of truth?

Ibn al Walīd's Strategy

Upon the death of ibn Rawāhah, Thābit ibn Arqam, a tribesman of Banū 'Ajlān, picked up the Prophet's banner and asked the Muslims to appoint a leader. Many nominated him, but he declined. The people then asked Khālid ibn al Walīd to assume command. Khālid accepted despite the disintegration of Muslim power and the disorganization of their ranks. Making full use of his great military experience and unique wisdom and foresight in battle, he first commanded the Muslims to reorganize their ranks and recoup their forces. He allowed only skirmishes with the enemy in order to gain time. Soon night came and the two armies disengaged until the following morning. During the night, Khālid carefully laid out his plan. He sent a number of men toward the rear deploying them in such a way as to give the impression the next morning that massive reinforcements from Madīnah were arriving to join the battle. The ruse worked. Recalling their losses and the Muslims' fierce acts of war on the previous day, the Byzantines decided to abandon the battlefield. The Muslims, pleased by the withdrawal of the enemy, withdrew toward Madīnah. It was a battle in which the Muslims were not victorious. Neither did they lose.

Muslim Disappointment and Muhammad's Assurance

As soon as Khālid and the army reached Madīnah, Muhammad and the Muslims went out to meet them, Muhammad carrying on his arm 'Abdullah, the son of Ja'far, the second commander of the Muslim force. Upon learning of the news, the people flung dust in the face of the Muslim soldiers and accused them of fleeing in the face of the enemy and abandoning the cause of God. The Prophet of God argued with his people that the soldiers did not flee but simply withdrew in order, with God's will, to advance again. Despite this justification on the part of Muhammad of the Muslim army, the people were not willing to forgive them their withdrawal and return. Salāmah ibn Hishām, a member of this expedition, would neither go to the mosque for prayer nor show himself in public in order to avoid being chastized for fleeing from the cause of God. Were it not for the fact that these same men, especially Khālid ibn al Walīd, later distinguished themselves in battle against the same enemy, their reputations would have remained forever stained.

Muhammad was deeply saddened by the death of Zayd and Ja'far. After hearing the sad news, he went to the latter's house where his wife, Asmā', daughter of 'Umays, had baked her bread, washed and dressed up her children, and awaited the return of her husband. The Prophet embraced Ja'far's children and cried. Asmā' immediately grasped what the Prophet was about to say to her and said: "O Prophet of God, woe to me if you should cry! Have you heard any news about Ja'far and his companions?" The Prophet answered: "Yes indeed, and they have fallen this very day." The Prophet cried and sobbed and Asmā' began to cry and shout in mourning. Before leaving the house, Muhammad commanded the people who assembled to take care of Ja'far's family and to provide food for them. Upon meeting the daughter of his client, Zayd, he picked her up and cried on her shoulder. When those who saw them expressed astonishment, he explained to them that it was all too natural. The martyrs were not only his people, but his own personal friends.

According to one version, the remains of Ja'far were carried to Madīnah where he was buried three days after the return

of Khālid and the army. On that day, the Prophet commanded
the Muslims to stop mourning their lost ones. To reassure the
bereaved relatives, he announced that God had given Ja'far,
instead of the two arms he lost on the battlefield, two wings
with which to fly to Paradise.

The Campaign of Dhāt al Salāsil

A few weeks after the return of Khālid, Muḥammad sought to
make up the losses in Muslim prestige in the northern parts
of the Peninsula which the previous engagement with the
Byzantines had caused. He therefore commissioned 'Amr ibn
al 'Āṣ to rouse the Arabs to march against al Shām. He chose
'Amr for this task because the latter's mother belonged to one
of the northern tribes, and he hoped that 'Amr could use this
connection to facilitate his mission. As he arrived at a well
called al Salāsil, in the land of Judham, fearing the enemy might
overtake him, he sent word to the Prophet asking for more
forces. The Prophet sent Abū 'Ubaydah ibn al Jurrāḥ at the
head of a corps of Muhājirūn which included Abū Bakr and
'Umar. The Prophet feared that 'Amr, new as he was in his
conversion to Islām, might disagree with Abū 'Ubaydah, one of
the earliest and oldest among the Muhājirūn. He therefore
advised Abū 'Ubayah when he assigned to him the leadership of
the expedition not to disagree with 'Amr. When Abū 'Ubaydah
and his men joined forces with 'Amr, the latter reminded Abū
'Ubaydah that he had come not as a commander but only as a
relief force to operate under 'Amr's command. Abū 'Ubaydah
was a very affable, ascetic, and humble man, and he instantly
assured 'Amr that he stood under the Prophet's commandment
to obey 'Amr at all costs and under all circumstances. 'Amr led
the army in prayer as well as in battle. With his reinforcements,
he not only engaged the enemy but dispersed and routed them,
thereby recovering the Muslim prestige lost in the campaign
of Mu'tah.

At the same time, Muḥammad was thinking of Makkah and of
its affairs. In this regard, he was bound by the Treaty of Ḥudaybiyah for two years, and he meant to abide by its terms. Therefore, the only engagements he allowed his forces in the south
were small skirmishes designed merely to calm down the tribes
inclined toward rebellion. This was not difficult to do, and many
delegations were already arriving in Madīnah from all corners

of Arabia to declare their conversion. It was during this interval that the Quraysh violated the Treaty of Ḥudaybiyah, thereby triggering the chain of events which led to the conquest of Makkah and the establishment of Islām therein. Unlike any other conquest, the Muslim conquest of Makkah conferred upon it the greatest sanctity ever enjoyed by any city.

24

The Conquest of Makkah

Effects of the Previous Campaign

After the Campaign of Mu'tah, the Muslim army led by Khālid ibn al Walīd returned to Madīnah neither victorious nor vanquished, but happy to be able to return at all. Their return affected the Byzantines, the Muslims of Madīnah, and the Quraysh in the most diverse ways. The Byzantines were glad that the Muslim army, despite its small size compared to their one or two hundred thousand, had withdrawn; and they gave thanks that the war did not last long. Regardless of whether the satisfaction of the Byzantines was due to the cessation of a war so fierce that nine swords had fallen apart in Khālid ibn al Walīd's hand, or to that of a war fought with such strategy that untold forces were thought to reinforce the Muslim army, the tribes living in the outskirts of al Shām were left stupefied in admiration of the Muslim exploit. Farwah ibn 'Amr al Judhamī, commander of a Byzantine army division, was at the same time chieftain of one of those tribes. Soon after Mu'tah, he proclaimed his conversion to Islām. He was arrested by order of Heraclius and accused of high treason; however, he was told that Heraclius would let him go free if he were to repent and return to Christianity. Indeed, he was promised the return to his position as army commander. Farwah refused and insisted on following the faith of Islām and was hence put to death. As a result of his execution, Islām spread widely among the tribes adjoining al 'Irāq and al Shām under Byzantine suzerainty.

Spread of Islām in the North

The chaos and insecurity attending the Byzantine Empire further encouraged the people to convert to the new faith of Islām. Its situation was truly chaotic. Entrusted by the emperor with paying the members of the armed forces their wages, one of Heraclius' governors discharged the soldiers with the announcement that the emperor had no money. Adding insult to injury, he said: "My Emperor has neither money nor food to distribute among his dogs." It was natural that such men would become disillusioned regarding Heraclius and his state and that the new order of Islām would shine with more brilliant light in their eye. It is no wonder that such men felt more inclined to it and thus followed the new guidance to divine truth. The foregoing explains, though necessarily only in part, the conversion to Islām of thousands from the tribe of Sulaym, under the leadership of al 'Abbās ibn Mirdās; of the tribes of Ashja' and Ghatafān, the old allies of the vanquished Jews of Khaybar; and of those of 'Abs, Dhubyān and Fazārah. Thus, it may be said that the campaign of Mu'tah caused the consolidation of the Muslim front north of Madīnah all the way to the frontiers of al Shām.

The effect of that Campaign upon the morale of the Muslims in Madīnah, however, was different. We may recall that as soon as Khālid and the army returned to Madīnah without the proofs of victory, they were called deserters. Many soldiers and commanders felt so humiliated that they stayed at home in order not to be seen and insulted in public. The campaign of Mu'tah gave the Quraysh the impression that the Muslims and their power had now been destroyed and that both their dignity and the fear they previously inspired in others had all but disappeared. This made the Quraysh incline strongly to the conditions prevalent before the Treaty of Hudaybiyah. They thought that they could now launch a war against which the Muslims were incapable of defending themselves, not to speak of counterattacking or making retaliation.

Quraysh's Violation of Her Treaty

The Treaty of Hudaybiyah prescribed that any non-Makkans wishing to join the camp of Muhammad or that of the Quraysh may do so without obstruction. On the basis of this provision, the tribe of Khuzā'ah joined the ranks of Muhammad, and that of Banū Bakr joined the Quraysh. Between Khuzā'ah and Banū Bakr a number of old unsettled blood feuds had to be suspended on account of the new arrangement. With the Quraysh now believing that Muslim power had crumbled, Banū al Dīl, a clan of Banū Bakr, thought that the occasion had come to avenge themselves aganist Khuzā'ah. In this, they were encouraged by Quraysh, especially by 'Ikrimah ibn Abū Jahl and others who furnished them with arms and equipment. While Khuzā'ah tribesmen were camping one day near a well of theirs called al Watīr, Banū Bakr launched a surprise attack against them. The Khuzā'ah party fled to Makkah and took refuge in the house of Budayl ibn Warqā', complaining that the Quraysh and their Banū Bakr allies violated their treaty with the Prophet. After running in full haste toward Madīnah, 'Amr ibn Sālim al Khuzā'ī related to Muhammad and the Muslims in the mosque what had happened and asked for assistance. The Prophet of God answered: "Certainly, O 'Amr ibn Sālim, we shall come to your rescue." Another group of Khuzā'ah tribesmen followed him to Madīnah together with their Makkan host, Budayl ibn Warqā', and confirmed their predecessor's report. Realizing that this flagrant violation by the Quraysh of their treaty was forcing his hand to conquer Makkah, the Prophet sent word to the Muslims all over the Peninsula to mobilize at once. The objective, however, he kept as a secret.

Quraysh's Fears

The wise elders of Quraysh realized the danger to which 'Ikrimah and his youthful companions had exposed Makkah for their action was a clear violation of the Hudaybiyah Treaty. Should Muhammad decide to avenge his Khuzā'ah allies against the Makkans, the holy city would be exposed to the strongest danger. What should they do? It occurred to them to send Abū Sufyān to Madīnah to reaffirm the peace treaty and seek a prolongation of its two year term to ten. Abū Sufyān, chief statesman and leader of Makkah, proceeded to Madīnah to conduct negotiations. On his way there, he met Budayl ibn Warqā' and his companions near 'Usfān, and feared that Muhammad might have preceded him to this place with an army bent on revenge, thus making his mission all the more difficult. Budayl denied that he had seen Muhammad before, but the shrewd Abū

Sufyān could tell from the refuse of Budayl's horse that he had
recently been in Madīnah. He therefore decided that upon arrival
to Madīnah, he had better see his daughter, Umm Ḥabībah,
the Prophet's wife, rather than Muhammad himself.

The Failure of Abū Sufyān's Efforts

Umm Ḥabibah knew well the Prophet's emotions regarding the
Quraysh, though she did not know of his plans for Makkah.
Such was the case with all Muslims in Madīnah. Entering into
his daughter's quarters, Abū Sufyān was about to sit upon the
mattress of the Prophet when Umm Ḥabībah moved it away.
When he asked her whether she had done so in order to save
her father from the mattress or the mattress from her father,
she replied: "This is the mattress of the Prophet of God—May
God's peace and blessing be upon him. You are an associationist
and hence impure. You may not therefore be allowed to sit on the
Prophet's mattress." Abū Sufyān was enraged by this reply and
left the house, saying to his daughter, "By God, after you left
my house, you must have become utterly mad." His strategy
exposed, he proceeded to see Muhammad. The Prophet, however,
refused to give him an audience. Abū Sufyān decided to go to
Abū Bakr and ask him to intervene with the Prophet. Again, his
request was turned down. He then approached 'Umar ibn al
Khaṭṭāb, who rejected him with the harsh rebuke: "Do you
expect me to intervene with the Prophet of God for you? By
God, if nothing is left for me but the sand of the desert, I will
still fight you." Abū Sufyān went to 'Alī ibn Abū Ṭālib and
talked to him in the presence of his wife Fāṭimah. 'Alī spoke
to him gently and apologized that nobody could change the mind
of Muhammad once it was made up. Finally, the mighty delegate
of Quraysh begged Fāṭimah to allow him to use her son, al
Ḥasan, in his search for support among the people of Madīnah
as a means of convincing Muhammad to prolong the peace.
Fāṭimah answered that nobody could dissuade the Prophet of
God by this method. As the gates closed in the face of Abū Sufyān
one after another, he returned to 'Alī and sought his advice.
'Alī replied that he knew of no measure which would alleviate
the situation. He told him, however, that since he was the chief
of Banū Kinānah, he could invoke his own tribal connections
for a while and quickly return home. 'Alī informed Abū Sufyān
that he did not think even that measure would work but that

Abū Sufyān could turn to it *faute de mieux*. Abū Sufyān went to the Mosque and there proclaimed on behalf of his tribe his willingness to make peace with the people. He then mounted his horse and returned to Makkah. His heart was full of sorrow and his pride badly wounded, partly by his own daughter and partly by the rejection of those who, prior to their emigration from Makkah, had longed for the least bit of consideration or compassion from the great and mighty leader.

Abū Sufyān returned to Makkah and reported to his people the frustration of his efforts. He informed them of his proclamation in the Mosque of Madīnah and of Muḥammad's refusal to come to any terms of peace. The Makkans chastized him for allowing himself to be so contemptuously treated and continued their deliberations on the fate of their city.

Muslim Preparations for War

It was Muhammad's plan not to give the Quraysh the time to prepare for war. Armed by his confidence in Muslim power and in God's assistance, he sought to surprise the enemy before they could build up their defenses. His aim was to conquer without bloodshed. He therefore first commanded the people to get ready and informed them of his plans for Makkah later. He asked the Muslims to hurry and prayed that Quraysh would not find out his plan before it was too late.

While the Muslim army prepared to leave Madīnah, Ḥāṭib ibn Abū Balta'ah wrote a letter informing the Quraysh about the Muslim move and gave it to a woman called Sārah, a client of some members of the house of Banū 'Abd al Muttalib. He commanded her to take it to Makkah and to hand it over to the Quraysh leaders. Ḥāṭib was one of the foremost Muslims. How then could he now turn informant for the enemy? Apparently, there are sides of the human soul which remain weak despite the great strength achieved by other sides, and man remains forever at the mercy of his weaknesses despite his conscious effort to overcome them. At any rate, Muhammad, soon learned of Ḥāṭib's attempt and sent 'Alī ibn Abū Ṭalib and al Zubayr ibn al 'Awwām to intercept the messenger. The latter was arrested and her horse and saddle searched, but no letter was found. 'Alī threatened her that unless she produced the letter voluntarily, he would be forced to search her own person and to unveil her body in the process. When the woman realized how serious 'Alī was, she unloosened her pigtails, brought out the letter and handed it over to 'Alī. The woman was returned to Madīnah, and Ḥāṭib was called to account. In his own defense, Ḥāṭib said: "O Prophet of God, by God I swear that I am still a believer in God and in His Prophet. My faith has not changed by one jot or tittle. But I am a man here in the Muslim camp devoid of relatives, family or clan, whereas in Makkah, I have children, family, and relatives whom I want no evil to befall." Upon hearing his reply, 'Umar ibn al Khaṭṭāb asked the Prophet's permission to strike his neck on the grounds that he had apostatized. The Prophet answered: "O 'Umar, perhaps God has looked favorably on the men who fought at Badr and has permitted them to do whatever they wish; for their merit with God is truly great." Ḥāṭib was one of those who fought at Badr. In this connection, the following verse was revealed: "O Men who believe, do not take My and your enemies as friends. Show such people no amity."[1]

The Muslims' March on Makkah

The Muslim army proceeded from Madīnah to Makkah bent upon conquering that city and seizing the sanctuary which God had declared a place of peace, security, and religious sanctification to all mankind. This army had more men than Madīnah had ever seen before, since the tribes of Sulaym, Muzaynah, Ghaṭafān, and others had joined the Muhājirūn and the Anṣār in such numbers and with such armaments that the wide expanses of the desert were filled with them. As the force moved forward it covered the desert from horizon to horizon and no end of it could be seen. They moved fast, and at every station many more tribes joined their ranks and added to their armaments and equipment. Every soul was filled with the faith of Islām and entertained no doubt that God's help will bring them victory. Muhammad led this army at the forefront. His greatest concern was to seize the holy house without shedding any unnecessary blood. By the time the army arrived at al Zahrān, four miles from Makkah, its number had reached ten thousand. Until then, the Quraysh knew nothing about it, and its leaders continued to consult with one another, to agree and to disagree regarding the measures to be taken by them to meet Muslim anger. Al 'Abbās ibn 'Abd al Muṭṭalib, uncle of the Prophet, withdrew from the conversation of the Quraysh leaders, took all members of his family, and went out in the direction of Madīnah. At al Juhfah he met Muḥammad and converted to Islām.[2] It is rather likely that a group of the Banū Hāshim heard a rumor regarding the Prophet's new expedition and sought to join him before the battle began. Two other Makkans came to join the ranks of the Muslims at Nīq al 'Uqāb, both cousins of the Prophet: Abū Sufyān ibn al Ḥārith ibn 'Abd al Muṭṭalib and 'Abdullah ibn Abū Umayyah ibn al Mughīrah. The Prophet, however, refused to grant them their request, replying to Umm Salamah, who approached him on their behalf, that he had no need for either cousin. The first had previously injured the Prophet, and the second, the Prophet's brother-in-law, had broadcast all sorts of libels and calumnies about him. When a report of the Prophet's decision reached the ears of Abū Sufyān, he swore that either Muḥammad would grant him this permission or he would take his son and strike out aimlessly into the desert and perish of thirst and hunger. Muḥammad felt compassion toward him and his son, and permitted them to be received within the Muslim ranks. They entered his audience and were converted to Islām.

Al 'Abbās ibn 'Abd al Muṭṭalib saw that the armies of his nephew were disturbingly preponderant in power and numbers. Although a Muslim, he felt quite apprehensive for what might befall his own native city should this hitherto unrivalled army advance on it with hostile intention. After all, the city he had just left behind was full of his own people, friends and relatives, and he did not consider those relationships terminated by his entry into Islām. Perhaps he intimated some of these fears to the Prophet when he asked, "What would the Prophet do in case Quraysh asked for a guarantee of its own security?" And perhaps Muḥammad was pleased that al 'Abbās had broached the subject with him. It might even be conjectured that the Prophet thought of using al 'Abbās as a delegate to the Quraysh that his apprehensiveness might be transmitted to the Makkans. Such measure would prevent the shedding of blood and enable the Muslims to enter Makkah without war. The sanctity of the city would thus be saved and its picture in the Arab mind as a place of security, refuge, and peace would be preserved. In fact, al 'Abbās was soon sent back to Makkah, riding on the Prophet's own white mule. When he approached the locality of al Arāk, al 'Abbās looked for anyone from Makkah, be it a lumberman or herdsmen, with whom he might send a message informing the Makkan leadership of the Muslim's preponderant armies and

advising them to come out to meet the Prophet and reconcile
themselves to him before he should take Makkah by storm.

Abū Sufyān's Audience with the Prophet

The Quraysh, for their part, felt gravely apprehensive ever
since the Muslims arrived at al Zahrān. They sent Abū Sufyān,
Budayl ibn Warqā', and Ḥakīm ibn Ḥazzām, the relative of Khadījah, to reconnoiter the field and assess the danger. While riding
in the area on the Prophet's white mule, al 'Abbās overheard a
conversation between Abū Sufyān and Budayl ibn Warqā'. To
Abū Sufyān's exclamation that he had never seen any lights
or encampments as wide and great as those which he had just
beheld that night, Budayl answered that the said lights and encampments must belong to Khuzā'ah tribe, now aroused to
do battle. Abū Sufyān rejected this view of Budayl, affirming
that Khuzā'ah was known to be much fewer in number and much
poorer than to afford all such lights and camps. Overhearing
the voice of Abū Sufyān and recognizing it for what it was,
al 'Abbās called out to him using his title "Abū Ḥanẓalah". Abū
Sufyān, who recognized the voice, answered by using the title
of al 'Abbas, "Abū al Faḍl". Al 'Abbās said: "Watch out, O
Abū Sufyān! What you see is the Prophet of God leading his
people. Woe to the Quraysh tomorrow morning, when his armies
storm their city." Abū Sufyān answered: "Oh the misery of it!
What shall we do?" Al 'Abbās invited him to mount on his
mule, sent his companions back to Makkah and returned with him
to the Muslim camp. As the Muslims recognized the mule of the
Prophet, they let it pass unhurt with Abū Sufyān on its back.
It ran between rows of thousands of Muslims who had built
enormous bonfires. As the mule passed by the fire of 'Umar ibn
al Khaṭṭāb, 'Umar recognized Abū Sufyān and surmised that
al 'Abbās was about to take Abū Sufyān under his protection.
He hurried to the tent of the Prophet and asked the latter
to permit him to strike the neck of Abū Sufyān. Al 'Abbās
entered the tent of the Prophet saying: "O Prophet of God,
I have extended my protection to this man on account of the
urgent need of this hour of the night." After what must have
been a hot discussion between 'Umar and al 'Abbās, Muḥammad
said: "O 'Abbās, take your guest to your tent and bring him
over in the morning."

On the next day, Abū Sufyān was brought to the Prophet and,
in front of a court composed of the elders of the Muhājirūn and

al Anṣār, the following conversation took place. Addressing himself to Abū Sufyān, the Prophet said: "Is it not time for you to know that there is no God but God, O Abū Sufyān?" Abū Sufyān answered: "How great, noble, and generous you are, O Prophet of God! By God I swear that if God had an associate, such had ample time to prove himself. But he didn't." The Prophet said: "Woe to you, O Abū Sufyān, is it not time for you to learn that I am the Prophet of God?" Abū Sufyān answered: "How great, noble and generous you are, O Prophet of God! While I entertain no more doubt that God has any associate, I am still not so sure about this claim." At this point, al 'Abbās intervened and asked Abū Sufyān to convert to Islām and to witness, before he was put to death, that there is no God but God and that Muḥammad is the Prophet of God. Faced with the threat, Abū Sufyān converted and recited the confession of faith. Al 'Abbās then turned to the Prophet—God's peace be upon him—and said: "O Prophet of God, Abū Sufyān is a proud man. Would you not grant him some privilege?" The Prophet answered: "Yes, indeed! Whoever enters the house of Abū Sufyān shall be secure; whoever remains in his own house shall also be secure; and whoever enters the Mosque shall be secure."

The Historians' Estimate of These Reports

The veracity of the foregoing event is agreed upon by all historians and biographers. Some of them question whether these events took place accidentally or by previous arrangement. They point to the fact that when al 'Abbās sought the Prophet, he meant to travel to Madīnah, but we find him confronting the Muslim army at al Juḥfah. They also point to the fact that Budayl ibn Warqā' and Abū Sufyān ibn Ḥarb left Makkah in order to reconnoiter, whereas we do know that the same Budayl had gone to Madīnah and related to the Prophet how he encountered Khuzā'ah on the road and learned from the Prophet that the Banū Khuzā'ah had become the Prophet's allies. How, then, is this consistent with the view that Abū Sufyān had left Makkah without prior knowledge that Muḥammad and his army were already on the road to Makkah? Some historians therefore suggest that some prearrangement, whether little or much, must have taken place before these events unfolded, and that it was under some such prearrangement that al 'Abbās went out to meet Muḥammad. They point out that such an arrangement between Makkans and Muslims is implicit in the meeting of al 'Abbās and Abū Sufyān in the night. Abū Sufyān stood in need of no argument to convince al 'Abbās that Quraysh had no more means to stop Muḥammad, especially since he had been in Madīnah seeking to extend the term of the Ḥudaybiyah Treaty without success. These historians and biographers suggest that Abū Sufyān must have thought that if he could cooperate with the Prophet and prepare for the Muslim conquest of Makkah, his position of leadership in Makkan society would be safeguarded. That such a prearranged agreement did not go beyond Muḥammad and the few persons concerned, the evidence of 'Umar's request to kill Abū Sufyān eloquently proves. At any rate, it is conjecture for us to judge. But we certainly may decide, and do so with utmost conviction, that regardless of whether these events took place incidentally or by previous arrangement, they prove beyond doubt Muḥammad's skill, sure insight, and precision in winning the greatest victory of Islāmic history without war or bloodshed.

The March on Makkah Continued

The conversion of Abū Sufyān did not dissuade Muḥammad from taking all necessary precautions before entering Makkah. Although understood that victory is a gift of God granted to whomsoever He pleases, it is still true that God does not grant His gift except to those who prepare for it perfectly and who avail themselves of every possible precaution to achieve it. Only in this way can it be explained why the Prophet ordered that Abū Sufyān be held at the gate of the valley in the outskirts of Makkah. He deemed it desirable that Abū Sufyān watch the Muslim armies at close range and describe them to his people accurately. But he was careful not to give the enemy any time to mobilize an army or to prepare any kind of opposition before the Muslims had entered the city. As the tribes passed by Abū Sufyān, he was in no way so much impressed as by the "green company" in which Muḥammad stood surrounded by the Muhājirūn and al Ansār. So close were their ranks and so well equipped that all one could see was a solid mass of iron. After they passed, Abū Sufyān said to al 'Abbās: "O Abū al Faḍl, no force can stand in the face of this. By God, the dominion of your nephew has become truly great." He then rushed toward Makkah calling to his people at the top of his voice: "O men of Quraysh, here comes Muḥammad with an army such as you have never seen before. Put up no resistance. Whoever enters into my house shall be secure; whoever remains in his own house shall be secure; and whoever enters the Mosque shall be secure."

Muḥammad advanced with the army until he reached Dhū Ṭuwā. From there he realized that Makkah lay in front of him devoid of any army to give him battle. He stopped his forces, stood over this mount, and bent himself in prayers and thanksgiving. He was grateful to God that he had enabled him to conquer the first theatre of revelation. The sanctuary of the holy House was now to be opened to all the Muslims in peace and security. At the same time, Abū Quḥāfah who had not yet been converted to Islām like his son, asked a granddaughter of his to take him over to the mount of Abū Qubays. Being blind, he asked his granddaughter what she saw once they got to the top. She answered, "A black mass is all I see." He said, "That must be the cavalry." She said, "By God the black mass is spreading out." He said, "The cavalry must have been given orders to march over Makkah. Take me quickly to my home." Before they reached Makkah, however, the Muslim cavalry had entered the city and intercepted him on the road.

Deployment of the Muslim Forces

Muḥammad praised God and thanked him for the conquest of Makkah. Nonetheless, he continued to take every precaution. He had divided the army into four groups and commanded them all not to engage in any fighting or shed any blood except in cases of extreme emergency. He gave the command of the left wing to al Zubayr ibn al 'Awwām and ordered him to enter Makkah from the north. He gave the command of the right to Khālid ibn al Walīd and ordered him to enter Makkah from the south. He gave the command of the Madīnese to Sa'd ibn 'Ubādah and ordered him to enter Makkah from the west. As for Abū 'Ubaydah ibn al Jarrāḥ, he gave him the command of the Muhājirūn and ordered him to enter Makkah from the north near Hind Mountain and joined his own company to the Muhājirūn. While about to march, Sa'd ibn 'Ubādah was heard saying: "Today is the day of battle, the day of the great war, the day when all taboos will be lifted." Had he been permitted to proceed, this general would have violated the Prophet's commandment that no blood should be shed in Makkah. Hence, as soon as the Prophet learned of his attitude, he relieved him of the command of the forces and appointed his son, Qays, to replace him. The son was less active than the father on account of his voluminous size, but he was of a far more gentle disposition.

The armies entered and occupied Makkah without opposition. Only the front assigned to Khālid ibn al Walīd put up any resistance. That area, the south of Makkah, was populated by the most hostile and antagonistic members of Quraysh. Many of them were among the attackers of Khuzā'ah who, together with their Banū Bakr allies, had violated the Treaty of Hudaybiyah. Not moved by the call of Abū Sufyān, they prepared for battle. Those of them ready to fight were led by Safwān, Suhayl, and 'Ikrimah ibn Abū Jahl. When Khālid's army entered their quarter, they showered it with arrows. Khālid, however, quickly dispersed them, losing two of his men and killing thirteen of the enemy, according to one version, and twenty-eight according to another. It is even said that the two soldiers missing from Khālid's army were not lost in battle but had strayed into the wilderness and lost their way. Safwān, Suhayl, and 'Ikrimah took to flight as soon as they realized the futility of their stand, leaving their own men whom they had incited to resistance at the mercy of Muslim arms. Standing with a group of Muhājirūn on a Makkan height and surveying the various quarters of the city he had just conquered without violence, Muhammad noticed toward the south the shining of swords in battle with the local inhabitants. The Prophet became angry and repeated his command that there should be no fighting. He was soon told the facts of the case and accepted God's judgment in the matter.

The Muslims Enter Makkah

The Prophet camped on a height opposite the mountain of Hind and in the proximity of the graves of Abū Tālib and Khadījah. He was asked whether he wanted to rest in his old house in Makkah and answered, "No! They have leveled it." The Prophet then retired to his tent grateful to God for this glorious and victorious return, and for bringing to its knees the cruel city which had tortured and banished him. For a moment, he turned his gaze toward the valley of Makkah as well as to the surrounding hills. He recalled that in those hills he often found refuge from the persecution of Quraysh; that one of them, Hirā', was the scene of his periodical retreats. Vividly, he represented to himself the moment when, in the cave of that same mountain, the first verses of the Qur'ān were revealed; he could hear the holy words resound in his ears:

$$اِقْرَأْ بِاسْمِ رَبِّكَ الَّذِى خَلَقَ ۝ خَلَقَ الْإِنْسَانَ مِنْ عَلَقٍ ۝ اِقْرَأْ وَرَبُّكَ الْأَكْرَمُ ۝ الَّذِى عَلَّمَ بِالْقَلَمِ ۝ عَلَّمَ الْإِنْسَانَ مَا لَمْ يَعْلَمْ ۝$$

"Read! Read in the Name of your Lord, Who created man from a clot! Read! For your Lord is the Most gracious. He has taught man to read and to write! He has taught man that which he does not know!"[3]

The Prophet was naturally attracted by the view of Makkah spread out in expanding circles before him between these hills, at the center of which stood the sanctuary and its holy House. Muḥammad, moved by the sight of Makkah and by the remembrance of God's revelation, let tears fall from his eye as he thanked God, praised Him, and witnessed that there is no truth and no power except in Him. He felt that his task as leader was coming to a natural conclusion. So agitating were all these feelings that he was unable to settle down to rest or, indeed, even to restrain himself within the tent. Mounting his she-camel, al Qaṣwā', he rode toward the Ka'bah where he circumambulated the House without dismounting. He then dismounted and called upon 'Uthmān ibn Ṭalḥah to open the Ka'bah for him. Muḥammad stood at the door surrounded by the many worshippers who had found their way to the holy House. He delivered a speech to the people present in which he said, quoting the Qur'ān:

$$يَا أَيُّهَا النَّاسُ إِنَّا خَلَقْنَاكُمْ مِنْ ذَكَرٍ وَأُنْثَى وَجَعَلْنَاكُمْ شُعُوبًا وَقَبَائِلَ لِتَعَارَفُوا إِنَّ أَكْرَمَكُمْ عِنْدَ اللّٰهِ أَتْقَاكُمْ إِنَّ اللّٰهَ عَلِيمٌ خَبِيرٌ ۝$$

"O men, We have created you from male and female and constituted you into peoples and tribes that you might know and cooperate with one another. In the eye of God, highest among you is the most virtuous. God is omniscient and all-wise."[4] He continued: "O Men of Quraysh, what do you think I am about to do with you?" "Everything good," they answered, "for you are a noble brother and a noble nephew of ours." Muḥammad went on: "Rise, then, and go. For you are free."

With this word, Muḥammad gave a general amnesty to all Quraysh and all the Makkans.

The Prophet's General Amnesty

Oh, the beauty of pardon and forgiveness on the part of the mighty and powerful! How great is the soul of Muḥammad which rose above hatred and above revenge, which denied every human feeling and ascended to heights of nobility man had never reached before! There were the Quraysh among whom were people whom Muḥammad well knew had plotted to kill him, had persecuted him, and inflicted upon him and his companions all kinds of injury and harm, who fought him at Badr and at Uḥud, who blockaded him in the Campaign of al Khandaq, who incited the Arab tribes to rise against him, and who would even then tear him apart if only they had the power. There, the whole of Quraysh stood totally under Muḥammad's hand, indeed under his feet, totally subject to his command. Indeed, their very life depended upon the first word emerging from his lips. All these thousands of men, of Muslims in battle array, stood on the ready waiting for that one word to wipe out the whole of Makkah and its people within minutes. Muḥammad, however, was no less than Muḥammad! He was no less than the Prophet of God! No alienation, antagonism, or hostility could find any permanent abode in his heart. His heart was absolutely free of injustice, of malice, of tyranny or false pride. In the most decisive moment, God gave him power over his enemy. But Muḥammad chose to forgive, thereby giving to all mankind and all the generations the most perfect example of goodness, of truthfulness, of nobility and magnanimity.

Cleansing the Ka'bah of Its Images

When Muḥammad entered the Ka'bah, he saw that its walls were painted with pictures of angels and prophets. His eyes fell upon a picture of Ibrahīm holding the divination arrows and a pigeon made out of twigs. He seized the pigeon, broke it into pieces and threw it to the ground and, looking at the picture of Ibrahīm, he said: "Accursed be the Makkans! They have made our ancestor an idolater and a diviner. What does Ibrahīm have to do with divination arrows? He was neither a Jew nor a Christian nor yet an associationist, but a *ḥanīf*, and a Muslim." On the walls of the Ka'bah, the angels were pictured as beautiful women. Turning to them, Muḥammad denied that angels had any such bodily forms, that they were either male or female. He commanded the obliteration of all pictures and images. Attached with lead to the walls of the Ka'bah were the idols which the Quraysh worshipped as the associates of God; the idol Hubal stood in the center of the Ka'bah. Muḥammad designated every one of these idols with his stick and recited the verse of the Qur'ān:

$$ وَقُلْ جَآءَ الْحَقُّ وَزَهَقَ الْبَاطِلُ إِنَّ الْبَاطِلَ كَانَ زَهُوقًا ۞ $$

"Say, the truth is now manifest. Falsehood is truly confuted. And it is right that it should be."[5]

The idols were then torn down and broken, and the holy House was purified. That which Muḥammad had called for during the last twenty years was now accomplished before the first day of the conquest of Makkah was over. That which Makkah had opposed most strongly was now a fact of history. The destruction of the idols and the wiping out of paganism in the holy sanctuary was now completed before the very eyes of Quraysh. The Makkan idols, the objects of reverence and worship inherited from the ancestors, crumbled to bits under the hammering blows of Muḥammad.

Al Anṣār's Fears and the Prophet's Reassurance

As the Anṣār of Madīnah witnessed all this, and as they saw Muḥammad on top of al Ṣafā mountain invite the Makkans to embrace Islām, they feared he might now abandon Madīnah and reestablish himself in his native city. Some of them inquired of one another, seeking to reassure themselves whether or not this was the case. Their apprehension was not out of place. Victor in his own home town where stood the sanctuary, the holy House of God and center of worship, it was quite likely that the Prophet would now make Makkah his capital. Muḥammad had hardly finished his prayer and preaching when he inquired concerning their fears. When, after long hesitancy, they intimated to him their concern, the Prophet said: "Never, by God! I have covenanted to join you in life and death. I shall remain true to my covenant." Evidently, neither relatives, nor native city, nor even the holy sanctuary itself could dissuade Muḥammad from honoring a pledge he once gave to those who stood by him at his hour of need. His word given at the conclusion of the Covenant of 'Aqabah was to be honored in exemplary faithfulness and loyalty, and the occasion proved to be just what the moral teacher needed. When the Ka'bah was purified of its idols, the Prophet ordered Bilāl to mount to its top and from there to recite the *adhān,* to give the call to worship. The Muslims gathered and, led by Muhammad, performed the prayer. From that time until today, for fourteen long centuries without interruption, Bilāl as well as his countless successors have recited the *adhān* calling men to prayer five times a day from that same spot on top of the Ka'bah. For fourteen long centuries since that day, Muslims all over the globe have worshipped God and invoked His blessing upon His Prophet, their face turned toward this holy House which Muhammad cleansed on that day of its images and idols and reconsecrated to the One Almighty God.

Quraysh, resigned to its fate, felt reassured by Muhammad's general pardon. They watched the Muslims go about their city with great surprise, not without a measure of fear and caution. Seventeen Makkans were excepted from Muhammad's general amnesty and were ordered executed even if found clutching to the coverings of the Ka'bah. Some of them went into hiding and others ran away from the city altogether. They all stood convicted of atrocious crimes they had committed. One of these men was 'Abdullah ibn Abū al Sarh who once converted to Islām and wrote down the revelation for Muhammad, but who then apostatized, returned to Quraysh, and there spread tales about his falsification of the revelation. Another convict was 'Abdullah ibn Khatal who converted to Islām, killed one of his clients, apostatized, and commanded his two slave women, one of whom was called Fartanā, to castigate Muhammad in song. Both slave women were indicted and ordered executed with their master. Another was 'Ikrimah ibn Abū Jahl, the most persistent enemy, who could not accept the Muslim conquest of Makkah and put up strong resistance in the face of Khālid ibn al Walīd on the southern front.

Pardon Extended to The Convicts

As soon as he entered Makkah, Muhammad ordered that no blood should be shed and that only the seventeen people would receive their just punishment. While some of the seventeen condemned hid, others ran away from Makkah with their families. As the situation settled down and the news of the Prophet's clemency and all-embracing forgiveness became fully known and appreciated by all, some companions dared to think that even the condemned could also be forgiven. 'Uthmān ibn 'Affān, brother-in-nursing of Ibn Abū al Sarḥ, approached the Prophet in this regard and sought an order for the safe passage of his *protégé*. Muḥammad was silent for a long time sunk in thought, but he then consented to grant forgiveness. Umm Ḥakīm, daughter of al Ḥārith ibn Hishām and the wife of 'Ikrimah ibn Abū Jahl who ran away to Yaman, converted to Islām and sought pardon for her husband directly from Muḥammad. She was granted it. She then went to Yaman and returned with her husband. Muḥammad also forgave Ṣafwān ibn Umayyah who accompanied 'Ikrimah on his escape toward the sea and thence to Yaman. Both had been caught just before their ship was to sail. Muḥammad also forgave Hind, wife of Abū Sufyān, who chewed the liver of Ḥamzah, uncle of the Prophet, after his martyrdom at the Battle of Uḥud. Indeed, most of the men condemned to death had been forgiven. Only four were executed: al Ḥuwayrith who tempted Zaynab, the Prophet's daughter, when she returned from Makkah to Madīnah; two Muslims guilty of murder in Madīnah who escaped to Makkah and apostatized; and one of the slave women of Ibn Khaṭal who used to castigate the Prophet in song. The other slave-woman ran away, but was brought back and later forgiven.

Reconsecration of Makkah: The City as Inviolate

Following the conquest of Makkah, the Khuzā'ah tribe discovered a Hudhayl tribesman in their midst who was still a pagan and killed him. Upon hearing the news, the Prophet was so angry that he delivered a speech in which he said: "O men, God made Makkah a holy place on the day heaven and earth were created. Makkah is therefore holy, holy, holy to the end of time. No man believing in God and the Day of Judgment may therefore shed any blood or destroy any tree in its precincts. Makkah has never been desecrated by anyone before me and it shall never be desecrated by anyone after me. Only for the brief hour of conquest and because of God's wrath upon its people, it was permitted to me to enter it with arms. But now Makkah fully enjoys her previous holiness. Let the present inform the absent. Whoever argues with you that the Prophet of God fought in Makkah, answer him that God had desanctified the city for His Prophet but not for anyone else, and surely not for you, O Tribesmen of Khuzā'ah! All killing must stop, for it is evil crime and brings no advantage when indulged in. You have killed a man, and I shall have to pay his bloodwit to his people. Henceforth, the heirs of a victim shall have the choice between executing the murderer or receiving bloodwit." Muhammad immediately paid the bloodwit of the Khuzā'ah tribesman to his people. By his disposal of the case in this manner and his general proclamation concerning murder and retaliation, Muhammad struck a further example of clemency and justice. The force of Islām's appeal to the Makkans became irresistible, and they began to convert. The town crier proclaimed: "Whoever believes in God and the Day of Judgment will destroy on this day every idol and vestige of paganism in his home." The Prophet commissioned some Khuzā'ah men to repair the walls of the holy city, thereby giving further proof of his respect for it. Under the circumstances, the love and esteem for Muhammad could only increase. Muhammad told the Makkans that he loved them the most, that they were the highest in his regard, and that he would have never left them had they themselves not rejected and banished him. With this praise, the Makkans' esteem for Muhammad broke all bounds.

Abū Bakr brought his own father, Abū Quhāfah, the old blind man who went up to the mount of Abū Qubays guided by his daughter to find out what was happening before the Muslims entered the city, and placed him in the presence of the Prophet. When seeing him, Muhammad reproached Abū Bakr for bringing the old man over and said that it was he, Muhammad, that should have come to Abū Quhāfah. Paying no attention to Abū Bakr's rejoinder that it was his father's duty to come to the Prophet and not vice versa, he asked the man to sit by him, wiped his face for him and invited him to enter into Islām. Abū Quhāfah converted and became an ardent Muslim. Through this noble behavior of the Prophet, this magnanimous conduct, Muhammad succeeded in winning over a people who had nursed for him the strongest hatred. Thereafter, the Makkans revered the person of Muhammad, embraced Islām, and wholeheartedly subjected themselves to his rule.

Ibn al Walīd and the Tribe of Jadhīmah

Muḥammad resided in Makkah fifteen days during which he organized its affairs and instructed its people in Islām. During this period, he sent forth delegations to call men peaceably to Islām to destroy the idols without shedding any blood. Khālid ibn al Walīd was sent to Nakhlah to destroy al 'Uzzā, goddess of Banū Shaybān. His task accomplished, ibn al Walīd proceeded to Jadhīmah. There, however, the people took up arms at his approach. Khālid asked them to lay down their arms on the grounds that all people had accepted Islām. One of the Jadhīmah tribesman said to his people: "Woe to you, Banū Jadhīmah! Don't you know that this is Khālid? By God, nothing awaits you once you have laid down your arms except captivity, and once you have become captives you can expect nothing but death." Some of his people answered: "Do you seek to have us all murdered? Don't you know that most men have converted to Islām, that the war is over, and that security is reestablished?" Those who held this opinion continued to talk to their tribesmen until the latter surrendered their arms. Thereupon, ibn al Walīd ordered them to be bound, and he killed some of them. When he heard of the news, the Prophet lifted his arms to heaven and prayed: "O God, I condemn what Khālid ibn al Walīd has done." The Prophet gave funds to 'Alī ibn Abū Ṭālib and sent him to look into the affairs of this tribe, cautioning him to disregard all the customs of pre-Islām. Upon arrival, 'Alī paid the blood-wit of all the victims and compensated the property owners for their damages. Before leaving, he surrendered the rest of the money which the Prophet had given him to the tribe just in case there were any other losses which may have escaped notice at the time.

During the two weeks which Muḥammad spent in Makkah, he wiped out all the traces of paganism in the city. All the offices attached to the holy House were abolished except two: the *sidānah* which the Prophet assigned to 'Uthmān ibn Ṭalḥah, his children, and progeny after him till the end of days, and the *siqāyah*, which he assigned to his uncle al 'Abbās. Thus Umm al Qurā[6] embraced Islām and raised high the torch of genuine monotheism, illuminating the whole world for generations and centuries to come.

25

Campaigns of
Ḥunayn and al Ṭā'if

After its conquest, the Muslims remained in Makkah for two weeks during which they showed their joy over the victory which God had granted to them. They gave thanks that such a great victory had been achieved with such little bloodshed. They hurried to the sanctuary every time Bilāl delivered the *adhān* calling them to prayer. They strove to be near the Prophet wherever he went. The Muhājirūn visited their old houses and their relatives and friends whom God had guided to the truth after the conquest. Everybody was satisfied that Islām was now firmly established and that the greater part of the holy war had been victorious. Fifteen days of their stay in Makkah had hardly passed when news broke out which shook the Muslims out of their joy and feeling of security. They learned that Hawāzin, the tribe living a few miles to the southeast of Makkah, had mobilized its forces and was marching against the Muslims in Makkah. This tribe had learned of the conquest of Makkah by the Muslims and of the subsequent destruction of the idols of the Ka'bah. Apparently, their men feared that the time would soon come for the Muslims to fight them on their own ground. Anxious to prevent such a tragedy, they thought this hour of Muslim intoxication with victory the right time to mobilize their forces for an attack. Their purpose, however, was the larger one of wrecking the Muslims' general plan of uniting all the tribes of the Peninsula under the banner of Islām.

Mālik ibn 'Awf's March against the Muslims

It was toward this end that Mālik ibn 'Awf al Naḍrī succeeded in uniting the Hawāzin and Thaqīf tribes and rallying the tribes of Nasr and Jusham in one front opposing the Islāmic movement as a whole. Only the Ka'b and Kilāb clans of Hawāzin refused to join the new alliance. Durayd ibn al Ṣimmah, of the Jusham tribe, was a very old man, too old to fight, but he was extremely wise and had the advantage of an extensive military experience and career. The anti-Islāmic alliance had mobilized all its members, men, women, and children, and carried to battle all the treasures it possessed. It completed its mobilization in the valley of Awṭās. When Durayd, who was blind, heard the braying of donkeys and lowing of cattle mixed in with the crying of children and the bellowing of goats, he asked Mālik ibn 'Awf why he had brought women, children, and treasures to the front. Mālik answered that he meant thereby to encourage the fighting men and to incite them to greater self-exertion in war. Durayd answered: "But what do we do in case of defeat? Does the vanquished ever keep anything he brings to the battlefield? If we are to be victorious, surely such victory will be brought about not by the women or children but by the fighting men and their swords, arrows, and javelins. But if we should lose the war, then we would be shamed and scandalized by the capture of our families and treasures." Mālik disagreed with Durayd, and the people followed the former. Mālik was a youth of thirty years, a man of strong will and firm resolution. Durayd, anxious to safeguard the newly forged unity, decided, against his better judgment, to go along with the majority. Mālik commanded his people to stand by on the tops of the Sulaym hills at the entrance to the valley and, at the proper signal, to fall upon the Muslims like one man and break their ranks as they passed in file through the canyon. Such a plot would reduce the Muslim ranks to a rabble, and the Muslims would not be able to distinguish their own soldiers from the enemy. They would be vanquished; and with their defeat, their victory over Makkah would be cancelled and to the tribes of Hawāzin and Ḥunayn would belong the honor of destroying a power which came close to engulfing the whole

Peninsula. The tribes obeyed the orders of Mālik and dug themselves in on the sides of the canyon.

The Muslims March to Ḥunayn

As for the Muslims, they went forth under the leadership of Muhammad with such power and such numbers that they themselves had never seen before. There were twelve thousand of them, ten thousand of which were those who conquered Makkah and two thousand who were newcomers from Quraysh including Abū Sufyān. Their war equipment was excellent and their armies were preceded by their cavalry and camel corps carrying their provisions and ammunition. Theirs was an army the like of which the Arabian Peninsula had never seen before. It consisted of many tribes, and each tribe had its own banner which it carried high above its ranks. It was a sight convincing any spectator of Muslim invincibility. Indeed, many Muslims told one another: "To say the least, our numerical strength has today made us invincible." They arrived at Ḥunayn in the evening and camped at the entrance of the valley until dawn. At dawn the following day the army began to move, and Muhammad, riding his white mule, was in the rear while Khālid ibn al Walīd, commanding a group of soldiers from Banū Sulaym, was in the vanguard.

Muslim Defeat

As the Muslims passed through the canyon of Ḥunayn, Mālik ibn 'Awf ordered his army to attack in the darkness before dawn, first with arrows and then with a general charge. The Muslims' ranks broke up and were stricken with panic. Some of them ran out of the canyon as fast as they could in search of safety. Witnessing what had befallen the Muslims, Abū Sufyān felt no little pleasure at the defeat of his previous enemies who until now had been celebrating their victory over Makkah. He said, "The Muslims will not be defeated until they are thrown into the sea." Shaybah ibn 'Uthmān ibn Abū Ṭalḥah, whose father was killed at Uḥud, said, "Today is my day of vengeance from Muhammad." Likewise, Kaladah ibn Ḥanbal said, "Today, the fate of the Muslims is cast," only to be answered by his brother Ṣafwān: "Silence! Cursed be your tongue. By God, to be lorded over by a man from Quraysh is better than by a man of Hawāzin." These remarks were exchanged while Muslim ranks were falling apart, and soldiers, fleeing in face of the enemy, were bypassing the Prophet in the rear unaware of his presence.

Muḥammad's Resoluteness and Bravery

What would Muḥammad do? Would he allow the sacrifices of twenty years to be lost in this moment of pre-dawn darkness? Could he think that God had abandoned him in this hour? Such could never be! Better death and annihilation. Better that Muḥammad die in the thick of battle! At any rate, when one's hour has struck, to what purpose is delaying or advancing it a little? Muḥammad therefore held his ground and was surrounded by a number of Muhājirūn, Anṣār, and immediate relatives. As his men passed by, he called out to them and sought to rally them back to the ranks. But they neither heard nor wanted to hear. The sudden onslaught of Hawāzin and Thaqīf robbed them of their senses. This terrible picture the Muslims had of the enemy was not exaggerated. From the sides of the canyon the tribesmen of Hawāzin poured down in overwhelming numbers. Their leader rode a red camel and held a black banner attached to a long spear which he plunged into the chest of every Muslim that came anywhere near him. Hawāzin and Thaqīf tribesmen, as well as their allies, fought in the same way. It was a sea of drawn spears. At one moment, Muḥammad almost plunged with his mule into enemy lines to stop their torrent of blows. Abū Sufyān ibn al Ḥārith ibn 'Abd al Muṭṭalib held back the reins of the mule and prevented it from carrying the Prophet forward.

Al 'Abbās's Call for Regrouping

Al 'Abbās ibn 'Abd al Muṭṭalib was a man of large stature who had a very resonant voice. He called loudly enough to reach all the Muslims: "O Anṣār Company! O Men who opened their homes and helped Muḥammad! O Muhārijrūn Company! O Men who pledged their allegiance under the tree! Muḥammad is still alive. Charge forward with him." Al 'Abbās repeated his call until the whole valley reverberated with its echo. Then, the miracle happened. The covenanters of al 'Aqabah and the Muhājirūn heard. They remembered Muḥammad and their oaths of allegiance to him as well as their sacrifices in the cause of Islām.

The other Muslims also heard and realized that Muḥammad was still there, alive, holding his ground, and fighting the enemy just as he had held his ground and fought the enemy at the Battle of Uhud. Suddenly, they were gripped by a consciousness of shame at their conduct and of apprehension at what might befall their Prophet and God's religion in case the associationists carried the day. Al 'Abbās's call continued to reverberate through the valley; the Muslims' hearts were immediately touched and their wills kindled. There and then, from every corner and quarter came the resounding cry, "At Your command, O God, at Your command!" The Muslims returned to battle and fought with utmost resolution and gallantry.

Muslim Counterattack and Victory

Muḥammad was reassured as he saw them return to the battlefront. In the meantime, the whole Hawāzin camp had come out of their trenches in the hills and confronted the Muslims face to face in the valley. At that time, too, the darkness was dissipated by sunrise. Around the Prophet a few hundred soldiers stood and repelled the attacks of the Hawāzin. Their ranks began to swell as the fleeing Muslims returned. The Ansār began to call to one another, "Rally forth to battle." They quickly reorganized themselves according to tribes and clans while Muḥammad watched the progress of the battle. As the Muslim soldiers refilled their ranks and began to march shoulder to shoulder together, the Prophet proclaimed: "Now the battle has begun. God will not fail the Prophet and will fulfill the promise He gave him." Then, turning to al 'Abbās and asking for a handful of pebbles, the Prophet threw the pebbles in the face of the enemy with the war cry, "Woe to the enemies of God!" With this, the Muslims charged, throwing themselves upon their enemies. They were convinced that theirs would be the victory and the fate of the martyr would even be greater than that of the surviving victor. The battle raged and men fell on all sides. Soon Hawāzin, Thaqīf, and their allies realized that their efforts were vain and that they faced annihilation. They turned around and started to flee, leaving behind them their women, children, and all their properties: 22,000 camels, 40,000 goats, and 4,000 ounces of silver. The captives which numbered 6,000, were transported under Muslim protection to the valley of al Ji'rānah where they were held until the Muslims returned from their

pursuit of the enemy and from their blockade of Thaqīf tribe
in the city of al Ṭā'if.

The Muslims' Pursuit of Their Enemies

The Muslims gave their enemy close pursuit, and they were
further encouraged by the Prophet's proclamation that whoever
killed an associationist would receive his victim's booty. Ibn al
Dughunnah overtook a camel carrying an open palanquin which
he thought might be carrying a woman whom he could take
captive. He brought the camel to its knees, looked into the palanquin and discovered an old man unknown to him. The old man
asked his pursuer what he wanted. Ibn al Dughunnah answered,
"I wish to kill you," and hit him with his sword. The blow
was so light that the old man was not even cut. Aware of the
shame that had befallen him and his people, the old man had
no desire to live; he addressed his attacker in these words of
disdain and pride: "Woe to your mother who taught you how
to bear arms! Take my sword from my saddle and strike with
it. Hit neither the chest nor the head but apply all your strength
to one blow against the neck. In this way I used to kill my
own enemies in days gone by. And if your miserable mother
should ask you whom you killed in this fashion, tell her that
you have killed Durayd ibn al Ṣimmah. By God, it was a wretched
day on which I extended my protection to your women and
saved them by my arm." When Rabī'ah ibn al Dughannah returned and told the story to his mother, she cried in agonies
of conscience and said to her son: "To fire with both your arms!
What crime have they perpetrated! Durayd sought to remind
posterity of our obligation to him. By God, it was he who
granted freedom to three of your own mothers in one day; myself,
my mother, and the mother of your father." The Muslims followed
Hawāzin all the way to the plain of Awṭās where they inflicted
upon them the most terrible defeat, capturing all their women and
property. Only then did they return to Muḥammad. Mālik ibn
'Awf al Nadrī gave the Muslims some resistance but then ran
away with his people and some Hawāzin tribesmen to Nakhlah.
From there he escaped to al Ṭā'if where he took refuge.

Thus, Muslim victory was complete. The unbelievers were
vanquished after they had almost defeated the Muslim army.
The advantage they had secured by their surprise attack in pre-
dawn darkness was shattered when the Prophet called his men

back to their ground. The steadfastness of Muḥammad and of
the small number of believers that surrounded him turned the
tide and proved the Muslims invincible. In this regard, the
following verses were revealed:

لَقَدْ نَصَرَكُمُ اللّٰهُ فِى مَوَاطِنَ كَثِيرَةٍ ۙ وَيَوْمَ حُنَيْنٍ ۙ إِذْ أَعْجَبَتْكُمْ كَثْرَتُكُمْ فَلَمْ تُغْنِ
عَنْكُمْ شَيْئًا وَضَاقَتْ عَلَيْكُمُ الْأَرْضُ بِمَا رَحُبَتْ ثُمَّ وَلَّيْتُمْ مُدْبِرِينَ ۝ ثُمَّ أَنْزَلَ اللّٰهُ
سَكِينَتَهُ عَلَى رَسُولِهِ وَعَلَى الْمُؤْمِنِينَ وَأَنْزَلَ جُنُودًا لَمْ تَرَوْهَا وَعَذَّبَ الَّذِينَ كَفَرُوا ۚ
وَذٰلِكَ جَزَآءُ الْكَفِرِينَ ۝ ثُمَّ يَتُوبُ اللّٰهُ مِنْ بَعْدِ ذٰلِكَ عَلَى مَنْ يَشَآءُ ۗ وَاللّٰهُ غَفُورٌ
رَحِيمٌ ۝ يَٰأَيُّهَا الَّذِينَ آمَنُوا إِنَّمَا الْمُشْرِكُونَ نَجَسٌ فَلَا يَقْرَبُوا الْمَسْجِدَ الْحَرَامَ بَعْدَ
عَامِهِمْ هٰذَا ۚ وَإِنْ خِفْتُمْ عَيْلَةً فَسَوْفَ يُغْنِيكُمُ اللّٰهُ مِنْ فَضْلِهِ إِنْ شَآءَ ۚ إِنَّ اللّٰهَ عَلِيمٌ
حَكِيمٌ ۝

"God has given you victory on many occasions as well as on the
Day of Ḥunayn. The numerical superiority of which you were so
proud did not avail you. The tide overwhelmed you and you ran
away in face of the enemy. But God brought down His peace
upon the Prophet and believers. He sent forth soldiers whom you
could not see to fight on the Prophet's side, and inflicted upon the
unbelievers the great punishment they deserved. However, God
accepts the repentance of whomsoever He pleases. He is merciful and forgiving. O Men who believe, the unbelievers are impure. They shall hence not enter the holy Mosque. In case you
fear a reduction of your incomes as a result of this proscription,
remember that God gives you of His bounty. For God is all-wise
and all-knowing."[1]

The Price of Victory

Victory was not cheaply achieved. The Muslims paid a very
high price. True, they could have done it at much lesser loss
had they not fallen back at the beginning and occasioned Abū
Sufyān's derisive remark that they would be thrown into the
sea. Although the source books of biography have not listed all
the casualties of the battle, they did mention that two tribes
of Muslims were almost totally annihilated, and that the Prophet

held a funerary prayer for them in which he asked God to let them enter Paradise. Partially offsetting this tremendous cost in human lives was the unquestioned supremacy the victory brought to the Muslims. Moreover, victory brought more captives and booty than the Muslims had ever seen before. As long as the war itself is an honorable one, victory, its final objective, must be achieved regardless of prices. That is why the Muslims did not mind the initial loss, celebrated the victory, and awaited the distribution of the booty.

Muḥammad, however, had other plans. Seeking to make the victory still more spectacular, he commanded the Muslims to march immediately. Mālik ibn 'Awf, leader of the enemy alliance, had taken refuge in the city of al Ṭā'if with the tribe of Thaqīf, his allies against Muḥammad. Full justification was therefore provided for the next Muslim move. Observing the same strategy employed at Khaybar following the Battle of Uḥud, and at Qurayẓah following the campaign of al Khandaq, the Prophet ordered the army to march against al Ṭā'if. Perhaps Muḥammad remembered on that day how, many years before the Hijrah, he came to al Ṭā'if calling its people to Islām; how he was met with derision, driven away and pelted with stones; and how he sought shelter from its street children inside the closed vineyard. Perhaps he remembered how at that time he was alone, weak, and devoid of all support except God's; and how he had nothing but the great mountain-moving faith which filled his soul. Today, Muḥammad found himself going again to the same city but at the head of a Muslim army the like of which Arabia had never seen before.

The Siege of al Ṭā'if

The city of al Ṭā'if, capital of the Thaqīf tribe and refuge of Mālik ibn 'Awf, loomed before Muḥammad and his companions as the next objective. It was a fortified city and, like most Arab towns in that period, had gates which shut out the undesirable intruder. Its people had wide military experience, especially in the art of siege. Their great wealth had enabled them to make their fortifications the strongest in the world. As the Muslims approached al Ṭā'if, they passed by Liyyah where stood a fortress of Mālik ibn 'Awf. The fortress as well as a nearby building belonging to a tribesman from Thaqīf were destroyed. The army was commanded to put up camp in the vicinity, and the Prophet called his companions together to map out a strategy. Ṭā'if, on the other hand, learning of their approach, observed Muslim movements from the top of its fortresses and towers, and showered the Muslims with volleys of deadly arrows. It was not possible for the Muslims to storm these strong fortresses with their old weapons. New means of waging war, destructive and innovative weapons were needed. It was suggested that perhaps they could starve Ṭā'if into surrender by simply maintaining the siege. Those who favored a frontal attack could not find the necessary means with which to launch it. One immediate decision had to be taken at once, namely, to move the Muslims' camp and forces beyond the reach of al Ṭā'if's arrows. Once this danger was removed, the Muslims thought they could afford the leisure requisite for a sound decision as to strategy. At the Prophet's command, the Muslims erected their tents at a distance from the fortresses. There they built a mosque which was handed over to the city after its surrender and conversion to Islām. This preliminary measure was unavoidable considering that the arrows of Ṭā'if had accounted for the deaths of 18 Muslims and the wounding of a great number, including one of the sons of Abū Bakr. In the same locality two red tents were erected for the Prophet's wives, Umm Salmah and Zaynab, who had accompanied him throughout this expedition. It was near his tents that Muhammad used to call men to prayer, and, perhaps, it was precisely in that spot that the mosque of Ṭā'if was subsequently built.

Bombardment of al Ṭā'if by Catapult

The Muslims encamped and waited for new orders. Some tribesmen spoke to the Prophet in favor of a prolonged siege, claiming that nothing the Muslims had would help them scale Ṭā'if's fortifications. Time alone, they argued, would eventually force Ṭā'if's people out of their safe foxholes. Muhammad, however, found it difficult to return without having achieved a victory over Ṭā'if. Banū Daws, one of the tribes living to the south of Makkah, were fully acquainted with the use of the catapult and had experience in tank-led assaults upon high fortifications. Al Ṭufayl, one of its leaders, who had accompanied Muhammad ever since the conquest of Khaybar, stood at the Prophet's side always on the ready to fulfill his wishes. At Muhammad's command, al Ṭufayl speeded to his tribe with a request for their assistance, and they responded by bringing with them their tools of war. Reaching al Ṭā'if four days after the Muslim siege began, they put their catapult to immediate use. They also brought their tanks into the battlefield, and sent a number of their men under their cover to the fortified walls. The soldiers of Ṭā'if, however, were clever enough to force the men of Banū Daws to flee. Having heated pieces of iron to red hot temperatures, they threw these missiles onto the tanks and put them to flame. The Muslim soldiers which the tanks were covering had to flee or be burnt alive. As they emerged from under their tanks, they were shot at with arrows and a number of them were killed. Having failed at this new effort, the Muslims became convinced that there was no way to storm the fortresses of Ṭā'if.

Destruction of al Ṭā'if's Orchards

What was left for them to do? Muḥammad pondered this question for a long while. Suddenly, the thought occurred to him that he had achieved victory over Banū al Nadīr and forced their evacuation simply by destroying their orchards. The vineyards of Ṭā'if were far more important than the orchards of Banū al Nadīr and were known throughout Arabia for their produce. It was due to them that the city of al Ṭā'if acquired the reputation of being a little paradise in the desert. Without further ado, Muḥammad gave the order, and the Muslims began systematically to cut down and burn the orchards. Upon discovering this destruction and realizing that Muḥammad really meant to spare none of their vineyards, the Ṭā'if tribesmen sent to him pleading that they would rather give away their vineyards to Muḥammad, or to those citizens of al Ṭā'if—and there were large numbers of them—who were bound to Muḥammad in blood relationships. Muḥammad stopped his men temporarily and called out to the besieged city that he would set free any man who surrendered to him. Twenty people responded to his appeal. From them he learned that enough ammunition and provisions were available that the city could withstand the siege for a very long time. Considering that his own men were anxious to return home and enjoy the fruits of their victory over Hawāzin—indeed, that their patience would be at an end if the siege were prolonged—Muḥammad ordered the Muslims to withdraw. With the arrival of the new moon (the month of Dhū al Qi'dah) the siege had become one month old, and the holy season during

which no war was permitted had begun. Muhammad returned
to Makkah with his army, visiting the holy places and performing
the lesser pilgrimage or *'umrah*. He announced that he would
resume the war against al Ṭā'if at the expiration of the holy
months.

Hawāzin Captives Liberated and Returned to Their Tribe

In their withdrawal to Makkah, the Muslims turned in the
direction of al Ji'rānah where they had left their booty and
captives. There, they stopped long enough to divide their spoils.
The Prophet separated one-fifth for himself and distributed the
rest among his companions. Before they finished, a delegation
from the Hawāzin tribe who had already accepted Islām appealed
to Muhammad to return to them the women, children, and
property that the Muslim army had seized. They complained that
they were anxious to see their families and that they had suffered enough from this war. Muhammad met this delegation in
person and listened attentively as one of them said: "O Prophet
of God; the captives in the wards of your army are themselves
your relatives. Among them are your aunts on your father or
mother's side and your nurse-mothers who held you in their
arms as a baby. Had our women played similar roles to al
Ḥārith ibn Abū Shimr, or to al Nu'mān ibn al Mundhir, and
had any of these kings inflicted upon us what you have inflicted,
he would have granted every request of ours if we but asked
for his mercy and compassion and reminded him of his obligation.
You, on the other hand, are the most merciful and compassionate
and the least needful of being reminded of your obligations." The
Hawāzin delegation did not err in reminding Muhammad of his
blood relationship to them. Among the captives, an older looking
woman whom the soldiers had treated roughly shouted in their
faces: "Woe to you! Learn that I am the sister of your leader
by virtue of having had the same wet nurse as he." The soldiers
did not believe her and brought her to Muhammad to verify
her story. The Prophet immediately recognized her. She was al
Shaymā', daughter of al Ḥārith ibn 'Abd al 'Uzzā. Muhammad
went out to meet her and spread out his mantle for her to sit
on. After reassuring her of his devotion and respect, Muhammad
asked the old lady whether she chose to stay in his camp or to
return to her people. When she chose to return, Muhammad gave
her some gifts and returned her to her people unharmed. It

was natural for Muḥammad, considering his relationship to the Hawāzin Muslims who came pleading for mercy, that he granted their request. Such loyalty, remembrance, and considerateness to anyone who had shown him any respect or consideration, were second nature with Muḥammad. Gratitude was with him a matter of course, and compassion for the wounded-at-heart was innate. After hearing their plea, Muḥammad asked: "Which are more precious to you, your women and children or your property? They answered, "O Prophet of God, if you are giving us a choice between our relatives and our property, we take the former." Muḥammad said: "All that I have set aside for me and for Banū 'Abd al Muṭṭalib is yours. After the noon prayer, rise in the midst of the worshippers and plead: 'We appeal to all the Muslims in the name of the Prophet of God, and to the Prophet of God in the name of all the Muslims for the return of our women and children.' I shall then publicly declare that I relinquish my share as well as my tribe's share." The delegation followed the advice of the Prophet and pleaded as he taught them. No sooner than they did, the Prophet declared his plan as he had promised them. Thereupon, the Muhājirūn rose and said: "Anything that is ours belongs automatically to the Prophet of God and is hereby relinquished." Al Ansār and all the Muslims did likewise except al Aqra' ibn Ḥābis, speaking for Tamīm; 'Uyaynah ibn Ḥisn, speaking for himself; and al 'Abbās ibn Mirdās, speaking for Banū Sulaym. The last named was immediately contradicted by his people. The Prophet said: "Anyone among you who has declined to give up his right in this instance has my word that if he does, I will make it up to him sixfold on the next campaign." Thus, all the captives of Hawāzin were returned and the tribe converted to Islām *en masse.*

The People's Fear of Losing Their Booty

Muḥammad inquired from the Hawāzin delegation concerning Mālik ibn 'Awf al Nadrī and learned that he was still in al Ṭā'if. The Prophet asked the delegation to inform Mālik that should he surrender and convert to Islām, Muḥammad would return to him his family and property as well as make a gift to him of 100 camels. Upon hearing of this promise and invitation of the Prophet, Mālik did not hesitate to steal out of al Ṭā'if on his mare under cover of night. Upon arrival at the Prophet's camp, he proclaimed his conversion to Islām, picked up his family, his property, and the prize of 100 camels and then went home. Indeed, the people even feared that should Muhammad continue such giveaways to the defectors from the other camp, soon there would be little left of the booty. They therefore insisted that each Muslim should receive his share, and they whispered one to another to this effect. As this whispering reached the ears of Muhammad, he pulled out a hair of the camel nearest him, lifted it up for his people to see and said: "O Men! By God, no part of your booty shall come to me that exceeds my legitimate share by as much as this hair, and this very share of mine I hereby return to you." The Prophet then asked everyone to return what he had taken that Muhammad might redistribute it to each according to his due. The Prophet proclaimed that anyone unjustly taking anything however little, would be guilty of eternal shame and hellfire.

Muhammad made this proclamation while enraged against those of his followers who had picked up his mantle thinking that it was part of the spoils of war. However, they returned it to him after he called out to them: "Return my mantle to me, O Men. By God, even if your cattle were as numerous as the trees of Tihāmah, I would still divide it all among you in absolute fairness and justice, without avarice, fear, or deception. That which I have given away belongs to the fifth which is my due." It was out of the fifth which was due him that Muhammad distributed some spoils to those who were previously Islām's strongest and most hostile enemies. He gave, for instance, 100 camels each to Abū Sufyān, to his son Muʿāwiyah, to al Hārith ibn al Hārith ibn Kaladah, to al Hārith ibn Hishām, to Suhayl ibn ʿAmr, and to Huwaytib ibn ʿAbd al ʿUzzā as well as to each of the nobles and chieftains of the tribes which he had won over after the conquest of Makkah. He gave 50 camels each to the lesser notables of the same tribes. Those who were so rewarded counted a few score, but the effect of this giving was far reaching. The Prophet of God was praised as the exemplar of hospitality and mercy by the very people who until recently—indeed, until the day before—had been fighting him with all their power. Now, they joined in an eloquent chorus of praise and gratitude. There was no request which Muhammad did not manage to fulfill for them. When ʿAbbās ibn Mirdās complained that Muhammad had given more favorable treatment to ʿUyaynah, to al Aqraʿ, and others than to him, the

Prophet sent his companions to give him more until he was perfectly satisfied.

Al Anṣār and the Reconciliatory Gratuities

The reconciliation of the enemies of yesterday which the Prophet had just effected caused al Ansār to murmur that the Prophet had done what he did because the people involved were his own tribesmen and people. Sa'd ibn 'Ubādah reported this murmur to the Prophet but sided with them and justified their complaint. The Prophet commanded him to bring his people together. When they were assembled, the Prophet said: "O Ansār! It has been reported to me that you were personally angry, that you do not approve of my distribution of the booty. Do tell me, when I came to you, did I not find you languishing in misguidance and error and did not God guide you to the truth through me? Did I not find you in a state of need and did not God make you affluent? Did I not find you enemies of one another and did not God reconcile your hearts?" Confused, al Ansār answered: "Indeed! God and his Prophet have been very generous and very loving;" and they fell into silence. Muḥammad continued: "Will you not then say more than this, O Ansār? By God, had you replied, 'Rather, it was you Muḥammad, who were under our obligation. Did you not come to us belied by your fellow men and did we not believe in you? Did you not come to us vanquished and defeated and did we not come to your rescue? Did you not come to us banished and repulsed and did we not give you shelter? Did you not come to us in want and need and did we not give you of our bounty?' Had you replied to me in this vein you would have said nothing but the truth and I would have had to agree. O Ansār, are you angry because I have given away some goods to those whom I sought to win to Islām? Because I deemed their faith confirmable by material goods whereas I deemed yours to be based on solid conviction, to be candid beyond all dissuasion? Are you not satisfied, O Ansār, that all the people return from this conquest loaded with goods and camels whereas you return with the Prophet of God? By Him who dominates Muḥammad's soul, except for the fact of my birth, there is no people to whom I love to belong beside al Ansār. If all mankind went one way, and al Ansār went another, I would certainly choose the way of al Ansār. O God, bless al Ansār, their children, and their grandchildren. Show

Your mercy to them and keep them under Your protection."

The Prophet said these words out of great affection for all the men of al Anṣār who had pledged their loyalty and allegiance to him, who had helped him, who had reinforced his ranks and found their strength in him. Indeed, he was so moved by his feelings for them that he cried. The Anṣār cried with him and declared their contentment.

Thus the Prophet showed that he was above the temptation of wealth. Although the booty of the Ḥunayn War surpassed anything he had ever seen, he showed that he had no wish for it. Rather he made of it a means for reconciling the hearts of those who had been associationists. He hoped that they might find in the new faith some happiness in this world besides the happiness of the hereafter. If in distributing this wealth Muhammad encountered such difficulties that the Muslims almost accused him of injustice, and if by giving liberally to those whose hearts he sought to soften he had infuriated al Anṣār, he also proved his justice, farsightedness and such deep wisdom in administering the affairs of his people that he was able to cause the thousands to return home happy, contented and prepared to lay down their lives in the cause of God. The Prophet left al Ji'rānah to visit the holy places in Makkah. After performing the 'umrah, or lesser pilgrimage, he appointed 'Attāb ibn Usayd governor of Makkah, and Mu'ādh ibn Jabal to teach the religion and the Qur'ān. Together with al Anṣār and al Muhājirūn, Muhammad returned to Madīnah to await the birth of his son Ibrahīm and to enjoy a moment of peace and security before undertaking the next expedition to Tabūk on the frontiers of al Shām.

26

Ibrahīm and the
Wives of the Prophet

Effect of the Conquest of Makkah upon the Peninsula

Muhammad returned to Madīnah after his conquest of Makkah, his victory at Ḥunayn, and his siege of al Ṭā'if. He had convinced all that no power could match his power within the Arabian Peninsula and that no tongue might henceforth vituperate him or spread any false information regarding himself or his cause. Both al Ansār and al Muhājirūn returned heartened with joy that God had crowned His prophet's endeavor with such success; that He enabled Muḥammad to conquer the city of the holy Mosque, that He guided its people to Islām; and that He inspired all Arab tribes to pledge their allegiance, loyalty and obedience to him. They all returned to Madīnah in order to settle down in peace. Muḥammad had taken care to appoint 'Attāb ibn Usayd as governor of Umm al Qurā, or Makkah, and Mu'ādh ibn Jabal as teacher of the people in matters of religion and in the Qur'ān. This victory, the like of which the whole history of Arabia and all its traditions have never known, left a profound impression upon the Arabs. Whether lords and masters of land and cities, men to whom it had never occurred that a day might come when they would be subject to Muḥammad or accept his faith as their religion, or poets who labored as mouthpieces of those masters in exchange for their patronage and protection, or, finally, simple tribesmen for whom personal freedom was till death the most priceless possession, the Arabs were all strongly affected by the conquest of Makkah, Ḥunayn and the siege of al Ṭā'if. To one and all, it now seemed that the poetry of the poets, the mastery of the chieftains, and the personal freedom of the tribesmen were all to no avail before the tremendous power of Muhammad and his followers.

Conversion of Ka'b ibn Zuhayr

Muhammad's success among the Arabs of the Peninsula influenced them so profoundly that Bujayr ibn Zuhayr wrote a letter to his brother, Ka'b, after the Prophet's withdrawal from al Ṭā'if, informing him that Muhammad had killed a number of men in Makkah who had slandered his reputation by spreading false rumors concerning him. Bujayr, after informing his brother that a number of these men had run away in all directions, advised him to hurry to Madīnah to give himself up and repent. He assured him that the Prophet would not kill anyone who came to him repentent and warned him that unless he was prepared to do so, he should escape to the most distant place on earth to remain alive. Bujayr had indeed told the truth. Muhammad commanded the execution of only four persons, one of whom was a poet who had vituperated the Prophet severely, and two of whom had hurt his daughter, Zaynab, when with her husband's permission, she sought to emigrate to Makkah to join her father. Ka'b recognized the veracity and timeliness of his brother's advice; and, anxious not to spend the rest of his life as an outlaw, he hurried to Madīnah, spent the night at a friend's house, and came to the Prophet in the morning at the mosque to declare his conversion and pledge his allegiance. In the Prophet's presence, Ka'b recited his famous poem which opened with the verse: "Great distance now separates me from Su'ād. My heart is orphaned and bereaved. It awaits the sacrifice which will ransom my beloved." The Prophet forgave him and he became a good Muslim.

Conversion of Zayd al Khayl and Others

Another consequence of the same influence was that the tribes began to come to the Prophet to pledge their allegiance. Such was the case of a delegation headed by Zayd al Khayl who came to Madīnah to pledge allegiance of the tribe of Ṭay'. Muhammad gave the delegation a fair welcome, conversed with their leader, and was so well pleased with him that he said: "No Arab has ever been praised before me but that when I finally met him

I discovered that his eulogy surpassed his reality, except Zayd al Khayl concerning whom I had heard less than I have found." The Prophet then changed the name of his guest from Zayd al Khayl (meaning literally, "increase of horses") to Zayd al Khayr ("increase of goodness"), and the whole tribe of Tay' entered into Islām under Zayd's leadership.

'Adiyy ibn Ḥātim al Ṭā'iy was a Christian who felt the strongest hatred for Muḥammad. As he witnessed the rise of the Prophet and the Muslims and the spread of their dominion over the Peninsula, he loaded his goods, family, and children on his camel and joined his fellow Christians in al Shām. Indeed, 'Adiyy escaped at the very time that 'Alī ibn Abū Ṭālib destroyed, at the Prophet's command, the·idol of Ṭay' and seized a number of captives, including the daughter of Ḥātim and sister of 'Adiyy and a large amount of booty. 'Adiyy's sister was brought to Madīnah and was held in the captives' quarters by the Mosque's gate. As the Prophet passed through the gate one day, she said to him from behind the bars: "O Prophet of God! My father has perished and my supporter has deserted. Be merciful to me, that God may be merciful to you." When the Prophet learned that her supporter was 'Adiyy ibn Ḥātim al Ṭā'iy, the escapee, he refused to talk to her. She tried once more, and this time she succeeded. In conversation, the Prophet mentioned to her her father's old prestige and noble reputation in pre-Islāmic days. He praised him for the good name his hospitality had given to all Arabs. The Prophet then granted her her freedom, gave her respectable clothes and pocket money to satisfy her other needs, and sent her to her people with the first al Shām-bound caravan. Upon joining her brother, she mentioned to him the noble treatment Muḥammad had accorded her. 'Adiyy was so impressed by the Prophet's chivalry that he returned with her to Madīnah and joined the ranks of Islām immediately.

Likewise, following the conquest of Makkah, the victory of al Shām, and the siege of al Ṭā'if, the great and the poor, the tribes and the individuals, all came to Muḥammad to acknowledge his mission and to convert to Islām. In the meantime, Muḥammad remained in Madīnah and, feeling reassured that God has given him victory, he enjoyed a measure of peaceful existence.

Muḥammad's Bereavement

The measure of peaceful existence which Muḥammad enjoyed was not to last. His daughter, Zaynab, was seriously ill. After

al Ḥuwayrith and Habbār hurt her when she attempted to emigrate from Makkah, Zaynab suffered from a miscarriage from
which she never recovered. With her loss, Muḥammad's only
surviving child was Fāṭimah, for Umm Kulthūm and Ruqayyah
had passed away earlier. Muḥammad was saddened by the loss
of Zaynab. He surely appreciated her compassionate disposition
and loyalty to her husband, Abū al 'Āṣī ibn al Rabī', whom she
had ransomed after his fall as captive at the Battle of Badr
with jewelry her father had given her on her wedding. It did
not matter that she, a Muslim, sought to ransom her husband,
an unbeliever; nor that this unbeliever husband had fought
against her father in a battle in which, had the Quraysh been
victorious, Muhammad would have surely lost his life. The
Prophet praised Zaynab's good disposition and strong loyalty
to her husband, and bemoaned her suffering from sickness during
the whole time since her emigration from Makkah. It is no
wonder that he felt bereaved at her loss. He felt the same deep
concern for the well-being and happiness of others. It was his
nature to sympathize with every sufferer, every bereaved, and
to take the trouble to go everywhere within and outside of
Madīnah to visit the sick, console the destitute, and reassure
the wounded. The hand of fate had here touched his own daughter.
His tragedy was not the first of its kind, but the fifth, as he
had previously lost two of his daughters and two sons. If he
had found in God's favorable disposition toward him a measure
of consolation, he surely well deserved it.

The Birth of Ibrāhīm, Muḥammad's Son

Soon, Muḥammad's loss was to be compensated. Māriyah, his
Coptic wife, gave birth to a son whom Muḥammad called
Ibrāhīm after the ancestor-father of the Arabs as well as of
ḥanīfism and Islām. Until that day, and since the Archbishop
of Alexandria had presented her to the Prophet, Māriyah had
the status of a slave. She did not enjoy the benefits of a living
quarter by the mosque as did the other wives of the Prophet,
"the Mothers of Believers." Muḥammad had provided Māriyah
with a second-story residence in one of the outskirts of Madīnah,
called today Mashrabat Umm Ibrāhīm. Her house, which was
surrounded with vineyards, was where Muḥammad used to visit
her every now and then. He had chosen her for himself and gave
her sister Sīrīn to Ḥassān ibn Thābit. Muḥammad did not expect

to have any more children as none of his wives except the late Khadījah had ever conceived, though some of them were quite young and capable of bearing children. When Māriyah gave birth to Ibrahīm, the event brought to Muḥammad, a man past sixty years of age, great joy and filled his heart with reassurance and jubilation. By giving birth to a child, the status of Māriyah was raised in the Prophet's esteem; he now looked upon her as a free wife, indeed, as one enjoying a most favored position.

Jealousy of the Prophet's Wives

It was natural that this change would incite no little jealousy among his other wives who continued to be barren. It was also natural that the Prophet's esteem and affection for the newborn child and his mother increased that jealousy. Moreover, Muḥammad had liberally rewarded Salmā, the wife of Abū Rāfi', for her role as midwife. He celebrated the birth by giving away a measure of grain to all the destitute of Madīnah. He assigned the newborn to the care of Umm Sayf, a wet nurse, who owned seven goats whose milk she was to put at the disposal of the newborn. Every day Muḥammad would visit the house of Māriyah in order to take another look at his son's radiant face and to reassure himself of the newborn's continued health and growth. All this incited the strongest jealousy among the barren wives. The question was, how far would these wives be able to bear the constant challenge?

One day, with the pride characteristic of new parents, the Prophet carried his son on his arm and walked into 'Ā'ishah's quarters in order to show him to her. He pointed out to her his great resemblance to his offspring. 'Ā'ishah looked at the baby and said that she saw no resemblance at all. When the Prophet observed how much the child was growing, 'Ā'ishah responded waspishly that any child given the amount of milk which Ibrahīm was getting would grow just as big and strong as he. Indeed, the birth of Ibrahīm brought such disaffection to the wives of the Prophet as would go beyond these and similar unfriendly answers. It reached such proportions that revelation itself voiced a special condemnation. Undoubtedly, the whole affair had left its imprint on the life of Muḥammad as well as on the history of Islām.

Such far-reaching effects were natural in the circumstances. For Muḥammad had granted to his wives a position hitherto

unknown in Arabia. 'Umar ibn al Khaṭṭāb said, "By God, in
pre-Islāmic days, we never gave consideration to our women. It
was only after God had revealed in their regard what He did
that we started to do so. My wife came once seeking to dissuade
me from doing what I had planned to do. When I answered
her that this was none of her business, she said: 'How strange
of you, 'Umar ibn al Khaṭṭāb! You refuse to be told anything
whereas your daughter may criticize her husband, the Prophet
of God—May God's peace and blessing be upon him—and do
so so strongly that he remains worried the whole day long.'
Upon hearing this, I took my mantle and went straight to my
daughter, Ḥafsah, and said to her: 'O my daughter, is it true
that you criticize the Prophet of God and do so so strongly that
he remains worried the whole day long?' Ḥafsah answered: 'Indeed, I and his other wives do criticize him.' I said: 'You had
better be warned that this will bring both the punishment of
God and the wrath of His Prophet upon you. O Daughter, do
not be deceived by that woman who became too proud of herself because of her beauty or Muhammad's love for her.' I left
my daughter and went to visit Umm Salamah, another wife of
the Prophet and a close relative of mine. Upon asking her the
same question, Umm Salamah replied: 'How strange of you,
O Ibn al Khaṭṭāb! Are you going to interfere in everything, even
in the Prophet's own domestic affairs?'" 'Umar continued: "With
this I was utterly rebuffed and I abandoned every thought I had
entertained." Muslim has related in his *Ṣaḥīḥ* that Abū Bakr
once sought the permission of the Prophet to visit him, and so
did 'Umar. Upon entrance into the Prophet's living quarters,
they found him sitting still and silent, surrounded by his wives.
After announcing that he was about to break the silence with a
story which he hoped the Prophet would find entertaining, he
said: "O Prophet of God, if the daughter of Khārijah,[1] *i.e.*, my
wife, were ever seen or heard asking me for money, I would
surely pull her hair." The Prophet laughed, saying, "Here are
my wives surrounding me and asking me for money." Immediately, Abū Bakr rose to his daughter 'Ā'ishah and pulled
her hair and so did 'Umar to his daughter, Ḥafsah. Both Abū
Bakr and 'Umar said to their daughters: "Do you dare ask
the Prophet of God what he cannot afford to give?" They
answered: "No, by God, we do not ask him any such thing."
Actually, Abū Bakr and 'Umar had sought to see the Prophet
because the latter was conspicuously absent at the previous

prayer in the mosque, and the Muslims had asked one another the cause of his absence. It was in connection with this conversation between Abū Bakr and 'Umar and their daughters that the following verse was revealed:

$$يَٰٓأَيُّهَا ٱلنَّبِىُّ قُل لِّأَزْوَٰجِكَ إِن كُنتُنَّ تُرِدْنَ ٱلْحَيَوٰةَ ٱلدُّنْيَا وَزِينَتَهَا فَتَعَالَيْنَ أُمَتِّعْكُنَّ وَأُسَرِّحْكُنَّ سَرَاحًا جَمِيلًا وَإِن كُنتُنَّ تُرِدْنَ ٱللَّهَ وَرَسُولَهُ وَٱلدَّارَ ٱلْءَاخِرَةَ فَإِنَّ ٱللَّهَ أَعَدَّ لِلْمُحْسِنَٰتِ مِنكُنَّ أَجْرًا عَظِيمًا$$

"O Prophet, tell your wives that in case they want the pleasures of this world and its ornaments, you will give them their freedom and send them on their way in fairness that they may elsewhere seek what they desire. But if they want God, His Prophet, and the other world, then remind them that God has prepared for the virtuous among them a great reward."[2]

The Wives' Plotting

As a matter of fact, the wives of the Prophet went as far as to plot against their husband. Muḥammad was in the habit of visiting them immediately after the midafternoon prayer. According to one report, he once visited Ḥafṣah (or Zaynab, daughter of Jaḥsh according to another version) and paid her an unusually long visit. This made all the other wives jealous. 'Ā'ishah reported: "Ḥafṣah and I plotted together that any wife whom the Prophet—May God's peace and blessing be upon him —will visit will complain to him that she finds his breath undesirable, and will ask him whether he has eaten any *maghāfīr* (*i.e.*, sweets with bad smells, and the Prophet could not stand bad smells). As he entered upon one of his wives, she asked him that question to which he answered: "No, but I have taken some honey at the quarters of Zaynab, which I will never do again." Having agreed to the plot of 'Ā'ishah and Ḥafṣah, Sawdah related that when the Prophet approached her, she asked him whether he ate any *maghāfīr* to which he answered, "No." She asked him: "Where then does this bad odor come from?" Muḥammad replied: "Ḥafṣah gave me a little honey, so then it must be that the bees that made that honey had picked it up from the blooms of the awful tree which produces the *maghāfīr*."

When he entered upon 'Ā'ishah, the latter repeated to him the question of Sawdah, which he heard again from Ṣafiyyah, whereupon he vowed never to touch that honey again. Upon hearing the other wives' reports, Sawdah said: "May God be praised! We have deprived him of something he truly likes." 'Ā'ishah, however, looked askance at Sawdah and asked her to keep quiet.

Since the Prophet granted to his wives such an unusual position at a time when Arab women amounted to nothing at all in society, it was natural for his wives to abuse the liberty which none of their peers had known before, a liberty which went so far as to enable any of them to criticize the Prophet so severely as to spoil his disposition the rest of the day. He often ignored some of his wives, and avoided others on many occasions, precisely in order to discourage their abuse of his compassion. Even so, one of them was so moved by jealousy as to exceed all limits of decency. But when Māriyah gave birth to Ibrāhīm, they were incensed. They lost all the composure and self-mastery which Muhammad had for years been trying to instill into them. It was for this reason that 'Ā'ishah had gone to the extreme of denying all resemblance between him and his son, a denial which amounted to an accusation of adultery on the part of the innocent Māriyah.

Their Rebellion

One day Ḥafṣah went to her father's house complaining about this situation. While the Prophet was in her room, Māriyah came to him and stayed with him some time. Upon Ḥafṣah's return she found the Prophet and Māriyah in her quarters and, as she waited for them to come out, her jealousy broke all bounds. When, finally, Māriyah left the quarters and Ḥafṣah entered, she said to the Prophet: "I have seen who was here. By God, that was an insult to me. You would not have dared do that if I amounted to anything at all in your eyes." At the moment Muhammad realized that such deep-lying jealousy might even move Ḥafṣah to broadcast what she had seen among the other wives. In an attempt to please her, Muhammad promised that he would not go unto Māriyah if she would only refrain from broadcasting what she had seen. Ḥafṣah promised to comply. However, she could not keep her promise as jealousy continued to affect her disposition. Hence, she intimated the secret to 'Ā'ishah, who in turn reported it to the Prophet. He took it as evidence of Ḥafṣah's failure to keep her promise. Perhaps the affair did not stop with Ḥafṣah and 'Ā'ishah but spread to the other wives. Perhaps, too, all of them had noticed the high esteem in which Māriyah was held and sympathized with 'Ā'ishah and Ḥafṣah's opposition to the Prophet. There is nothing unusual in the whole story, such gossip and petty jealousies being commonplace between man and his many wives. A man's affection belongs where he puts it within his household, and the controversy which the daughters of Abū Bakr and 'Umar had woven around the Prophet's affection for Māriyah was utterly groundless. Previously we had seen that some disaffection had risen between the Prophet and his wives on various occasions because of the pocket money he allocated to them, or because of the honey Zaynab used to serve. Therefore, they had all the more reason to feel slighted and no little alienated when they discovered their husband's inclination toward 'Ā'ishah or his esteem for Māriyah.

An explosion was soon to come. One day, while the Prophet was staying with 'Ā'ishah, his other wives delegated Zaynab, daughter of Jaḥsh, to go in and, in their name, to accuse him of injustice and unfairness to them, and to plead that his love for 'Ā'ishah was a violation of the code which he himself had set down of a day and night for each of his wives. On the other hand, realizing that the Prophet did not care very much for her charms, and being no longer anxious to please him, Sawdah had given up her day and night to 'Ā'ishah. But Zaynab was not satisfied with expressing the other wives' indignation at this apparent injustice. She attacked 'Ā'ishah personally. The latter was anxious to defend herself, but kept still in response to the Prophet's reconciliating pleas. Seeing that 'Ā'ishah was defenseless, Zaynab went to excess in her accusations, and the Prophet finally had to permit his favorite wife to take her defense into her own hands. 'Ā'ishah spoke out with great eloquence in refuting Zaynab's claims. The Prophet listened with obvious satisfaction and admired the perspicacity of Abū Bakr's daughter.

Indeed, favoritism for some of his wives had created such controversy and antagonism among the "Mothers of the Believers" that Muḥammad once thought of divorcing some of them, but they soon agreed to let him distribute his favors as he pleased. When Māriyah gave birth to Ibrāhīm, their jealousy was at its strongest, especially in the case of 'Ā'ishah. Certainly, Muḥammad's leniency and gentleness encouraged rebellion, and the new status which he had conferred upon women in society fanned their vanity. Muḥammad, however, was not free to spend his time dealing with household problems. The need soon came to be felt for a decisive lesson to reestablish discipline and to liberate him for teaching the message and fulfilling the mission of his prophethood. Hence, he decided to ignore his wives and, indeed, to threaten them with divorce. A lesson had to be taught to them, and the time had apparently come for a decision. Either these women were to return to reason or they would be given their freedom in a mutually convenient divorce.

The Prophet's Separation from His Wives

Muḥammad isolated himself from all his women for a full month and refused to talk about them to anyone. Nor did anyone dare talk to him concerning them. During this month, his mind was absorbed by his mission and the requirement of carrying the message of Islām beyond the Arabian Peninsula. Abū Bakr, 'Umar, and his other in-laws as well, were deeply concerned over the sad fate that awaited the "Mothers of the Believers" now that they had exposed themselves to the anger of the Prophet and the consequent punishment of God. It was even said that Muḥammad had divorced Ḥafsah, 'Umar's daughter, after she had divulged the secret she had promised to keep. The marketplace of Madīnah hummed with rumors about the impending divorce of the Prophet's wives. The wives, for their part, were repentent and apprehensive. They regretted that their jealousy of one another had carried them away, that they had abused and harmed their gentle husband who was to each one of them at all times an elder brother, a compassionate father, a nearest kin, and the best of everything that might be hoped for in this life and the next. Muḥammad spent most of his time in a storeroom he owned, placing his servant Rabāḥ at its doorstep as long as he was inside. Therein he used to sleep on a very hard bed of coarse date branches.

'Umar's Reconciliation of the Prophet and His Wives

At the end of the month during which Muḥammad vowed to separate himself from his wives, the Muslims were despondent over the prospect of Muḥammad's domestic affairs. Many signs of dejection and sorrow were apparent on their faces as they gathered in the mosque. 'Umar ibn al Khaṭṭāb sought out the

Prophet in his isolation. He went to the storeroom and called
out to his servant, Rabāḥ, asking for permission to enter. Rabāḥ
went in to speak to the Prophet but came out silent, a sign
that Muḥammad did not wish to see anyone. 'Umar asked once
more. Once more Rabāḥ went in and came out silent. At this,
'Umar raised his voice that the Prophet might hear and, repeating
his request for an audience, said: "O Rabāḥ, seek permission
for me to see the Prophet of God. I fear that he thinks that I
have come to intercede for my daughter, Ḥafsah. By God, if he
were to ask me to strike off her head, I would do so without
hesitation." The Prophet then permitted him to enter. He came
in, sat down as his eyes roved around the room, and began to
cry. Muḥammad asked him why he was crying. Actually 'Umar
cried out of severe shock at seeing the Prophet lying on the
only piece of furniture in the room, the miserable straw mat,
whose pattern of weaving had imprinted itself on the Prophet's
side. He cried out of compassion for the Prophet's isolation in a
room absolutely empty except for a little barley, a skin, and a
small container of water. After hearing 'Umar's explanation,
Muḥammad taught him a lesson on the necessity of renouncing
the pleasures of the world in order to achieve inner peace. 'Umar
then said: "O Prophet of God, what difficulties do your wives
present? If you have truly lost them through divorce, you still
have God, His angels Jibrīl and Mikhā'īl, Abū Bakr and me,
and all the Muslims on your side." He kept on talking to the
Prophet in this vein until the latter felt pleased and even smiled.
As the Prophet's mood changed for the better, 'Umar told him
about the despondency of the Muslims gathered in the mosque
and their bemoaning of his separation from his wives. The
Prophet explained that he had not divorced his wives but that
he meant only to teach them a lesson. 'Umar immediately asked
for and was granted permission to inform the Muslims waiting
in the mosque. He hurried thither to announce the good news that
the Prophet of God—May God's peace and blessing be upon him
—had not divorced his wives. It was in connection with this
incident that the following verses of the Qur'ān were revealed:
"O Prophet, why do you forbid yourself that which God has made
legitimate for you, namely, to seek to please your wives? God
is certainly compassionate and merciful. God has made it legitimate for you to release yourself from your vows. He is your
Lord, and He is the All-Wise and All-Knowing. The Prophet
had intimated information to one of his wives, but she did not

keep the secret. When God brought knowledge to the Prophet of her insincerity, and the Prophet blamed her for it, her asking who had told him the news thus divulged her secret. The Prophet answered that God, the All-Knowing and Omniscient, had informed him of the deed. If the insincere wife and her insincere confidante were to repent to God and purify their thoughts, then they would be forgiven. But if they persist in striving against him, then God will compensate him with His friendship, with that of Jibrīl, Ṣāliḥ, the believers and angels, who will assist him in his plight. In case he should divorce his wives, God might even replace them with better ones, with women who are Muslims, believing, pious, repentant, and virtuous, whether widowed or virgins."[3] With this revelation, the whole affair was brought to a close. The wives of the Prophet, having regained their wisdom and common sense, returned to their husband repentant, pious, and confirmed in their faith. Once reconciled by their repentance, Muhammad returned to his wives and his domestic life resumed its peace—the necessary prerequisite for any man with a mission to perform.

The Judgment of Critical Historiography

In my opinion, the foregoing is the true account of the story of Muhammad's self-imposed isolation from his wives, of the choice he gave them, of the incidents which led to his isolation as well as of its causes and consequences. This account is confirmed by all the evidence of the books of Qur'ānic exegesis and of Hadith, as well as by the accounts of various biographies. The fact remains, however, that not one of these biographies has presented all these data in the proper sequence, beginning with the causes and ending with the consequences in the manner we have done here. Most of the biographers have passed by this matter too quickly and too simplistically. They give the impression that they found the material too rough to handle. Some accounts have pondered the story of the honey and *maghāfīr* at length but have omitted to point to the affair of Hafsah and Māriyah. As for the Orientalists, they regard the story of Hafsah and Māriyah and the former's divulgence to 'Ā'ishah of the secret she promised to keep as the cause of all that had happened. Their purpose is precisely to add to their already alienated readers further occasion to condemn the Arab Prophet by presenting him as a shameless runner after women. It is also my considered opinion that the Muslim historians are not justified in ignoring these incidents, or in omitting to examine all the data available with a view to giving them an objective interpretation. That is what we have sought to do here, though only in part. While the mistake of the Muslim historians was to underestimate the importance of these events, that of the western Orientalists is to exaggerate their importance, to violate historiographic precision, and to vent their Christian prejudice. Genuine historical criticism will not attribute to any man as great as Muḥammad such a petty conduct as would be implied by referring his self-imposed exile solely to Ḥafsah's divulgence of a domestic secret to 'Ā'ishah. In fact, Muḥammad had nothing to hide since the women in question were all his own legitimate wives. Indeed, whatever the nature of that domestic secret, it is too insignificant to cause Muḥammad to threaten to divorce all his wives. Genuine historical criticism would also refuse to explain these events as due to the "honey" affair. A man as great, forbearing, and compassionate as Muḥammad, as all historians and biographers acknowledge, would not regard such incidents as justifying a whole month's isolation, let alone divorce. The critical attitude is satisfied only when all these incidents are arranged in such historical sequence as would not violate the causal interrelationships between them. Only such history-writing satisfies the requirements of objectivity and presents its data as elements in factual interrelationships acceptable to reason. The arrangement we have given these events seems to us to have achieved precisely this, and to accord perfectly with what is known of Muḥammad's wisdom, greatness, determination and farsightedness.

Refutation of the Orientalists' Claim

Referring to some of the verses at the beginning of *sūrah* "Al Taḥrīm" quoted above, some orientalists argue that none of the holy books of the Orient make any mention of domestic problems such as those of Muḥammad. I do not think we need to quote here the similar stories and accounts of other scriptures. Suffice it to mention here the People of Lot and their argument with the two angelic visitors of Lot, the story of Lot's wife and her vagrancies. Indeed, the Torah does tell the story of Lot's two daughters, of their deliberately intoxicating their father with wine that he might commit incest and save their seed, and how they then suffered the punishment they deserved. We may say that in fact, contrary to the Orientalists claim, all the holy books have told stories about the prophets and have given accounts of what happened to them so that they might serve as examples for the education of mankind. Likewise, the Qur'ān tells many stories for the same purpose, stories which God related to His prophets for the best of purposes. The Qur'ān was not revealed for Muhammad's benefit alone but for that of all men. Muhammad is a prophet and a messenger preceded by many prophets and messengers, some of whose tales the Qur'ān took upon itself to tell. That the Qur'ān should find it fitting to tell some of the stories of Muhammad's life and to give some account of his biography to provide examples for the education of Muslims, and that it should find it fitting to give aspects of Muhammad's wise, pious, and virtuous conduct so that the Muslims might find in him an example to emulate, is no different from the contents and purpose of any other holy book. Moreover, what the Qur'ān reported about Muhammad is not different in content or purpose from what it reported of the lives of the former prophets. If, therefore, it is now asserted that Muhammad isolated himself from his wives, not for any single reason deducible from that fact, nor for Hafsah's divulgence to 'Ā'ishah of Muhammad's legitimate love for Māriyah—a right which belongs to any man toward his free and slave wives—this would not be far from the truth. But it does expose the Orientalists whose claim stands on the shallowest grounds and whose historiography flies in the face of the biographical data common to all holy scriptures.

Minaret of the National Mosque, Masjid Negara, Kuala Lumpur, Malaysia.

27

Campaign of Tabūk and the Death of Ibrahīm

Institution of Zakāt and Kharāj

All the foregoing conflicts between the Prophet and his wives did not in the least affect the conduct of public affairs. After the conquest of Makkah and the conversion of its people, the cause of Islām confronted less danger than hitherto. The whole Peninsula had begun to feel the passing of inter-Arab war. The holy sanctuary held as sacred by the Arabs, to which they had performed pilgrimages for generations, had become an integral institution of the new religion. Its attendant functions of *sidānah*, *rifādah*, and *siqāyah*[1] had been equally integrated into the order of Islām as Makkah passed under the control of Muḥammad. The conquest of Makkah therefore led to a strengthening of public Muslim life and civil order, and the Muslims felt more confident as their power increased everywhere throughout the Peninsula. With the widening of Muslim society, public functions naturally demanded an increase in public expense. It was therefore inevitable that the Muslims be asked to pay *zakāt* of *al 'ushr;*[2] and that the Arabs who decided to maintain their pre-Islāmic faith to pay whatever *kharāj*[3] was imposed upon them. Taxes are always uncomfortable, and taxpayers might always complain or even rebel against them. Nonetheless, the new order imposed by the new religion on the Peninsula necessitated a large public expense, impossible to meet without the additional incomes from *zakāt al 'ushr* and *kharāj*. For this purpose, soon after his return from Makkah, Muḥammad sent his collectors to levy and

443

collect a tenth of the income of the tribes now converted to
Islām. He commanded the collectors explicitly to restrict themselves to the incomes, never to touch the people's capitals. These
collectors went in different directions to fulfill their duty.

The tribes welcomed the collectors and remitted to them the
amounts due wholeheartedly with the exceptions of a branch of
the tribe of Banū Tamīm and another of Banū al Mustaliq which
refused to pay. While the collector, 'Uyaynah ibn Hisn, was in
the neighborhood making collections, a branch of Banū Tamīm,
called Banū al 'Anbar, jumped upon him with their arrows
and swords and threw him out of their territory even before
he had asked them to remit their due. When 'Uyaynah ibn Hisn
told the news to Muhammad, he was sent right back at the
head of fifty riders to reestablish order. 'Uyaynah launched a
surprise attack against the Banū al 'Anbar, captured over fifty
men, women, and children and seized some of their wealth. The
Prophet received the captives and the seized properties and kept
them in Madīnah. Some of the Banū Tamīm had been converted
to Islām a long time before and had fought alongside the Prophet
in the battles of Makkah and Hunayn while others were still
unconverted. When these Muslims knew what their relatives,
the Banū al 'Anbar, had done and what had happened to them,
they sent a delegation of notables to seek the Prophet. They
asked for an audience in the Mosque of Madīnah calling out to
the Prophet to come out to meet them. This impropriety disturbed
the Prophet so much that he decided not to see them. Soon,
however, the time of prayer arrived and 'Utārid ibn Hājib called
the Prophet to lead the worship in the mosque as was his custom.
After prayer, the delegation approached the Prophet and related
to him what 'Uyaynah had done with their people. They took
especial pains to remind him of his comradeship in arms with
those of them who had joined Islām as well as of their high esteem
among the Arabs. They then said to him, "We have come here in
order to compete with your followers in poetic eloquence and
rhetoric. Would you please permit our poet to recite some of
his poems for you?" 'Utārid ibn Hājib, their orator, rose and
delivered his speech. When he finished, the Prophet of God
called Thābit ibn Qays to respond; when he finished, al Zabriqān
ibn Badr, their other poet, rose and recited his eulogy in verse,
whereupon Hassān ibn Thābit responded in verse also. When
this contest was ended, al Aqra' ibn Hābis said, "I swear that
this man (i.e., Muhammad) is surely going to win, for his orator

is more eloquent and his poet more poetic than ours. Indeed, the voices of the Muslims are higher than our voices." With this confession, the tribesmen converted to Islām, and the Prophet set the captives free and enabled them to return home.

When the Banū al Muṣṭaliq saw the tax collectors run away, they feared the consequences and immediately sent word to the Prophet explaining to him that the *zakāt* collector has nothing to fear from their quarter and that the whole affair with Banū al 'Anbar was a regrettable misunderstanding.

Indeed, not one of the provinces of the Arabian Peninsula failed to feel the power of Muḥammad. Every tribe or clan that attempted to resist faced the Prophet's overwhelming power and was compelled either to convert to Islām and pay the *zakāt* or submit to Muslim political power and pay the *kharāj*.

The Threat of Byzantine Invasion and Muslim Reaction

While still engaged in bringing security and order to the distant regions of the Peninsula, the news reached Muḥammad that Byzantium was mobilizing an army to invade the northern approaches of Arabia to avenge the last engagement at Mu'tah. It was also rumored that this imperial army would seek to stamp out the nascent power of the Muslims who now stood at the frontier of both the Byzantine and Persian empires. At once and without hesitation, the Prophet decided that the imperial army must be met and destroyed so completely that the Byzantines would not think again of attacking Arabia or interfering in its affairs. It was autumn, but the desert heat, being greater in the beginning of autumn than in summer, was all the more deadly. Moreover, a long distance separated Madīnah from al Shām. Any venture to cross it required great amounts of water and provisions. Inevitably, therefore, Muḥammad had to tell the people of his plan if they were to prepare themselves adequately. Equally, it was necessary this time to alter his old diversionary strategy of ordering the army to march in the opposite direction, for no such expedition as he was preparing for could be kept a secret. Indeed, Muḥammad sent messengers to all the tribes asking them to mobilize the greatest army ever, and to the Muslims of large means everywhere to give liberally for the equipment of the army. The Muslim force, the Prophet decided, should be so large and preponderous as to overwhelm an enemy long known for their numbers and military equipment.

The Muslim's Response to Muḥammad's Call to Arms

How were the Muslims to receive this new call to leave their families and properties in the height of summer heat, to venture in desolate and waterless deserts, and to confront an enemy powerful enough to defeat Persia and even too mighty to be defeated by the Muslims? Would their Islāmic conviction, love for the Prophet, and loyalty to God's religion inspire them to give up wealth, armour, and life, and to do so in such proportion as to instil terror in the heart of such an enemy? Or, would the discomforts of desert and summer heat, of thirst and hunger, force them to sit back and refuse to move? In those days, Muslim ranks included two kinds of people: those who entered Islām with hearts full of guidance and light and minds certain of their convictions, and those who did so in search of material gain or out of fear of Muslim arms. Those who belonged to the former group volunteered their own persons and offered all the equipment they could muster. They put themselves and their wealth entirely at the Prophet's disposal. Among them were the poor who walked on foot and the wealthy who provided for themselves and others. All hoped for martyrdom and closeness to God. The other group complained and looked for excuses to justify their recalcitrance. Secretly, they derided Muḥammad's call to arms and ridiculed its timing and strategy. These were the *munāfiqūn* about whom *Sūrah* "Al Tawbah" had spoken. How great was its call to *jihād!* And how terrible the punishment it promised to he who failed to answer the Prophet's call!

Al Munāfiqūn

Some of the *munāfiqūn* counseled one another not to venture out in the desert at that time. In response to them, God said:

وَقَالُوالَاتَنْفِرُوا فِى الْحَرِّ قُلْ نَارُجَهَنَّمَ أَشَدُّ حَرًّا لَوْ كَانُوا يَفْقَهُونَ ۞ فَلْيَضْحَكُوا قَلِيلًا وَلْيَبْكُوا كَثِيرًا ۚ جَزَآءً بِمَاكَانُوا يَكْسِبُونَ ۞

"They counseled against venturing out in the desert heat. Answer: 'The fire of hell is hotter, if only they knew.' They laugh now, but their pleasure is short lived. They shall weep far more, and they will have deserved every bit of it."[4]

The Prophet asked an older tribesman of Banū Salamah: "Uncle, will you fight the Byzantines?" The man answered: "O Prophet of God, permit me to stay behind and do not tempt me. For I am known to be a ladies' man and I am especially weak in front of Byzantine women." Commenting upon him, the Qur'ān said: "Among the *munāfiqūn* some impertinently begged to be permitted to stay behind so as not to be exposed to temptation. In temptation shall be their undoing. Then will they be cast into hell."[5] Those who in secret hated Muḥammad and resented his leadership seized the opportunity to strengthen the *munāfiqūn's* suspicion and disobedience. Fearing that they might get bolder unless they were shown some firmness, and learning that they were meeting in the house of a Jew called Suwaylim, the Prophet angrily sent Ṭalḥah ibn 'Ubaydullah to deal with them. Ṭalḥah and his companions put Suwaylim's house on fire while the *munāfiqūn* were meeting inside. As the flames· engulfed the house, one of them jumped from the roof and broke his leg. The others escaped without injury, but they never dared to meet again in Madīnah.

Recruitment of Jaysh al 'Usrah

This firmness in dealing with the *munāfiqūn* was not devoid of effects on all fronts. Even the wealthy Muslims came out to spend more liberally of their wealth in equipping the army. 'Uthmān ibn 'Affān alone spent one thousand Dīnārs. Many others spent of their wealth each according to his means. Those who were capable of equipping themselves did so on their own. But there were many others who offered all they had: their energies and their lives. The Prophet took as many of them as he could equip and apologized to the rest. These wept in sorrow at their poverty and were for this reason called *al bakkā'ūn,* or "the weepers." The army was finally assembled and counted thirty thousand men. Because of the difficulties encountered in its mobilization, this army was given the name *Jaysh al 'Usrah,* or the "hardship army."

The Muslims' March

While Muḥammad was busy settling the affairs of Madīnah—handing over the reins of government to Muḥammad ibn Maslamah, appointing 'Alī ibn Abū Ṭālib as guardian of his household and giving to each the necessary instructions—he left the army under the command of Abū Bakr. The latter led the assembled men in prayer, and when the Prophet returned, he handed the command back to him. Responding to Muḥammad's call, 'Abdullah ibn Ubayy came out at the head of a little band of soldiers and asked for permission to march alongside the Muslim army. The Prophet, however, preferred that 'Abdullah stay in Madīnah, for he was not quite sure of his good faith. At Muḥammad's command, the army began its march, raising great dust and making a tremendous roar. The people of Madīnah hurried to the rooftops to see this great mass of men, animals, and equipment move toward al Shām. They were anxious to catch a glimpse of this large mass of humanity venturing out against heat, thirst, and all kinds of hardship in order to fulfill their duty to God and to win His pleasure, the pleasure which they had deemed worthier than all the good things they had left behind. Indeed, the sight of this army on the march pioneered by ten thousand cavalrymen and the stupefied people of Madīnah watching it, moved to action those whom the very command of the Prophet failed to stir. Such was the case of Abū Khaythamah who, after seeing the Muslim army, went straight to his house where each of his two wives had cooked for him a delicious meal, drew some fresh water to drink, and sprinkled the tent and surroundings to cool off the place. Abū Khaythamah could not advance into his own house a single step before exclaiming, "The Prophet of God is battling the heat, sand, and thirst of the desert and I, Abū Khaythamah, languish in the cool, eat delicious food, and enjoy the company of beautiful women? No, by God, that cannot be! Prepare for me quickly some provisions that I may join him." He shot off like an arrow. There were probably many more who did likewise after realizing the shame that would befall them if they remained in the city.

Encampment at Al Ḥijr

The army arrived at al Ḥijr where the rock-hewn remains of Thamūd stood, and the Prophet commanded the army to dismount for a watering and a brief rest. When it was time to leave, he ordered against drinking the water or using it for ablutions. "If you have used any of it to knead bread," he said, "give your dough to the camels and do not eat it. Let no one go out into the open desert alone." Muḥammad knew that the place was desolate and often struck by blinding sandstorms. Two men disobeyed and went out of camp. One was carried away by the wind and the other buried in the sand. When morning came and the people saw that the sandstorm had filled the well with sand, they panicked. Soon rain fell upon them from a passing cloud. They drank, filled their skins, and felt reassured. Some of them thought this was a miracle. Others thought it was only a passing cloud.

Byzantine Withdrawal, Covenants of Peace with the North

The army then marched in the direction of Tabūk. News of its approach had already reached the Byzantines who immediately withdrew to the safety of their hinterland. When Muḥammad learned of their fear and withdrawal, he saw no reason to pursue them within their territory. Instead, he roamed over the border inviting all either to fight or befriend him. His purpose was to secure the frontiers of Arabia. Yūḥannā ibn Ru'bah, Governor of Aylah, received such an invitation. He came in person carrying a golden cross, presented gifts, declared his submission, and handed over the keys of his island to the Prophet. So did the people of al Jarbā' and Adhruh, and they all paid the *jizyah*. The Prophet gave each of them a covenant which read as the following document given to Yūḥannā. "In the name of God, the Merciful, the Compassionate. This is a covenant of security granted under God by Muhammad, the Prophet of God, to Yūḥannā ibn Ru'bah and the people of Aylah. Their ships, vehicles, and routes on land and on sea are secure under God's guaranty and Muhammad's. So are all those who accompany them whether of the peoples of al Shām, Yaman, or beyond the seas. Whoever among them perpetrates a crime shall be liable for it in his own person, and it shall be legitimate for Muhammad to confiscate his wealth. It shall not be legitimate to prevent any one of them from using a well or a road on land or sea which they have been in the habit of using." When the Prophet applied his seal to the document, he presented Yūḥannā with a mantle woven in Yaman and showed him every courtesy, respect, and friendship. It was further agreed that Aylah would remit a yearly *jizyah* of three hundred Dīnārs.

Ibn al Walīd's Campaign against Dūmah

With the withdrawal of the Byzantines and the binding of the frontier provinces with treaties and covenants of peace, Muḥammad had no reason to march any further. The only one he feared was Ukaydir ibn 'Abd al Malik al Kindī, the Christian prince of Dūmah. This prince was suspected of preparing to launch a treacherous attack as soon as the Byzantine forces could return. Taking no chances, Muhammad sent Khālid ibn al Walīd with five hundred cavalrymen to deal with this threat and commanded the army to return to Madīnah. Khālid hurried to Dūmah and, discovering that its king was out on a hunting trip with his brother Hassān, attacked it without finding any appreciable resistance outside the city; its gates, however, remained tightly closed. Khālid seized Ukaydir and his brother Hassān as they returned home. He killed Hassān and threatened to kill Ukaydir unless the gates of the city were opened. Ukaydir and his city yielded. After seizing two thousand camels, eight hundred goats, four hundred loads of grain, and four hundred coats of arms, Khālid carried them, together with his captive, Prince Ukaydir, to Madīnah. Muhammad offered Islām to Ukaydir, and the latter converted. He was then reinstated on his throne and became the Prophet's ally.

The Muslims' Return

Leading all these thousands of troops back to Madīnah across the wide wastes which separate it from al Shām required no little feat of leadership on the part of Muhammad. Not many of them understood the Prophet's purpose or saw the value of the treaties he concluded with Aylah and other northern states. Evidently they could not appreciate the fact that Muhammad has thereby guaranteed the frontiers of Arabia and created buffer zones between it and Byzantium. All they saw was the plain fact that they had crossed long desert wastes full of hardships, lingered in the vicinity of Tabūk some twenty days, and returned without a fight, without capturing anyone, or seizing anything. Was this reason enough to justify their leaving Madīnah at harvest time? Some of them began to whisper to one another derisive remarks about the whole expedition. Others, more faithful, reported the rumors to the Prophet. Muhammad dealt with the guilty, sometimes harshly and sometimes with leniency, his purpose being to maintain discipline in the body of the army. When the army was just about to enter Madīnah, Khālid ibn al Walīd caught up with and joined them, together with his captive Ukaydir and the booty he seized from Dūmah. Ukaydir wore a golden, brocaded garment which caught the attention of everyone in Madīnah.

The Recalcitrants

Upon the Muslims' return, those who failed to answer the call to mobilize and remained behind came to give account of their failure. They were given such harsh judgment that all those of questionable faith, including those soldiers who derided the outcome of the campaign just concluded, trembled in fear or changed their minds. The recalcitrants presented their reasons which were anything but spurious. The Prophet listened and, for the most part, let them go free pending God's final judgment. Three others told the truth frankly but repentantly. They were Ka'b ibn Mālik, Murārah ibn al Rabī', and Hilāl ibn Umayyah. Muhammad ordered them to be boycotted by the Muslims for fifty days, after which they were forgiven and rehabilitated within the community. In this regard the following verses of the Qur'ān were revealed: "God has forgiven the Prophet, and the Muhājirūn and Ansār who followed him on the 'hardship expedition.' Some of them had almost swerved away from faith. But they repented and God has forgiven them. He is the Merciful, the Compassionate. The three men who remained behind were accused, indicted, and castigated by their own consciences; they came forth repentant, however, as they realized that there is no escape from Him except by His judgment and mercy. God has accepted their repentance and forgiven them, that they may lead a new life. God is the Forgiver, the Merciful."[6]

Severe Treatment of the Munāfiqūn

From then on, Muhammad dealt more and more severely with the *munāfiqūn,* whose presence and influence among the Muslims became increasingly grave and demanded decisive solution. Muhammad did not doubt God's promise to give His religion victory and His word power, or that the Muslims would soon increase in very large numbers. Previously, when Islām was limited to the confines of Madīnah and its vicinity, it was possible for him personally to supervise all Muslim affairs. Now that Islām had spread to the farthest reaches of Arabia and stood ready to cross its frontiers, any leniency toward the *munāfiqūn* might lead to grave consequences. Hence, there was all the more reason for the Prophet to eradicate this source of potential disruption. A group of *munāfiqūn* built a mosque at Dhū Awān, an hour's ride from Madīnah, wherein to meet to concoct and plan their divisive strategy and misinterpret and misrepresent the words of God to the people. Before he left for the campaign of Tabūk, the Prophet was even asked by them to dedicate their mosque. The time, however, was pressing and the Prophet asked to be excused. After his return, the Prophet learned more about this group and their purposes, and hence ordered their mosque assigned to the flames. The *munāfiqūn* shook with fear and went into hiding. Henceforth, there remained only their elder, 'Abdullah ibn Ubayy, to lead and protect them.

'Abdullah, however, did not live long after Tabūk. He fell ill two months later and died. To the knowledge of everyone, 'Abdullah nursed the strongest hatred and resentment for the Prophet ever since the Hijrah. This notwithstanding, Muhammad was careful enough to let no Muslim inflict any harm upon him. Indeed, more. When he learned of 'Abdullah's death, Muhammad was quick to conduct a funeral service for him, to pray for him, and to see to it that he was given proper burial. With 'Abdullah's passing, however, the *munāfiqūn* lost their strongest pillar, and most of them hurried thereafter to repentance and genuine faith.

The Prophet's Last Campaign

With the campaign of Tabūk, the word of God became supreme throughout the whole Peninsula. Arab frontiers became secure and the peoples of Arabia began to enter Islām *en masse* and to merge into greater unity under Muhammad. The campaign of Tabūk was the last one the Prophet conducted. Henceforth, he remained in Madīnah contented with what God had done for him. His son, Ibrahīm, who was then sixteen or eighteen months old, was to him a source of constant joy. Whenever he finished with the day's official engagements and receptions, and satisfied himself that his duties to God, family, and friends were fulfilled, he would sit with his son, fondling and playing with him. He watched his son grow, become daily more resembling his father and, like any other father, Muhammad became more and more attached to him. Throughout these months the child was in the care of his nurse Umm Sayf, to whom Muhammad gave some goats to complement her milk supply.

Illness and Death of Ibrahīm

Muhammad's attachment to his son had nothing to do with either his faith or with his mission. Repeatedly, he used to say: "We, the prophets, have nothing to pass on as inheritance to

anyone. Any wealth we may leave behind must go for charity."
Muḥammad's case was purely one of a common human emotion,
though in him, it has reached its highest and noblest expression.
In the Arab, this human emotion expressed itself in causing him
to see in his male progeny a form of eternity. It explains fully
Muḥammad's love for his son, however strong it may have been.
Indeed, Muḥammad had more reason for such strong attachment
since he had lost his two sons, al Qāsim and al Ṭāhir, at a
tender age, and his daughters—even after they grew to maturity,
married, and bore children—so that only Fāṭimah remained of all
his progeny. Naturally, these sons and daughters who passed
away one after the other and were buried by Muḥammad's own
hand left their father with a severe sense of bereavement. It
was natural that a father so bereaved would feel excessive joy
and the strongest personal pride and hope at the birth and
growing of a son.

The promise and hope which Ibrahīm represented were not to
last long. Soon, the child fell seriously ill. He was moved to a
date orchard near Mashrabat Umm Ibrahīm, where his mother
and Sīrīn, her sister, looked after him. When his state worsened
and it became apparent that he will not live long, Muḥammad
was called. He was so shocked at the news that he felt his
knees could no more carry him, and asked 'Abd al Rahman ibn
'Awf to give him his hand to lean upon. He proceeded immediately
to the orchard and arrived in time to bid farewell to an infant
dying in his mother's lap. Muḥammad took the child and laid
him in his own lap with shaking hand. His heart was torn
apart by the new tragedy, and his face mirrored his inner pain.
Choking with sorrow, he said to his son, "O Ibrahīm, against
the judgment of God, we cannot avail you a thing," and then
fell silent. Tears flowed from his eyes. The child lapsed gradually,
and his mother and aunt watched and cried loudly and inces-
santly, but the Prophet never ordered them to stop. As Ibrahīm
surrendered to death, Muḥammad's hope which had consoled
him for a brief while completely crumbled. With tears in his
eyes he talked once more to the dead child: "O Ibrahīm, were the
truth not certain that the last of us will join the first, we
would have mourned you even more than we do now." A moment
later he said: "The eyes send their tears and the heart is
saddened, but we do not say anything except that which pleases
our Lord. Indeed, O Ibrahīm, we are bereaved by your departure
from us."

Aware of Muḥammad's sorrow, the wise among the Muslim

sought to remind the Prophet that he himself had commanded
against indulgence in self-pity after a bereavement. Muḥammad,
however, answered: "I have not commanded against sadness, but
against raising one's voice in lamentation. What you see in me
is the effect of the love and compassion in my heart for my lost
one. Remember that whoever feels no compassion toward others
will not receive any compassion." These may not have been
his exact words, but the meaning remains the same. Muḥammad
tried to sublimate his sadness and lighten his sorrow, and, looking
toward Māriyah and Sīrīn, he said to them in appeasement that
Ibrahīm would have his own nurse in Paradise. Umm Burdah,
or according to another version, al Faḍl ibn 'Abbās, washed the
body of the child in preparation for burial. He was carried on
a little bed by the Prophet, his uncle al 'Abbās, and a number
of Muslims to the cemetery of Abū Bakr where, after a funeral
prayer recited by the Prophet, he was laid down to rest. As
Muḥammad ordered the grave closed, he filled it with sand,
sprinkled some water, and placed a landmark on it. He then said:
"Tombstones do neither good nor ill, but they help appease the
living. Anything that man does, God wishes him to do well."

The death of Ibrahīm coincided with the eclipse of the sun,
a phenomenon the Muslims saw as a miracle. They went about
saying that the sun was eclipsed in sadness over the death of
Ibrahīm. The Prophet heard them. Would his exceeding love for
Ibrahīm and deep sorrow over his loss not enable him to find
in such rumors a measure of consolation? Would he not at
least keep his silence and thus allow the people to believe what
they had taken to be a miracle? Certainly not. Such an attitude
surely belongs to those who exploit the ignorance and credulity
of the people; for those whom suffering and sorrow push beyond
reason and common sense. It does not belong to the man of
genuine wisdom, nor a fortiori, to the great Prophet. Hence,
looking to those who claimed the sun was in eclipse because
of the death of Ibrahīm, Muḥammad said, "The sun and the moon
are signs of God. They are eclipsed neither for the death nor
birth of any man. On beholding an eclipse, therefore, remember
God and turn to Him in prayer." What greatness! Even in his
moment of greatest personal disaster this Prophet preserved
his cool presence of mind. He remained fully conscious of his
message and most serious in his commitment to it. And even
the Orientalists could not hide their admiration and wonder
when they came across this fact in the life of Muḥammad. Even

they could not fail to acknowledge the genuineness of the man who insisted on truth even in face of the greatest personal adversity.

One wonders what the attitude of the wives of the Prophet was toward the loss of Ibrahīm and Muḥammad's strong sense of bereavement. Muḥammad himself found consolation in God, in the divine assistance he received in the fulfillment of His message, and in the successful spread of Islām that was shown by all the delegations that appeared in Madīnah from every direction with the rise of each new day. So wide was the spread of the religion of God and so many peoples entered its ranks that this year, the 10th of the Hijrah, was called "the Year of Deputations." It is also the year in which Abū Bakr made the pilgrimage to Makkah.

28

The Year of Deputations and Abū Bakr's Leadership of the Pilgrimage

The Effects of the Campaign of Tabūk

With the campaign of Tabūk the word of God was fulfilled throughout the Arabian Peninsula. Muḥammad had firmly secured it against all attacks. In fact, as soon as he returned to Madīnah from Tabūk, the associationists of Arabia began to ponder their fate. The Muslims who accompanied Muḥammad on his march toward al Shām suffered many hardships, bore the heat and thirst of the desert, and returned somewhat disappointed, nay resentful, that they were not given a chance to fight and to enjoy the fruits of victory. The Byzantines had withdrawn to the interior where they stood better fortified. Nonetheless, their withdrawal before a marching Arab army left the tribes severely shaken, anxious over the fate of their pagan religion and of their society. The tribes of southern Arabia, of Yaman, Ḥaḍramawt, and ʻUmān were specially affected in this manner. The Byzantines, they thought, were those who vanquished the Persians, recaptured the cross and reinstated it in Jerusalem with imperial pomp and grandeur. This happened at a time when Persia held dominion over Yaman and the surrounding countryside, territories which Persia had ruled for many decades. Since the Muslims were now close to Yaman—indeed close to every quarter of the Peninsula—why should these territories not join the greater unity under the banner of Muḥammad, the aegis of Islām? Such a step would at least save them from the imperialism of both Byzantium and Persia. So they thought regarding their relations with the outside world. On the internal front the princes of the territories and the tribal chieftains knew very well that Muḥammad would confirm any leader or sovereign in his leadership or sovereignty if he but converted to Islām. Why then, they thought, should they not join this greater unity, which would bring them clear advantage without prejudice to their particular structure of power? And so it was. The tenth year of the Hijrah was indeed the "Year of Deputations," in which men entered into the religion of God *en masse*. The Campaign of Tabūk and the withdrawal of the Byzantines before the Muslims brought forth results as great as the conquest of Makkah, the Muslim victory at Ḥunayn, or the blockade of al Ṭā'if.

Conversion of 'Urwah ibn Mas'ūd and His Murder

Fortunately, it was al Ṭā'if, the city which resisted the Prophet despite the long blockade and which the Muslims had had to bypass without conquering, that came first to declare its allegiance to Muḥammad after Tabūk. 'Urwah ibn Mas'ūd, one of the chieftains of the tribe of Thaqīf, was absent in Yaman during the Prophet's blockade of his city following the Battle of Ḥunayn. Upon his return to al Ṭā'if and his realization of the Prophet's victory in Tabūk, he hastened to Madīnah to declare his conversion as well as his commitment to call his fellow tribesmen unto the religion of God. 'Urwah was not ignorant either of Muḥammad or of the power which the latter had so far achieved, for he was one of the notables of Arabia who entered the negotiations regarding the peace of Ḥudaybiyah on behalf of Quraysh. 'Urwah's conversion reassured the Prophet that the voice of Islām would reach the tribesmen of Thaqīf inside al Ṭā'if. Aware of Thaqīf's attachment to their goddess al Lāt, and of their determination to die in defense of their idol, Muḥammad warned 'Urwah that his tribesmen would fight him. 'Urwah, however, felt too sure of his position and influence with his people. He answered: "O Prophet of God, my people love me more than they do their own eyes." 'Urwah proceeded to Thaqīf and preached Islām to his people. They consulted among themselves and gave him no reply. In the morning, 'Urwah ascended to the top of

his high house and from there gave the Islāmic call to prayer.
It was then that the Prophet's prediction came to be realized.
Deeming 'Urwah's behavior utterly dishonorable, his people
attacked him with arrows on all sides and killed him. As his
relatives panicked around him, 'Urwah told them just before
he breathed his last that: "This is indeed an honor granted to
me by God, the honor to die as a martyr in His cause. For my
case is identical to that of all the other martyrs who gave up
their lives at the gates of this city while the Prophet of God—
May God's peace and blessing be upon him—was laying siege
to it." He then asked to be buried together with those martyrs
who were buried in that area.

Thaqīf's Delegation to the Prophet

'Urwah had not laid down his life in vain. The tribes which
lived in the neighborhood of al Ṭā'if on all sides had already
been converted to Islām. Thaqīf's quick disposal of one of its
chieftains was regarded by the surrounding tribes as a hideous
and contemptible crime. Naturally, this led to the decline of
security in the area, for no Thaqīf's tribesmen crossed the
territories of these tribes without exposing himself to the gravest
dangers. Soon Thaqīf realized that unless it reached peace
with the Muslims, its fate would be doomed. The tribesmen
consulted with one another and approached an elder of theirs
called 'Abd Yā Layl to go to the Prophet and negotiate with
him. 'Abd Yā Layl feared to meet a fate not unlike that of his
predecessor 'Urwah ibn Mas'ūd. He therefore declined to go to
Muḥammad unless Thaqīf would delegate him five more chieftains belonging to different clans and capable of committing
those clans to whatever decision the five would reach with
Muḥammad. Thaqīf agreed and their delegation was formed.
As they approached Madīnah, al Mughīrah ibn Shu'bah met
them first at the outskirts of the city. When he discovered their
purpose, he hastened to the Prophet to inform him. Abū Bakr
met him on the road and, finding out the cause of his hurry,
pleaded with al Mughīrah to give him the pleasure of announcing the great news to the Prophet. It was therefore Abū Bakr
who made the announcement to the Prophet.

The delegation consisted of proud chieftains who had the
greatest esteem for their city and people. They remembered too
well—and of course resented—the Prophet's blockade of their city.

Despite al Mughīrah's instruction of them in Islāmic protocol, they refused to greet the Prophet except in the pre-Islāmic manner. Furthermore, they requested that a special tent be put up for their use within the mosque of Madīnah, for they trusted no one to be their host. It was Khālid ibn Sa'īd·ibn al 'Ās who played the role of middleman between them and the Prophet of God; and it was he who had to taste of every food which the Prophet furnished to them in order to convince them that it had not been poisoned. Finally, on their behalf, Khālid informed Muḥammad of their preparation to convert to Islām on condition that the Prophet exempt them from prayer and promise not to destroy their idol, al Lāt, for three years. Muḥammad strongly rejected their proposal. They changed their proposal to two years, and then to one year, and indeed to one month after their return home. But Muḥammad rejected all their terms. This was naturally to be expected of a prophet calling man to the religion of God, the One, the Mighty, of a prophet committed to stamp out all idolatry. How could he spare any idol, no matter how cherished it might be by its own devotees? On this matter, there can be no middle ground. Either man believes or he is victim to doubt and suspicion. Doubt and conviction do not unite, just as faith and unbelief are ever disparate. The sparing of al Lāt would definitely imply that Thaqīf would mingle its worship of God with that of the idol. That is plain associationism, condemned by God in clear and unequivocal terms. That is unfaith. Thaqīf also pleaded for exemption from prayer. This, too, Muḥammad rejected, saying: "There is no good in a religion in which prayer is ruled out." Finally, Thaqīf accepted Islām on Muḥammad's terms. They agreed to both the destruction of al Lāt and the institution of regular prayers. They demanded, however, that they be exempted from having to destroy their own idol with their own hands. Since they were new converts and since they still had the task of convincing their fellows to accept the terms they were bringing back from Muḥammad, their request was natural and could well be understood. It was too much to ask them to destroy with their own hands idols which they themselves had been worshipping the day before, idols which their people honored as the object of their ancestors' worship, and to do so at a time when their people's confidence in them was absolutely necessary if their call to Islām was to succeed. Hence, Muḥammad was not adamant on this point. For him, it was all one whether al Lāt was destroyed by Thaqīf tribesmen or by others. What was important to him was that the idol was soon to be destroyed and that Thaqīf was henceforth to turn to the worship of God alone. Addressing himself to the delegation, the Prophet—May God's blessing be upon Him—said: "As for the destruction of your idols with your own hands, we exempt you from it." Muhammad appointed 'Uthmān ibn Abū al 'Āṣ, the youngest among them, as leader despite his youth; for he sensed in him the strongest desire to learn the Qur'ān and the most brilliant mind for studying the law. Abū Bakr and other early Muslims attested to 'Uthmān's competence. The delegation remained in Madīnah as guests of the Prophet during the rest of Ramaḍān, fasting with the Prophet and eating of the food which he presented to them at sunset and before dawn. When it was time for them to leave and return home, Muhammad counseled their leader, 'Uthmān ibn Abū al 'Āṣ, saying, "Be brief when leading the prayers, and measure the people by the weakest among them. Remember that among them are the old men, the youth, the weak, and the deprived."

Destruction of the Idol al Lāt

The delegation returned home accompanied by Abū Sufyān ibn Harb and al Mughīrah ibn Shu'bah, who knew the tribe of Thaqīf and felt toward its people great friendship and compassion. They were assigned by the Prophet the job of destroying al Lāt. Abū Sufyān and al Mughīrah approached the sanctuary, and the latter began the job of destruction while the women of Thaqīf stood around moaning and crying. Not one tribesman, however, dared to stop al Mughīrah in the fulfillment of his duty, for everyone had ratified beforehand the agreement the delegation had concluded with the Prophet. Al Mughīrah further seized the wealth of al Lāt and its jewelry and, at the direction of the Prophet and in agreement with Abū Sufyān, settled the debts of 'Urwah and al Aswad. With the destruction of al Lāt and the conversion of al Ṭā'if, the conversion of the Ḥijāz was complete. Muhammad's power expanded from the frontiers of Byzantium in the north to al Yaman and Ḥadramawt in the south. The territories of South Arabia were all preparing to join the new religion and integrate themselves into a system of defense. That is why delegations from all corners proceeded to Madīnah to declare allegiance to the new order and to convert to the new faith.

Jāmiʻ Mosque, Nairobi, Kenya.

Abū Bakr Leads the Pilgrimage

As these delegations followed one another to Madīnah, the months went by until it was time again for pilgrimage. Until that time, the Prophet—May God's blessing be upon him—had not performed the pilgrimage in exactly the same way as it is performed today. It will be remembered that the previous pilgrimages had all been performed under extraordinary circumstances. Would the Prophet go out to perform the pilgrimage this year in gratitude for the victory God had granted him over the Byzantines, or for the conversion of al Ṭā'if and the numerous peoples who sent all these delegations to Madīnah? Many persons in the Arabian Peninsula did not believe either in God or His Prophet. Unbelievers, Jews, and Christians were still in their places. The unbelievers continued to observe their ancient custom of going on pilgrimage to the Ka'bah during the holy months. But the unbelievers were anathema. Would the Prophet therefore not remain in Madīnah until God's word was more completely fulfilled, until express permission from above were granted him for the purpose? Thus the Prophet reasoned, and he instructed Abū Bakr to lead the pilgrimage in his place.

Abū Bakr proceeded to Makkah together with three hundred Muslims. There was apprehension that the years would follow one another while the unbelievers continued to perform pilgrimage to the holy sanctuary and mingle with the Muslims in religious worship. After all, there was a general pact between Muhammad and the Arabs that none should be prevented from reaching the Holy House if he so desired, that none should be attacked during the holy months. Likewise, the relations with various Arab tribes were governed by pacts whose terms had not yet expired. As long as these pacts had not expired, the associationists had the same right to perform the pilgrimage to the Holy House as the Muslims. For sometime yet, the Muslims would have to continue to see pre-Islāmic worship performed side by side with theirs around the Ka'bah.

True, most of the idols worshipped by the Arabs had by then been destroyed, as were the idols and images of the Ka'bah. The pilgrimage institution was, however, still confused. In the sacred months the sanctuary of Makkah was the scene of idolators worshipping their gods as well as of Muslims in revolt against idolatry. A religious institution with a texture such as this is in contradiction with itself. It may be possible to understand the pilgrimage of Jews and Christians to Palestine because it is the land of promise for the former and the birthplace of Jesus Christ for the latter. But it is incomprehensible that two systems of worship meet in the same sanctuary, the one destroying the idols of that sanctuary and the other worshipping the idols destroyed. Hence, it was necessary to stop the associationists from entering a sanctuary just cleansed of associationism and ridden of its idols and images. Thus, the *Sūrah* of "Barā'ah" was revealed at the right time but too late for implementation in this pilgrimage. The Hajj season had begun and already thousands of associationists had converged upon Makkah as they were accustomed to do for generations. Though this was obviously not the time to implement the revelation, it was time to proclaim it and to let the associationists know that, henceforth, no covenant between Muslims and associationists would be valid unless it specified a given term. In this case, the covenant would be honored for the duration of its term.

For this purpose, the Prophet sent 'Alī ibn Abū Ṭālib to Makkah to join Abū Bakr and to address the congregation of pilgrims assembled at 'Arafāt. He was entrusted with the duty to proclaim the commandments of God and His Prophet. When the two met, Abū Bakr asked: "Do you come to us as commander or messenger?" 'Alī answered, "Indeed as messenger," and informed Abū Bakr of his mission. When the pilgrims congregated at Minā, 'Alī rose and delivered the following address, quoting the Qur'ān:

> "This is a complete absolution from God and His Prophet regarding all obligation arising from pacts made with the associationists. The unbelievers may travel throughout the land for four months in freedom and security. Certainly, they cannot frustrate the plans of God, nor will they escape His final humiliation of them. This proclamation from God and His Prophet is for the benefit of all people on the day of the greater pilgrimage. God and His Messenger are clear of all obligation toward the associationists. It is better for them that they repent; but if they do not and turn away, they should know that they will not frustrate God's plan. Rather, to them belong the tidings of a severe and painful punishment. [These verses constitute a general and a particular absolution of obligations incumbent upon the Muslims

toward the associationists. —Tr.] The "particular" absolution will not apply in those cases where those who covenanted with the Muslims have not subsequently violated their covenant nor aided anyone against the Muslims. Such covenanters shall enjoy the benefit of their pact until it expires. God loves the righteous. As for the others, when the holy months have passed, then you are free to kill the associationists wherever they may be, to take them prisoners, to beleaguer and blockade them, and to lie in wait for them at every place of ambush. However, if they repent, observe prayer, and pay the *zakāt,* let them go free, for God is forgiving and merciful. And at any rate, if any of them ask for your protection, grant it to him so that he may hear the words of God. Extend your protection to him until he reaches his home in safety, remembering that he is ignorant and needs your mission. As for the others, how can there be any covenant between them and God and His Prophet? Certainly, those with whom a pact of peace has been concluded near the holy sanctuary are protected thereby, and the Muslims are obliged to remain true to their covenant as long as the associationists are true to theirs. God loves the righteous; but the others can have no peace. Should they prevail against you, they will honor neither blood tie nor covenant of peace. They will delude you with sweet words while their hearts are full of perfidy and resentment. It was they who bartered God's word for a mean price; it was they who put obstacles in the way of men seeking the pleasure of their Lord. Evil indeed is everything they have done. They honor neither relation nor covenant. It is they who are the transgressors. Nonetheless, if they repent, hold prayer, and pay the *zakāt,* then treat them as your brethren in the faith. Thus do We explain Our word to men with knowledge. But if they break their oath after their covenant and attack your religion, then fight these leaders of unfaith, these scions of ungodliness, for they are unworthy of their covenants. Fight them that they may desist from their path of error. As for you, the Muslims, will you hesitate to fight a people who have broken their oath, who have expelled the Prophet, and who were the first to open hostilities against you? Will you fear them? Is not God worthier of your fear, you who call yourselves true believers? Fight them then so that God may inflict upon them His punishment through you, that He may humiliate them and give you victory, and that He may avenge the believers for the wrongs they have suffered and dissipate the wrath of their hearts. God will then forgive whomsoever He pleases, for He is All-Knowing and All-Wise. Or, would you think that you would be abandoned and forsaken, assuming that God did not know which of you truly strive for His sake or which of you faithfully refuse to regard as their friend anyone but God, His Prophet, and the believers? Would you think that God is not well aware of everything you do? The associationists have no right to visit the mosques of God to bear witness against themselves of their own unbelief. It is they whose works shall be in vain and who will dwell eternally in the fire. The mosques of God are for those who believe in Him, in the Day of Judgment, and who hold the prayers, pay the *zakāt*, and fear only God. Only they may be counted among the righteous. True, the unbelievers have been responsible for providing food and drink to the pilgrims and for maintenance of the sanctuary. But would you confuse the moral worth of these services with the believers' faith in God and the Day of Judgment, with their fighting in the cause of God? Surely, they are unequal. The unjust are not guided by God. The worth of those who believed, who emigrated and fought for the sake of God, and who spent of their wealth and laid down their lives, is far greater with God. Theirs will be the true triumph. To them God will grant His mercy, His pleasure, and His gardens full of lasting bliss. God's reward is surely the greatest. O Men who believe, do not take your parents and brothers as friends as long as they prefer unfaith to faith. Whoever among you befriends them will do wrong. Remember, if parents, sons, wives and relatives, clans and tribes, wealth and property, prosperity and affluence which you fear might be adversely affected, a trade recession, and dwellings and material things you wish to preserve—if these are dearer to you than God or His Prophet and self-exertion in His cause, then God's judgment will soon fall upon you. Such immoral people are not guided by God. God has given you victory on many occasions, but when you became too proud of your numbers, that is on the day of Hunayn, your numbers availed you nothing. The earth with all its vastness became too small for you and you had to run away, vanquished and in retreat. Then did God send

His peace upon His Prophet and the believers. He sent down
His hosts to fight on their side, hosts which you did not see.
Then did the unbelievers meet their due punishment. Then,
too, did God forgive whomsoever He wills. For He is most
forgiving and merciful. O Men who believe! The associationists are anathema. After this year they shall not approach
the holy Mosque. Do not fear the economic consequences of
this proclamation. God will give you of His bounty as He
pleases. Surely God is All-Knowing and All-Wise. Fight,
therefore, those 'People of the Book' who do not believe
either in God or in the Day of Judgment, who do not
forbid that which God and His Prophet have forbidden, nor
follow the religion of truth, until they pay the *jizyah* and
acknowledge their subjection. The Jews claim Ezra to be
the son of God, and so do the Christians claim Jesus to be
the son of God. That is what they actually claim in their
own words. By claiming this they surpass even the unbelievers of old in unbelief. God's curse be upon them wherever they turn. They have taken their rabbis, priests, and
monks as lords beside God, and so have they regarded the
Messiah, son of Mary. But they were never commanded to
worship any but God alone, the One, besides whom there
is no other. Praised be God above their associations! Evidently they seek to extinguish the divine light by what they
claim. But God will not be frustrated and His light will
illumine the world in spite of them. It is He who sent His
Prophet with genuine guidance and the religion of truth;
and it is He who will make this religion prevail over all
other religions, however much the unbelievers may resent it.
O Men who believe, many of the rabbis, priests, and monks
devour the wealth of the people by false means and turn men
away from the true path of God. Many of them hoard gold
and silver and do not spend it in the cause of God. To such
of them as do this will belong painful and strict punishment.
Their punishment shall be a scorching fire, a fire branding
their foreheads, sides, and backs, and they will be told
that such punishment is reward for what they have hoarded,
a taste of what they themselves have treasured. Remember
also that God reckoned the months to be twelve, ever since
He created heaven and earth, and that four of them are
sacred. That is the right religion. Do not therefore wrong
yourselves during these months by committing any act of

aggression. When the sacred months are over, then fight the
associationists in all-out war just as they fight you. Know
that God is always on the side of the pious and the virtuous."[1]

'Alī delivered all these verses from *Sūrah,* "Al Taubah,"[2] which
we have quoted in full for a reason which will soon become
apparent. After he finished his recitation of the Qur'ān, he continued in his own words: "O Men, no unbeliever will enter
Paradise; no associationist will perform pilgrimage after this
year; and no naked man will be allowed to circumambulate the
Holy House. Whoever has entered into a covenant with the
Prophet of God—May God's peace and blessing be upon him—
will have his covenant fulfilled as long as its term lasts." 'Alī
proclaimed these four instructions to the people and then gave
everybody four months of general peace and amnesty during
which anyone could return safely home. From that time on no
associationist performed the pilgrimage and no naked man circumambulated the Holy House. From that day on, the Islāmic
state was established.

The Moral Foundations of the Islāmic State

It was precisely for the purpose of clarifying the foundation
of the Islāmic state that we have quoted the verses of *Sūrah* "Al
Tawbah" at length. This was equally the purpose of 'Alī's recitation, namely, to enable all the Arabs to understand this foundation. That is why the Prophet had asked him, according to a
number of sources, to recommend that these verses be recited
to the people each in his own house and quarter. If one were
to give close and conscientious examination to the opening pages
of this *Sūrah,* he would be convinced that it contains all that
constitutes the moral base of any nascent state. The revelation
of this *Sūrah* of the Qur'ān at a time following the last of the
Prophet's campaigns, after conversion of the people of al Ṭā'if,
of Ḥijāz, Tihāmah and Najd, after all these territories and many
of the tribes of the south had made common cause with
Muḥammad and Islām, was meant to clarify the moral foundation
on which the new state was to be erected. It was then necessary,
as it is now, for the state to have a general moral ideology in
which its people believe and for the sake of which they would
be prepared to fight with all their power and energy. The *Sūrah*
in question seems to be saying to the Muslims in particular and

to mankind in general that there is no ideology greater than faith in God alone, in God devoid of associates.

No idea, no faith and no conviction of any kind can exercise greater power over the soul of man than that soul's entry into communion with reality as a whole, with reality at the point of its greatest and most sublime manifestation—in short, with God. Here, man is without master except God; his conscience is without judge except God. The *Sūrah* seems to be laying down the principle that those who flout this general conviction which ought to be the foundation of the state are the rebels, the immoral, and the nucleus of subversion and hateful destruction. Such ones should be entitled to no covenant and the state ought to fight them. If their rebellion against the general faith of the state is overt, then they should be fought and brought to subjection. If it is not overt, as was the case with the people of Tabūk, then they should pay the *jizyah* in acknowledgment of their subjection.

A close but unbiased consideration of the problem from the historical and social points of view will enable us to appreciate the moral which the foregoing verses of the *Sūrah* were supposed to teach. Those who hastily have jumped to conclusions condemning Islām and its Prophet do not consider this aspect of the matter and regard these very strong verses of the *Sūrah* as a call to fanaticism and intolerance inconsistent with genuine civilization. They take the verses calling for fighting the associationists and killing them wherever they may be found without compassion or mercy as a call to raise the political state on a foundation of power and tyranny. Such false claims one often reads in the books of western Orientalists. They are the claims of those who have no talent for social and historical criticism even though, sometimes, they themselves be Muslims. They are claims which fly in the face of historical truth and run counter to every fact of social life. The prejudice with which such claims are advocated compel their authors to interpret the pertinent verses of this and other *Sūrahs* of the Qur'ān in violence to the whole biography of the Prophet. Their interpretation contradicts the logic of the life of the great Prophet and the sequence of events from the day God commissioned him to prophethood to his death.

The Principle of Freedom in Western Civilization

In order to establish the foregoing point, it behooves us to inquire what is the moral foundation of the dominant civilization

of modern times and then to compare it with the foundation
on which Muḥammad sought to base the civilization of Islām.
The moral foundation of contemporary civilization is the limitless
freedom of opinion, a freedom which cannot be limited except
by due process of law. On this account, freedom of opinion is a
first principle which men are prepared to defend, whatever the
sacrifice, and to realize in their societies, whatever the cost,
including war. The advocates of this freedom regard this principle as one of their greatest glories. They boast of it and call
themselves greater than all previous generations and periods on
its account. It is because of their commitment to this principle
that the above mentioned Orientalists call Islām's condemnation
of those who believe neither in God nor in the Day of Judgment
a will to fanaticism incompatible with freedom. But the fallacious
nature of this point of view becomes flagrantly obvious when one
realizes that the value of an opinion lies in the ability to express,
to propagate, and to implement it. Islām did not call for fighting
the Arab associationists who acknowledged the dominion of
Muḥammad and did not propagate their unbelief or display their
pagan rituals. Likewise, the dominant civilization of today wages
a war to the knife against any ideology which runs counter to its
own, and does so more resolutely and fiercely than the Muslims
fought the Arab associationists. Indeed, it imposes upon its own
"People of the Book" (i.e., those who reside in its midst but
disagree with its basic premises) that which is a thousand times
worse than the jizyah of Islām.

The West's War against Communism

To illustrate this point, we may refer to the fight against
slavery. In its war against those of its members who adhered
to the institution of slavery, modern western civilization gave
no heed to the fact that those adherents believed in their
institution, that they did not regard slavery as taboo. By this we
do not mean that Islām approves of slavery, though it must be
remembered that Islām did not require us to fight anything but
that which God had clearly and unequivocally condemned. The
two cases are not dissimilar. Therefore, rather than invoking this
case, let us look at Europe, the contemporary carrier of dominant
western civilization together with America and all those countries of South and East Asia which run in her orbit. Europe has
fought Bolshevism and continues to do so with the strongest de-

termination. We, too, in Egypt are also prepared to cooperate with the western countries in fighting Bolshevism. But Bolshevism is only an economic view, an ideological opinion which runs counter to that of the dominant western countries. Can one therefore say that the call of Islām to fight the unbeliever who violates his own covenant after it has been given is a call to fanaticism, an "empty liberalism," and at the same time say that the call to fight Bolshevism, the destroyer of the West's economic system, is one which upholds the principle of freedom of faith and opinion and which respects and honors that freedom?

The West's War against Nudism

Furthermore, in more than one European country it has been thought that moral discipline cannot be separated from bodily discipline, that hiding some parts or organs of the human body under clothing is more sexually arousing, and hence, more corrupting than the exposure of the whole human body in total nakedness. The advocates of this view began to implement it and founded resorts in a number of cities where those who want to discipline themselves to total nakedness can pursue their desire without hindrance. However, as soon as this view began to spread, the rulers of most of the countries concerned decided that the practice constituted a grave threat to the morality of the majority. They thus declared these "health centers" out of bounds and fought the advocates of nudism. They propagated laws forbidding the organization or construction of any nudist centers. And were nudism to envelop a whole nation, there is no doubt but that nation would become the object of a new war waged against it by all other nations on the grounds that it constituted a denial of the morality of man. Many a nation was threatened with war by other nations on account of its toleration of slavery, prostitution, or commerce in narcotics. How could such wars be justified? Surely, they could be justified solely on the grounds that freedom, despite its absoluteness, is a value only as long as it is limited to those bounds protecting the community from harm. Wherever the exercise of freedom exceeds those limits, it is deemed a threat to the social, economic, and moral health of the community, an evil worthy of being combated on all fronts. In such an instance, all public exercise of freedom is stopped, and the opinion itself whose freedom is in question is fought. The degree of brutality to which such a war may have to resort is determined by the nature of the threat which the ideological principle in question poses for the particular community.

Legislation May Restrict Freedom

Such is the social truth acknowledged by the dominant civilization of today. Were we to cite every expression and effect of this truth among the various nations, these pages would hardly suffice. Generally speaking, it may be safely asserted that every piece of legislation designed to combat a social, economic, or political movement is a denial of the freedom of opinion and an act of war against that movement. Such denial of freedom to that to which freedom gives birth can be tolerated only on the grounds'that the free implementation of those principles entails harm to society. If, therefore, we are to appreciate Islām's war against associationism and its adherents, and its resolution to pursue the fighting till surrender, it is necessary to consider the social implications of associationism. Without such consideration, it is not fair to pass judgment on the legitimacy of the war. Now, if it can be established that associationism brought great harm to human society in all stages and periods, then Islām's call to war against it is not only legitimate but obligatory.

Social Aspect of Associationism

The associationism which was prevalent when Muhammad— May God's peace and blessing be upon him—began to call men to the religion of God was not only a matter of idol worship. Even if it were so, fighting it would still be obligatory. For it is an insult to the human mind, to the dignity of man, that any member of society should worship a stone. But that is not all. Associationism represented a system of traditional customs, beliefs, and practices; indeed, a total social structure which was far worse than slavery, Bolshevism, or any other social evil in the Twentieth Century. Associationism implied the burial of daughters alive and limitless polygamy whereby a man could marry thirty, forty, one or three hundred women. It implied the most cruel forms of usury and the most degrading license and immorality. The society of Arab pagans of Muhammad's time was truly one of the worst that has existed on earth. We ask every man of reason the following question: If a certain nation today were to adopt for itself the same system of beliefs and customs as the pagan Arabs, including the burial of daughters alive, limitless polygamy, slavery with or without cause, economic exploitation and usury, would an internal movement that seeks to destroy that order and alter its system be accused of fanaticism and violation of freedom? Suppose a social group neighboring the degraded community, realizing its own exposure to the contagion of such social evils as dominated their neighbors, were to challenge them to a war. Would such a war be justified or not? Would it not be even better justified than World War I in which millions of men were slaughtered for no other reason except the gluttony and recklessness of the colonialist states? If this argument is valid, what is the value of the Orientalists' criticism of the Qur'ānic verses from *Sūrah* "Al Tawbah" which we have just brought to the attention of the reader? What would be the point of their critique of Islām's call to combat associationism and its adherents who seek to establish the evil order which we have just described?

Legitimacy of the War against Associationism

If such was the historical truth of that pattern of life which was prevalent in the Arabian Peninsula under the banner of associationism and paganism, it is not without implications for the historical truth of the life of the Prophet. It must be recalled that, ever since his commission to prophethood thirteen years before, Muhammad had been calling men to the religion of God with argument and the kindest of words. All the campaigns which he undertook against his enemies were purely defensive. In none of them had he been guilty of aggression. On the contrary, he undertook those campaigns in defense of his Muslim converts, of their freedom to preach the religion in which they believed and which they cherished more than their lives. The stringent call to fight the associationists because they were anathema and had violated the covenant and amnesty freely concluded between them and the believers was in fact revealed to the Prophet after the last of his campaigns, *viz.* the campaign of Tabūk. Islām arose in a land saturated with associationism and unbelief, a land in which associationism had established its destructive economy and immoral social system. If, therefore, the Prophet commanded the Muslims to ask Arabia to exchange its order for one allowing that which God legitimitized and forbidding

that which He proscribed, no fair observer could but agree to
rise against the associationists and to pursue the fight against
them to victory. Such victory is the victory of truth and goodness, of the religion which is all God's.

ʿĀmir ibn al Ṭufayl

'Alī's recitation of the Qur'ānic *Sūrah* "Al Tawbah," and his
calling Muslim attention to the divine order that henceforth no
unbeliever would enter Paradise or would perform pilgrimage, and no naked man would circumambulate the Holy House,
brought forth the best of fruits. Above all, it removed all hesitancy in the minds of those tribes which had not yet resolved to
enter into Islām. Moreover, the territories of Yaman, Mahrah,
Baḥrayn, and Yamāmah immediately joined the ranks of Islām.
No one was left to oppose Muḥammad nor to contend with him
except a few deluded individuals. One of them was ʿĀmir ibn
al Ṭufayl, who refused to convert. His people had enlisted him to
serve as a member of their delegation to the Prophet proclaiming
their conversion. When the delegation obtained audience with
the Prophet, ʿĀmir refused to go forward. He even proclaimed
himself the Prophet's equal. Muḥammad invited him to a talk
and tried to convince him of the truth of Islām—to no avail.
'Āmir walked out threatening with war: "By God", he swore,
"I shall fill your spaces with men and cavalry." Muḥammad
prayed God to restrict ʿĀmir. On his way home, the persistent
unbeliever was struck with cancer in his neck and died in an
inn belonging to a woman from the tribe of Banū Salūl. It is
reported that he expired while lamenting, "O Banū ʿĀmir, do you
leave me to be stifled to death by a lump in my neck as big as a
camel's lump here in the house of a woman of Banū Salūl?"

Another persistent associationist was Arbad ibn Qays. He,
too, refused to convert and returned to Banū ʿĀmir where he
perished by lightning shortly after his arrival at the marketplace.
However, neither ʿĀmir nor Arbad, whether dead or alive, could
stop their people from joining Islām. Worse yet was the case
of Musaylimah ibn Ḥabīb who accompanied the delegation of
his tribe, the Banū Ḥanīfah of Yamāmah, to the Prophet. His
companions assigned him the job of watching their horses while
they entered the court of the Prophet to present their submission
and receive his blessing. They did not forget him, but they
mentioned his case to Muḥammad, and the latter ordered that he

be given exactly what his companions received. Indeed, Muhammad praised him for agreeing to stay behind and watch his people's property. But when Musaylimah heard of this, false pride took possession of him and he claimed to be himself a prophet. He not only started to argue that God had associated him with Muhammad in prophethood but as well to compose rhymes and verses in imitation of the Qur'ān. He recited such verses as "God blessed the pregnant woman. He brought forth from her the breath of life, embedded within a well-padded womb." Musaylimah proclaimed wine and adultery legitimate, and he absolved men from the obligation of prayer. He preached widely but was met with ridicule. Except for these individual cases, Arab groups from all corners of the Peninsula, led by some of the greatest men of the period such as 'Adiyy ibn Hātim and 'Umar ibn Ma'dī Karib, entered the religion of God. The kings of Himyar sent a messenger to the Prophet declaring their conversion to Islām, and the Prophet accepted their conversion and wrote to them explaining their rights and obligations under God. It was then that Muhammad sent some of the early converts to teach the new Muslims in the south the institutions of their faith and to deepen their understanding of it.

The Other Deputations

Unlike some early biographers, we shall not spend time relating the details of the delegations of tribes who came to declare their entrance into the faith. In his *al Tabaqāt al Kubrā*, the historian Ibn Sa'd devoted fifty long pages to those details. Suffice it here to mention only their names. These were: Muzaynah, Asad, Tamīm, 'Abs, Fazārah, Murrah, Tha'labah, Muhārib, Sa'd ibn Bakr, Kilāb, Ru'ās ibn Kilāb, 'Uqayl ibn Ka'b, Ja'dah, Qushayr ibn Ka'b, Banū al Bakkā', Kinānah, Ashja', Bāhilah, Sulaym, Hilāl ibn 'Āmir, 'Āmir ibn Sa'sa'ah, Thaqīf; the Rabi'ah group of 'Abd al Qays, Bakr ibn Wā'il, Taghlib, Hanīfah, Shaybān; the Yamanī tribes of Tay', Tujīb, Khawlān, Ju'fiyy, Sudā', Murād, Zubayd, Kindah, al Sadif, Khushayn, Sa'd Hudaym, Baliyy, Bahrā', 'Udhrah, Salāmān, Juhaynah, Kalb, Jarm, al Azd, Ghassān, al Hārith ibn Ka'b, Hamdān, Sa'd al 'Ashīrah, 'Ans, al Dāriyyīn, al Rahāwiyyīn branch of Madhhaj, Ghāmid, al Nakha', Bajīlah, Khath'am, al Ash'arayn, Hadramawt, Azd 'Umān, Ghāfiq, Bāriq, Daws, Thumālah, al Huddān, Aslam, Judhām, Mahrah, Himyar, Najrān, and Jayshān. There remained not one of the tribes of the Peninsula, or of its clans, but had entered into Islām.

Such was the fate of the associationists who lived in the Arabian Peninsula. They hastened to enter into Islām and to abandon the worship of idols until the countryside was cleansed of idols and idol-worship. All this was accomplished after the campaign of Tabūk and willingly and in freedom without a single soul being coerced or a single drop of blood being spilled. But what did the Jews and Christians do with Muḥammad, and what did the latter do to them?

29

The Farewell Pilgrimage

Ever since 'Alī ibn Abū Ṭālib recited the opening verses of the *Sūrah* "Al Tawbah" to the Muslims and associationists who came to perform the pilgrimage under the leadership of Abū Bakr, and ever since the announcement that henceforth no associationist would enter paradise or perform the pilgrimage, no naked man would circumambulate the Holy House, and that whoever had a covenant with the Prophet of God—May God's peace and blessing be upon him—would have his covenant honored till its expiration, the unbelievers of the Arabian Peninsula realized that their idol worship would have to come to an end. They awoke to the fact that unless they themselves put an end to idolatry, they would eventually have to take up arms against God and His Prophet. This situation applied particularly to the southern regions of the Peninsula, al Yaman and Ḥadramawt, because al Ḥijāz and all the territories of the north had already entered into the new faith and stood under its protection.

Islām's Distinction between Paganism and the Religions of the Book

In the south, associationism and Christianity divided the land. As we have seen in the preceding chapter, most associationists announced their entry into God's religion and sent their delegations to Madīnah to proclaim it. The Prophet accorded these delegations all the welcome possible, thereby hastening the entrance of others and confirming the new converts in the faith. Muhammad's restitution to each prince of his princedom and to each leader of his leadership made all these new converts extremely keen to protect their new status. As for the People of the Book, whether Jews or Christians, the following verses from *Sūrah* "Al Tawbah," read by 'Alī on that momentous occasion had become known to them.

قَاتِلُوا الَّذِينَ لَا يُؤْمِنُونَ بِاللَّهِ وَلَا بِالْيَوْمِ الْآخِرِ وَلَا يُحَرِّمُونَ مَا حَرَّمَ اللَّهُ وَرَسُولُهُ وَلَا يَدِينُونَ دِينَ الْحَقِّ مِنَ الَّذِينَ أُوتُوا الْكِتَبَ حَتَّى يُعْطُوا الْجِزْيَةَ عَنْ يَدٍ وَهُمْ صَاغِرُونَ ۞

"Fight, therefore, those 'People of the Book' who do not believe either in God or in the Day of Judgment, who do not forbid that which God and His Prophet have forbidden, nor follow the religion of truth until they pay the *jizyah* and acknowledge their subjection. O Men who believe, many of the rabbis, priests and monks devour the wealth of the people by false means and turn men away from the true path of God. Many of them hoard gold and silver and do not spend it in the cause of God. To such as these will belong painful and strict punishment. Their punishment shall be a scorching fire, a fire branding their foreheads, sides and backs, and they will be told that such punishment is the reward for what they have hoarded, a taste of what they themselves have treasured."[1]

Faced with these verses from *Sūrah* "Al Tawbah" with which the whole Qur'ānic revelation came to an end, many historians ask themselves whether or not the revelation of Muhammad— May God's peace and blessing be upon him—has not changed tone in regard to the People of the Book. Some western Orientalists even claim that these verses have put the People of the Book on a level with the unbelieving associationists; that after achieving victory over paganism with the assistance of Judaism and Christianity, as was demanded by the proclamation that Islām confirmed the religion of Jesus, Moses, Abraham and the earlier prophets, Muḥammad had turned his wrath against the Jews who opposed him and fought them until they evacuated the Peninsula. During this time, so the claim runs, Muḥammad pretended friendship with the Christians and recited verses which praised their genuine faith and friendliness, such as:

لَتَجِدَنَّ أَشَدَّ النَّاسِ عَدَاوَةً لِلَّذِينَ آمَنُوا الْيَهُودَ وَالَّذِينَ أَشْرَكُوا وَلَتَجِدَنَّ أَقْرَبَهُمْ مَوَدَّةً لِلَّذِينَ آمَنُوا الَّذِينَ قَالُوا إِنَّا نَصَارَىٰ ذَٰلِكَ بِأَنَّ مِنْهُمْ قِسِّيسِينَ وَرُهْبَانًا وَأَنَّهُمْ لَا يَسْتَكْبِرُونَ ۝

"You will find the Jews and the associationists more hostile to those who believe. You will find those who say 'We are Christians' the friendliest to those who believe, for many of them are monks and priests, and they are humble."[2]

But now, the claim continued, Muḥammad has turned his wrath against Christianity and sought to destroy its adherents as he did those of Judaism before. Arguing from these premises, a number of Orientalists have blamed Muḥammad for regarding Christianity on a level with unfaith. They invoke the fact that Christians had protected his followers when they took refuge in Abyssinia. They also invoke the facts that Muḥammad had approved of the religion of the people of Najrān and other Arab Christians and that he allowed them to follow their rituals of worship. Finally, the western Orientalists claim that it was this turnabout in the strategy of Muḥammad which established the continuing hostility between Muslims and Christians. Their purpose is to impute to the Prophet a strategy which, they claim, made any reconciliation between the followers of Jesus and Muḥammad very difficult, if not impossible.

On the face of it, this argument seems appealing and logical. Those to whom it is intended might even incline to see in it some if not all the truth. However, a careful investigation of the situation, context, and causes of revelation of the said verses leaves no reason for doubt that the attitude of Islām and Muḥammad toward the scriptural religions was always one and the same. The Messiah, son of Mary, is of the spirit of God. He is God's word, given unto Mary. In his lifetime, the Messiah was a servant of God to whom God revealed the Book, whom He commissioned as a prophet, blessed, commanded to hold the prayers, and always to pay the *zakāt*. From the beginning of Muḥammad's prophethood to its end, the Qur'ānic revelation maintained that God is One, that He was not born, that He did not give birth to anyone, and that None is like unto Him.

Such is the spirit of Islām. Such has been its foundation from the very first moment. And such will the spirit of Islām remain for all eternity. A delegation of the Christians of Najrān went to the Prophet and argued with him in the matter of God as well as in the matter of Jesus' prophethood a long time before the revelation of *Sūrah* "Al Tawbah." They asked Muḥammad, "If Mary is the mother of Jesus, who was his father?" In this connection, the following verse was revealed:

"The example of Jesus is for God like that of Adam. He created him of clay and commanded him to be and he was. This is the truth from your Lord. Do not, therefore, have any doubt concerning it. Whosoever argues with you to the contrary now that certain knowledge has come to you, answer. 'Let us call our sons and yours, our women and yours, ourselves and yours to pray to God and seek His guidance. May His curse fall upon the liars.' This is the true knowledge and the true narrative; there is no God but God, and He is the Glorious, the All-Wise. But if they disagree, remember that God knows the propagators of falsehood. Say: 'O People of the Book, let us join together in upholding a noble principle common to both of us, namely, that we shall not worship any God but God, that we shall not associate aught with Him, and that we shall not take one another as lords besides God. If they disagree then tell them, 'Remember, as for us, we are indeed Muslims.' "³

In this *Sūrah* of "Āl 'Imran," the text irrefutably indicts the People of the Book with discouraging the Muslims from believing in God and throwing obstacles in the path to Him. It asks them directly why they do not believe in this new revelation when it reaffirms the same truth which Jesus, Moses, and Abraham received from God, in its pristine purity, before it was tampered with and edited following the prejudices, ulterior motives, and vain desires of man. In many other *Sūrahs* of the Qur'ān the same argument is repeated against the People of the Book. In *Sūrah* "Āl 'Imran," for instance, as in the *Sūrah* "Al Mā'idah," God said:

لَقَدْ كَفَرَ الَّذِينَ قَالُوا إِنَّ اللهَ هُوَ الْمَسِيحُ ابْنُ مَرْيَمَ وَقَالَ الْمَسِيحُ يَبَنِي إِسْرَائِيلَ اعْبُدُوا
اللهَ رَبِّي وَرَبَّكُمْ إِنَّهُ مَنْ يُشْرِكْ بِاللهِ فَقَدْ حَرَّمَ اللهُ عَلَيْهِ الْجَنَّةَ وَمَأْوَاهُ النَّارُ
وَمَا لِلظَّالِمِينَ مِنْ أَنْصَارٍ لَقَدْ كَفَرَ الَّذِينَ قَالُوا إِنَّ اللهَ ثَالِثُ ثَلَاثَةٍ وَمَا مِنْ إِلَهٍ إِلَّا
إِلَهٌ وَاحِدٌ وَإِنْ لَمْ يَنْتَهُوا عَمَّا يَقُولُونَ لَيَمَسَّنَّ الَّذِينَ كَفَرُوا مِنْهُمْ عَذَابٌ أَلِيمٌ أَفَلَا
يَتُوبُونَ إِلَى اللهِ وَيَسْتَغْفِرُونَهُ وَاللهُ غَفُورٌ رَحِيمٌ مَا الْمَسِيحُ ابْنُ مَرْيَمَ إِلَّا رَسُولٌ قَدْ خَلَتْ مِنْ
قَبْلِهِ الرُّسُلُ وَأُمُّهُ صِدِّيقَةٌ كَانَا يَأْكُلَانِ الطَّعَامَ انْظُرْ كَيْفَ نُبَيِّنُ لَهُمُ الْآيَاتِ ثُمَّ انْظُرْ
أَنَّى يُؤْفَكُونَ

"Those who claim that God is one of three have lied and committed unbelief. There is no God but God, the One. If they do not stop from propagating this lie, a severe punishment will fall upon them. But if they repent to God and seek His mercy, God is most pardoning and merciful. The Messiah, son of Mary, is only a prophet, one among many prophets who preceded him. His mother was a faithful believer but a human like him. Both ate worldly food. Is this not sufficient evidence to convince them? But see how they persist in going astray!"[4]

In the same *Sūrah*, God also says: "And when God asked Jesus, son of Mary, 'Did you tell the people to take you and your mother as two deities beside God?' Jesus answered, 'Praise be to God. How can I say that which is not true?'"[5] It was in the much earlier *Sūrah* "Al Mā'idah," not in "Al Tawbah," the last to be revealed, that the verse is to be found which the Christian historians use as evidence for their allegation that Muḥammad turned toward Christianity following the change of his political fortunes. This is the verse, "You will find the Jews and the associationists more hostile to those who believe. You will find those who say 'We are Christians' the friendliest to those who believe, for many among them are monks and priests, and they are humble."[6] And yet, while they take this part of the *Sūrah* for evidence, they deliberately omit consideration of the evidence of its other parts.

On the other hand, the verses of *Sūrah* "Al Tawbah" which mention the People of the Book, do not discuss their faith in Jesus, the son of Mary. Rather, they discuss their association of

other beings with God, their unjust economic exploitation of the
people, and their hoarding of gold and silver. Islām undoubtedly
regards such practices on the part of the People of the Book as
violating the religion of Jesus. Therefore, Islām does well to
criticize them as making legitimate that which God had forbidden and of being guilty of those practices which usually belong
to those who believe neither in God nor in the Day of Judgment.
Nonetheless, Islām was careful enough to remind them that
their faith in God, despite all their evil and immoral practices,
would intercede for them in God's judgment. It reassured them
that their faith in God would lift them above the pagans and
would enable them, even though they declare God to be one
of three and tolerate that which God forbade, to get by with
merely paying the *jizyah* and acknowledging subjection.

More Deputations to the Prophet

It was precisely this call, which was proclaimed by 'Alī at
the pilgrimage led by Abū Bakr, that brought in its trail the
conversion of the South Arabians. Their delegations then followed
one another to Madīnah as we have said earlier. Among these
were the delegations of associationists as well as of People of
the Book. The Prophet used to give the best welcome to anyone
who sought him, and to reinstitute the princes and leaders in
their positions of power upon conversion to Islām. Al Ash'ath
ibn Qays led the delegation of Kindah which consisted of eighty
horsemen. Seeking the Prophet, they entered the mosque clad
in silken mantles, and with decorated eyes and faces. When the
Prophet saw them in this condition, he said: "Have you not
entered Islām?" They answered, "Certainly." Muḥammad then
retorted: "What is all this silk around your necks?" Immediately
every one of them tore his mantle to bits. Al Ash'ath said in
apology to the Prophet: "O Prophet of God, we are noblemen,
sons of noblemen. But so are you! You would, then, understand
our will to self-distinction." The Prophet smiled and related the
story to al 'Abbās ibn 'Abd al Muṭṭalib and Rabī'ah ibn al
Ḥārith. Along with al Ash'ath there came Wā'il ibn Ḥujr, of
Kindah, who was the ruler of the coastlands of Ḥaḍramawt.
He, too, converted to Islām, was confirmed in his rulership and
asked to collect the tithe from his citizens for transfer to the
Muslim collectors. Mu'āwiyah ibn Abū Sufyān was commanded
to accompany Wā'il home. On the way, accustomed to behaving

as royalty, Wā'il refused to let Mu'āwiyah ride with him or even to lend him his sandals that he might protect his feet from the hot sand. He thought it sufficient condescension on his part to allow Mu'āwiyah to walk in the shadow of his camel. Despite the violation of the egalitarianism and fraternity of Islām, Mu'āwiyah acquiesced in order to help Wā'il and his people secure their new faith.

Arab Unity under the Banner of Islām

When Islām spread in Yaman, the Prophet sent Mu'ādh to teach its people the ethic and law of the new faith. He advised Mu'ādh, "Make things easy and do not raise obstacles. Reconcile and do not alienate. Some People of the Book will ask you, 'What is the key to Paradise?' Answer, 'It is to witness that there is no God but God; that He is alone and without associates!'" Mu'ādh travelled to Yaman together with a number of early converts and tax collectors, all commissioned to teach the people and to judge between them by the law of God and His Prophet. As Islām spread from one corner of the Arabian Peninsula to another, its people from the extreme north to the extreme south became one *ummah*, unified under the banner of Muhammad, the Prophet of God—May God's peace and blessing be upon him! Everybody acknowledged one and the same religion, Islām; and all turned together to the worship of one God, without associates. Only twenty years before, the same people were hostile tribes, warring with one another, and robbing one another's property and wealth. Now that they all joined Islām's ranks, the country was cleansed of the abomination of paganism and became reconciled to live under the shadow of divine judgment. Thus, intertribal hostility was eradicated, and there was neither aggression nor injustice. Henceforth, no one was to draw his sword except to defend the greater country or to put an end to aggression against the religion of God.

Conversion of Arab Christians to Islām

A group of Christians from Najrān opted to keep their faith and not to follow the example of Banū al Hārith, the majority of whom had joined Islām. To these the Prophet sent Khālid ibn al Walīd to preach to them the faith and to bring them into the *pax Islāmica* that had just covered the Peninsula end to end. They responded favorably to his call and entered Islām.

Khālid then arranged for a delegation of them to visit Madīnah where the Prophet met them with friendly welcome. Another group from Yaman found it difficult to subject themselves to the dominion of Islām for the provincial reason that Islām arose in Hijāz rather than in their country. Since they had never been subjected to Hijāz, which had on many occasions been the object of military campaigns by the people of Yaman, the latter were too proud to submit. To them the Prophet sent 'Alī ibn Abū Tālib to call them to Islām, but they attacked him. Tender of age though he was, and commanding no greater force than three hundred horsemen, 'Alī vanquished them. For a second time they regrouped their forces and fought. But again 'Alī surrounded them and broke their resistance. Finally, they submitted and converted to Islām in good faith. They listened to the teachings of Mu'ādh and his companions. Their delegation to Madīnah was the last one which the Prophet met before his death.

The Prophet Prepares for Pilgrimage

While 'Alī was preparing to return to Makkah, the Prophet was preparing to undertake the pilgrimage and advising his companions to do likewise. The month of Dhū al Qi'dah was almost at an end, to be followed by Dhū al Hijjah, the month of pilgrimage. Up until that time, the Prophet had not performed the pilgrimage ritual in full, though he had performed the lesser pilgrimage on two previous occasions. The ritual of the pilgrimage had to be established in its entirety so that the Muslims might learn and follow it. As soon as the people knew of the Prophet's intention and heard his call to march with him on pilgrimage, the whole Peninsula reverberated with the call, and thousands and thousands of people from all corners poured into Madīnah. From every town and village, from every mountain and valley, from every plain and desert across the wide Peninsula, the people arrived to perform the pilgrimage. It was as if this vast expanse of land had all been illuminated by the dazzling light of God and His Holy Prophet. Around Madīnah tents were set up to accommodate the new visitors, numbering 100,000 or more, who had risen up in response to the call of their Prophet, Muhammad the Prophet of God—May God's best blessing and peace be upon him. All these men came as brethren, in love and respect for one another, and united in the true bond of friendship and Islāmic brotherhood, whereas but yesteryear they had been the most hostile of enemies. These thousands upon thousands of men crisscrossed the streets of Madīnah, all manifesting the smiles of faith, the certainty of conviction, and the confidence and pride of true religion. Their convocation was an inspiring evidence of the victory of truth, of the wide reach of the light of God, and of the deep bond of truth and righteousness which had cemented them one to the other so that they stood like one great fortress.

The Muslims March for Pilgrimage

On the twenty-fifth of Dhū al Qiʿdah of the year 10 A.H., the Prophet set forth toward Makkah accompanied by all his wives, each riding her own carriage. He was followed by a great multitude, numbering 90,000 according to some historians, 114,000 according to others. These men marched with consciences deeply moved by faith, with hearts full of joy and contentment at their intended accomplishment of pilgrimage to the holy sanctuary of God. They reached Dhū al Ḥulayfah at the end of the day and there they spent the night. On the following morning, the Prophet put himself into a sacral state and the Muslims followed his example. Everyone shed his clothes and put on two pieces of unsewn white cloth, the simplest of all garments. In this way, they expressed the absolute egalitarianism of Islām in its most eloquent and highest sense. Muḥammad turned to God with all his heart and mind praying, "At your service, O God! At your service! You have no associates! At your service, O God! Praise be to God! Thanks be to God! At your service, O God! You have no associates! At your service, O God! You have no associates, O God! At your service, O God!" And all the Muslims repeated these words after him. Deserts, valleys, and mountains reverberated with this prayer. The sky itself reverberated with the call of those pious, believing, and worshipping souls. Thus the procession continued on its way to Makkah, its thousands and hundreds of thousands filling the air with the sound of this prayer. At every mosque on the way to Makkah, the procession would stop to pray, and the voices of the thousands would rise proclaiming the unity of God, their praise and blessing in anticipation of the great day of pilgrimage that awaited them. Everyone was impatient to reach the sanctuary of God that he revered and honored more than anything else in the world. Undoubtedly, the deserts, mountains, and valleys, the trees, birds and skies were moved by what they witnessed in this great call, the like of which they had never heard before! They and the Peninsula had been blessed by the advent of this illiterate Prophet, Muhammad, the Servant of God and His Apostle.

Desacralization after the 'Umrah or Lesser Pilgrimage

When the procession reached Sarif, midway between Makkah and Madīnah, Muḥammad said to his companions: "Those of you who do not have any sacrificial animals with them may perform the lesser pilgrimage. But those who do, must perform the complete ritual." The procession continued and reached Makkah on the fourth of Dhū al Ḥijjah. Upon arrival, the Prophet, followed by the Muslims, hastened to the Ka'bah. There, the Prophet went to the Black Stone and kissed it. Then he circumambulated the holy sanctuary seven times, the first three of which he did at a trotting pace, just as he had done in the lesser pilgrimage. He then proceeded to the Sanctuary of Ibrahīm where he performed a prayer. Returning back to the Black Stone, he kissed it once more and then left the temple area for the Mount of al Ṣafā, and from there performed the Sa'y between that mount and the mount of Marwah.[7] He then announced to the Pilgrims that whoever did not have an animal to sacrifice should now desacralize himself and bring his pilgrimage ritual to a close. Some pilgrims hesitated, and this angered the Prophet. He repeated his command. When he entered his tent, the anger visible on his face, 'Aishah inquired about it. He answered, "How can I be otherwise when my commands are not obeyed?" As a visiting companion inquired again, adding, "Whoever angers the Prophet of God will taste of the fire," the Prophet said, "Is it not strange that I command the people and find them hesitant to obey? If it were permissible to come to pilgrimage without animals to sacrifice, I too would have been content to perform the lesser pilgrimage and desacralize at this moment." So relates Muslim.[8] When the news of the Prophet's anger reached the people, thousands of them terminated their pilgrimage regretfully. Even the wives of the Prophet, including his daughter Fāṭimah, did likewise. Only those people who had brought sacrificial animals with them kept themselves in the sacral state.

'Alī's Return from Yaman

While the Muslims were performing their pilgrimage, 'Alī returned from his campaign in Yaman. Before entering Makkah, and upon hearing that the Prophet of God was leading the pilgrimage, 'Alī put himself in a sacral state and wore the pilgrim garments. Upon finding that his wife Fāṭimah, had desacralized herself, he asked for an explanation. He was told that the Prophet had commanded that only lesser pilgrimage was permitted to those who did not bring their sacrificial animals with them. 'Alī went to the Prophet and there related to him the news of his campaign in Yaman. When he finished, the Prophet asked him to circumambulate the holy sanctuary and then to desacralize himself like the rest. 'Alī retorted: "Prophet of God, I have recited exactly the same prayers as you have." The Prophet said. "Even so, desacralize yourself as your companions have done." 'Alī rejoined again: "Prophet of God, when I put myself in the sacral state, I recited: 'O God, I intend to perform this pilgrimage in identically the same manner as Your Prophet, Servant, and Apostle Muḥammad.'" The Prophet then asked 'Alī whether he had any sacrificial animals and, when 'Alī answered in the negative, Muḥammad gave him some of his own. For this reason, 'Ālī kept his sacral state and performed the ritual of pilgrimage in its complete form.

Performance of the Pilgrimage Ritual

On the eighth day of Dhū al Ḥijjah, the day of al Tarwiyah, Muḥammad went to Minā and spent the day and night in that locality. There, he performed all the prayers incumbent during that period. The following day, Muḥammad recited his dawn prayer and, at sunrise, proceeded on his camel, al Qaswā', to the Mount of 'Arafāt, followed by all the pilgrims. As he ascended the mountain, he was surrounded by thousands of his companions reciting the *talbiyah* and the *takbīr*.[9] The Prophet naturally heard their recitations but made no effort either to stop them or to encourage them. He commanded some of his companions to put up a tent for him on the east side of the mountain at a spot called Namirah. When the sun passed the zenith, he ordered his camel to be saddled, and rode on it until he reached the valley of 'Uranah.

The Prophet's Last Sermon

It was there that he, while sitting on his camel, delivered his sermon in a loud voice to his people. Rabī'ah ibn Umayyah ibn Khalaf repeated the sermon after him sentence by sentence.

He began by praising God and thanking Him, and then turning to the people, he said:

"O Men, listen well to my words, for I do not know whether I shall meet you again on such an occasion in the future. O Men, your lives and your property shall be inviolate until you meet your Lord. The safety of your lives and of your property shall be as inviolate as this holy day and holy month. Remember that you will indeed meet your Lord, and that He will indeed reckon your deeds. Thus do I warn you. Whoever of you is keeping a trust of someone else shall return that trust to its rightful owner. All interest obligation shall henceforth be waived. Your capital, however, is yours to keep. You will neither inflict nor suffer inequity. God has judged that there shall be no interest and that all the interest due to 'Abbās ibn 'Abd al Muṭṭalib shall henceforth be waived. Every right arising out of homicide in pre-Islāmic days is henceforth waived. And the first such right that I waive is that arising from the murder of Rabī'ah ibn al Ḥārith ibn 'Abd al Muttalib. O Men, the devil has lost all hope of ever being worshipped in this land of yours. Nevertheless, he still is anxious to determine the lesser of your deeds. Beware of him, therefore, for the safety of your religion. O Men, intercalation or tampering with the calendar is evidence of great unbelief and confirms the unbelievers in their misguidance. They indulge in it one year and forbid it the next in order to make permissible that which God forbade, and to forbid that which God has made permissible. The pattern according to which the time is reckoned is always the same. With God, the months are twelve in number. Four of them are holy. Three of these are successive and one occurs singly between the months of Jumādā and Sha'bān. O Men, to you a right belongs with respect to your women and to your women a right with respect to you. It is your right that they not fraternize with any one of whom you do not approve, as well as never to commit adultery. But if they do, then God has permitted you to isolate them within their homes and to chastise them without cruelty. But if they abide by your right, then to them belongs the right to be fed and clothed in kindness. Do treat your women well and be kind to them, for they are your partners and committed helpers. Remember that you

have taken them as your wives and enjoyed their flesh
only under God's trust and with His permission. Reason well,
therefore, O Men, and ponder my words which I now convey
to you. I am leaving you with the Book of God and the
Sunnah of His Prophet. If you follow them, you will never
go astray. O Men, harken well to my words. Learn that
every Muslim is a brother to every Muslim and that the
Muslims constitute one brotherhood. Nothing shall be legitimate to a Muslim which belongs to a fellow Muslim unless
it was given freely and willingly. Do not, therefore, do
injustice to your own selves. O God, have I conveyed Your
message?"

As the Prophet delivered his speech, Rabī'ah repeated it sentence by sentence and asked the people every now and then
whether or not they had understood the Prophet's words and
committed them to memory. In order to make sure that the
people understood and remembered, the Prophet used to ask his
crier to say: "The Prophet of God asks, 'Do you know which
day is this?" The audience would answer, "Today is the day of
the greater pilgrimage." The Prophet then would say, "Tell them
that God has declared inviolate your lives and your property
until the day you will meet your Lord; that he has made the
safety of your property and of your lives as inviolate as this
day." At the end of his speech, the Prophet asked, "O God, have
I conveyed your message?" And the people answered from all
corners, "Indeed so! God be witness."

When the Prophet finished his sermon, he dismounted and
waited until noon, at which time he performed both the noon
and the midafternoon prayers. He then mounted his camel and
proceeded to al Sakharāt where he recited to the people the concluding divine revelation: "Today I have completed for you your
religion, and granted you the last of my blessings. Today I have
accepted for you Islām as the religion."[10] When Abū Bakr heard
this verse he realized that with the completion of the divine
message, the Prophet's life was soon to come to a close.

The Prophet left 'Arafāt and spent his night at Muzdalifah.
In the morning, he visited first the sanctuary of al Mash'ar, and
then Minā on the road to which he threw pebbles against the
symbol of Satan. When he reached his tent, he sacrificed sixty-
three camels, one for each year of his life. 'Alī sacrificed the rest
of the animals which the Prophet had brought with him from

Madīnah. The Prophet then shaved his head and declared his pilgrimage completed. This pilgrimage is sometimes called "the Farewell Pilgrimage." Others have called it the "Pilgrimage of the Annunciation" and others, the "Pilgrimage of Islām." In truth, the Prophet's pilgrimage was all these at once. It was the "Farewell Pilgrimage" because Muhammad saw Makkah and the holy sanctuary for the last time. It was also the "Pilgrimage of Islām" because God completed His religion for the benefit of mankind and granted to them His total blessing. Finally, it was also the "Pilgrimage of the Annunciation" because the Prophet had completed his announcement and conveyance to the people of what he has been commanded by God to announce and to convey. Muhammad was truly only an announcer, a conveyor, and a warner sent to a people who see the truth and believe.

Sulṭān Ḥasan and Rifā'ī Mosques, Cairo, Egypt.

The Prophet's
Sickness and Death

Effects of the "Farewell Pilgrimage"

The "Farewell Pilgrimage" completed, tens of thousands of pilgrims began their return home. Those who came from the desert returned to the desert; those who came from Tihāmah returned hence, and those who came from the south, from Yaman, Ḥaḍramawt and neighboring territories, did likewise. The Prophet and his immediate companions set out in the direction of Madīnah. When they reached it, they settled down confident that peace had covered the entire Peninsula. Henceforth, it was natural that Muḥammad became preoccupied with the conditions of those countries under the dominion of Byzantium and Persia, especially al Shām, Egypt, and 'Irāq. Now that the people have converted to Islām in such large groups, that their delegations had already declared in Madīnah their obedience and committed their peoples to serve under its banner and, finally, now that all the Arabs have united in this "Farewell Pilgrimage," the Arabian Peninsula became secure in its entirety. Indeed, there was no reason for any of the Arab kings and princes to withdraw or to violate loyalty to the Prophet or to his religion. Under no other regime did they enjoy more power and internal autonomy than under that which the unlettered Prophet had instituted. Bādhān, the Persian governor of Yaman, was reinstated in his governorship as soon as he converted to Islām. In recognition

of this, Bādhān preserved the unity of Arabia and threw off
the yoke of the Zoroastrian Persians. Whatever little rumblings
took place in the Peninsula never came close to resembling
rebellion, and they did not occupy the Prophet or raise in him
any apprehension for the future. The dominion of the new religion
had firmly spread over all parts of the Peninsula; all faces were
turned to the living and eternal God, and all hearts truly believed
in the One, the Almighty.

The Prophetic Pretenders

It was natural, therefore, that the pretenders to prophethood
who arose at the time were not the object of anxiety or care on
Muhammad's part. True, some of the tribes in the outlying
distances hastened to listen to any pretender, especially after
they had heard of the Prophet of God and of the success of his
mission. Obviously, such tribes wished they had the same good
fortune as the Prophet's tribe, Quraysh. Precisely because of
their distance from Makkah and from the headquarters of the
new religion, such tribes did not yet fully absorb the new religion.
However, this new religion, this honest and candid call to God,
struck its roots firmly everywhere else. To resist it would not be
easy. The anecdotes of Muhammad's travails and sacrifices for the
sake of his mission had already spread to the horizons, and everyone knew that none but Muhammad ibn 'Abdullah was capable
of such sacrifice. Every false pretension, however, must sooner
or later be exposed; and no pretender to prophethood can meet
with any long lasting success. Tulayhah, for instance, the leader
of Banū Asad and one of the greatest war heroes, a real lord
of the desert, pretended that he, too, was a prophet and an
apostle. He claimed that his true prophesying about the exact
location of water when his people were lost in the desert, and
almost perished from thirst, was the proof of his prophethood.
But he remained afraid of contradicting Muhammad or withdrawing his loyalty to him as long as the Prophet lived. He
therefore rebelled only after Muhammad's death. It was Ibn al
Walīd that led the Muslim forces in suppressing the rebellion of
Tulayhah. Upon his defeat, Tulayhah once more joined the ranks
of Islām and henceforth led a virtuous life. On the other hand,
neither Musaylimah nor al Aswad al 'Ansī fared any better
than Tulayhah as long as the Prophet lived. The former sent to
the Prophet—May God's blessing be upon Him—a message saying, "I, too, am a prophet like you. To us belongs half the earth,

and to Quraysh belongs the other half, if Quraysh were only just." When Musaylimah's two messengers delivered this message of their master to Muḥammad, the Prophet told them that, were it not for the conventional security granted to messengers, he would have ordered them executed. He then asked them to convey to Musaylimah the reply that Muḥammad heard his message and realized its lies. The earth belongs to none but God, and God grants it to whomsoever He chooses among His worthy and righteous servants. Peace belongs to the right-guided."

As for al Aswad al 'Ansī, the Governor of Yaman after the death of Bādhān, he began to practice magic and to call people to believe in him until he had achieved a measure of strength. Then he marched from the south toward Yaman and expelled Muḥammad's governors from the territory. He marched on Najrān and killed its governor, the son of Bādhān who inherited the office from his father. Al Aswad then married the widow of the fallen ruler and brought the whole area under his dominion. All this, however, did not worry Muḥammad nor did it call, in his judgment, for more than a word to his governors and agents in Yaman to pull al Aswad down. The Muslims of the area fulfilled the command of the Prophet by themselves, turned the tables on al Aswad and ended his regime. And it was his own wife who put an end to his life in vengeance for the blood of her first husband.

The Prophet's Concern for the Northern Front

Muḥammad's care and preoccupation, therefore, were directed toward the north, not toward the south of Arabia. This was especially so following his return from the "Farewell Pilgrimage." In fact, ever since the campaign of Mu'tah, when the Muslims returned without conquest after the clever and strategic withdrawal of Khālid ibn al Walīd, Muḥammad had been giving to Byzantium a good portion of his thought and careful planning. He was convinced that Muslim power at the northern frontier with al Shām should be firmly established if those who had been evacuated from the Peninsula and who had emigrated to Palestine were not to return and attack again. It was in consequence of this care that Muḥammad mobilized a very massive army when he heard that the Byzantines were about to advance on the northern frontier, and he himself led that army all the way to Tabūk. The Byzantines had withdrawn toward the interior upon hearing of the march of that army. This notwithstanding, Muḥammad continued to plan for the day when the lords of Christendom who dominated the world through Byzantium might be stirred to attack in resentment against those who had brought Christianity to an end in Najrān and other places in Arabia. Consequently, the Muslims did not stay long in Madīnah following their return from the farewell Pilgrimage in Makkah. The Prophet had immediately ordered the mobilization of a large army and commanded it to march on al Shām. That is why he sent along with that army a number of the elders of Islām, the earliest Muhājirūn, among whom were Abū Bakr and 'Umar. That is why he gave the command of the army to Usāmah ibn Zayd ibn Ḥārithah.

The Prophet's Counsel to Usāmah

Usāmah ibn Zayd, the commander of the army, was then a young man hardly twenty years of age. His appointment and precedence over the elders of Islām, the early Muhājirūn, and greater companions of the Prophet, would have caused quite a stir among the people had it not been for everybody's genuine faith in the Prophet's judgment and calculation. By appointing him, the Prophet sought to place him in the same command in which his father fell in the campaign of Mu'tah. The Prophet had wanted to give Usāmah cause for pride in victory tantamount to a reward for the martyrdom of his father. Moreover, such an appointment was sure to stir within the soul of the youth the greatest resolution, determination, and bravery. It was also meant as an example for the youths of Islām to carry the burden of great responsibility. Muḥammad commanded Usāmah and his army to enter the approaches of al Balqā' and al Dārūm in Palestine, in the vicinity of Mu'tah where his father had fallen. He also commanded him to fight the enemy in the early hours of dawn, to fight them fearlessly, and to shower them with fire. He also commanded him to surprise the enemy, never to let the news of his advance reach them beforehand. Once victory was achieved, Usāmah was to return home quickly and not to extend his stay in those lands.

The Prophet's Illness

Usāmah and his army set up their headquarters at al Jurf, in close proximity to Madīnah, and there began their preparation for the long trip to Palestine. While they were getting ready, the Prophet of God fell ill and the seriousness of his ailment prevented their going forth. One may ask with surprise how the sickness of the Prophet of God could prevent an army from undertaking a campaign which he himself had ordered. One must remember, however, that for that army to go to al Shām, it had to cross wide deserts and empty places, a matter that was not at all easy and would take many long days. It was not easy for the Muslims, considering their great love for the Prophet, to leave Madīnah while he suffered from grave illness. Those same men knew that the Prophet never suffered from any serious ailment. Nothing had adversely affected his health throughout this period except a brief lack of appetite in 6 A.H. falsely attributed to Jewish magic, and a little discomfort following his eating a bite of poisoned lamb in 7 A.H. Furthermore, the rhythm of his life and the logic of his teachings always protected him against disease. He always ate little and satisfied himself with the barest and simplest necessities. His clothes and his house were always perfectly clean, for Muhammad not only saw to it that the duties of ablutions were perfectly carried out at all times, but he even used to say: "Were it not for my fear of imposing hardship on my people, I would have made it a duty for them to brush their teeth five times a day." On the other hand, the ritual of prayer and daily exercise which Muhammad observed as well as his sense for economy in the pursuit of pleasure, his refrain from indulgences of all kinds, and his general unconcern for things of this world which always kept him at a distance from them, but in communion with cosmic life and the secrets of existence—all these aspects of his character protected him against disease and gave him good health. His strong natural, construction and innate inclination to moral goodness consolidated his immunity against disease.

Now that he had fallen seriously ill, however, it was natural for his friends and companions to become concerned and anxious, fearing that the untold energies he spent during the last twenty years of life may have been begun to take effect upon him. Ever since he had proclaimed his prophethood in Makkah and begun to call men to worship God alone, to abandon the idols of the ancestors, Muhammad had met such great opposition and hardship that his companions had to flee to Abyssinia and he himself to the seclusion of the mountains in the outskirts of Makkah. His flight from Makkah to Madīnah, following the covenant of 'Aqabah, took place under the most trying and dangerous of conditions. Muḥammad did not know what awaited him in Madīnah before he arrived there under cover of night. When he did arrive there, he immediately became the object of Jewish plotting and intrigue. After God gave him victory following all these trials and permitted men from all corners to join the new faith, Muḥammad's duties multiplied to a tremendous extent. The keeping of the peace, the leadership of the community, the establishment of its institutions, the continuous wars he had to fight, and the attacks he had to repel would have broken the back of the strongest man.

What situation could have been more tragically trying than that in which Muḥammad found himself at the Battle of Uḥud when the Muslims ran away from their enemy and Muḥammad ascended the hill alone pursued by Quraysh's soldiers; when, under a shower of enemy arrows and stones, he fell wounded, with his teeth broken? What position could be more frightening than that in which the Prophet found himself at the Battle of Ḥunayn when the Muslims fell back at dawn before their attacking enemies when so determined was their retreat that Abū Sufyān could say that "Only the sea could make them turn back again"; when in the midst of this retreating stream of people Muḥammad held his ground and called unto the Muslims: "Where to? Where to? Come back! Come back to me!" until they returned and were victorious. Moreover, there was the burden of mission, the tremendous burden of revelation, the self-exhausting spiritual effort to keep in communion with the reality of the universe, with the supernal plenum—an effort the Prophet was reported to have described as more horrendous than the destiny of doom which befell Hūd and other ancient civilizations. Muḥammad's companions were witnesses to all this. They had seen him bear his burdens uprightly and with determination, never faltering. Now that he had fallen ill after such a splendid career, it was natural for them to want to postpone their march to al Shām for a while, until they could reassure themselves of God's disposition.

The Prophet's Visit to the Cemetery

In the meantime, another event took place which added to the companions' anxiety. At the beginning of his illness, Muḥammad suffered from sleeplessness. On one night, as the days were long and hot and the nights short and breezy, Muḥammad felt like going out of his house for a walk around the city. Only his servant, Abū Muwayhibah, accompanied him on this promenade. But where would he go? He went to Baqī' al Gharqad where all the cemeteries of the Muslims lay on the outskirts of Madīnah. According to the reports, he stood between the graves of his fallen companions and addressed them in the following words: "Peace be upon you who are in these graves. Blessed are you in your present state to which you have emerged from the state in which the people live on earth. Subversive attacks are falling one after another like waves of darkness, each worse than the previous one." Abū Muwayhibah related that the Prophet had told him upon arrival at Baqī' al Gharqad: "I have been commanded to pray for those who lie in this terrain. Won't you come with me?" After praying for the dead buried in that cemetery, when it was time to return home, the Prophet approached Abū Muwayhibah and said to him: "O Abū Muwayhibah, I have been given the keys of this world and eternity in it, and now I am being offered Paradise, and meeting with my God. I am asked to choose between them." Abū Muwayhibah said: "What would I not give for your sake, O Master! Is it not possible to have both? Do take the keys of this world, eternity in it, as well as Paradise." Muḥammad answered: "No, by God, O Abū Muwayhibah. I have chosen Paradise and meeting with my Lord."

Abū Muwayhibah must have reported what he had seen and heard. The Prophet began to complain from his sickness the morning following the night on which he had visited the cemetery of al Baqī'. It was then that the people became concerned and the army of Usāmah did not move. True, the report of Abū Muwayhibah is doubted by many historians who believe that Muḥammad's sickness could not have been the only reason that prevented the army from marching to al Shām, that another cause was the disappointment of many, including a number of elderly Muhājirūn and Ansār, with respect to the leadership assigned to the army. They based their judgment on facts that are given in the sequel. Although we do not wish here to dispute their judgment concerning the report of Abū Muwayhibah, we do not find reason to justify their denial of the event altogether. Whatever the value of the report, it is not necessary to deny the event of the Prophet's visit to the cemetery of Baqī al Gharqad, his prayer for its dead, or his realization that the hour of meeting with his Lord was soon to strike. In our age, science does not deny the possibility of communication between spirits. It subsumes such communication under the category of psychic phenomena. There have been many men endowed with strong and sensitive perception who knew that their hour was close, and many witnesses to this effect can be produced. Furthermore, communication between the living and the dead, the connection between the past and the present in a manner not limited by either space or time is today regarded as indubitable fact, although man's nature being what it is, it is not given for us to perceive its forms. There is hence no reason to deny the event of the Prophet's visit to the cemetery of Baqi' as out of place considering Muhammad's spiritual and psychic power of communication with the realms of reality and his awareness of spiritual reality that surpasses that of ordinary men.

Muhammad's Congenial Mood

On the following morning, Muhammad found 'A'ishah, his wife, complaining of a headache and holding her head between her hands, murmuring, "O My head!" Having begun to feel pain, Muhammad answered, "But rather, O 'A'ishah, my own head!" However, the pain was not strong enough to put him to bed, to stop his daily work, or to prevent him from talking kindly to his wives and joking with them. As 'A'ishah continued to complain from her headache, Muhammad said to her: "It wouldn't be too bad after all, O 'A'ishah, if you were to die before me. For I would then pray for you and attend your funeral." But this only aroused jealousy in the youthful 'A'ishah, who answered: "Let that be the good fate of someone else besides me. By God, should that ever happen to me, your other wives would still be there to give you company." The Prophet smiled, but did not follow up the conversation because of an attack of pain. As soon as the pain subsided, he got up and visited with his wives just as he had always done. The pain returned with stronger force, however, so that Muhammad could not bear it any longer. He was in the quarters of Maymūnah, his wife, when he found it necessary to call the members of his house and to ask all of them to attend to him in the quarters of 'A'ishah. His wives agreed to nurse him there. He moved out of Maymūnah's quarters, his head wrapped, leaning on 'Alī ibn Abū Ṭālib on one side and on al 'Abbās, his uncle, on the other. His legs could hardly carry him. He entered the quarters of 'Ā'ishah and there lay down.

Attacks of Fever

His fever increased in the first days of his sickness so that he felt as if he were on fire. When the attacks of fever subsided, the Prophet walked to the mosque to lead the prayers. He continued to do so for several days but felt too weak to talk to his companions or to listeñ to them. But he could hear their gossip about his appointment of a very young man to command the elder Muhājirūn and Ansār in the coming campaign against al Shām. Despite the gradual deterioration of his health and the aggravation of his pain, he felt it necessary to address the people on that subject.

Sortie to the Mosque

One day he asked his wives and servants to pour on him seven goatskins of water from various wells. The water was brought from different wells as he commanded and poured over him as he sat in a tub belonging to Ḥafṣah. He then put on his clothes, wrapped his head, and went to the mosque. Standing at the pulpit, he praised God, prayed for the martyrs of Uḥud, and addressed the congregation in the following words: "O Men, carry out the expedition under Usāmah. Your complaint against his generalship is of the same kind as your complaint against the generalship of his father before him. By God, Usāmah is as fit for the generalship as was his father." Muḥammad stopped for a while, and there was absolute silence. He then resumed his address, saying: "Has he not made the better choice who, when given the option of taking this world, the other world, or properly acquiescing in whatever is with God, chooses the last alternative?" Muḥammad fell silent again, and the people were absolutely motionless. With his deep perception and sensitivity Abū Bakr realized that Muḥammad was here referring to himself. His loyalty to the Prophet and profound feeling for his person overwhelmed Abū Bakr, who could not hold back his tears. Deeply moved and crying, he said: "But we would give our own lives and the lives of our children for you, O Muḥammad!" Fearing the spread of Abū Bakr's contagious affection among

the congregation, Muhammad said softly: "O Abū Bakr!" He
then commanded all the gates of the mosque to be closed except
the one which led to the quarters of Abū Bakr. When this was
done, he said: "I do not know of anyone whose companionship
is preferable to me than yours. Of all the people of the world,
I would choose only Abū Bakr as a permanent friend and constant companion. His has been the friendship and fraternity of
true faith! And it will last until God brings us together again."
Muhammad left the pulpit to return to 'Ā'ishah's quarters. As
he did, he turned to the people and said: "O Muhājirūn, be good
to al Ansār. The Muslim community increases every day, but
the number of al Ansār remains the same. Al Ansār have been
my own people, my trustworthy people among whom I have
taken shelter. Be good to the virtuous among them, reward the
pious, and forgive the wrongdoers."

Muhammad proceeded to the house of 'Ā'ishah nearly exhausted by the effort he had exerted. When a man is ill, suffering from high fever, to get out of bed and go to the Mosque after
having had to cool his body with seven skins of water is hard
enough. How much more exacerbating must this brief outing
have been for Muhammad when at the same time he had to confront such momentous matters as Usāmah's mobilized army and
the threatened fate of al Ansār as well as of the Arab *ummah*,
newly cemented together by the religion of Islām? The following
day, Muhammad tried to get out of bed and lead the prayers in
the Mosque as usual. When he found his effort futile, he ordered
that Abū Bakr lead the prayers in his place. 'Ā'ishah was anxious
for her husband to lead the prayers himself. She thought that
nothing would better allay the fears of the people than for them
to see the Prophet resume his daily functions. She therefore
apologized for her father, Abū Bakr, saying that his voice was
too soft and that he would break down and cry whenever he
recited the Qur'ān. Realizing his incapacity to rise from bed,
the Prophet ordered once again that Abū Bakr lead the prayers.
When 'Ā'ishah insisted on her objection, the Prophet shouted in
anger: "How obsessive are women! Order Abū Bakr to lead the
prayers at once."

On another day, when Abū Bakr was absent, Bilāl called the
Muslims to prayer and invited 'Umar to lead them. As 'Umar's
loud voice reached the ear of the Prophet next door, he took this
as another flouting of his previous command. He said: "Where
is Abū Bakr? God and the believers do not agree that Abū Bakr

be not the leader." It was this incident that convinced the people that Muḥammad has indeed appointed Abū Bakr as his successor, for leadership of the prayers was the foremost sign of succession to the Prophet.

The Prophet's Whisper to Fāṭimah

After this, the Prophet's sickness and pain increased. His fever was so high that it could be felt by his wives and servants upon touching the blankets which covered him. Fāṭimah, his daughter, whom he loved deeply as his only surviving offspring, visited him every day. Whenever she entered his room, the Prophet would cry, kiss her, and give her his own chair. One day when she entered the room, he greeted her saying, "Welcome, my daughter." But it was she who kissed him. He asked her to sit by him on his bed and whispered to her twice, first making her cry and then making her laugh. 'Ā'ishah sought to discover what was said; but Fāṭimah refused to give away what she took to be a secret. It was not until after he died that Fāṭimah divulged what he had then told her, namely, that he was to die of that same sickness—which caused her to cry—and that she would be the first member of his family to join him after death— which made her smile. In order to cool down his fever, Muḥammad dipped his hand in a container by his bed, filled every now and then with cold water, and wiped his face. At times, the high fever gave him convulsions. Recovering from one of those attacks, he overheard his daughter, Fāṭimah, say with deep sorrow: "Oh, the terrible pain my father is suffering!" At this Muḥammad said, "Your father will suffer no more pain after this day," meaning that he was to meet his Lord before the day was over.

The Prophet's Wish to Write a Testament

Anxious to lighten his pain, his companions reminded him that he had counseled them not to complain when sick. He apologized to them, saying that his pains surpassed whatever any two of them could bear together. While under a strong attack of fever and surrounded by visitors, he asked that pen and ink and paper be brought. He said he would dictate something for his followers' benefit, assuring them that if they adhered to it, they would never go astray. Some of the people present thought that since the Prophet—May God's peace and blessing be upon him—was severely ill and since the Muslims already had the Qur'ān, no further writing was necessary. It is related that that thought belonged to 'Umar. The people present disagreed among themselves, some wishing to bring writing materials and take down what the Prophet would dictate, and others thinking that any further writing besides that of the Book of God would be superfluous. Muḥammad asked them all to leave, saying, "It does not become you to disagree in my presence." Ibn 'Abbās felt concerned that the people would lose something important if they did not hasten to bring the writing materials, whereas 'Umar held firmly to his judgment which he based upon God's own estimate of His Holy Book: "In this scripture, We have left out nothing."[1]

As the news of the deteriorating health of the Prophet spread, Usāmah and a number of his aides left their encampment at al Jurf for Madīnah seeking reassurance concerning the Prophet's health. Usāmah entered the quarters of 'Ā'ishah unable to speak. But when Muḥammad saw Usāmah, he lifted his hands toward the sky before placing them on Usāmah's shoulders, as a sign of prayer for him.

Members of the Prophet's household saw fit at this stage to give him some medicine which Asmā', a relative of Maymūnah, had learned to prepare during her stay in Abyssinia. Taking advantage of Muḥammad's loss of consciousness, they poured the medicine into his mouth. When he came back to himself, he asked who had given him the medicine and why. His uncle, al 'Abbās, explained that they had prepared it and given it to him because they feared he had pleurisy. The Prophet said, "That is a disease which God would not inflict upon me." He then ordered everyone in the house except his uncle, al 'Abbās, to taste it. Even Maymūnah, who was then fasting, was forced to taste it.

At the beginning of his illness, Muḥammad had in his house seven Dīnārs; he feared he might die while some money was still in his possession. He therefore commanded his relatives to give the money away to the poor. However, their preoccupation with his sickness and constant attendance upon him, in addition to their concern for his deteriorating health, caused them to forget to execute his order. When he came to himself on Sunday, on the eve of the day of his death, he inquired whether they had fulfilled his order. 'Ā'ishah answered that the money was still in her possession. He asked her to bring it forth to put on the palm of his hand. He then said: "What spectacle is this of Muḥammad, if he were to meet God in this condition?" The money was given forthwith to the poor.

Muḥammad spent a peaceful night in which his fever seemed to subside. It was as if the medicine which his relatives had prepared for him had somewhat alleviated the disease. In the morning he was even able to go to the mosque although his head was still wrapped and he needed to lean on 'Alī ibn Abū Ṭālib and al Faḍl ibn al 'Abbās for support. Abū Bakr was leading the prayer at the time of Muḥammad's entry into the mosque. As the Muslims saw the Prophet come in, they were so overjoyed at his recovery that they almost allowed their prayer to be interrupted. Abū Bakr raised his voice in the recitation signaling that the prayer must go on and not be interrupted. Muḥammad was extremely pleased with what he saw, and Abū Bakr knew well that the people would not have been diverted from prayer by the arrival of any other man. As Muḥammad came close to Abū Bakr to join in the prayer, the latter moved himself away from his position of leadership so that the Prophet might take over. Muḥammad, however, pushed him back into place saying, "You lead." He sat beside Abū Bakr and prayed in a sitting position. When he finished, he joined the congregation and talked to them with a clear voice audible even outside the mosque. He said: "O Men, the fire is ready. Subversive attacks are advancing like the waves of darkness. By God, I shall not be held responsible for aught of this. I have never allowed anything but that which the Qur'ān has made legitimate, and I have never forbidden aught which the Qur'ān has not forbidden. God's curse is upon those who take graves for their mosques."[2]

Muslim Joy at the Prophet's Apparent Recovery

The Muslims were so overjoyed at the signs of recovery in the health of their Prophet that Usāmah ibn Zayd even asked for permission to march on al Shām. Indeed, even Abū Bakr came forward to say: "O Prophet of God, it is evident that God has granted you His blessing and given you good health just as we all wished and prayed. I had promised the Daughter of Khārijah [meaning his wife] to spend the day with her. May I take leave of you?" The Prophet granted him leave, and Abū Bakr went to al Sunḥ on the outskirts of Madīnah, where his wife resided. 'Umar and 'Alī returned to their business as usual.

The Muslims dispersed in joy and happiness after their days of despondence over the news of Muhammad's illness. Muhammad returned to the quarters of 'Ā'ishah made happy by the happiness of his fellow Muslims who filled the mosque to see him and who anxiously awaited to hear of his news. But he felt quite weak. 'Ā'ishah helped her husband in with a heart full of awe and sympathy, wishing she could offer him her own life and energy to replace his waning strength.

The Interlude of Wakefulness before Death

The Prophet's visit to the mosque turned out to be only an interlude of wakefulness which precedes death. After he returned home, every minute saw further deterioration of his health. There was no doubt that he had only a few hours to live. How did he spend these last few hours of his life? What was his last vision? Did he spend those precious moments reviewing the career he had lived since God had commissioned him to prophethood and appointed him a guide to mankind? Did he recall the hardships he suffered, the joys he experienced, and the spiritual and military victories he achieved? Or did he spend his last moments praying to God and asking for mercy with all his soul and all his mind as he used to do throughout his life? Or was he too weak to review anything and too unconscious even to pray? The reports vary widely. Most reports tell that on that day, i.e., June 8, 632 C.E., one of the hottest days in Arabia, Muhammad asked for a pitcher of cold water in which he dipped his hands and wiped his face. Most reports state that a man from the clan of Abū Bakr entered the quarters of 'Ā'ishah carrying a toothbrush in his hand. Muhammad looked at him in a way expressive of his desire to obtain the toothbrush. 'Ā'ishah took the toothbrush from her relative and worked it out until it became pliable and handed it over to Muhammad who used it to brush his teeth.

"Rather, God on High and Paradise"

The same reports also tell that as the agonies of death became stronger, the Prophet turned to God in prayer saying: "O, God, help me overcome the agonies of death." 'Ā'ishah reported that his head was in her lap during the last hour. She said, "The

Prophet's head was getting heavier in my lap. I looked at his face and found that his eyes had become fixed. I heard him murmur, 'Rather, God on High and Paradise.' I said to him, 'By Him who sent you as a Prophet to teach the truth, you have been given the choice and you chose well.' The Prophet of God expired while his head was on my side between my lungs and my heart. It was my youth and inexperience that made me let him die in my lap. I then placed his head on the pillow and rose to bemoan my fate and to join the other women in our bereavement and sorrow."

Did Muḥammad truly die? That is the question over which the Arabs differed greatly at the time, indeed so greatly that they almost came to blows. Thanks to God's will and care, the division was quickly stamped out and the religion of the Ḥanīfs, God's true religion, emerged unscathed.

Interior of the Ulu Jāmi', Bursa, Turkey.

The Prophet's Burial

Muslim Shock at the News of Death

It was therefore in 'Ā'ishah's quarters, while his head lay in her lap that the Prophet—May God's peace and blessing be upon him—chose the company of God on High. When this happened, 'Ā'ishah laid his head down on a pillow and joined the other women of the house who rushed to her upon hearing the news and began to cry in bereavement and sorrow. The Muslims at the mosque were taken by surprise by the sudden noise. In the morning, they had seen the Prophet and were convinced his health was improving so much that Abū Bakr, it will be remembered, sought permission to go and visit his wife at al Sunḥ.

'Umar Belies the News

Upon hearing the news and hardly believing it, 'Umar returned quickly to the Prophet's quarters. Upon arrival, he went straight to Muḥammad's bed, uncovered and looked at his face for a while. He perceived its motionlessness and deathlike appearance as a coma from which he believed Muḥammad would soon emerge. Al Mughīrah tried in vain to convince 'Umar of the painful fact. 'Umar, however, continued to believe firmly that Muḥammad did not die. When al Mughīrah insisted, 'Umar said to him in anger, "You lie." The two went to the mosque together while 'Umar was proclaiming at the top of his voice, "Some hypocrites are pretending that the Prophet of God—May God's peace and blessing be upon him—has died. By God I swear that he did not die: that he has gone to join his Lord, just as Moses went before. Moses absented himself from his people fourteen consecutive nights and returned to them after they had declared him dead. By God, the Prophet of God will return just as Moses returned. Any man who dares to perpetrate a false rumor such as Muḥammad's death shall have his arms and legs cut off by this hand."

At the mosque, the Muslims heard these proclamations from 'Umar—they were shocked and stupefied. If Muḥammad truly died, woe unto all those who saw him and heard him, who believed in him and in the God Who sent him a conveyor of true guidance and religion. Their bereavement would be so great that their hearts and minds would break asunder. If, on the other hand, it were true that Muḥammad had not died but had gone to join his Lord, as 'Umar claimed, that was reason for an even greater shock. The Muslims should then await his return which, like that of Moses, would be all the more reason for wonder. The Muslim crowds sat around 'Umar and listened to him, inclined as they were to agree with him that the Prophet of God did not die. At any rate, they could not associate death with the man whom they had beheld in person only a few hours before and whose clear and resonant voice they had heard pray and invoke God's mercy and blessing. Moreover, they could not convince themselves that the friend whom God had chosen for the conveyance of His divine message, to whom all the Arabs had submitted, and to whom Chosroes and Heraclius were also soon to submit, could possibly die. They could not believe that a man could die who had shown such power as had shaken the world for twenty consecutive years and had produced the greatest spiritual storm of history. The women, however, were still beating their faces and crying at Muḥammad's house, a sure sign that Muḥammad had really died. Yet, here in the mosque, 'Umar was still proclaiming that Muḥammad had not died; and that he had gone to join his Lord as Moses had done; that those who spoke of Muḥammad's death were hypocrites who would suffer the cutting of their arms and necks by Muḥammad upon his return. What would the Muslims believe? As they recovered from their severe shock, hope began to stir within them in consequence of 'Umar's claim that Muḥammad was to return, and soon they almost believed their own wishes. Their wishful thinking had apparently painted for them the sky a beautiful blue.

Enter Abū Bakr

As they wavered between believing 'Umar or the indubitable meaning of the women's crying, Abū Bakr heard the news and returned from al Sunḥ. He looked through the door of the mosque and saw the Muslims being addressed by 'Umar, but he did not tarry there. He went straight to the quarters of 'Ā'ishah and asked for permission to enter. He was answered that there was no need that day for permission. He entered and found the Prophet laid down in a corner and covered with a striped cloth. He approached, uncovered the face and kissed it, saying, "How wholesome you are, whether alive or dead!" He then held the Prophet's head in his hands and looked closely at the face which showed no sign whatever of death's attack. Laying it down again, he said, "What would I not have sacrificed for you! The one death which God has decreed for you, as for any other man, to taste, you have now tasted. Henceforth, no death shall ever befall you." He covered the head with the striped cloth and went straight to the mosque where 'Umar was still proclaiming loudly that Muhammad had not died. The crowds made a way for him to the front, and as he came close to 'Umar he said to him: "Softly, O 'Umar! Keep silent!" But 'Umar would not stop talking and continued repeating the same claim. Abū Bakr rose and made a sign to the people that he wished to address them. No one could have dared impose himself upon the congregation in such manner except Abū Bakr, for he was the ever trustworthy friend of the Prophet, whom Muhammad would have chosen from among all men. Hence, it was natural that the people hastened to respond to his call and move away from 'Umar.

Muḥammad Is Truly Dead

After praising and thanking God, Abū Bakr delivered the following brief address: "O Men, if you have been worshipping Muhammad, then know that Muhammad is dead. But if you have been worshipping God, then know that God is living and never dies." He then recited the Qur'ānic verse,

وَمَا مُحَمَّدٌ إِلَّا رَسُولٌ قَدْ خَلَتْ مِنْ قَبْلِهِ الرُّسُلُ أَفَإِنْ مَاتَ أَوْ قُتِلَ انْقَلَبْتُمْ عَلَى أَعْقَابِكُمْ
وَمَنْ يَنْقَلِبْ عَلَى عَقِبَيْهِ فَلَنْ يَضُرَّ اللهَ شَيْئًا وَسَيَجْزِي اللهُ الشَّاكِرِينَ "

"Muḥammad is but a prophet before whom many prophets have come and gone. Should he die or be killed, will you abjure your faith? Know that whoever abjures his faith will cause no harm to God, but God will surely reward those who are grateful to him."[1]

Realizing that the people were withdrawing from him and going to Abū Bakr, 'Umar fell silent and listened to Abū Bakr's speech. Upon hearing Abū Bakr recite the Qur'ānic verse, 'Umar fell to the ground. The certainty that the Prophet of God was truly dead shattered him. Beguiled by 'Umar's speech, the people listened to Abū Bakr's statement and to the Qur'ānic verse as if it was given to them for the first time. They had forgotten that there was any such revelation. Abū Bakr's stark words dissipated all doubt and uncertainty. His Qur'ānic quotation reassured the Muslims that their holding fast to God Who never dies would more than compensate for Muḥammad's passing.

Further Thoughts on Muḥammad's Death

Did 'Umar exaggerate when he convinced himself that Muḥammad had not died, when he tried to cause the people to believe likewise? The answer must be in the negative. In like vein, men of science tell us that the sun will continue to rise in the morning until a certain day when it will explode and disappear. Does anyone of us accept such a claim without entertaining a doubt as to its validity and truth? Does not everyone of us ask himself, "How could the sun explode, disappear, and go away, the sun by whose light and warmth everything in the world lives? How could it explode and disappear and the world continue thereafter even for one day?" And yet, was the light of Muḥammad any less brilliant than that of the sun or his warmth and power any less strong than those of the sun? The sun is source of much good. But was not Muḥammad the source of as much and equal good? The sun stands in communion with all beings. But was not the soul of Muḥammad equally in communion with all being? Does not his blessed memory still fill the whole universe with its grace and beauty? No wonder then that 'Umar was not convinced that Muḥammad could have died, and in truth, in one sense Muḥammad did not die and will not die.

Having seen him that morning when he went to the mosque and, like all other Muslims, having thought that the Prophet had recovered his health, Usāmah ibn Zayd returned to al Jurf

with those of his colleagues who had accompanied him to Madīnah
in search of reassuring news. He ordered the army to prepare
to march to al Shām; but before the army proceeded forth, it
heard the news of the Prophet's death. Usāmah ordered the army
to return to Madīnah. He hung his command flag on the door
of 'Ā'ishah's quarters and decided to wait until the Muslims
recovered from their shock.

At Banū Sā'idah's Court

In fact, the Muslims were wondering which step to take.
After hearing Abū Bakr and knowing for certain that Muḥammad
had died, they dispersed. Some of the al Anṣār gathered around
Sa'd ibn 'Ubādah in the courtyard of Banū Sā'idah. 'Alī ibn Abū
Ṭālib, al Zubayr ibn al 'Awwām, and Ṭalḥah ibn 'Ubaydullah
gathered in the house of Fāṭimah; and al Muhājirūn, together
with the Usayd ibn Ḥuḍayr as well as Banū 'Abd al Ashhal,
gathered around Abū Bakr. Soon a man came to Abū Bakr and
'Umar to inform them that al Anṣār were gathering around
Sa'd ibn 'Ubādah. The informant added that the two leaders
should go out and reorganize Muslim leadership before the
division of the Muslim community got any worse. Since the
Prophet of God—May God's peace and blessing be upon him—
was still laid out in his house and unburied, it was surely unbecoming that the Muslims begin to divide among themselves.
'Umar pleaded with Abū Bakr to go with him immediately to
al Anṣār and see what they were doing. On the way thither,
they were met by two upright and trustworthy Anṣār men who,
when questioned, remarked that al Anṣār were contemplating
separatist ideas. When the two Anṣār men questioned Abū Bakr
and 'Umar in turn and learned from them that they were going
to al Anṣār's gathering, they advised them not to go but to try
to settle the Muhājirūn's own affairs. 'Umar was determined
to go and Abū Bakr was not difficult to persuade on this point.
They came to the courtyard of Banū Sā'idah and found that
al Anṣār had gathered around a man wrapped up in a blanket.
'Umar ibn al Khaṭṭāb asked who the man was, and he was told
that that was Sa'd ibn 'Ubādah suffering from a serious sickness.
'Umar and Abū Bakr, joined at this moment by a number of
Muhājirūn, took their seats in the assembly. Soon, a speaker rose
and addressed al Anṣār in the following words after praising
God and thanking Him: "We are al Anṣār—i.e., the helpers
of God and the army of Islām. You, the Muhājirūn, are only

a brigade in the army. Nonetheless, a group of you have gone to the extreme of seeking to deprive us of our natural leadership and to deny us our rights."

Actually, this complaint had always been on al Anṣār's lips, even during the Prophet's lifetime. When 'Umar heard it being voiced again, he could hardly restrain himself. Indeed, he was ready to put an end to this situation once and for all by the sword, if needed. Fearing that harsh treatment might aggravate rather than improve matters, Abū Bakr held 'Umar back and asked him to act gently. He then turned to al Anṣār, saying: "O men, we, the Muhājirūn, were the first men to convert to Islām. We enjoy the noblest lineage and descendence. We are the most reputable and the best esteemed as well as the most numerous of any group in Arabia. Furthermore, we are the closest blood relatives of the Prophet. The Qur'ān itself has given us preference. For it is God—May He be praised and blessed—Who said, 'First and foremost were al Muhājirūn, then al Anṣār, and then those who have followed these two groups in virtue and righteousness.'[2] We were the first to emigrate for the sake of God, and you are literally 'al Anṣār', *i.e.*, the helpers. However, you are our brethren in religion, our partners in the fortunes of war, and our helpers against the enemy. All the good that you have claimed is truly yours, for you are the most worthy people of mankind. But the Arabs do not and will not recognize any sovereignty unless it belongs to the tribe of Quraysh. The princes shall be from among us, whereas your group will furnish the viziers." At this, a member of al Anṣār became furious and said: "Rather am I, the experienced warrior! On my arm every verdict shall rest. And my verdict is that the people of Quraysh may have their prince as long as we, too, may have our own." Abū Bakr repeated his proposition that the princes of the Muslims must be of the Quraysh whereas their vizers must be of al Anṣār. Taking the hand of 'Umar ibn al Khaṭṭāb as well as that of Abū 'Ubaydah ibn al Jarrāh, who were sitting on either side of him, Abū Bakr said, "Either one of these two men is acceptable to us as leader of the Muslim community. Choose whomsoever you please."

Nomination of Abū Bakr to the Caliphate

At that moment, all the men present began to talk at the same time, and the meeting itself was on the verge of disintegration. With his usual clear and loud voice, 'Umar said: "O Abū

Bakr, stretch forth your hand and I will give you my oath of fealty. Did not the Prophet himself command you to lead the Muslims in prayer? You, therefore, are his successor. We elect you to this position. In electing you, we are electing the best of all those whom the Prophet of God loved and trusted." 'Umar's words touched the hearts of the Muslims present, as they truly expressed the Prophet's will up to and including the last day of his life. On that day they had witnessed his insistence that Abū Bakr lead the prayer even in his presence. Thus, the difference between al Muhājirūn and al Anṣār was dissolved, and members of both camps came forward to give their oath of fealty.

Abū Bakr's Election

On the following day, as Abū Bakr took his place at the pulpit of the mosque, 'Umar ibn al Khaṭṭāb rose before the congregation and said, after offering due praise to God: "Yesterday, I presented to you a novel idea. I drew it neither from the Book of God, nor from any memory I have of the Prophet of God. It just occurred to me that the Prophet of God would continue to lead us in this world forever and that he would survive us all. But now I know better. God has left us His Holy Book, the Repository of His Prophet's guidance. If we hold closely to it, God will surely guide us to the same felicity to which he guided His Prophet. God has consolidated you together under the leadership of the best man among you, of the companion of the Prophet of God—May God's peace and blessing be upon him—who was blessed by God with the honor of the Prophet's company in the cave when the Makkans were following in close pursuit. Rise and give him your oath of fealty." All the men rose and pledged their loyalty to Abū Bakr. That was the public bay'ah,[3] following the private bay'ah in the courtyard of Banū Sā'idah.

Inaugural Speech of the First "Rāshidūn" Caliph

Thereafter, Abū Bakr rose and delivered a speech which may be regarded as one of the most illustrious embodiments of wisdom and sound judgment. After thanking God and praising Him, Abū Bakr said:

> "O Men! Here I have been assigned the job of being a ruler over you while I am not the best among you. If I do well in my job, help me. If I do wrong, redress me. Truth-

fulness is fidelity, and lying is treason. The weak shall be strong in my eyes until I restore to them their lost rights, and the strong shall be weak in my eye until I have restored the rights of the weak from them. No people give up fighting for the cause of God but God inflicts upon them abject subjection; and no people give themselves to lewdness but God envelops them with misery. Obey me as long as I obey God and His Prophet. But if I disobey God's command or His Prophet's, then no obedience is incumbent upon you. Rise to your prayer, that God may bless you."

The Quest for a Burial Site

Throughout the Muslims' disputing of the question of succession at the courtyard of Banū Sā'idah and in the mosque, the Prophet's remains were lying on his bed surrounded by his next of kin. After the election of Abū Bakr, the people came to the Prophet's house to prepare for his funeral and burial. There was disagreement as to where the Prophet was to be buried. Some Muhājirūn advised that he ought to be buried in Makkah, his native town, in the proximity of his own relatives. Others advised that he ought to be buried in Jerusalem where the Prophets were buried before him. The latter was certainly a baffling view considering that Jerusalem was in the hands of the Byzantines, and the relations between them and the Muslims were most hostile, especially since the Mu'tah and Tabūk campaigns. Indeed, an army which the Prophet himself had mobilized and placed under the leadership of Usāmah was supposed to fight them and avenge the Muslim defeat in those campaigns. At any rate, the proposals to bury the remains in Makkah or in Jerusalem were both rejected. The Muslims resolved to bury him in Madīnah, the city which gave him shelter and assistance and which was the first one to raise the banner of Islām. Once this decision was made, they proceeded to look for a proper location for burial. Some advocated burial in the mosque where he used to address the people, preach the faith, and lead them in prayer. They thought that the most appropriate place was either the very spot of ground where the pulpit stood or the spot next to it. This opinion, however, did not meet with approval. 'Ā'ishah had related that in his last days, whenever his pain increased, the Prophet used to uncover his face to curse such people as had taken the grave of their prophets as places of worship. Abū Bakr solved the issue when he proclaimed that he

had heard the Prophet say that prophets should be buried
wherever they die. This opinion carried the day.

Preparing the Body for Burial

Washing the Prophet's body before burial was performed by
his next of kin, by 'Alī ibn Abū Ṭālib, al 'Abbās ibn 'Abd al
Muṭṭalib and his two sons, al Faḍl and Qutham, as well as by
Usāmah ibn Zayd. Usāmah ibn Zayd and Shuqrān, the Prophet's
client, poured the water while 'Alī washed the body, covered as
it was by Muḥammad's nightgown. It was decided that the
Prophet's body should not, under any circumstance whatever,
be fully exposed. As they performed their washing, contrary to
what is usual in such cases, the body emitted beautiful smells,
so that 'Alī said continually: "By God, what would I give for
you! How sweet you are and how wholesome you are, both alive
and dead!" Some western Orientalists sought to explain this fair
scent emitted from the body of the Prophet by calling it the
result of the perfume which he used so lavishly, remembering
that he once declared it one of the good things he truly loved
in this world. When the washing was completed, the Prophet's
body was wrapped in three shrouds: two made in Ṣuhār and the
third in Ḥibarah in Yaman. When this operation was completed,
the body was left where it was and the doors were flung open
for the Muslims to enter from the mosque, to take a last look
at their Prophet, and to pray for him.[4] Undoubtedly, they
emerged deeply moved and conscious of their terrible bereavement.

The Funeral Prayer

The room was practically full when Abū Bakr and 'Umar
entered the room and joined the Muslims in a funerary prayer
for the Prophet. The prayer was performed without a leader.
When it was over, Abū Bakr began to pray aloud, saying: "Peace,
mercy, and blessings of God be upon you, O Prophet of God.
We witness that the Prophet of God and His apostle conveyed
the message entrusted to him by his Lord and that he exerted
himself and fought in His cause until God gave victory to His
religion. We equally witness that the Prophet of God and His
apostle fully performed his promise and that he commanded us
to worship none but God alone who has no associates." At the
end of every phrase, the Muslims responded together, "Amen,

Amen." When this prayer was complete, the men left and the women and children took turns taking a last look at the Prophet. One and all, every man, woman and child, emerged from that room torn with sorrow and crushed by a sense of bereavement for the loss of the Prophet of God, the Seal of His apostles. They were full of apprehension that some calamity might befall the religion of God in the future.

A Grave Moment of History

No man can today reconstruct this thirteen-centuries-old scene in his imagination without being filled with awe and reverence. The anguishing view of this body laid down in a corner of the room which was to become a grave the following day and which until the day before reverberated with Muḥammad's vitality, mercy, and light, filled the hearts of the faithful mourners with apprehension. It could not have been otherwise. For, there lay the man who had called men to truth, to the path of righteousness and had struck for them the highest example of goodness, mercy, courage, chastity, purity, and justice. As the crowds of Muslims passed by his bier despondent, disheartened, and dispirited, every man, woman, and child among them saw in the body that lay motionless before him his own father, brother, friend, trustworthy companion, Prophet, and Apostle of God. To recall that hour is surely to reconstruct a pathetic scene. Even as he writes about it, this author is seized by the grip of its terror and can hardly overcome the consequent anguish.

Confusion of the Men of Little Faith

It was natural for the Muslims to be apprehensive of the future. Indeed, as soon as the news of the Prophet's death spread in Madīnah and reached the Arab tribes in the surrounding area, Jews and Christians sprang to their feet, hypocrisy took a new lease on life, and the faith of many weak Arabs fell into confusion. The Makkans sought to abjure Islām, and they did so to the extent of instilling fear in 'Attāb ibn Asīd, their governor appointed by the Prophet to rule them. Suhayl ibn 'Amr, following the news of the Prophet's death, stood up in their midst and said: "The Prophet's death shall increase the power of Islām and strengthen it. Whoever attacks us or abjures our cause, we shall strike with the sword. O People of Makkah! you were the last to enter Islām. Do not, therefore, be the first to desert it. Have faith that God will bring you final victory just as the Prophet of God—May God's peace and blessing be upon him—has promised you." Only then did the Makkans change their minds.

The Prophet's Burial

The Arabs knew two ways of digging graves. The Makkans made their graves flat at the bottom while the Madīnese made them curved. Abū 'Ubaydah ibn al Jarrāh was the gravedigger for the Makkans, and Abū Ṭalhah Zayd ibn Sahl was gravedigger for the Madīnese. The Prophet's relatives could not choose between them. The Prophet's uncle, al 'Abbās, sent two men to call the two gravediggers for a consultation. Only one was found and could respond to the call, and that was Abū Ṭalhah, the Madīnese. He therefore was commissioned to dig a grave for the Prophet of God as he knew best. When evening came and the Muslims had taken leave of the body of their Prophet, Muḥammad's relatives prepared for the burial. They waited until a quarter or a third of the night had passed before proceeding with the burial. In the grave, they spread out a red mantle that once belonged to the Prophet, and the men who had washed the body lowered it to its last repose. They built over it a bridge with bricks and then covered the grave with sand. 'Ā'ishah said: "We did not learn of the burial of the Prophet of God—May God's peace and blessing be upon him—until midnight or later"; and so did Fāṭimah report. The Prophet was buried on Tuesday night, 14th of Rabī' I, two days after his death, in the year 10 A.H.

'Ā'ishah and the Grave Room

'Ā'ishah lived thereafter in her quarters, next door to the Prophet's grave, contented with her proximity to this holy precinct. When Abū Bakr died, he was buried in the immediate vicinity of the Prophet's grave, as was 'Umar ibn al Khaṭṭāb thereafter. It is related that 'Ā'ishah used to visit the grave room without veil until 'Umar was buried therein, i.e., during the time it contained only the grave of her father and husband. But after 'Umar's burial, she entered the room only when fully veiled.

Expediting Usāmah's Army on Its March

As soon as the burial of the Prophet was completed, Abū Bakr commanded that the army of Usāmah begin its march on al Shām in execution of the commandment the Prophet of God had issued in his last days. Some Muslims objected to this measure just as they had during the sickness of Muḥammad. 'Umar joined the ranks of these objectors on the grounds that the Muslim forces ought not to be dispersed in this grave hour. Abū Bakr, however, did not hesitate to follow the commandment left unfulfilled by the Prophet at his death. He refused to give credit to those who counseled that an older and more experienced general in war than Usāmah be appointed to lead that army. Al Jurf remained the rallying place for the army, and Usāmah remained its leading general. Abū Bakr went out in person to see the army off on its march. It was there that Abū Bakr asked Usāmah to absolve 'Umar ibn al Khaṭṭāb from his duty to go forth in the army so that he might remain in Madīnah in close proximity to Abū Bakr who needed his advice in his first days of administration. Twenty days after the army began its march northward, the Muslims launched their attack against al Balqā' and avenged the Muslims' setback in Mu'tah where Usāmah's father fell under Byzantine arms. The war cry in that campaign was "O Victor! Give death to the enemy!" Thus Abū Bakr and Usāmah fulfilled the commandment of the Prophet, and the army returned to Madīnah victorious. Usāmah was at its head, riding the very horse on which his father died at the Battle of Mu'tah, and carrying high the banner which the Prophet of God had entrusted to him in person.

Prophets Leave No Inheritance

After the death of the Prophet, his daughter Fāṭimah asked Abū Bakr to return to her the land the Prophet kept for himself at Fadak and Khaybar. Abū Bakr, however, answered her by quoting her father's words: "We, the Prophets, do not leave any inheritance for anyone. Whatever we do leave shall be given out in charity." Continuing with his own words, Abū Bakr said: "However, if it was the case that your father had made a grant to you of this property, then I shall certainly honor your word to this effect and fulfill for you his commandment." At this,

Fāṭimah answered that her father had not made any such grant to her at all, but that Umm Ayman had informed her that that might have been Muhammad's purpose. Abū Bakr therefore resolved that the lands of Fadak and Khaybar should be kept by the public treasury of the Muslims as state domain.

Muhammad's Great Spiritual Legacy

Thus Muhammad left this world just as he had entered, without material shackles. His only inheritance left to mankind was the religion of truth and goodness. He had paved the ground and laid the foundation for the great civilization of Islām which had covered the world in the past and would cover the world in the future. It was a civilization in which *tawḥīd*, or the unitization of God, was the cornerstone; and an order in which the word of God and His commandments are always uppermost, while those of unfaith are nethermost. It was a civilization purged absolutely clean of all paganism and of all idolatrous forms and expressions, a civilization in which men were called upon to cooperate with one another for the good and moral felicity of all men, not for the benefit of any group or people. Muhammad left to this world the Book of God, a guidance and mercy to mankind, while the memory of his own life gave the highest and noblest example for man's emulation. One of the last sermons which the Prophet delivered to the people during his illness contained the following words: "O Men! If I have lashed the back of anyone, let him come forward and lash my back in return. If I have insulted anyone, let him come forth and take satisfaction of me. If I have dispossessed anyone of any wealth, let him come forth and seize his wealth from me. If there be any such men as these, let them come forth without fear of retaliation or hatred, for neither of these become of me." Only one man came forth to make a claim, that Muhammad owed him three dirhams; he was paid in full by Muhammad on his deathbed. The Prophet left this world an inheritance of a great spiritual legacy whose light continues to illumine the world and will continue to illumine the world until God completely fulfills His promise and gives victory to His religion over all the religions despite all unbelievers. May God's peace and blessing be upon Muhammad!

Conclusion in
Two Essays

I. ISLĀMIC CIVILIZATION AS
DEPICTED IN THE QUR'ĀN

Islāmic and Western Civilizations

Muḥammad left a great spiritual legacy which enveloped the world in its light and guided man's civilization throughout many centuries, a legacy which will envelop the world again and guide man's civilization once more until the light of God has filled the universe. The legacy of Muhammad had such great effect in the past and will have great or greater effect in the future precisely because Muḥammad established the religion of truth and laid the foundation of the only civilization which guarantees the happiness and felicity of man. The religion which Muḥammad conveyed and the civilization which he established at his Lord's command for the benefit of mankind are inseparable from each other. Islāmic civilization has been raised on a foundation of science and rationalism, and that is the same foundation on which western civilization of today is based. Moreover, Islām as a religion has based itself on personalist thinking and intentional logic. The relation between religion and its propositions on the one hand, and civilization and its foundation on the other, is binding and firm. Islām links metaphysical thought and personal feelings with the rules of logic and the precepts of science, with a bond that all Muslims must discover and grasp if they are to remain Muslims. From this aspect, the civilization of Islām is radically different from that of western civilization which dominates the world today. The two are different in their description of life as well as the foundation on which they base such description. The difference between the two civilizations is so essential that they have developed in ways which are radically contradictory to each other.

The West and the Struggle between Church and State

The difference is due to a number of historical causes to which we have alluded in the prefaces to the first and second editions of this work. In western Christendom, the continuing struggle between the religious and secular powers, or—to use the contemporary idiom—between church and state, led to their separation and to the establishment of the state upon the denial of the power of the church. The struggle to which this will to power led has left deep effects upon the whole of western thought. The first of these effects was the separation of human feeling and reasoning from the logic of absolute reason and the findings of positive science based on sensory observation and evidence.

The Economic System as Foundation of Western Civilization

The victory of materialist thinking was largely due to the establishment of western civilization primarily upon an economic foundation. This situation led to the rise in the West of a number of worldviews which sought to place everything in the life of man and the world at the mercy of economic forces. Many an author in the West sought to explain the whole history of mankind—religious, esthetic, philosophic or scientific—in terms of the waves of progress or retrogression which constitute the economic history of the various peoples. Not only has this thinking pervaded historiography; it has even reached philosophy. A number of western philosophies have sought to found the laws and principles of morality on bases of pragmatism and utilitarianism. As a result of this fixation of thought in the West, all these theories, despite their perspicacity and originality, have been limited in scope to the realm of material benefits. In other words, all the laws of morality were based on a material foundation and in satisfaction of what was regarded as a necessary consequence of scientific research and evidence. As for the spiritual aspect, western civilization regarded it as purely individual, rationally incapable of being the object of any group consideration. From this followed the absolute freedom of belief which the West has sanctified. The West has honored the freedom of belief far more than it has the freedom of morals; and it has honored the freedom of morals far more than the freedom of economic activity. The latter it has tied hand and foot by public laws, and commanded that every western state and army prevent any violation of economic laws with all the power and coercive means at its disposal.

Incapacity of Western Civilization to Bring Happiness to Man

In this author's opinion, a civilization which founds itself upon economic activity and erects its moral system on that activity as a base, and yet gives no weight in public life to faith, is incapable of achieving for mankind the happiness that men seek. Indeed, a civilization which so regards human life is bound to bring upon mankind all the calamities which have befallen our world in the recent centuries. Under its aegis, any attempt to prevent war and to establish universal peace will prove futile and vain. As long as man's relation to man is based upon the loaf of bread and the struggle which man wages against his fellows in order to get it for himself, a struggle the success of which depends upon the animal power which each one of us can marshal for the purpose, it is indubitable that every man will watch for the best occasion to cheat his fellow out of his loaf of bread. Every man will regard his fellow man as his enemy rather than his brother; and personal morality will have nothing but the animal in us on which to stand. This is true though man's animality may remain hidden until need uncovers it, for only utility is consonant with such a moral foundation. Charity, altruism, love, brotherhood—in short, all the principles of nobler morality and the values of higher humanity—will forever pass over a consciousness disciplined by such a civilization just as water passes off the back of a duck.

The actualities of the contemporary world furnish empirical evidence for my claim. Competition and struggle are the first principles of the economic system and are the most salient characteristics of western civilization. This is the case regardless of whether the system is individualistic or socialistic. In the former, the worker competes with his fellow worker, the capitalist with his fellow capitalist, and worker and capitalist are committed enemies of each other. The devotees of this view regard struggle and competition as the forces of man's good and progress. They regard these forces as the source of motivation for the pursuit of perfection and the division of labor, as well as for a just criterion for the distribution of wealth. The socialist system, on the other hand, sees in the struggle between the classes a means to destroy those classes and bring the destiny of society under control of the workers. This system is regarded by socialism as the necessary logic of nature. But as long as struggle and competition for wealth are the essence of life, and as long as class struggle is the law of nature, then it is equally the law of nature that the nations of the world struggle and prey upon one another in order to realize their purposes. Nationalism thus arose as a necessary consequence to this economic anthropology. But if it is natural for the nations to struggle and compete with one another for wealth, and if colonialism is a natural consequence of this necessary system, how are wars ever to be avoided and how is peace ever to be achieved? In this Christian twentieth century we have witnessed sufficient evidence to convince anyone that a world founded upon such a civilization may dream of, but never realize, peace. Because of it, peace will forever be a false mirage and an impossible desideratum.

The Groundwork of Islāmic Civilization

Unlike western civilization, the civilization of Islām is built upon a spiritual base in which man is first and foremost called upon to recognize ultimate reality and to realize his position in the world with regard to that reality. Whenever man's consciousness of this relation reaches the point of certainty and conviction, that conviction will demand of him ever to discipline himself, to cleanse his soul, and to nourish his heart as well as his mind with the sublime principles of magnanimity, contentment, brotherhood, love, charity, and piety. On the basis of such principles man will then organize his economic life. Such progression is the foundation of Islāmic civilization as the revelation of Muḥammad conceived it. It is first and foremost a spiritual civilization. In it, the spiritual order constitutes the groundwork of the system of education, of personal and social morality. The principles constituting the moral order in turn constitute the groundwork of the economic system. It is therefore not permissible in this civilization that any moral principle be sacrificed for the sake of the economic system.

In this author's opinion, it is this conception peculiar to Islāmic civilization that is capable of bringing mankind to a sure realization of happiness and felicity. Should it ever become firmly established in the minds of men, and should it come to dominate this world as western civilization has come to dominate it today, mankind will lead a different life. The current ideologies will be washed away, and nobler moral principles will take over the solution of the chronic crises of the present world. In both East and West, men have been trying to find solutions to these crises without anyone's realizing—not excluding the Muslims themselves—that Islām offers to them certain and guaranteed solutions. The western people are today groping for a new spiritual seriousness which might save them from the paganism in which they have allowed themselves to fall and from the worship of wealth which has been at the root of their misery and interminable wars. The western peoples are seeking to discover this new spiritual seriousness in the religions of India and the Far East, when it has been right here close to them all the time, established once and for all, and clearly elaborated in the Qur'ān, as well as given its highest examplification in the life and sayings of the Prophet Muhammad.

It is not my intention to predict here the role of Islāmic civilization or to analyze its system. Such work would by itself occupy a volume of this size or even larger. But I do think it imperative to characterize that civilization in general now that I have pointed to the spiritual basis on which it stands. Therefore, I hope to give an idea of the nature of Muhammad's call and thereby to pave the road for further and more complete research and study.

No Competition between Church and State in Islām

Before I do this, however, it behooves me to point to the fact that the history of Islām has been free of any struggle between religious and secular authorities, that is, between church and state. This fact has protected Islāmic history from the effects that struggle has left upon western thought. This salutory influence upon Islām and upon its history and thought is primarily due to the fact that it has never known anything called church or religious authority along the lines of Christianity. No Muslim, even if he should be a caliph, has any right to impose anything in the name of Islām. He can neither forgive nor punish any violation of such commandments imposed in the

name of religion. Moreover, no Muslim may, even if he should
be a caliph, impose upon the people anything other than that
which God imposed in His Book. Indeed, in front of God, all
Muslims are equal; none may be distinguished from the others
except in virtue and piety. No ruler in Islām is entitled to the
Muslim's obedience in a matter involving a violation of a divine
commandment, or of that which has not been expressly commanded by God. We should recall here the inaugural speech of
Abū Bakr following his election to the caliphate: "Obey me as
long as I obey God and His Prophet. But if I disobey God's command or His Prophet's, then no obedience is incumbent upon you."
Despite all the crass exercises of the will to political power
and all the civil wars and rebellions which the history of the
Islāmic state has witnessed, the Muslims have remained true
to this great personal freedom which their religion had established
for them. Theirs has always been a freedom which assigned to
reason the role of judge in everything, whether in religion or in
the matter of conviction and faith itself. The Muslims have
held strongly to this freedom even in the face of those kings
and princes who claimed that they were the lieutenants of God
on earth, not of His Prophet, and who wielded in their hands
the keys of life and death. Witness the turbulent events during
the reign of al Ma'mūn when the issue was whether or not
the Qur'ān was created. The caliph believed one thing, but the
Muslims differed from him despite the certainty of the punishment and wrath that awaited them.

Islām Makes Reason the Final Judge

Islām made reason the judge in everything, whether in religion
or in conviction and faith itself. God said: "And the case of
those who disbelieve is like that of a person who hears the
sound of a call but who does not distinguish any word or idea.
To talk to them is like talking to the deaf, dumb, and blind.
Those who disbelieve simply do not use their reason and neither
do they understand."[1] Commenting on this verse, Shaykh
Muḥammad 'Abduh wrote: "This verse clearly asserts that taqlīd[2]
without reason or guidance is the prerogative of the disbelievers,
that man is not a convinced Muslim unless he has reasoned
out his religion, known it in person, and become personally
convinced of its truth and validity. Whoever, therefore, has
been brought up so as to acquiesce without reason and to act

without knowledge and wisdom—even though he may be virtuous
—is not a convinced Muslim. Religious conviction does not
have for its purpose the subjugation of man to the good as if
he were an animal. Rather, its purpose is that man may, by
the use of reason and the pursuit of knowledge, rise to the level
where he will do the good because he fully knows that it is in
itself good and acceptable to God, and avoid the evil because
he fully knows its undesirable consequence and harm."

The foregoing claims of Shaykh Muḥammad 'Abduh given in
exegesis of this verse are all to be found in the Qur'ān itself
in a number of other verses. The Qur'ān has called upon men
to look into the universe and to discover its construction and
structure. It commanded men to do so in the conviction that
their investigation of the structure of the universe would lead
them to the discovery of God as well as of His unicity—May He
be adored! God—to Whom is the praise—says: "In the creation
of heaven and earth, in the succession of day and night, in the
phenomena of the ships sailing across the seas with goods for the
welfare of men, in the fall of rain water from heaven to quicken
a dead earth, in populating the earth with all species of animals,
in the ordering of winds and clouds between sky and earth—
in all these there are signs and pieces of evidence for men who
reason."[3] Further, God says:

و اٰيَةٌ لَهُمُ الْاَرْضُ الْمَيْتَةُ ۖ اَحْيَيْنٰهَا وَ اَخْرَجْنَا مِنْهَا حَبًّا فَمِنْهُ يَأْكُلُونَ ۞ وَجَعَلْنَا فِيهَا جَنّٰتٍ
مِنْ نَّخِيْلٍ وَّ اَعْنَابٍ وَّ فَجَّرْنَا فِيهَا مِنَ الْعُيُونِ ۞ لِيَأْكُلُوا مِنْ ثَمَرِهٖ وَمَا عَمِلَتْهُ اَيْدِيهِمْ ۖ
اَفَلَا يَشْكُرُونَ ۞ سُبْحٰنَ الَّذِيْ خَلَقَ الْاَزْوَاجَ كُلَّهَا مِمَّا تُنْبِتُ الْاَرْضُ وَمِنْ اَنْفُسِهِمْ وَمِمَّا
لَا يَعْلَمُونَ ۞ وَاٰيَةٌ لَّهُمُ الَّيْلُ ۖ نَسْلَخُ مِنْهُ النَّهَارَ فَاِذَا هُمْ مُّظْلِمُونَ ۞ وَالشَّمْسُ تَجْرِيْ لِمُسْتَقَرٍّ لَّهَا ۖ
ذٰلِكَ تَقْدِيرُ الْعَزِيْزِ الْعَلِيْمِ ۞ وَالْقَمَرَ قَدَّرْنٰهُ مَنَازِلَ حَتّٰى عَادَ كَالْعُرْجُونِ الْقَدِيْمِ ۞ لَا الشَّمْسُ
يَنْبَغِيْ لَهَا اَنْ تُدْرِكَ الْقَمَرَ وَلَا الَّيْلُ سَابِقُ النَّهَارِ ۖ وَكُلٌّ فِيْ فَلَكٍ يَسْبَحُونَ ۞ وَاٰيَةٌ لَّهُمْ اَنَّا
حَمَلْنَا ذُرِّيَّتَهُمْ فِي الْفُلْكِ الْمَشْحُونِ ۞ وَخَلَقْنَا لَهُمْ مِّنْ مِثْلِهٖ مَا يَرْكَبُونَ ۞ وَاِنْ نَّشَأْ نُغْرِقْهُمْ فَلَا
صَرِيْخَ لَهُمْ وَلَا هُمْ يُنْقَذُونَ ۞ اِلَّا رَحْمَةً مِّنَّا وَمَتَاعًا اِلٰى حِيْنٍ ۞

"Of Our signs and pieces of evidence which We have
presented to man are the phenomena of a dead earth

quickened and caused to give forth grain, gardens of date
trees and vines, and fountains of fresh water with which
We have covered the earth that man may eat and drink
his fill. All these are not merely the work of man's hands;
but will men not feel grateful? Will they not give thanks
to God, saying, 'Praise be to God Who created from earth
and from that which grows and remains hidden in the earth
all the creatures that live in pairs, and all that they pro-
create of themselves.' Of our signs and evidence are the
phenomena of night from which We cut off all light, causing
man to stand in darkness; of the sun which runs in its orbit,
an orbit well defined by the All-Knowing and Almighty; of
the moon for which We have appointed various stages of
growth and decline until it appears as an old shriveled tree
branch. It is of Our signs and evidence that neither sun
overtakes the moon nor night overtakes the day but that
each runs in a well-defined and ordered course. As further
signs and clearer evidence, We have made it possible for
laden ships to sail across the seas carrying men and their
offspring. Were it not for divine providence, men would fall
into the sea, no one would hear their cries, and they would
perish. They are saved only by Our mercy. We wish them to
enjoy their pleasures for a prescribed time."⁴

Indeed, the call to look into the universe to discover its laws and
to arrive at the conviction that God is its creator is repeated a
hundred times in the various *Sūrahs* of the Qur'ān. All these
Qur'ānic invitations are directed to man's rational faculties in
the expectation that he will consider, search for and discover the
truth, so that his religious conviction might be rational and truly
supported by the facts. The Qur'ān constantly warns its readers
not to adopt uncritically and blindly the ideas and principles of
the forefathers, but to have faith in man's personal capacity to
reach the truth.

The Power of Īmān

Such is the nature of *īmān*, or religious conviction, to which
Islām has called. It has nothing to do with blind faith. Instead,
it is involved with the conviction of the enlightened mind, the
instructed reason which has considered and weighed the alter-
natives, pondered and reconsidered the evidence on all sides,

researched and rediscovered and finally reached the certainty that God—May He be adored—is. Surely any man who considers the evidence with both heart and reason will be guided to religious conviction. Indeed, the more closely a man looks at the evidence, the longer he contemplates and the larger his scope of investigation becomes so that his awareness considers the whole of time, space, and all the eternally changing universes which they include, the more he will be convinced of his littleness *vis-à-vis* the well patterned, well-ordered, and well-governed worlds, of the shortcoming of his knowledge to grasp them or to enter him into meaningful relation to them without the assistance of a power surpassing his senses and reason, the more capable he will become of defining his place within the total realm of being. All this is the precondition of his entering into relation with the universe and of his encompassing with his consciousness and vision the whole of being. This enlarged vision is the strength given by religious conviction alone.

Īmān *in God*

Īmān, or religious conviction, then, is a spiritual intuition by which man's consciousness is filled whenever it seeks the universe and realizes that the infinity of space and time is unreachable, and whenever it seeks to encompass all being within itself, realizing that every species in existence lives, changes, and dies in accordance with laws and patterns, and that all existence realizes the divine pattern and fulfills the cosmic laws of its Lord and Creator. To look for God—May He be adored—as immanent in all existence and in contact with it, rather than as absolutely separate from it, is a futile search leading to error rather than to truth, harming rather than blessing the investigator. Moreover, it does not add to man's knowledge. Writers and philosophers have often exhausted themselves seeking evidence for God's immanence without avail, while others have sought to grasp the essence of the Creator Himself—all to no purpose. Some writers and philosophers have acknowledged that the success of such searches are forever impossible.

But if our reason falls short of achieving such knowledge, that very shortcoming can be the source of a greater realization, namely, the certain religious knowledge of God. This certitude of ours that God exists, that He knows, provides for, and governs everything, that He is the Creator, the Forgiver unto Whom everything returns, can also convince us that it cannot ever be possible for us to know the nature of God Himself. If to this day we do not understand the nature of electricity, even though our very eyes have seen its effects, nor the nature of ether, though we grant that its waves or quanta carry sound and light, how vain it is not to accept the existence of God when we constantly behold His original creations and effects, or to go about denying Him until we can know His very nature! God is transcendentally beyond anything anyone may say in description of Him. As a matter of fact, those who try to describe God under one form or another are precisely those whose consciousness is incapable of rising to the level requisite for grasping that which lies beyond human life. It is they who should be accused of seeking to measure being and the Creator of being with their own relative standards gathered from their own little knowledge of being. On the other hand, those who have true knowledge and wisdom will pause at these divine statements: "And when they ask you concerning the Spirit, answer, 'The Spirit belongs to God.' Given the little knowledge that you have, your minds must fall short of understanding its nature."[5] The consciousness of such men becomes filled with certitude and conviction regarding the Creator of the Spirit, the Maker of the whole universe. They do not allow themselves to become involved in futile and vain controversy.

Īmān, *the Basis of Islām*

The Qur'ān differentiates between conversion to Islām before or after such religious certitude and conviction. God says, "Some Arabs of the desert claimed that they have achieved religious conviction. Say, 'You have not achieved such conviction; you have been converted to Islām and have acquiesced in it, but religious certitude and conviction have not yet found their way to your heart and consciousness.' "[6] Such Islāmization is an acquiescence arising from the call of ulterior motive, desire, fear, admiration, or reverence. It is not the acceptance by a consciousness which has understood and known full well that it has reached certitude and conviction. The subject of such Islāmization has not been guided to his conviction through examination of the universe, grasping of its laws and patterns, and the movement of his thought from that knowledge to the recognition of the Creator of the universe. It is rather the acquiescence of a man in satisfaction of an ignoble desire or in blind imitation of his parents or community. Thus, religious conviction and certitude have not entered into his heart despite his acquiescence to Islām.

Many such Muslims exist who seek to cheat God and the true Muslims, but they succeed in cheating only themselves, little do they know. Their hearts are diseased, and their disease blinds their minds still further. Those men who convert to Islām without religious conviction but because of an ulterior motive, desire or fear, continue to have weak souls throughout their lives. Their faith remains doubtful, their commitment shaky, and their wills ever ready to submit to men upon command. On the other hand, those whose minds and hearts have reached conviction of God by means of investigation of the universe possess a genuine conviction which calls them to submit to God alone, to none other than Him. Neither do such men think of their Islām as a favor they have granted to anyone. "Rather, God grants you the favor of guiding you to religious conviction if only you are genuine."[7] Whoever, therefore, in conviction of God's existence and Lordship over the universe, opens himself to determination by Him alone, has reason neither to fear nor to grieve. Such men fear neither poverty nor humilation in this world because religious certitude is the greatest wealth and the greatest glory. Glory does indeed belong to God and to the true believers who are contented and certain of their faith.

The soul which is happy and contented with such *imān* finds its fulfillment only in the search for the secrets of the world, the laws of the cosmos, and the pattern of the universe—all to the end that it may consolidate its communion with God. The means it employs for its search is scientific investigation, rational analysis, and consideration of all that is in creation. That is precisely what the Qur'ān calls for and what the early Muslims practiced. That is the scientific method currently pursued in the West. The purpose of such pursuit, however, differs in Islām from western civilization. In the former, its purpose is to enable man to make the pattern of God in the universe the law and pattern of his own existence. In the latter, the purpose is to exploit the knowledge of cosmic laws for the material benefit of man. The foremost purpose of science in Islām is the achievement of firm and certain knowledge of God, a knowledge which strengthens man's conviction of Him—May He be adored—by its own comprehensiveness and certainty. Equally, it is a pursuit which seeks to achieve such better knowledge not for the in-

dividual alone but for the community as a whole. Spiritual
perfection is not merely an individualistic matter, but rather the
very foundation of the human community throughout the world.
Islām therefore regards the pursuit of knowledge and understanding of the universe as a human duty, a duty incumbent upon all
men as individuals as well as groups. Mankind must therefore
seek this spiritual perfection even more conscientiously and
systemically than it has sought to understand the nature of
material things, and it ought to use the secrets of the material
world and the laws and pattern of the universe as a means to
attain spiritual perfection rather than as a means for achieving
material mastery over things.

Divine Assistance to Discover the Pattern of the Universe

In order to attain this spiritual perfection, it is not sufficient
to rely upon our own formal logic. Having reached the highest
level possible through that logic, it is necessary to prepare our
own hearts and minds for what lies beyond. This is possible
by seeking God's assistance and by turning one's heart and soul
toward the divine Being. By worshipping Him and asking for
His assistance it is possible, once the highest levels of logic
have been reached, to discover the secrets of the universe and the
patterns of existence. This process is what is meant by communion with God, by gratitude for His blessings, and by prayer
to Him for further guidance. God said:

وَإِذَا سَأَلَكَ عِبَادِي عَنِّي فَإِنِّي قَرِيبٌ ۖ أُجِيبُ دَعْوَةَ الدَّاعِ إِذَا دَعَانِ ۖ فَلْيَسْتَجِيبُوا لِي وَ
لْيُؤْمِنُوا بِي لَعَلَّهُمْ يَرْشُدُونَ ۚ

"And if My servants ask you of Me, tell them that I am near and
that I respond to the caller who calls upon Me. Tell them then
to pray to Me, to believe in Me. That is the way to wisdom."[8]

He also said: "Seek further assistance by patience and prayer.
The latter overtaxes none but the irreverent and the proud. It
is a force of genuine assistance for those who know that they will
someday confront their Lord and that to Him they shall finally
return."[9]

Nature of Islāmic Prayer

Prayer, then, is communion with God in the certitude that He exists and is receptive to a solicitation for His assistance. Its purpose is not the bodily movements of kneeling and prostration nor the verbal recitation of the Qur'ān, not the prescribed *takbīr* and *ta'zīm*.[10] Rather, it is meant to fill the soul with *īmān* and the heart with reverence and recognition of God's holiness. Every element in the Muslim's prayer is designed to achieve this dual purpose. It is the worship of God for the sole sake of God, the recognition of God's face as the light of heaven and earth. He—May He be adored—said:

$$\text{لَيْسَ الْبِرَّ اَنْ تُوَلُّوا وُجُوهَكُمْ قِبَلَ الْمَشْرِقِ وَالْمَغْرِبِ وَلٰكِنَّ الْبِرَّ مَنْ اٰمَنَ بِاللّٰهِ وَ}$$
$$\text{الْيَوْمِ الْاٰخِرِ وَالْمَلٰٓئِكَةِ وَالْكِتٰبِ وَالنَّبِيّٖنَ وَاٰتَى الْمَالَ عَلٰى حُبِّهٖ ذَوِى الْقُرْبٰى وَالْيَتٰمٰى}$$
$$\text{وَفِى الرِّقَابِ ۚ وَاَقَامَ الصَّلٰوةَ وَاٰتَى الزَّكٰوةَ ۚ وَالْمُوفُونَ بِعَهْدِهِمْ وَالْمَسْكِيْنَ وَابْنَ السَّبِيْلِ وَ}$$
$$\text{السَّآئِلِيْنَ اِذَا عَاهَدُوا ۚ وَالصّٰبِرِيْنَ فِى الْبَأْسَآءِ وَالضَّرَّآءِ وَحِيْنَ الْبَأْسِ اُولٰٓئِكَ الَّذِيْنَ صَدَقُوا ۚ}$$
$$\text{وَاُولٰٓئِكَ هُمُ الْمُتَّقُوْنَ}$$

"Righteousness does not consist in your turning your faces toward east or west. Instead, it involves *īmān* in God, in the Day of Judgment, in the Book, in the prophets, and spending of one's wealth out of love of Him for the welfare of the relative, the orphan, the deprived, the wayfarer, the poor, and for ransoming the captive. Righteousness also consists of the holding of prayer, the paying of *zakāt*, the fulfillment of promises and covenants made, patience in good or ill, and steadfastness in war. Those who fulfill these values are the genuine in faith; they are the pious, the righteous."[11]

The man with genuine *īmān*, therefore, is the man who turns with his whole heart to God in prayer, making God the witness of his own piety. It is he who implores His help in the fulfillment of the duties of life, solicits His guidance and blessing in his search for the secrets of the world and for the laws and pattern of the cosmos during his prayer as well as at any other time.

Hence, the Muslim is fully conscious of his insignificance before almighty God on high. We are capable of achieving such a view of the earth's insignificance when we ascend in an airplane a few thousand meters into the sky and begin to see the mountains, rivers, and cities as small marks upon a vast canvas. We see them delineated in front of our eyes as if they were mere lines on a map made out of paper. The earth looks flat; mountains and buildings lose their elevation, and wells and rivers their depression. The whole appears to be no more than patches of color moving and waving and intermingling with one another the higher we ascend into space. Our very earth is only a little planet among thousands of other heavenly bodies and systems, and these are only a very small pocket in the infinite magnitude of being. How small and little we therefore are! How weak and insignificant in relation to the Creator of all this being and to its Ruler and Provider whose very greatness stands beyond our grasp!

Equality before God

How worthy we are when we turn our heart to His sublime holiness and majesty, soliciting Him to strengthen us and guide us to the truth to realize the profound equality which characterizes all men in such weakness! How inevitable is then our realization of the absolute equality of mankind, an equality impervious to any amount of wealth or power achievable on earth, but deeply transformable by *imān* in God, by submission to Him, by righteousness, virtue, and piety! What a tremendous distance separates this kind of equality, this genuine equality before God, from equality before the law of man which western civilization has recently been professing so loudly! Indeed, western civilization is not far from denying equality before the law when its people deny the privileges of such equality to this or that group of men. How unlike each other are the two egalitarianisms! On the one hand is the equality before God, touched and held most concretely in the hour of prayer and reached by each man deliberately in the exercise of his own mind and free thought. On the other hand, we have an equality before the law, achieved in the struggle and competition for the acquisition of wealth. By definition, equality before the law does not rule out cheating, hypocrisy, and untruth; and it allows the culprit to escape the jurisdiction of the law if he is only creative enough to find ways and means of outwitting the legislator, the judge, or his own victim.

On the other hand, equality before God calls for genuine fraternity and brotherhood because it imposes upon all a realization of their fraternity in service to God and in the worship of the One Master. Such brotherhood is based on conscientious evaluation of the fact, free investigation, and critical research, all imposed by the Qur'ān. Surely, no liberty, no equality, and no fraternity are greater than this one, where all men stand in front of God in one line prostrating their heads to Him, acknowledging His transcendence and unity, and kneeling and praying to Him without the slightest distinction between one and the other. No equality is greater than that which belongs to such a community whose every member actually seeks divine assistance in repentence and awe, asking for forgiveness and mercy, without any distinction whatever to differentiate the one from his fellowmen except his virtuous actions, his righteousness and piety. This kind of fraternity and equality purifies the hearts of men and cleanses them from the stain of matter. This condition alone guarantees happiness to mankind and leads it to certain knowledge of God's pattern in the world as long as God Himself is willing to lead men with His own light.

Nature of Islāmic Fasting

Men are not all equal in their capacities to fulfill the piety and virtue which God has made incumbent upon them. Our bodies may weigh down our spirits so as to make them incapable of moving and rising toward God. Our will to material need and welfare may overcome our humanity unless we keep up the exercise of our spirit and constantly turn to God in our prayers rather than being satisfied with the mechanical performance of kneeling, prostration, and recitation. Hence it is our duty wherever possible to stop all activities which tend to weigh us down, to shackle our spirit, or to give dominance to our material welfare over our humanity. Hence, Islām imposed fasting as a means for achieving virtue and piety. God has said: "O Men who believe, fasting has been imposed upon you as it has been imposed on those that have gone before you that you may achieve virtue and piety."[12] Piety, virtue, and righteousness are all equivalent. The righteous are those who are pious, who prove their *īmān* in God on the Day of Judgment, and who, by following the angels, the Book and the prophets, fulfill the requisites of the above-mentioned verses.

But if the purpose of fasting is that the body may not weigh down the spirit and that matter may not overcome humanity, to abstain from food and drink from dawn till sunset and then to indulge in the enjoyment of all kinds of pleasures is surely to deny that purpose. Indulgence in pleasures is by itself immoral and vicious, regardless of whether it is preceded by fasting or not. The case is even worse if man fasts all day and then surrenders himself greedily to that of which he has been deprived. Such conduct is tantamount to bringing God to witness that the fast was not made in purification of the body and strengthening of humanity. Such a man does not fast in freedom, convinced of the advantage of fasting for his spiritual life, but in order to fulfill a duty, the meaning of which his mind is incapable of grasping. More likely, he regards fasting as a privation and a violation of the freedom which he will recapture at the end of the day. His case is not unlike that of the person who does not steal because the law forbids him to, not because he regards himself above stealing and denies it to himself as well as to others, in full exercise of his freedom.

Fasting Is Not Self-Privation

In fact, to regard fasting as privation, or as an attack upon man's liberty, is to misunderstand it and to make of it something utterly futile and vain. The truth is that fasting is a purification of the soul. It is demanded by reason and should be entered into freely if man is to recapture his freedom of willing and thinking which his material demands have denied or lessened. Once such freedom is gained, man may rise to the level of genuine *īmān* in God. This is the purpose of the divine statement which follows the imposition of fasting upon men of faith of past or present, namely: "Fasting is to be performed on prescribed and numbered days. But if a man is ill or suffers from the hardships of travel, fasting may be postponed to other days. To those who are exempted from fasting because of hardship, the feeding of a poor man is imposed as expiation. At any rate, whoever willingly performs the good deed will be benefitted. To fast is certainly better for you than not to fast, if only you had the wisdom to know."[13]

It may seem strange to claim that a person can recapture his freedom of will and freedom of thinking if he should undertake to fast in deliberate pursuit of his spiritual welfare. But this strangeness is really the result of a confusion which modern thought has brought to our idea of freedom. Modern thought has pulled down the spiritual and psychic frontiers of freedom, and preserved only its material frontiers whose guardianship and protection it entrusted to the arms of the law. According to this modern thinking, man is not free to attack the wealth of his neighbor nor his person, but he is free in all that pertains to his own person even if he were to transgress the limits of reason or of morality.

The facts of life tell otherwise. They tell that man is the slave of habit; that, for instance, man is accustomed to eat his food in the morning, at noon, and in the evening. Therefore, his being asked to eat food only in the morning and evening is considered an attack upon his freedom. The truth is that it is only an attack upon his enslavement to his habit, so to speak. Some men accustom themselves to smoking so heavily that they can very well be said to have become the slaves of their habit. If they are asked to spend an entire day without smoking, it will be regarded as an attack upon their freedom, whereas in fact it is only an attack upon their enslavement to their habit. Likewise, others have accustomed themselves to drinking coffee or tea or other drinks at certain times. If they are asked to change these times, it will be regarded as an attack upon their freedom. But slavery to habit and custom is corruptive of the will, of the genuine exercise of true freedom. Moreover, it is corruptive of sane thinking, for it subjugates thinking to the material requirements to which the body has become accustomed. That is why many people have had recourse to varying kinds of fasting which they observe at different intervals of the week or the month. But God seeks no hardship for men. That is why He prescribed for them a definite number of days during which all men must fast without distinction. That is why He allowed them to expiate for their failure to fast, and granted the sick and the traveler express permission to postpone their fasting to other days.

The prescription of fasting for a definite number of days further consolidates the Muslim's feeling for and consciousness of equality with other men before God. This is the effect of complete abstinence from dawn to sunset undertaken not as physical but as spiritual exercise imposed equally on all. The same sense of equality is experienced in the communal fasting as that which communal prayer fosters so well. It is during their fast that the feeling of Muslim fraternity is at its greatest strength, for men are not then affected by the usual differences in enjoyment of the material goods of this life which separate them from one another. Fasting consolidates freedom, equality, and fraternity in man just as strongly as does prayer.

If we undertake fasting freely and in the consciousness that God's commandments can never differ from those of reason as long as it perceives the final purpose of life, we can appreciate how much fasting liberates us from the yoke of habit and contributes to the development of our will and capacity for freedom. We may remember that what man prescribes for himself with God's permission by way of spiritual and psychic limitations upon his own freedom in seeking to liberate himself from his habits and passions is the best guarantee for his reaching the highest levels of religious conviction. If, in matters of religion, *taqlīd* constitutes no religious conviction at all but mere acquiescence to the proposed claim without conviction of its truth, *taqlīd* in fasting is self-privation and a limitation of one's personal freedom, a totally different affair from that fasting which liberates man from the chains of habit and furnishes him with the greatest psychic nourishment and spiritual *élan*.

Nature of Islāmic Zakāt

Through prayer and fasting exercises which rest on a base of the widest and deepest possible scientific knowledge of the world, man may reach awareness of the pattern of the cosmos and a penetration of its secrets. In consequence, man may discover his place as well as that of his fellow men in the cosmos. His love for them and their love for him will increase with this realization. In service to God, they will cooperate with one another for the good and reinforce one another's piety; the strong will protect the weak, and the rich will share their bounty with the poor. But that is precisely the *zakāt*. To do more than it requires is charity. The Qur'ān joins *zakāt* to prayer in many places. Some of the following verses have already been quoted: "But righteousness consists in being convinced of the existence and unity of God, of the reality of the Day of Judgment, of the angels, the Book, the Prophets; in giving of one's wealth lovingly to the next of kin, the orphan, the destitute, the wayfarer, the poor, the slave; and in holding the prayer and giving the *zakāt*."[14] The Most High also says: "Observe the prayer and remit the *zakāt* and kneel with those who pray."[15] Further, God—May He be adored—says: "Those believers have done well and achieved felicity who hold their prayers with reverence, abstain from gossip, and complete their payment of *zakāt*,"[16] etc., etc.

Concerning *zakāt* and charity, the Qur'ān talks at length, clearly and emphatically. It has classified charity among the highest virtues deserving of the greatest rewards; indeed, it has placed charity alongside the conviction of God, thus leading us to believe that the two are equal. Addressing His angels regarding a man who violated the duty of charity, God said:

$$\text{خُذُوهُ فَغُلُّوهُ ۞ ثُمَّ الْجَحِيمَ صَلُّوهُ ۞ ثُمَّ فِي سِلْسِلَةٍ ذَرْعُهَا سَبْعُونَ ذِرَاعًا فَاسْلُكُوهُ ۞ إِنَّهُ كَانَ لَا يُؤْمِنُ بِاللَّهِ الْعَظِيمِ ۞ وَلَا يَحُضُّ عَلَى طَعَامِ الْمِسْكِينِ ۞}$$

"Take him away. Fetter him and cast him into the fire that he may broil therein. Bind him in long and heavy chains that he may not move. For he did not believe in God Almighty, nor did he urge the feeding of the poor."[17]

Similarly, God said: "And give glad tidings to the humble, whose hearts are filled with reverential fear whenever God is mentioned, who patiently endure whatever befalls them, who observe the prayer and spend of that which We have provided for them."[18] Further, God—May He be blessed and adored—says: "Those who spend of their wealth at night and during the day, in secret and in public, have their reward with God. They have reason neither to fear nor to grieve."[19]

Islām and the Manners of Giving

Not satisfied with mentioning charity, nor with prescribing for it the same reward as for faith in God and the observance of prayer, the Qur'ān furnishes norms for the manner of giving in charity. It says: "If you give alms openly and to the public at large, it is good and you have done well. But if you give

it to the poor and you do so in secret, it is better for you."
God also says:

قَوْلٌ مَعْرُوفٌ وَمَغْفِرَةٌ خَيْرٌ مِنْ صَدَقَةٍ يَتْبَعُهَآ أَذًى وَاللهُ غَنِيٌّ حَلِيمٌ ۔
يَأَيُّهَاالَّذِينَ اٰمَنُوالَاتُبْطِلُواصَدَقٰتِكُمْ بِالْمَنِّ وَالْأَذٰى

"A word of kindness and an act of forgiveness are superior
to an act of charity followed by injury or harm. God is self-
sufficient and forebearing. O Men who believe, do not vitiate
and annul your charitable deeds by taunting or injuring those
to whom you give."[20]

God—May He be praised—specified the people who may be
recipients of charity: "Rather, alms belong to the poor, the des-
titute, the protectors, those whose hearts need to be reconciled.
They are for the freeing of slaves and debtors, for the cause of
God, and for the wayfarers. To give alms is a duty imposed by
God, the Omniscient, the All-Wise."[21]

Zakāt as Act of Worship

Zakāt and charity, therefore, constitute two of the major
duties and pillars of Islām. It may be asked whether the performance of these duties is a matter of worship or merely of
ethics and moral refinement. Without doubt the answer is worship. The believers are brethren; no man's īmān is complete
until he wishes for his neighbor that which he wishes for himself. The believers love one another by virtue of God's light and
grace. The duties of zakāt and charity are intimately related to
this fraternal feeling. They are not pieces of moral sophistication
nor elements of the Islāmic theory of contracts. In Islām, that
which pertains to brotherhood pertains equally to īmān, or religious conviction of God; and all that pertains to īmān is worship.
That is why zakāt is one of the five pillars of Islām, and why,
after the death of the Prophet, Abū Bakr required the Muslims
to pay it. When some Muslims failed to do so, the immediate
successor of Muḥammad regarded their failure as a fault of faith,
a preference for wealth, and a violation of the spiritual system
revealed in the Qur'ān—in short, as abjuration of Islām itself.

Hence, Abū Bakr conducted the Riddah War in order to confirm the establishment of the message of Islām in its totality, a message which has remained a cause for pride forever.

The Will To Wealth

To regard *zakāt* and charity as duties essentially related to *īmān*, i.e., to faith as religious conviction of God, is to regard them as part of the spiritual system which ought to govern the civilization of the world. Such regard is, indeed, the highest wisdom which can guarantee happiness to man. The pursuit and acquisition of wealth, and its use as an instrument for the dominion of man over man, have always been and still are the cause of the misery of the world, of revolutions, and of wars. The worship of wealth was and still is the cause of the moral deterioration which has enveloped the world and of which human society continues to suffer. It is the acquisition, pursuit, and hoarding of wealth which has destroyed human fraternity and planted enmity between man and man. Were men to follow a higher vision and had they a nobler bent of mind, they would have realized that fraternity is more conducive to happiness than wealth, that to spend wealth on the needy is worthier with God and with men than the subjugation of men to its dominion. Were they truly convinced of God, they would realize this fraternity toward one another; and they would fulfill, as the least requirement of such a fraternity, the duties of rescuing the needy, assisting the deprived, and putting an end to the misery and suffering brought about by poverty and want. Granted, some highly civilized countries in our day do establish hospitals and communal buildings for rescuing the poor, for sheltering the homeless and assisting the deprived in the name of humanity and mercy. Still, were these constructions and communal services founded upon fraternal feeling and love in God for the neighbor as an expression of praise for His bounty, they would constitute nobler efforts and lead more truly to the happiness of all men. God said:

وَابْتَغِ فِيمَآ اٰتٰىكَ اللّٰهُ الدَّارَ الْاٰخِرَةَ وَلَا تَنْسَ نَصِيبَكَ مِنَ الدُّنْيَا وَ اَحْسِنْ كَمَآ اَحْسَنَ اللّٰهُ اِلَيْكَ وَلَاتَبْغِ الْفَسَادَ فِى الْاَرْضِ اِنَّ اللّٰهَ لَايُحِبُّ الْمُفْسِدِيْنَ"

"In all that God has provided for you, seek the higher value and do not forget to seek your share of this world. Do good as God has done good to you; and do not spread corruption in the world. God loves not the agent of corruption."[22]

Nature of Islāmic Pilgrimage

Brotherhood reinforces men's love for one another. In Islām, it is not legitimate to limit the exercise of this love to the frontiers of one's homeland, nor even to one's race or continent. Fraternal love must have no spatial limits whatever. That is why Islām commands that men from all corners of the world know, defend, and fraternize with one another, that their love for one another in God may be strengthened and their conviction of God may be confirmed. The instrument proper for such exercise is the congregation of men from all corners of the earth in one place and for one purpose. The best locality for such a convocation is precisely the place where the light of this great love has broken through, namely God's sanctuary in Makkah. This assembly is the Islāmic pilgrimage. As the believers gather and perform the rites of pilgrimage, it is their duty to lead such lives as would provide the most illustrious living example of conviction and faith in God and of a sincere openness to determination by His will. God—May He be praised—said: "Pilgrimage is during well-known months. Whoever performs the pilgrimage during these months shall engage in no gossip, corruption, vain controversy, or transgression. Everything you do is known to God. Equip yourself therefore with good deeds remembering that the best of deeds is piety. Fear Me, therefore, and fulfill My will, O Men of understanding."[23]

On this great and unique occasion when the believers perform the pilgrimage aiming at fraternizing with one another and thus strengthening their conviction of God, all distinctions between man and man must fall to the ground. All men must feel that they are equal before God, and all must turn their minds and hearts to Him in response to His call and fulfillment of His command. They should approach the pilgrimage fully convinced of His unicity and deeply grateful for His bounty. But what bounty and what felicity are greater than *īmān* in God, the source of all good and all bounty? May He be adored! Before the light which such *īmān* brings, all the worries and concerns of life dissolve; all its vanity, whether of wealth, children, political power or glory, utterly vanishes. By virtue of this light, man becomes capable of apprehending the truth, goodness, and beauty of this world, the eternal laws and immutable pattern on which the world is founded. It is this general convocation, namely the pilgrimage, that embodies the meaning of equality and brotherhood among all the believers and does so in the most comprehensive, clear, and sublime manner.

The Metaphysic of Morals in Islām

These are the fundamental principles of Islām and its duties as revealed to the Prophet Muḥammad—May God's peace be upon him. They constitute the five pillars of Islām as the above mentioned verses of the Qur'ān show. They are the cornerstones of Islāmic spiritual life. Now that these principles and duties have been enumerated, it is easy to infer from them the schemata of Islāmic morality. These belong to a level so high, so sublime, that they have never been matched by any human civilization in any period of history. In this regard, the Qur'ān has given rules and ideals of conduct which, if duly observed, fulfilled, and made to constitute the guiding principles of life, would enable man to attain moral perfection. These principles were not all recorded in the same chapter of the Qur'ān but in many chapters. The reader has no sooner read a *sūrah* of the Qur'ān than he feels himself elevated to the apex of moral advancement, an apex which had never been reached and will never be reached by any other civilization. Sufficient is the Qur'ānic raising of the whole discipline of the soul on a spiritual foundation stemming from the conviction of God. Sufficient is the Qur'ānic demand that mind and heart of man be nourished exclusively from this source and without regard either to material welfare or to any utilitarian value that might accrue from such conduct.

The Qur'ānic Notion of the Perfect Man

In all ages and among all peoples, poets and writers, philosophers and dramatists have depicted the perfect man. Nonetheless, no picture of perfect man is to be found anywhere which dares compare with this sublime picture which the Qur'ān has depicted in the *sūrah* "al Isrā'," though it constitutes only a small portion of the wisdom revealed by God to His Prophet.

This *surah* by no means aims at giving a full description of the perfect man but only at reminding men of a fraction of the duties imposed upon them. God says:

وَقَضَىٰ رَبُّكَ أَلَّا تَعْبُدُوٓا إِلَّآ إِيَّاهُ وَبِٱلْوَٰلِدَيْنِ إِحْسَٰنًا إِمَّا يَبْلُغَنَّ عِندَكَ ٱلْكِبَرَ أَحَدُ
هُمَآ أَوْ كِلَاهُمَا فَلَا تَقُل لَّهُمَآ أُفٍّ وَلَا تَنْهَرْهُمَا وَقُل لَّهُمَا قَوْلًا كَرِيمًا ۝ وَٱخْفِضْ لَهُمَا
جَنَاحَ ٱلذُّلِّ مِنَ ٱلرَّحْمَةِ وَقُل رَّبِّ ٱرْحَمْهُمَا كَمَا رَبَّيَانِى صَغِيرًا ۝ رَّبُّكُمْ أَعْلَمُ بِمَا فِى نُفُوسِكُمْ
إِن تَكُونُوا صَٰلِحِينَ فَإِنَّهُ كَانَ لِلْأَوَّٰبِينَ غَفُورًا ۝ وَءَاتِ ذَا ٱلْقُرْبَىٰ حَقَّهُ وَٱلْمِسْكِينَ وَ
ٱبْنَ ٱلسَّبِيلِ وَلَا تُبَذِّرْ تَبْذِيرًا ۝ إِنَّ ٱلْمُبَذِّرِينَ كَانُوٓا إِخْوَٰنَ ٱلشَّيَٰطِينِ وَكَانَ ٱلشَّيْطَٰنُ
لِرَبِّهِ كَفُورًا ۝ وَإِمَّا تُعْرِضَنَّ عَنْهُمُ ٱبْتِغَآءَ رَحْمَةٍ مِّن رَّبِّكَ تَرْجُوهَا فَقُل لَّهُمْ قَوْلًا
مَّيْسُورًا ۝ وَلَا تَجْعَلْ يَدَكَ مَغْلُولَةً إِلَىٰ عُنُقِكَ وَلَا تَبْسُطْهَا كُلَّ ٱلْبَسْطِ فَتَقْعُدَ مَلُومًا مَّحْسُورًا
۝ إِنَّ رَبَّكَ يَبْسُطُ ٱلرِّزْقَ لِمَن يَشَآءُ وَيَقْدِرُ إِنَّهُ كَانَ بِعِبَادِهِ خَبِيرًا بَصِيرًا ۝ وَلَا تَقْتُلُوٓا
أَوْلَٰدَكُمْ خَشْيَةَ إِمْلَٰقٍ نَّحْنُ نَرْزُقُهُمْ وَإِيَّاكُمْ إِنَّ قَتْلَهُمْ كَانَ خِطْـًٔا كَبِيرًا ۝ وَلَا
تَقْرَبُوا ٱلزِّنَىٰٓ إِنَّهُ كَانَ فَٰحِشَةً وَسَآءَ سَبِيلًا ۝ وَلَا تَقْتُلُوا ٱلنَّفْسَ ٱلَّتِى حَرَّمَ ٱللَّهُ إِلَّا بِٱلْحَقِّ
وَمَن قُتِلَ مَظْلُومًا فَقَدْ جَعَلْنَا لِوَلِيِّهِ سُلْطَٰنًا فَلَا يُسْرِف فِّى ٱلْقَتْلِ إِنَّهُ كَانَ مَنصُورًا ۝
وَلَا تَقْرَبُوا مَالَ ٱلْيَتِيمِ إِلَّا بِٱلَّتِى هِىَ أَحْسَنُ حَتَّىٰ يَبْلُغَ أَشُدَّهُ وَأَوْفُوا بِٱلْعَهْدِ إِنَّ
ٱلْعَهْدَ كَانَ مَسْـُٔولًا ۝ وَأَوْفُوا ٱلْكَيْلَ إِذَا كِلْتُمْ وَزِنُوا بِٱلْقِسْطَاسِ ٱلْمُسْتَقِيمِ ذَٰلِكَ خَيْرٌ
وَأَحْسَنُ تَأْوِيلًا ۝ وَلَا تَقْفُ مَا لَيْسَ لَكَ بِهِ عِلْمٌ إِنَّ ٱلسَّمْعَ وَٱلْبَصَرَ وَٱلْفُؤَادَ كُلُّ أُو۟لَٰٓئِكَ
كَانَ عَنْهُ مَسْـُٔولًا ۝ وَلَا تَمْشِ فِى ٱلْأَرْضِ مَرَحًا إِنَّكَ لَن تَخْرِقَ ٱلْأَرْضَ وَلَن تَبْلُغَ ٱلْجِبَالَ
طُولًا ۝ كُلُّ ذَٰلِكَ كَانَ سَيِّئُهُ عِندَ رَبِّكَ مَكْرُوهًا ۝

"Your Lord commands you to worship none but Him and to be kind to your parents. Should any one of them be under your care until he reaches old age, do not say to him as much as 'Fie' and do not speak harshly to him but rather speak kindly. Humble yourself to your parents in love, and pray: 'May God have mercy on them as they nursed me when I was young.' Your Lord knows well that which is in your soul, especially whether or not you are truly virtuous. God forgives those who repent. Give the next of kin his due, as well as the poor and the wayfarer, but do not be a spendthrift. The spendthrifts are associates of the devil, and the latter is disobedient to God. Even if you have to avoid your parents on account of your fulfillment of God's call, give them a kind and compassionate explanation. Do not hold your hand back when it is time to give, nor give all you have so that you throw yourself in need. God spreads His bounty to whomsoever He wishes. He measures it carefully, for He cares for His servants and knows their need. Do not kill your children for fear of poverty. We shall provide for them as well as for you. Moreover, to kill them is a great misdeed. Do not commit adultery. It is an evil and its consequences are always bad. Do not kill any man—That is God's prohibition!—except after due process of law. To the heir of whoever is killed unjustly, a right of revenge is established. But he may not take that revenge wantonly, for his right shall be recognized. Do not touch the wealth of the orphan, unless it be to increase it. Be true to your covenants, for to covenant is a serious and responsible affair. Fill the measure when you measure, and when you weigh, weigh with the true weight; for that is better and more rewarding. Do not claim that of which you have no knowledge, and remember that as cognitive faculties, your hearing, sight, and heart were given to you for a responsible function. Do not walk around with impudence and false pride, for you will never measure up to the mountains of the earth. All these actions are evil and deemed undesirable by your Lord."[24]

What sublimity! What perfection! What magnanimity and purity! Every one of the foregoing verses causes the reader to fall down in reverence and awe, combining as it does the moving appeal of moral value, the sublimity of expression, the beauty of form, the nobility of meaning, and the highest vividness of description. How I wish the occasion permitted an elaboration of this passage! But it does not, for to do justice to a passage even as short as the foregoing would require a whole volume.

The Qur'ān on Self-Discipline

Indeed, even if we were to limit ourselves to a discussion of only a portion of what the Qur'ān contains by way of self-discipline and morality, much more would be needed than a mere chapter of a book. Suffice it to say, therefore, that no writing has ever called man to do the good works and elevated the virtuous life as the Qur'ān has done; that no book has elevated the human soul to the level to which the Qur'ān has raised it; and that no book has emphasized virtue, mercy, fraternity and love, cooperation and harmony, charity and kindness, loyalty and trustworthiness, sincerity and good intention, justice and forgiveness, patience and forbearance, humility and submission, virtue and goodness, the commandment to good and the forbiddance of evil with as much power, persuasion, and sublimity as the Qur'ān has done. No book has ever spoken against weakness and fear, favoritism and jealously, hatred and injustice, lying and libel, avarice and prodigality, false witness and perjury, aggression and corruption, cheating, treason, and all vice as profoundly and persuasively as the revelation which came to the Arab Prophet. The reader will find no *surah* in the Qur'ān in which the call to virtue, the commandment to good, the forbiddance of evil, and the pursuit of perfection are not central. Every *surah* raises the reader to the highest level of moral awareness and tension. Let us mark well God's statement regarding tolerance: "Respond to the evil deed with a good one. . . . The good deed is certainly not the equivalent of the evil one. Repel the evil deed with the good one. Instantly, your enemy will be transformed into a warm friend."[25] This toleration to which the Qur'ān calls, however, does not proceed from weakness but from magnanimity of spirit, a will to compete in good deeds and to avoid lowly ones. God says: "And if you are greeted, respond with a better greeting or, at least, with the same."[26] Further, God says: "And when you punish, inflict the same punishment as was meted out to you. But if you refrain out of patience, it is better for you."[27] All these verses clearly establish that the Islāmic call to tolerance is at the same time a call to virtue unspoiled by any weakness. It is indeed the consequence of a self-transcendence that is pure and unalloyed.

Tolerance from strength and virtue, to which the Qur'ān calls, is founded upon brotherhood which Islām places at the root of its civilization and which it holds to be absolutely universal. Islāmic brotherhood integrates justice and mercy without weakness or sufferance. It arises from equality in right, goodness and virtue, unaffected by utilitarian advantage. Under its aegis, the Muslim prefers his fellows to himself even though they be far inferior to him. He fears God and none other; consequently, the Muslim is the model of pride, dignity, and self-respect. And yet he is the model of humility and modesty. He is truthful and fulfills a covenant once he has entered into it. He is as patient when tragedy strikes as when he receives good fortune and new power. Faced with calamity, he thinks, feels, and prays: "We are all God's, and to Him we shall all return." He never abases himself to anyone, and yet he has no false pride. God has protected him against avarice and stinginess when they are directed toward himself. He never reports falsely about God or about His servants; he never approves of adultery and always seeks to avoid transgression and crime. If he ever goes into a rage, he seeks God's mercy and forgiveness, sublimates his rage and fury, and forgives his offenders. He avoids suspicion, spying, and reporting secretly about his fellows. He does not violate the wealth of his fellows, nor allow the rulers to do so unjustly. He stands beyond jealousy, strategy, deceit, gossip, and every kind of misdemeanor.

Morality and Utilitarianism

These virtues and the ethical system which they constitute are all founded on the spiritual system revealed in the Qur'ān which is essentially related to īmān in God. As we have said earlier, this characteristic is the most important feature of Islāmic morality. It guarantees the grasp of the human soul by these values and ideals, as well as saves that system from all corruption. Morality founded upon utility and mutual advantage is quickly corrupted as soon as the moral subject is convinced that his personal advantage does not suffer in consequence of his immorality. In such morality, it is most often the case that the subject is double-faced, showing an appearance different from what he holds deep within him. He would, for instance, seek to appear trustworthy while giving himself the right to use another's confidence as a means for increasing his advantage. He would seek to appear truthful but would not restrain from false pretense as long as this added to his advantage. A morality founded upon such standards falls down as the winds of temptation begin to blow. Its subject is often found pursuing ulterior motives and ever running after the satisfaction of his own prejudices.

This essential moral weakness is most conspicious in our present-day world. How often have we heard of great scandals occurring in this or that part of the civilized world, scandals all traceable to the pursuit of wealth and power on the part of their subjects, and on the weakness of their will to possess true *īmān* and noble morals. Many of these people who fall to the nethermost depths in morality and perpetrate the worst crimes have started out with high morals based upon utilitarianism. They regarded success in life as based upon the observance of these high morals; and so they observed them in order to succeed, not because moral practice is a necessary part of their personal path which they ought to follow even though it might incur serious disadvantage. Hence, when they realized that some deviation from moral uprightness did in fact bring forth a measure of success within the civilization of this age, they allowed themselves to swerve. Many of them have been able to keep their personal code of behavior hidden from the public and, therefore, have never been exposed to scandal. They continue to be respected and esteemed. Others, less adept, have been exposed and have fallen into scandalous involvements which often have ended in personal ruin or suicide.

To found morality on utility and advantage, therefore, is to expose it to eventual but certain calamity. On the other hand, to found it on a spiritual system such as the Qur'ān has revealed is to guarantee its permanent strength, its moving appeal, and power to determine man's ethics. The intention behind a deed is itself the measure of its moral worth, the genuine rubbing stone against which it should be tested. The man who buys a lottery ticket designed to build a hospital does not buy it with the intention of doing good and being charitable but in pursuit of material gain. Such act is not moral. Likewise, the man who gives to the insistent beggar in order to rid himself of the nuisance caused, is not on a par with the man who gives to the poor who not only do not insist when they ask, but do not ask at all out of a deep sense of dignity, shame, and self-respect. Furthermore, the man who tells the truth to the judge in fear of the punishment the law metes out to perjurers is not equivalent to the man who tells the truth because he believes in the virtue of truthfulness. A system of morals based upon utility and mutual advantage therefore cannot have the strength of a morality which the subject believes to be essentially related to his human dignity and to his *īmān* in God, a morality founded upon the spiritual system on which his *īmān* in God is itself founded.

The Wisdom of Prohibition of Alcohol and Gambling in Islām

The Qur'ān, seeking to preserve the jurisdiction of reason in morality, thus has kept morality immune to all that might vitiate its judgment in matters of faith or morals. Consequently, it has regarded alcohol and gambling as anathema, the inspiration of the devil. Even though they might bring some advantage in their wake, their crime and evil are greater than their advantage; hence, they ought to be avoided. Gambling, for instance, takes such possession of the mind of the gambler that its victim can think of nothing else and can make no other use of his time. It tempts him away from the fulfillment of any moral obligation. On the other hand, alcohol dissolves reason as well as wealth, to use the terms of 'Umar ibn al Khaṭṭāb when he prayed that God might reveal His judgment in its regard. It is natural for the mind to err in its judgment when intoxicated; it is easy for the mind, once it has gone astray, to tolerate the pursuit of crime and evil instead of warning man against them.

The Qur'ān and Science

The ethical system of the ideal state revealed in the Qur'ān does not deprive man of the enjoyments of the good things of life, precisely because both privation and overindulgence may lead to the same consequences: neglect of the cosmos as a whole and of the pursuit of cosmic knowledge. The Islāmic system strongly rejects man's total surrender to enjoyment of affluence and comfort even as it rejects his surrender to privation and abstinence in which he loses himself in subjective psychic pursuits. On the contrary, Islām seeks to make its people a community of the golden mean, to orient them toward pure virtue, to develop their knowledge of the cosmos, and to master all that it contains. The Qur'ān continually speaks of the cosmos and of what it contains in a way directing us toward increasing our knowledge of it. It speaks about the new moons, about the sun and the moon, day and night, the earth and the creatures that roam over it, the sky and the stars which adorn it, the sea whose surface is crisscrossed with ships sailing in pursuit of God's bounty, of the animals we take as beasts of burden and others as ornaments, and of all that the earth contains for knowledge and art. In speaking about all these, the Qur'ān asks man not only to look into them and study them but to enjoy their effects and to feel grateful to God for His bounty. With such discipline as the Qur'ān has enjoined, and by following its insistent call to seek cosmic knowledge, man may fufill his destiny. If he responds to the 'call of the Qur'ān and fulfills its requisite rational contemplation of the cosmos, he bases his economic and social system upon solid and worthy foundations.

The Islāmic Economic System

Were economic and social systems to be based upon such moral and spiritual foundations, man would be able both to achieve happiness and to put an end to human suffering and misery on earth. The high ethical principles which the Qur'ān poses as the very content of its creed, as well as its faith, command men to remove any shortcoming or misery in the world which it is possible to remove. A person disciplined by these principles and gripped by their ethic will condemn selfish interests, the basis of present economic life and the source of misery for all mankind. That is why Islām categorically forbids charging interest for loans. God said, "Those who appropriate interest are like men possessed of the devil."[28] Further, the Qur'ān says, "The interest which you impose seeking to increase your wealth will not bring about any increase in the sight of God. Rather, it is the zakāt which you pay for the sake of God alone, that brings about such increase of your fortune."[29]

The Evils of the Interest System

The prohibition of interest is a basic principle of Islāmic civilization. It guarantees and safeguards the happiness of mankind. In its least offensive sense, interest is a system which enables the unproductive man to share in the fruits of someone else's labor for no reason but that he lent him money. The argument advanced in its favor is that the money lent enabled the producer to produce his fruits and that without it, it would not have been possible for the producer to earn what he did. Even if this advantage were the only consequence of interest, it would not be justified. For, were the money lender capable of usufructing his money for himself, he would not have lent it to someone else. And were that money to remain in its coffer, it would not produce any fruits at all. Rather, it would probably be gradually consumed by its owner. If, therefore, the capitalist allows another man to usufruct his money, hoping thereby to win a share in its fruits, he should certainly be entitled to a share of the fruits—should there be such—rather than imposing a definite interest charge for his money. If the operation proves successful and economically profitable, the owner of the capital should receive the share agreed upon. If it should turn out to be a failure and a loss, however, then he, too, should share a proportionate part of the burden. On the other hand, to impose a definite interest charge for the use of capital regardless of whether or not the use of such capital has been productive is illegitimate exploitation.

It is futile to object here that capital is entitled to its rent because it is used like any other commodity, be it a piece of land or a mule, and that interest is really the equivalent of rent. The renting of movable and immovable property is vastly different from renting money; the latter may bring about mutual benefit and usufruct as well as pure exploitation and crime. Man does not rent a piece of land, a house, a beast of burden, or any immovable property except in order to use it to his advantage. Otherwise, he is insane, and his commitments are not responsible. It is otherwise with money. Money is for the most part lent for purposes of trade. But trade is always exposed to profit and loss. The renting of immovable or movable property is hardly ever exposed to loss except in rare, indeed exceptional, cases falling outside the realm of normal legislation. Where it does happen that the rent of movable or immovable property exposes the user to loss, the legislator usually intervenes between the landowner and the lessees in order to relieve such injustice and prevent exploitation by the landowner. Such has been the repeated practice of the world everywhere. On the other hand, the imposition of a definite interest rate of seven or nine percent, more or less, is not affected by whether the usufruct of the money in question has realized a profit or a loss. Where the result of the usufruct is a loss, to demand the interest is surely to commit a crime. It is on this account that hatred and immoral competition arise between men in place of fraternity and love. This source of misery is the primary cause of the repeated crises which the world community has been witnessing in recent times.

The foregoing is perhaps the least offensive description of interest. In other pictures the money lender is better compared to a wild beast rather than to anything human. Consider the case of the man who needs money for a purpose other than production. It is possible that a man may fall in need and seek financial assistance to feed himself and his family for an interval, pending his finding a job or his engaging in some productive activity. To come to the assistance of such a man is one of the first duties of humanity. This is precisely what the holy Qur'ān demands. Is not the charging of interest in such cases a heinous crime, an offense deserving the same punishment as murder? And is it not a crime still more sinister to tempt those who are not shrewd in the management of their own affairs in order to get them to borrow money on interest and thereby rob them of the little wealth they possess? To tempt and to trap a man with interest is no less a crime than the lowliest theft. Surely it deserves the same if not greater punishment.

Interest and Colonialism

It was interest and the demand for the profit it entails to the lender which engulfed the world in all the calamities of colonialism. In most cases, colonialism began with a number of capitalists, whether individuals or corporations, lending money to the colonized at interest and infiltrating the colony's system with the aim of gaining control over its resources. When the borrowing people woke up and sought to liberate themselves from the money lender's clutches, the creditors appealed to their own governments to intervene and protect what then came to be called their national interest. The latter then arrived with their armies and fleets and imposed themselves as colonial powers seeking to protect the interests of their own citizens. The colonial power then imposed its rule, deprived the people of their liberty and began to control whatever God gave the people of His bounty in their own land. Their happiness thus vanished. Misery, suffering, and poverty engulfed them. Ignorance and misguidance stifled their minds. Their morals deteriorated and their *imān* became dissolute. They thus fell below the level of humanity and reached a degree of inferiority that no man believing in God would accept for himself. No man believing that God alone is worthy of worship will allow his fate to be so controlled by someone else as to bring about his own loss and suffering.

Colonialism is indeed the source of wars. It is the source of the misery which has befallen the whole of mankind in the present age. As long as interest is legitimate and real, as long as it is the basis of economic life and colonialism the dominant factor in international relations, there is no hope for the establishment of fraternity and love. Such a condition cannot be reached unless civilization is rebuilt upon the foundation which Islām has provided and which revelation has recorded in the Qur'ān.

Islāmic Socialism

The Qur'ān also contains a system of socialism which has never yet been the object of research. It is a socialism which is not based on the competition of capital or class war, as the socialism of western civilization today. Rather it is based on moral principles guaranteeing fraternity between the classes and fostering mutual security and cooperation for the good and felicity of their members instead of crime and transgression. It is relatively easy to appreciate this Qur'ānic socialism based upon brotherhood and institutionized in *zakāt* and charity. It does not allow one class to dominate another or one group to impose its will upon another. The civilization depicted in the Qur'ān knows no such dominion or imposition. It rests entirely upon genuine fraternity deriving from unswerving *īmān* in God, a conviction which makes the recognition of God tantamount to giving to the poor and the deprived that which they need by way of nourishment, clothing, shelter, medicine, education, and upbringing, without even making them feel that they have been the object of charity. Under this system, misery will vanish and men may hope God will complete His bounty and grant them the happiness they desire.

No Abolition of Private Property

Islāmic socialism does not demand the annulment of private property, as is the case with western socialism. The facts are that even in Bolshevik Russia, as well as in any socialist country, the doing away with private property has not been fruitful. On the other hand, it goes without saying that all public utilities should become common property for the people. The definition of public utilities should be left for the state to conclude. As may be expected, men may disagree on such definition, as was the case in the first century of Islām. Some of the Prophet's companions demanded that all the creations of God should be

included in the definition of public utilities. They regarded the
land and all that it contained on a par with water and air,
and thus not subject to becoming the property of anyone. They
regarded every man as entitled to its fruits in proportion to
his effort and capacity. Other companions saw the question differently. They deemed the land capable of becoming the property
of individuals and, like the immovable properties, capable of
being exchanged.

The Final Groundwork of Islāmic Socialism

At any rate, one basic socialist principle that was agreed upon
by all the Prophet's companions is passing today as a matter
of course in the socialist countries of Europe: that every man
is duty-bound to put to full use all his capacities for the sake
of the community; and that *is* the duty of the community to
guarantee to every individual all his basic needs. Every Muslim
was entitled to draw from the public treasury all that was
required to satisfy his survival needs and those of his family
as long as he did not find work to do, or as long as the work
he did was not sufficient to satisfy these wants. As long as
morality is governed by the principles of the Qur'ān, no one
may tell a lie and claim that he is out of work when in reality
he is just lazy and unwilling to exert himself. Nor will anyone
claim falsely that his income is insufficient. In the first century
of Islām, the caliphs and leaders of the Muslim community
took it upon themselves to inspect the conditions of their subjects
in order to insure themselves that no basic need remained unsatisfied.

Socialism Is Brotherhood

From this basic discussion, the reader will realize that the
socialism of Islām is not a socialism of capital and distribution
but one founded upon. fraternity in the spiritual, moral, and
economic spheres of life. If a person's *īmān* is not regarded
as complete until that person has wished for his fellow that
which he wishes for himself, it can be deduced safely that
no *īmān* is complete unless its subject has urged the feeding
of the hungry and has spent privately and publicly of what God
has provided, with a view to serving the commonweal. The more
altruistic a person becomes, the closer he comes to realizing
internal peace and happiness. If God has so constituted men

that some stand above others in capacities and achievements, and if God has given of his bounty differently to whomsoever He chooses, it is certain that there will be no end to evil in this world until the young respects the older, the older shows mercy to the younger, the richer gives to the poorer, and all have done so purely for the sake of God and in praise of Him as well as of His bounty.

It is not necessary in this connection to give the details of the laws of inheritance, of wills, of contracts, trade, and other areas of the Qur'ānic economic system. Even the briefest reference to any one of these topics, whether social or jurisprudential, would require many more chapters. It is sufficient to note that the contribution of Islām in any one of these fields is still unsurpassed by any other kind of legislation. Indeed, one can only react with surprise when he considers some of the details of this Islāmic contribution—e.g., the command always to write down one's contracts unless it be a case of irreversible trade; the arbitration of disputes between husband and wife by representatives of either party in order to avoid dissolution of the marriage; the commandment to reconcile any two disputing factions within the state and to all the Muslims to fight that faction which resists the efforts, judgment or instrument of reconciliation. One is surprised at the novelty of such provisions of Islāmic law. And when compared with the provisions of other bodies of law, one invariably reaches the conclusion that that legislation is indeed the highest which has sought to fulfill the Qur'ānic principles. It should, however, surprise no one—considering that the foregoing principles regarding interest and Islāmic socialism are the bases of the Qur'ānic economic system and that this legislation is the highest that has ever been reached by man in any period—that Islāmic civilization is not only truly worthy of mankind but is also the only one that can guarantee man's happiness.

Probable Western Objections

After reading our presentation of the bases and structure of Qur'ānic civilization, some western writers may deem them too utopian to be fulfilled by man and, hence, not destined to endure even when successfully realized. Such thinkers hold man to be motivated by fear and hope, prejudice and pressure, just like any other animal except that man adds to his equipment the faculty of speech. To expect humanity to follow a system such

as that provided by Islām for civilization is either impossible
or extremely difficult. The utmost that we may expect in ordering
the life of human society is the regulation of human passion
and greed and the orientation of human fear and hope from the
economic aspect alone. What is beyond these desiderata is beyond
the capacity of human society. The Islāmic system, formulated
by the Qur'ān and described in this chapter, did not survive in
Islāmic history beyond the days of the Prophet and his immediate
successors. This phenomenon constitutes for these thinkers
further proof of the utopian nature of that system and its not
having enveloped the world. They cite this failure to survive
and to spread itself over the world as proof of its unfitness.

Refutation

To refute this claim, it is sufficient to note the acknowledgment of its adherents that the Islāmic system was indeed realized
during the period of the Prophet and that of his immediate
successors. Muhammad was indeed the highest exemplar of that
system and his application of it the highest instance of its feasi-
bility. His immediate successors followed his example and
carried his own application of it to perfection. Under the influence
of various Israelitisms[30] and provincialisms,[31] that system was
gradually dissolved by intrigue and corruption. Slowly but surely,
men allowed material considerations to overrule the spiritual,
and animal passion to elbow out the humane until mankind
reached the situation of the present day in which it suffers from
the most terrible miseries.

The Example of Muhammad

Muhammad's example was the best application of Islāmic
civilization as elaborated in the Qur'ān. From this work, the
reader may remember how the Prophet extended his fraternity
to all men without distinction. In Makkah, he regarded himself
and his fellows absolutely on a par in poverty and suffering.
Indeed, he assumed the greater share of privation and suffering
for their sake. When he emigrated to Madīnah, he established
this fraternity between the Muhājirūn and Ansār so firmly that
he granted the privileges and obligations incumbent upon real
blood relationship to all. In that period, the fraternity of believers
was based upon mutual love and the common will to raise the

foundations of the new civilization. It was fed and reinforced by a genuine *īmān* in God, a faith and a conviction whose strength carried Muḥammad to communion with God Himself—May He be adored. At the campaign of Badr, Muḥammad called upon God to give him the promised victory and prayed to Him saying, that should the Muslims be defeated at Badr, God would not be worshipped in Arabia. This is strong evidence of that communion with the Divine. Indeed, many such stands which Muḥammad took on other occasions point to his constant communion with God. These were moments other than those of revelation. It was this communion with the Divine based on his true *īmān* in God which enabled Muḥammad not to fear death but, indeed, to seek it. This was only as it should be, for the man of genuine conviction never fears death but welcomes it. Every life has a term, and death will reach its object wherever it may be. No man may escape. It was this conviction that enabled Muḥammad to stand firmly on his ground when the Muslims ran away in panic at the outbreak of hostilities at Ḥunayn. When practically surrounded with death, Muḥammad paid no attention to it and called his men to rally forth around him. It was this *īmān* that made him give liberally without fear of poverty or privation and enabled him to do good to the orphan, the wayfarer, the deprived, and the suffering. In brief, it enabled him to rise to the highest pinnacle of every Qur'ānic virtue. All this, as well as the Muslims' close observance of his example in the first period of their history, caused Islām to spread in the years immediately following the death of Muḥammad and to establish itself by planting the seeds of Islāmic civilization in every land. Finally, it was this *īmān* that transformed corrupt and decadent peoples into strong and progressive states seeking knowledge and advancement, discovering the secrets of the universe, and developing creativity in every field of human endeavor. These same states can vie successfully even with the accomplishments of the modern age, the so-called 'Age of Light and Science,' an age so unsuccessful in bringing about happiness to mankind because of an *īmān* weak in God and strong in matter.

The Misguided 'Ulamā'

However, like any other civilization of Western Asia and Europe, Islāmic civilization was corrupted by the prejudices engendered by provincialism or Israelitism. This corruption is

attributable to the fact that a number of 'ulamā', who are
normally expected to be the heirs of the Prophets, preferred
power to the truth, worldly glory to virtue, and used their
knowledge and leadership to misguide the community of the
people and their young in the same way as do the 'ulamā' of this
age. Such 'ulamā' however are the devil's associates. Upon them
will fall the greatest responsibility on the Day of Judgment.
It is the first duty of every modern 'ālim, true to God and to his
knowledge, to fight the misguiding 'ulamā' and combat the evil
propaganda they spread. If such 'ulamā' have any kind of place
in Christendom where the church and science have to fight each
other and compete for power, they have utterly no place in the
Islāmic world where religion and science are close associates,
where religion without science is deemed unbelief and ungodly,
and where science without religion is deemed delusion. Had
mankind entered into the civilization of Islām as the Qur'ān
depicts it, had the Mongols not destroyed its great centers, and
had the insincere converts to Islām not taken their Islām as a
means for subjecting the community of Muslims to their dominion, a dominion based on the opposite of Islāmic fraternity,
the world would have had a different destiny. Mankind would
not have been subject to the miseries it finds itself under today.

Islāmic Civilization and the Future

I am nonetheless certain that Qur'ānic civilization will conquer
the world if a group of 'ulamā' rise today to call for it in a
progressive, open, and scientific manner. This civilization addresses itself to both the heart and reason. It appeals to all
men and to all people; no vested interests and no prejudices will
be able to prevent their movement toward it. Nor is it required
that such 'ulamā' have any more than a genuine īmān, and that
they sincerely call men to God. Then will mankind find their
happiness in this fraternity in God as they found it in the
Prophet's time.

The accomplishments of the period of the Prophet and of that
of his immediate successors constitute evidence for my claim,
advanced in the preface to this work, that scientific research
into the spiritual revolution which Muḥammad initiated in this
world will guide mankind to the new civilization toward which
it has been groping. There is no doubt whatever in this regard.

Western men of knowledge object to this claim by deploring the spirit dominating Islāmic civilization. On the basis of these objections, they accuse Islām of causing the decay and degradation of the Muslim peoples. The most important of these objections is the claim that the determinism of Islām weakens the will of its people, disables them from participating in the struggle for existence, and brings about their decadence and subjugation. To expose the falsity of this claim and other claims will be the purpose of the second essay in this conclusion.

II. ISLĀMIC CIVILIZATION AND THE WESTERN ORIENTALISTS

Irving and Islāmic Determinism

Washington Irving, one of the greatest writers the United States of America produced in the nineteenth century, is a real credit to his people. He has written a biography of the Arab Prophet in which the material is presented in an eloquent and captivating manner. Although his treatment is well taken at times, it is prejudiced at others. His book ends with a conclusion in which he presents the principles of Islām and what he has taken to be the historical sources of those principles. After mentioning imān in God, in His angels, Books, prophets, and the Day of Judgment, Washington Irving wrote:

> "The sixth and last article of the Islām faith is PREDESTINATION, and on this Mahomet evidently reposed his chief dependence for the success of his military enterprises. He inculcated that every event had been predetermined by God, and written down in the eternal tablet previous to the creation of the world. That the destiny of every individual and the hour of his death were irrevocably fixed, and could neither be varied nor evaded by any effort of human sagacity or foresight. Under this persuasion the Moslems engaged in battle without risk; and, as death in battle was equivalent to martyrdom, and entitled them to an immediate admission into paradise, they had in either alternative, death or victory, a certainty of gain.
> "This doctrine, according to which men by their own free will can neither avoid sin nor avert punishment, is con-

sidered by many Mussulmen as derogatory to the justice
and clemency of God; and several sects have sprung up, who
endeavor to soften and explain away this perplexing dogma;
but the number of these doubters is small, and they are
not considered orthodox.

"The doctrine of Predestination was one of those timely
revelations to Mahomet that were almost miraculous from
their seasonable occurrence. It took place immediately after
the disastrous battle of Ohod, in which many of his followers,
and among them his uncle Hamza, were slain. Then it was,
in a moment of gloom and despondency, when his followers
around him were disheartened, that he promulgated this
law, telling them that every man must die at the appointed
hour, whether in bed or in the field of battle. He declared,
moreover, that the angel Gabriel had announced to him
the reception of Hamza into the seventh heaven, with the
title of Lion of God and of the Prophet. He added, as he
contemplated the dead bodies, 'I am witness for these,
and for all who have been slain for the cause of God, that
they shall appear in glory at the resurrection, with their
wounds brilliant as vermilion and odoriferous as musk.'

"What doctrine could have been devised more calculated
to hurry forward, in a wild career of conquest, a set of
ignorant and predatory soldiers, than assurance of booty
if they survived, and paradise if they fell? It rendered almost
irresistible the Moslem arms; but it likewise contained the
poison that was to destroy their dominion. From the moment
the successors of the Prophet ceased to be aggressors and
conquerors, and sheathed the sword definitely, the doctrine of
predestination began its baneful work. Enervated by peace,
and the sensuality permitted by the Koran—which so distinctly separates its doctrine from the pure and self-denying
religion of the Messiah—the Moslem regarded every reverse
as preordained by Allah, and inevitable; to be borne stoically,
since human exertion and foresight were vain. 'Help thyself
and God will help thee,' was a precept never in force with the
followers of Mahomet; and its reverse has been their fate.
The crescent has waned before the cross, and exists in Europe, where it was once so mighty, only by the suffrage, or
rather the jealously of the great Christian powers, probably
ere long to furnish another illustration, that 'they that take
the sword shall perish with the sword.' "[1]

Falsity of Irving's Criticism

These are the words of Washington Irving. They are the words of a man whose study fell short of grasping the spirit of Islām and of its civilization. Hence, his false interpretation of the problem of divine providence and predestination. Perhaps Irving had some excuse in that some of the Islāmic books which he may have read do in fact point in the direction of his interpretation. As for the Qur'ān, the dictum "God helps them that help themselves" is far too weak to be even comparable to its emphatic call for self-reliance, its thunderous warning that men will receive exactly what their deeds and intentions had earned for them. God said:

$$\text{قُلْ يَـٰٓأَيُّهَا النَّاسُ قَدْ جَآءَكُمُ الْحَقُّ مِن رَّبِّكُمْ فَمَنِ اهْتَدَىٰ فَإِنَّمَا يَهْتَدِى لِنَفْسِهِ}$$
$$\text{وَمَن ضَلَّ فَإِنَّمَا يَضِلُّ عَلَيْهَا}$$

"Say, O Men, the truth has come to you from your Lord. Whoever is guided thereby is so to his own credit; whoever is not so guided is so to his own discredit."

In another passage God said: "Whoever is guided by the truth will earn the advantage thereof, and whoever goes astray will earn the disadvantage thereof. Do not extrapolate responsibility. No punishment is due until a prophet has been duly sent and men have been duly warned; . . . whoever seeks the advantage of the other world will receive the same and more of it. Whoever seeks the advantage of this world will receive the same, but he will have no share in the other. . . . God does not change the conditions of a people until that people have changed their conditions by themselves."[2]

The Qur'ān and Determinism

It is, therefore, a clearly Qur'ānic position that man's will and action are the sole determinants of his worth, of his punishment or reward. Emphatically, God has urged man to go forth into the world to seek its fruits and to enjoy them. He commanded self-exertion in His cause in very strong terms as may be seen from many verses quoted in this book. This is all irreconcilable with Irving's claim, which has been repeated by a number of other westerners, that Islām is a religion of lethargy and reliance, that it teaches its adherents that they can in no way influence whatever befalls them, whether good or evil, and hence that there is no point in their trying to do so. This claim argues that will and efficacy are exclusive prerogatives of God; that man's efforts come to naught when the divine decree orders otherwise; and that if it were decreed that somebody would become rich, strong, or a believer, this would surely come to pass without any effort or action on his part. The verses we have already cited all run counter to these claims.

It may also be possible that these western writers and thinkers attribute the lethargy and reliance of the Muslims in the recent period of their history to the Qur'ānic verses which pertain to divine providence in the manner of the following: "No man may expire, except by permission of God and at a prefixed term. . . . every people has a term; so that whenever that term arrives, that people must fulfill that which is proper thereto at its time, neither before nor after it. . . . whatever calamity befalls the earth or your own persons is predetermined before it happens. Such determination is easy for God. . . . Say, 'Nothing shall befall us except that which God has predetermined for us. He is our Lord; and upon Him the believers will rely.' "³ But if this is the line of their reasoning, then they have misunderstood the meanings of these verses and others like them. Misunderstanding these verses, they think Islām calls for resignation, whereas the Qur'ān meant to stress the solid bond between God and His dedicated servants. The fact is that Islām is a religion which calls for exactly the opposite, for dynamism and personal initiative, self-exertion and sacrifice, self-respect and dignity, while it founds its civilization on brotherhood and mercy. Islām is the one religion which does so *par excellence!*

Scientific Determinism

As a matter of fact, these and like verses point to a scientific truth recognized by most western philosophers and men of science in which determinism is ascribed to the general pattern of the cosmos as a whole rather than to God, the Almighty and Omniscient. This view is narrower, more rigid, and less amenable to the good of mankind than the philosophic view deducible from the Qur'ān, as we shall see in the sequel. Scientific determinism teaches that man has no freedom except in the narrowest and most insignificant fields and that this little freedom is relative and is evident only as a practical consequence of social needs, but not from any established scientific or philosophical reality. It is not a principle but a provision. For without some provision for freedom of choice, it would be impossible for society to find a basis for its legislation, for the regulations it imposes on all its members under threat of criminal and civil sanction. True, some men of science and jurisprudence do not regard punishment or sanction as based on either determinism or on freedom, and they explain punishment as a response on the part of society to the need for self-preservation, just as an individual would react for his own self-preservation. It is all one for society when it reacts in self-preservation, whether the individual criminal has been free or determined in the perpetration of his crime. Nonetheless, freedom of action is still the foundation for most jurists. Their evidence therefor is the principle that the person devoid of freedom and choice, such as the insane, the child, and the moron, are never judged as the conscious man who distinguishes between good and evil.

If we go beyond these practical considerations of legislation and jurisprudence to reach a scientific and philosophical principle, we are led to conclude in favor of determinism. No man, for instance, has any choice as to the period in which he is born, nor of the nation, community, environment, nor parents to whom he is born. Just as no man chooses his parents, no man chooses them as poor or rich, perfect or imperfect; neither has he chosen his sex nor the happenings which surround his life and determine it to any great extent. The French philosopher Hyppolite Taine expressed this view with the dictum, "Man is the product of his environment." Many philosophers and scientists have adopted this view, insisting that if it were possible to know the laws and secrets of human life to the same extent as we have discovered the laws of movement of the heavenly bodies, it would become possible to predict precisely the destiny of every man and nation, just as astronomers predict with precision an eclipse of the sun or of the moon.

All this notwithstanding, no one in the West or in the East has claimed that this determinist view prevents man from seeking success in life or the nations of the world from bringing themselves up to a position of affluence and prosperity. No one claims that this determinist view leads to the deterioration and decadence of the people who believe in it. This fact remains true in spite of the westerner's subscription to determinism as not being counteracted by such strong religious pronouncements as the Qur'ānic verses quoted in this chapter, which assert that "Man acquires nothing but what he himself has earned; none of his deeds is lost and each will count on the Day of Judgment."[4] This point alone constitutes evidence that the western Orientalists' claim that determinism in Islām had led to the deterioration and decay of the Muslim peoples is nothing but a piece of sheer prejudice.

Rather, the determinism of Islām stresses far more than that of the West the need for self-exertion and personal initiative in the actualization of material and ethical values. Both systems are agreed that the cosmos has immutable patterns to which everything in the world is necessarily subject and that man is as subject to these patterns as is all of nature. Further, western determinism subjects man to determination by his environment and inheritance from his parents to such a degree that no escape from natural law is possible. It subjects man's will to this determination so that it is impossible for man to change himself. On the other hand, the Qur'ān calls upon every man to govern his will by the judgment of reason and to orient it toward the ethical good. It teaches that even if the good has been predetermined to be the consequence of man's given endeavor, man cannot reach it haphazardly or without effort.

The Absolute Need for Deliberate Self-Change

God—May He be adored—said, "God does not change the conditions of a people until that people have changed their conditions by themselves."[5] It is hence within the capacity of men to think out and to ponder their course in life once God has guided them to their duties. God does this by means of His revealed Books, by His prophets—who show men the road of goodness and truth—or by calling men to look into the universe in order to grasp its laws and the will of God imperative therein, by stirring within them the innate will to know. Whoever believes that the final disposition is God's, and directs himself toward it, will not reach except that which God had predetermined for him. If, therefore, it has been predetermined for a man to fall on the battlefield of truth and goodness that God commanded us to realize, such man has no reason to fear. He and the like of him live with their Lord and enjoy His bounty. What philosophy of progress, advancement and self-exertion, and freedom of the will compares with this philosophy of Islām? Where in it is the lethargic reliance upon fate which Irving and his fellow Orientalists claim?

Tawākul, or lethargic reliance upon God, has nothing to do with *tawakkul*, or trust in God. Trust in God does not consist in man's lethargic immobility and lack of response to the commandment of his Lord but in the serious and active pursuit of that commandment. That is why God says, "And if you have resolved on a certain course, then put your trust (*tawakkul*) in God."[6] Resolution and will, therefore, must precede *tawakkul* or trust in God. Indeed, when a man does resolve to put his trust in God, he will surely reach his objective by God's grace. We may even say that if man seeks God's sake alone, if he fears Him alone, and if he follows His path alone, he will reach the good by reason of God's necessary pattern in the cosmos. This divine pattern, it must be remembered, is immutable and necessary. In his pursuit of the good, therefore, man must reach his objective since that is the pattern of God in the cosmos regardless of whether he survives his pursuit or perishes in the process. The good thus achieved by man is from God. The bad that he achieves is his own work, earned by following a path other than God's. The good is all in God's hands; evil and misguidance are both the inspiration of the devil and his handwork.

As for God's knowledge of all that happened in the world before its creation, the fact is that "Nothing, not even an atom in heaven and earth, or even anything smaller than that or bigger, escapes God's knowledge and attention. Everything is clearly laid out on the divine tablet."[7] This statement simply means that God has provided for creation immutable patterns necessarily followed by everything which is or happens therein. And if, as we said earlier, scientists claim that positive science can predict the future of every individual and every nation with certainty if the secrets and laws of human life be known, just as it is possible to predict the eclipse of the sun or the moon, we should also admit that faith in God demands that we stand ever certain of His knowledge of everything before creation. An engineer who lays down a plan for a house or a palace and observes this plan in the erection of the building, knows how long the building will stand and what its various parts may suffer from exposure to the elements.

Likewise, economists claim that their knowledge of economic laws enables them to predict with certainty any future prosperity or crisis in the economic life of the world. Once such an assertion is granted, then there is all the more reason to say that God does indeed know everything big or small in this world and that to deny divine knowledge is unacceptable sophistry. Such knowledge of God, however, does not and need not prevent men from planning their own course of action, from exerting themselves in the pursuit of truth and goodness, or from seeking to avoid misguidance. The knowledge of God is not open to man. But man will reach and know the truth at the end, however distant that end may seem today. God has taken upon Himself to show mercy. He accepts the repentence of His servants and is very forgiving. Since God's mercy envelops everything, man should not despair of receiving guidance to the truth and to the good as long as he constantly studies the universe and seeks to discover its laws. No man may despair of God's mercy, since his study of the cosmos will, in the final analysis, guide him to the path of God. But woe to him who denies his humanity, who is too proud to study the universe, and who fails to seek God's guidance! Such a man offends God and does not seek His face! Such a man has his heart and mind sealed! To him belongs hellfire and evil destiny!

Will then the western Orientalists see the loftiness of Islāmic determinism and the wide scope it leaves open for human freedom of action? Will they realize the falsity of their claim that Islāmic determinism demands self-immobilization, acceptance of humiliation, and satisfaction with submission to any but God? Certainly, Islāmic determinism leaves the gate wide open for hope in God's mercy and forgiveness to anyone who repents and changes for better. What then becomes of their claim that Islāmic determinism demands of the Muslim to regard whatever evil befalls him as an inscrutable divine decree that he must suffer in patience, however damaging or humiliating it may be? Such a claim stands at the farthest possible remove from Islāmic determinism, which calls upon man always to exert himself in the pursuit of God's pleasure and to trust in God only after he has resolved upon a course of action. If man does not achieve the good today, he is commanded to keep on striving that he may achieve it on the morrow. He should fix his hope upon God that He may guide his path, accept his repentance, and forgive him. In this hope, man has the best impulsion to continue his search, his exertion and his pursuit, and will hence come nearer to realizing the utmost level of God's pleasure, the God Whom he worships, Whose help he asks for, and Who is the source of all guidance and unto Whom everything shall return.

The strength of thought which these noble teachings provide is tremendous, and the wide horizons they lay open before them are breathtaking. They regard man as sure to reach the good if, in his action, he seeks nothing but the face of God; and in case man is led astray by the devil, his repentance is acceptable to God as long as his reason and judgment overwhelm his passion and return him to the straight path. The straight path is itself the pattern of God in creation, a pattern discoverable by reason and heart through investigation of God's creation and constant self-exertion in the search for nature's laws. If, despite all this assurance, some men continue not to recognize God, to spread corruption on earth, and to remain blind to the values of brotherhood and immune to their moving appeal, they will sooner or later come to tragedy. Their fate, however, would only constitute God's didactic example to the rest of mankind. That is the justice of God and His mercy to all, which are not affected by the erring of the misguided few who finally receive that which their misdeeds had earned for them.

But, it may be asked: Since every man's hour is written already, why do men act when they know that death is lying in wait for them, that when their term comes, their fate will be fulfilled on the hour? Why do men think and search, exert themselves and work when some are predetermined to happiness and felicity and others to suffering and misery? This is a repetition of the question which we have just answered. We are repeating it deliberately in order to raise another issue, namely that of man's last hour. That which God predetermined as man's last hour was indeed part of the pattern of the cosmos before there was even a cosmos, before God created the world by commanding it to be. This point is evidenced in the divine statement, "God has taken upon Himself to show mercy."[8] This statement means that mercy is an attribute of God and hence part of the cosmic pattern, not an exertion of His will. God says that "We shall impose no punishment until We have sent a prophet."[9] If, therefore, a people have gone astray without God having sent them a prophet, the divine pattern prescribes that none of them shall suffer any punishment. God's knowledge of the effect of His pattern in the cosmos is evident to anyone who believes that God is the Creator of the cosmos. But if God does send a prophet to a certain people, and the cosmic pattern and God's will prescribe that some of them persist in going astray despite the call to wisdom and guidance, their evil is upon themselves and their suffering will be an example for the rest.

Misguidance Is Injustice to Oneself

It may not be claimed that those who persist in their misguidance have been punished or have suffered an injustice because their misguidance was predetermined for them. Such an assertion would be naive, not deceptive, because the least amount of reasoning leads to the conclusion that whoever goes astray does indeed do injustice to himself. To clarify this argument, it is sufficient for us to consider the example of the compassionate father of a child standing close to a fire. If the child seeks to touch the fire, the father moves him away from it, explaining that it would burn him otherwise. But if he brings his child close to the fire again, the father would do so under the assumption that his child's fingers being burnt will give him a direct sensation of fire, a realization which will persist in his memory throughout his life. Once the child becomes an adult and touches the fire, or throws himself into it, he surely deserves the burns thus inflicted. His father is not to blame, and no one would expect the father to stand between his grown son and the fire in order to stop such a happening. A similar case is that of the father who explains to his son the evils of alcohol and of gambling. If, after attaining maturity, the child violates the commandment of his father and suffers for it, his father may not be declared unjust toward him, even though it may have been within his capability to prevent his son by force from drinking or gambling. Indeed, it would even be the duty of his father not to interfere and prevent such violation if the son's violation provides a moral and example to his brethren and relatives. If one considers as relatives and brethren the hundreds and thousands who inhabit the cities where temptations necessarily abound, it is good and just that some violators do suffer the consequences of their deeds so that the moral health of the community may be preserved, however regretful their personal suffering may be to the community. This example is an elementary case of justice as we apprehend it in our human community. How stronger should it be when we consider the universe as a whole, the millions upon millions of creatures in infinite space and time! Whatever punishment may fall upon any individual or people as the result of their injustice is indeed just in the purview of that vast cosmic picture which our imagination can hardly represent.

Our Personal Ethical Ideals

If we impute injustice to a father who leaves his erring son to meet the consequences which have been predetermined for his misconduct, we should impute injustice to ourselves when we kill the flea in fear of its sting or in fear of contagion with the disease which it may carry and which may be calamitous to us as well as to the community in which we live. Following that reasoning, we should not be surprised if injustice is imputed to ourselves when we break up and dissolve the stones in our liver or kidney in fear of the pain or discomfort which such stones bring, or when we cut off a member or organ of our body in fear of its disease spreading to the rest of the body and bringing about its death. If we do not kill the flea, break up the stone, or cut off the member or organ, and, in consequence, we suffer pain, contagion, calamity, or death, we blame only ourselves on the grounds that the road to cure was wide open.

But so is the road of repentence for the guilty. It is only the ignorant who submit to pain and misery in the belief that it has been predetermined for them. This kind of submission is nothing short of stupidity and naïveté on their part. But we do kill the flea, break and remove the stone, and cut off the sick organ and yet consider all this perfect justice when it is predetermined in the matter of the cosmos that the flea shall sting and thus carry contagion to man, that the stone shall disturb the organ and cause it to malfunction, that the sick organ shall communicate its sickness to the whole body and thus bring about death. How do we who make such judgments feel so certain of their validity and truth, and yet fail to recognize the implied limitation of justice to our own person and its non-extension to the human community as a whole? Indeed, how do we choose to ignore the cosmos as a whole, as it really is? To do so is an unjustified piece of idiocy and stupidity, a case of extreme narrowmindedness and low intelligence.

Good Works Are Acts of Worship

And what is the flea, the stone, or man himself when compared to the large universe? Indeed, what is humanity itself in this regard? The universe is so great that our mind, incapable of imagining it, turns to such concepts as eternity, infinity, and the like in order to give us an incomplete picture of it, a picture as incomplete as our knowledge is little. Our knowledge is indeed limited, but despite its limitation, it is still great enough to guide us to the divine pattern in the universe, and to understand that divine pattern as orderly, immutable, and determined. God has given us faculties of knowledge, hearing, sight, and a heart that we may learn with them the creative work of His own hand and the patterns He has imbedded in the cosmos. Such knowledge is prerequisite to religious feeling and thinking. We must know God and know His work if we are to praise Him, to thank Him, and to do the good which He commands. To do the good in conviction or *īmān* is the noblest form of worship that any rational creature can offer to God.

Death, Conclusion, and Beginning of Life

As for death, it is the end of one life and the beginning of another. Consequently, it is feared only by those who deny the other life or fear it on account of their ill conduct in this life. Such men never wish for death because they know what awaits them. Those who wish for death sincerely and fearlessly are the true believers, the truly convinced, and the doers of good deeds in the world.

God—May He be adored—says:

$$\text{الَّذِى خَلَقَ الْمَوْتَ وَالْحَيٰوةَ لِيَبْلُوَكُمْ اَيُّكُمْ اَحْسَنُ عَمَلًا ۚ وَهُوَ الْعَزِيْزُ الْغَفُوْرُ ۙ}$$

"He who created death as well as life that you may prove who of you is the better in deed is the Almighty and the Merciful."[10]

Further, addressing His Prophet, He said—May He be praised—: "No human has ever been granted everlasting life. If you will certainly die, will they not? Every man shall taste of death, and the evil and good which befall you are a trial for you. To earth will be your return."[11] Further, He says: "Those unto whom the Torah has been revealed but who have not observed its commandments are like a donkey carrying a load of books. Wretched are the people who deny the revelations of God. God does not guide the unjust in their injustice. Say, 'O Jews, if, as you pretend, you are the friends of God and His elect of all mankind, wish for death that you may prove your sincerity.' But they never wish for death, for rejoining their Lord; and that is because they know that their arms have wrought evil and injustice. God knows the unjust."[12] God also says, "It is He who terminates your life by night, Who knows every violation you have committed by day, Who will resurrect you after a prescribed term, return you to Himself, and confront you with all the deeds that you have wrought on earth."[13]

These verses are extremely emphatic in their rejection of the Orientalists' claim that Islāmic determinism implies immobolization and unconcern for work and acquisition. God created life and death that men may prove who among them is the better worker of deeds. The theater of human achievement is this life; reward and punishment come after death. If men do not work, if they do not strike out into the earth and seek therein God's bounty, if they do not earn and hence do not give in charity of that which God has provided for them, nor perform any good to others, however little their means may be, they have disobeyed God. It is no excuse for them that they have nothing to give, for their duty is to go out and earn. Failure to perform one duty constitutes no justification of their failure to perform another. On the contrary, those who earn and give are the more righteous in God's sight and the more deserving of rewards in the other world. Through good and evil works God gives us the chance to prove ourselves. Upon us devolves the duty of rationally distinguishing between them. Not an atom's weight of good nor an atom's weight of evil done in this world will be lost on the Day of Judgment. If nothing befalls us except what has been predetermined by God, we should concern ourselves all the more to discern the good that we may realize it in the world. It makes no difference whatever whether God chooses to terminate our lives at the prime of youth, vitality, wisdom, and glory, or at old age when we become senile and lapse into childish ignorance. The measure of a life is certainly not the number of years one lives, but the good works which one does that nothing can obliterate. Those who die in the cause of God are alive with their Lord, and they are alive among us inasmuch as we continue to remember them. Many are the men who have written their names indelibly on history because they dedicated themselves to the good. Among us, surely, they are still alive, even though they may have died hundreds of years ago.

"And when their term arrives, men shall meet their death at its prescribed hour, neither before nor after."[14] This, indeed, is the truth. It alone accords with the pattern of the universe. Man has an hour which he cannot outlive, just as the sun and the moon have their terms and their eclipse always occurs according to law, without fail. It is more likely that man's awareness that his life will terminate will incite him to hasten the performance of good deeds and to exert all possible effort. Moreover, the fact that man does not know when his hour will strike will stir his anxiety enough to prepare for that eventuality. Everyday we witness new evidence that man's hour is determined and, when it strikes, inevitable. Some people die suddenly without apparent reason; others fall sick and fight for their lives for decades until they reach a decrepit old age. A number of medical men today claim that the agent which brings about man's death is innate to him and that the period this agent requires to achieve its objective would not be impossible to calculate if the agent itself could be isolated and identified—a problem of no little difficulty—though not impossible. God, who is omniscient, knows the hour of every man by reason of the immutable and eternal pattern he has imbedded in the cosmos as a whole.

Prophets Are Always Folkmen

It is the method of His mercy—May He be adored—that He will inflict no punishment until He has sent a prophet to guide men to the truth and to show them the path to the good. If God were to punish men for the injustices they commit, immediately upon their commission of them, no creature would be left alive on earth. But He defers judgment to a future but definite term in order to give them a chance to listen to the prophet, to follow his guidance, and to resist the appeal of lowly life. The prophets whom God has sent were neither royal nor wealthy. They belonged neither to the rank of the great and glorious nor to that of the men of science. Rather He has chosen His prophets from among the populace. Ibrahīm was a carpenter, and so was his father. Jesus was a carpenter in Nazareth. Many others were shepherds, and so was the Seal and last of them, Muḥammad—May God's peace and blessing be upon him. God chooses His prophets from among the populace in order to teach that the truth is not the exclusive monopoly of the rich or the strong but is available to whosoever seeks it for its own sake and for its own sake alone. The eternal truth is that man does not fulfill his *īmān* until he has desired for his fellow man that which he has loved for himself, and has acted and lived in accordance with the principle. "The worthier among you in the sight of God is the more pious, the more virtuous. . . . Work and realize the good, for God will reckon your achievement" and you will be given exactly what you have earned.[15] The great truth is that God is, and that there is no God but He.

Death is the terminus of one life and the commencement of another. It is the terminus of this life and the beginning of the life beyond. We know but little about this life, namely, that which is accessible to our senses, that to which our reason leads us, and that which our intuitive faculties enable us to behold. As for the life beyond, we do not know anything about it except what God has revealed to us. Of the patterns of the cosmos, many are not given to us that are known to the Omniscient, the Great and Glorious God Who sees all. Sufficient unto us therefore is what God related in His Holy Book concerning the life beyond. He told us that it is the House of Judgment, of Reward and Punishment. Let us then prepare ourselves in this life by our deeds and our resolution to take our affairs into our own hands. Let us put our trust in God and await His just reward. What lies beyond these considerations belongs to God alone.

After all this, will Washintgon Irving, and the Orientalists and non-Orientalists who follow in his footsteps, realize how deeply erroneous is their understanding of the determinism of Islām? Our foregoing discussion has been limited to what the Holy Qur'ān has said on the matter. That is precisely because we do not wish to open a controversy by bringing in the opinions of the Ṣūfīs, the *mutakallimūn*, the philosophers, and other Muslim schools. Irving is in deep error when he claims that divine judgment, providence, and man's final hour were all given in those Qur'ānic passages that were revealed after the Battle of Uḥud and the martyrdom of Ḥamzah. Actually, many of the

verses that we have quoted in this discussion are Makkan and
were revealed before the Hijrah and before any battles were
fought by the Muslims. As a matter of fact, Irving and his
like fall into error because they fail to give adequate scientific
consideration to such an important and grave problem as determinism. They understand Islām under categories which accord
with their Christian or Western inclinations and prejudices, and
then they construct a patchwork of so-called evidence to prove
their prejudice, thinking that they can really convince their
readers and hoping that no one will take to task their argument
and analyze their reasoning.

The Philosophic Value of Islāmic Determinism

Had the Orientalists understood Islāmic determinism in the
manner we have described, they would have appreciated its
philosophic worth and profound value. For Islāmic determinism
regards life in a manner coherent with the most advanced,
precise, philosophical, and scientific theories which human thought
has achieved in its long and progressive history. The Islāmic
philosophic idea is synthetic. It does not exclude scientific determinism, nor does it deny the world as will and idea or the
doctrine of emergent evolution.[16] Rather, Islāmic determinism
includes all these views within its system as aspects of the
pattern of the cosmos and life. This is not the place to elaborate
this point in detail. Nonetheless, we shall try to state it as
succinctly and as clearly as possible, hoping that the reader will
agree that the greatness, comprehensiveness, and depth of this
idea is comparable with any other theory known or discovered
until now, and that it leaves the door wide open for any great
advance human thought may achieve in the future.

Before we begin our brief statement, two observations are in
order and should not be forgotten. First, it is not the intention
of this author to contradict any Christian theory. The revelation
of Jesus has been confirmed by Islām, as we have had many
occasions to see in the course of this work. Islām sought to
synthesize the prophecies and divine messages which had gone
before and to provide for them a climax and a crowning. As
the Gospel substantiates Jesus Christ's claim to his disciples,
"Think not that I am come to destroy the law . . . I am not come
to destroy but to fulfill,"[17] just so the Qur'ān confirmed the
Muslim's *imān* in Ibrahīm, Moses, Jesus, and all the preceding

prophets. Islām came as a synthesis of all the previous divine revelations, as a correction and reproof of all the tampering with scripture done by the followers of those prophets. The second point is that the philosophical theory deducible from the Qur'ān has been discovered by others before but in a different way than that which I am following in these pages. I have reached it in the way I have because I have opened myself to the guidance of the Qur'ān and followed a modern scientific method. If God has guided me to the truth, to Him belongs the praise and the gratitude. And if I have missed the truth in some of my reasoning, then it is all the more cause to pray for my mistakes to be corrected by men of knowledge. But that too is to praise God and to be grateful for His blessing.

The first principle the Qur'ān firmly establishes is that God has implanted in the universe immutable patterns and eternal laws. The universe does not only consist of our earth and all that is on it, nor is it limited to all that our senses can reach by way of stars and other heavenly bodies. The universe consists of all that God has created, whether sensory or non-sensory, past, present or future. If we only attempt to imagine God's creation, we will realize that our knowledge is indeed small. The space which stands between us and the stars of heaven, electricity which fills this space as well as our earth, the great vastness of space which separates us from the sun and the stars and other systems of heavenly bodies yet farther than the sun and separated from us by thousands of light years, and the infinity of space lying still beyond these which is beyond our imagination but known to God—all this runs according to changeless and immutable laws. All that we have scientifically known about creation is still very scant; in it the actual has been mixed up with the imaginary. Indeed, the real component of our so-called knowledge is little by comparison with the fictitious. However, it constitutes all that we genuinely know of the universe and serves as foundation for what we call the laws of the universe and of life, and puts a critical brake on our overhasty will to generalize. If, for a moment, we were to lift this brake, our imagination would seek to encompass the whole and the result would be the greatest flowering of science fiction. Supposing, for instance, that the inhabitants of Mars were to build a broadcasting station of a force of one hundred million kilowatts in order to bring to us, the inhabitants of the earth, details of what was taking place on their planet and show it to us by means of television. Would it then be possible for man on earth to restrain his imagination, considering that Mars is not the most distant of the planets nor the most difficult with which to have communication?

Everything in this vast universe, of which we know so little, exerts some influence on our world and everything it contains. If any one of these heavenly bodies were to change its course or structure in some measure, however little, the pattern of our universe would be equally affected by such a change, and our own short and insignificant life that is already determined by our environment would equally be affected. Naturally, our life is more deeply affected by the greater cosmic forces and changes; even so, in suffering their effects, we may achieve the good as well as its opposite. The final result is not only a function of the influences we suffer, but of our preparation for receiving such influences and our mastery of ourselves in disposing of their effects. Many an identical pattern has determined many people in different ways, propelling some to good, others to evil, with all the variant degrees between them. In this life, good and evil are the effects of a dialectical relation between the elements and factors of the cosmos and the human soul. Thus, both good and evil may be said to result from the immutable pattern of the cosmos and follow necessarily from its existence, just as the positive and the negative are necessary implications of the existence of electricity, and microbes and germs are necessary implications of human bodily life.

Nature of Good and Evil

Nothing, therefore, is evil in itself or good in itself but is so in relation to the purpose which it serves and the consequences which it brings about. What is sometimes regarded as evil may at other times be absolutely necessary, or absolutely good. Many of the devices that in war time serve to annihilate millions of humans and destroy man's greatest monuments may during peace furnish the greatest advantages. Dynamite, for instance, is absolutely necessary for the construction of tunnels, of railways, and for the discovery of mines and the realization of their priceless treasures. Even poison gas that hostile nations hurl at one another in the most shameful and calamitously irresponsible acts of war can be put to many advantageous uses during peace— such as the use of chlorine gas to purify water and to detect other harmful and dangerous gases.

Men have always been tempted to think that some insects, birds, and animals are absolutely useless. Study and research have changed these prejudices by showing the good purpose each of these species serves. Indeed, some countries have even promulgated legislation for the protection of these species in appreciation of the service they render to mankind. The zoologists have observed that animals can live in peace with their environments as long as their environments do not interfere with the discharge of their natural functions and that they do not harm other creatures except in self-defense or under alien pressures.

Ethical Nature of Human Deeds

As for us humans, our deeds are likewise neither good nor evil in themselves but have value only with reference to the purpose that they serve and the consequence that they achieve. Is not homicide a crime and hence forbidden? Nonetheless, God says, "And do not kill anyone; for God has forbidden it, unless it be a case of right, and after due process of law."[18] Killing by right, therefore, is morally unassailable. God said, "In punishment, great value—indeed a whole life—may be realized, O Men of thought!"[19] The executioner who kills the condemned convict, the man who kills another in self-defense, the soldier who kills in defending his homeland, and the believer who kills resisting those who would force him to abjure his faith, all these are guilty of neither disobedience nor crime when they commit homicide. They are fulfilling a divine duty imposed upon them by God and are deserving of righteous merit. What is true of homicide may also be true of many other deeds of men, as far as good and evil are concerned. The scientist who discovers a destructive force and the technologist who produces the instruments with which to deliver it, whether for the purpose of defending the homeland or for peacetime use, indeed every human operation on earth—none of these is good or evil in itself, but only in reference to the purpose it seeks to realize and the actual consequence it brings about.

The Gateway of Repentance

Such is the will of God and His pattern for the universe. Since God created men with different endowments and hence with varying preparation for understanding this pattern, some men exhaust all their energies usufructing and exploiting the very spot of the environment in which they are born and in which they grow. Some men are endowed with technological skills, others are endowed with faculties necessary for the professions, the arts and the sciences—all of which together are necessary if man is to be guided to the divine pattern. Since knowledge of the divine pattern is absolutely necessary for man if he is to lead a life of righteousness, God has granted to some individuals the gift of prophethood. He has selected some to convey His message to men, to show them the good and the evil. To others, he has granted the faculties with which to pursue science and logic that they may, as heirs to the Prophet, guide mankind to what it ought to do and not to do. Moreover, God has endowed every man with the necessary intellectual and emotional faculties for understanding and grasping the teachings thus offered, for disciplining himself in truth and wisdom and fulfilling in life God's imperative: in short, for doing good and avoiding evil. If, all this notwithstanding, some men fail to understand and commit evil, and if the community punishes them for their misdeeds in order to safeguard itself against their harm, this need not hinder their repentence and return to the straight path. Whoever commits a misdeed in ignorance or weakness, corrects himself, changes his orientation, and returns to God obedient and repentant, God will surely forgive and accept. Hence, the criminal or author of any misdeed ought to learn from the wisdom of the past in order to purify himself; he ought to use this wisdom to enable himself to be rehabilitated. God, the Merciful and Forgiving, will accept his repentance.

This presentation of the moral issue of human life has the merit of synthesizing many philosophical views hitherto deemed beyond conciliation. It clearly recognizes a purposive, efficacious will in all that is. "All being," God says, "is such that if We desire any part of it to exist, We command it to be and it will be."[20] It regards the universe as inclusive of all that is perceivable by sense as well as that which is not so perceivable and as subject to immutable natural laws that, despite the limitation of our capacities, are still discoverable by rational effort, the more so the more we exert ourselves in their study and pursuit. Moreover, it regards the universe as one whose foundation is the good. Though evil is ubiquitous and oft seems to prevail, our view regards the constant victory of good over evil as constitutive of the universe's emergent evolution, the progressive perfection the world has so far achieved through its long history.

Man's Spiritual Development

The reader will recognize that our presentation assumes human progress toward perfection, and regards it as the ideal of the highest philosophical system possible. Furthermore, the Qur'ān regards spiritual development as the central principle of God's creation of the earth and all that is in it. God created heaven and earth in six days, it asserts, and then rested on His throne. Were these six days equivalent to our days on earth? Or were they such that "One day with your Lord is like a thousand years of your reckoning?"[21] This is not the place to discuss whether such statements imply a theory of evolution, or whether the Qur'ān regards evolution as the law of the cosmos. Further, it asserts that God created Adam and Eve and asked the angels to serve them and that all angels did so except Satan who was not moved by the fact that God had told Adam all the names. God said:

> " 'O Adam, reside with your wife in the Garden. Eat of such of its fruits as you wish, but do not come near this tree and thus be guilty of injustice.' Seeking to misguide them and to make them aware of their shame, Satan told them that God had forbidden them the fruit of that tree in order to prevent them from becoming angelic or eternal. He pledged to them that he only meant to give them good counsel. Thus, by deception he caused them to transgress. After they tasted of the fruit of the tree, their shame became manifest and they covered themselves with leaves. Their Lord called out to them: 'Have I not forbidden you the fruit of this tree and warned you of Satan's grave hostility to you?' They answered, 'O God, we have transgressed and thereby wronged ourselves. If You do not have mercy on us and forgive us, surely our fate will be that of the lost.' God said, 'Go forth! Some of you will henceforth be enemies of the others. On earth, you will have but a temporary abode. Therein you will spend your lives: you will die and will be raised again.' O, Men, We have provided for you clothes and raiment with which to cover your bodies. But the raiment of piety and good deeds is far superior. This is another sign and evidence from your Lord that you might remember and observe. O Men, let not Satan deceive you anymore, as he succeeded in forcing

your ancestors out of the Garden by seeking to show them their shame. Satan and his legion keep a constant eye upon you. You have no awareness of them. Their nature is to be the friends and guides of those who have no faith and no conviction."[22]

Adam and Eve departed from the Garden, and their progeny became hostile to one another. They strove and still strive the length of their lives. The powers and faculties with which God had endowed them help them in their effort, but they shall continue to struggle on earth until God's purpose is fulfilled.

Cruelty and prejudice, strife and competition characterize the first attempts of human life on earth. God said:

"And relate to them the true story of the two sons of Adam. Each one of them made an offering to God but only one was accepted. The son whose offering was not accepted said to the other, 'I shall kill you.' The other answered, 'God accepts the offering only of those who are righteous. Should you attack and kill me, I shall not attack you because I fear God, the Lord of the Universe. If you do what you say, yours will be a double guilt—that of being unrighteous in the first place and that of killing me in the second. You will surely then deserve the right punishment as all other unjust men, namely the fire.' Induced by his passion, the son of Adam killed his brother and reaped the fate of the lost. God then sent a raven which scratched into the ground, thereby showing him how to bury the corpse of his brother. As he interred his brother, remorse gripped him and he repented for what he had done, realizing that he was not even as worthy as the raven who had just taught him how to dispose of the dead. On this account We have prescribed, as We did for the Children of Israel, that whoever kills a man for a purpose other than self-defense or legitimate punishment for misdoing is as guilty as he who kills the whole of mankind; and, likewise, that whoever saves a life has saved the lives of all mankind. Repeatedly have Our messengers come to men with clear evidence of this, but many of them still perpetrate their injustice in the world."[23]

Jealousy, cruelty, resentment, and hostility are all amply evident in the story of this fratricide. The righteous victim, on the other hand, did not respond with forgiveness and pardon when his brother threatened to kill him. Rather, his response was that he wished to have him carry the double burden of his own misdeeds and of the murder he was contemplating and thus earn the punishment of hell. Undoubtedly, the man spoke in concert with human nature and its overwhelming inclination to seek to punish evil rather than magnanimously to forgive it.

The children of Adam multiplied and spread over the earth. God sent them prophets to remind and warn them of Him. But they persisted in going astray; their spiritual life was dead, and their minds utterly blocked to the truth. God sent Noah to call his people to the worship of the One God, and he warned them saying: "I fear for you the punishment of a painful death." But his people paid him little heed. Following Noah, many prophets came and many divine messages were conveyed, all calling to the worship of God alone. Gradually stagnation became the rule, and men's minds became utterly closed to the divine call. Indeed, they took the creatures of the world for Gods; and whenever a prophet was sent to them by their Lord, they either belied or killed him. Nonetheless, the stagnation of men was repeatedly shaken by prophets, sent from God, who planted good seeds. Although these were slow to grow, they were not without significant effects; for, is truth ever wholly lost? If men happen to be so vain as to avoid the message of truth or to ridicule its conveyor, they will still ponder that message when they are alone and consider what it says. At any rate, those who have apprehended the divine messages have always been few, and these few have often been guilty of false pride.

In ancient Egypt, the priesthood knew and believed the monotheistic truth, but they taught the people something else and multiplied for them their gods. They regarded this practice as necessary for safeguarding their authority and glory. So attached were they to their own powers that they opposed Moses and his brother Aaron's calling them to God and their seeking Pharaoh's permission for the Children of Israel to follow them. Further, the Qur'ān relates the stories of the prophets who followed one another across the centuries while the great majorities of their people persisted in their misguidance. In the Qur'ānic accounts of the prophets of the past, one significant point ought to be underlined. First, however, we must recall the history of Moses and Jesus and the subsequent history of Muḥammad—May God's blessing be upon him.

The Judgment of Reason and Belief in Miracles

The point to be noted is the separation of, or what seems to be the discrepancy between, reason and its logique on one hand, and faith built upon acceptance of miracles and extraordinary events on the other. God confirmed every one of His prophets with some miracle in order to enable him to win the confidence of his people. However, only a few men believed in their prophets or took them seriously. Men's minds were still too undeveloped to understand that God is the Creator of everything, that He is One, that He is the just Lord of the universe, and that there is no God but He. Before God chose to send Moses, the latter had run away from Egypt in fear and found security in the desert with the tribe of Midyan into which he also married. Before God permitted him to return, "He was called from the right side of the valley, from the blessed spot, out of the tree: 'O Moses, verily, I am God, Lord of the universe.' Moses was told to lay down his staff; but when he saw it move as if it were a serpent, he ran away without turning back. Again he was called to approach. He was ordered to search inside his garment, to shed away his fear, and compose himself. God then said to him: 'This is the judgment of your Lord which you will convey to Pharaoh and his government; namely, they have become a truly corrupt people.' "[24]

Pharaoh's magician priests did not respond favorably to Moses' call until his rod devoured all their rods. Only then did they prostrate themselves and declare their faith in God, the Lord of Aaron, and of Moses. Nonetheless, the Children of Israel persisted in their misguidance. Indeed, they even asked Moses to show them God with their own eyes; and as soon as he passed away, they returned to the worship of the calf. Following Moses, their prophets came to call them to God, but they killed them unjustly. When they did return to the worship of God, they expected a Messiah who would return to them a political kingdom and the material power with which to rule the world. This series of events is not so far removed from us that it remains lost in the darkness of early history. Barely twenty-five centuries old, this event clearly shows man's preference of selfishness over reason and his desire for material things over the things of spirit.

A few centuries later, Jesus, confirmed by God's holy spirit, came calling men to God. Since Jesus was a Jew, the Jews first thought of him as their Messiah and expected him to return to the Jews their lost kingdom in the promised land. The hardships they suffered under Roman rule had made them all the more anxious to achieve such a political kingdom. They waited, however, in order to find out more precisely what Jesus was about. Did Jesus appeal to the logic of reason alone? No. Rather, it was a miracle that opened the road to his persuasion of them. If the Christian stories are not mistaken, it was the miracle of transforming the water into wine at the wedding of Cana that first drew public attention to Jesus. Thereafter came the miracles of the loaves of bread and fishes, of curing the sick, and of resurrecting the dead that made it possible for him to teach the public by appealing to their hearts, feelings, and emotions. Reason and its logic played a very minor role in his teaching. Nonetheless, Jesus proved more successful than his predecessors. He had combined his appeal to feeling, mercy, forgiveness, and love with a call to God, devoid of critical evidence and rational proof. Whenever people suspected his cause, God permitted him to perform a new miracle and thus regain their loyalty and appreciation. His miracles included the curing of the leper, giving sight to the blind and raising the dead. They produced such a strong appeal among his followers that some of them thought that he was the Son of God, and others that he was God incarnate coming to expiate the sins of men. This evidence clearly shows that men were not mature enough to comprehend by force of reason alone the supreme truth regarding the Creator—May He be adored—namely, that He is One, Eternal, Unbegotten and Unbegetting, and that nothing is like unto Him.

The Rational Sciences

Long before the times of Moses and Jesus, the science of ancient Egypt as well as its philosophy and law had passed to Greece and Rome, which had then spread their dominion. It was Egypt that contributed to Greek philosophy and literature their noblest ideas. The new rationalist awakening thus produced, warned and convinced the people that miracles constitute no argument at all. It was in consequence of this that Greek philosophy contributed to the multiplication of Christian doctrines and hence to sectarianism diversification in Egypt, Palestine and al Shām, as we had occasion to see earlier. But it was God's pattern that reason shall constitute the apogee of human life, as long as it is not composed of empty logic, not devoid of feeling and spirit, and as long as it martials all these faculties in a synthesized effort to discover the secrets of the universe and achieve intimate knowledge of the cosmic pattern. Thus, it was decreed by God that soon the Prophet of Islām would rise to call men to the truth through reason, complemented by feeling and spirit, and that the one miracle of such a gnoseological synthesis should be the Holy Book revealed to His Prophet Muhammad. With Muhammad's revelation and teaching, God completed for men their religion and granted them His blessings. With it, He climaxed all prophethood, concluded all revelation, and sealed it. But all this took place only after the prophets' great and continuous effort and the messengers' guiding of mankind in its spiritual deportment until it could reach the height of the Islāmic call to faith and conviction in one God alone.

To complement and buttress this new conviction in the Divine "Unicity," the duties discussed in the first part of this conclusion were instituted. All were designed to enable the believer to reach this pinnacle of vision. It is also man's duty always to strive after a vision of God's pattern in creation. That is what the Muslims strove to do in the early centuries of their history until they began to decline.

The arguments so far adduced refute the western Orientalists' interpretation of Islāmic determinism and the Qur'ānic position on fate and the last hour. They prove without a shadow of doubt that Islām is a religion of striving and activism in all the theaters of life—the spiritual, the scientific, the religious, and the worldly. They prove that God's immutable pattern in the cosmos is that man will get what his own deeds have earned for him and that God—May He be adored—will commit no injustice to anyone. Rather, it is men who commit injustice to themselves. Indeed, men do injustice to themselves when they think that they can achieve God's blessing through stagnation and inactivity, through *tawākul* or lazy dependence, disguised as *tawakkul* or trust in God.

Material Wealth and Children

Although these arguments have proved this point without a doubt, I am unable to overlook one other argument that I consider extremely important. It is the argument implied in the divine statement:

اَلْمَالُ وَالْبَنُونَ زِينَةُ الْحَيوةِ الدُّنْيَا وَالْبَقِيتُ الصّٰلِحٰتُ خَيْرٌ عِنْدَ رَبِّكَ ثَوَابًا وَخَيْرٌ أَمَلًا ۞

"Wealth and children are the ornaments and joy of this life; but the good deeds, imperishable as they are, weigh more with your Lord. They are indeed better, and provide a sound basis for greater hopes."[25]

Nothing in the world incites us to greater exertion, striving, and work than the acquisition of wealth. In its pursuit, most men spend the greatest part of their energies. Indeed, they often outdo themselves. One look at our modern world is sufficient to perceive the strenuous persistence, the hardships, the wars, the revolutions, and the disturbances that occur all for the sake of wealth. For its sake monarchies become republics, blood is shed, and men lay down their lives. So much for wealth. As for children, they are pieces of our flesh groping the earth in front of us! What hardship will we not gladly bear for their sake! What bitterness will not taste sweet as long as it leads to their security, health and happiness! Every hardship we encounter on the road to their happiness becomes easy; every conflict becomes harmony. And there are men who for the sake of wealth and children would do that which would otherwise be impossible. Indeed, some people are so committed to such a pursuit that they would sacrifice their own happiness and even their lives.

Wealth and children, therefore, do constitute "the joy and ornament" of this world. An ornament is nothing, however, by comparison to the essence. No one would sacrifice the essence for the sake of an ornament except the ignorant and the insane, vain women and deluded youths. Vain women would expose their health to danger that they might appear beautiful for a few hours or less; and deluded youths would squander their wealth that their companions may applaud and acclaim them as masters. Such people are no less mad than those who pursue wealth and children, the ornaments and joy of this life, at the cost of everything else. To repeat, wealth and children do constitute a joy and an ornament. But the essence of life is the doing of righteous deeds which are imperishable. It is for the sake of this imperishable righteousness that we ought to devote the greater part of our effort and striving.

The nobility of purpose served by the last quoted verse of Holy Scripture is truly arresting. What it purports to say is

that if it is natural that man spend his effort and blood for
the sake of an ornament, he should spend his whole soul and
mind for the sake of the essence; that he should make the
ornament subject to the essence and, finally, that he should
dedicate his own life, his wealth, and his children to the pursuit
of this essence which consists of righteous deeds. For the latter
weigh more with God. Righteousness is the worthier ideal. Its
merit is greater and its promise is nobler. It is the higher hope
of mankind.

How did the thinking of Muslims change so radically from
this sane, healthy, and clear logic to the very opposite? We
referred to this question accidentally in the first part of this
conclusion when we discussed the change that the Muslims under-
went as result of being conquered by foreigners at the close of
the 'Abbāsī regime.

Shaykh Muḥammad 'Abduh's Views

In the preface to the second edition we also mentioned how
the government changed from being based upon consultation
in the earliest period to a sheer contest of power during the
Umawī period, and finally to rule by divine right during the
'Abbāsī period. On this point, let us quote the late professor
and leader, Shaykh Muḥammad 'Abduh, who wrote in his book,
Al Islām al Nasrāniyyah, the following passage:

"The religion of Islām was once purely Arab. Science was
once Greek and then became Arab too. Subsequently, one of
the 'Abbāsī caliphs committed a political mistake when he
abused the tolerance of Islāmic political theory. Suspecting
that an army composed largely of Arabs might readily lend
its support to a caliphal contender supporting the cause
of 'Alī, he sought to build for himself an army of aliens,
particularly of Turks and Daylams, whom he thought he
could rule by his authority, win with his largesse, and
keep loyal to him against all his enemies. Islāmic law is
tolerant enough to allow the Muslim ruler to take such
measures, and it was on this account that Muslim society
fell under dominion of foreign elements.

"Thus, an 'Abbāsī caliph sought to secure himself on the
caliphal throne and secure that throne for his progeny. He
may have done well for himself and his children, but woe

to him for what he did to his people and his religion. He increased the number of aliens in his army and appointed aliens to command it. But no sooner had he done so than these soldiers and their captains seized the upperhand, monopolized the political power, and subjected caliph, people, and state to their whims. These were still brutes not yet disciplined by Islām. Their hearts had not yet been sensitized to religious value. Rather, these frontiersmen came to the world of Islām with crudeness, ignorance, and injustice. Islām was for them a cover; little of it penetrated their consciousness, and only the superficial aspects of it influenced their thinking. Many of them even carried their own gods around with them but prayed with the Muslim masses in order to consolidate their power over them. Later, the world of Islām fell prey to the Tatars who held it in subjection for generations and who saw no other impediment to their sovereignty and power than knowledge which would make the people aware of the state of their masters and expose the immorality of their conduct. As a result, they became openly hostile to knowledge and to Islām itself, which promotes knowledge and requires its cultivation as an act of worship. As for knowledge, science, and wisdom, their cultivators were maltreated and most of them denied any assistance or subsidy. They encouraged their own protagonists to introduce themselves into the ranks of the men of knowledge, to wear their gowns, and pretend to belong to their circles. From this position, these protagonists began to teach in the name of religion such doctrines as would make knowledge hateful to the people and cause men to avoid striving for it. Their propaganda posed as piety, for they claimed that their new doctrines were designed but to safeguard the religion. They claimed that the religion was incomplete and they had set out to complete it; that it was diseased and they had set out to cure it; that it was floundering and they had set out to consolidate it; that it was about to collapse, and they had set out to rescue and support it.

"These newcomers to Islāmic leadership wished to imitate some of the pageantry of pagans and Christians, and, therefore, they adopted some of their customs which were inconsistent with Islām. They convinced the ignorant masses that the new practices added glory and aggrandizement to the ritual of Islām. Demagogery is the resort of the unjust ruler. By recoursing to it, they instituted the celebrations with which we have been plagued. By prescribing the worship of saints and of their own leaders they divided the Muslim community, thus enabling it to fall into complacency and ignorance. They decided that the later generations may never question anything passed down by the former, and they defended this conservatism as a principle of faith precisely in order to freeze man's thinking and to stop deliberation. Throughout the provinces of the Islāmic world, they sent their mouthpieces and instructed them to teach such tales, stories, and reports as would convince the masses that public affairs were none of their concern, that all community and state affairs are the jurisdiction of the ruler alone, and that whoever interferes in the ruler's jurisdiction has overstepped the boundaries laid down by the religion. These mouthpieces also taught the masses that corruption, insecurity, hardship, and privation are not the responsibility of the rulers but the fulfillment of prophecies regarding the end of time; that it is futile to seel to change any state, any situation or verdict; that it is salutory to relinquish all responsibilities to God and the rulers, and that the Muslim is responsible only for the upkeep of himself and his immediate family. They found support for their claims in the letter of some prophetic, many spurious and fabricated, traditions which they were quick to exploit for their own purpose, interpreting them only in order to indoctrinate the people with their fictions and delusions. A whole army of such false teachers spread among the Muslims, and the puppet rulers in every province helped them to spread their poison. They misinterpreted the Islāmic doctrine of divine decree so as to frustrate human will and to choke every striving for action. The peoples' ignorance of their religion, their naiveté, their inclination to the path of least resistance, and their desire to satisfy their passions persuaded the Muslims to accept those lethal superstitions and fables. As a result, the truth fell under the darkness of falsehood, and in the people's minds principles which diametrically contradicted their religion and ran counter to its precepts became the rule of the day and were accepted without hesitation.

"This policy of spreading the darkness of ignorance, injustice, and prejudice is responsible for the corruption of Islām, for mixing the Islāmic with the unIslāmic in an unholy concoction of faith and superstition. It robbed the Muslim of his will and of the hope which once prompted him to pierce the heavens. It caused him to imitate the despair of the non-Muslims. Most of what goes today under the name of Islām is not Islām at all. It may only have preserved the outer shell of the Islāmic ritual of prayer, fasting, and pilgrimage, as well as some sayings which have been, however, perverted by allegorical interpretations. All these sinister accretions and superstitions that found their way into Islām brought about the stagnation that now passes under the name of religion. Accursed be that policy and its men for what they falsely attribute to God and His religion. All that is today blameworthy among the Muslims is not of Islām. It is something else which falsely carries that name."[26]

Muslim Views in the Age of Decline

It was this situation, so well analyzed by Shaykh Muḥammad 'Abduh, that led to the propagation among the Muslims of contradictory principles which their authors claimed to be Islāmic and falsely attributed to the Prophet. One of these principles is the doctrine of determinism which later Muslims interpreted in a way which runs counter to the Qur'ānic spirit. In the foregoing pages, we have seen how the Qur'ān understood that doctrine. Departing from that understanding, the advocates of those specious doctrines taught the virtues of surrender and stagnation. They preached that each man's life is not the result of striving and planning but is predetermined so that man cannot affect its outcome. Such is the false determinism which enables the western critics of Islām to impute to Islām that of which it is innocent. Another such principle is the contempt of matter and condemnation of its pursuit. This was the view of the Greek stoics which spread at certain periods among some Muslims despite its contradiction to the whole tenor of the Qur'ānic message expressed in the command, "And do not forget to pursue your share of this world."[27]

Despite its contradiction of the Qur'ān, this principle even produced a large body of literature in the 'Abbāsī period and thereafter. The Qur'ān in fact calls for the reasonable satisfaction of all wants. It does not tolerate self-deprivation any more than it tolerates indulgence and license. And yet, Irving falsely supposes that Islām engulfed the Muslims in luxury, distracted them from self-exertion in war and, indeed, brought the Muslim peoples to the state of decline in which they find themselves today.

Islām and Christianity: A Comparison

The American author contends that Christianity calls men to purity and charity and that it is, on this account, the opposite of what he thinks Islām is. This is not the place to compare Islām and Christianity on this point, because, fundamentally, the two religions are in agreement. Comparison in this manner would lead to futile controversy and to a profitless competition between Christianity and Islām. However, I do wish to observe that between Jesus—May God's blessing be upon him—and Christianity, as far as this call to stoicism and asceticism is concerned, there is a clear difference. Jesus was certainly no stoic. His first miracle was the transformation of the water into wine at Cana where he was a guest. Obviously, Jesus had not wished that the people go without drinking wine. Neither did he turn down the invitation of the Pharisees to sit at their lavish banquet, for he did not wish the people to deprive themselves from enjoying the blessings of God. Likewise, Muhammad emphasized the need for pursuing one's share of this world. On the other hand, it is true that Jesus used to call the rich to give charitably to the poor and to love the latter in good heart. In this, however, the Qur'ān has given voice to the greatest and most eloquent expression ever known to man. The reader may recall that we have quoted from the Qur'ān in connection with the zakāt and sadaqāt which we discussed earlier. Sufficient for us in reply to Irving and his like to say that the Qur'ān has called for charity, temperance, moderation, goodness, and love regarding everything.

"They That Take the Sword..."

There remains the last sentence of Washington Irving's statement. It is that by which the West indicts us with that which it had better indict itself, namely, the sword. The crime is indeed that of the western world, not ours. It is its stain of shame, the sinister seed which will finally destroy its false pride and civilization. Irving says: "That the crescent has waned before the cross, and exists in Europe where it was once so mighty, only by the sufferance or rather the jealously of the great Christian powers, probably ere long to furnish another illustration, that 'they that take the sword shall perish with the sword.' "

"They that take the sword shall perish with the sword." This verse of the New Testament Irving directs accusingly toward Islām in the name of Christianity. How strange! Perhaps Irving might have had some excuse had he hurled his accusation a hundred or so years ago when the imperialism of the West (as we like to call it) or of Christendom (as Irving likes to call it) had not reached the terrible degree of greed and covetousness, of conquest and aggression by the sword which it has reached today. When Field Marshall Allenby captured Jerusalem in 1918 in the name of the Allies, he made this terrible proclamation standing on the steps of the Dome of the Rock: "Today the Crusades have come to an end." Doctor Peterson Smith, in his book on the life of Jesus, wrote, "This capture of Jerusalem was indeed an eighth Crusade in which Christianity had finally achieved its purpose." And it may even be true to say that the capture of Jerusalem was not a purely Christian effort, but that it was equally the effort of the Jews, who used the Christians in order to realize the old diaspora dream of making the Land of Promise a national home for the Jews.

Islām Has Never Taken Anything by the Sword

"They that take the sword shall perish with the sword." If these words of the New Testament are true at all, and truly applied to any nation, they certainly apply today to the nations of Christian Europe more than any other. Islām did not take the sword and therefore will not be taken with the sword. Rather it is Christian Europe which has taken the sword throughout the modern period, and it is Christian Europe which gives itself utmost license in the enjoyment of pleasure and comfort which Irving falsely imputes to Islām and to the Muslims. Today, Christian Europe is playing exactly the same role which the Mongols and Tatars played in the past in relation to Islām. The latter had put on the appearance of Islām and conquered its territories without paying any heed to Islāmic teaching at all. Jesus's judgment fell rightly upon them as they brought corruption and disintegration to their Muslim subjects. Indeed, Chris-

tian Europe stands today even more guilty than those Tatars
and Mongols of the past. The countries which the latter conquered
quickly entered into Islām as soon as they were able to see its
simplicity and greatness. Europe, however, does not conquer in
order to spread a faith, nor in order to spread a civilization. What
it wants is to colonize; to this end it has made the Christian faith
a tool and instrument. That is why the European missions never
succeeded, for they were never sincere and their propaganda
served ulterior motives. They did not meet with any success at
all in the Muslim countries—and indeed they never will—because
the greatness of Islām—its simplicity, its rational and scientific
character—leave no room in the minds of its adherents for any
alien religious propaganda at all.

"They that take the sword shall perish with the sword." That
is true. If this dictum was once true of the late Muslims who
conquered for the sake of conquest and colonization, not in
self-defense nor in defense of the faith, it is all the more true
of this Christian West which conquers and vanquishes the peoples
of the earth in order to colonize and to exploit. As for the early
Muslims, during the time of the Prophet and of his immediate
successors, they did not conquer for the purpose of conquest
and colonization but in defense of their faith when it was
threatened by Quraysh, Arab tribes, Byzantines, and Persians.
Throughout their conquests, they never imposed their religion
on anyone, for it was a cardinal principal of their faith that
"there shall be no coercion in religion."[28]

Forced by the needs of defense against persistent attack, the
Muslims' conquests were never motivated by the will to colonize.
The Prophet left the kings of Arabia and her princes on their
thrones with their territories, economies, and political structures
virtually untouched. In conquering, the Muslims sought the freedom to preach the faith. If the Islāmic faith spread, it was simply
because it of itself was strong by virtue of the truth which
it proclaimed, the universalist nondiscrimination between Arab
and non-Arab which it commanded and its adherents practiced,
and the strict monotheism by which Islām enabled man to have
no master except the one true God. It was because of these innate
strengths of the Islāmic faith that it spread throughout the
earth, just as any genuine truth would spread. When the Tatar
latecomers to Islām fought only for the purpose of conquest and
took men by the sword, they, too, were soon taken by the sword.
But Islām never took anything or anyone by the sword, and no
one will take it by the sword. On the contrary, Islām conquered

the minds, hearts, and consciences of the people by its innate strength. Consequently, the Muslim people have seen many governments, dictators, and tryants, none of which has changed their faith and religion in the least. Today, Europe is still the ruler of the Muslim peoples and the tyrannic administrator of their affairs. But her tyranny will not change the Muslims' faith in God. And as she has taken the Muslims by the sword, she cannot and will not escape the destiny of being taken by the sword. Matthew's principle will once more prove true, but this time to mete out to Christian Europe her due.

The Muslim League of Nations

We have said that the Prophet reinstated the princes and kings to their thrones and kingdoms. Toward the end of the Prophet's life the Arabian Peninsula was truly a league of Arab-Islāmic nations. None of them was a colony either of Makkah or of Yathrib. By virtue of their strong faith in God, the Arabs were all equal to one another before Him. They acted together like one man against anyone who was against them or sought to sway them away from their religious faith. Up to the age of decline, the Muslim peoples remained a league of nations, and the seat of the caliphate was the headquarters of their league. The caliphate never claimed for itself any authority over the Muslim spirit, nor did it ever monopolize knowledge and the search for enlightenment. No Muslim nation submitted to any spiritual authority except that of God. The Muslim capitals were all capitals of science, knowledge, art, and industry. This felicity continued until the Muslims changed their view of Islām, denied its noble principles, violated the brotherhood of the faithful, and forgot that man's faith is never complete until he has desired for his fellow man what he desires for himself. It was then that prejudice did its evil work and destructive contests for power tore up the Muslim brotherhood as the sword became sole judge. But whoever takes with the sword shall be taken by the sword.

After the 15th century, Christian Europe arose to a new life of the spirit which might have brought benefit to all mankind except for the corruption that had quickly found its way to it. Hence, Christianity began to split into many factions. It was in this relatively recent period of its rise that Christian Europe faced a Muslim World that had forgotten its Islām, and took it by the sword. Europe continued to take the Muslim people by the sword, and, indeed, made the sword the sole judge between it and the Muslim people. But when the sword rules, we can then bid farewell to reason, to science, to goodness, to love, to faith, and, indeed, to mankind and to humanity.

It is the rule of the world by the sword which is the cause of the spiritual and psychic crisis from which the world suffers and groans. Those countries which rule the world by the sword realized this unfortunate truth as a result of World War I. They thus sought to bring peace to the world, and, for this purpose, they established the League of Nations. The whole point of the League of Nations is summed up in this verse of the Qur'ān:

وَإِن طَآئِفَتَانِ مِنَ الْمُؤْمِنِينَ اقْتَتَلُوا فَأَصْلِحُوا بَيْنَهُمَا فَإِن بَغَتْ إِحْدَاهُمَا عَلَى الْأُخْرَى فَقَاتِلُوا الَّتِي تَبْغِي حَتَّى تَفِيءَ إِلَى أَمْرِ اللَّهِ فَإِن فَآءَتْ فَأَصْلِحُوا بَيْنَهُمَا بِالْعَدْلِ وَأَقْسِطُوا إِنَّ اللَّهَ يُحِبُّ الْمُقْسِطِينَ ۝ إِنَّمَا الْمُؤْمِنُونَ إِخْوَةٌ فَأَصْلِحُوا بَيْنَ أَخَوَيْكُمْ ۚ وَاتَّقُوا اللَّهَ لَعَلَّكُمْ تُرْحَمُونَ ۝

"And if two factions of believers fight each other, reconcile them in peace. If, thereafter, one aggresses upon the other, then fight the aggressor until it returns to the command of God. If it heeds that command, reconcile that faction again with justice, for God loves justice and those who judge accordingly. The faithful are brothers of one another. Reconcile them therefore as brothers. Fear God that you may be shown mercy."[29]

The Spirit of World Peace Still Missing

Nonetheless, peace did not rule the world after World War I, for the foundation upon which the dominant civilization is based is that of colonialism, and colonialism is in turn based upon the competition of one nationalism against another and upon domination of the weak by the strong. It is the right of the vanquished people, indeed their first duty, to seek to destroy the yoke of the tyrant. Consequently, colonialism has bred and nurtured the germs of rebellion and war. As long as colonialism is the rule, peace will never be established and wars will be continuous. Colonizing or colonized, the nations of the world will continue to regard one another with suspicion and, in fact, to lie in wait for one another. How then can there be peace? Peace will come to this world only when men everywhere change that which is within themselves; that is to say, when they begin to believe truly in peace, when they base their world views upon peace, and when they agree with one another to defend peace against every attempt at disturbing it.

But all this will happen only when colonialism is no more the basis for world order, when the strong of the earth will regard it as their first duty to come to the assistance of the weak, when the affluent will give to the deprived, when the big will show mercy to the small, and when the more learned will teach the ignorant. Peace will indeed reign over the world when the dominant powers spread knowledge throughout the earth to the end of serving mankind rather than of exploiting them in the name of knowledge or industry or technology. When the whole world comes to believe in this principle and all men come to feel that the earth is their own homeland—that they are all brothers of one another, each of them wishing for his brothers that which he wishes for himself—then will clemency, tolerance and fellowship grow among them. Then will they address one another in a language different from that in which they speak today; they will trust one another though they may be separated by wide spaces. They will all do the good for the sake of God. Then and only then will hatred and resentment dissolve, truth be supreme, peace rule the world, and God be pleased with mankind, and mankind with Him.

World Peace Founded Only on Tolerance

God says:

$$\text{اِنَّ الَّذِينَ اٰمَنُوْا وَالَّذِينَ هَادُوْا وَالنَّصٰرٰى وَالصَّابِئِينَ مَنْ اٰمَنَ بِاللّٰهِ وَالْيَوْمِ الْاٰخِرِ وَ عَمِلَ صَالِحًا فَلَهُمْ اَجْرُهُمْ عِنْدَ رَبِّهِمْ وَلَاخَوْفٌ عَلَيْهِمْ وَلَا هُمْ يَحْزَنُوْنَ}$$

"Those who believe, and those who are Jews, Christians, Sabeans, all those who believe in God and in the Day of Judgment and do the good works, all of them have their merit with their Lord. They have no reason to fear nor will they grieve."[30]

Has the world known any tolerance wider than this? Whoever believes in God, in the Day of Judgment, and in doing good works will have his merits with his Lord. No difference separates the believer from those whom the Islāmic call has not reached, whether Jews, Christians, or Sabeans.[31]

God—May He be adored—further says: "Of the people of the Book, some believe in God, in what has been revealed to you, and what has been revealed to them. These revere God and fear Him and do not exchange the revelations of God for a mean price. To them belongs their reward with their Lord. God is quick to take account."[32] How far is all this from our world dominated as it is by western civilization? How far is the tolerance of Islām from the national and religious fanaticisms of the West and all the wars and catastrophes which it has contributed to human history!

The Sublime Life of Muḥammad

It is this high and noble spirit of tolerance that should dominate the world if the world is to live in peace and men are to live in happiness. It is this spirit that makes every study of the life of Muḥammad, to whom God revealed these genuine truths, and of every scholarly study undertaken only for the sake of knowledge, capable of achieving a mastery of such cosmic and spiritual principles as will guide humanity to the new civilization it seeks. Every deep research undertaken in such a study will expose secrets many men believed for a long time to be forever closed to scientific investigations, but on which the investigations of psychology have shed illuminating light. The life of Muḥammad, as we have had occasion to see, is a human life that realized in itself the highest ideals of which man is capable. On this account, the Prophet's life constitutes a good example and true guidance to whosoever wishes to reach human perfection through faith and the work of virtue. What highness and nobility can compare with that which made the life of Muḥammad—even before his commission to prophethood—the example of truthfulness, dignity and trustworthiness, just as it made that life after the commission to prophethood one long poem of self-sacrifice in the cause of God—the cause of truth and goodness, the final end of all prophethood? Muḥammad exposed his life to death many times; his people sought to tempt him with wealth, sovereignty, and all things desired by men; but he resisted them all. He remained the best of all men in nobility, ethical virtue, and dedication to the cause of God.

This human life of Muḥammad attained exalted levels of vision and nobility, of power and magnanimity such as no other life has realized. It was a human life which kept itself in communion with the cosmos from eternity to eternity, and with the Creator of the cosmos by His grace and mercy. Were Muḥammad not exactingly truthful in the conveyance of his Lord's message, some thinkers throughout the centuries would have come up with some evidence to this effect, and some principle taught by Muḥammad would have been exposed as untrue. But 1,350 years[33] have passed while that which Muḥammad conveyed from his Lord continues to be the model of truth and genuine guidance. Sufficient is it to mention in support of this that what God revealed to Muḥammad, to the effect that he was the last of the prophets and messengers of God, has never been successfully overthrown by anybody else's claim to be a prophet and a messenger of God. Throughout the world during all these centuries many men have achieved the greatest possible heights of power and excellence in all aspects of life. None of them, however, has been given the gift of prophethood, of conveying a message from God. Before Muḥammad, however, the prophets and the messengers were many, each of whom warned his people that they had gone astray, and each one sought to bring them back to the religion of truth. Yet none of them claimed that he was sent to all men or that he was the last of the prophets. But Muḥammad made this claim which was revealed to him by God, and the centuries have proved his claim to be true. What Muḥammad conveyed was no fabrication but a true report of a divine message meant to provide guidance and to bring mercy to all mankind.

In conclusion, let me say that the utmost purpose I have hoped my book to achieve is that it may have prepared the road for further researches and studies in these matters. Such researches and studies, we hope, will be wider in scope and deeper in insight than this book. In writing these pages, I have exerted all the effort of which I am capable and explored all the field that my vision could, with God's grace, encompass. God says:

لَا يُكَلِّفُ اللّٰهُ نَفْسًا إِلَّا وُسْعَهَا، لَهَا مَا كَسَبَتْ وَعَلَيْهَا مَا اكْتَسَبَتْ، رَبَّنَا لَا تُؤَاخِذْنَا إِنْ نَسِينَا أَوْ أَخْطَأْنَا، رَبَّنَا وَلَا تَحْمِلْ عَلَيْنَا إِصْرًا كَمَا حَمَلْتَهُ عَلَى الَّذِينَ مِنْ قَبْلِنَا، رَبَّنَا وَلَا تُحَمِّلْنَا مَا لَا طَاقَةَ لَنَا بِهِ، وَاعْفُ عَنَّا، وَاغْفِرْ لَنَا، وَارْحَمْنَا، أَنْتَ مَوْلَانَا فَانْصُرْنَا عَلَى الْقَوْمِ الْكَافِرِينَ

"God only holds a man responsible to the extent of his capacity. He holds every man responsible for what he has done whether good or ill. O God! Grant to us that we may not forget, that we may not fall into error. O God! Grant to us that we may not have to bear the great burden of those who have gone before us. O God! Grant to us that we may not have to bear a burden beyond our capacity. Grant us Your forgiveness, and have mercy on us. You alone are our Lord and Master. Help us therefore to achieve victory over the Godless."[34]

Notes and References

FOREWORD

1. *'Ummah'* is not translatable into English. It "is not merely the 'nation' of the English language, nor *'la nation'* of post-revolution France and European nationalism. It adds to the utilitarian, practical connotation of the former, and the rationalistic idealistic meaning of the latter, the cosmological sense of being the eternal reality in which 'nations' in the foregoing senses may come and go, and the religio-axiological sense of being the real-existent substrate of divine will" (Fārūqī, I. R., *On Arabism, 'Urūbah and Religion*, Amsterdam: Djambatan, 1962, p. 15). —Tr.

2. *See* Preface to the First Edition, p. xl.

3. *Kalām* is the discipline of Islāmic thought. The English concept of "theology" is inadequate because *kalām* includes logic, epistemology and metaphysics and is always presented as critical, not dogmatic, thought. "Philosophy" is equally inadequate on account of the confusion its use might imply, namely, the assumption that all there is to philosophical thought in Islām is the tradition which begins with al Kindī (d. 873 c.e.) and ends with ibn Rushd (d. 1198 c.e.). —Tr.

4. *Sunnah* means the example of the Prophet as normative concretization of the principles of Islām. —Tr.

5. *Mutakallimūn* are those scholars who engage in *kalām*. —Tr.

6. *Isrā'* refers to the night journey Muḥammad undertook from Makkah to Jerusalem—whence he ascended to heaven—and back.—Tr.

595

7. *See* p. vli.
8. *See* p. xlii.

PREFACE TO FIRST EDITION

1. Al Shām or Diyār al Shām refers to the territories presently known as Lebanon, Syria, Palestine and Jordan. —Tr.
2. *I.e.*, China. —Tr.
3. *Zakāt* means the sharing of one's legitimately earned wealth with the community. It is not equivalent to charity because it is levied under penalty of law, has a definite ratio to wealth and is, in Islām, institutionalized. It is not a "poor-tax" because its uses are not limited to those of the poor but extend to the general welfare of the community and state. —Tr.
4. In his book, Dr. Butler says that the name of this general was Khuriam, that "Shahrbaraz," "Shahrbarāz" and "Shirawazayh" by which this general has been known in other books are mistranscriptions of the Persian name "Shahr-Wazar," literally "the king's boar" and signifying as a title "great courage." A figurative representation of this title appeared on the seal of ancient Persia as well as of Armenia (*The Arab Conquest of Egypt*, p. 53.)
5. Qur'ān, 30:1–7.
6. Qur'ān, 5:82.
7. Qur'ān, 3:45–49.
8. Christian scholars have invariably attacked Islām on the ground that it has missed the nature of trinitarianism. They impute to the Qur'ān and to Muḥammad the charge of having misunderstood the trinity as consisting of Father, Mary and Jesus. *E.g.*, Gibb's statement that "the doctrine of the divine Sonship of Jesus is emphatically repudiated, in terms which betray the crassly anthropomorphic form in which it had been presented or presented itself to the Arabs . . . Mohammed had no direct knowledge of Christian doctrine" (Gibb, H. A. R., *Mohammedanism*, London: Oxford U. Press, 1954, p. 45). "A more serious confusion occurs, however, when Mary, the mother of Jesus, is admitted to the Trinity in the place of the Holy Spirit—Qur'ān 5: 76–79, 116 (Donaldson, D. M., *Studies in Muslim Ethics*, London: S.P.C.K., 1953, p. 57). Like statements may be read in Guillaume, A., *Islam*, Edinburgh, Penguin paperback, 1956, p. 52–53; Cragg, K., *The Call of the Minaret*, New York: Oxford University Press paperback, 1964, p. 253; etc., etc. These charges are utterly groundless. The Qur'ān certainly criticized and condemned trinitarianism—as in 5:171; 5:73; etc. It has certainly criticized and condemned the doctrine of *theotokos* or "mother of God" as in 5:75–79, 116. These are two distinct criticisms the Qur'ān has directed at Christianity. But it has nowhere identified the persons of the trinity as consisting of God, the Father; Jesus, the son; and Mary, the mother. The Qur'ānic position is simply that whoever and whatever the persons of the trinity may be, trinitarianism and theotokos are blasphemous compromises of divine trancendence and unity. Combining the two Qur'ānic condemnations, some

exegetes had regarded "The Mother of God" as part of "The Trinity." If this is a mistake, it belongs to those exegetes, not to the Qur'ān. Even so, it is not necessarily a mistake. The exegetes' works constitute evidence of the current tenets of faith of their contemporaries; and there is no apriori evidence that some Near Eastern Christians have not identified the Trinity in these terms. Indeed, there is but one small step from the Christian assertion that "the Logos took human nature to Himself in the womb of the Virgin Mary—that Godhead and Manhood were united in the Incarnate logos in one Person," to use Cyril's words, to the assertion that "theotokos" implies the unity of the mother with the embryo in her womb, and hence that the Incarnation creates a bond between mother & logos separable only in theory. (See for further detail F. J. Foakes Jackson, *The History of the Christian Church to* C.E. *461*, London: George Allen & Unwin Ltd., 1st pub. 1891, rep. 1957, pp. 459 ff.) This need not be a mistake; indeed it is quite probable that some Near Eastern Christians had held such a view, since in this, as well as in many other passages, the Qur'ān is simply reporting what is being heard.

9. Arabic *mushrikūn*, those who associated other gods with God.
10. Qur'ān, 5:17–18.
11. Qur'ān, 5:72–73.
12. Qur'ān, 5:116–118.
13. Qur'ān, 112:1–4.
14. Qur'ān, 19:35.
15. Qur'ān, 3:59.
16. Qur'ān, 4:48.
17. Qur'ān, 4:157–158.
18. Qur'ān, 31:33.
19. Arabic *tawhīd*, the Islāmic doctrine of divine unity. The English "monotheism" is not specific enough and is applied to Christianity precisely where Islām would charge its inapplicability. Hence, our new term. —Tr.
20. Emil Dermenghem, *The Life of Mahomet*, translated by Arabella Yorke, New York: The Dial Press, 1930, pp. 119–121.
21. Theosophy is a doctrine founded by Madame Plawatzki, of the U.S.A., and derived from the religions of India, from Buddhism and Brahmanism especially. It is also called "religion of wisdom." A society embracing this new faith was founded in America and Madame Plawatzki has been its president. Branches of this society have arisen in many European countries. As soon as the founder passed away, the Theosophic Society divided into three main groups. However, they all believe in the unity of being and of life and observe a kind of Ṣūfī discipline aimed at reaching Nirvana of Buddhism. Such a state is reached only when the subject achieves, by means of discipline and exercise, a total separation of the spirit from the concerns of material life and when the soul rises to such heights of holiness and purity that it joins the spirits on high. Theosophy also calls for universal fraternity among mankind, an order in which race, language and all other impediments would dissolve away.
22. One of the sources of Islāmic law. Creative interpretation of the principles and precepts of Islām. —Tr.
23. According to Webster, where it is spelled "ulema," "a body of scholars

trained in Moslem religion and law," or "sometimes, erroneously, a
Moslem learned man or theologian." —Tr.

24. Rational conviction of religious truth, possibly only as a category of
critical natural theology such as Islām provides. Colloquially convertible
with "faith." —Tr.

25. Dr. Haykal is here referring to France's expulsion of the Jesuit,
Dominican, Franciscan, and other missionary orders. —Tr.

PREFACE TO SECOND EDITION

1. Qur'ān, 61:6.
2. *Ibid.*
3. Dr. Haykal translated this term so as to mean "recitation" rather than
"composition," in conformity with the Islamic position. —Tr.
4. Sir William Muir, *The Life of Mahomet*, London: Smith, Elder and
Company, 1878, pp. 551–562.
5. *See* p. 355.
6. Qur'ān, 33:56.
7. 1574–1624 C.E., great grammarian, court clerk, and qāḍī who lived in
Safad, Ṣaidā, Beirut and Jerusalem.
8. Arabic *"adab al Qur'ān."*
9. Qur'ān, 16:103.
10. Qur'ān, 53:19–20.
11. Literally "hypocrite;" as a special name it applied to the Zoroastrians
and Manichaeans who pretended to embrace Islām but remained true to
their old gods. —Tr.
12. The Law of Islām.
13. *See* p. x.
14. *Al Manār*, May 3, 1935, p. 793.
15. Qur'ān, 17:90–93.
16. Qur'ān, 6:109–111.
17. Qur'ān, 26:43–48.
18. *See* pp. 50–51.
19. *See* pp. 285–289.
20. *The Ṣaḥīh* of Muslim, Istanbul, 1332 A.H., Vol. VII, p. 60.
21. Rule of consultation, or consent. Presently used as equivalent to representative government or democratic rule.
22. The Shu'ūbiyyah movement (hence the adjective shu'ūbī) comprehends
all the fissiparous tendencies of the non-Arab Muslims in the Islamic
Empire. The movement was begun in the Umawī period predominantly by
Persians, but it came to include many other national, ethnic, cultural
and religious minorities. The movement fomented the rebellion which
brought the Umawī dynasty and period to an end, but it was itself
dissipated with the triumph of Islām and the Arabic language in the
succeeding two centuries.
23. Qur'ān, 15:9.
24. Qur'ān, 60:40.

CHAPTER 1

1. As in the Qur'ānic verse: "As to their saying, 'We did kill the Messiah, Jesus, Son of Mary, the Apostle of God;' whereas they slew him not, nor crucified him, but it was made to appear to them as if they did. Those who differ therein are certainly in a state of doubt about it. They have no definite knowledge thereof but only follow a conjecture. None of them knows for sure that he was killed. Rather, God raised him unto Himself. God is Mighty and Wise." 4:156–7. —Tr.

2. The term "al Rūm" used in pre-Islāmic (Qur'ān, 30:2) times, as well as later, refers to Rome, the Roman Empire and the East Roman Empire or Byzantium. Arab historians say "Roman" when they mean "Byzantine." —Tr.

3. 476 C.E.

4. *Heeren's Researches: Africa*, Vol. I, p. 23, quoted by Muir, *op. cit.*, pp. ii–iii.

5. Perhaps the author meant the Euphrates, for it is hard to see why a west-bound caravan should travel alongside the Tigris. —Tr.

6. The narrow plain alongside the East coast of the Red Sea, separating the latter from the Ḥijāz mountain chain and the desert beyond. —Tr.

7. Qur'ān, 85:5–9.

8. This fact is confirmed by most historians in a number of works of history and reference. It is confirmed by the *Encyclopædia Britannica* and the *Historian's History of the World*. In his book, *The Life of Muḥammad*, Dermenghem accepts it as true. Al Ṭabarī reports from Hishām ibn Muḥammad that when the Yamanī Christians solicited the Negus's assistance against Dhū Nuwās, informed him of what the Jewish King did to the Christians and showed him a partially burnt Evangel, the Negus said: "My men are many but I have no ships. I shall write to the Byzantine Emperor to send me ships with which to carry the men over to Yaman." The Negus wrote to the Byzantine Emperor and sent him the partially burned Evangel. The Emperor responded by sending many ships. Al Ṭabarī adds: "Hishām ibn Muḥammad claims that when the ships arrived, the Negus sent his army therein and landed them on the shores of Mandib" (Al Ṭabarī, ibn Jarīr, *Tārīkh al Rusul wa al Mulūk*, Cairo: Al Maṭba'ah al Ḥusayniyyah, Vol. II, pp. 106, 108).

9. Literally, "the man with the cut lip."

10. Some historians give a different explanation of the conquest of Yaman by Abyssinia. They claim that trade moved along connected links between Abyssinia, Yaman, and Ḥijāz; that Abyssinia then had a large commercial fleet operating on the shores of the Red Sea. The Byzantines were anxious to conquer Yaman in order to reap some of its produce and wealth. Anxious to conquer Yaman for Byzantium, Aelius Gallus, Governor of Egypt, equipped and prepared the army on the shore of the Red Sea, sent it to Yaman, and occupied Najrān. The Yamanīs put up a stiff resistance and were helped by the epidemic which ravaged the expeditionary force and compelled a withdrawal to Egypt. A number of other attempts to conquer Yaman were made by the Byzantines, but

none of them succeeded. It was this long history of conflict which opened the eyes of the Negus and prompted him to avenge his fellow Christians against the Yamanī Jews; it also explains why he prepared the army of Aryāt, sent it to conquer Yaman (525 C.E.). —Tr. The Abyssinians ruled the country until the Persians forced them out of the Peninsula.

11. Al Shām refers to the lands otherwise known as Syria, Lebanon, Palestine, and Jordan. —Tr.

CHAPTER 2

1. Qur'ān, 21:62–63
2. Qur'ān, 6:76–79.
3. Haykal here reports a typical case of Israelitism in the Muslim tradition. With little variation the story of Genesis had passed into Muslim legends through Jewish converts to Islām. —Tr.
4. Genesis 22:2 also calls Isaac Abraham's "only son," thus corroborating the claim and making the Bible's declaration of Isaac as the sacrificial son a very likely emendation of the Biblical text. —Tr.
5. Unfortunately, Haykal has not shown how this implication follows from the claim in favor of Ismaʿīl. —Tr.
6. Qur'ān, 37:102–107.
7. Qur'ān, 3:96–97.
8. Qur'ān, 2:125–127.
9. Qur'ān, 11:53.
10. Qur'ān, 17:15.
11. For definitions of these terms, see pp. 31–32.
12. Ibid.
13. The author is using the pre-Islāmic and Islāmic names of the same city interchangeably. Pre-Islāmic "Yathrib" had, upon the Prophet's emigration thereto and the establishment therein of the first Islāmic polity, become "Madīnah al Nabī" (literally, the city of the Prophet) and "Madīnah" for short. —Tr.
14. Qur'ān, 105:1–5.
15. Literally, "man with a book or scripture," following the Qur'ānic appellation for Jews and Christians, "People of the Book," or "scripturists."
16. "Sidānah" is synonymous to "ḥijābah." For a definition of this and "siqāyah," see pp. 31–32.

CHAPTER 3

1. Qurān, 94:1–3.
2. "Most Arab among you" (Arabic, "aʿrabukum") could well have been rendered "most eloquent among you." To be an Arab, or "to arabize"

means to speak forth eloquently in Arabic, without stammering or grammatical mistakes, and with literary beauty. *'Urūbah* or Arabness is always something which admits of many degrees, the more Arab being always the man in better command of the Arabic language, Arabic diction, style, letters and all forms of literary beauty. Ya'rub, (literally, "he arabizes" or "speaks eloquent Arabic") was the name of the first Arab King, whom legend declares to be the first to have spoken in Arabic. As far as history goes, the Arabs have regarded the desert Arabic purer and more classical and beautiful than that of the towns; the tribes were graded in *'Urūbah* according to their racial purity as means for the preservation of the purity of Arabic. Hence, the Prophet's statement. —Tr.

3. Waraqah ibn Nawfal was a *ḥanīf* (an ethical monotheist of pre-Islāmic times). He was the relation of the Prophet's wife, Khadījah, from whom she sought advice regarding Muḥammad's reports about revelation. (*See* p. 77.)

4. A village located between Madīnah and Jaḥfah, twenty-three miles south of Madīnah.

5. Qur'ān, 93:6–7.

6. At the yearly market of 'Ukāẓ (near Makkah), held during the holy months, poets from all tribes competed with one another in poetry. They recited their compositions in public and the greatest was given the prize of having his composition written down and "hung" on the walls of the Ka'bah. According to al Mufaḍḍal (d. 189 A.H./805 C.E.), Imru' al Qays (d. 560 C.E.), Zuhayr (d. 635 C.E.), al Nābighah (d. 604 C.E.), al A'shā (d. 612 C.E.), Labīd (d. 645 C.E.), 'Amr ibn Kulthūm (d. 565 C.E.) and Ṭarafah (d. 565 C.E.) were authors of the greatest poems of pre-Islāmic days, accorded this special honor. Hence, their name "*al mu'allaqāt*," literally "the hanging poems." Other early historians of Arabic literature claimed that the *mu'allaqāt* were eight, adding to the seven above-mentioned a poem of 'Antarah. Other pre-Islāmic and early Islāmic (up to 50 A.H./672 C.E.) poems, numbering 42 in all, were divided into six groups of seven poems each—the whole of pre-Islāmic poetry adding up to seven groups of seven poems each—arranged according to their literary merit, poetic eloquence and force. They included: *al mujamharāt* by 'Ubayd, 'Antarah, 'Adiyy, Bishr and Umayyah, *al muntaqayāt* (literally, "the selected poems") by al Musayyib, al Muraqqash, al Mutalammis, 'Urwah, al ' Muhalhil, Durayd and al Mutanakhkhil; *al mudhahhabāt* (literally, "The golden poems," or "written in gold") by Ḥassān ibn Rawāḥah, Mālik, Qays ibn al Khātim, Uḥayḥah, Abū Qays ibn al Aslat and 'Amr ibn Umru' al Qays; *al mashūbāt* (literally, "the poems touched by Islām as well as pre-Islāmic unbelief"), *al malḥamāt* (literally, "the epic poems"). For further details, see any literary history of the Arabs, or Muḥammad 'Abd al Mun'im Khafājī, *al Ḥayāh al Adabiyyah fī al 'Aṣr al Jāhilī*, Cairo: Maktabat al Ḥusayn al Tijāriyyah, 1368/1949. —Tr.

7. Literally, "the immoral war." —Tr.

8. Quss ibn Sā'idah al Iyādī, Archbishop of Najrān.

9. Literally, "the alliance for charity." —Tr.

CHAPTER 4

1. Most of the scholars who have investigated the geneological descendents of Muhammad and his family agree that the sons of the Prophet—may God's peace and blessing be upon him—given him by Khadījah were two: al Qāsim and 'Abdullah, who was also called "the pure" and "the good." It has also been reported that his sons were three or even four.
2. Title given to each of the wives of the Prophet.
3. *See* p. 97.
4. Qur'ān, 29:7-8.
5. Qur'ān, 96:1-5.

CHAPTER 5

1. Qur'ān, 73:1-7.
2. Qur'ān, 93:1-11.
3. Arabic *"mawlā,"* the person standing under protection. This was the position of the manumitted slave. —Tr.
4. Unfortunately, in this as in many other cases, Haykal has quoted the author and placed his words between quotation marks but has not indicated the source. —Tr.
5. Qur'ān, 26:214-216; 15-94.
6. Qur'ān, 111:1-3.
7. Qur'ān, 102:1-8.
8. Qur'ān, 7:188.
9. Qur'ān, 79:24.
10. Qur'ān, 99:7-8.
11. Qur'ān, 32.
12. Qur'ān, 19:29-33.

CHAPTER 6

1. Qur'ān, 53:19-20.
2. Qur'ān, 17:73-75.
3. Non-Muslims concealing their unbelief, falsely pretending that they are members of the ummah; mostly Zoroastrians and Manichaeans. —Tr.
4. Qur'ān, 22:52-53.
5. Qur'ān, 17:73-75; *see* p. 106.
6. Qur'ān, 22:52-53; *see* p. 107.
7. "Muhammad saw some of his Lord's greatest signs. Would you consider, after al Lāt and al 'Uzzā, Manāt, the third goddess? But would you give God the females and keep for yourselves the males? That is indeed an unjust division. But they are all mere names which you and your ancestors have named and for which God gave no authority. In this claim of yours you followed naught but conjecture and your own wishful thinking, while true guidance has arrived to you from your Lord" (Qur'ān, 53:18-23).

8. Literally, unitization of God or conviction of His unity, transcendence and absolute uniqueness. Often the term applies to Islām as a whole, to Islāmic theology and to monotheism. —Tr.

CHAPTER 7

1. Qur'ān, 16:103.
2. Qur'ān, 80:1–16.
3. Qur'ān, 49:14.
4. Qur'ān, 43:31–32.
5. Qur'ān, 80:33–42.
6. Qur'ān, 70:8–18.
7. Qur'ān, 69:18–37.
8. Qur'ān, 50:30; 4:56.

CHAPTER 8

1. Qur'ān, 17:73–75.
2. *Al Isrā'* means the night journey the Prophet was reported to have taken from Makkah to al Masjid al Aqṣā, the distant mosque, or Jerusalem. *Al Mi'rāj* means the Prophet's ascension to heaven and his visit to paradise and hell, later to serve as model for Dante's *La Divina Comedia*. See M. Asin Palacios, *La escatologia musulmana en la Divina Comedia*, Madrid, 1919; 2nd edition, Madrid, 1943. —Tr.
3. Qur'ān, 17:60.
4. Emile Dermenghem, *The Life of Mahomet*, New York: Lincoln Mac-Veagh, 1930, pp. 132–135.
5. Qur'ān, 18:110.
6. Qur'ān, 4:48.
7. The Arabic text has "spiritual" at both poles of the comparison, which I assume to be a misprint. —Tr.
8. *Al Ṣiddiq, i.e.,* he who believes the truth to be true. —Tr.

CHAPTER 9

1. Qur'ān, 41:34.
2. Literally, "the helpers," the name given by Muḥammad to the first Muslims of Madīnah who gave assistance to the cause at the time of its greatest peril. Later on, the name was to apply to all the Muslims of Madīnah in contrast to al *Muhājirūn*—literally, "the emigrants"—applied to those Muslims of Makkah who emigrated before or after the Prophet to Madīnah. —Tr.
3. See note 2, *supra.*

CHAPTER 10

1. E. Dermenghem, *op. cit.*, p. 149.
2. Qur'an, 8:30; 9:40.
3. The word is originally the Greek *"drachme,"* a silver coin of varying value. —Tr.
4. Six and a half miles south of the city. —Tr.

CHAPTER 11

1. Qur'ān, 22:39.
2. Qur'ān, 8:39.
3. The allusion here is to Constantine who began to show favors toward Christianity in 312 C.E. and decreed the Edict of Toleration in 313. He supported both paganism as well as Christianity. To the end of his life he bore the title of *pontifex maximus*, being the chief priest of the pagan state cult and classed among the gods by the Roman Senate. He was not baptized until the latter part of his life. —Tr.
4. Qur'ān, 2:194.
5. Qur'ān, 2:179.
6. A dish made out of layers of bread often topped with meat, rice, and soaked with gravy. —Tr.
7. Qur'ān, 2:57; 28:77.
8. Qur'ān, 112:1–3.
9. *I.e.*, al Aws and al Khazraj.
10. Qur'ān, 2:87–89.
11. Qur'ān, 2:245.
12. Qur'ān, 3:181.
13. Qur'ān, 5:49–50.
14. Qur'ān, 2:144.
15. Qur'ān, 2:142–143.
16. Qur'ān, 2:136.
17. Qur'ān, 3:64.

CHAPTER 12

1. A *dīnār* is a golden coin, equivalent to twenty silver *dirhims*. —Tr.
2. *Munāfiqūn*, literally, the pretenders; applied to the insincere idolaters who joined the ranks of Islām for ulterior motives. —Tr.
3. Qur'ān, 2:190.
4. Qur'ān, 2:217.
5. Matthew, 10:34.
6. Qur'ān, 2:256, 190.
7. Matthew, 17:20.

CHAPTER 13

1. Qur'ān, 8:7.
2. Qur'ān, 8:65, 8:66.
3. Qur'ān, 8:12, 17.
4. Qur'ān, 8:41.
5. Qur'ān, 21:67; 14:36.
6. Qur'ān, 5:118.
7. Qur'ān, 71:26; 10:88.
8. Qur'ān, 8:67.
9. *Ibid.*

CHAPTER 15

1. The locality halfway between Makkah and Madīnah on the coastal route.
2. The Qur'ān called the insincere Muslims *"munāfiqūn"* or pretenders. —Tr.
3. Qur'ān, 56:25–26.
4. According to another version, it was Sa'd ibn Abū Waqqās that was so attracted.
5. Qur'ān, 16:126–127.
6. Significantly, this is the same question which Western Islāmicist Wilfred Cantwell Smith thinks confutes Muslims in modern times because of its novelty. See his *Islam in Modern History*, Princeton, New Jersey, Princeton University Press, 1957, ch. II, where he argues that the view that Islām's movement in history is God-willed and God-incepted—such as Islām holds—leads in case of frustration, loss or defeat, to the absurdity either that God's will is being frustrated or that the movement in question is not God-willed. Smith omits here to consider that the unfolding of God's will in history is, in Islām, not the working of blind necessity but that of free men whose responsible decisions are the very stuff of divine will, so that defeat or victory are attributable to them rather than to God. It was this moralism of the Muslims that saved them after their defeat at Uhud and at the hands of Crusaders and Tatars in the Middle Ages. And it is likely to save them, too, after their defeat by an imperialist West in modern times. —Tr.

CHAPTER 16

1. Qur'ān, 59:5.
2. Qur'ān, 59:11–13.
3. Qur'ān, 59:22–24.
4. Qur'ān, 3:168–75.

CHAPTER 17

1. Qur'ān, 33:37.
2. Title attributed to all wives of the Prophet. —Tr.

3. Qur'ān, 4:3.
4. Qur'ān, 4:129.
5. Qur'ān, 49:13.
6. Qur'ān, 33:36.
7. Qur'ān, 33:4.
8. Qur'ān, 33:37.
9. *Ibid*.

CHAPTER 18

1. Qur'ān, 4:51–52.
2. Qur'ān, 33:10–13.

CHAPTER 19

1. Qur'ān, 5:3.
2. John, 8:7.
3. Qur'ān, 33:58–62.
4. Qur'ān, 24:30–31.
5. Qur'ān, 33:53.
6. Qur'ān, 33:32–33.
7. Qur'ān, 63:7–8.
8. Qur'ān, 24:11, 16–17.
9. Qur'ān, 24:4.

CHAPTER 20

1. Qur'ān, 2:217.
2. Qur'ān, 8:34–36.
3. Pilgrimage to the Sanctuary of Makkah at a time other than that prescribed for it by custom and the Qur'ān. —Tr.
4. A group of strong bowmen from Arabia—i.e. Abyssinians—so called for their dark complexion. Another possible explanation for their name is that it refers to Ḥubshī, a mountain south of Makkah.
5. Qur'ān, 48:18.
6. It was customary for the pilgrim in pre–Islāmic Arabia to shave his head as evidence of desacralization after a complete performance of the religious function of pilgrimage. When the performance of the religious function had been interrupted or any one of its rituals for some reason missed, the pilgrim would only cut his hair short rather than shave it. He thereby gave evidence of his awareness that his religious function had not been completely fulfilled and of the need to repeat the same function in the following season. —Tr.
7. Qur'ān, 48:1–30.
8. Qur'ān, 60:10.

CHAPTER 21

1. *See* p. 355.
2. Qur'ān, 2:219.
3. Qur'ān, 4:43.
4. Qur'ān, 5:90–91.
5. Qur'ān, 5:93.
6. Recognizing that there has been a large variety of views regarding the voweling and meaning of the term *"al arīsiyyīn,"* the author appended a footnote in which he preferred its meaning as "subjects." This view was based on the *Nihāyat* of Ibn al Athīr and other dictionaries of the Arabic language, q.v. *Rūm.* Another meaning of the term, which does not at all seem improbable, is "Arians." In this case the Prophet would seem to be giving Heraclius the alternative of accepting the monotheism of Islām or of remaining a trinitarian Christian. In the latter case, the emperor would fall under a new indictment of heresy regarding the truth of Jesus Christ which Islām was teaching in consonance with Arianism. —Tr.
7. Qur'ān, 48:15.
8. Not personally, but as chief of state. —Tr.
9. The old city of Emessa in Syria.
10. That is, Hagia Sophia. —Tr.
11. The year in question was 7 A.H./629 C.E. —Tr.

CHAPTER 22

1. Two hills outside of Makkah, between which Hāgar ran a number of times to and fro in search of water for her thirsty son, Isma'īl. It was part of the pre-Islāmic pilgrimage as well as the Islāmic pilgrimage to Makkah to reenact this anxious running between these two hills and thereby pay tribute to Isma'īl, the common ancestor, founder of Makkah and co-builder of the Ka'bah with his father, Ibrahīm. —Tr.

CHAPTER 24

1. Qur'ān, 60:1.
2. Some biographers relate that al 'Abbās met the Muslim army at Rābigh. Others assert that al 'Abbās had reached Madīnah before Muhammad resolved to march against Makkah, that he converted to Islām in Madīnah and accompanied the Muslim army on its march. This latter view, however, is refuted by the historians as a fabrication injected into the biography of Muhammad in order to please the 'Abbāsī rulers during whose reign the biographies of the Prophet were first written down. The refutation of the historians is confirmed by the fact that if the claim were true, al 'Abbās, as the last notable of Makkah to join

the ranks of Islām, would have been the first to be visited by Abū
Sufyān for the purpose of extending the Treaty of Ḥudaybiyah. It
would seem that despite his defense of his nephew when the latter was
at Makkah, al 'Abbās did not join Islām. Al 'Abbās was a Makkan
tradesman and, like all other tradesmen of the city, feared the disastrous consequences Islām would bring to his business.
3. Qur'ān, 96:1–5.
4. Qur'ān, 49:13.
5. Qur'ān, 17:81.
6. *I.e.*, Makkah. —Tr.

CHAPTER 25

1. Qur'ān, 9:25–28.

CHAPTER 26

1. As in the *Ṣaḥīḥ* of Muslim. In the account of Ṭabarī there is no mention
   of a wife of 'Umar by this name. In *Rūḥ al Ma'ānī* of Allūsī, the same
   statement by 'Umar names "The daughter of Zayd" instead.
2. Qur'ān, 30:28–29.
3. Qur'ān, 30:1–5.

CHAPTER 27

1. *See* pp. 31–32.
2. *I.e.*, "the tax of the tenth," levied on the Muslims' annual incomes at
   the rate of 10%. —Tr.
3. *I.e.*, income tax levied on the annual incomes of non-Muslims at varying
   rates not exceeding 10%. —Tr.
4. Qur'ān, 9:81–82.
5. Qur'ān, 9:49.
6. Qur'ān, 9:117–118.

CHAPTER 28

1. Qur'ān, 9:1–36.
2. The *sūrah* in question is Qur'ān 9. It is known by either of the two
   titles "Al Tawbah" (repentence) and "Barā'ah" (absolution). —Tr.

CHAPTER 29

1. Qur'ān, 9:29, 34–35.
2. Qur'ān, 5:82.
3. Qur'ān, 3:59–64.

4. Qur'ān, 5:73–75.
5. Qur'ān, 5:11.
6. Qur'ān, 5:82.
7. *I.e.*, running to and fro between the two mountains. This part of the pilgrimage ritual is a re-creation of Hagar's desperate running on the same plain in search of water for her son Ismā'īl. —Tr.
8. Muslim ibn al Ḥajjāj, 817–865 C.E., compiler of the *Ṣaḥīḥ*, the second canonical collection of *Ḥadīth*. —Tr.
9. The invocations which include either "At your service, O Lord" or "God is Great" as dominant theme. —Tr.
10. Qur'ān, 5:4.

CHAPTER 30

1. Qur'ān, 6:38. There can be little doubt that this story is a fabrication of later times, specifically, of the eighth century C.E./second century A.H., when at the height of the *ḥadīth* movement, controversy arose as to the place of *ḥadīth* in the framework of Islāmic Law and ideas. It is not likely that Muḥammad's closest and most trusted companions or the members of his house would have refused to fulfill a wish their Prophet was making on his death bed. Nor is it likely that the Prophet's *Sunnah* would have constituted a problem at all, or one necessitating such hard contradiction between the written and the oral traditions. —Tr.
2. Here again, there can be little doubt of the spuriousness of this report. It is evidently anachronistic and must have come from a much later time than the Prophet's. Firstly, it is not possible that the Prophet had such a low and pessimistic esteem of his time. At his death the Prophet stood at the height of power, having welded Arabia into one powerful unity, strong enough to venture beyond its borders. No Arab tribe or person was strong enough to wage "subversive attacks" against the Islāmic polity. Secondly, no justification could be adduced for the Prophet's public defense of himself because he was under serious attack from no one. No one in his senses could have accused the Prophet of violating the legislation of the Qur'ān. Thirdly, no Muslims had at that time built mausoleums for anyone, including the Prophet, and no one had used grave–sites or cemeteries as mosques. The Prophet's condemnation is hence pointless. Granted, then, that this *ḥadīth* was not the Prophet's but that of later Muslims, it becomes a source of historical information about its time. Only the late Umawī and early 'Abbāsī times could have presented "subversive attacks" against the regime in power; only then could some caliphs have been indicted for violating the Qur'ānic legislation; and only then, if not even much later, did Muslims begin the practice of building mausoleum–mosques mostly under Ṣūfī and Persian inspiration. —Tr.

CHAPTER 31

1. Qur'ān, 3:144.
2. Qur'ān, 9:100.

3. In Islāmic political theory, *"bay'ah"* means the investment of the caliph with political authority. It consists of a "private" and "public" investment. The former amounts to nomination of the caliph by a number of supporters; the latter to confirmation of the private *bay'ah* by the electorate at large. It is only when the two *bay'ahs* have taken place and have been accepted by the caliph that he is said to have legitimately acceded to the caliphate. —Tr.

4. The reader may be thrown off by this usage of "pray upon" instead of the commonplace "pray for." In the Muslim practice nobody "prays for" the Prophet in the sense that one prays for a departed loved one. Prayer upon the Prophet is much more formal and is commanded by the Qur'ān (33:56). It is a main part of Muslim worship to use the Qur'ānic "pray upon" in invoking God's blessing upon His Prophet. —Tr.

ESSAY I OF CONCLUSION

1. Qur'ān, 2:171.
2. Imitation of the ancestors, conservatism. —Tr.
3. Qur'ān, 2:164
4. Qur'ān, 36:33–44.
5. Qur'ān, 17:85.
6. Qur'ān, 49:14.
7. Qur'ān, 49:17.
8. Qur'ān, 2:186.
9. Qur'ān, 2:45–46.
10. The reference is here to the phrases, *Allahu Akbar* (God is Greatest) and *Subhāna Rabbī al 'Azīm* (Praise to my Lord Almighty) repeated many times in the course of the Islāmic prayer.
11. Qur'ān, 2:177.
12. Qur'ān, 2:183.
13. Qur'ān, 2:184.
14. Qur'ān, 2:277.
15. Qur'ān, 2:43.
16. Qur'ān, 23:1–4.
17. Qur'ān, 69:30–34.
18. Qur'ān, 22:34–35.
19. Qur'ān, 2:274.
20. Qur'ān, 2:271, 263–64.
21. Qur'ān, 9:60.
22. Qur'ān, 28:77.
23. Qur'ān, 2:197.
24. Qur'ān, 17:23–38.
25. Qur'ān, 23–96; 41:34.
26. Qur'ān, 4:86.
27. Qur'ān, 16:126.
28. Qur'ān, 2:275.
29. Qur'ān, 30:39.

30. An "Israelitism" is usually a spurious interpretation of, or a fabricated addition to, an Islāmic religious text, the Qur'ān being naturally excluded. While most "Israelitisms" had to do with Islāmic doctrine, tradition, and semitic history, their purpose was always to subvert the faith from within. They are supposed to be the work of Jews of the first two centuries who ostensibly converted to Islām but who nursed for it the strongest hatred. —Tr.

31. Provincialism, or "shu'ūbiyyah," is the name given by Muslim historians to every centrifugal movement in the Islāmic empire, such as Persian nationalism, Turkish nationalism, Coptic nationalism, etc. —Tr.

ESSAY II OF CONCLUSION

1. Washington Irving, *Mahomet and His Successors*, Philadelphia, J. B. Lippincott and Co., 1871, Vol. I, pp. 360–362.
2. Qur'ān, 10:108; 17:15; 42:20; 13:11.
3. Qur'ān, 3:145; 7:34; 57:22; 9:51.
4. Qur'ān, 53:40
5. Qur'ān, 13:11.
6. Qur'ān, 3:159.
7. Qur'ān, 34:3.
8. Qur'ān, 7:12.
9. Qur'ān, 17:15.
10. Qur'ān, 6:2.
11. Qur'ān, 21:34–35.
12. Qur'ān, 62:5–7.
13. Qur'ān, 6:60.
14. Qur'ān, 7:13.
15. Qur'ān, 49:13; 4:106. The author does not quote these words in the manner proper to Qur'ānic words, but uses them as his own—a perfectly permissive literary feature in Arabic. The last part of the sentence not included within quotation marks sounds Qur'ānic in construction and phrasing, but it is not of the Qur'ān. —Tr.
16. "Scientific Determinism," "The World as Will and Idea," and "Emergent Evolution" are philosophic systems advanced by the positivist philosophers, Schopenhauer and Henri Bergson.
17. Matthew, 5:17.
18. Qur'ān, 6:151; 17:33.
19. Qur'ān, 2:179.
20. Qur'ān, 16:40.
21. Qur'ān, 22:47.
22. Qur'ān, 7:19–27.
23. Qur'ān, 6:27–32.
24. Qur'ān, 28:30–32.
25. Qur'ān, 18:46.
26. Muhammad 'Abduh, *Al Islām wa al Naṣrāniyyah Ma'a al 'Ilm wa al Madaniyyah*, Cairo, n.d., pp. 122–125.

27. Qur'ān, 28–77.
28. Qur'ān, 2:256.
29. Qur'ān, 49:9–10.
30. Qur'ān, 2:62.
31. Commenting on this verse, al Ṭabarī wrote in his exegesis: " 'Those who believe' refers to the people who believed in the Prophet of God.' 'The Jews' refers to those who gave themselves this name as a derivation from their statement, 'We have returned to You,' that is, 'we have repented.' 'The Christians,' are the followers of Jesus. They were called by this name—naṣārā—in derivation from the name, Nazareth, the village of Jesus in Palestine. According to another view, the derivation was one of Jesus' statements, 'And who are my helpers—anṣār—in God?' 'The Sabeans' are, according to one view, those who worship the angels. According to another view, the Sabeans were a people who believed that there is no God but God but had neither scripture nor prophet. Their religion may be characterized by no other statement except that there is no God but God. According to a third view, the Sabeans were a people without religion." Al Ṭabarī explained the verse as follows: "Those who believe in God and in the reality of resurrection after death, in the Day of Judgment, who do the good works in obedience to God—such men have their merit with their Lord; that is, they have the merit earned by their good works. As for the statements 'they have no reason to fear' and 'neither shall they grieve,' the meaning which God—May He be adored—intended is that those people have no reason to fear any of the terrors of the Day of Judgment, nor will they grieve for all the good things of the world which they left behind when they come to know all the bliss which God has reserved for them in Paradise." Following these comments, al Ṭabarī mentioned that this verse was revealed in reference to those Christians who guided Salmān al Fārisī and converted him to their religion, announcing to him that an Arab prophet would come forth and asking Salmān to verify the identity of such prophet with given signs and to follow him if he could find him. After Salmān converted to Islām, he told the Prophet about those Christians, and the Prophet replied: "O Salmān, those people belong to Hell." Salmān was grieved, and on this account, God revealed the verse: "Those who believe, the Christians, etc." According to another view, God had revoked this verse with another verse, namely, "Whoever seeks another religion besides Islām, it will not be accepted of him" (Qur'ān 3:85). However, al Ṭabarī adds: "What we have mentioned at the beginning is the closer to the commonsense meaning of the revelation because God—May He be praised—could not have restricted merit for the good works and faith to some of His creatures rather than to others. The predicate of the verse therefore belongs to every subject mentioned therein, including the Muslims." A confirmation of this view of al Ṭabarī is that it may be said in regard to the verse, "Whoever seeks another religion besides Islām, it will not be accepted of him." It applies to those Muslims who seek another religion besides Islām, after they have been born into Islām or come to believe in it. As to those who are born in another religion, and those whom the

Islāmic call has not reached without falsification, their case will be like that of those who have gone before the advent of Muḥammad and his prophethood, and who have not come to know of his message as it is and without falsification. (See further Ibn Jarīr al Ṭabarī, *Kitāb al Tafsīr*, Vol. 1, pp. 253–57.)

32. Qur'ān 3:199.
33. The current year is Islām's one thousand, three hundred, eighty-seventh year, A.H. —Tr.
34. Qur'ān 2:286.

Supplementary Readings in the English Language on the Life of the Prophet

Abu'l-Fadl, Mirza (ed. and tr.). *Muhammad in the Hadees*, or *Sayings of the Prophet Mohammad*. Allahabad: Abbas Manzil Library, 195—.

Ahmad, Fazl. *Muhammad, the Holy Prophet*, "Heroes of Islam Series." Lahore: Ashraf, 1960.

Ahmad, Syed Khan Bahadur. *Essays of the Life of Mohammed and Subjects Subsidiary Thereto*, Vol. I. London: Trubner, 1870.

Ali, Muhammad. *The Living Thoughts of the Prophet Muhammad*. London: Cassell, 1947.

———. *Muhammad and Christ*. Madras: S.P.C.K. Press, 1921.

———. *Muhammad the Prophet*. Lahore: Ahmadiyya Anjuman-i-Isha'at-i-Islam, 1933.

Ali, Syed Ameer. *A Critical Examination of the Life and Teachings of Mohammed*. London: William, 1873.

———. *The Spirit of Islam, A History of the Evolution and Ideals of Islam with a Life of the Prophet*. Amplified and revised ed.; London: Chattos and Windus, 1964.

Amin, Muhammad (ed.). *The Sayings of Prophet Muhammad*. Lahore: Lion Press, 1960.

———. *Wisdom of Prophet Muhammad*. Lahore: Lion Press, 1960.

Andrae, Tor. *Mohammed: The Man and His Faith*, translated by Theophil Menzel. New York: Barnes and Noble, 1957.

Azzam, Abdel Rahman. *The Eternal Message of Muhammad*, translated from the Arabic by Caesar E. Farah, with an introduction by Vincent Sheean. New York: Devin-Adair Co., 1964.

Bodley, Ronald Victor Courtenay. *The Messenger: The Life of Muhammed.* Garden City, New York: Doubleday and Co., Inc., 1946.

Bosworth-Smith, R. *Mohammed and Mohammedanism.* London: Murray, 1889.

Bush, Rev. George. *The Life of Mohammed; Founder of the Religion of Islam, and of the Empire of the Saracens.* New York: J. & J. Harper, 1830.

Carlyle, Thomas. *On Heroes, Hero-Worship, and the Heroic in History* (lecture II). London: J. Fraser, 1841, and various other editions.

Draz, Muhammad 'Abd Allah. "Muhammad" in *Islam, The Straight Path*, ed. by Kenneth W. Morgan. New York: The Ronald Press, 1958.

Draycott, Gladys M. *Mohomet Founder of Islam.* New York: Dodd, Mead and Co., 1916.

Essad Bey. *Mohammed: A Biography*, translated by Helmut L. Ripperger. New York and Toronto: Longmans, Green and Co., 1936.

Foster, H. Frank. "An Autobiography of Mohammed," *The Moslem World*, XXVI (1936), 130–152.

Galwash, A. A. "The Life of Prophet Mohammad," *The Religion of Islam.* 5th ed.; Cairo: Imprimerie Misr, 1958.

al Ghazzālī, Abū Ḥāmid Muḥammad. *Ihyā' 'Ulūm al Dīn*, Book XX, edited and translated by L. Zolondek. Leiden: E. J. Brill, 1963.

Gibb, H. A. R. *Mohammedanism, An Historical Survey.* London: Oxford University Press, 1953.

Glubb, Sir John Bagot. *The Life and Times of Muhammad.* London: Hodder and Stoughton, and New York: Stein and Day, 1970.

Guillaume, Alfred. *New Light on the Life of Muhammad.* Manchester: Manchester University Press, 1960.

Gulick, Robert. *Muhammad, the Educator.* Lahore: Institute of Islamic Culture, 1953.

Hakim, Khalifa Abdul. *The Prophet and His Message.* Lahore: Institute Of Islamic Culture, 1972.

Hamadeh, Muhammad Maher. "Muhammad the Prophet: A Selected Bibliography." Unpublished Ph.D. dissertation, Michigan University, 1965.

Hashmi, Rahm Ali. *Mohammad, the Benefactor of Humanity*, translation and condensation of the Urdu *Mohsin-e-insaniyat* by Naeem Siddiqi. Delhi: Board of Islamic Publications, 1971.

Hilliard, Frederick Hadaway. *The Buddha, the Prophet, and the Christ.* London and New York: G. Allen and Unwin and Macmillan, 1956.

Hosain, Saiyid Safdar. *The Early History of Islam: An Impartial Review of the Early Islamic Period Compiled from Authentic Sources.* Karachi: Mushtaq Ali K. Laddhani, 1971.

Husain, Athar. *Prophet Muhammad and His Mission.* Bombay and New York: Asia Publishing House, 1967.

Ibn Hishām, 'Abd al-Malik. *The Life of Muhammad: A Translation of ibn Ishāq's Sīrat Rasūl Allah.* London and New York: Oxford University Press, 1955.

Ibn Sa'd, Muḥammad. *Kitāb al-Ṭabaqāt al Kabīr,* translated by S. Moinul Haq assisted by H. K. Ghazanfar. Karachi: Pakistan Historical Society, 1967.

Imamuddin, S. M. *A Political History of Muslims: Prophet and Pious Caliphs.* Dacca: Najmah, 1967.

Iqbal, Afzal. *Diplomacy in Islam: An Essay on the Art of Negotiations as Conceived and Developed by the Prophet of Islam.* Lahore: Institute of Islamic Culture, 1962.

Irving, Washington. *Life of Mahomet.* London: J. M. Dent and Sons, and New York: E. P. Dutton and Co., 1911.

————. *Mahomet and His Successors,* edited by Henry A. Pochmann and E. N. Feltskog. Madison: University of Wisconsin Press, 1970.

Jeffery, Arthur. *Islam: Muhammad and His Religion.* New York: Liberal Arts Press, 1958.

Johnstone, P. DeLacy. *Muhammad and His Power.* New York: Charles Scribner's Sons, 1901.

Khan, Inamullah. *Maxims of Mohummud.* Karachi: Umma Pub. House, 1965.

Lane-Poole, Stanley. *The Prophet and Islam,* abridged from 1879 edition. Lahore: National Book Society, 1964.

Liu Chai-Lien. *The Arabian Prophet: A Life of Mohammed from Chinese and Arabic Sources,* translated by Isaac Mason. Shanghai: Commercial Press, Ltd., 1921.

Margoliouth, D. S. *Mohammed and the Rise of Islam.* London: G. P. Putnam's Sons, 1905.

Merrick, J. L. (tr.). *Life and Religion of Mohammed as Contained in the Sheeah Traditions of the Hyat-ul-Kuloob.* Boston: Phillips, 1850.

Mohy-ud-Din, Ata. *The Arabian Prophet: His Message and Achievements.* Karachi: Ferozsons, 1955.

Muir, Sir William. *The Life of Mohammad from Original Sources,* a new and revised edition by T. H. Weir. Edinburgh: J. Grant, 1923.

Nadvi, Muzzaffar Uddin. *An Easy History of the Prophet of Islam.* Lahore: M. Ashraf, 1954.

Pike, Edgar Royston. *Mohammed, Prophet of the Religion of Islam.* 2nd ed.; London: Weidenfeld, 1968.

Rahnama, Zayn al 'Abidin. *Payambar: The Messanger,* translated by L. P. Elwell-Sutton. Lahore: Sh. M. Ashraf, 1964–65.

Rodinson, Maxime. *Mohammed,* translated by Anne Carter. New York: Pantheon Books, 1971.

Sarwar, Hafiz Ghulam. *Muhammad the Holy Prophet.* Lahore: Sh. Muhammad Ashraf, 1964.

Shibli Numani, Muhammad. *'Allamah Shibli's Sīrat al-Nabī,* translated by Fazlur Rahman. Karachi: Pakistan Historical Society, 1970.

Siddiqui, Abdul Hameed. *The Life of Muhammad.* Lahore: Islamic Publications, 1969.

Smith, Reginald Bosworth. *Mohammed and Mohammedanism,* lectures delivered at the Royal Institution of Great Britain in 1874. London: Smith, Elder and Co., 1874.

Sprenger, Aloys. *Life of Mohammad from Original Sources.* Allahabad, 1851.

Stobart, James William Hampson. *Islam and Its Founder.* London: Society for Promoting Christian Knowledge; and New York: Pott, Young, and Co., 1877.

Suhrawardy, Sir Abdullah al-Mamun. *The Sayings of Muhammad.* London: J. Murray, 1954.

Wahab, Syed Abdul. *The Shadowless Prophet of Islam: Being a Treatise on the Spiritual Aspect of the Prophet's Life and Spiritualism of Islam as Taught by Him.* Lahore: Sh. Muhammad Ashraf, 1962.

Waheeduddin Fakir, Syed. *The Benefactor,* translation of *Mohsin-e-Azam and Mohsanin,* English text revised by Faiz Ahmed Faiz. Karachi: Lion Art Press, 1964.

Watt, William Montgomery. *Muhammad at Mecca.* Oxford: Clarendon Press, 1960.

————. *Muhammad at Medina.* Oxford: Clarendon Press, 1966.

————. *Muhammad: Prophet and Statesman.* London: Oxford University Press, 1961.

Wessels, Antonie. *A Modern Arabic Biography of Muhammad: A Critical Study of Muhammad Husayn Haykal's Ḥayāt Muḥammad.* Leiden: E. J. Brill, 1972.

Widengren, George. *Muhammad, the Apostle of God, and His Ascension.* Uppsala: Lundequistska Bokhandeln, 1955.

Index of Proper Names